California Real Estate Practice

SECOND EDITION

Robert L. Herd

Bruce A. Southstone

CENGAGE
Learning™

Australia • Brazil • Japan • Korea • Mexico • Singapore • Spain • United Kingdom • United States

CENGAGE Learning

California Real Estate Practice, Second Edition
Robert L. Herd and Bruce A. Southstone

Vice President/Editor-in-Chief: Dave Shaut

Acquisitions Editor: Sara Glassmeyer

Developmental Editor: Arlin Kauffman, LEAP

Editorial Assistant: Michelle Melfi

Senior Marketing and Sales Manager: Mark Linton

Content Project Management: Pre-Press PMG

Production House/Compositor: Pre-Press PMG

Production Technology Analyst: Starratt Alexander

Senior Manufacturing Buyer: Charlene Taylor

Senior Art Director: Jennifer Wahi

Copyeditor: Pre-Press PMG

Cover Designer: Jeff Bane, CMB Design, Ltd.

Cover Images: (top) Shutterstock/Sklep Spozywczy; (center) Shutterstock/Vika Sabo; (bottom) Shutterstock/Chris Rodenberg Photography

Permissions Acquisition Manager/Text: Mardell Glinkski-Schultz

Permissions Acquisition Manager/Photo: Deanna Ettinger

Library of Congress Control Number: 2009944105

ISBN-13: 978-0-538-74055-5

ISBN-10: 0-538-74055-8

Cengage Learning
5191 Natorp Boulevard
Mason, OH 45040
USA

Cengage Learning products are represented in Canada by Nelson Education, Ltd.

For your course and learning solutions, visit **academic.cengage.com**

Purchase any of our products at your local college store or at our preferred online store **www.cengagebrain.com**

Printed in the United States of America
2 3 4 5 6 7 13 12 11

Brief Contents

Contents

3 ETHICS, FAIR HOUSING, AND RESPA 53

4 DISCLOSURES 93

5 LEAD GENERATION OR PROSPECTING FOR CLIENTS AND CUSTOMERS   145

6 WORKING WITH BUYERS   167

Preface

A NEW BEGINNING

The housing market has undergone volatile changes in recent years, the impacts of which have demanded better performance from those in the field. While the real estate market has always seen and will always experience booms and busts, the combined fallout in the finance, banking, and construction industries did not help an already fragile situation. We open with this statement because that is where we are—at the beginning. Or a new beginning, at least. Real estate has been and continues to be one of the most exciting and rewarding career paths we know. The opportunity to work with others in brokering the foundation of their dreams has pushed us to want to better ourselves so that we can better serve them.

MEASURABLE OUTCOMES

The real estate market can be tough—and rewarding. With this book we hope to prepare students to encounter the challenges and see their way through them. That is one of the primary reasons we added Student Learning Outcomes (SLOs) to the start of the chapters in this edition. SLOs demonstrate what a student can do with the knowledge, skills, and abilities acquired from a specific course of study. This second edition is offered in the sincere hope that the student learning outcomes produce measurable increases in professional performance. While it is true learning objectives require basic thinking skills, outcomes require a higher order of thinking, that is, analysis, synthesis, and/or evaluation.

LICENSE REQUIREMENTS

The state of California and its Department of Real Estate require applicants for the salesperson license to show, among other

requirements (see BPC §10153), an understanding of California real estate as evidenced by successful completion of three college-level courses of study in Real Estate Principles, Real Estate Practice, and one course from a list of approved courses. This California Real Estate Practice text meets the practice requirement.

For the California brokers license one must successfully complete eight required college-level courses, one of those being Real Estate Practice.

THE SECOND EDITION

Since publication of California Real Estate Practice, 1st Edition, real estate as practiced in California has continued to change and evolve as it has since its earliest beginnings. This second edition underwent significant revision to bring it current in terms, principles, and technology in use today. California real estate is a work in progress, and therefore constant adjustment in both detail and practice are necessary to maintain a level of knowledge and professional competence sufficient to meet the high standards of consumer protection demanded by professional standards, the state of California, and the Department of Real Estate.

We have also made a concerted effort to minimize the confusing use of the word "agent." Generally speaking, an *agent* is one who is authorized to represent another (called the principal) in dealings with a third party. However, California real estate law has limited those who, for compensation, may legally act as *agents* in real estate and related transactions to those holding a valid California real estate broker license. Hence, by definition, there can be only one person who qualifies as a "real estate agent" who can legally represent the public for compensation and that would be the employing broker at each firm.

All other "licensees," whether broker associate or salesperson, working under an employing broker's license, and being therefore an agent of that broker, will be referred to in this text as a either licensee, listing licensee, selling licensee, salesperson or seller's or buyer's representative, not as "agent" since that position is already held by the employing broker. We will use the term *agent* when specifically referring to a firm's employing broker. Of course, the terms *escrow agent* or *insurance agent* are another matter. Our intent here is to minimize wherever possible the persistent misuse of terms.

In deference to the fact that a majority of licensees nationally are women and to avoid the repetitious use of gender specific pronouns,

we use the feminine where a gender specific pronoun is required. It should be understood that we are referring to both genders.

NEW TO THE SECOND EDITION

Global changes to the second edition include additions of real estate law, references to civil code, Business and Professions Code, and Regulations of the Real Estate Commissioner, inclusion of Student Learning Objectives for each chapter, and update of all forms where necessary throughout.

Other significant changes by chapter include the following:

- Chapter One: Extensive rewrite and reorganization to include discussion of myths of common usage, agent vs. licensee, and other terms.
- Chapter Two: Revised figures and inserts. Revised and updated California DRE license requirements.
- Chapter Three: Inclusion of NAR Code of Ethics and reference to AB 957, Buyer's Choice Act.
- Chapter Four: Inclusion of updated forms, DA Disclosure and Consent form, rewrite of section on agency, TDS, AIDS disclosure and Combined Hazards Book.
- Chapter Five: Inclusion of information on electronic media.
- Chapter Six: Revised lender underwriting requirements, income debt ratios, and agency disclosure.
- Chapter Seven: Inclusion of new forms, discussion of updated forms, and order of presentation.
- Chapter Eight: Revised discussion of the Listing Presentation Manual.
- Chapter Nine: Expanded discussion of Buyer Representation Agreements and limited agency broker.
- Chapter Ten: Update of IDX, VOW, internet advertising, social networking, and presenting co-op offers.
- Chapter Thirteen: Revised RESPA information.
- Chapter Sixteen: Addition of section on REO and Foreclosure termination notice.

INSTRUCTIONAL SUPPORT

Instructors who adopt this book receive access to an online Instructor's Manual written by the authors. Each chapter is supported with

chapter rationale, overall focus of classroom discussions, lecture outline, classroom discussion topics, and supplemental learning activities or quizzes. Plus, there is a 50-question Mid-Term Exam and a 100-question Final Exam.

Online WebTutor™ support for WebCT™ and BlackBoard® is also provided. Designed to accompany this textbook, WebTutor is an eLearning software solution that turns everyone in your classroom into a front-row learner. Whether you want to Web-enhance your class, or offer an entire course online, WebTutor allows you to focus on what you do best—teaching. More than just an interactive study guide, WebTutor™ is an anytime, anywhere online learning solution providing reinforcement through chapter quizzes, multimedia flashcards, e-mail discussion forums, and other engaging learning tools.

Classroom PowerPoint® presentation slides also support each chapter outlining learning objectives, emphasizing key concepts and highlighting real-world applications to help further engage learners and generate classroom discussion.

These instructional support materials are available online only to adopters from the text companion site www.cengage.com/realestate/herd.

ACKNOWLEDGMENTS

When I was asked to write a second edition of this textbook, I asked myself, "What can I do to make it clearly the very best textbook out there? What can I do to make it a valuable cutting-edge resource?" The answer came in the form of Bruce Southstone, a practicing California broker, director of the California Association of REALTORS®, and community college real estate instructor. Bruce and I have nearly 70 years of real estate experience between us, and our collaboration gives the reader many useful suggestions about how to handle the everyday issues faced by a licensee.

It was a pleasure to work with Bruce because his tenure as a college instructor brought a very sharp academic viewpoint to the material conveyed in this book and balances well with what each of us has experienced as working brokers. He is a stickler for detail and regularly cites useful civil code sections and commissioner's rules for the reader to earmark for handy future reference—something I believe you and your students will certainly appreciate.

We hope you enjoy reading this book as much as we did writing it and what you learn will enhance your knowledge, your ability to better represent your clients, and your ability to earn an excellent living while doing so.

I would also like to express our appreciation to those who served as reviewers and who provided insightful comments and valuable suggestions.

George Devine
University of San Francisco

Hal Bouley
Coastline Community College

About the Authors

Bob Herd started his real estate career in early 1972 with a small real estate company on the San Francisco Peninsula.

Although no formal training programs or systems were available in those days, Bob used some good initial training from his branch manager, his natural ability to interact with people, and his keen intuition about human nature to sell more than sixty homes his first and second years in the business. He was awarded the coveted "Top Salesperson" award in 1974 from the real estate association to which he belonged. Although Bob opened his own highly successful company in 1974, he still remained very active in sales, and under his training and guidance, one of his agents won the "Top Salesperson" award every year for the next six years, except in 1979.

Over the course of his career, which spans more than thirty-eight years, he has been a salesperson, broker owner, branch manager, and regional manager for some of the largest real estate companies in the San Francisco Bay area. Whether he was in a sales position or a non-selling management position, he always maintained and nurtured in his associates a keen sense of the ever-evolving sensible, human nature–based style of professionally handling the needs of customers and clients.

Bob has been a licensed California broker since 1974 and holds the Certified Real Estate Brokerage Manager (CRB), Certified Residential Specialist (CRS), and Graduate, REALTORS® Institute (GRI) designations. You may contact Bob by e-mail at rlherd@comcast.net.

Bruce Southstone is a licensed California real estate broker with more than twenty years of experience in California real estate sales, sales management, training, consulting and coaching. Bruce is an

adjunct instructor in real estate at Cabrillo College and he is an orientation instructor for the Santa Cruz Association of REALTORS®. He has taught real estate sales and practice for several large independent and franchise companies and has coached many individuals to a higher level of professional achievement in real estate. Currently he is general manager of Coast Country Real Estate, in Soquel, California.

Bruce served as president of the Santa Cruz Association of REALTORS® in 2002, was named REALTOR® of the Year in 2004, and received the Lifetime Achievement Award from the Santa Cruz Association of REALTORS® in 2008. At present he is a member of MLS Listings, Inc., Rules Committee.

A director of the California Association of REALTORS® since 1999, he served on numerous committees and as regional chair for Region #10 (San Benito, Santa Cruz, and Monterey Counties) in 2005. He continues to serve as a 2010 C.A.R. Director, regional representative for Professional Standards and C.A.R. Nominating Committee member.

Bruce holds the Certified Real Estate Brokerage Manager (CRB), Certified Residential Specialist (CRS), and Graduate Realtor® Institute (GRI) designations. You may contact Bruce by e-mail at retext@brucesouthstone.com.

Chapter

1

IMPORTANT PHRASES AND TERMS

Attitude

Broker

Consumer
   protection

Independent
   contractor

MLS

National
   Association of
   REALTORS®

SOI

Successive
   approximation

Starting Your Real Estate Career

Upon completion of this chapter, the student will be able to:

- Restate the requirements for a California Real Estate Salesperson license.
- Recognize the value of ethical conduct to the real estate professional.
- Explain the value that a real estate licensee brings to the consumer.
- Identify the two things a licensee has to sell.
- Create a personal business plan.
- Formulate personal real estate goals.

1.1 THE REAL WORLD OF REAL ESTATE

Many consumer surveys indicate that the biggest shortcoming among real estate professionals is a general failure to communicate effectively with clients, customers, and each other. For communication to be effective, there must be a common language and common understanding of terms and concepts. Most students taking a course in California Real Estate Practice have been exposed to many new terms and concepts during their study of Real Estate Principles. Terms and their precise meanings have a tendency to change over time. Because real estate, like other professions, is a work in progress, it is imperative that every licensee stay current with the nuances in terms and usage in the industry.

We feel obligated to clarify some of the more prevalent misunderstandings that have come into common usage. Such clarification

will aid all licensees in communicating with each other and with consumers.

It is very important that we establish and agree on the primary purpose of the real estate professional. What do we hope to accomplish by doing what we do? Some, who have worked in this industry for years, are not clear about why they are in this business. Many believe they are here solely to "make money." Of course, they can't mean that literally because "making money" is a function reserved to the federal government. What they really mean is that they are in this business to "earn money." The definition of the word *earn* is "to gain or get in return for one's labor or service"; service, then compensation. It seems such a small point, but it is critical that every licensee understand the sequence of events here: service, then compensation. Our purpose is service and the fee received is a byproduct of the labor or service provided.

Now we must ask, if our purpose is service and our goal is earning money, what is the purpose of the Department of Real Estate and the licensing structure? Is there a common goal here that can be integrated harmoniously? The common goal is **consumer protection**. If every licensee were to embrace the goal of providing service that facilitates the sale or purchase of property while protecting the clients' interests, we would have the ultimate in harmonious relationships. By using the knowledge gained through the licensing process to protect the interest of the client, the licensee will also protect themselves, their firm, and the reputation of the industry as a whole. Now there's a win/win combination.

What constitutes service to one broker may not fit the definition of service to another. Therefore, the definition of "service" is the variable that makes it nearly impossible to assume that "all licensees provide the same service."

Reality and consistency are as elusive in the world of real estate as in any other. Constant change makes it so. This field is in a constant state of change. The value of the land, as well as the needs of the people who live on it, may be different today than yesterday. Values and customer needs vary constantly. Because of this, licensees need to be aware of the changing needs of buyers and sellers and the necessity for flexibility in their services and marketing practices. For example, because each property and each buyer are unique, accurate pricing or appraising is more an art than an exact science. There are no two properties that are identical. Even adjoining properties offer different benefits and burdens.

Strength or weakness in the real estate marketplace is determined by perceived value that, in turn, creates supply and demand. Some of the reasons for the broad range of perceived values that exist today are:

- *Buyer and seller knowledge* – The Internet gives buyers and sellers access to a vast amount of real estate information; however, even if sales data is available, it is often misinterpreted by both buyers and sellers. The inability to interpret the data can often lead both buyers and sellers to overpay or underprice the homes they buy or sell. The GIGO (garbage in, garbage out) rule applies to real estate marketing as well as to computers. Providing accurate information to clients and customers along with proper interpretation of the data is one of the most important services offered by the knowledgeable licensee.

- *Motivation* – Motivation will almost always have a major influence on the seller's asking price, the price offered by the buyer, and the price finally accepted by the seller. A particular home may meet every one of a buyer's needs, but the fear of losing out to another offer may cause that buyer to offer a premium well above the seller's asking price. Another buyer may be less motivated or only mildly interested in the same home and may offer less than the seller's asking price. Sometimes the motivation to accept employment in another city is strong enough to cause the seller to accept less for her home than, say, a seller whose motivation for selling is to purchase a larger, more expensive home. For many sellers, getting the highest price for their home may not be their primary goal and, for many buyers, offering the lowest price may not be their primary goal.

- *Product differentiation* – No property is exactly like another. Even in "cookie cutter" tract homes with exactly the same floor plan, there are differences such as location (one backs up to a main highway while another is on a quiet street), amenities (one has a remodeled kitchen while another has the original kitchen), square feet, architectural style, maintenance, external influences such as barking dogs, and a stunning view. When the property is appraised, the appraiser factors all of these variables into an analysis of what the property is worth, but the appraiser's conclusion is still only an estimate of value. The actual price a property is sold for is generally set by the buyers, not the sellers. The sellers can ask any price that they want, but if no buyer meets that price the property remains unsold.

- *The ability of the real estate licensee* – Most buyers and sellers rely on information provided by a real estate professional. Even the "For Sale by Owner" needs the pricing information from the Multiple Listing Service (MLS) in order to price her property competitively. On occasion a licensee will represent a seller whose property is in an area or of a type where the licensee has no experience or knowledge. When this happens, the licensee may suggest an asking price or range that is inappropriately high or low that may have the effect of underpricing or discouraging interest by overpricing. While most licensees are interested in selling property (not just listing property), there are a few who may purposely suggest an unobtainably high selling price in order to beat the competition for the listing. This is clearly a violation of the **National Association of REALTORS®** Code of Ethics as well as laws relating to misrepresentation.

- *Terms* – Because most real estate purchases are financed, there is interdependency between real estate values and the availability of low-cost financing. When interest rates are low, financing is not really an issue with most buyers. When rates rise, however, an astute seller can get a higher price for a property by offering below market financing, although it's necessary to become familiar with all of the risks associated with doing so. This financing can be in the form of a first or second loan or a seller credit to the buyer for all or part of the buyer's closing costs. The availability of purchase from lenders is a critical factor in the viability of markets worldwide.

There are also times when different rules apply to different segments of the real estate marketplace. Different price ranges may have different supply/demand rules all in play at the same time, even in the same marketplace: homes in the lower price range may be selling briskly while nearby higher priced homes are taking a long time to sell because of lower demand.

The **MLS** provides current information on competitive pricing in the marketplace. This allows you to more accurately assess a given property's comparable market value and then to convey that information to your client or customer so they can make better decisions about listing price or what to offer for a given property.

As a licensee, you must be able to clearly explain the services you offer. You must be able to show the seller/buyer how your service can be of benefit.

Before dispelling and clarifying a few of the more prevalent myths currently embraced by many consumers and professionals

alike, we need to define a few basic terms. Here are a few definitions from the California Business and Professions Code (BPC) to aid in a common understanding of this discussion:

- BPC 10011 "Licensee," when used without modification, refers to a person, *whether broker or salesman*, licensed under any of the provisions of this part. (emphasis added)
- BPC 10012 "Broker," when used without modification, refers to a person licensed as a broker under any of the provisions of this part.
- BPC 10013 "Salesman," when used without modification, refers to a person licensed as a salesman under any of the provisions of this part.

1.2 BUSTING A FEW MYTHS

Myth number one: California Real Estate Salespersons sell real estate. After all, that is what it says on the license. This myth has been (and will continue to be until clarified) the cause of much misunderstanding between buyers, sellers, and licensees. *The real estate licensee has only two things to sell and neither is real estate.*

Think about it. The actual seller of real property is the owner, not the licensee. The **broker** acts on behalf of the seller and the licensee acts on behalf of the broker. Per the listing contract, the seller is the "principal" and the *broker* is the "agent" acting on her behalf. *It is the employing broker who, by law, is the only one allowed to receive compensation for effecting the sale or transfer of real property (BPC 10131).* Because the broker is the only one authorized by law to collect a fee for real estate services, the licensee must be employed by a licensed broker and therefore collects fees and other compensation only through that employing broker—never directly from buyers, sellers, or others.

The logical progression is as follows: The property owner or buyer (the principal) hires an "agent" (the *broker*) to represent her in the sale or purchase of property. That broker hires a licensed real estate salesperson (the licensee) to represent her in dealings with the public. The licensee is never the direct representative of the principal; the licensee always represents the broker who represents the client. In other words, *the broker is the "agent" of the seller or buyer.* The licensee is the "agent" of the broker. Why is this distinction important? Because licensees have misunderstood their relationship to the client by referring to them as "my client"; they are not the

licensee's clients, they are clients of the broker. The licensee's client is the broker. This concept becomes critically important when the licensee decides to change broker affiliations. The listings taken by a licensee, as well as the buyers being represented (directly, through a Buyer Representation Agreement or, indirectly, through a Calif. Purchase Agreement) stay with the broker. When any other disposition occurs, it is because the broker and licensee have negotiated an alternate agreement.

You can see from this discussion how misuse of the term *agent* can lead to universal misunderstanding by brokers, licensees, clients, and customers. It has become standard usage in the industry and by the public to refer to all licensees as "agents." Although technically correct (all licensees do represent others), we must be very careful to clearly understand who is representing whom. Because there can be only one "agent" with every firm, that "agent" is, by definition, a licensed California Real Estate Broker. Licensees, whether broker associate or salesperson, work under and offer their services through the "employing broker." It's the broker who may legally offer to sell, lease, and rent property for compensation, not the salesperson. Properties are listed (and contracts written) in the name of the seller or buyer and the broker, not the salesperson licensee. *The authors, when referring to salespersons or broker associates working under an employing broker, will use the term licensee.*

Because it is important that you know what service you offer the consumer, you need to be very clear on this point: You have only two things to sell—your time and your knowledge. Time and knowledge (that is, the knowledge required to obtain a real estate license and the "local" knowledge required to be able to give the principals good and proper advice) are the essence of the service you offer. Many careers have met their untimely demise as a result of failure to understand this concept.

It is interesting that many consumers and some licensees believe that all licensees offer the same service: another myth. Although "activity for which a license is required" may be the same, the real "service" of time and knowledge are not likely to be identical for any two or more licensees.

Success or failure is not something that happens to you—it's a choice. The single most important component of that choice is belief. Your belief system will determine your success. Because success is a concept and not an object, you must have a clear idea of what you mean by success before you can develop a plan to achieve it. In other words, you must define what success means to you. When you have created your own clear image of what success is to you: *Your*

beliefs become your thoughts, your thoughts become your words, your words become your actions, your actions become your habits, your habits become your values, and your values become your destiny (Mahatma Gandhi). Logically then, a change in belief would change a destiny.

As a new licensee, there will be many times when you may be tempted to doubt your knowledge and abilities. The more confident you are in your knowledge of any subject, the more confidence you will feel and the more you will project. The authors sincerely encourage every licensee to maximize their confidence by maximizing their knowledge and ability. Your community college can be of great assistance in providing specific instruction in many aspects of business and real estate. Take advantage of this valuable resource.

The California Real Estate Broker License is a very good start toward professional competence. The added knowledge and confidence gained through studying for and passing the California Real Estate Broker Exam is the least we owe the people we serve. Although the broker's license is a good start, education and the acquisition of real estate knowledge does not end there. Beyond the broker's license, there are other professional designations that can enhance your knowledge and expertise.

1.3 THE ATTITUDE OF PROFESSIONALISM

"If you think you can do a thing or think you can't do a thing, you're right," said Henry Ford. Real estate is no exception to this rule. As with most human endeavor, belief is a critical component of accomplishment and plays a major role in determining individual and collective reality. Your attitude, positive or negative, will dictate how others perceive you and how you perceive yourself.

Getting started will be much more difficult if you believe it will be difficult. A negative attitude will almost certainly guarantee a negative result and consequent need for a career change.

There is no substitute for a strong belief in yourself. Do whatever is necessary to put yourself in a positive environment. Surround yourself with as many successful people as you can. Successful people have positive attitudes and are fun to be around. You will find that success, like negativity, can be catching.

You will be making your presentations and using your knowledge outside the office. In order to do that, you must bring your positive attitude with you into the field. Your broker will not be watching over you every minute of every day. For the positive, "yes, I can" attitude to be there, it must be nurtured and cultivated

by you. Many motivational programs on CD and other media are available if you need quick inspiration. Keep a few of your favorites in your car and play them often.

To keep a positive attitude, ask yourself the following questions. If your answer to any of them is "no," take steps to reaffirm who you are and your role as a service provider and representative of other people.

- *Are you able to handle your own inner fear?* Fear can keep you from taking the bold steps needed to call or see people and help them with their real estate needs. More people fail as real estate professionals due to an unfounded fear of rejection than any other reason.

- *Are you persistent?* When a client says no, do you just quit asking or do you take it as a signal to probe for more information? Often, when clients say "no," they are really telling you that they don't have enough information to make a decision. If you just give up, hoping you won't offend them, you may well be keeping them from achieving the result that they truly desire. Only a small percentage of your potential clientele will agree with you or ultimately do a transaction with you, but the service you provide to that small percentage can make you an excellent living and you will help a lot of people, so keep probing.

- *Are you self-confident?* There is no substitute for the confidence that comes with professional knowledge and competence. Your clients want you to lead them to what they believe to be a logical conclusion, even before they believe it themselves. If you lack self-confidence, it will be seen as uncertainty and your clients will perceive you as lacking knowledge about the issues at hand. You need to have a deep reservoir of local real estate knowledge so when you are asked for advice or direction by your clients, your knowledge and preparation will reflect your professionalism. You can't fake this. If you don't have a ready answer to every question, tell them you will find the answer and get back to them. No one expects you to know everything, but knowledge is one place where more is better.

- *Are you enthusiastic?* Enthusiasm can be highly contagious. Enthusiastic licensees have an insatiable thirst for knowledge about every aspect of the real estate business and are always looking for ways to improve how they represent others. When you are truly enthusiastic about your work, it rubs off on your clients and they begin to mirror your enthusiasm. Find something about this business that you can get enthusiastic about.

- *Are you a problem solver?* Matching motivated buyers and sellers in a real estate transaction will bring many differences into the light. Most can be dealt with creatively, given sufficient understanding by the licensee. This means asking many questions. Approach all differences of opinion with an open mind. Each party will tend to see the solution that works for them; it's your job to help the client see the "harmony" in the solution. Here is where your creativity and negotiating skills can shine. We sell time and knowledge to people who need advice and direction when they are buying or selling real property.

- *Are you adept at handling objections?* One of the most difficult clients to represent is the one who never raises any objections but doesn't commit to buy or sell.

1.4 GOAL SETTING

You must ask yourself two important questions: Who am I? and What do I want? Most people avoid the first question because they believe the answer to be obvious; it is not. Who you are is not defined by what you do. That's what our culture would have you believe. Who you are is, perhaps, a philosophical question beyond the scope of this text, but each one of us needs an answer to this question.

As the comedian says, "I always wanted to be somebody ... I guess I should have been more specific." Getting specific about who you are and what you want is the first step toward achievement. It is difficult to achieve what one cannot define.

What do you want to achieve in this life with the time you have available? From the macro to the micro, large to small, lifetime goals to tasks of the present moment, each individual must create their own goal. Since this is a text on California Real Estate Practice, we will assume you have worked through your lifetime goals and are now at the micro level of determining what you will achieve as a real estate licensee.

Goals establish the baseline you will use to measure your progress. A number of factors must be considered when setting goals because these factors will profoundly affect your ability to meet or exceed them. Among the more obvious are:

- *Personal motivation* – Just how motivated are you to succeed in the real estate business? Some people go into this business thinking they will "give it a try." If "trying" is your goal, you will surely succeed at that, but "trying" is not achieving. Many

others will have a strong desire to become the very best at what they do and will not settle for less. Your **attitude** is the single biggest factor in deciding your fate as a real estate professional.

- *Personal finances* – Although some new licensees may establish a meaningful earnings pattern very quickly, some can take a year or longer to become established, depending on economic and other market conditions. Any well-thought-out business plan contains reserves for contingencies. You should be able to support yourself through savings or other income for a minimum of six to twelve months. Financial reserves that will sustain both you and your family for less than a year may cause you to focus your attention on day-to-day survival rather than on your plan to become successful in real estate.

- *Economic and market conditions* – Supply and demand has a marked influence on the activity of any product or service industry. Health of the national and local economies affects marketability of most products and services including real estate. Starting a successful career in real estate can be done in virtually any market condition, but it can be much easier when capable buyers are abundant. If you enter the profession during a period of increased demand for real estate, you can expect the number of licensees to increase and competition among those licensees to become more intense. The opposite is also true. A decline in demand will reduce the number of licensees, creating an environment where only the most determined service providers prevail.

- *Personal support from family and friends* – You need a support group. The added incentive that comes from the support of family and friends can be critical to success in any field. It is particularly important in real estate to enjoy the support of family and friends as this is the group that will make up a major portion of your sphere of influence (SOI).

To be effective, goal setting must be an exact, not an abstract, exercise, or it loses much of its meaning and effectiveness. As an example, an abstract goal would be: I will see "For Sale by Owners" this week. A much more effective and specific goal would be: I will talk with each "For Sale by Owner" on Elm Street between 3:00 P.M. and 6:00 P.M., this Wednesday, Thursday, and Friday.

To be most effective, your goals must be in writing, on 3 × 5 cards and placed in conspicuous places: for example, your car visor, your bathroom mirror, or on the first page of your daily planner.

Goals must be realistic and achievable. This means that you must believe them to achieve them. If goals are set too high, to

the point where you subconsciously feel they are unobtainable, you may become discouraged or depressed and give up prematurely. Your broker, branch manager, or a successful licensee mentor may be a helpful resource for additional information on goal setting. Goals will vary with the individual. Some licensees are motivated by the number of personal calls they make, and some get more excited by the number of transactions closed. Fortunately, there are some licensees who take pride in providing the best service possible to clients and customers alike. It is this type of licensee who understands that excellent service brings more satisfied consumers, which leads to more business, more referrals, and ultimately, more income. Remember, the money earned is a by-product of the amount and quality of the service performed. More and better quality service will inevitably translate into more income and more referrals.

Setting short-, medium-, and long-term goals with personal rewards for achieving each one can help break down the process into achievable bites. Though a goal may appear to be completely out of reach, small steps with appropriate course corrections can provide the means to achieve almost any goal. The method used is one of **"successive approximation"**—the process of making small but precise course corrections. For instance, a sailboat, because it cannot sail directly into the wind, must reach its destination by making a zigzag pattern across its intended course. If you have a clearly defined goal or aiming point, you can reach it just like a guided missile reaches its target: through constant course corrections.

As an added incentive to stimulate performance, you might decide to reward yourself with a new car, computer, cell phone, or other helpful piece of equipment after closing a predetermined number transaction.

Goals must be tied to a specific time line with precise dates for completion built into the plan. Time is of the essence in your quest for success. You want to be able to help enough people so that you can devote full time to your service profession. Those interested in buying and selling homes want results in a reasonable amount of time; ideally in less than three months (six months at the outside). Licensees are not paid for their service until the service has been performed. That usually means a property has actually changed hands and the deed has been recorded or a lease has successfully been negotiated.

We won't be recommending or endorsing any specific types of cars or other equipment, but it should be obvious that you do need a clean car (preferably a four-door sedan) in excellent

mechanical condition with four good tires. The type of car is not nearly as important as its cleanliness and reliability. You should be confident that if you decide to drive this car across the country on the spur of the moment, you could do so without worry or hesitation; after all, you will be showing property to a wide variety of clients and customers; you have a responsibility for their safety while they are in your car.

We understand there are exceptions to every rule. We know there are licensees out there who show property using a motorcycle or two-seat sports car; but it's just not the preferred method nor is it one we would recommend.

Long-term goals can be fun and will help you prepare for your retirement. Perhaps you could set a long-term goal of investing in your first home or your first income property when you reach a certain level of production.

Accountability is extremely important. If you really want to hold yourself accountable for achieving your goals, tell someone special in your life about them. Ask that person to question you often about how you are progressing. That's real motivation.

Be sure to set goals that you can fully control. For instance, if you set a goal of obtaining two listings this month, you are relying on the timing of other people (potential sellers) to list with you now, and this may not be realistic. A better system is to tie goals to activities, rather than end results. While you are fully in control of the activities you perform, results are really controlled by other people. If you set a goal to make twenty-five contacts on Monday, Wednesday, and Friday of each week, in time you will get business from those activities; however, if you set a goal of obtaining three listings a month from your lead generating activities, you may end up with a number of people who have committed to list with you, but no actual listings at the end of the month. Over time, goals that are tied to fundamental lead generating or client acquisition activities and are carried out on a regular basis will help you to quickly become far more successful.

Other examples of goals include:

Short term
- Collect thirty business cards (five per day). Asking others for their business card gives you an opportunity to offer yours in return.
- Research a geographic area and get the owners list from a title company.
- Personally meet with three For Sale by Owners.

Intermediate term

- Find buyers for $3,000,000 worth of property this year.
- Take three Graduate REALTORS® Institute (GRI) courses and commit to obtaining the designation.
- Purchase a new automobile within eighteen months.
- Take two courses toward my broker license each year.
- Purchase a rental home every two years.

Long term

- Open a real estate firm within seven years.
- Purchase a ten-unit apartment house within six years.
- Obtain my broker license within three years.

Goal setting not only gives new meaning and importance to time, it helps bring a true sense of accomplishment and satisfaction into an otherwise intrinsic world and acts as a barometer of our success along the way.

1.5 PLANNING

"Plan your work, and work your plan" is an old saying that almost every successful real estate professional takes to heart. Your broker will expect you to know what to do. For tax purposes, the Internal Revenue Service may consider you to be an **independent contractor**, but the state of California sees you as an employee of your employing broker. Although required by regulation to supervise your work, your broker will not be watching your every move. However, you will be evaluated according to the results you produce. Your ultimate success will be the result of the quality of the service you provide and how well you protect the interests of your broker, your clients, and yourself. You and you alone will be responsible for how much money you earn, which will be a direct result of how effectively you spend your *time* and apply your *knowledge*.

Planning is the process of putting in writing the most efficient use of your time. It is a list of the activities you intend to accomplish on any given day, week, month, or year.

Whether you adopt your own system and style of planning, or adopt one of the many systems available for real estate professionals, the important thing is to plan your work and then work your plan. Each and every task that must be done on any given day should be reduced to writing, no matter how insignificant it may seem. Then, once your day's tasks are in front of you, you can prioritize them, giving the least significant tasks the lowest priority.

Planning combined with self-discipline will soon make you keenly aware of time-wasting activities and the importance of your time. Once you are aware of these things, you will begin to see better results in the form of more appointments, listings, and closed sales. In the beginning, you will have more time available for generating leads of people who may be interested in buying or selling because you have fewer, if any, clients or customers; however, as you engage in productive activities, you will start to generate a larger and larger list of people who need your services. If you don't plan carefully, you will soon find yourself with more tasks than time. Now you must begin to eliminate ineffective methods and systems and really become a master planner.

The National Association of REALTORS® surveyed its members several years ago to learn how much time an average licensee spent in front of clients each day. The answer was alarming! The average licensee spent only fourteen minutes a day with clients. Is there any correlation between this very poor use of time and the high attrition rate among new licensees? Probably.

If there is a marked difference between successful and unsuccessful licensees, it is in how they plan and actually spend their time. Successful licensees come into the office with a written agenda for the day. They immediately start to work on that agenda without lingering over coffee with others or making small talk in the kitchen for extended periods of time. The real power of starting your day in a focused manner is that you will carry that momentum with you for the rest of the day.

What is your time worth?

Remember, in the real estate business, as in any service business, time is money. Doing the following will help you realize the value of your time:

There are 1,952 working hours in a year including 244 days at 8 hours per day. Your desired annual income divided by 1,952 = the dollar value of your time.

Example: If sales licensee Margie Wright makes $60,000 per year, her hourly wage is just under $31 per hour ($60,000/1,952 hours). For purposes of estimating, it is easier to round the 1,951 hours to an even 2,000; then, $60,000 divided by 2,000 equals $30, which is close enough considering the fact that most successful real estate professionals work more than 40 hours a week.

In actuality, you only have a fraction of that time to interact with clients and customers—maybe even a little less than 400 hours. So if you recalculate using only "client contact" hours, you begin to see the real value of the time spent in touch with decision makers. With this newly found knowledge, here are some things you can do to increase the value of the hours you do have available to be in communication with customers:

- Increase the number of calls you make.
- Increase the number of appointments you get from calling.
- Increase the number of closing questions asked per appointment.
- Increase the number of prospects you meet each week.
- Increase the number of referrals you receive.
- Increase the amount of repeat business you receive.

As mentioned earlier, you need to plan your work day every day, preferably the night before. After only a short time in the real estate business, it can often become difficult to preplan days off and vacations as it seems that the more successful you become, the more people seek you out.

To be as productive as possible, you will be wise to segment your time into categories. Many real estate professionals use A, B, C, and D categories.

A time: Time spent with decision makers that involves making a listing presentation, writing a purchase contract, or showing property to prospective buyers.

B time: Time spent prospecting for new leads, clients, and customers. Also, time spent preparing for property showings.

C time: Time spent seeing new listings, doing escrow work, and doing other work that supports listings, sales, and open escrows.

D time: Time spent on any non-work-related issues and personal time. This includes time off and vacations, which are important to avoid burnout.

It is easy to see that the more time that you spend doing *A time* activities, the higher your income will be. When you combine this with an ever-increasing amount of skill and knowledge, it only follows that your income will increase dramatically! There will probably come a time when you will want to hire a part-time or full-time licensed assistant to conduct much of the *B time* and *C time* activities for you.

As your effectiveness as a licensee grows, so does your hourly worth, and the old saying that "If you don't have as assistant, you are one" will loom large in your career.

Now that you have a clear understanding of the value of your time, you are ready to obtain a daily planner. Many types are available to you. Be sure to keep your planner with you at all times because you will often encounter situations where you are away from the office and need to schedule an appointment with someone.

Planners vary from the rather sophisticated cell phone/electronic planner combination and iPhone and Palm Pilot–type PDAs (Personal Data Assistants) to the *Week at a Glance* planners available in every stationery store. There are also several fine computer programs such as *Microsoft Outlook*.

These are often hard to use and keep updated if all you have is a nonportable desktop computer because you have to print each day out from the computer every morning and you are not always at the computer to enter new data and appointments.

Remember that you will seldom complete all of the tasks you have in your planner each day. If you don't complete a task, just advance it to the next day and increase its priority, if appropriate. You will have new things to do and new opportunities coming to you along the way every day that will often require you to push back something you had planned. This is perfectly normal, so don't be frustrated by it. The important thing is to *use* your planner, whatever type it may be, and always do what is necessary to take care of *A time* activities as soon as possible.

Every few days, review the activities that have been in your planner for the past few days. See what you did or did not accomplish and critique yourself. By doing this, you increase your awareness of the value of your time. One rule to make each day much nicer and more productive is to do the most unpleasant tasks as early in the day as possible. That way the work you dislike the most is behind you and you don't have to worry about it all day.

1.6 YOUR REAL ESTATE BUSINESS PLAN—PREPARATION IS EVERYTHING

There is overwhelming evidence that the failure of the vast majority of new licensees can be traced to a failure to create and execute a business plan.

Most new licensees do not have a large client base, and without one, they have no one to sell to, so they don't earn any money, get discouraged, and quit, often out of fundamental necessity.

It is essential that new real estate professionals take the time to become technically proficient; however, they also need to learn quickly what "client acquisition" or "lead generating" techniques are most effective and incorporate those activities into their daily work plan. Where does one get that client base?

It has been estimated that each of us know 250 to 300 people, each of those 250 to 300 people know 250 to 300 people, and so on. Success depends on how many of these people the new licensee can find who would be willing to pay for the services she offers. The task is called "lead generation." Finding as many people as you can who are motivated to buy or sell a home in the next 90 days and who need your expert assistance as a real estate licensee should be your goal. How you propose to do that will be your business plan. A real estate licensee without a plan is similar to a ship without a specific destination. Any course is equally effective if you don't know where you are going.

It is relatively easy to obtain a Real Estate Salesperson license in California. Becoming a successful licensee is another thing entirely. If you take three college level real estate courses including Real Estate Principles, Real Estate Practice, plus an elective such as Real Estate Finance or Real Estate Law, and pass the state exam with a score of 70 percent or higher, you will qualify for a California Real Estate Salesperson license. In terms of classroom hours, three courses or approximately 135 class hours are required to qualify to sit for the salesperson license exam. Approximately 360 class hours are required for the broker exam. Compared to other California state licenses, the required educational prerequisite is minimal. For example, the California cosmetology license requires 1,600 hours of classroom instruction, barber 1,500, and manicurist 400, and none of these people deal with transactions potentially involving millions of dollars.

One reason for the high attrition rate among real estate licensees is that although the requirements to qualify for the license are relatively minimal, the requirements for sustained success are formidable and include having a detailed business plan. New licensees come into this business with little or no business planning knowledge or experience and little or no capital to sustain them through the six to twelve months or longer that it may take to become self-sufficient in this business.

After the initial office orientation, for example, the fax and coffee machines, computer ports, and the introduction of staff, many firms begin their "in-house training." It goes something like this: "Well, now that you've met the staff and know where everything

is, there's your desk and there's your phone, let's see what you can do." At the end of the training, you must have a plan.

Below is a sample one-month business plan. It is fairly general; however, it is designed to get you in front of prospective buyers and sellers as much as possible. Feel free to add, change, or make adjustments to allow the plan fit your particular needs and geographic area. Do not succumb to the temptation to delete the activities that get you in front of decision makers. There will be some people who do not need your knowledge or service at this point in time and they will let you know. Do not interpret this as personal rejection. It's not personal, it's just business.

Business Plan

Week 1

- Activate your real estate license, if necessary.
- Attend all training classes.
- Join the local real estate organization and MLS.
- Have the staff give you a tour of the office.
- Order business cards and any promotional materials.
- Get Open House signs from your office if they have them or purchase your own.
- Get your desk assignment.
- Obtain your e-mail and voice-mail accounts and codes.
- Have a studio-quality headshot photo taken for your business cards and promotional materials.
- Purchase all necessary office supplies.
- Meet with your broker or branch manager to discuss building your SOI database. Your goal is to build this list to at least 300 people.
- Obtain and read several times the purchase contract and listing contract that your firm uses. Write down any issues that you do not fully understand and ask your broker to clarify them for you.
- Obtain and study any alternate listing and purchase contracts in use by adjoining counties or regions.
- Preview at least four of the office or company's listing inventory each day.
- Begin to plan your annual budget.
- Attend the office meeting.

Week 2

- Attend all training classes.
- Preview at least four of the office listings daily.
- Meet with your broker, branch manager, or mentor to finalize your SOI mailings and database. If you plan to market to a geographical area, research subdivision(s) you will target. Remember, number of

sales in a specific area is far more important than the individual selling price.

- Start your computer research of potential geographic areas via the MLS and drive by the areas you are considering. Meet with your broker/manager to discuss your findings.
- Order a list of names and addresses from your title company.
- Read the purchase agreement two more times. Memorize paragraph numbers and their subjects.
- Obtain some type of electronic database and start to enter your SOI.
- Schedule an Open House for yourself for the following Sunday. (If you do not yet have a listing, ask your broker/manager to assist you in getting another licensee's listing to hold open.)
- Write and send at least five personal notes a day to your SOI being sure to include your business card.
- Prepare Open House flyers.
- Mail or drop off at least fifty Open House invitations with flyer.
- Refine your annual budget.
- Start to prepare your personal website, if applicable.
- Attend the office meeting.

Week 3

- Attend training classes as scheduled.
- On Monday, send thank-you notes or e-mails to prospects you met at your Sunday Open House. Personal notes are preferred.
- Preview at least four office listings per day.
- Enter new names to your SOI database.
- Tuesday evening, call the people you met on Sunday and ask for a showing or listing appointment with them.
- Meet with your broker/manager to discuss your annual goals. Decide how you want to "keep score," for example, volume of sales, total earnings, or number of transactions.
- Research properties to show to your buyers.
- Show properties and write contracts.
- Make listing presentations.
- Arrange an Open House for next Sunday.
- Start to assemble your listing presentation.
- Prepare Open House flyers.

Week 4

- Attend all training classes.
- Preview at least four office listings per day.
- On Monday, send personal or e-mail thank-you notes to new leads or customers you met at your Sunday Open House.
- On Tuesday or Wednesday, call all of the new leads or customers from your Open House and ask for showing or listing appointments.

- Research properties to show to your buyers and make any necessary appointments with licensees or sellers for showing.
- Show properties.
- Research homes for CMA (Comparative Market Analysis) and conduct listing presentations.
- Call and see For Sale by Owners (check the Do-Not-Call List first).
- Call expired listings (check the Do-Not-Call List first). Make an appointment to see the home if possible.
- Take floor time as appropriate (be prepared).
- Call twenty SOI people per week (four per day, on average). Ask for referrals.
- Do escrow work as needed.
- Schedule an Open House for next Sunday.
- Prepare Open House flyers.
- Build and refine your listing presentation manual.
- Sign up for floor time for next month.
- Write to absentee owners about their property.

(Note: Week 4 is a good example of a week-to-week operational guide of daily activities.)

This basic plan may be used as a guideline each month. As you grow and mature as a real estate professional, you will replace "training classes" with "continuing education." You will also add activities that keep you in touch with your new and growing group of satisfied customers and clients so they start to send you referrals.

1.7 ADDITIONAL PREPARATION FOR THE PROFESSIONAL

Learn Office Policies and Procedures

The Regulations of the Real Estate Commissioner, Article 4, Section 2725, states in part: "A broker shall exercise reasonable supervision over the activities of his or her salespersons. Reasonable supervision includes, as appropriate, the establishment of policies, rules, procedures and systems to review, oversee, inspect and manage." These policies are usually published internally in an Office Policies and Procedures Manual. Many firms incorporate the Office Policies and Procedures Manual into their Broker Salesperson contract that you sign when you affiliate with the firm. You should ask for a copy and study it so you know the office rules and regulations.

Become Computer Literate

Computer literacy is an absolute must in today's real estate environment. You should at least have a good working knowledge of:

- MLS property search basics, including the ability to search the MLS database for a three-bedroom, two-bath home with a three-car garage in a certain subdivision at a list price of $450,000 to $550,000.
- How to use the MLS data to obtain and print out listing and sales information.
- How to create and send an e-mail message and attach a file to an e-mail.
- How to use word-processing software.
- How to use software to create flyers and property brochures for your listings and marketing materials.

Tax Knowledge

You are a real estate professional, not a tax professional. Unless you are prepared to be legally held to the standard of care of a currently licensed tax professional, do not make tax recommendations. That being said, it will be extremely helpful to have a good understanding of various types of taxes so that you can make the appropriate referral to a tax specialist if one is required. You should know things such as:

- Real property taxes and any special benefits available to homeowners.
- Income tax benefits available to homeowners and how they differ from investment property.
- Income tax benefits available to income and investment property owners and how they vary from those available to homeowners, including tax-deferred exchanges of "like kind" properties.

As a real estate professional, you have an obligation to be knowledgeable regarding the information necessary to obtain a real estate license. Real estate tends to draw new licensees from a diverse array of other professions. Some licensees have advanced degrees in other professions including, but not limited to, accounting, engineering, general contracting, law, and medicine. Offering advice and opinion beyond that required to obtain a real estate license may expose you and your broker to an unacceptable level of liability beyond the scope of your profession and may not be covered by your employing broker's Errors and Omissions (E & O) insurance policy. Before offering advice or opinion outside the area of real

estate consult with your broker; remember, your broker represents the client and you represent your broker.

Equipment Needed

You will not always be at your office when you write a purchase contract or take a listing. You will need a number of things with you or available at your office to be prepared for what each day will bring. The items you should consider having available are:

- *A daily planner* – This may be anything from the often-used *Day (or Week) at a Glance* to some sort of handheld PDA. Many title companies give out very nice yearly planners to real estate licensees on a complimentary basis, so don't be afraid to ask for one. Keep you planner with you at all times.

- *Business cards* – Your company will have its own format for business cards, but there is often some latitude for personal numbers or notations about languages you speak and so on. Make the most of them but do not put so much information on you card that it looks too busy and unprofessional.

- *Your automobile* – You should have a fairly modern four-door vehicle. Keep it clean, uncluttered, and well maintained. If you smoke, don't do it in your car as the smell is offensive to most people (especially, former smokers). It is also reasonable to ask other people not to smoke in your car. Use an air freshener, if necessary. Two-door automobiles are discouraged as they are very tiring to enter and exit several times while viewing properties.

- *In the car* – Have a method of storing the following items:
  1. Large folder or plastic bag for forms to prevent them from being folded or sun-damaged.
  2. Pen.
  3. Flashlight.
  4. 100-foot tape measure or an electronic measuring device for your client to use, not you.
  5. For Sale sign and stake, if your company doesn't have them installed for you.
  6. Digital camera (watch out for car heat that may affect picture quality).
  7. Business cards.
  8. Financial calculator that can do amortization schedules.
  9. Basic tools such as a hammer, a set of both Phillips and standard screwdrivers, and nuts and bolts for signs and sign riders.

10. Current map of your marketing area, even if you have a GPS.

11. Handheld recorder to record your thoughts and ideas as well as things that you will enter into your escrow communication log later. (Optional)

Some time ago, cell phones were large, bulky things that only the "big hitters" could afford. Today, it is hard to imagine working without one. For example, you are showing a property to a client and drive by a For Sale sign you didn't know existed, so you use your cell phone to call the listing office for information about the home and show it to your client. Also, some lock box companies have programs that allow cell phones to double as lock box keys. Text telephones (for the hearing impaired) essentially have given way to the Internet as a way to communicate. Most cell phone models have voice-activated dialing, which is highly recommended as dialing or speaking on a cell phone while driving can be very distracting, dangerous, and illegal. Most real estate companies have policies against it.

As a professional courtesy, it is best to turn your cell phone off when you are in a classroom environment or with clients.

Although nearly every real estate firm has its own toll-free number today, many agents have adopted their own 800 numbers to directly channel prospective buyers and sellers without going through the company. The cost is relatively inexpensive. A personal toll-free number is especially effective if the number is shown on the licensee's personal website so the public can view the licensee's listings and call them directly for more information or for a showing appointment.

About You

As the saying goes, "You never get a second chance to make a first impression." Your appearance is a nonverbal statement about you and your firm. What message do you wish to convey? What type of clientele will you be assisting? It is generally good advice to dress as you would expect a person to dress that performed the services of a professional counselor—one that you expected would charge a substantial fee for their service. The way you dress, smell, and act will directly affect how your clients respond to you and feel about working with you.

Watch the use of garlic and other strong or potentially offensive-smelling foods prior to working with clients, and keep

perfume or aftershave to a minimum. Some people have allergies and are extremely sensitive to odors and chemicals.

Be approachable and easy to be around; the more you smile and relax around your clients, the more relaxed they will be. Their experience with you should be something they look forward to with pleasure.

Above all, take care of yourself. If you let it, this business will consume all of your time, leaving you no time to exercise, eat right, and get enough sleep. It will also prevent you from working efficiently. Take time to keep your "machine" running smoothly.

1.8 BECOMING A REAL ESTATE PROFESSIONAL

Is there pride in being a real estate professional? There certainly is! As a real estate licensee, you are at the focal point in what is often the largest single investment a family or person ever makes in life: a home. Buyers are buying much more than a roof over their head, they are buying a lifestyle, a statement of what they are about, and often an environment in which to raise their children. Sellers are not just selling bricks and mortar; they are selling memories and comfort. It is true that you help thousands and thousands of dollars to change hands, but you are also the purveyor of emotions and therefore you hold the true essence of why people really are in your care. You should and must take great responsibility and great pride in doing it well.

SUMMARY

The real estate professional is constantly aware of the need for clear communication with clients, customers, and other licensees. The product, or service provided, is time and knowledge; service for a fee through the vehicle of property sale, acquisition, or use. Consumer protection while satisfying client needs is the goal of every transaction.

Licensees understand the various myths that have become accepted by the public and clients alike and know that they represent the buyer or seller indirectly through their employing broker. Real estate licensees have only two things to sell: *time* and *knowledge*. This is a service for fee business and the service must come first. Because time and knowledge are the value-added

service provided, these are rarely, if ever, exactly duplicated in every licensee. Therefore, it is unlikely that any two licensees will be offering identical service. From the client perspective, facilitation of the transaction (purchase, sale, or lease) may be the goal, but to have ultimate value this must be done while protecting the clients' interests.

Because confidence comes from knowledge, continuing education must be an ever-present goal of every licensee. If you think you can or think you can't, you are right.

The job of the real estate professional includes maintaining a positive attitude, handling inner fear with confidence, being persistent in the search for knowledge, being enthusiastic, solving problems, handling objections, and accepting failure as a learning experience. Essentially, the job is to create harmony out of chaos wherever possible.

Your attitude is everything. A positive attitude will evoke a favorable response from your clients, whereas a negative attitude will cause you to be perceived as unsure of what you are doing and will hurt your business.

Establishing goals will help to keep you focused and aware of the progress that you are making and should include short-, intermediate-, and long-term goals. You should create a business plan with the help of your broker/manager or a mentor and stick to it as closely as you can, but be prepared to make changes in it if you find that your interests or plans change. By planning your work and working your plan, you will maximize the time you spend developing as a real estate professional. It is wise to remember that you should never go to bed at night until your next day is planned in writing and in your appointment book.

As the essence of your job is matching people and property, you must learn the inventory as soon as possible and continue to preview new listings to stay keenly aware of what property is available in your marketplace at all times. You must also have a good working knowledge of the real estate taxation issues that can affect your clients so that you may make any necessary referral to a tax professional.

Remember, you never get a second chance to make a good first impression, so dress appropriately and take care of your physical well being and health because your health and emotional state can affect your productivity.

CLASS DISCUSSION TOPICS

1. Describe and evaluate your local market. Is it stratified? Are there many layers? If so, how?

2. What are your goals? Describe your top long-, intermediate-, and short-term goals. Do they complement each other in any way?

3. Take a day from your daily planner and evaluate it for effectiveness. Were all of the *A time* activities completed? If not, why?

4. What steps do you need to take to become computer-literate about the necessary real estate programs that you will need to know?

5. Discuss the proper use of cell phones when you are with a client or in a group setting.

6. Whom do you actually represent: the client, the broker, or the customer? Why? Who is the "agent"?

CHAPTER 1 QUIZ

1. The real estate market could best be described as being
   A. perfect
   B. not influenced by emotion
   C. uninfluenced by external factors
   D. stratified

2. Product differentiation means
   A. the difference between a mobile home and a manufactured home
   B. that similar homes can be entirely different because of amenities, location, and condition
   C. stick-built homes are different from prefab homes
   D. none of the above

3. When interest rates are high, a seller can enhance the value of her home by
   A. seeking only an all-cash sale
   B. painting the exterior of the home
   C. offering low-cost seller financing
   D. none of the above

4. A salesperson's use of the MLS
   A. expands her knowledge of the local marketplace
   B. allows a more accurate assessment of a given property's true market value
   C. allows the licensee's customer to make a more informed buying decision
   D. all of the above

5. Salespersons sometime work in teams for all of the reasons *except*

    A. more members mean better availability of someone to meet buyers' and sellers' needs

    B. better cash flow because of a greater likelihood that someone on the team is selling something every month

    C. having fewer people available to help in an area where help is needed

    D. better utilization of each team member's time

6. Successful real estate teams

    A. put the partnership agreement in writing

    B. make the term of the partnership for a relatively short, finite time period, unless extended by mutual consent

    C. clearly set out the duties and responsibilities of each member of the team

    D. all of the above

7. All of the following can affect your attitude, except

    A. being around negative agents in your office

    B. a strong belief in yourself

    C. listening to motivational tapes and CDs

    D. the number of licensees in your office

8. Which of the following is not an exact goal?

    A. I will make personal visits to four For Sale by Owners on Tuesday.

    B. I will send a mailing to my entire farm area on Friday of next week.

    C. I will have lunch with a successful licensee in my office this week.

    D. I will start to telephone prospect soon.

9. To be effective, goals should be

    A. specific

    B. attainable

    C. in writing and visible to you

    D. all of the above

10. When planning each day, you should

    A. not go to bed at night until your next day is planned and in writing in your appointment book

    B. prioritize your activities to maximize the time spent with decision makers, or *A time*

    C. minimize the amount of *D time* activities

    D. all of the above

Chapter

2

Choosing the Right Broker

STUDENT LEARNING OUTCOMES

Upon completion of this chapter, the student will be able to:

- Identify the requirements for an independent contractor as defined by the Internal Revenue Code.
- Compare the job descriptions for a variety of real estate specialties.
- Recognize desirable attributes of an employing broker.
- Analyze and interpret the broker/salesperson contract.
- Recognize three real estate advanced designations.

2.1 GENERAL BROKERAGE

Most real estate professionals represent people who are either buying or selling a home. They may represent either the buyers only or the sellers only, which is called **single agency**. With written consent from both parties, they may represent both the buyers and the sellers at the same time, which is called **dual agency**. The job description of a real estate professional is twofold. She may spend a great deal of time obtaining listings, and through advertising, Open House, and other means, seeking buyers for those properties. The licensee may also seek to meet and represent buyers in their property purchases. In short, the job is one of continuous "lead generation." The licensee must generate a list of potential sellers and buyers of real estate who may need the services of a knowledgeable professional. You will learn how lead generation has largely shifted away from activities such as Open House, cold calling, and "floor time" to maintaining a presence on many different Internet sites such as **Facebook**, **Twitter**, and **YouTube**.

Real estate brokers and salespersons can expand their efforts on behalf of buyers and sellers through the use of a regional or state-wide Multiple Listing System (MLS). The MLS exists so that brokers can share their listings with each other. This greatly expands the number of properties available to any given licensee. It also gives sellers exposure to a larger group of potential buyers and gives buyers a much larger selection of homes from which to choose. Entry of a property into the MLS constitutes the publication of an offer of compensation to all members of the respective MLS and to members of nearby MLS associations that may have reciprocal agreements of cooperation.

There are many other types of real estate activities for brokers or licensees, including, but not limited to:

- *Residential income property* – Brokers and salespersons often choose this type of multifamily housing as a secondary brokerage activity, right behind their home sales activity. Proper training in appraisal techniques, government regulations, and Internal Revenue Code Section 1031, which deals with tax-deferred exchanges of investment property, is a *must* before getting involved in this type of brokerage. You should also have a basic knowledge of property management issues.

- *Commercial property* – Commercial brokers and salespeople tend to specialize in this area because of an interest in, and thorough knowledge of, the needs and demands of commercial buyers. They often specialize in only one type of commercial sales such as retail shopping centers, office buildings, and mini-storage developments. Like residential property, a high degree of technical knowledge and expertise is required to function effectively in any of these specialized areas, especially commercial real estate sales.

- *Industrial property* – This highly specialized market involves the acquisition, sale, or exchange of factories, warehouses, research and development parks, and manufacturing plants. While sales are not abundant, the high prices paid for such real estate generates large commissions and fees. Industrial property buyers are usually owner/users who will use the facilities they purchase in the operation of their business and not just as an investment.

- *Manufactured home parks (previously known as mobile home parks)* – These so-called *parks* contain spaces that are rented to either owners of mobile homes, now called manufactured homes, or park owners who buy manufactured homes, install them on the pads, and rent both the home and the pad to the public. Real estate professionals may solicit buyers and sellers for manufactured homes that have been purchased by a user

and registered for a year or more, or are already in place on an existing pad or plot of land, but they may not sell new manufactured homes. Selling a new one requires a license from the Department of Housing and Community Development. As housing costs increase, manufactured homes fill an ever-growing need for low-cost housing.

- *Land and farm brokerage* – This specialty requires a reasonable knowledge of farming, zoning, crop rotation, and water rights. Many, if not most, brokers and sales licensees who specialize in this type of property cover a very wide territory and often work with investors and/or developers.

- *Lot sales* – Many licensees represent builders or subdividers in the sale of lots to the public. Some lots are held for investment and appreciation, whereas others are purchased by builders to create new residential subdivisions. Many real estate brokerage firms deal in the sale of lots and land of all sizes. In California, large parcels of vacant land are becoming scarce, especially in or near the coastal areas and near the major coastal cities.

- *Site sales* – This specialty often involves an employer/employee relationship with the builder or developer. Licensees work out of an on-site sales trailers or model homes that have been converted into sales offices. Generally not involved in listing property on behalf of sellers, these salespersons show lots and "spec" homes to potential buyers and write purchase contracts. This type of position often calls for a "draw," a monetary allowance paid to the site sales licensee by the builder or developer as an advance against future commissions earned from new home sales.

- *Auction sales* – A number of brokerage firms specialize only in auction sales, which are being used to sell all types of real estate. Auction sales have become much more in demand due to the recent increase in the number of *short sales* and *foreclosures*.

- *Property management* – Covered in detail in Chapter 16, property management firms often tend to specialize in only one type of property, such as retail shopping centers, apartment complexes, mini-storage facilities, office buildings, and resort properties.

- *Licensees specializing in leasing* – Although many property management firms have leasing specialists on staff, they are not necessarily property managers. Each licensee has her own specialized knowledge. Leasing fees are usually a percentage of the gross rental income received per the lease agreement. Like commercial brokerage and property management, there are also subspecialties such as office, retail, or medical within the leasing field.

- *Loan brokerage* – Loan brokers perform a function that is quite similar to real estate brokers; they find investors with money and match them up with people who need real estate financing. Unlike mortgage bankers, who loan their own funds as well as investors' funds, mortgage brokers do not loan their own money; they simply act as a "matchmaking" service. (Note: In August 2008, congress passed the Housing and Economic Recovery Act, HR 3221 bill covering, among many other things, a national licensing and regulatory program for mortgage loan originators [MLO] called the Secure and Fair Enforcement for Mortgage Licensing Act of 2008 or SAFE Act. This legislation will affect all loan originators, including real estate licensees arranging seller financing or other loans. See Chapter 11.)
- *Appraisal* – Since the mid-1980s, an appraiser must be certified by the state that she works in and she must acquire a license in that state. A large number of former real estate licensees are now certified appraisers.

2.2 CHOOSING THE RIGHT BROKER

Your success as a real estate professional greatly depends your ability to choose the right broker. Although the first offer of employment may be the best, it may also not be the right move for you. Making the right choice can help prevent wasting a great deal of time spent in a nonlearning environment that can result in becoming cynical about your new career, even to the point of leaving the real estate business.

When you consider the fact that over 50 percent of new licensees leave the business before the end of the first year and that over 87 percent leave before the end of the third year, you can see just how important your choice of broker can be. If you do not want to be an "attrition statistic," then you must pick your broker with great care!

Another major contributing factor to the high failure rate among real estate professionals is a lack of training. The real estate brokerage business, like most others, has a group of success patterns that you will need to learn.

Too often a new licensee is given a set of business cards and a desk, some rudimentary training (and maybe not), and told to observe the experienced and successful licensees. At times they are given basic tasks to perform such as telephone solicitation, or equally onerous, knocking on doors. These assignments are often given without training, supervision, or feedback. These are activities

rife with the chance for significant fines for violation of the "Do Not Call" statutes or, in rare cases, physical assault. Many new licensees are enticed by the offer of very high commission splits from these types of brokerage firms and they do not yet understand that 80 or 100 percent of nothing is nothing.

Many firms have formal training schools that all new licensees are required to attend. Some have **mentor** programs whereby the new licensee is assigned to a knowledgeable, experienced salesperson for the earlier of six months, three transactions, or some other criteria. This is a better way to enter the real estate brokerage business as the licensee shadows someone attending to the day-to-day tasks of prospecting, presenting offers, and so on. By closely following a successful salesperson, you will truly and comfortably learn your craft while in a learn-by-doing environment. Experienced licensees will also be there for you when you have questions.

The amount of training varies widely from company to company. While some companies have almost no training, some have mentors, sales meetings, audio and video training, books, and CDs; some conduct role-playing exercises; and some have formal training schools.

During the first few months in the real estate business, there simply is no substitute for training, and lots of it. When you interview brokers, ask about their training programs, their training library, and their availability when you have questions. You will also want to know the availability and accessibility of the broker or sales manager.

Ask if the firm has any formal type of continuing education or skill enhancement, including gaining an Internet presence, and if there will be an administrative staff assistant to answer telephone calls and help with files and listings. Be an active participant in your interviews. Before your first interview, reread this section and write down your personal list of questions that are important to you and your success, then get answers to each question from the brokers you interview.

Often overlooked by some new licensees is the dynamism of the broker under consideration. Does the broker/manager show signs of a true leader or is she passive and subdued? The broker who demonstrates good leadership talents during an interview is very often the type of person who is always thinking of ways to vault her office one step ahead of the competition and always seems prepared for every shift in the marketplace. If you see these traits, ask questions that can further expose the broker's style of leadership.

You may wish to ask for references from the firm's current sales staff, as well as the high, low, and average earnings of the existing licensees. Find out all you can about the existing sales and administrative staff to determine the type of environment, which must be positive. If you affiliate with a broker whose sales staff is mediocre to poor, you will feel the negative effects of it. A brokerage firm with good management, a supportive administrative staff, and good initial and ongoing training will greatly enhance your chances for success.

Most licensees immediately affiliate with a broker who specializes almost exclusively in residential real estate simply because the majority of real estate sales are residential. You may, however, be drawn toward commercial real estate, in which case you need to be very careful. Although the commissions in commercial real estate can be very large, it can often take more than a year to earn any money and the chances of getting short of money and becoming discouraged are very high unless you have a working (and understanding) spouse, significant savings, or other means of paying your living expenses for a protracted time.

Even if you want a career in commercial real estate, it is still best to become experienced in residential real estate first. Get familiar with working with clients and customers and how to conduct an escrow. If you still want to transfer to commercial real estate, you will have the basic skills in place to give you a better chance of success at your new endeavor.

If you are already an experienced real estate professional, you have a different set of issues to consider. You will be more concerned about **commission splits**, **ongoing training**, and the company's Internet presence. Most firms today have more than one commission split to choose from. Often referred to as a graduated split, the percentage of the total commission received by the broker is paid to you in ever-larger percentages as your annual earnings increase. Many brokers also have some form of **100 percent commission plan**. Licensees working under this plan will likely be at a lower commission split, usually in the range of 50 to 60 percent until they reach a threshold earnings level. At that time they receive 100 percent of the commission received by the broker in each transaction that they are involved in, minus some type of transaction fee for the balance of their fiscal year, at which time it would start over. These types of commission splits came into being as a way for real estate brokerage firms that had conventional commission splits, as noted previously, to compete with the 100 percent commission brokers.

Under the 100 percent type of commission split program, the sales associate actually pays the broker to belong to the office. The associate also pays a "broker supervision fee" and pays for all forms and supplies that she uses plus a pro rata share of the cost to run the office. In return, she is paid 100 percent of the commission earned from each transaction. This type of firm is usually not a good idea for a new licensee because the expenses start right away. It usually takes some time to start generating commission income.

There are also offices that pay a new licensee 80 or 90 percent of the commission right from the start, while only charging a small monthly fee to affiliate with the office. These firms generally have many licensees, minimal broker supervision or mentor availability, and a modest amount of company-paid advertising or other support for licensees. These firms tend to take on a large number of part-time licensees as well. As a new licensee, you need as much support and training as you can get. Don't be lured by a high commission split. A well-run, active firm with lots of training and support is the surest place to gain the experience that you need while developing your client base and educating yourself.

Ongoing education and training may also be obtained through your local real estate association, the **California Association of REALTORS®**, the **National Association of REALTORS®**, and national speaker's bureaus. Many large, multioffice companies provide regular training seminars, the majority of which offer continuing education credits toward your real estate license renewal. The Brokerage Firm Comparison chart shown in Figure 2.1 may be helpful in evaluating brokerage firms during your hiring interviews.

What Should the New Licensee Look for in a Brokerage Firm?

- A large proportion of successful licensees.
- Longevity of salespeople.
- A good supply of various training materials for your use.
- A strong Internet presence.
- Management and mentors who are available to help you and truly interested in your success.
- Compatibility with and proper support for the type of real estate brokerage that you wish to pursue.
- An office where you feel welcome and secure. If you are not comfortable, it will show up in your attitude and your sales.

FIGURE 2.1   Brokerage Firm Comparison Chart

Type of Real Estate Agency

1. _____
2. _____
3. _____

Broker-provided benefits	Broker 1	Broker 2	Broker 3
1. New licensee training program	_____	_____	_____
2. Ongoing training program	_____	_____	_____
3. Mentor system	_____	_____	_____
4. Voice mail	_____	_____	_____
5. E-mail	_____	_____	_____
6. Fax machine	_____	_____	_____
7. Computer/MLS training	_____	_____	_____
8. MLS access	_____	_____	_____
9. Company/office website	_____	_____	_____
10. Advertising program	_____	_____	_____
11. Weekly meeting/property tour	_____	_____	_____
12. Availability of forms/stationery	_____	_____	_____
13. Open House availability	_____	_____	_____
14. Open House signs/flags	_____	_____	_____
15. Toll-free number	_____	_____	_____
16. Floor time offered/required	_____	_____	_____
17. Start-up expenses	_____	_____	_____
18. Ongoing expenses	_____	_____	_____
19. Reserved geographic areas	_____	_____	_____
20. Success of current sales staff	_____	_____	_____
21. Selling versus nonselling broker	_____	_____	_____
22. Any part-time licensees?	_____	_____	_____
23. Strong Internet presence	_____	_____	_____

2.3 BROKER/SALESPERSON RELATIONSHIPS

It is mandatory that an employing broker have a written contract with her licensees. Although some real estate professionals are hired as salaried employees, it is not very common. Most licensees are hired as independent contractors (Figure 2.2).

Despite the nature of the independent contractor agreement, salespersons and associate brokers (brokers working for other brokers) are considered **employees** of the employing broker by the state of California and not **independent contractors** because Section 10177(h) of the Business and Professions Code requires that brokers supervise their salespeople. The ability to supervise salespeople under

FIGURE 2.2 Independent Contractor Agreement

CALIFORNIA ASSOCIATION OF REALTORS®

INDEPENDENT CONTRACTOR AGREEMENT
(Between Broker and Associate-Licensee)
(C.A.R. Form ICA, Revised 4/09)

This Agreement, dated _____, is made between _____
_____ ("Broker") and
_____ ("Associate-Licensee").
In consideration of the covenants and representations contained in this Agreement, Broker and Associate-Licensee agree as follows:

1. BROKER: Broker represents that Broker is duly licensed as a real estate broker by the State of California, ☐ doing business as
_____ (firm name), ☐ a sole proprietorship, ☐ a partnership, or ☐ a corporation.
Broker is a member of the _____
Association(s) of REALTORS®, and a subscriber to the _____
Multiple Listing Service(s). Broker shall keep Broker's license current during the term of this Agreement.

2. ASSOCIATE-LICENSEE: Associate-Licensee represents that: **(i)** he/she is duly licensed by the State of California as a ☐ real estate broker, ☐ real estate salesperson, and **(ii)** he/she has not used any other names within the past five years, except
_____. Associate-Licensee shall keep his/her license current during the term of this Agreement, including satisfying all applicable continuing education and provisional license requirements.

3. INDEPENDENT CONTRACTOR RELATIONSHIP:
   A. Broker and Associate-Licensee intend that, to the maximum extent permissible by law: **(i)** This Agreement does not constitute an employment agreement by either party; **(ii)** Broker and Associate-Licensee are independent contracting parties with respect to all services rendered under this Agreement; and **(iii)** This Agreement shall not be construed as a partnership.
   B. Broker shall not: **(i)** restrict Associate-Licensee's activities to particular geographical areas, or **(ii)** dictate Associate-Licensee's activities with regard to hours, leads, open houses, opportunity or floor time, production, prospects, sales meetings, schedule, inventory, time off, vacation, or similar activities, except to the extent required by law.
   C. Associate-Licensee shall not be required to accept an assignment by Broker to service any particular current or prospective listing or parties.
   D. Except as required by law: **(i)** Associate-Licensee retains sole and absolute discretion and judgment in the methods, techniques, and procedures to be used in soliciting and obtaining listings, sales, exchanges, leases, rentals, or other transactions, and in carrying out Associate-Licensee's selling and soliciting activities; **(ii)** Associate-Licensee is under the control of Broker as to the results of Associate-Licensee's work only, and not as to the means by which those results are accomplished; **(iii)** Associate-Licensee has no authority to bind Broker by any promise or representation; and **(iv)** Broker shall not be liable for any obligation or liability incurred by Associate-Licensee.
   E. Associate-Licensee's only remuneration shall be the compensation specified in paragraph 8.
   F. Associate-Licensee who only performs as a real estate sales agent, shall not be treated as an employee for state and federal tax purposes. However, an Associate-Licencee who performs loan activity shall be treated as an employee for state and federal tax purposes unless the activity satisfies the legal requirements to establish an independent contractor relationship.
   G. The fact the Broker may carry workers' compensation insurance for Broker's own benefit and for the mutual benefit of Broker and licensees associated with Broker, including Associate-Licensee, shall not create an inference of employment.
   (Workers' Compensation Advisory: Even though Associate-Licensees may be treated as independent contractors for tax and other purposes, the California Labor and Workforce Development Agency considers them to be employees for workers' compensation purposes. According to that Agency: **(i)** Broker must obtain workers' compensation insurance for Associate-Licensees and **(ii)** Broker, not Associate-Licensees, must bear the cost of workers' compensation insurance. Penalties for failure to carry workers' compensation include, among others, the issuance of stop-work orders and fines of up to $1,000 per agent, not to exceed $100,000 per company.)

4. LICENSED ACTIVITY: All listings of property, and all agreements, acts or actions for performance of licensed acts, which are taken or performed in connection with this Agreement, shall be taken and performed in the name of Broker. Associate-Licensee agrees to and does hereby contribute all right and title to such listings to Broker for the benefit and use of Broker, Associate-Licensee, and other licensees associated with Broker. Broker shall make available to Associate-Licensee, equally with other licensees associated with Broker, all current listings in Broker's office, except any listing which Broker may choose to place in the exclusive servicing of Associate-Licensee or one or more other specific licensees associated with Broker. Associate-Licensee shall provide and pay for all professional licenses, supplies, services, and other items required in connection with Associate-Licensee's activities under this Agreement, or any listing or transaction, without reimbursement from Broker except as required by law. Associate-Licensee shall work diligently and with his/her best efforts to: **(i)** sell, exchange, lease, or rent properties listed with Broker or other cooperating Brokers; **(ii)** solicit additional listings, clients, and customers; and **(iii)** otherwise promote the business of serving the public in real estate transactions to the end that Broker and Associate-Licensee may derive the greatest benefit possible, in accordance with law. Associate-Licensee shall not commit any unlawful act under federal, state or local law or regulation while conducting licensed activity. Associate-Licensee shall at all times be familiar, and comply, with all applicable federal, state and local laws, including, but not limited to, anti-discrimination laws and restrictions against the giving or accepting a fee, or other thing of value, for the referral of business to title companies, escrow companies, home inspection companies, pest control companies and other settlement service providers pursuant to the California Business and Professions Code and the Real Estate Settlement Procedures Acts (RESPA). Broker shall make available for Associate-Licensee's use, along with other licensees associated with Broker, the facilities of the real estate office operated by Broker at _____
and the facilities of any other office locations made available by Broker pursuant to this Agreement.

ICA REVISED 4/09 (PAGE 1 OF 3)

Broker's Initials (_____)(_____)
Associate-Licensee's Initials (_____)(_____)

Reviewed by _____ Date _____

EQUAL HOUSING OPPORTUNITY

INDEPENDENT CONTRACTOR AGREEMENT (ICA PAGE 1 OF 3)

FIGURE 2.2 *(Continued)*

5. **PROPRIETARY INFORMATION AND FILES:** **(A)** All files and documents pertaining to listings, leads and transactions are the property of Broker and shall be delivered to Broker by Associate-Licensee immediately upon request or termination of this Agreement. **(B)** Associate- Licensee acknowledges that Broker's method of conducting business is a protected trade secret. **(C)** Associate-Licensee shall not use to his/her own advantage, or the advantage of any other person, business, or entity, except as specifically agreed in writing, either during Associate-Licensee's association with Broker, or thereafter, any information gained for or from the business, or files of Broker.

6. **SUPERVISION:** Associate-Licensee, within 24 hours (or ☐ _____) after preparing, signing, or receiving same, shall submit to Broker, or Broker's designated licensee: **(i)** all documents which may have a material effect upon the rights and duties of principals in a transaction, **(ii)** any documents or other items connected with a transaction pursuant to this Agreement in the possession of or available to Associate-Licensee; and **(iii)** all documents associated with any real estate transaction in which Associate-Licensee is a principal.

7. **TRUST FUNDS:** All trust funds shall be handled in compliance with the Business and Professions Code, and other applicable laws.

8. **COMPENSATION:**

    A. TO BROKER: Compensation shall be charged to parties who enter into listing or other agreements for services requiring a real estate license:

        ☐ as shown in "Exhibit A" attached, which is incorporated as a part of this Agreement by reference, or

        ☐ as follows: _____

        _____

        Any deviation which is not approved in writing in advance by Broker, shall be: **(1)** deducted from Associate-Licensee's compensation, if lower than the amount or rate approved above; and, **(2)** subject to Broker approval, if higher than the amount approved above. Any permanent change in commission schedule shall be disseminated by Broker to Associate-Licensee.

    B. TO ASSOCIATE-LICENSEE: Associate-Licensee shall receive a share of compensation actually collected by Broker, on listings or other agreements for services requiring a real estate license, which are solicited and obtained by Associate-Licensee, and on transactions of which Associate-Licensee's activities are the procuring cause, as follows:

        ☐ as shown in "Exhibit B" attached, which is incorporated as a part of this Agreement by reference, or

        ☐ other: _____

        _____

    C. PARTNERS, TEAMS, AND AGREEMENTS WITH OTHER ASSOCIATE-LICENSEES IN OFFICE: If Associate-Licensee and one or more other Associate-Licensees affiliated with Broker participate on the same side (either listing or selling) of a transaction, the commission allocated to their combined activities shall be divided by Broker and paid to them according to their written agreement. Broker shall have the right to withhold total compensation if there is a dispute between associate-licensees, or if there is no written agreement, or if no written agreement has been provided to Broker.

    D. EXPENSES AND OFFSETS: If Broker elects to advance funds to pay expenses or liabilities of Associate-Licensee, or for an advance payment of, or draw upon, future compensation, Broker may deduct the full amount advanced from compensation payable to Associate-Licensee on any transaction without notice. If Associate-Licensee's compensation is subject to a lien, garnishment or other restriction on payment, Broker shall charge Associate-Licensee a fee for complying with such restriction.

    E. PAYMENT: **(i)** All compensation collected by Broker and due to Associate-Licensee shall be paid to Associate-Licensee, after deduction of expenses and offsets, immediately or as soon thereafter as practicable, except as otherwise provided in this Agreement, or a separate written agreement between Broker and Associate-Licensee. **(ii)** Compensation shall not be paid to Associate-Licensee until both the transaction and file are complete. **(iii)** Broker is under no obligation to pursue collection of compensation from any person or entity responsible for payment. Associate-Licensee does not have the independent right to pursue collection of compensation for activities which require a real estate license which were done in the name of Broker. **(iv)** Expenses which are incurred in the attempt to collect compensation shall be paid by Broker and Associate-Licensee in the same proportion as set forth for the division of compensation (paragraph 8(B)). **(v)** If there is a known or pending claim against Broker or Associate-Licensee on transactions for which Associate-Licensee has not yet been paid, Broker may withhold from compensation due Associate-Licensee on that transaction amounts for which Associate-Licensee could be responsible under paragraph 14, until such claim is resolved. **(vi)** Associate-Licensee shall not be entitled to any advance payment from Broker upon future compensation.

    F. UPON OR AFTER TERMINATION: If this Agreement is terminated while Associate-Licensee has listings or pending transactions that require further work normally rendered by Associate-Licensee, Broker shall make arrangements with another associate-licensee to perform the required work, or Broker shall perform the work him/herself. The licensee performing the work shall be reasonably compensated for completing work on those listings or transactions, and such reasonable compensation shall be deducted from Associate-Licensee's share of compensation. Except for such offset, Associate-Licensee shall receive the compensation due as specified above.

9. **TERMINATION OF RELATIONSHIP:** Broker or Associate-Licensee may terminate their relationship under this Agreement at any time, with or without cause. After termination, Associate-Licensee shall not solicit: **(i)** prospective or existing clients or customers based upon company- generated leads obtained during the time Associate-Licensee was affiliated with Broker; **(ii)** any principal with existing contractual obligations to Broker; or **(iii)** any principal with a contractual transactional obligation for which Broker is entitled to be compensated. Even after termination, this Agreement shall govern all disputes and claims between Broker and Associate-Licensee connected with their relationship under this Agreement, including obligations and liabilities arising from existing and completed listings, transactions, and services.

Broker's Initials   (_____)(_____)
Associate-Licensee's Initials (_____)(_____)

ICA REVISED 4/09 (PAGE 2 OF 3)

Reviewed by _____ Date _____

EQUAL HOUSING OPPORTUNITY

INDEPENDENT CONTRACTOR AGREEMENT (ICA PAGE 2 OF 3)

FIGURE 2.2 *(Continued)*

10. DISPUTE RESOLUTION:
    A. Mediation: Mediation is recommended as a method of resolving disputes arising out of this Agreement between Broker and Associate-LIcensee.
    B. Arbitration: All disputes or claims between Associate-Licensee and other licensee(s) associated with Broker, or between Associate-Licensee and Broker, arising from or connected in any way with this Agreement, which cannot be adjusted between the parties involved, shall be submitted to the Association of REALTORS® of which all such disputing parties are members for arbitration pursuant to the provisions of its Bylaws, as may be amended from time to time, which are incorporated as a part of this Agreement by reference. If the Bylaws of the Association do not cover arbitration of the dispute, or if the Association declines jurisdiction over the dispute, then arbitration shall be pursuant to the rules of California law. The Federal Arbitration Act, Title 9, U.S. Code, Section 1, et seq., shall govern this Agreement.

11. AUTOMOBILE: Associate-Licensee shall maintain automobile insurance coverage for liability and property damage in the following amounts $_____ /$_____. Broker shall be named as an additional insured party on Associate-Licensee's policies. A copy of the endorsement showing Broker as an additional insured shall be provided to Broker.

12. PERSONAL ASSISTANTS: Associate-Licensee may make use of a personal assistant, provided the following requirements are satisfied. Associate-Licensee shall have a written agreement with the personal assistant which establishes the terms and responsibilities of the parties to the employment agreement, including, but not limited to, compensation, supervision and compliance with applicable law. The agreement shall be subject to Broker's review and approval. Unless otherwise agreed, if the personal assistant has a real estate license, that license must be provided to the Broker. Both Associate-Licensee and personal assistant must sign any agreement that Broker has established for such purposes.

13. OFFICE POLICY MANUAL: If Broker's office policy manual, now or as modified in the future, conflicts with or differs from the terms of this Agreement, the terms of the office policy manual shall govern the relationship between Broker and Associate-Licensee.

14. INDEMNITY AND HOLD HARMLESS; NOTICE OF CLAIMS: A. Regarding any action taken or omitted by Associate-Licensee, or others working through, or on behalf of Associate-Licensee in connection with services rendered or to be rendered pursuant to this Agreement: (i) Associate-Licensee agrees to indemnify, defend and hold Broker harmless from all claims, disputes, litigation, judgments, awards, costs and attorney's fees, arising therefrom and (ii) Associate-Licensee shall immediately notify Broker if Associate-Licensee is served with or becomes aware of a lawsuit or claim regarding any such action. **B.** Any such claims or costs payable pursuant to this Agreement, are due as follows:
    ☐ Paid in full by Associate-Licensee, who hereby agrees to indemnify and hold harmless Broker for all such sums, or
    ☐ In the same ratio as the compensation split as it existed at the time the compensation was earned by Associate-Licensee
    ☐ Other: _____
_____

Payment from Associate-Licensee is due at the time Broker makes such payment and can be offset from any compensation due Associate-Licensee as above. Broker retains the authority to settle claims or disputes, whether or not Associate-Licensee consents to such settlement.

15. ADDITIONAL PROVISIONS: _____
_____

16. DEFINITIONS: As used in this Agreement, the following terms have the meanings indicated:
    (A) "Listing" means an agreement with a property owner or other party to locate a buyer, exchange party, lessee, or other party to a transaction involving real property, a mobile home, or other property or transaction which may be brokered by a real estate licensee, or an agreement with a party to locate or negotiate for any such property or transaction.
    (B) "Compensation" means compensation for acts requiring a real estate license, regardless of whether calculated as a percentage of transaction price, flat fee, hourly rate, or in any other manner.
    (C) "Transaction" means a sale, exchange, lease, or rental of real property, a business opportunity, or a manufactured home, which may lawfully be brokered by a real estate licensee.

17. ATTORNEY FEES: In any action, proceeding, or arbitration between Broker and Associate-Licensee arising from or related to this Agreement, the prevailing Broker or Associate-Licensee shall be entitled to reasonable attorney fees and costs.

18. ENTIRE AGREEMENT: All prior agreements between the parties concerning their relationship as Broker and Associate-Licensee are incorporated in this Agreement, which constitutes the entire contract. Its terms are intended by the parties as a final and complete expression of their agreement with respect to its subject matter, and may not be contradicted by evidence of any prior agreement or contemporaneous oral agreement. This Agreement may not be amended, modified, altered, or changed except by a further agreement in writing executed by Broker and Associate-Licensee.

Broker:

(Brokerage firm name)

By _____

Its Broker/Office manager (circle one)

(Print name)

(Address)

(City, State, Zip)

(Telephone)   (Fax)

Associate-Licensee:

(Signature)

(Print name)

(Address)

(City, State, Zip)

(Telephone)   (Fax)

Published and Distributed by:
REAL ESTATE BUSINESS SERVICES, INC.
a subsidiary of the California Association of REALTORS®
525 South Virgil Avenue, Los Angeles, California 90020

R E B S | I N C

ICA REVISED 4/09 (PAGE 3 OF 3)

Reviewed by _____ Date _____

INDEPENDENT CONTRACTOR AGREEMENT (ICA PAGE 3 OF 3)

Source: Reprinted with permission of California Association of REALTORS®.

an independent contractor agreement is recognized as being untenable. Almost all real estate professionals work under an independent contractor agreement with their employing broker. According to the *Real Estate Reference Book,* "An independent contractor is one, who in rendering services, exercises an independent employment or occupation and is responsible to the employer only as to the results of her work." This means that an independent contractor is responsible only to her employing broker for the results of the work carried out and is not under the direction or control of an employer. A real estate broker's employer could be a buyer, seller, tenant, or lessee.

The Internal Revenue Service (IRS) provides guidelines that allow licensees to qualify as independent contractors for tax purposes if the following three criteria are met:

• The salesperson is licensed as a real estate broker or salesperson.
• Financial reimbursement to the salesperson is based solely on sales, not on hours worked.
• There is a written contract that states that the salesperson shall be treated as an independent contractor for tax purposes.

If the above criteria are met, employing brokers are not required to contribute to their licensee's Social Security accounts, which currently saves the employing broker about 7.5 percent of the salesperson's earnings, nor are they required to withhold income taxes from a salespersons' earnings. All of the salespersons are required to file their own estimated tax returns and pay the employer and employee portions of the Social Security tax.

Despite a contract to the contrary, if the broker actually does exercise a great deal of control over a salesperson, that person might be considered an employee for tax purposes anyway. Figure 2.3 will help you to understand the factors indicating control.

The fact that a real estate salesperson is treated as an independent contractor by the IRS does not relieve the employing broker from responsibility for the wrongful acts of the salesperson while acting on behalf of the broker. Because of this potential liability, some employing brokers require the licensees who work for them to carry a certain level of automobile insurance and to name the employing broker as a name insured under the policy. In these litigious times, it has also become the norm for nearly all employing brokers to require that the licensees working in their office participate in a malpractice insurance policy more commonly known as an Errors and Omissions (E & O) insurance policy. This policy offers protection for both the employing broker and the licensee. It should be noted that "E & O" insurance policies *do not* cover acts of fraud or malfeasance.

FIGURE 2.3 Employee or Independent Contractor Checklist for IRS Guidelines

Control Considerations	Employee	Independent Contractor
Note: The factors listed below are only possible indicators of a worker's status. Each case is determined individually.		
Must employer instructions be complied with about when, where, and how work is to be performed?	Yes	No
Is training mandated by the employer?	Yes	No
Does the worker hire, supervise, and pay others to perform work for which she is responsible?	No	Yes
Are the worker's hours set by the employer?	Yes	No
Must the work be performed on the employer's property?	Yes	No
Must tasks be performed on the employer's property?	Yes	No
Must tasks be performed in a certain order set by the employer?	Yes	No
Are regular reports required of the worker?	Yes	No
Is the worker paid hourly, weekly, or monthly?	Yes	No
Is payment for work performed in a lump sum?	No	Yes
Are the worker's business and travel expenses paid by the employer?	Yes	No
Does the worker rent her own office or work space?	No	Yes
Does the worker make her services available to the general public?	No	Yes
Does the worker have the right to quit the job at any time, whether or not all tasks are complete?	Yes	No
Are the tools and materials required for the job furnished by the employer?	Yes	No
Will the worker realize a profit or loss as a result of her services?	No	Yes
Does the individual work for more than one firm at a time?	No	Yes
Does the employer have the right to fire the worker?	Yes	Yes

While unemployment insurance coverage is not required, since real estate professionals as independent contractors are not eligible for any benefits, **workers' compensation insurance** is a requirement and all employing brokers must have a policy in place. The employing broker may not pass this cost for this coverage on to the employee. Also, employing brokers are exempt from minimum wage laws if all of the licensees working for them are paid by commission only.

2.4 CONTINUED AND ADVANCED TRAINING

While your initial training is of paramount importance to a successful start in real estate, you should continually upgrade your real estate knowledge for the balance of your career. Your local association of REALTORS® as well as your local community college can be a real asset in maintaining a high level of professional competence. Both offer a wide variety of courses applicable to enhancing professionalism. The continuing education required by the Department of Real Estate for license renewal every four years should be considered a bare minimum. It has been said that the only thing about real estate that never changes is that it never stops changing. Virtually all of the top real estate professionals in the country are constantly seeking to increase their skills and overall knowledge of the business. You must remember that as real estate professionals, we do not sell real estate; sellers sell real estate and buyers buy it. *We sell time and knowledge* to sellers and buyers so they can make good, intelligent decisions when they sell or buy.

There are many ways to get the education you need on a continuing basis, including the seminars mentioned earlier. Your local community college offers many courses appropriate to enhancing your professional real estate education. The education divisions of the National Association of REALTORS®, the California Association of REALTORS®, and your county or regional association all have books, CDs, DVDs, and tapes, and they all sponsor continuing education courses. On the national level, *REALTOR® Magazine*, published by the National Association of REALTORS®, offers many fine articles that will help you to succeed. Your state and local associations also have similar publications available.

All well-run real estate offices have some continuing training as a regular part of their weekly office meetings. You will learn new ways of doing things all the time. Part of your job will be to evaluate these various new ideas and concepts to see if you would be comfortable using them, and then thoroughly learn each one, so that when the time arises using them will be automatic.

The practice of **role-playing** has been an effective tool used by most successful licensees. New salespersons seem to be reluctant to practice new techniques using this process, but this is a mistake. Shakespeare said it first, *"All the world's a stage, And all the men and women merely players; They have their exits and entrances, And one man in his time plays many parts"* (*As You Like It*, Act I, Scene VII). So you see, role-playing is simply a part of what all of us do every day. Role-playing new ideas will help make using them sound natural and automatic rather than stilted and memorized. If you hear an idea that you like, don't be shy about asking another new or newer licensee in the office if he or she will role-play with you. Your office or company may have a training director who will provide new training and ideas to you and may offer to role-play with you and critique you on how well you are doing. Don't be bashful about asking someone's help with this. You may think you are the only one in the office that a certain idea is new to, but there are surely several other licensees who would like to enhance their newfound skills through role-playing.

The successful licensees in your office are a wealth of great ideas and most of them are quite willing to share them with you. If you really want to "learn from the pros," develop a good relationship with a successful licensee in your office and shadow her as much as possible and ask questions. They will be flattered by your attention and you will have obtained a wonderful new mentor. This kind of relationship is especially beneficial during your "formative" months and will accelerate your learning—especially if you have a broker or branch manager who is too busy to give you a lot of individual attention.

Learn about new and different ways to generate leads, hold an Open House, meet and work with For Sale by Owners, handle incoming ad and sign calls during floor time, and consider taking the *Electronic Professional* (ePRO) course offered by the National Association of REALTORS®. You can try each one out for a reasonable amount of time to see how each one fits your particular style and how effective each one is at getting you new business. Also, keep in mind that you should use each new technique as soon as you can so that it is fresh in your mind. The authors highly recommend role-playing with another licensee until you become comfortable with the dialogue. Your delivery will be much more effective than attempting to fumble through it, unrehearsed.

Community colleges often offer real estate courses and business courses on general sales techniques that are applicable to the real estate profession, so be sure to check with them. There are also many private business schools with similar offerings. If you are the stay-at-home type, you might want to look into taking courses via the Internet or courses that are available by correspondence.

As a real estate licensee, you will be required to take a certain number of continuing education classes every four years to renew your license. The important issue here is to start early and take courses that you know will expand your knowledge of real estate and finance. You will be required to take forty-five clock hours, of which fifteen hours are from DRE-approved continuing education courses in ethics, fair housing, agency, trust fund handling, and risk management as well as a minimum of eighteen clock hours of consumer protection courses, and the remaining fifteen hours are in courses related to consumer service or consumer protection. By starting early, you will be able to choose what you really want to learn or learn more about. If you wait until the last minute, like way too many people do, you will be forced to take a three-day "crash course" from one of the license training schools, and your course topics will be mandated in a package deal. Remember, *we sell time and knowledge*, not real estate, so pick your renewal classes early and carefully.

Many national sales trainers offer available courses geared strictly to real estate salespersons. Some of these include excellent, cutting-edge sales techniques and business plans that can really help to boost your sales activity immensely. The best way to find out which ones are the most effective is to ask one or more seasoned licensees in your office, your broker, or branch manager.

Survival Training

Earlier in this book, we talked about the high fallout rate of real estate licensees (50 percent by the end of year one and 87 percent by the end of year three). Far and away, the two biggest reasons for this high attrition rate are a lack of training and the lack of a business plan.

From your first day as a real estate professional, you need to be on a quest for knowledge, customers, and clients, in that order. Your "formal" training period will last from a few days at some companies, to well over a month or two at others. Your training program should continue throughout your entire career. Training of only a few days, without being assigned to a mentor or some other form of guidance by an experienced professional, is an open invitation to failure in most cases.

Whatever the circumstances of your training and ongoing guidance as a new licensee, you should be prepared to spend far more than the average eight-hour day "learning and doing." If available, use your office library or the public library to check out tapes, CDs, or books on real estate sales, or at least sales. Spend some time each day in a learning mode, even after your formal classroom training, and couple it with time spent in "client acquisition mode" during

which you are doing activities that get you in front of For Sale by Owners, or other potential sellers and buyers.

Another critical step in your success is to learn as much as you can as quick as you can about the inventory of properties in your market area. It's important to learn about all of the different neighborhoods as far as current home values are concerned, but there is much more to it than that. You need to know where the shopping centers are and about schools, including how they rate academically. Find out where the different religious facilities are located, and if there are cultural facilities in your area learn as much about them as you can. In this age of two-income families, it will serve you well to know the location of any day-care centers in your market areas for buyers moving into a new area. The internet will help in gathering this information.

Any resource materials available to you are only as good and as effective as you make them. Any number of low-producing real estate salespeople out there have hundreds of dollars worth of tapes and CDs that remain unopened and unused. It takes a real commitment on your part to balance continued learning with doing.

The undisputed best method of internalizing new sales techniques and strategies is to role-play each new one as you learn it. Whether you are on a listing appointment, writing a contract with a buyer, presenting a contract to the sellers, or handling an ad or sign call from an interested party, your ability to put fear behind you and speak naturally and effectively with people depends a great deal on how comfortable you are with what you are talking about and how often you have done it before. Role-playing offers you the opportunity to practice, drill, and rehearse until you reach an effective comfort level with each of the many situations you will encounter.

There are two types of *role-playing*. The first is to role-play with one or more licensees taking turns practicing the skill. This can actually be fun, plus it gives you a chance to hear objections, deal with them effectively, and then get feedback from the others in your group. The second method is simply to visualize yourself in a sales situation (such as presenting an offer to a seller) and then verbalizing what you would say. If you do this in front of a mirror, you will see your facial expressions and body language as well. We would also suggest calling your own voice-mail or your home answering machine and role-play situations so that you can hear your voice as others do over the phone. This can be very enlightening!

The overall effectiveness of your role-playing efforts is greatly enhanced if you follow it with a critique session. Be sure to assess

what you, or another person, if you are in a group, did right, and what needs improvement.

Role-playing helps to alleviate fear. If you are not sure of yourself in any given situation, you will have a fear of failure in the back of your mind. This often shows in your voice inflection and/or your body language or attitude and often appears to other people as a lack of self-confidence. People who are about to make a huge financial decision using your input will sense this and it will put them off. If you have role-played this situation many times, you are far more likely to appear as a self-confident, caring professional, and people will perceive you that way.

2.5 PROFESSIONAL DESIGNATIONS

Little else in the real estate profession synchronizes as well with the premise that what we sell is knowledge as the subject of professional designations. Several designations are available to practitioners, on both the state and the national level.

These designations are earned by taking a course of study and, in many cases, taking a comprehensive examination. Some designations require a minimum number of closed transactions as well.

The most well-known example of a state-level professional designation is the Graduate REALTORS® Institute (GRI) designation. This involves several classes that are often given at state conventions and at the local real estate association level.

On the national level, there are a number of professional designations. Five of the most common are:

- Certified Residential Specialist (CRS)
- Certified Residential Brokerage Manager (CRB)
- Certified Commercial Investment Member (CCIM)
- ePRO (a REALTOR® who has successfully completed the National Association of REALTORS® Technology Certification Program)
- Seniors Real Estate Specialist (SRES)

There are several others that deal with specialized knowledge and expertise in dealing with land specialties, industrial real estate, and appraisal, to name a few.

A recent study by the National Association of REALTORS® found that real estate licensees with professional designations make on average far more money than their counterparts who do not hold some type of professional designation.

Since selling knowledge is our business, and it is, professional designations are your surest path to far better earnings and better client representation. You can find out more about these and other professional designations on the National Association of REALTORS® website (www.realtor.org). You will need your NRDS (*National REALTOR® Database System*) number to gain access to the site.

SUMMARY

Although the majority of real estate licensees are involved with residential property listing and sales activities, other areas of activity include:

- Residential income property
- Commercial property
- Land and farm brokerage
- Subdivision/Lot sales
- Manufactured home sales
- Industrial property
- Auctions
- Property management
- Leasing
- Property auctions
- Appraisal

Real estate professionals are considered employees of brokers by the state of California for almost all purposes, but most work as independent contractors. If the salesperson or associate broker meets the IRS test criteria to be an independent contractor, there is no withholding tax deducted from the salesperson's commission checks, and the responsibility for payment of Social Security taxes belongs to the licensee.

Choosing a broker or brokerage firm is an extremely important decision. The emphasis on training and education should be of paramount importance to the new licensee. Training should consist of classroom study, field training through a mentor, solo or group role-playing, and panel discussions.

Professional designations can be obtained through the state and national real estate associations. On average, licensees with professional designations earn far more money than their noncertified counterparts.

CLASS DISCUSSION TOPICS

1. What area of real estate would you want to specialize in? Are you interested in a particular type of real estate, a geographic area, or both? Why?

2. Describe what you know about the training available at the various real estate firms in your area. Who's one is the best, and why?

3. What are the advantages to the designated broker of having her licensees work as independent contractors?

4. As a group, list the top five characteristics of a successful office. Put them in order of importance.

5. Role-play with another classmate how you would handle an incoming sign call on a property that is already under contract. You act as the duty salesperson and your classmate can be the potential buyer.

6. Have two students role-play an interview between a broker and a new licensee.

CHAPTER 2 QUIZ

1. In what area of real estate are most licensees engaged?
   A. Land sales
   B. Subdivision home sales
   C. Commercial property
   D. Residential property

2. Which two of the following are the most effective aids to the real estate salesperson in representing buyers and sellers?
   A. The Internet
   B. The Multiple Listing Service
   C. Open House
   D. None of the above

3. Which one of the following criteria must be met for the IRS to treat real estate salespersons as independent contractors?
   A. The worker is required to undergo training.
   B. Payment is made only when and if the job is fully completed.
   C. The worker does not make her services available to the public.
   D. The worker's business and travel expenses are paid by the employer.

4. When choosing a broker, a new licensee should be most interested in which of the following offices?
   A. An office that has excellent initial and ongoing training
   B. An office that offers a 100-percent commission plan
   C. An office that has only a couple of successful salespeople
   D. An office that has a very busy selling broker

5. When choosing a broker, a new licensee should
   A. interview several brokers.
   B. speak with several licensees in each office before accepting a position.
   C. use a comparison chart.
   D. All of the above.

6. Which of the following is not true of role-playing?
   A. Role-playing can only be used for interpersonal activities, not telephone techniques.
   B. Role-playing situations are as limitless as our imaginations.
   C. Role-playing can involve more than one person.
   D. Group role-playing with honest critiques after each session are a very effective way to learn.

7. Independent contractors working for an employing broker
   A. must pay their own as well as the employer's part of the Social Security tax.
   B. are excluded from any type of litigation.
   C. are not responsible to the employing broker for their actions.
   D. are not considered employees by the federal government.

8. What is the most effective type of training?
   A. Classroom training
   B. CDs and tapes
   C. Books
   D. Role-playing

9. As real estate professionals, the real product we sell is
   A. time and knowledge, to people who want to buy, sell, or lease real estate.
   B. homes.
   C. all types of real estate.
   D. None of the above.

10. What are the advantages of professional designations?
    A. More knowledge, which leads to greater self-confidence
    B. Greater credibility to your customers and clients
    C. Higher earnings
    D. All of the above

Chapter

3

IMPORTANT PHRASES AND TERMS

1988 Fair Housing
Amendments Act

Americans with
Disabilities Act

Blockbusting

Civil Rights Act
of 1866

Civil Rights Act
of 1870

Civil Rights Act
of 1964

Civil Rights Act
of 1968

Diversity training

Ethics

Fair Employment
and Housing Act

Golden Rule

National
Association of
Real Estate
Brokers

RESPA of 1974

REALTORS® Code
of Ethics

Redlining

Rumford Act

Sexual harassment

Steering

Testers

Thing of value

Unruh Act

Ethics, Fair Housing, and RESPA

STUDENT LEARNING OUTCOMES

Upon completion of this chapter, the student will be able to:

- Differentiate REALTOR® versus real estate licensee.
- Define and discuss acts prohibited by fair housing laws.
- Describe real estate activities permissible under RESPA.
- Compare and contrast referral and finer fees.
- Define and recognize steering, blockbusting, and redlining.

3.1 WHAT IS ETHICS?

The word **ethics** is derived from two Greek words: ethikos, which means *moral*, and ethos, which means *character*. Ethics has nothing to do with what is or is not legal. We have laws that set minimum standards of acceptable behavior and create "legal boundaries" for people in our society to live within. Ethics has to do with standards of moral character. The **Golden Rule**, or, "do unto others as you would have them do unto you," is the keystone of ethical behavior.

If you adhere closely to the tenets of ethical conduct, you will have a far more rewarding career, a far better reputation, and much more repeat and referral business. Plus, you will never have to worry about any action being taken against you by any real estate association for unethical activity.

There is a big difference between being unethical and breaking the law. Ethics precedes the law. If you conduct yourself ethically, you will probably never break the law. Laws change but ethics do not.

For example, in past years, many appraisers were appraising property for the value they were told the client needed, not the

actual value of the properties. As a result, properties were turning over several times very quickly and always for new and higher prices with new bank loans. These appraisals were unfounded and purposely overstated to meet the clients' needs. Although it was not considered illegal to perform such appraisals, it was certainly unethical to breach the trust that was placed in the appraisers by the stockholders of the lending institutions that made the loans, who eventually lost hundreds of millions of dollars. Some bank owners and major investors who used these unethical appraisers to make huge profits eventually went to prison for a number of years.

Simply put, good ethics is good business. It is well documented in the real estate business that nothing spreads as fast as a bad reputation. If you conduct yourself in an ethical manner, your reputation will quickly produce a loyal following of satisfied customers and clients who will become the hallmark of your business. Salespeople who put compensation before service or "doing the deal" before ethical practice soon pay for those choices through:

- a constant struggle to find new clients who don't know their reputation.
- censure from a Professional Standards Ethics Hearing Panel.
- actions of the Department of Real Estate to suspend or revoke their licenses.

3.2 CODES OF ETHICS
REALTORS® Code of Ethics

Although any number of professional organizations, including the American Bar Association, have codes of ethics, the **REALTORS® Code of Ethics** is based on the Golden Rule and by nature acts as an excellent guide to ethical behavior. The word REALTOR® is a registered trademark of the National Association of REALTORS® (NAR) and may only be used by its members. Even real estate licensees who are not REALTORS® are encouraged to read and abide by the Code of Ethics in their dealings with others. Some courts have found the Code of Ethics to be the standard of care expected of a real estate licensee. Although we are including the text of the NAR 2010 Code of Ethics (see Figure 3.1), the reader should be aware that the code is subject to annual revision by NAR. Always refer to the most current annual edition.

Realtists®

Up until the mid-1940s, African Americans were denied the right to join nearly all professional groups or associations. In 1947, a

FIGURE 3.1   2010 NAR Code of Ethics

Code of Ethics and Standards of Practice of the NATIONAL ASSOCIATION OF REALTORS®

Effective January 1, 2010

Where the word REALTORS® is used in this Code and Preamble, it shall be deemed to include REALTOR-ASSOCIATE®s.

While the Code of Ethics establishes obligations that may be higher than those mandated by law, in any instance where the Code of Ethics and the law conflict, the obligations of the law must take precedence.

Preamble

Under all is the land. Upon its wise utilization and widely allocated ownership depend the survival and growth of free institutions and of our civilization. REALTORS® should recognize that the interests of the nation and its citizens require the highest and best use of the land and the widest distribution of land ownership. They require the creation of adequate housing, the building of functioning cities, the development of productive industries and farms, and the preservation of a healthful environment.

Such interests impose obligations beyond those of ordinary commerce. They impose grave social responsibility and a patriotic duty to which REALTORS® should dedicate themselves, and for which they should be diligent in preparing themselves. REALTORS®, therefore, are zealous to maintain and improve the standards of their calling and share with their fellow REALTORS® a common responsibility for its integrity and honor.

In recognition and appreciation of their obligations to clients, customers, the public, and each other, REALTORS® continuously strive to become and remain informed on issues affecting real estate and, as knowledgeable professionals, they willingly share the fruit of their experience and study with others. They identify and take steps, through enforcement of this Code of Ethics and by assisting appropriate regulatory bodies, to eliminate practices which may damage the public or which might discredit or bring dishonor to the real estate profession. REALTORS® having direct personal knowledge of conduct that may violate the Code of Ethics involving misappropriation of client or customer funds or property, willful discrimination, or fraud resulting in substantial economic harm, bring such matters to the attention of the appropriate Board or Association of REALTORS®. *(Amended 1/00)*

Realizing that cooperation with other real estate professionals promotes the best interests of those who utilize their services, REALTORS® urge exclusive representation of clients; do not attempt to gain any unfair advantage over their competitors; and they refrain from making unsolicited comments about other practitioners. In instances where their opinion is sought, or where REALTORS® believe that comment is necessary, their opinion is offered in an objective, professional manner, uninfluenced by any personal motivation or potential advantage or gain.

The term REALTOR® has come to connote competency, fairness, and high integrity resulting from adherence to a lofty ideal of moral conduct in business relations. No inducement of profit and no instruction from clients ever can justify departure from this ideal.

In the interpretation of this obligation, REALTORS® can take no safer guide than that which has been handed down through the centuries, embodied in the Golden Rule, "Whatsoever ye would that others should do to you, do ye even so to them."

Accepting this standard as their own, REALTORS® pledge to observe its spirit in all of their activities whether conducted personally, through associates or others, or via technological means, and to conduct their business in accordance with the tenets set forth below. *(Amended 1/07)*

Duties to Clients and Customers

Article 1

When representing a buyer, seller, landlord, tenant, or other client as an agent, REALTORS® pledge themselves to protect and promote the interests of their client. This obligation to the client is primary, but it does not relieve REALTORS® of their obligation to treat all parties honestly. When serving a buyer, seller, landlord, tenant or other party in a non-agency capacity, REALTORS® remain obligated to treat all parties honestly. *(Amended 1/01)*

- **Standard of Practice 1-1**
  REALTORS®, when acting as principals in a real estate transaction, remain obligated by the duties imposed by the Code of Ethics. *(Amended 1/93)*

- **Standard of Practice 1-2**
  The duties imposed by the Code of Ethics encompass all real estate-related activities and transactions whether conducted in person, electronically, or through any other means.

  The duties the Code of Ethics imposes are applicable whether REALTORS® are acting as agents or in legally recognized non-agency capacities except that any duty imposed exclusively on agents by law or regulation shall not be imposed by this Code of Ethics on REALTORS® acting in non-agency capacities.

  As used in this Code of Ethics, "client" means the person(s) or entity(ies) with whom a REALTOR® or a REALTOR®'s firm has an agency or legally recognized non-agency relationship; "customer" means a party to a real estate transaction who receives information, services, or benefits but has no contractual relationship with the REALTOR® or the REALTOR®'s firm; "prospect" means a purchaser, seller, tenant, or landlord who is not subject to a representation relationship with the REALTOR® or REALTOR®'s firm; "agent" means a real estate licensee (including brokers and sales associates) acting in an agency relationship as defined by state law or regulation; and "broker" means a real estate licensee (including brokers and sales associates) acting as an agent or in a legally recognized non-agency capacity. *(Adopted 1/95, Amended 1/07)*

- **Standard of Practice 1-3**
  REALTORS®, in attempting to secure a listing, shall not deliberately mislead the owner as to market value.

- **Standard of Practice 1-4**
  REALTORS®, when seeking to become a buyer/tenant representative, shall not mislead buyers or tenants as to savings or other benefits that might be realized through use of the REALTOR®'s services. *(Amended 1/93)*

NATIONAL ASSOCIATION OF REALTORS®

The Voice for Real Estate

REALTOR®

Real Strength.
Real Advantages.

FIGURE 3.1 *(Continued)*

- **Standard of Practice 1-5**
REALTORS® may represent the seller/landlord and buyer/tenant in the same transaction only after full disclosure to and with informed consent of both parties. *(Adopted 1/93)*

- **Standard of Practice 1-6**
REALTORS® shall submit offers and counter-offers objectively and as quickly as possible. *(Adopted 1/93, Amended 1/95)*

- **Standard of Practice 1-7**
When acting as listing brokers, REALTORS® shall continue to submit to the seller/landlord all offers and counter-offers until closing or execution of a lease unless the seller/landlord has waived this obligation in writing. REALTORS® shall not be obligated to continue to market the property after an offer has been accepted by the seller/landlord. REALTORS® shall recommend that sellers/landlords obtain the advice of legal counsel prior to acceptance of a subsequent offer except where the acceptance is contingent on the termination of the pre-existing purchase contract or lease. *(Amended 1/93)*

- **Standard of Practice 1-8**
REALTORS®, acting as agents or brokers of buyers/tenants, shall submit to buyers/tenants all offers and counter-offers until acceptance but have no obligation to continue to show properties to their clients after an offer has been accepted unless otherwise agreed in writing. REALTORS®, acting as agents or brokers of buyers/tenants, shall recommend that buyers/tenants obtain the advice of legal counsel if there is a question as to whether a pre-existing contract has been terminated. *(Adopted 1/93, Amended 1/99)*

- **Standard of Practice 1-9**
The obligation of REALTORS® to preserve confidential information (as defined by state law) provided by their clients in the course of any agency relationship or non-agency relationship recognized by law continues after termination of agency relationships or any non-agency relationships recognized by law. REALTORS® shall not knowingly, during or following the termination of professional relationships with their clients:
1) reveal confidential information of clients; or
2) use confidential information of clients to the disadvantage of clients; or
3) use confidential information of clients for the REALTOR®'s advantage or the advantage of third parties unless:
   a) clients consent after full disclosure; or
   b) REALTORS® are required by court order; or
   c) it is the intention of a client to commit a crime and the information is necessary to prevent the crime; or
   d) it is necessary to defend a REALTOR® or the REALTOR®'s employees or associates against an accusation of wrongful conduct.
Information concerning latent material defects is not considered confidential information under this Code of Ethics. *(Adopted 1/93, Amended 1/01)*

- **Standard of Practice 1-10**
REALTORS® shall, consistent with the terms and conditions of their real estate licensure and their property management agreement, competently manage the property of clients with due regard for the rights, safety and health of tenants and others lawfully on the premises. *(Adopted 1/95, Amended 1/00)*

- **Standard of Practice 1-11**
REALTORS® who are employed to maintain or manage a client's property shall exercise due diligence and make reasonable efforts to protect it against reasonably foreseeable contingencies and losses. *(Adopted 1/95)*

- **Standard of Practice 1-12**
When entering into listing contracts, REALTORS® must advise sellers/landlords of:
1) the REALTOR®'s company policies regarding cooperation and the amount(s) of any compensation that will be offered to subagents, buyer/tenant agents, and/or brokers acting in legally recognized non-agency capacities;
2) the fact that buyer/tenant agents or brokers, even if compensated by listing brokers, or by sellers/landlords may represent the interests of buyers/tenants; and
3) any potential for listing brokers to act as disclosed dual agents, e.g., buyer/tenant agents. *(Adopted 1/93, Renumbered 1/98, Amended 1/03)*

- **Standard of Practice 1-13**
When entering into buyer/tenant agreements, REALTORS® must advise potential clients of:
1) the REALTOR®'s company policies regarding cooperation;
2) the amount of compensation to be paid by the client;
3) the potential for additional or offsetting compensation from other brokers, from the seller or landlord, or from other parties;
4) any potential for the buyer/tenant representative to act as a disclosed dual agent, e.g., listing broker, subagent, landlord's agent, etc., and
5) the possibility that sellers or sellers' representatives may not treat the existence, terms, or conditions of offers as confidential unless confidentiality is required by law, regulation, or by any confidentiality agreement between the parties. *(Adopted 1/93, Renumbered 1/98, Amended 1/06)*

- **Standard of Practice 1-14**
Fees for preparing appraisals or other valuations shall not be contingent upon the amount of the appraisal or valuation. *(Adopted 1/02)*

- **Standard of Practice 1-15**
REALTORS®, in response to inquiries from buyers or cooperating brokers shall, with the sellers' approval, disclose the existence of offers on the property. Where disclosure is authorized, REALTORS® shall also disclose, if asked, whether offers were obtained by the listing licensee, another licensee in the listing firm, or by a cooperating broker. *(Adopted 1/03, Amended 1/09)*

Article 2

REALTORS® shall avoid exaggeration, misrepresentation, or concealment of pertinent facts relating to the property or the transaction. REALTORS® shall not, however, be obligated to discover latent defects in the property, to advise on matters outside the scope of their real estate license, or to disclose facts which are confidential under the scope of agency or non-agency relationships as defined by state law. *(Amended 1/00)*

- **Standard of Practice 2-1**
REALTORS® shall only be obligated to discover and disclose adverse factors reasonably apparent to someone with expertise in those areas required by their real estate licensing authority. Article 2 does not impose upon the REALTOR® the obligation of expertise in other professional or technical disciplines. *(Amended 1/96)*

- **Standard of Practice 2-2**
(Renumbered as Standard of Practice 1-12 1/98)

- **Standard of Practice 2-3**
(Renumbered as Standard of Practice 1-13 1/98)

- **Standard of Practice 2-4**
REALTORS® shall not be parties to the naming of a false consideration in any document, unless it be the naming of an obviously nominal consideration.

FIGURE 3.1 *(Continued)*

- **Standard of Practice 2-5**

  Factors defined as "non-material" by law or regulation or which are expressly referenced in law or regulation as not being subject to disclosure are considered not "pertinent" for purposes of Article 2. *(Adopted 1/93)*

Article 3

REALTORS® shall cooperate with other brokers except when cooperation is not in the client's best interest. The obligation to cooperate does not include the obligation to share commissions, fees, or to otherwise compensate another broker. *(Amended 1/95)*

- **Standard of Practice 3-1**

  REALTORS®, acting as exclusive agents or brokers of sellers/landlords, establish the terms and conditions of offers to cooperate. Unless expressly indicated in offers to cooperate, cooperating brokers may not assume that the offer of cooperation includes an offer of compensation. Terms of compensation, if any, shall be ascertained by cooperating brokers before beginning efforts to accept the offer of cooperation. *(Amended 1/99)*

- **Standard of Practice 3-2**

  To be effective, any change in compensation offered for cooperative services must be communicated to the other REALTOR® prior to the time that REALTOR® submits an offer to purchase/lease the property. *(Amended 1/10)*

- **Standard of Practice 3-3**

  Standard of Practice 3-2 does not preclude the listing broker and cooperating broker from entering into an agreement to change cooperative compensation. *(Adopted 1/94)*

- **Standard of Practice 3-4**

  REALTORS®, acting as listing brokers, have an affirmative obligation to disclose the existence of dual or variable rate commission arrangements (i.e., listings where one amount of commission is payable if the listing broker's firm is the procuring cause of sale/lease and a different amount of commission is payable if the sale/lease results through the efforts of the seller/landlord or a cooperating broker). The listing broker shall, as soon as practical, disclose the existence of such arrangements to potential cooperating brokers and shall, in response to inquiries from cooperating brokers, disclose the differential that would result in a cooperative transaction or in a sale/lease that results through the efforts of the seller/landlord. If the cooperating broker is a buyer/tenant representative, the buyer/tenant representative must disclose such information to their client before the client makes an offer to purchase or lease. *(Amended 1/02)*

- **Standard of Practice 3-5**

  It is the obligation of subagents to promptly disclose all pertinent facts to the principal's agent prior to as well as after a purchase or lease agreement is executed. *(Amended 1/93)*

- **Standard of Practice 3-6**

  REALTORS® shall disclose the existence of accepted offers, including offers with unresolved contingencies, to any broker seeking cooperation. *(Adopted 5/86, Amended 1/04)*

- **Standard of Practice 3-7**

  When seeking information from another REALTOR® concerning property under a management or listing agreement, REALTORS® shall disclose their REALTOR® status and whether their interest is personal or on behalf of a client and, if on behalf of a client, their representational status. *(Amended 1/95)*

- **Standard of Practice 3-8**

  REALTORS® shall not misrepresent the availability of access to show or inspect a listed property. *(Amended 11/87)*

- **Standard of Practice 3-9**

  REALTORS® shall not provide access to listed property on terms other than those established by the owner or the listing broker. *(Adopted 1/10)*

Article 4

REALTORS® shall not acquire an interest in or buy or present offers from themselves, any member of their immediate families, their firms or any member thereof, or any entities in which they have any ownership interest, any real property without making their true position known to the owner or the owner's agent or broker. In selling property they own, or in which they have any interest, REALTORS® shall reveal their ownership or interest in writing to the purchaser or the purchaser's representative. *(Amended 1/00)*

- **Standard of Practice 4-1**

  For the protection of all parties, the disclosures required by Article 4 shall be in writing and provided by REALTORS® prior to the signing of any contract. *(Adopted 2/86)*

Article 5

REALTORS® shall not undertake to provide professional services concerning a property or its value where they have a present or contemplated interest unless such interest is specifically disclosed to all affected parties.

Article 6

REALTORS® shall not accept any commission, rebate, or profit on expenditures made for their client, without the client's knowledge and consent.

When recommending real estate products or services (e.g., homeowner's insurance, warranty programs, mortgage financing, title insurance, etc.), REALTORS® shall disclose to the client or customer to whom the recommendation is made any financial benefits or fees, other than real estate referral fees, the REALTOR® or REALTOR®'s firm may receive as a direct result of such recommendation. *(Amended 1/99)*

- **Standard of Practice 6-1**

  REALTORS® shall not recommend or suggest to a client or a customer the use of services of another organization or business entity in which they have a direct interest without disclosing such interest at the time of the recommendation or suggestion. *(Amended 5/88)*

Article 7

In a transaction, REALTORS® shall not accept compensation from more than one party, even if permitted by law, without disclosure to all parties and the informed consent of the REALTOR®'s client or clients. *(Amended 1/93)*

Article 8

REALTORS® shall keep in a special account in an appropriate financial institution, separated from their own funds, monies coming into their possession in trust for other persons, such as escrows, trust funds, clients' monies, and other like items.

Article 9

REALTORS®, for the protection of all parties, shall assure whenever possible that all agreements related to real estate transactions including, but not limited to, listing and representation agreements, purchase

FIGURE 3.1 *(Continued)*

contracts, and leases are in writing in clear and understandable language expressing the specific terms, conditions, obligations and commitments of the parties. A copy of each agreement shall be furnished to each party to such agreements upon their signing or initialing. *(Amended 1/04)*

- **Standard of Practice 9-1**

  For the protection of all parties, REALTORS® shall use reasonable care to ensure that documents pertaining to the purchase, sale, or lease of real estate are kept current through the use of written extensions or amendments. *(Amended 1/93)*

- **Standard of Practice 9-2**

  When assisting or enabling a client or customer in establishing a contractual relationship (e.g., listing and representation agreements, purchase agreements, leases, etc.) electronically, REALTORS® shall make reasonable efforts to explain the nature and disclose the specific terms of the contractual relationship being established prior to it being agreed to by a contracting party. *(Adopted 1/07)*

Duties to the Public

Article 10

REALTORS® shall not deny equal professional services to any person for reasons of race, color, religion, sex, handicap, familial status, or national origin. REALTORS® shall not be parties to any plan or agreement to discriminate against a person or persons on the basis of race, color, religion, sex, handicap, familial status, or national origin. *(Amended 1/90)*

REALTORS®, in their real estate employment practices, shall not discriminate against any person or persons on the basis of race, color, religion, sex, handicap, familial status, or national origin. *(Amended 1/00)*

- **Standard of Practice 10-1**

  When involved in the sale or lease of a residence, REALTORS® shall not volunteer information regarding the racial, religious or ethnic composition of any neighborhood nor shall they engage in any activity which may result in panic selling, however, REALTORS® may provide other demographic information. *(Adopted 1/94, Amended 1/06)*

- **Standard of Practice 10-2**

  When not involved in the sale or lease of a residence, REALTORS® may provide demographic information related to a property, transaction or professional assignment to a party if such demographic information is (a) deemed by the REALTOR® to be needed to assist with or complete, in a manner consistent with Article 10, a real estate transaction or professional assignment and (b) is obtained or derived from a recognized, reliable, independent, and impartial source. The source of such information and any additions, deletions, modifications, interpretations, or other changes shall be disclosed in reasonable detail. *(Adopted 1/05, Renumbered 1/06)*

- **Standard of Practice 10-3**

  REALTORS® shall not print, display or circulate any statement or advertisement with respect to selling or renting of a property that indicates any preference, limitations or discrimination based on race, color, religion, sex, handicap, familial status, or national origin. *(Adopted 1/94, Renumbered 1/05 and 1/06)*

- **Standard of Practice 10-4**

  As used in Article 10 "real estate employment practices" relates to employees and independent contractors providing real estate-related services and the administrative and clerical staff directly

supporting those individuals. *(Adopted 1/00, Renumbered 1/05 and 1/06)*

Article 11

The services which REALTORS® provide to their clients and customers shall conform to the standards of practice and competence which are reasonably expected in the specific real estate disciplines in which they engage; specifically, residential real estate brokerage, real property management, commercial and industrial real estate brokerage, land brokerage, real estate appraisal, real estate counseling, real estate syndication, real estate auction, and international real estate.

REALTORS® shall not undertake to provide specialized professional services concerning a type of property or service that is outside their field of competence unless they engage the assistance of one who is competent on such types of property or service, or unless the facts are fully disclosed to the client. Any persons engaged to provide such assistance shall be so identified to the client and their contribution to the assignment should be set forth. *(Amended 1/10)*

- **Standard of Practice 11-1**

  When REALTORS® prepare opinions of real property value or price, other than in pursuit of a listing or to assist a potential purchaser in formulating a purchase offer, such opinions shall include the following unless the party requesting the opinion requires a specific type of report or different data set:

  1) identification of the subject property
  2) date prepared
  3) defined value or price
  4) limiting conditions, including statements of purpose(s) and intended user(s)
  5) any present or contemplated interest, including the possibility of representing the seller/landlord or buyers/tenants
  6) basis for the opinion, including applicable market data
  7) if the opinion is not an appraisal, a statement to that effect *(Amended 1/10)*

- **Standard of Practice 11-2**

  The obligations of the Code of Ethics in respect of real estate disciplines other than appraisal shall be interpreted and applied in accordance with the standards of competence and practice which clients and the public reasonably require to protect their rights and interests considering the complexity of the transaction, the availability of expert assistance, and, where the REALTOR® is an agent or subagent, the obligations of a fiduciary. *(Adopted 1/95)*

- **Standard of Practice 11-3**

  When REALTORS® provide consultive services to clients which involve advice or counsel for a fee (not a commission), such advice shall be rendered in an objective manner and the fee shall not be contingent on the substance of the advice or counsel given. If brokerage or transaction services are to be provided in addition to consultive services, a separate compensation may be paid with prior agreement between the client and REALTOR®. *(Adopted 1/96)*

- **Standard of Practice 11-4**

  The competency required by Article 11 relates to services contracted for between REALTORS® and their clients or customers; the duties expressly imposed by the Code of Ethics; and the duties imposed by law or regulation. *(Adopted 1/02)*

Article 12

REALTORS® shall be honest and truthful in their real estate communications and shall present a true picture in their advertising, marketing, and other representations. REALTORS® shall ensure that their

FIGURE 3.1   *(Continued)*

status as real estate professionals is readily apparent in their advertising, marketing, and other representations, and that the recipients of all real estate communications are, or have been, notified that those communications are from a real estate professional. *(Amended 1/08)*

- **Standard of Practice 12-1**

  REALTORS® may use the term "free" and similar terms in their advertising and in other representations provided that all terms governing availability of the offered product or service are clearly disclosed at the same time. *(Amended 1/97)*

- **Standard of Practice 12-2**

  REALTORS® may represent their services as "free" or without cost even if they expect to receive compensation from a source other than their client provided that the potential for the REALTOR® to obtain a benefit from a third party is clearly disclosed at the same time. *(Amended 1/97)*

- **Standard of Practice 12-3**

  The offering of premiums, prizes, merchandise discounts or other inducements to list, sell, purchase, or lease is not, in itself, unethical even if receipt of the benefit is contingent on listing, selling, purchasing, or leasing through the REALTOR® making the offer. However, REALTORS® must exercise care and candor in any such advertising or other public or private representations so that any party interested in receiving or otherwise benefiting from the REALTOR®'s offer will have clear, thorough, advance understanding of all the terms and conditions of the offer. The offering of any inducements to do business is subject to the limitations and restrictions of state law and the ethical obligations established by any applicable Standard of Practice. *(Amended 1/95)*

- **Standard of Practice 12-4**

  REALTORS® shall not offer for sale/lease or advertise property without authority. When acting as listing brokers or as subagents, REALTORS® shall not quote a price different from that agreed upon with the seller/landlord. *(Amended 1/93)*

- **Standard of Practice 12-5**

  REALTORS® shall not advertise nor permit any person employed by or affiliated with them to advertise real estate services or listed property in any medium (e.g., electronically, print, radio, television, etc.) without disclosing the name of that REALTOR®'s firm in a reasonable and readily apparent manner. *(Adopted 11/86, Amended 1/10)*

- **Standard of Practice 12-6**

  REALTORS®, when advertising unlisted real property for sale/lease in which they have an ownership interest, shall disclose their status as both owners/landlords and as REALTORS® or real estate licensees. *(Amended 1/93)*

- **Standard of Practice 12-7**

  Only REALTORS® who participated in the transaction as the listing broker or cooperating broker (selling broker) may claim to have "sold" the property. Prior to closing, a cooperating broker may post a "sold" sign only with the consent of the listing broker. *(Amended 1/96)*

- **Standard of Practice 12-8**

  The obligation to present a true picture in representations to the public includes information presented, provided, or displayed on REALTORS®' websites. REALTORS® shall use reasonable efforts to ensure that information on their websites is current. When it becomes apparent that information on a REALTOR®'s website is no longer current or accurate, REALTORS® shall promptly take corrective action. *(Adopted 1/07)*

- **Standard of Practice 12-9**

  REALTOR® firm websites shall disclose the firm's name and state(s) of licensure in a reasonable and readily apparent manner.

  Websites of REALTORS® and non-member licensees affiliated with a REALTOR® firm shall disclose the firm's name and that REALTOR®'s or non-member licensee's state(s) of licensure in a reasonable and readily apparent manner. *(Adopted 1/07)*

- **Standard of Practice 12-10**

  REALTORS®' obligation to present a true picture in their advertising and representations to the public includes the URLs and domain names they use, and prohibits REALTORS® from:

  1) engaging in deceptive or unauthorized framing of real estate brokerage websites;

  2) manipulating (e.g., presenting content developed by others) listing content in any way that produces a deceptive or misleading result; or

  3) deceptively using metatags, keywords or other devices/methods to direct, drive, or divert Internet traffic, or to otherwise mislead consumers. *(Adopted 1/07)*

- **Standard of Practice 12-11**

  REALTORS® intending to share or sell consumer information gathered via the Internet shall disclose that possibility in a reasonable and readily apparent manner. *(Adopted 1/07)*

- **Standard of Practice 12-12**

  REALTORS® shall not:

  1) use URLs or domain names that present less than a true picture, or

  2) register URLs or domain names which, if used, would present less than a true picture. *(Adopted 1/08)*

- **Standard of Practice 12-13**

  The obligation to present a true picture in advertising, marketing, and representations allows REALTORS® to use and display only professional designations, certifications, and other credentials to which they are legitimately entitled. *(Adopted 1/08)*

Article 13

REALTORS® shall not engage in activities that constitute the unauthorized practice of law and shall recommend that legal counsel be obtained when the interest of any party to the transaction requires it.

Article 14

If charged with unethical practice or asked to present evidence or to cooperate in any other way, in any professional standards proceeding or investigation, REALTORS® shall place all pertinent facts before the proper tribunals of the Member Board or affiliated institute, society, or council in which membership is held and shall take no action to disrupt or obstruct such processes. *(Amended 1/99)*

- **Standard of Practice 14-1**

  REALTORS® shall not be subject to disciplinary proceedings in more than one Board of REALTORS® or affiliated institute, society, or council in which they hold membership with respect to alleged violations of the Code of Ethics relating to the same transaction or event. *(Amended 1/95)*

- **Standard of Practice 14-2**

  REALTORS® shall not make any unauthorized disclosure or dissemination of the allegations, findings, or decision developed in connection with an ethics hearing or appeal or in connection with an arbitration hearing or procedural review. *(Amended 1/92)*

FIGURE 3.1 (Continued)

- **Standard of Practice 14-3**

  REALTORS® shall not obstruct the Board's investigative or professional standards proceedings by instituting or threatening to institute actions for libel, slander, or defamation against any party to a professional standards proceeding or their witnesses based on the filing of an arbitration request, an ethics complaint, or testimony given before any tribunal. (Adopted 11/87, Amended 1/99)

- **Standard of Practice 14-4**

  REALTORS® shall not intentionally impede the Board's investigative or disciplinary proceedings by filing multiple ethics complaints based on the same event or transaction. (Adopted 11/88)

Duties to REALTORS®

Article 15

REALTORS® shall not knowingly or recklessly make false or misleading statements about competitors, their businesses, or their business practices. (Amended 1/92)

- **Standard of Practice 15-1**

  REALTORS® shall not knowingly or recklessly file false or unfounded ethics complaints. (Adopted 1/00)

- **Standard of Practice 15-2**

  The obligation to refrain from making false or misleading statements about competitors, competitors' businesses, and competitors' business practices includes the duty to not knowingly or recklessly publish, repeat, retransmit, or republish false or misleading statements made by others. This duty applies whether false or misleading statements are repeated in person, in writing, by technological means (e.g., the Internet), or by any other means. (Adopted 1/07, Amended 1/10)

- **Standard of Practice 15-3**

  The obligation to refrain from making false or misleading statements about competitors, competitors' businesses, and competitors' business practices includes the duty to publish a clarification about or to remove statements made by others on electronic media the REALTOR® controls once the REALTOR® knows the statement is false or misleading. (Adopted 1/10)

Article 16

REALTORS® shall not engage in any practice or take any action inconsistent with exclusive representation or exclusive brokerage relationship agreements that other REALTORS® have with clients. (Amended 1/04)

- **Standard of Practice 16-1**

  Article 16 is not intended to prohibit aggressive or innovative business practices which are otherwise ethical and does not prohibit disagreements with other REALTORS® involving commission, fees, compensation or other forms of payment or expenses. (Adopted 1/93, Amended 1/95)

- **Standard of Practice 16-2**

  Article 16 does not preclude REALTORS® from making general announcements to prospects describing their services and the terms of their availability even though some recipients may have entered into agency agreements or other exclusive relationships with another REALTOR®. A general telephone canvass, general mailing or distribution addressed to all prospects in a given geographical area or in a given profession, business, club, or organization, or other classification or group is deemed "general" for purposes of this standard. (Amended 1/04)

Article 16 is intended to recognize as unethical two basic types of solicitations:

First, telephone or personal solicitations of property owners who have been identified by a real estate sign, multiple listing compilation, or other information service as having exclusively listed their property with another REALTOR®; and

Second, mail or other forms of written solicitations of prospects whose properties are exclusively listed with another REALTOR® when such solicitations are not part of a general mailing but are directed specifically to property owners identified through compilations of current listings, "for sale" or "for rent" signs, or other sources of information required by Article 3 and Multiple Listing Service rules to be made available to other REALTORS® under offers of subagency or cooperation. (Amended 1/04)

- **Standard of Practice 16-3**

  Article 16 does not preclude REALTORS® from contacting the client of another broker for the purpose of offering to provide, or entering into a contract to provide, a different type of real estate service unrelated to the type of service currently being provided (e.g., property management as opposed to brokerage) or from offering the same type of service for property not subject to other brokers' exclusive agreements. However, information received through a Multiple Listing Service or any other offer of cooperation may not be used to target clients of other REALTORS® to whom such offers to provide services may be made. (Amended 1/04)

- **Standard of Practice 16-4**

  REALTORS® shall not solicit a listing which is currently listed exclusively with another broker. However, if the listing broker, when asked by the REALTOR®, refuses to disclose the expiration date and nature of such listing; i.e., an exclusive right to sell, an exclusive agency, open listing; or other form of contractual agreement between the listing broker and the client, the REALTOR® may contact the owner to secure such information and may discuss the terms upon which the REALTOR® might take a future listing or, alternatively, may take a listing to become effective upon expiration of any existing exclusive listing. (Amended 1/94)

- **Standard of Practice 16-5**

  REALTORS® shall not solicit buyer/tenant agreements from buyers/tenants who are subject to exclusive buyer/tenant agreements. However, if asked by a REALTOR®, the broker refuses to disclose the expiration date of the exclusive buyer/tenant agreement, the REALTOR® may contact the buyer/tenant to secure such information and may discuss the terms upon which the REALTOR® might enter into a future buyer/tenant agreement or, alternatively, may enter into a buyer/tenant agreement to become effective upon the expiration of any existing exclusive buyer/tenant agreement. (Adopted 1/94, Amended 1/98)

- **Standard of Practice 16-6**

  When REALTORS® are contacted by the client of another REALTOR® regarding the creation of an exclusive relationship to provide the same type of service, and REALTORS® have not directly or indirectly initiated such discussions, they may discuss the terms upon which they might enter into a future agreement or, alternatively, may enter into an agreement which becomes effective upon expiration of any existing exclusive agreement. (Amended 1/98)

- **Standard of Practice 16-7**

  The fact that a prospect has retained a REALTOR® as an exclusive representative or exclusive broker in one or more past transactions does not preclude other REALTORS® from seeking such prospect's future business. (Amended 1/04)

FIGURE 3.1 *(Continued)*

- **Standard of Practice 16-8**

  The fact that an exclusive agreement has been entered into with a REALTOR® shall not preclude or inhibit any other REALTOR® from entering into a similar agreement after the expiration of the prior agreement. *(Amended 1/98)*

- **Standard of Practice 16-9**

  REALTORS®, prior to entering into a representation agreement, have an affirmative obligation to make reasonable efforts to determine whether the prospect is subject to a current, valid exclusive agreement to provide the same type of real estate service. *(Amended 1/04)*

- **Standard of Practice 16-10**

  REALTORS®, acting as buyer or tenant representatives or brokers, shall disclose that relationship to the seller/landlord's representative or broker at first contact and shall provide written confirmation of that disclosure to the seller/landlord's representative or broker not later than execution of a purchase agreement or lease. *(Amended 1/04)*

- **Standard of Practice 16-11**

  On unlisted property, REALTORS® acting as buyer/tenant representatives or brokers shall disclose that relationship to the seller/landlord at first contact for that buyer/tenant and shall provide written confirmation of such disclosure to the seller/landlord not later than execution of any purchase or lease agreement. *(Amended 1/04)*

  REALTORS® shall make any request for anticipated compensation from the seller/landlord at first contact. *(Amended 1/98)*

- **Standard of Practice 16-12**

  REALTORS®, acting as representatives or brokers of sellers/landlords or as subagents of listing brokers, shall disclose that relationship to buyers/tenants as soon as practicable and shall provide written confirmation of such disclosure to buyers/tenants not later than execution of any purchase or lease agreement. *(Amended 1/04)*

- **Standard of Practice 16-13**

  All dealings concerning property exclusively listed, or with buyer/tenants who are subject to an exclusive agreement shall be carried on with the client's representative or broker, and not with the client, except with the consent of the client's representative or broker or except where such dealings are initiated by the client.

  Before providing substantive services (such as writing a purchase offer or presenting a CMA) to prospects, REALTORS® shall ask prospects whether they are a party to any exclusive representation agreement. REALTORS® shall not knowingly provide substantive services concerning a prospective transaction to prospects who are parties to exclusive representation agreements, except with the consent of the prospects' exclusive representatives or at the direction of prospects. *(Adopted 1/93, Amended 1/04)*

- **Standard of Practice 16-14**

  REALTORS® are free to enter into contractual relationships or to negotiate with sellers/landlords, buyers/tenants or others who are not subject to an exclusive agreement but shall not knowingly obligate them to pay more than one commission except with their informed consent. *(Amended 1/98)*

- **Standard of Practice 16-15**

  In cooperative transactions REALTORS® shall compensate cooperating REALTORS® (principal brokers) and shall not compensate nor offer to compensate, directly or indirectly, any of the sales licensees employed by or affiliated with other REALTORS® without the prior express knowledge and consent of the cooperating broker.

- **Standard of Practice 16-16**

  REALTORS®, acting as subagents or buyer/tenant representatives or brokers, shall not use the terms of an offer to purchase/lease to attempt to modify the listing broker's offer of compensation to subagents or buyer/tenant representatives or brokers nor make the submission of an executed offer to purchase/lease contingent on the listing broker's agreement to modify the offer of compensation. *(Amended 1/04)*

- **Standard of Practice 16-17**

  REALTORS®, acting as subagents or as buyer/tenant representatives or brokers, shall not attempt to extend a listing broker's offer of cooperation and/or compensation to other brokers without the consent of the listing broker. *(Amended 1/04)*

- **Standard of Practice 16-18**

  REALTORS® shall not use information obtained from listing brokers through offers to cooperate made through multiple listing services or through other offers of cooperation to refer listing brokers' clients to other brokers or to create buyer/tenant relationships with listing brokers' clients, unless such use is authorized by listing brokers. *(Amended 1/02)*

- **Standard of Practice 16-19**

  Signs giving notice of property for sale, rent, lease, or exchange shall not be placed on property without consent of the seller/landlord. *(Amended 1/93)*

- **Standard of Practice 16-20**

  REALTORS®, prior to or after their relationship with their current firm is terminated, shall not induce clients of their current firm to cancel exclusive contractual agreements between the client and that firm. This does not preclude REALTORS® (principals) from establishing agreements with their associated licensees governing assignability of exclusive agreements. *(Adopted 1/98, Amended 1/10)*

Article 17

In the event of contractual disputes or specific non-contractual disputes as defined in Standard of Practice 17-4 between REALTORS® (principals) associated with different firms, arising out of their relationship as REALTORS®, the REALTORS® shall submit the dispute to arbitration in accordance with the regulations of their Board or Boards rather than litigate the matter.

In the event clients of REALTORS® wish to arbitrate contractual disputes arising out of real estate transactions, REALTORS® shall arbitrate those disputes in accordance with the regulations of their Board, provided the clients agree to be bound by the decision.

The obligation to participate in arbitration contemplated by this Article includes the obligation of REALTORS® (principals) to cause their firms to arbitrate and be bound by any award. *(Amended 1/01)*

- **Standard of Practice 17-1**

  The filing of litigation and refusal to withdraw from it by REALTORS® in an arbitrable matter constitutes a refusal to arbitrate. *(Adopted 2/86)*

- **Standard of Practice 17-2**

  Article 17 does not require REALTORS® to arbitrate in those circumstances when all parties to the dispute advise the Board in writing that they choose not to arbitrate before the Board. *(Amended 1/93)*

- **Standard of Practice 17-3**

  REALTORS®, when acting solely as principals in a real estate transaction, are not obligated to arbitrate disputes with other

FIGURE 3.1   *(Continued)*

REALTORS® absent a specific written agreement to the contrary. *(Adopted 1/96)*

• **Standard of Practice 17-4**

Specific non-contractual disputes that are subject to arbitration pursuant to Article 17 are:

1) Where a listing broker has compensated a cooperating broker and another cooperating broker subsequently claims to be the procuring cause of the sale or lease. In such cases the complainant may name the first compensated broker as respondent and arbitration may proceed without the listing broker being named as a respondent. When arbitration occurs between two (or more) cooperating brokers and where the listing broker is not a party, the amount in dispute and the amount of any potential resulting award is limited to the amount paid to the respondent by the listing broker and any amount credited or paid to a party to the transaction at the direction of the respondent. Alternatively, if the complaint is brought against the listing broker, the listing broker may name the first cooperating broker as a third-party respondent. In either instance the decision of the hearing panel as to procuring cause shall be conclusive with respect to all current or subsequent claims of the parties for compensation arising out of the underlying cooperative transaction. *(Adopted 1/97, Amended 1/07)*

2) Where a buyer or tenant representative is compensated by the seller or landlord, and not by the listing broker, and the listing broker, as a result, reduces the commission owed by the seller or landlord and, subsequent to such actions, another cooperating broker claims to be the procuring cause of sale or lease. In such cases the complainant may name the first cooperating broker as respondent and arbitration may proceed without the listing broker being named as a respondent. When arbitration occurs between two (or more) cooperating brokers and where the listing broker is not a party, the amount in dispute and the amount of any potential resulting award is limited to the amount paid to the respondent by the seller or landlord and any amount credited or paid to a party to the transaction at the direction of the respondent. Alternatively, if the complaint is brought against the listing broker, the listing broker may name the first cooperating broker as a third-party respondent. In either instance the decision of the hearing panel as to procuring cause shall be conclusive with respect to all current or subsequent claims of the parties for compensation arising out of the underlying cooperative transaction. *(Adopted 1/97, Amended 1/07)*

3) Where a buyer or tenant representative is compensated by the buyer or tenant and, as a result, the listing broker reduces the commission owed by the seller or landlord and, subsequent to such actions, another cooperating broker claims to be the procuring cause of sale or lease. In such cases the complainant may name the first cooperating broker as respondent and arbitration may proceed without the listing broker being named as a respondent. Alternatively, if the complaint is brought against the listing broker, the listing broker may name the first cooperating broker as a third-party respondent. In either instance

the decision of the hearing panel as to procuring cause shall be conclusive with respect to all current or subsequent claims of the parties for compensation arising out of the underlying cooperative transaction. *(Adopted 1/97)*

4) Where two or more listing brokers claim entitlement to compensation pursuant to open listings with a seller or landlord who agrees to participate in arbitration (or who requests arbitration) and who agrees to be bound by the decision. In cases where one of the listing brokers has been compensated by the seller or landlord, the other listing broker, as complainant, may name the first listing broker as respondent and arbitration may proceed between the brokers. *(Adopted 1/97)*

5) Where a buyer or tenant representative is compensated by the seller or landlord, and not by the listing broker, and the listing broker, as a result, reduces the commission owed by the seller or landlord and, subsequent to such actions, claims to be the procuring cause of sale or lease. In such cases arbitration shall be between the listing broker and the buyer or tenant representative and the amount in dispute is limited to the amount of the reduction of commission to which the listing broker agreed. *(Adopted 1/05)*

• **Standard of Practice 17-5**

The obligation to arbitrate established in Article 17 includes disputes between REALTORS® (principals) in different states in instances where, absent an established inter-association arbitration agreement, the REALTOR® (principal) requesting arbitration agrees to submit to the jurisdiction of, travel to, participate in, and be bound by any resulting award rendered in arbitration conducted by the respondent(s) REALTOR®'s association, in instances where the respondent(s) REALTOR®'s association determines that an arbitrable issue exists. *(Adopted 1/07)*

The **Code of Ethics** *was adopted in 1913. Amended at the Annual Convention in 1924, 1928, 1950, 1951, 1952, 1955, 1956, 1961, 1962, 1974, 1982, 1986, 1987, 1989, 1990, 1991, 1992, 1993, 1994, 1995, 1996, 1997, 1998, 1999, 2000, 2001, 2002, 2003, 2004, 2005, 2006, 2007, 2008 and 2009.*

Explanatory Notes

The reader should be aware of the following policies which have been approved by the Board of Directors of the National Association:

In filing a charge of an alleged violation of the Code of Ethics by a REALTOR®, the charge must read as an alleged violation of one or more Articles of the Code. Standards of Practice may be cited in support of the charge.

The Standards of Practice serve to clarify the ethical obligations imposed by the various Articles and supplement, and do not substitute for, the Case Interpretations in *Interpretations of the Code of Ethics.*

Modifications to existing Standards of Practice and additional new Standards of Practice are approved from time to time. Readers are cautioned to ensure that the most recent publications are utilized.

group of African American real estate brokers founded the **National Association of Real Estate Brokers** and adopted the registered trademark **Realtist®** to designate its members. Like the NAR, the National Association of Real Estate Brokers strives to enhance the professionalism of the real estate profession.

3.3 FAIR HOUSING AND ANTIDISCRIMINATION LEGISLATION

The federal government as well as state governments have passed extensive legislation affecting fair housing issues. The Real Estate Commissioner's Rules and Regulations and the California Business and Professions Code also contain many references to discrimination in housing as it pertains to real estate licensees. The astute licensee takes the time to seek out these issues and become familiar with them. Doing so is an act of elevating oneself to a higher degree of professionalism, in addition to being the right thing to do in one's dealings with others.

Federal Laws That Affect Real Estate

The purpose of this section is to review the history of antidiscrimination legislation as it pertains to housing issues, why it is needed, and the real estate professional's role in seeing that these laws are carefully followed during the entire home buying or selling process.

The original draft of the Declaration of Independence contained language that condemned slavery, but it was removed just prior to the creation of the final, signed document to ensure the consensus of all of the states. However, the statement, "We hold these truths to be self-evident, that all men are created equal, that they are endowed by their Creator with certain unalienable Rights, that among these are Life, Liberty, and the pursuit of Happiness," was retained.

While the economy of the South had become very dependent on slave labor, strong antislavery sentiment had grown. Because technology and the Industrial Revolution made growing cotton so profitable, Congress in the early 1800s was under considerable pressure to protect this lucrative industry while addressing the issue of slavery at the same time. The result, in 1820, was the Missouri Compromise, which allowed Missouri to enter the Union with no slavery restrictions while Maine would enter as a free state. It was also decided that the western territories would be free.

In 1857, the U.S. Supreme Court handed down the *Dred Scott* decision, essentially requiring the federal government to keep out of any slavery issues, as they were strictly a matter for the states. This mandate negated the Missouri Compromise as being unconstitutional by

stating that Congress had exceeded its authority by prohibiting slavery in the territories.

It is also interesting to note that the Constitution contained a provision that, in determining how many Congressional representatives a state could have, a slave was to be considered three-fifths of a person. The courts also stated that slaves were considered to be property, that the Constitution guaranteed property rights, and that "Negroes" were not entitled to rights as U.S. citizens.

Anger over the Dred Scott decision in the north was a major factor leading to the Civil War.

To see how the political thinking of the country evolved over the years, let's look at several pieces of legislation that affect how we, as a country, changed the way we view discrimination and fair housing.

Thirteenth Amendment

The Thirteenth Amendment to the U.S. Constitution abolished slavery but did not address the rights of former slaves.

Civil Rights Act of 1866

The intent of the **Civil Rights Act of 1866** was to provide equal treatment of former slaves, and states in part that all citizens of the United States "shall have the same right, in every State and Territory … to inherit, purchase, lease, sell, hold, and convey real and personal property … as is enjoyed by white citizens."

This act applied to race only and could be enforced by anyone who was discriminated against, without exception. Legal remedies included injunction, compensatory, and punitive damages.

Fourteenth Amendment

The Fourteenth Amendment to the Constitution was passed after the Civil Rights Act of 1866 to protect the rights granted in the 1866 Act by providing permanent constitutional protection, thus preventing a later Congress from repealing the act and taking away the rights it afforded.

The Fourteenth Amendment states: "All persons born or naturalized in the United States, and subject to the jurisdiction thereof, are citizens of the United States and the State wherein they reside. No State shall make or enforce any law which shall abridge the privileges or immunities of citizens of the United States; nor shall any State deprive any person of life, liberty, or property without due process of law; nor deny any person within its jurisdiction the equal protection of the laws."

This language is very broad in scope, not limited to race or any other specific issue, and may be interpreted as comprehensive civil rights protection.

Civil Rights Act of 1870

Because some attorneys felt that the Fourteenth Amendment effectively replaced the Civil Rights Act of 1866 and that it was no longer law, a statement was "tacked on" to another voting rights act that became known as the **Civil Rights Act of 1870**. The purpose of this act was to prevent later courts from nullifying the remedies granted in the 1866 Act. The actual legislation reads: "and be it further enacted that the act to protect all persons in the United States in their civil rights and furnish the means of their vindication, passed April nine, eighteen hundred and sixty-six, is hereby reenacted."

In a matter of only a few years, Congress had addressed Civil Rights issues on three separate occasions, making the protections granted broader on nearly every occasion. Even though the Civil Rights Act of 1866 was passed twice, to ensure that it would withstand future legal challenges, it was effectively rendered all but useless by court decisions that limited its enforcement to government property. Both the Civil Rights Act of 1866 and the Fourteenth Amendment were largely ineffective in providing equal rights for almost one hundred years.

Executive Order 11063

On November 21, 1962, President John F. Kennedy issued an order that prohibited discrimination in housing wherever federal funds were involved. The order affected all property sales that involved FHA and VA loans, as well as other programs subsidized by the federal government. It stated that "the executive branch of the government, in faithfully executing the laws of the United States which authorize federal financial assistance, directly or indirectly, for the provision, rehabilitation, and operation of housing and related facilities, is charged with an obligation and duty to assure that those laws are fairly administered and that benefits thereunder are made available to all Americans without regard to their race, color, creed, or national origin." Thus began the modern-day focus by the federal government to put teeth into antidiscrimination laws as they relate to civil rights and fair housing.

Civil Rights Act of 1964

The **Civil Rights Act of 1964** made John Kennedy's 1962 executive order a matter of law and is considered one of the first of the

modern civil rights acts. Although not as comprehensive as later acts, it prohibited discrimination in all federally assisted programs.

Civil Rights Act of 1968

The **Civil Rights Act of 1968** prohibited discrimination in housing based on race, religion, color, and national origin. Sexual discrimination was added by Congress in 1974. The act prohibits the following:

- Discrimination by brokers toward clients and customers.
- Discrimination as to access to Multiple Listing Service (MLS).
- **Steering** is directing people of protected classes away from or toward particular areas.
- **Redlining** is the refusal by a lender to loan within certain areas.
- Refusal to show, rent, or sell through the false representation that a property is not available.
- Discriminatory sales or loan terms.
- **Blockbusting** is inducing panic selling in an area or neighborhood by representing that property values will decline or the crime rate will increase due to the entry of minority group members to the area.
- Retaliatory acts against persons making fair housing complaints and intimidation to discourage complaints.
- Discriminatory advertising, which is prohibited in all cases, even when it relates to activities that are exempt from the act.

There has been much concern and frustration on the part of real estate licensees regarding what actually constitutes discriminatory advertising. Essentially, advertising that describes the property is usually acceptable while advertising that describes the buyer, especially a buyer from a protected class, is almost always discriminatory. Advertising a property as being near the Jewish Synagogue, for instance, would be considered discriminatory as it can be deemed steering of an ethnic or religious nature. Advertising that indicates a preference for a particular sex or age group suggesting that members of other protected categories are not welcome would probably be considered discriminatory. When writing ads, keep the Golden Rule in mind and ask yourself, "How would I feel if I was a minority and read this ad?"

The U.S. Department of Housing and Urban Development (HUD) issued the following list of terms and phrases that it has indicated are *not* discriminatory in nature:

Master bedroom	Easter Bunny
Quiet streets	Walk to bus stop
Rare find	St. Valentine's Day
No bicycles allowed	Jogging trails
Desirable neighborhood	Merry Christmas
Family room	Happy Easter
Two-bedroom	Walk-in closets
Kosher meals available	Mother-in-law suite
Sober	Third-floor walkup
Santa Claus	Great view
Nonsmoking	Bachelor apartment

Several different entities issue lists of words they feel are either discriminatory or nondiscriminatory in nature. These lists often differ in what words may or may not be used, in part because different groups have different connotations of the same words. As a licensee, you are well advised to carefully adhere to the HUD list, as there may well be a conflict between it and the "private" lists.

Exemptions to the Civil Rights Act of 1968 include the following:

- Religious groups, which can discriminate in providing nonprofit housing, so long as the religion is open to everyone, regardless of race, sex, color, or national origin.

- Private clubs, which can discriminate or give preference to members when selling or leasing housing for noncommercial purposes.

- Owners of one to four residential units who occupy a unit can discriminate, provided that they do not use a real estate licensee when renting.

- Owners of single-family homes, who can discriminate when selling or renting without a real estate licensee, provided they do not own more than three such homes and are not in the business of renting.

Jones v. Mayer

In 1968, the Supreme Court held in the *Jones v. Mayer* case that the Civil Rights Act of 1866 applied to private property as well as real property, and that it could be enforced by the party being discriminated against. The court's decision was based on the Thirteenth Amendment to the Constitution. It is interesting to note that the

Thirteenth Amendment was drafted in its original form to perpetuate slavery but was changed, largely through the efforts of President Lincoln and the Republican Party, to abolish slavery.

1988 Fair Housing Amendments Act

The **1988 Fair Housing Amendments Act** is an important piece of legislation that further extends protection against housing discrimination to families and handicapped persons. It also gives HUD much greater enforcement powers and strengthens the enforcement mechanisms available to the government.

Adult-only designations are essentially a thing of the past, except for subdivisions or housing complexes where a minimum of 80 percent of the dwellings are occupied by at least one person who is at least fifty-five years old. This percentage may be further reduced by voluntary action of the controlling homeowners association, but it may not exceed the 80 percent limit set by the federal government. It is common today for homeowners associations to reduce the percentage to 75 percent so as to allow a buffer and further keep them from being in violation of the federal statute.

Creating a separate area within a condominium or apartment complex as an age-restricted area does not meet the federal standard of 80 percent and is illegal. This type of activity is considered steering, as it tries to place certain tenants in a particular area within a complex and violates the antisteering provisions of the law.

It is legal for apartment and condominium complexes to have rules for children's use of the facilities, such as being accompanied by an adult to the pool or spa area if they are under the age of twelve, provided that the rules are nondiscriminatory in nature and are applied fairly and evenly to everyone. If rules adopted by a complex are unreasonable, they are not enforceable.

Discrimination against handicapped persons is prohibited. The term *handicapped* refers to both physically and mentally handicapped persons. Landlords and sellers cannot discriminate against persons with HIV or AIDS as they are considered a handicap under the act. Guide dogs and support animals are protected under the act as well, and discrimination against them is strictly prohibited, including any requirement for additional security deposits.

If a handicapped person rents a property and must make alterations to accommodate the handicap, the property manager or landlord may not prohibit the renter from doing so, so long as she pays for the alterations; the landlord is under no obligation to pay for such alterations. The property manager or landlord can require the

tenant to restore the premises to their original condition upon vacating the premises, at their discretion.

In the event that someone files a complaint alleging housing discrimination against brokers, those brokers will find the burden of proof shifted to them to prove they did not discriminate, unless they have prominently displayed the Equal Housing Opportunity poster shown in Figure 3.2 in all of their rental offices.

Americans with Disabilities Act

The **Americans with Disabilities Act** (ADA) prohibits discrimination that would deny the equal enjoyment of goods, facilities, services, and accommodations in any existing place of public accommodation, based on an individual's physical or mental disabilities. A "place of public accommodation" applies to offices, stores, and other nonresidential, commercial public facilities.

Property management firms and virtually all owners and operators of such public facilities must make the facilities accessible to the extent readily achievable. "Readily achievable" is defined as easily accomplished without a great deal of expense. This would be based on the cost of compliance related to a property's value and on the financial abilities of the person or people involved. New construction, however, must be readily accessible unless it is impractical for structural reasons. Figure 3.3 lists some reasonable modifications to public facilities or services.

Employment discrimination is also protected by the ADA. If an employer has fifteen or more employees, she must alter the workplace to provide reasonable accommodations for handicapped employees unless it causes an undue hardship.

The act provides for civil penalties of $50,000 for the first discriminatory act and $100,000 for each subsequent violation, including compensatory damages and attorneys' fees.

California Fair Housing Laws

California has administrative regulations as well as several fair housing laws that deal with discrimination. Real estate professionals should take great care to become familiar with these acts and regulations to avoid the violation of more than one state and/or federal laws or regulations by committing just one act.

Unruh Act

The **Unruh Act** prohibits discrimination in all business establishments. It applies to all real estate licensees as well as any person

FIGURE 3.2   Equal Housing Opportunity Poster

U. S. Department of Housing and Urban Development

EQUAL HOUSING OPPORTUNITY

We Do Business in Accordance With the Federal Fair Housing Law

(The Fair Housing Amendments Act of 1988)

It is Illegal to Discriminate Against Any Person Because of Race, Color, Religion, Sex, Handicap, Familial Status, or National Origin

---

■ In the sale or rental of housing or residential lots

■ In advertising the sale or rental of housing

■ In the financing of housing

■ In the provision of real estate brokerage services

■ In the appraisal of housing

■ Blockbusting is also illegal

Anyone who feels he or she has been discriminated against may file a complaint of housing discrimination:
    1-800-669-9777 (Toll Free)
    1-800-927-9275 (TTY)

U.S. Department of Housing and Urban Development
Assistant Secretary for Fair Housing and Equal Opportunity
Washington, D.C. 20410

FIGURE 3.3   Reasonable Modifications to Public Facilities or Services

- Provide doors with automatic opening mechanisms.
- Lower public telephones.
- Provide ramps in addition to entry stairs.
- Install an intercom so customers can contact a second-floor business in a nonelevator building.
- Add grab bars to public restroom walls.
- Permit guide dogs to accompany customers.
- Provide a shopper's assistant to help disabled customers.
- Provide menus (and real estate listings) in a large-print or Braille format.

managing an apartment building or other business establishment. A person found guilty of violating this act may be fined for any personal damages plus $250. Age discrimination has been added to the provisions of the act in rental apartments and condominiums. Housing that is developed and designed for the special needs of senior citizens is exempt from this act.

Rumford Fair Housing Act

The **Fair Employment and Housing Act** (Government Code Sections 12900 et seq.), also known as the **Rumford Act**, prohibits discrimination in supplying housing accommodations on the basis of sex, color, race, religion, marital status, ancestry, or national origin. Anyone selling, renting, leasing, or financing housing must comply with the Rumford Act. An individual who violates this act may be reported to the Fair Employment Practices Commission within sixty days of the occurrence. Any violation of this act also violates the federal act. The Rumford Act predates the Civil Rights Act of 1968.

At Home with Diversity

The typical buyer in today's real estate market is very diverse in many different ways. The NAR and HUD have recognized this by creating a program called "At Home with Diversity." The purpose of this program is to expand homeownership opportunities for more Americans by training real estate professionals to actively and aggressively seek out potential homebuyers from all racial and cultural backgrounds. Licensees who take this training program will:

- Learn how attending diverse cultural and community events will help to expand their client bases.
- Learn how education in simple multicultural etiquette can lead to success with new clients and customers.
- Develop sound diversity practices and strategies to incorporate into their overall business plan.

3.4 THE CALIFORNIA BUSINESS AND PROFESSIONS CODE

In addition to compliance with federal and state fair housing laws, the behavior of real estate licensees is governed by the California Business and Professions Code. The code provides detailed antidiscrimination information, including a definition of the term *discrimination* as used within the code. It also contains sections dealing with behavioral guidelines for licensees and what constitutes grounds for disciplinary action in the event of noncompliance.

Section 125.6: Disciplinary Provisions for Discriminatory Acts

Under Section 125.6, every person who holds a license under the provisions of the code is subject to disciplinary action if she refuses to perform the licensed activity or makes any discrimination or restriction in the performance of the licensed activity because of an applicant's race, color, sex, religion, ancestry, physical handicap, or national origin.

Section 10177(l): Further Grounds for Disciplinary Action

Discrimination occurs if a licensee "solicited or induced the sale, lease, or the listing for sale or lease of residential property on the ground, wholly or in part, of loss of value, increase in crime, or decline of the quality of the schools, due to the presence or prospective entry into the neighborhood of a person or persons of another race, color, religion, ancestry, or national origin."

Section 2780: Discriminatory Conduct

Section 2780 prohibits discriminatory conduct by real estate licensees based on race, color, sex, religion, physical handicap, or national origin and includes:

a. Refusing to negotiate for the sale, rental, or financing.
b. Refusing or failing to show, rent, sell, or finance.
c. Discriminating against any person in the sale or purchase, collection of payments, or performance of services.
d. Discriminating in the conditions or privileges of sale, rental, or financing.

e. Discriminating in processing applications, referrals, or assigning licensees.
f. Representing real property as not available for inspection.
g. Processing an application more slowly.
h. Making any effort to encourage discrimination.
i. Refusing to assist another licensee.
j. Making an effort to obstruct, retard, or discourage a purchase.
k. Expressing or implying a limitation, preference, or discrimination.
l. Coercing, intimidating, threatening, or interfering.
m. Soliciting restrictively.
n. Maintaining restrictive waiting lists.
o. Seeking to discourage or prevent transactions.
p. Representing alleged community opposition.
q. Representing desirability of particular properties.
r. Refusing to accept listings.
s. Agreeing not to show property.
t. Advertising in a manner that indicates discrimination.
u. Using wording that indicates preferential treatment.
v. Advertising selectively.
w. Maintaining selective pricing, rent, cleaning, or security deposits.
x. Financing in a discriminatory manner.
y. Discriminating in pricing.
z. Discriminating in services.
aa. Discriminating against owners, occupants, or guests.
ab. Making an effort to encourage discrimination.
ac. Implementing discriminatory rule in multiple listings and other services.
ad. Assisting one who intends to discriminate.

Section 2781: Panic Selling

Section 2781 prohibits discriminatory conduct that creates fear or alarm to induce sale or lease because of the entry into an area of persons of another race, color, sex, religion, ancestry, or national origin.

Section 2725f: Duty to Supervise

Section 2725f requires a broker to take reasonable steps to be familiar with, and to familiarize her salespersons with, the federal and state laws pertaining to the prohibition of discriminatory process.

The Holden Act (Housing Financial Discrimination Act of 1977)

The Holden Act prohibits financial institutions from engaging in discriminatory loan activities or practices. Activities covered under this act include awarding building, improvement, purchase, or refinancing loans using the criteria of race, color, national origin, ancestry, sex, religion, or marital status. Discrimination based on the ethnic composition of the area surrounding a property (redlining) is also illegal.

3.5 COMMISSIONER'S RULES AND REGULATIONS

Article 10 of the Real Estate Commissioner's Rules and Regulations concerns the discriminatory activities of real estate licensees. Regulations 2780, 2781, and 2725f, which are contained within Article 10 and summarized earlier, list unacceptable discriminatory practices by licensees. According to Regulation 2780, real estate licensees may be disciplined by the Commissioner for conducting discriminatory activities.

Sometimes politics and other national issues can play a significant part in the passage of legislation in the United States. It was the assassination of Dr. Martin Luther King, Jr., in 1968 that finally led Congress to enact fair housing legislation at that time. Another issue was that the deaths in Vietnam at that time were falling most heavily on young, poor African and Hispanic Americans. While these groups were suffering the most casualties, on the home front they could not purchase or rent homes for their families due to unfair housing practices. It is bad business to be anything but "color blind" in your dealings with the public.

3.6 SEXUAL HARASSMENT

In today's work environment, you must be keenly aware of what may be regarded by others as being **sexual harassment.** Sexual harassment can be defined *by how your actions are viewed by others*, not necessarily by your intent, and if you are charged with sexual harassment, you may incur huge legal expenses to defend yourself as well as significant damage awards or settlement costs.

A claim of sexual harassment may also seriously harm your reputation in the workplace and your working relationship with your peers.

Always remember that you are licensed to fulfill the real estate needs of others—period.

The Golden Rule really applies here, so, in general:

- Avoid sexually oriented jokes and stories and keep your love life and gossip about the love life of others in your office to yourself.
- Take great care in touching others; your friendly pat may be mistaken for something that it wasn't intended to be.
- Be aware of the "space" requirements of various cultures. Although in some cultures it is perfectly all right to be very close and face-to-face, it may be seen as intimidation or sexual harassment in others.
- Romantic overtures, gestures, and entanglements are to be discouraged in the workplace. Repeatedly asking someone for a date may be deemed harassment, and even if you do start a relationship that does not end well, it can make for a very uncomfortable working relationship.

If a client or customer seems to be inviting sexual advances, ignore them. If you respond and you are wrong, you could end up facing sexual harassment charges or at least find yourself in an extremely embarrassing situation and lose a client.

3.7 REAL ESTATE SETTLEMENT PROCEDURES ACT

During the 1960s and early 1970s, companies involved with "settlement procedures" that were necessary to conduct an escrow for the purchase and sale of a property were often engaged in "buying" business from real estate brokers and others. Complaints to the federal government from consumers and from within the real estate and related industries caused Congress to charge HUD to start an investigation of the matter. Upon completion of HUD's findings, Congress enacted the **RESPA of 1974**. The Act was revised in 1980.

Although there was a flurry of initial activity, enforcement quickly became almost dormant; however, in 2003, under the Bush administration, HUD stepped up its enforcement activity considerably. By entering into a contract with an investigation firm in Arlington, Virginia, to conduct on-site reviews to monitor conformity, the department has nearly tripled its enforcement staff, which includes many ex-FBI agents who have actively taken on the role of **testers** as well as enforcers.

Who is covered by RESPA?

- Real estate brokers and salespersons.
- Mortgage bankers and mortgage brokers.
- Title and/or escrow companies and title agents.
- Home warranty companies.
- Hazard insurance agents.
- Appraisers.
- Home inspection and pest control inspectors.

RESPA does not apply to:

- Moving companies.
- Gardeners.
- Painters.
- Decorating companies.
- Home improvement companies.

RESPA Prohibitions

- RESPA prohibits a real estate broker or licensee from receiving a **thing of value** for referring business to a settlement service provider (SSP), such as a mortgage banker, mortgage broker, title company, or title agent.
- RESPA also prohibits SSPs from splitting fees received for settlement services, unless the fee is for a service actually performed. For example, while a real estate licensee may refer a client or customer to another licensee and legitimately collect a referral fee through their employing broker, that same licensee cannot fill out a loan application for a mortgage broker, do no other work on the loan, and collect all or a portion of any loan fee paid by the borrower.
- RESPA prohibits a seller or listing licensee from requiring that a buyer use and pay for a certain title insurance company or policy. No seller "shall require directly or indirectly, as a condition of selling the property, that title insurance covering the property be purchased by the buyer from any particular title company" (12 U.S.C. § 2608(a)). This can happen in northern California when the licensee opens an escrow for a new listing "with the buyer to come." Because title insurance companies and escrow companies are one and the same entity, by the seller opening the escrow before the buyer is acquired, the net effect is to indirectly force the buyer to use a particular title insurer. The seller or

seller's licensee who violates this law "shall be liable to the buyer in an amount equal to three times all charges made for such title insurance" (12 U.S.C. § 2608(b)). This would suggest that a seller or seller's licensee should not require the use of a particular title company even if the seller pays for the title policy.

With the passage of AB957 Buyer's Choice Act, by Assembly-member Cathleen Galgiani, on October 12, 2009, California buyers of short sale and foreclosed properties have the option of choosing their own local title and escrow company when purchasing bank-owned houses.

For non-RESPA transactions, such as those involving commercial property or vacant land, sellers are not expressly prohibited from demanding the use of a specific title company.

Exceptions to RESPA's Prohibitions

Not all referral arrangements fall under RESPA's referral restrictions. In fact, RESPA and its regulation feature a number of exceptions, including the following:

- **Promotional and educational activities**
  - Settlement Service Providers (SSPs), such as mortgage bankers, mortgage brokers, title insurance companies, and title agents, can provide normal promotional and educational activities under RESPA.
  - The above activities must not defray the expenses that the real estate licensee would otherwise have to pay.
  - The activities cannot be in exchange for or tied in any way to referrals.

- **Payments in return for goods provided or services performed**
  - A real estate licensee must provide goods, facilities, and services that are actual, necessary, and distinct from what they already provide.
  - The amount paid to a real estate licensee must be commensurate with the value of the goods provided and services performed. If the payment exceeds market value, the excess is considered a kickback that violates RESPA.
  - Payment for services rendered should not be based on whether the real estate licensee's services resulted in a successful transaction. Payment may not be tied to the success of the real estate licensee's efforts but must be a flat fee that represents fair market value.

- **Affiliated business arrangements**
  - Real estate licensees are permitted to own an interest in a settlement company, such as a mortgage brokerage or title company, so long as the real estate licensee:
    - Discloses her relationship with the joint venture company when it refers a customer to the mortgage broker or title company.
    - Does not require the customer to use the joint venture mortgage broker or title company as a condition for the sale or purchase of a home.
    - Does not receive any payments from the joint venture company other than a return on its ownership interest in the company. These payments cannot vary based on the volume of referrals to the joint venture company.

The joint venture mortgage broker or title company must be a bona fide, stand-alone business with sufficient capital, employees, and separate office space, and must perform core services associated with that industry.

Examples of Permissible Activities and Payments

- A title company provides a food tray for an Open House and posts a sign in a prominent location indicating that the event was sponsored by the title company, and its representative stays at the Open House and distributes brochures about the company's services.
- A mortgage lender sponsors an educational lunch for real estate licensees where employees of the lender are invited to speak. If, however, the mortgage lender subsidizes the costs of continuing education credits, this activity may be seen as defraying costs the licensee would otherwise incur and may be characterized as an unallowable referral fee.
- A title company hosts an event that various individuals, including real estate licensees, will attend and posts a sign identifying the title company's contribution to the event in a prominent location for all attending to see and distributes brochures regarding the title company's services.
- A hazard insurance company provides notepads, pens, or other office materials reflecting the hazard insurance company's name.
- A mortgage broker sponsors the hole-in-one contest at a golf tournament and prominently displays a sign reflecting the brokerage's name and involvement in the tournament.

- A real estate licensee and a mortgage broker jointly advertise their services in a real estate magazine, provided that each individual pays a share of the costs in proportion with her prominence in the advertisement.
- A lender pays a real estate broker fair market value to rent a desk, copy machine, and phone line in the real estate broker's office for a loan officer to prequalify applicants.
- A title company pays for dinner for a real estate licensee during which business is discussed, provided that such dinners are not a regular or expected service.

Examples of Prohibited Activities and Payments

- A title company hosts a monthly dinner and reception for real estate licensees.
- A mortgage broker pays for a keybox without including any information identifying the mortgage broker on the keybox.
- A mortgage lender provides lunch at an Open House but does not distribute brochures or display any marketing materials.
- A hazard insurance company hosts a "happy hour" and dinner outing only for real estate brokers and licensees who have referred business to them in the past year.
- A home inspector pays for a real estate licensee's dinner but does not attend the dinner.
- A title company makes a lump-sum payment toward a function hosted by the real estate licensee but does not provide advertising materials or make a presentation at the function.
- A mortgage broker buys tickets to a sporting event for a real estate licensee or pays for the licensee to play a round of golf.
- A title company sponsors a "getaway" in a tropical location, during which only an hour or two is dedicated to education and the remainder of the event is directed toward recreation.
- A mortgage lender pays a real estate licensee for taking the loan application and collecting credit documents only if the activity results in a loan.

Before you undertake any activity with a SSP or accept any payments, goods, or services from a SSP, you should speak with your employing broker or a real estate attorney who is familiar with RESPA. Make sure the activity complies with state and local laws. Some of these laws prohibit activities that are otherwise permissible under RESPA.

3.8 CASE STUDIES OF ETHICS, FAIR HOUSING, AND RESPA

The following case studies regarding compliance with ethical conduct, fair housing issues, and adherence to RESPA's guidelines will help you be a responsible public servant in your role as a real estate professional.

Case Study 1

Broker Mike Evans was contacted by Mary, an elderly widow who said she wanted to sell her home and move closer to her children. Even though she was anxious to move, Mary said she wanted to get as much for the property as she could, as it was all that she had. Evans did a market analysis that clearly showed a comparative value of $350,000. When Evans met with Mary, he told her, without presenting the research he had done, that she "could sell at $300,000 very quickly." He then listed the property and immediately presented her with an offer from one of his clients for that amount and told her she should sign it as it was "a good deal." The property never had any MLS exposure and it was a "hot market." Evans did not disclose his dual agency status. Analyze Evans's actions from an ethical perspective.

Analysis 1

The minute Mike Evans signed his name to the listing contract, a fiduciary relationship was created between him and Mary. He had the utmost duty of fidelity, loyalty, and honesty to her as well as a duty to protect and promote her best interests. It is clear that he violated every one of these canons of the Code of Ethics. Knowing that she was elderly, he probably should have recommended that she consult with one or more of her children prior to making any decisions. He also had a duty to share with her all of the information he had gathered about the property's value and the market conditions, and he certainly had a legal duty as well as an ethical one to disclose his role as a dual agent. The Golden Rule was tossed out the window by broker Evans. Legally speaking, he is very likely guilty of gross negligence as well, if Mary and/or her children should pursue the issue. Code of Ethics Article 1, Standard of Practice 1-3 and 1-5.

Case Study 2

Ralph Johnson wanted to buy a home in a particular subdivision where there were no listings available at the time. He signed a

Buyer/Broker Representation Agreement with Jim Foss, a local real estate licensee, and asked Jim to find him a home. After checking the National Do-Not-Call-List, Jim began cold-calling in the neighborhood and found a couple that was willing to sell if he "could get them their price" of over $500,000 net to them. Jim's commission was to be anything over that. Even though Jim's company charged an average of 6 percent of the sales price as a commission, Jim listed the home under those circumstances (often called a "net" listing) and showed the home to Ralph, stating that the sellers were firm at $570,000. Ralph really liked the home and agreed to pay the price. Did Jim violate any ethical standards? Did he violate the law?

Analysis 2

The first issue to address here is Jim's relationship with Ralph. Ralph signed a Buyer/Broker Representation Agreement with Jim. That created a fiduciary relationship between them and made Ralph's interests "of the utmost importance" to Jim. By increasing the price by more than double his company's normal compensation, Jim definitely did not act in his buyer–client's best interest nor did he make any attempt to negotiate this fee. In fact, Jim lied when he said the owners were firm at $570,000 when they were actually "firm at $500,000." It was Jim's fee of $70,000 that was firm. He could have secured the property for Ralph at a lesser price and still received reasonable compensation. When Jim took the listing, he also created a fiduciary relationship with the sellers, whereby he agreed to act in their best interest as well. By not informing the sellers of the actual fair market value and then securing a buyer for that amount plus a compensation charge based on negotiation with the seller, Jim placed his own interests ahead of the sellers thus breaching the contract as well as his ethical and fiduciary duty. Code of Ethics Article 1, Standard of Practice 1-12 and 1-13.

Case Study 3

Larry is very effective at listing property for sale. When he gets a low- or mid-priced listing, he always submits it to the MLS within two days as prescribed by the MLS rules and regulations. When he gets a more expensive listing, however, or one he knows is highly saleable, he convinces the owners that it would be best to take an exclusive listing only for their protection and privacy and not invite MLS participation by the other brokers.

When other brokers call about his signs or advertising on these "exclusive" listings, Larry tells them that the owner only wants his firm to work on the sale of the property and that at the owner's direction, he is not cooperating with other brokers. Is there anything unethical about his activities?

Analysis 3

This is a clear example of business conduct that goes completely against the Golden Rule as well as ethical conduct. By not cooperating on his higher-priced listings and refusing to share them with other brokers, Larry has greatly diminished the exposure and the competition for these listings. Because of Larry's selfish and unethical actions, his clients may very well receive lower sales prices for their homes. Violates Articles 3 and 12 of the Code of Ethics in addition to legal misrepresentation.

Case Study 4

Carla and her four children stopped at a real estate office that advertised rental services in the newspaper. She asked Louis, the licensee on duty, if his firm had any rentals she could look at since she wanted to get her children into a better school system. Louis told her all they currently had available was a studio apartment. He did not offer to have her fill out a rental or credit application.

Later that day, Bob and Eileen stopped at the office with their two children and asked about rentals in the same area where Carla had expressed an interest. Louis told them that although they had nothing right now, a nice three-bedroom house was coming up in the area in about a month. Louis offered to have them fill out a rental and credit report application and told them he would call as soon as the place became available. Has Louis violated any fair housing laws?

Analysis 4

The 1988 Fair Housing Amendments Act made familial status a protected class. The Civil Rights Act of 1968 also makes the "refusal to show, rent, or sell through the false representation that a property is not available," a federal violation. Louis, by his refusal to afford Carla the same courtesies and opportunities as he did to Bob and Eileen, is in violation of at least two federal fair housing

laws. While landlords may place a restriction on the number of occupants in a particular size unit, such as two persons per bedroom, any such restrictions must be applied fairly and equally to all parties. It should also be noted that, since Louis did not offer Carla the chance to fill out a rental application or have her credit investigated by his firm, he had absolutely no knowledge of her ability to qualify for the monthly rent on the home he told Bob and Eileen about.

Case Study 5

Broker Sally met Mr. and Mrs. Wong at an Open House last Sunday and is taking them out to see homes this Saturday. As they leave the parking lot, Sally says to the Wongs, "I found several homes in a mainly Chinese part of town that I thought you would be very interested in looking at. There are several Asian food stores and other Asian culture businesses nearby. I hope you like what I have found for you." Did Sally do anything wrong?

Analysis 5

She certainly did! Although Sally may have been well-meaning, she is in clear violation of the Civil Rights Act of 1968, which states that "steering, which is directing people of different races, religions, etc., away from or toward particular areas" is a violation of their civil rights. Sally made the mistake of assuming that because the Wongs were of Asian descent they automatically had a preference to live in a largely Asian neighborhood.

Sally had a duty to ask Mr. and Mrs. Wong about the items and issues important to them in their choice of neighborhoods and then show them homes in any and all neighborhoods that were a reasonable fit to their specific needs. Even if the Wongs stated that they only wanted to look at homes in that particular neighborhood, Sally still had a duty to explain to them that there were other neighborhoods they may find just as fulfilling to live in and then suggest they view those homes. Even if the Wongs said no, Sally would have fulfilled her duty.

Case Study 6

George is a loan agent for Michael's mortgage company. A broker referred Lionel and Teresa, an African American couple, to George

for financing on a home he had sold to them. Their credit FICO score was in the mid- to upper-500 range. This score was low due to the couple's credit problems, including car repossession. As it turned out, Lionel had been laid off from his job about three years prior and filed Chapter 7 bankruptcy a year later. While George carefully assembled the couple's file and tried to place it with several lenders, the best interest rate he could get was 8.75 percent for thirty years with a 2 percent loan origination fee. The going rate for loans of that type was 6.125 percent at the time. Was George discriminating against Lionel and Teresa because of their race? Did he violate their civil rights?

Analysis 6

Although Lionel and Teresa could obtain a loan that was only about 2.5 percent higher than the prevailing rate, it appears that George made a good-faith attempt to provide them with the best financing available to them. The reason for the higher interest rate and loan origination fee appears to be based on the couple's past credit history and not their race, so George does not appear to have violated their civil rights.

Case Study 7

Ken, a veteran of the war in Afghanistan, lost both of his legs in an explosion and gets around in a wheelchair. He went into broker Barry's real estate office and asked if there were any one-story rentals available. Barry told Ken that he was sorry, but, while they had some single-story homes available, they didn't have anything that would accommodate a wheelchair. He asked Ken to check back in a few weeks. Did Barry violate Ken's civil rights?

Analysis 7

Barry doesn't seem to understand the law as it applies to the rights of handicapped persons and property being made available to them. It isn't Barry who decides whether a rental property is or is not suitable for a person with a disability. Under the law, Ken may, at his own expense, make reasonable alterations to a property he rents to accommodate his wheelchair. He must also return the property to its original condition at his expense at the conclusion of the lease, unless the property owner wishes to leave the

improvements in place. Barry has violated Ken's civil rights under the 1988 Fair Housing Amendments Act.

Case Study 8

A title company, in an effort to gain the loyalty and referrals of the real estate community, paid for and created Internet virtual home tour software and made it freely available to the real estate licensees in the area. Is this a RESPA violation?

Analysis 8

HUD claims that the real estate licensees accepting virtual tours in exchange for the referral of business is in violation of Section 8 of RESPA. In two separate settlement agreements, brokers agreed to stop the practice and to notify their licensees in writing that accepting virtual tours at a discount or at no cost violates RESPA. The brokers agreed to make a combined $19,200 payment to the U.S. Treasury.

Note: In a HUD settlement with seven Austin-area title companies that provided these virtual tours as an incentive to refer business, the companies agreed that if they provide virtual tours in the future they would charge a fee that would, at a minimum, represent their actual costs. In addition, the title companies agreed to pay more than $130,000 in settlement payments.

Case Study 9

A mortgage broker sponsors a seminar to inform real estate professionals about its mortgage products and prequalification programs. Complimentary coffee, tea, and snacks are provided for all attendees. Is this a RESPA violation?

Analysis 9

A HUD ruling states that normal promotional and educational activities that are not conditioned on the referral of business are permissible. If the "education or training" had involved a dinner gala or a day at the country club for those "preferred" real estate professionals who work with that mortgage broker, the events would likely be considered violations of RESPA. They are not "normal" promotional and educational programs and they are being offered to select real estate professionals in return for the business they refer to the mortgage broker.

Case Study 10

A real estate licensee refers as many of her buyer–clients as she can to a particular lender. That lender pays for advertising, business cards, and promotional materials for that licensee's use. Is the licensee and/or the lender in violation of RESPA?

Analysis 10

HUD ruled that these activities violate RESPA because the advertising and promotional materials are considered "things of value" given to the real estate licensee in exchange for referral business.

Note: Joint advertising between a lender or other service provider and a real estate licensee is permissible as long as the cost of the advertising is reasonably allocated between the joint advertisers.

SUMMARY

Ethics, which deals with what is right and wrong, may differ from the law, which deals with what is legal and illegal, and sets minimum standards of acceptable conduct. The ultimate test of whether or not an act is ethical is its adherence to the Golden Rule.

The NAR and the National Association of Real Estate Brokers maintain professional ethical codes. These codes have been developed, implemented, and enforced in order to promote professionalism in the real estate and related industries.

The federal government first became involved with Federal Fair Housing legislation when it enacted the Civil Rights Act of 1866, which applied to racial discrimination. The act was reiterated in the Civil Rights Act of 1870, and in 1962, President John Kennedy issued Executive Order 11063, which prohibited housing discrimination where federal funds were involved, and that order was made law by the Civil Rights Act of 1964. In addition to race, under the Civil Rights Act of 1968, protection against discrimination was expanded to include national origin, color, and religion. The act has since been amended to include sex, physical handicaps, and familial status. Acts such as steering (directing persons to housing based on their race) and blockbusting (obtaining listings or sales based on a fear of loss of property value because of the entry of minority groups into a neighborhood) are specifically prohibited.

The ADA requires that owners and operators of places of public accommodations make the premises accessible to handicapped people to the extent readily achievable.

A **diversity training** program, developed by the NAR, helps licensees understand the customs and cultures of other nationalities

and how their diverse backgrounds affect their decision-making processes.

In California, the Unruh Act prohibits discrimination by a business establishment and is considered to be California's Fair Housing Act. The Holden Act prohibits financial institutions from engaging in discriminatory actions and practices. You can find details regarding discriminatory practices by California real estate licensees in the California Business and Professions Code and the Real Estate Commissioner's Rules and Regulations.

CLASS DISCUSSION TOPICS

1. Have you ever been subjected to discrimination of any kind? If so, describe the situation and discuss how it made you feel.

2. You overheard a licensee in your office telling someone over the telephone that she had two offers on her listing, one of which was her own, and that since hers was so good, she didn't tell the sellers about the other offer. What should you do?

3. You are showing property to a middle-aged couple. They ask you to pull over to the curb and just sit there for a while so they can observe the ethnic makeup of the people who pass by. Discuss how you should handle that situation.

4. Bill just got a new listing that is only a block away from the local synagogue. He feels that it is a major selling point and writes and submits an ad to you to approve that says: "This beautiful home is steps away from the Jewish Synagogue; don't miss this great opportunity!" Is Bill in violation of any antidiscrimination laws or Code of Ethics issues? If so, which ones?

5. Broker Jerry listed a thirty-home subdivision. He advertised that the homes were "selling fast." As buyers came in to the model home, they were shown a model of the subdivision that had "Sold" flags on quite a number of the lots. The truth was that only four homes had actually sold. What are the ethical and legal ramifications of Jerry's actions?

6. Richard and Sue were salespersons from competing offices. They were both asked to give a listing presentation to the Johnsons. The market data very clearly showed the Johnsons' home to be worth about $475,000. It was an average market with a reasonably good supply/demand ratio. Sue showed the comparables to the Johnsons and suggested an asking price of $489,000. Richard showed them the same data, but suggested, "because the market is so hot, you can probably get $525,000 and you should list at $525,000." Are either Richard or Sue guilty of a violation of the Code of Ethics?

7. Virgil, who is handicapped and gets around in a wheelchair, has made arrangements to meet friends at a local restaurant for dinner. When he arrives, the receptionist tells him that she is very sorry, but the front doors aren't wide enough to accommodate his wheelchair and it is too crowded inside for it as well. She suggests a restaurant down the street. Is the restaurant in violation of any civil rights issues, and if so, which one(s)?

8. Sammy has shown a number of homes to Gloria and Jeff who have declined them because of their proximity to traffic noise.

Sammy has just shown them a home they really want to buy. It is on a reasonably quiet, two-lane street, but Sammy knows that it is scheduled for widening into a four-lane major thoroughfare within the next two years. He sells the home to Gloria and Jeff without mentioning the street widening and the sellers do not disclose it in their Transfer Disclosure Statement. Has either Sammy or the sellers done anything wrong? If there was any wrongdoing by either party, was it unethical, illegal, or both?

9. Lisa, a title company representative, wants to get Geri's title and escrow business. She tells Geri that she will advertise in the local real estate magazine with her and take 20 percent of the page, letting Geri have the other 80 percent. Lisa states that she will pay 20 percent of the cost of the ad and have information about her company in that portion. Is Lisa violating the RESPA?

10. Bill is an insurance broker. He invites three real estate brokers to play golf with him at his club and he pays for their green fees and golf cart. They have a great time and during the game, Bill says that he really appreciates their business and that if they keep sending him referrals like they have been, that there's "plenty of golf matches to come." Has anyone in this foursome violated RESPA? If so, how?

CHAPTER 3 QUIZ

1. Which of the following best describes ethics?
   A. Doing what is right because it is right.
   B. Doing what is legal.
   C. Doing what meets your personal needs best.
   D. Doing what is expeditious.

2. The relationship that ethics has to law is
   A. the law is preceded by ethics.
   B. what is ethical is legal.
   C. if an act is illegal, it is also unethical.
   D. ethics and the law set minimum standards of behavior.

3. A broker who had a disabled employee widened the restroom doorway to accommodate a wheelchair. This work complied with the
   A. Fair Housing Amendment Act of 1988
   B. Rumford Fair Housing Act
   C. Executive Order 11063
   D. Americans with Disabilities Act

4. Which of the following would not be an unethical act?

   A. Having multiple offers on your own listing, including your own offer, and only telling the seller about your own offer.

   B. Taking the long route to show a home to someone so that you can show them the schools, parks, and other area amenities.

   C. Placing all of your listings immediately on the MLS, regardless of how "saleable" they are.

   D. Telling a licensee who calls about one of your listings that the property is sold, when it really isn't because you think you have a buyer for it yourself.

5. Which of the following words is considered discriminatory in an ad?

   A. Married couple's dream

   B. Near St. Bartholomew's Catholic Church

   C. Single Christian woman preferred

   D. All of the above

6. A broker is canvassing a neighborhood for listings by telling the occupants that minorities are moving in and prices will soon start to decline. His actions are

   A. illegal.

   B. unethical.

   C. blockbusting.

   D. All of the above.

7. A broker declined to show a home in a gated community to a young Hispanic family with four young children, even after the family had inquired about the home. The broker's action would be proper if

   A. elderly people occupied 73 percent of the homes.

   B. the broker considered the home to be too small for the family.

   C. there were no other children in the development.

   D. the development was restricted by the Covenants, Conditions, and Restrictions to occupants fifty-five years of age or older.

8. Which of the following is not a RESPA violation?

   A. A broker sharing advertising space on a pro rata basis with a lender, where they each pay their proportionate share of the cost.

   B. A home inspector who gives dinner certificates to several real estate licensees who use her services all the time.

   C. An insurance broker who buys theater tickets for a real estate licensee who sends her lots of business.

   D. None of the above.

9. A lender hosts a continuing education program for real estate professionals. Which of the following is a RESPA violation?

A. Have a representative present and promote the lender's services.

B. Defray the cost of the program tuition.

C. Hand out promotional material about the lender's services at the program.

D. Provide complimentary food and beverages.

10. A mortgage broker provides a snack tray and sodas for a real estate licensee's Open House. The mortgage broker does not appear at the Open House nor does he provide any marketing or promotional materials for the Open House. His actions are

A. unethical.

B. legal.

C. very kind.

D. a RESPA violation.

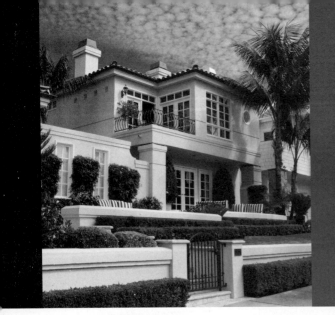

Chapter

4

IMPORTANT PHRASES AND TERMS

Agency disclosure

Agent's Inspection
    Disclosure

AIDS disclosure

Common interest
    subdivision

Dual agency

Earthquake safety
    disclosure
    statement

*Easton v.
    Strassburger*

Estoppel

Fiduciary
    relationship

Fiduciary
    responsibilities

Hazardous waste
    disclosure

Megan's Law

Military ordnance
    location

Principal

Public reports

Real Estate TDS

Red flag

Rescission rights

Seller Financing
    Addendum and
    Disclosure

Stigmatized
    property

Disclosures

Upon completion of this chapter, the student will be able to:

- Explain a licensee's fiduciary responsibility.
- Identify material facts requiring disclosure.
- Distinguish single versus dual agency.
- Employ proper agency disclosure timing and sequence.
- Recognize and implement proper disclosures.
- Describe buyer right to rescind under the TDS.

4.1 UNDERSTANDING MANDATED DISCLOSURES

Caveat emptor, or "buyer beware," has been around for centuries. It was the basis on which real estate transactions were conducted until the mid-1970s, when the California courts, legislators, and the Department of Real Estate (DRE) started enacting more and more consumer protection disclosure laws. Real estate law has always stressed full disclosure; however, many licensees did not understand when full disclosure was necessary and what it meant. As consumerism grew rapidly in the 1970s and beyond, many buyers and sellers began to sue real estate brokers and their licensees for nondisclosure issues. These new laws and regulations have led to more paperwork and better transaction management by real estate professionals in order to properly serve and protect the consumer.

The old real estate adage, "location, location, and location," has now been replaced by "disclose, disclose, and disclose."

Although commercial real estate transactions have their own set of disclosure issues, the issues discussed in this chapter deal primarily with one to four residential units and are general in nature. When faced with any situation involving a specific set of facts, you will need to consult your broker or a real estate attorney. Remember, full disclosure is the best way to protect your client, your broker, and you, as well as to avoid future litigation.

What does *full disclosure* really mean? It is the act of disclosing to a buyer fully and accurately all known material facts relevant to a decision maker in a transaction. A *material fact* is any fact relevant to a person making a decision. This is based on the logical notion that no fraud is committed if the decision maker has full and accurate information regarding a decision to purchase property. A material fact is any fact that would or could affect the decision of a party to a transaction to complete that lease, purchase, or sale. Usually many issues concerning a property must be disclosed to legally complete the sale or lease of the property. These issues affect not only the licensees but the principals as well. This is why a licensee must carefully consider all material facts, fully disclose them in a proper and timely manner, and advise her clients to do the same.

Full disclosure satisfies three things: (1) it protects the principals, including buyers, sellers, tenants, and landlords, (2) it establishes trust and confidence between the licensee and the principal, and (3) it satisfies both the licensee's and the principal's duties under the law. The importance of full, written disclosure cannot be overemphasized. There is much truth in the adage, "A verbal disclosure isn't worth the paper that it's not written on." Licensees must also be careful to see that the recipient of the disclosures not only receives them but also acknowledges receipt in writing. Because reading and understanding are two entirely separate things, it is important that licensees discuss and clarify with a seller or buyer anything that may not be clearly understood by the parties and then make a note of the discussion in their contemporaneous log. If understanding continues to elude the seller or buyer, they should be referred in writing to an appropriate professional.

Although any information conveyed to a principal may be considered a disclosure, certain disclosures are mandated. ("Mandate" is from the Latin *manus*, or *mandamus*, meaning a judicial or legal command.) A mandate is an order given by a court or other authoritative body that requires performance of specific duties. Mandated disclosures are disclosures deemed necessary by regulatory authority to protect principals and parties to a transfer of real property.

The disclosures that are mandated by law and DRE are determined by need, judicial precedent, and requirements of the contract. The California Association of REALTORS® (C.A.R.) forms that incorporate these disclosures are updated twice a year by the publisher (REBS, Inc.) in order to meet the ever-changing disclosure requirements necessary to protect the parties to a purchase, sale, or lease of real property. Hence, the use of outdated or generic forms may result in the omission of one or more disclosures. As a real estate professional practicing in California, you are not excused from making a disclosure because you used the wrong form. C.A.R. is relatively unique in that it has a User Protection Agreement offering to defend any claim, on appeal, that alleges any preprinted provision of its latest version of a pre-printed or computer generated form does not meet the statutory/regulatory requirements at the time of printing. As noted, C.A.R. will not support the use of other than the most current version of its forms. Be certain you are using the most current form in order to fully protect the interests of your broker, your client, and the consumer.

Beyond the so-called mandated disclosures, a real estate licensee has a duty to fully disclose, as well as a duty to guide her principal concerning the issues of what must be disclosed. If you are ever in doubt as to whether or not to disclose, you would be well advised to err on the side of over disclosure.

4.2 YOUR FIDUCIARY RESPONSIBILITIES AND DISCLOSURES

We cannot talk about a licensee's fiduciary responsibilities to a client without first analyzing the difference between a client and a customer. A client employs a representative to perform some service for compensation or fee; this person is also called a **principal**. In common real estate parlance in California, a client is the seller and the buyer is the prospect or customer. More and more frequently, in California, buyers are looking for direct representation as clients. As a licensee, when you enter into a contractual agreement with a principal on behalf of your employing broker, you create an agent/principal relationship that carries with it certain **fiduciary responsibilities**. The principal in such a **fiduciary relationship** is owed complete allegiance by the licensee or representative as well as the duties of honesty, loyalty, full disclosure (except that race, color, national origin, handicap, religion, familial status, and sex are not considered material facts and should not be disclosed even if asked), utmost care, obedience (to all lawful requests of the principal), and accounting.

The responsibility owed to a customer (or unrepresented third party to an agency relationship) is somewhat different. As a licensed representative of your employing broker, when you negotiate a contract for a principal with whom your broker does *not* have a representation agreement, they become your broker's customer and you owe them the duties of honesty, fair dealing, and full disclosure.

Great care must be taken here because the line separating client and customer can be fuzzy. Remember, written contracts are required in real estate transactions primarily to ensure legal enforceability of any compensation agreement between the broker and his principal. An oral agreement or action of the parties can create an agency, and hence a fiduciary relationship, and in doing so may create an ostensible or undisclosed dual agency without any written agreement.

A broker's fiduciary responsibility (and therefore, the licensee's fiduciary responsibility) to her principal must always place the interests of the client above her own so the actions of any representing licensee must be consistent with the interests of both principals. The licensee may not act in the best interests of another party to a transaction to the detriment of her principal, nor may the licensee act to her own benefit to the detriment of the principal; for example, a licensee, working in a fully disclosed **dual agency** capacity, representing both parties in a transaction, may not commit an act that clearly favors one party to the detriment of the other party. An illustration of "self-dealing" could be found in a situation where a licensee was directed by a principal to find a particular type of property to purchase, who then found such a property and bought it for her personal resale at a profit either to the client or to someone else at a higher price; that licensee would be in violation of the law and her fiduciary duty. Such circumstances place the licensee in competition with the principal and thus violate the fiduciary duty of loyalty to the client.

The act of a fully disclosed dual agency (where both parties are represented by the same broker) is presently legal in California as long as the parties agree to this arrangement in writing prior to the commencement of representation (see C.A.R. form, Disclosure and Consent for Representation of More Than One Buyer or Seller (DA), Figure (4.1)). Extreme care must be taken to avoid situations where dual agency occurs without prior written, informed consent as this is a violation of real estate law (specifically, Section 10176(d) of the Business and Professions Code).

The fiduciary duty of the licensee includes finding or discovery and full disclosure of *visible* defects and other material facts about

FIGURE 4.1 Disclosure and Consent for Representation of More Than One Buyer or Seller (DA)

DISCLOSURE AND CONSENT FOR
REPRESENTATION OF MORE THAN ONE BUYER OR SELLER
(C.A.R. Form DA, Revised 11/06)

A real estate broker, whether a corporation, partnership or sole proprietorship ("Broker"), may represent more than one buyer or seller provided the Broker has made a disclosure and the principals have given their consent. This multiple representation can occur through an individual licensed as a broker or through different associate licensees acting for the Broker. The associate licensees may be working out of the same or different office locations.

Broker (individually or through its associate licensees) may be working with many prospective buyers at the same time. These prospective buyers may have an interest in, and make offers on, the same properties. Some of these properties may be listed with Broker and some may not. Broker will not limit or restrict any particular buyer from making an offer on any particular property whether or not Broker represents other buyers interested in the same property.

Broker (individually or through its associate licensees) may have listings on many properties at the same time. As a result, Broker will attempt to find buyers for each of those listed properties. Some listed properties may appeal to the same prospective buyers. Some properties may attract more prospective buyers than others. Some of these prospective buyers may be represented by Broker and some may not. Broker will market all listed properties to all prospective buyers whether or not Broker has another or other listed properties that may appeal to the same prospective buyers.

Buyer and Seller understand that Broker may represent more than one buyer or seller and even both buyer and seller on the same transaction.

If Seller is represented by Broker, Seller acknowledges that Broker may represent prospective buyers of Seller's property and consents to Broker acting as a dual agent for both Seller and Buyer in that transaction.

If Buyer is represented by Broker, Buyer acknowledges that Broker may represent sellers of property that Buyer is interested in acquiring and consents to Broker acting as a dual agent for both Buyer and Seller with regard to that property.

In the event of dual agency, Seller and Buyer agree that: **(a)** Broker, without the prior written consent of the Buyer, will not disclose to Seller that the Buyer is willing to pay a price greater than the offered price; **(b)** Broker, without the prior written consent of the Seller, will not disclose to the Buyer that Seller is willing to sell property at a price less than the listing price; and **(c)** other than as set forth in (a) and (b) above, a Dual Agent is obligated to disclose known facts materially affecting the value or desirability of the property to both parties.

NON CONFIDENTIALITY OF OFFERS: Buyer is advised that Seller or Listing Agent may disclose the existence, terms, or conditions of Buyer's offer unless all parties and their agent have signed a written confidentiality agreement. Whether any such information is actually disclosed depends on many factors, such as current market conditions, the prevailing practice in the real estate community, the Listing Agent's marketing strategy and the instructions of the Seller.

Seller and/or Buyer acknowledges reading and understanding this Disclosure and Consent for Representation of More Than One Buyer or Seller and agrees to the dual agency possibility disclosed.

Seller/Buyer _____ Date _____

Seller/Buyer _____ Date _____

Real Estate Broker (Firm) _____ Date _____

By _____

THIS FORM HAS BEEN APPROVED BY THE CALIFORNIA ASSOCIATION OF REALTORS® (C.A.R.). NO REPRESENTATION IS MADE AS TO THE LEGAL VALIDITY OR ADEQUACY OF ANY PROVISION IN ANY SPECIFIC TRANSACTION. A REAL ESTATE BROKER IS THE PERSON QUALIFIED TO ADVISE ON REAL ESTATE TRANSACTIONS. IF YOU DESIRE LEGAL OR TAX ADVICE, CONSULT AN APPROPRIATE PROFESSIONAL.

This form is available for use by the entire real estate industry. It is not intended to identify the user as a REALTOR®. REALTOR® is a registered collective membership mark which may be used only by members of the NATIONAL ASSOCIATION OF REALTORS® who subscribe to its Code of Ethics.

Published and Distributed by:
REAL ESTATE BUSINESS SERVICES, INC.
a subsidiary of the California Association of REALTORS®
525 South Virgil Avenue, Los Angeles, California 90020

DA REVISED 11/06 (PAGE 1 OF 1) Print Date

| Reviewed by _____ Date _____ |

REPRESENTATION OF MORE THAN ONE BUYER OR SELLER (DA PAGE 1 OF 1)

Source: Reprinted with permission of California Association of REALTORS®.

a property that the principal should or would want to know in order to make a decision regarding the purchase or sale of property. Full disclosure also includes disclosing any potential problems with the intended use of a property as determined by zoning regulations. It also includes a duty to fully and honestly investigate and convey information as it relates to a property's value with relation to current market conditions.

As a licensee, you may not have a fiduciary duty to an unrepresented principal, but you still have the duty of honesty, care, and diligence because you and your broker could be liable for any material misrepresentations or acts of negligence. For example, you represent a seller on a residential property. You receive an offer to purchase from an unrepresented buyer. You have personal knowledge of negative neighborhood problems (such as a personal dispute with a neighbor or loud and disruptive parties). If you have knowledge of these facts, you must disclose them to any potential buyer whether or not they are represented. Failure to disclose any known fact that could have a foreseeable effect on the value of the home is a breach of the care and diligence owed to an unrepresented buyer, and legally actionable (*Alexander v. McKnight*).

If, during the course of an escrow, you discover new material facts your principal would want to know about, you have a duty to fully disclose the new facts in writing as soon as possible. For example, if during the escrow you discover that the street is scheduled for widening, where some of your client's property will be taken from him and much more traffic noise will be created, you have a duty to disclose this immediately. This additional disclosure provided later than, and separate from, the Transfer Disclosure Statement (TDS) has the effect of giving the buyer(s) an additional three-day right to rescind the contract (five days if the disclosure is delivered by mail). Obviously, the sooner a disclosure can be made, the better for all concerned.

For one to four residential units, as a licensee, you have a duty to conduct a reasonably diligent visual walk-through inspection of the property. This will be discussed more thoroughly later in this chapter. Although the law requires a visual inspection by the licensee for "one to four residential" units, commercial properties are generally exempt if the property contains five or more living units. The licensee is required to visually inspect the residential portion of a commercial property containing four or fewer units. However, any material fact should always be disclosed no matter how many units or what type of properties are under consideration.

4.3 AGENCY DISCLOSURE

Any time an attorney is asked to review a transaction on behalf of a disgruntled principal, she usually first looks at the "agency disclosure" issue. The attorney determines if the principal was duly informed (via the specific agency disclosure requirement in California Civil Code [CCC] Section 2079.13–24) of the type of agency relationships commonly available for that transaction. If the other party to the transaction was represented by another broker, "single agency" representation would be proper; however, if the same broker represented both parties, even through the use of two or more licensees within the broker's firm, a "dual agency" relationship would exist and must be agreed to in writing by all parties to the transaction.

Care must be taken to avoid what is referred to as an *ostensible agency* that may arise as a result of the actions of the parties rather than that of any specific agreement. For example, if an owner knows a broker is showing her property to a prospective buyer without a written contract, to do so the owner must take specific steps to stop the unauthorized showings. If she does not, the law considers that the parties have just cause to believe the licensee to be the owner's agent. If, on the surface, the agency appears to exist, it may be considered an ostensible agency and the owner may not (by **estoppel**) disclaim its existence. In this example, an undisclosed dual agency could have been created had the owner failed to openly repudiate an agency relationship.

Similarly, if a licensee representing a buyer aids and assists a For Sale by Owner (who may be selling a property to a buyer–client she is representing), the licensee could have created an ostensible agency as well as an undisclosed dual agency for which the licensee and broker could become liable.

On January 1, 1988, CCC Section 2079.13–24, which deals with agency relationships in real estate transactions involving one to four residential units, became law in California. It made it legally mandatory for any licensee who becomes involved in the purchase or sale of one to four residential units to provide the seller and buyer in a real estate transaction with a copy of the disclosure form specified. C.A.R. form Disclosure Regarding Real Estate Agency Relationships (AD) meets this requirement.

To understand the **agency disclosure**, licensees must understand the term *agency*. An *agency* is a relationship created when one person (the principal) directs another to act on her behalf, usually in business dealings with another (third party). The agency disclosure

form defines an "agent" as "a person acting under provisions of title 9 (commencing with section 2295) in a real property transaction, and includes a person who is licensed as a real estate broker under Chapter 3 (commencing with Section 10130) of Part 1 of Division 4 of the Business & Professions Code, and under whose license a listing is executed or an offer to purchase is obtained."

The words *employing broker* and *agent* are synonymous. Real estate salespersons commonly call themselves "agents," but (for the purpose of compensation) there is only one *agent* in a real estate company, whether it is a sole proprietorship, Limited Liability Company (LLC), or corporation and that is the designated broker. All agency activity is done under the license and auspices of the designated broker.

The CCC Section 2079.13b defines *associate licensee* as: "a person who is licensed as a real estate broker or salesperson … and who is either licensed under a broker or has entered into a written contract with a broker to act as the broker's agent … and to function under the broker's supervision in the capacity of an associate licensee. The agent (broker) in the real property transaction bears responsibility for her associate licensees. When an associate licensee owes a duty to any principal, or to any buyer or seller who is not a principal in a real property transaction, that duty is equivalent to the duty owed to that party by the broker for whom the associate licensee functions." Although a company may include any number of people who have a California real estate broker license, they, along with those employed as real estate salespersons, are licensees of the employing broker.

A licensee who lists a seller's property is referred to in common parlance as the **listing agent** and a licensee who represents the buyer is referred to as the **selling agent**. However, *listing agent* is defined in the CCC as "a person who has obtained a listing of real property to act as an agent for compensation." As the only person authorized by law to act as an agent for compensation is a licensed real estate broker, it follows that the broker is the listing agent and the associate licensee is an agent of the broker. Similarly, *selling agent* is defined in the CCC as "a listing agent who acts alone, or an agent who acts in cooperation with a listing agent, and who sells or finds and obtains a buyer for a property for which no listing exists and presents an offer to purchase to the seller." In common usage, a licensee who represents the seller is referred to as the "seller's agent" and a licensee who represents the buyer is referred to as the "buyer's agent or selling agent." In this text, we refer to all but the principal broker as "licensees."

Single agency is the practice of representing either the buyer or the seller in a transaction but never both. An agent (employing broker) that represents a buyer and a seller in the same transaction is working as a dual agent. It is important to remember that the issue of *agency* refers to the real estate broker client relationship and not to an individual licensee.

Under the previous system, it was the seller who paid the commission and that fact (and Multiple Listing Service [MLS] rules) required everyone to be the seller's agent. This is no longer the case. The person providing the compensation does not automatically create an agency relationship. It is common for a large multi-office company to have a situation where one of its licensees writes a purchase offer or lease agreement on a listing taken by another licensee from a different office but within the same firm. When both associate licensees in the same transaction work under the license of the same broker, a dual agency is created that requires both disclosure to and agreement of the parties.

Common-law agency holds that a fiduciary owes a duty (among others) of loyalty to the principal. Obviously, there would be a conflict of interest if the broker in a dual agency transaction represented a seller who wanted to receive the highest price and a buyer who wanted to pay the lowest price. It is for this reason that dual agency, as practiced in California, requires a duty of utmost care, integrity, honesty, and loyalty to both the seller and the buyer. In representing both buyer and seller, the licensee "may not, without the express permission of the respective party, disclose to the other party that the seller will accept a price less than the listing price or that the buyer will pay a price greater that the price offered." Any discussion of price or terms should be avoided. It is always an excellent policy for each licensee to keep good written records of conversations and actions taken (by keeping a contemporaneous log or transaction diary). Always maintain clear communication with the other licensee. Overall, there is no substitute for full written disclosure and a documentary record of every aspect of the transaction in any agency relationship.

Franchise operations can cause some confusion regarding the agency relationships. Because franchise offices are independently owned and operated, they may give the impression of being the same broker/agency in a transaction, when in fact they are each different companies owned by different brokers and thus constitute a separate agency representation despite the similar names of the companies.

Remember that once an agency relationship is created, as a representative of your employing broker, you have taken on a high degree of obligation as defined under the law.

FIGURE 4.2   Agency Relationship

Agency Relationship

Seller	Buyer
Broker	Broker
Listing agent	Selling agent
1. Seller's agent	1. Seller's agent
2. Dual agent	2. Buyer's agent
	3. Dual agent

Figure 4.2 shows the different types of agency relationships.

Keep in mind that C.A.R. model MLS rules, which have been adopted by most MLS, allow only three types of agency: seller's agent, buyer's agent, and agent representing both seller and buyer. Subagency is not one of the categories and is specifically excluded as an option in the agency disclosure form (CCC 2079.13(o)). MLS members are allowed to represent buyers in offers to purchase properties listed on the MLS "for, or in anticipation of compensation from the seller for representing the purchaser with no requirement or authorization to be a subagent of the seller."

The Disclosure Process

Disclose – Elect – Confirm (DEC) is the three-step process of giving proper disclosure to a principal in a purchase, sale, or lease.

Step One: Disclose

In this step, completed in writing on the AD form, the licensee must provide her principal with a copy of the agency disclosure form. This form outlines the three different types of agency relationships, including seller's agent, buyer's agent, and agent representing both seller and buyer or dual agency, and how they operate. The law requires that licensees provide this disclosure as soon as practicable but "prior to entering into the listing agreement." With a buyer, agency disclosure is required "as soon as practicable but prior to presenting the seller with an offer to purchase." Signatures of buyer or seller on this form simply acknowledge receipt of a copy of the disclosure and the portions of the CCC printed on the reverse side or a separate page (see Figure 4.3). The licensee should tell clients or customers that this disclosure is required by law and what they are signing is just a receipt and not their election of any particular type of agency.

FIGURE 4.3   Disclosure Regarding Real Estate Agency Relationships (AD Revised 04/06)

DISCLOSURE REGARDING REAL ESTATE AGENCY RELATIONSHIP
(As required by the Civil Code)
(C.A.R. Form AD, Revised 4/06)

When you enter into a discussion with a real estate agent regarding a real estate transaction, you should from the outset understand what type of agency relationship or representation you wish to have with the agent in the transaction.

SELLER'S AGENT
A Seller's agent under a listing agreement with the Seller acts as the agent for the Seller only. A Seller's agent or a subagent of that agent has the following affirmative obligations:
To the Seller:
    A Fiduciary duty of utmost care, integrity, honesty and loyalty in dealings with the Seller.
To the Buyer and the Seller:
    (a) Diligent exercise of reasonable skill and care in performance of the agent's duties.
    (b) A duty of honest and fair dealing and good faith.
    (c) A duty to disclose all facts known to the agent materially affecting the value or desirability of the property that are not known to, or within the diligent attention and observation of, the parties.
An agent is not obligated to reveal to either party any confidential information obtained from the other party that does not involve the affirmative duties set forth above.

BUYER'S AGENT
A selling agent can, with a Buyer's consent, agree to act as agent for the Buyer only. In these situations, the agent is not the Seller's agent, even if by agreement the agent may receive compensation for services rendered, either in full or in part from the Seller. An agent acting only for a Buyer has the following affirmative obligations:
To the Buyer:
    A fiduciary duty of utmost care, integrity, honesty and loyalty in dealings with the Buyer.
To the Buyer and the Seller:
    (a) Diligent exercise of reasonable skill and care in performance of the agent's duties.
    (b) A duty of honest and fair dealing and good faith.
    (c) A duty to disclose all facts known to the agent materially affecting the value or desirability of the property that are not known to, or within the diligent attention and observation of, the parties.
An agent is not obligated to reveal to either party any confidential information obtained from the other party that does not involve the affirmative duties set forth above.

AGENT REPRESENTING BOTH SELLER AND BUYER
A real estate agent, either acting directly or through one or more associate licensees, can legally be the agent of both the Seller and the Buyer in a transaction, but only with the knowledge and consent of both the Seller and the Buyer.
In a dual agency situation, the agent has the following affirmative obligations to both the Seller and the Buyer:
    (a) A fiduciary duty of utmost care, integrity, honesty and loyalty in the dealings with either the Seller or the Buyer.
    (b) Other duties to the Seller and the Buyer as stated above in their respective sections.
In representing both Seller and Buyer, the agent may not, without the express permission of the respective party, disclose to the other party that the Seller will accept a price less than the listing price or that the Buyer will pay a price greater than the price offered.
The above duties of the agent in a real estate transaction do not relieve a Seller or Buyer from the responsibility to protect his or her own interests. You should carefully read all agreements to assure that they adequately express your understanding of the transaction. A real estate agent is a person qualified to advise about real estate. If legal or tax advice is desired, consult a competent professional.
Throughout your real property transaction you may receive more than one disclosure form, depending upon the number of agents assisting in the transaction. The law requires each agent with whom you have more than a casual relationship to present you with this disclosure form. You should read its contents each time it is presented to you, considering the relationship between you and the real estate agent in your specific transaction.
This disclosure form includes the provisions of Sections 2079.13 to 2079.24, inclusive, of the Civil Code set forth on page 2. Read it carefully.
I/WE ACKNOWLEDGE RECEIPT OF A COPY OF THIS DISCLOSURE AND THE PORTIONS OF THE CIVIL CODE PRINTED ON THE BACK (OR A SEPARATE PAGE).

Buyer/Seller/Landlord/Tenant_____ Date _____
Buyer/Seller/Landlord/Tenant_____ Date _____

Agent _____ DRE Lic. # _____
                              Real Estate Broker (Firm)
By _____ DRE Lic. # _____ Date _____
         (Salesperson or Broker-Associate)

THIS FORM SHALL BE PROVIDED AND ACKNOWLEDGED AS FOLLOWS (Civil Code § 2079.14):
• When the listing brokerage company also represents Buyer, the Listing Agent shall have one AD form signed by Seller and one signed by Buyer.
• When Buyer and Seller are represented by different brokerage companies, the Listing Agent shall have one AD form signed by Buyer and the Buyer's Agent shall have one AD form signed by Buyer and one AD form signed by Seller.

Published and Distributed by:
REAL ESTATE BUSINESS SERVICES, INC.
a subsidiary of the California Association of REALTORS®
525 South Virgil Avenue, Los Angeles, California 90020

EQUAL HOUSING OPPORTUNITY

AD REVISED 4/06 (PAGE 1 OF 2)   PRINT DATE

Reviewed by _____ Date _____

DISCLOSURE REGARDING REAL ESTATE AGENCY RELATIONSHIP (AD PAGE 1 OF 2)

FIGURE 4.3   *(Continued)*

CIVIL CODE SECTIONS 2079.13 THROUGH 2079.24 (2079.16 APPEARS ON THE FRONT)

2079.13 As used in Sections 2079.14 to 2079.24, inclusive, the following terms have the following meanings:
(a) "Agent" means a person acting under provisions of title 9 (commencing with Section 2295) in a real property transaction, and includes a person who is licensed as a real estate broker under Chapter 3 (commencing with Section 10130) of Part 1 of Division 4 of the Business and Professions Code, and under whose license a listing is executed or an offer to purchase is obtained. **(b)** "Associate licensee" means a person who is licensed as a real broker or salesperson under Chapter 3 (commencing with Section 10130) of Part 1 of Division 4 of the Business and Professions Code and who is either licensed under a broker or has entered into a written contract with a broker to act as the broker's agent in connection with acts requiring a real estate license and to function under the broker's supervision in the capacity of an associate licensee. The agent in the real property transaction bears responsibility for his or her associate licensees who perform as agents of the agent. When an associate licensee owes a duty to any principal, or to any buyer or seller who is not a principal, in a real property transaction, that duty is equivalent to the duty owed to that party by the broker for whom the associate licensee functions. **(c)** "Buyer" means a transferee in a real property transaction, and includes a person who executes an offer to purchase real property from a seller through an agent, or who seeks the services of an agent in more than a casual, transitory, or preliminary manner, with the object of entering into a real property transaction. "Buyer" includes vendee or lessee. **(d)** "Dual agent" means an agent acting, either directly or through an associate licensee, as agent for both the seller and the buyer in a real property transaction. **(e)** "Listing agreement" means a contract between an owner of real property and an agent, by which the agent has been authorized to sell the real property or to find or obtain a buyer. **(f)** "Listing agent" means a person who has obtained a listing of real property to act as an agent for compensation. **(g)** "Listing price" is the amount expressed in dollars specified in the listing for which the seller is willing to sell the real property through the listing agent. **(h)** "Offering price" is the amount expressed in dollars specified in an offer to purchase for which the buyer is willing to buy the real property. **(i)** "Offer to purchase" means a written contract executed by a buyer through a selling agent which becomes the contract for the sale of the real property upon acceptance by the seller. **(j)** "Real property" means any estate specified by subdivision (1) or (2) of Section 761 in property which constitutes or is improved with one to four dwelling units, any leasehold in this type of property exceeding one year's duration, and mobile homes, when offered for sale or sold through an agent pursuant to the authority contained in Section 10131.6 of the Business and Professions Code. **(k)** "Real property transaction" means a transaction for the sale of real property in which an agent is employed by one or more of the principals to act in that transaction, and includes a listing or an offer to purchase. **(l)** "Sell," "sale," or "sold" refers to a transaction for the transfer of real property from the seller to the buyer, and includes exchanges of real property between the seller and buyer, transactions for the creation of a real property sales contract within the meaning of Section 2985, and transactions for the creation of a leasehold exceeding one year's duration. **(m)** "Seller" means the transferor in a real property transaction, and includes an owner who lists real property with an agent, whether or not a transfer results, or who receives an offer to purchase real property of which he or she is the owner from an agent on behalf of another. "Seller" includes both a vendor and a lessor. **(n)** "Selling agent" means a listing agent who acts alone, or an agent who acts in cooperation with a listing agent, and who sells or finds and obtains a buyer for the real property, or an agent who locates property for a buyer or who finds a buyer for a property for which no listing exists and presents an offer to purchase to the seller. **(o)** "Subagent" means a person to whom an agent delegates agency powers as provided in Article 5 (commencing with Section 2349) of Chapter 1 of Title 9. However, "subagent" does not include an associate licensee who is acting under the supervision of an agent in a real property transaction.

2079.14 Listing agents and selling agents shall provide the seller and buyer in a real property transaction with a copy of the disclosure form specified in Section 2079.16, and, except as provided in subdivision (c), shall obtain a signed acknowledgement of receipt from that seller or buyer, except as provided in this section or Section 2079.15, as follows: **(a)** The listing agent, if any, shall provide the disclosure form to the seller prior to entering into the listing agreement. **(b)** The selling agent shall provide the disclosure form to the seller as soon as practicable prior to presenting the seller with an offer to purchase, unless the selling agent previously provided the seller with a copy of the disclosure form pursuant to subdivision (a). **(c)** Where the selling agent does not deal on a face-to-face basis with the seller, the disclosure form prepared by the selling agent may be furnished to the seller (and acknowledgement of receipt obtained for the selling agent from the seller) by the listing agent, or the selling agent may deliver the disclosure form by certified mail addressed to the seller at his or her last known address, in which case no signed acknowledgement of receipt is required. **(d)** The selling agent shall provide the disclosure form to the buyer as soon as practicable prior to execution of the buyer's offer to purchase, except that if the offer to purchase is not prepared by the selling agent, the selling agent shall present the disclosure form to the buyer not later than the next business day after the selling agent receives the offer to purchase from the buyer.

2079.15 In any circumstance in which the seller or buyer refuses to sign an acknowledgement of receipt pursuant to Section 2079.14, the agent, or an associate licensee acting for an agent, shall set forth, sign, and date a written declaration of the facts of the refusal.

2079.17 (a) As soon as practicable, the selling agent shall disclose to the buyer and seller whether the selling agent is acting in the real property transaction exclusively as the buyer's agent, exclusively as the seller's agent, or as a dual agent representing both the buyer and the seller. This relationship shall be confirmed in the contract to purchase and sell real property or in a separate writing executed or acknowledged by the seller, the buyer, and the selling agent prior to or coincident with execution of that contract by the buyer and the seller, respectively. **(b)** As soon as practicable, the listing agent shall disclose to the seller whether the listing agent is acting in the real property transaction exclusively as the seller's agent, or as a dual agent representing both the buyer and seller. This relationship shall be confirmed in the contract to purchase and sell real property or in a separate writing executed or acknowledged by the seller and the listing agent prior to or coincident with the execution of that contract by the seller.
(c) The confirmation required by subdivisions (a) and (b) shall be in the following form.

| **(DO NOT COMPLETE. SAMPLE ONLY)** | is the agent of (check one): ☐ the seller exclusively; or ☐ both the buyer and seller. |
| (Name of Listing Agent) | |

| **(DO NOT COMPLETE. SAMPLE ONLY)** | is the agent of (check one): ☐ the buyer exclusively; or ☐ the seller exclusively; or |
| (Name of Selling Agent if not the same as the Listing Agent) | ☐ both the buyer and seller. |

(d) The disclosures and confirmation required by this section shall be in addition to the disclosure required by Section 2079.14.

2079.18 No selling agent in a real property transaction may act as an agent for the buyer only, when the selling agent is also acting as the listing agent in the transaction.

2079.19 The payment of compensation or the obligation to pay compensation to an agent by the seller or buyer is not necessarily determinative of a particular agency relationship between an agent and the seller or buyer. A listing agent and a selling agent may agree to share any compensation or commission paid, or any right to any compensation or commission for which an obligation arises as the result of a real estate transaction, and the terms of any such agreement shall not necessarily be determinative of a particular relationship.

2079.20 Nothing in this article prevents an agent from selecting, as a condition of the agent's employment, a specific form of agency relationship not specifically prohibited by this article if the requirements of Section 2079.14 and Section 2079.17 are complied with.

2079.21 A dual agent shall not disclose to the buyer that the seller is willing to sell the property at a price less than the listing price, without the express written consent of the seller. A dual agent shall not disclose to the seller that the buyer is willing to pay a price greater than the offering price, without the express written consent of the buyer. This section does not alter in any way the duty or responsibility of a dual agent to any principal with respect to confidential information other than price.

2079.22 Nothing in this article precludes a listing agent from also being a selling agent, and the combination of these functions in one agent does not, of itself, make that agent a dual agent.

2079.23 A contract between the principal and agent may be modified or altered to change the agency relationship at any time before the performance of the act which is the object of the agency with the written consent of the parties to the agency relationship.

2079.24 Nothing in this article shall be construed to either diminish the duty of disclosure owed buyers and sellers by agents and their associate licensees, subagents, and employees or to relieve agents and their associate licensees, subagents, and employees from liability for their conduct in connection with acts governed by this article or for any breach of a fiduciary duty or a duty of disclosure.

Seller's/Landlord's Initials (_____)(_____)
Buyer's/Tenant's Initials   (_____)(_____)

| Reviewed by _____ Date _____ |

EQUAL HOUSING OPPORTUNITY

AD REVISED 4/06 (PAGE 2 OF 2)

DISCLOSURE REGARDING REAL ESTATE AGENCY RELATIONSHIPS (AD PAGE 2 OF 2)

Source: Reprinted with permission of California Association of REALTORS®.

In addition to the AD form shown in Figure 4.3, licensees representing buyers must also provide the DA form. Paragraph 27B of the RPA-CA (Residential Purchase Agreement—California calls for this disclosure). Because the listing agreement (RLA, Figure 9.3 on page 250) makes similar disclosures in Paragraph 10, a separate disclosure DA is not required for sellers.

Step Two: Elect

Obviously, the actual "election" of the type of agency can occur only after the buyer has found a property to purchase. A seller cannot know whether single or dual agency would be appropriate until she knows who will represent the buyer. If the buyer's licensee is also the listing licensee, the relationship must be one of "dual agency." If the buyer is represented by a cooperating licensee (that is, an associate licensee employed by another broker), the type of agency elected would be an exclusive representation by each licensee, but again, this cannot be determined until the affiliation of the buyer's licensee is known.

Step Three: Confirm

Remember, the AD form shown in Figure 4.3 is not an election, only a disclosure. The actual election can be decided only after the property or buyer is known. The confirmation is the written record of this "election" and is available as a separate document: C.A.R. form **AC**, agency confirmation. AC may also be done through Paragraph 27C of the RPA-CA.

If dual agency is elected, the licensee will need the written, informed consent of all parties to the transaction that (if agency disclosure has been done properly) was obtained either through the RLA Listing Agreement for the seller or through the buyer's acknowledgment and signature on the DA form (See Figure 4.1).

Remember, it is the buyer's and seller's broker who is ultimately responsible to see that proper agency relationship disclosures have been made. However, be assured, the respective licensee will also be named in any litigation.

The selling licensee should always *confirm* the agency relationship in writing with the buyer either through the separate form or through the purchase agreement. If the buyer or seller is not represented by a licensee, depending on who represents whom, either a Buyer Non-Agency Agreement (BNA) or a Seller Non-Agency Agreement (SNA) may be appropriate.

Disclosure Timing

When should the licensee disclose the agency issue? CCC Section 2079.14 requires disclosure prior to entering into the listing agreement or, in the case of the selling licensee, "as soon as practicable prior to presenting the seller with an offer to purchase." Prompt disclosure is also required in the policies and procedures manual of most real estate offices. The timing of the three-step disclosure process may vary, depending on who is being represented and how. Let's take a general look at when to disclose, when to elect, and when to confirm.

Listing Licensee Who Does Not Represent the Buyer

In this case, the listing licensee must provide the agency disclosure to the seller "as soon as practicable prior to entering into the listing agreement."

Listing Licensee Who Represents Both Seller and Buyer

If only one licensee represents both seller and buyer, an agency disclosure must be given an acknowledgment of receipt received from each. If seller and buyer are represented by two associate licensees of the same firm, each licensee must provide the disclosure—the AD form to the seller and the DA form to the buyer—and receive an acknowledgment from their respective clients.

Selling Licensee Who Represents Buyer Only

"The selling agent shall provide the disclosure form to the buyer as soon as practicable prior to execution of the buyer's offer to purchase." The selling agent provides buyer with both AD and DA forms and receives signed acknowledgment of receipt. Figures 4.1 and 4.3 show a sample of AD and DA forms, respectively.

There is a great deal of misunderstanding among licensees as to how selling or buyer's agent/licensees are required to disclose agency to the seller. More than a few licensees have been heard to say, "Ah, the listing agent has already done that, why do I have to do it again?" The law (CCC 2079.14(b) and (c)) requires selling licensees to disclose agency not just to the buyer but to the seller (even though the listing agent may have already done so) before presenting the offer. Of the many reasons why this must be done, you need to know the two most important reasons:

1. The law says you must.
2. There may not always be a listing licensee (as in the case of a For Sale by Owner).

The AD form now allows the selling licensee or buyer's representative to provide the same AD form that was signed by the buyer

to the seller. The seller signs, acknowledging receipt of agency disclosure by the buyer's representative, in the designated box. Since this form is simply a disclosure no agency relationship is created. Agency is created through the confirmation of agency included in the RPA-CA purchase agreement.

It is, however, necessary that the buyer's (or selling agent) licensee provide the Agency Disclosure form "to the seller as soon as practicable prior to presenting the seller with an offer to purchase, unless the selling agent previously provided the seller with a copy of the disclosure ... [as in a dual agency 2079.14(b-c)] where the selling agent does not deal on a face-to-face basis with the seller [such as when the offer must be presented by the listing licensee] the disclosure form prepared by the selling agent may be furnished to the seller (and acknowledgement of receipt obtained for the selling agent from the seller) by the listing agent."

If agency disclosure under CCC Section 2079.14 is done right, two AD forms would have been provided: one to the seller before signing the listing, one to the buyer before writing an offer, and that same form is then presented to the seller for seller's signature before presenting the offer.

4.4 DEATH OR AIDS DISCLOSURE

A natural death on the property need not be disclosed; however, a murder or suicide should be disclosed for a minimum of three years from the date of the incident only. CCC Section 1710.2 provides that "No cause of action arises against an owner of real property or his or her agent, or any agent of a transferee of real property, for the failure to disclose to the transferee the occurrence of an occupant's death upon the real property or the manner of death where the death has occurred more than three years prior to the date the transferee offers to purchase, lease, or rent the real property, or that an occupant of that property was afflicted with, or died from, [AIDS]." **AIDS disclosure** is unnecessary; the licensee does not have to disclose that a former resident of the property ever had or died of AIDS. If a potential buyer asks you directly if a person ever died on the property of AIDS, the Department of Housing and Urban Development (HUD) does not provide a "correct" response but advises only that the licensee not respond. NAR, on the other hand, suggests that licensees not answer such queries as they are not considered material to the transaction. You may indicate to the client that any response from you or your firm may be a violation of federal or state housing laws.

Stigmatized Property

Stigmatized property may be perceived to be uninhabitable or undesirable for other than physical or environmental reasons. Many issues such as murder, suicide, molestations, satanic rituals, or a reputation of being haunted or an "unlucky" house to former residents are all examples of reasons a property could become stigmatized.

These and other similar issues may mean little to one person and a great deal to another. We also do not know how the courts would view the willful nondisclosure of such issues, so again the Golden Rule comes into play: If the issue is something you feel may possibly affect a buyer's decision, disclose it. If you are unsure, ask your broker.

Licensed Care Facilities

Opinion 95-907 of the California Attorney General makes it clear that a real estate licensee need not disclose the location of a licensed care facility that serves six or fewer people. A larger facility close to a one to four residential unit property that was being sold will probably require disclosure.

4.5 REAL ESTATE TRANSFER DISCLOSURE STATEMENT (TDS)

Under current law (CCC Sections 1102 through 1103.1), the purchaser of residential real property (including residential stock cooperatives) of four or less units is entitled to a **Real Estate Transfer and Disclosure Statement (TDS)** from the seller. The term *transfer* refers to the sale, exchange, real property sales contract (sometimes called a contract of sale or contract for deed), option, lease, or any other type of conveyance of real property from one person or entity to another. Since January 1, 1987, any seller, whether *represented by a licensee or not*, is required to give the buyer a written disclosure statement of the condition of the seller's property. The disclosure statement must identify (1) items in the home and whether these items are operational (part A); (2) significant defects of the home, if any (part B); and (3) all information regarding improvements and alterations as well as concerns with neighbors and the neighborhood (part C).

The buyer must receive a copy of the disclosure statement. If only one licensee is involved, she must deliver it to the buyer. If two licensees are involved, it is the responsibility of the selling licensee who obtained the offer to deliver it to the buyer. If no licensees are involved, the seller is responsible for the delivery to the buyer. If the seller has not completed the disclosure statement, the buyer must be notified in writing that she has the right to receive such a statement.

The disclosure statement must be fully executed and delivered as soon as practicable (the C.A.R. contract default calls for delivery of the TDS to the buyer within seven days of contract acceptance, or the licensee may opt for any number by filling in the blank) but before transfer of title. If the statement is delivered before the execution of a purchase agreement, the buyer has no right to cancel the offer on the basis of the TDS. If the statement is delivered to the buyer after execution of the purchase agreement, the transferee or buyer has three days after personal delivery (five days if delivery is by mail) to terminate her offer on written notice to the seller. The buyer is entitled to a full refund of any deposit that she has made. It should be obvious that because of the buyer's right to cancel the contract within three days of receipt of the TDS, or any revision or amendment made to the TDS, early delivery of all disclosures is advisable. If you represent a buyer, be careful to stay within these dates.

The three-page TDS form is shown in Figure 4.4.

4.6 AGENT'S INSPECTION DISCLOSURE— HOW AND WHY?

Every time a licensee takes a listing on one to four residential units, she should complete a Real Estate TDS. Even if the property is an exempt property, because it is an intra-family sale or has any of the exemptions listed later in this discussion, the listing agent, or her licensee, is still responsible for conducting an independent investigation and inspection of the property and must complete the **Agent's Inspection Disclosure** (Section III of the Real Estate TDS), as shown in Figure 4.4.

In California, you can't talk about the disclosure statement without talking about the *Easton v. Strassburger* case. On May 31, 1984, the California State Supreme Court refused to hear that case, officially making the decision of the appellate court case law. That case involved the failure of a real estate licensee to conduct a reasonable, visual inspection and investigation of a property and report any visible defects to the buyer. There were visible signs of land slippage on this sloped property when the sale took place and, not long after Easton moved in, the ground started sliding down the hill. The courts found that the licensees had been negligent in their duty to investigate and fully disclose visible defects in writing.

The importance of this case was that it imposed a greater duty of care on real estate licensees to be responsible, not only for what they know but for what they *should have known* by conducting a reasonably competent and diligent visual inspection. This case is

FIGURE 4.4   Real Estate Transfer Disclosure Statement (TDS Revised 10/03)

REAL ESTATE TRANSFER DISCLOSURE STATEMENT
(CALIFORNIA CIVIL CODE §1102, ET SEQ.)
(C.A.R. Form TDS, Revised 10/03)

CALIFORNIA
ASSOCIATION
OF REALTORS®

THIS DISCLOSURE STATEMENT CONCERNS THE REAL PROPERTY SITUATED IN THE CITY OF _____
_____, COUNTY OF _____, STATE OF CALIFORNIA,
DESCRIBED AS _____.

THIS STATEMENT IS A DISCLOSURE OF THE CONDITION OF THE ABOVE DESCRIBED PROPERTY IN COMPLIANCE
WITH SECTION 1102 OF THE CIVIL CODE AS OF (date) _____. IT IS NOT A WARRANTY OF ANY
KIND BY THE SELLER(S) OR ANY AGENT(S) REPRESENTING ANY PRINCIPAL(S) IN THIS TRANSACTION, AND IS
NOT A SUBSTITUTE FOR ANY INSPECTIONS OR WARRANTIES THE PRINCIPAL(S) MAY WISH TO OBTAIN.

I. COORDINATION WITH OTHER DISCLOSURE FORMS

This Real Estate Transfer Disclosure Statement is made pursuant to Section 1102 of the Civil Code. Other statutes require disclosures, depending upon the details of the particular real estate transaction (for example: special study zone and purchase-money liens on residential property).

Substituted Disclosures: The following disclosures and other disclosures required by law, including the Natural Hazard Disclosure Report/Statement that may include airport annoyances, earthquake, fire, flood, or special assessment information, have or will be made in connection with this real estate transfer, and are intended to satisfy the disclosure obligations on this form, where the subject matter is the same:

☐   Inspection reports completed pursuant to the contract of sale or receipt for deposit.
☐   Additional inspection reports or disclosures: _____
_____

II. SELLER'S INFORMATION

The Seller discloses the following information with the knowledge that even though this is not a warranty, prospective Buyers may rely on this information in deciding whether and on what terms to purchase the subject property. Seller hereby authorizes any agent(s) representing any principal(s) in this transaction to provide a copy of this statement to any person or entity in connection with any actual or anticipated sale of the property.

THE FOLLOWING ARE REPRESENTATIONS MADE BY THE SELLER(S) AND ARE NOT THE REPRESENTATIONS OF THE AGENT(S), IF ANY. THIS INFORMATION IS A DISCLOSURE AND IS NOT INTENDED TO BE PART OF ANY CONTRACT BETWEEN THE BUYER AND SELLER.

Seller ☐ is ☐ is not occupying the property.

A. The subject property has the items checked below (read across):

☐ Range	☐ Oven	☐ Microwave
☐ Dishwasher	☐ Trash Compactor	☐ Garbage Disposal
☐ Washer/Dryer Hookups		☐ Rain Gutters
☐ Burglar Alarms	☐ Smoke Detector(s)	☐ Fire Alarm
☐ TV Antenna	☐ Satellite Dish	☐ Intercom
☐ Central Heating	☐ Central Air Conditioning	☐ Evaporator Cooler(s)
☐ Wall/Window Air Conditioning	☐ Sprinklers	☐ Public Sewer System
☐ Septic Tank	☐ Sump Pump	☐ Water Softener
☐ Patio/Decking	☐ Built-in Barbecue	☐ Gazebo
☐ Sauna		
☐ Hot Tub	☐ Pool	☐ Spa
☐ Locking Safety Cover*	☐ Child Resistant Barrier*	☐ Locking Safety Cover*
☐ Security Gate(s)	☐ Automatic Garage Door Opener(s)*	☐ Number Remote Controls _____
Garage: ☐ Attached	☐ Not Attached	☐ Carport
Pool/Spa Heater: ☐ Gas	☐ Solar	☐ Electric
Water Heater: ☐ Gas	☐ Water Heater Anchored, Braced, or Strapped*	
Water Supply: ☐ City	☐ Well	☐ Private Utility or
Gas Supply: ☐ Utility	☐ Bottled	Other_____
☐ Window Screens	☐ Window Security Bars ☐ Quick Release Mechanism on Bedroom Windows*	

Exhaust Fan(s) in _____ 220 Volt Wiring in _____ Fireplace(s) in _____
☐ Gas Starter _____ ☐ Roof(s): Type: _____ Age: _____ (approx.)
☐ Other: _____
Are there, to the best of your (Seller's) knowledge, any of the above that are not in operating condition? ☐ Yes ☐ No. If yes, then describe. (Attach additional sheets if necessary): _____
_____

(*see footnote on page 2)

TDS REVISED 10/03 (PAGE 1 OF 3)   Print Date

Buyer's Initials (_____)(_____)
Seller's Initials (_____)(_____)

Reviewed by _____ Date _____

EQUAL HOUSING
OPPORTUNITY

REAL ESTATE TRANSFER DISCLOSURE STATEMENT (TDS PAGE 1 OF 3)

FIGURE 4.4   (*Continued*)

Property Address: _____   Date: _____

B. Are you (Seller) aware of any significant defects/malfunctions in any of the following? ☐ Yes ☐ No. If yes, check appropriate space(s) below.

☐ Interior Walls ☐ Ceilings ☐ Floors ☐ Exterior Walls ☐ Insulation ☐ Roof(s) ☐ Windows ☐ Doors ☐ Foundation ☐ Slab(s) ☐ Driveways ☐ Sidewalks ☐ Walls/Fences ☐ Electrical Systems ☐ Plumbing/Sewers/Septics ☐ Other Structural Components

(Describe: _____

_____

_____

_____)

If any of the above is checked, explain. (Attach additional sheets if necessary.): _____

_____

_____

_____

_____

_____

*This garage door opener or child resistant pool barrier may not be in compliance with the safety standards relating to automatic reversing devices as set forth in Chapter 12.5 (commencing with Section 19890) of Part 3 of Division 13 of, or with the pool safety standards of Article 2.5 (commencing with Section 115920) of Chapter 5 of Part 10 of Division 104 of, the Health and Safety Code. The water heater may not be anchored, braced, or strapped in accordance with Section 19211 of the Health and Safety Code. Window security bars may not have quick release mechanisms in compliance with the 1995 edition of the California Building Standards Code.

C. Are you (Seller) aware of any of the following:

1. Substances, materials, or products which may be an environmental hazard such as, but not limited to, asbestos, formaldehyde, radon gas, lead-based paint, mold, fuel or chemical storage tanks, and contaminated soil or water on the subject property . . . . ☐ Yes ☐ No
2. Features of the property shared in common with adjoining landowners, such as walls, fences, and driveways, whose use or responsibility for maintenance may have an effect on the subject property . . . . ☐ Yes ☐ No
3. Any encroachments, easements or similar matters that may affect your interest in the subject property . . . . ☐ Yes ☐ No
4. Room additions, structural modifications, or other alterations or repairs made without necessary permits . . . . ☐ Yes ☐ No
5. Room additions, structural modifications, or other alterations or repairs not in compliance with building codes . . . . ☐ Yes ☐ No
6. Fill (compacted or otherwise) on the property or any portion thereof . . . . ☐ Yes ☐ No
7. Any settling from any cause, or slippage, sliding, or other soil problems . . . . ☐ Yes ☐ No
8. Flooding, drainage or grading problems . . . . ☐ Yes ☐ No
9. Major damage to the property or any of the structures from fire, earthquake, floods, or landslides . . . . ☐ Yes ☐ No
10. Any zoning violations, nonconforming uses, violations of "setback" requirements . . . . ☐ Yes ☐ No
11. Neighborhood noise problems or other nuisances . . . . ☐ Yes ☐ No
12. CC&R's or other deed restrictions or obligations . . . . ☐ Yes ☐ No
13. Homeowners' Association which has any authority over the subject property . . . . ☐ Yes ☐ No
14. Any "common area" (facilities such as pools, tennis courts, walkways, or other areas co-owned in undivided interest with others) . . . . ☐ Yes ☐ No
15. Any notices of abatement or citations against the property . . . . ☐ Yes ☐ No
16. Any lawsuits by or against the Seller threatening to or affecting this real property, including any lawsuits alleging a defect or deficiency in this real property or "common areas" (facilities such as pools, tennis courts, walkways, or other areas co-owned in undivided interest with others) . . . . ☐ Yes ☐ No

If the answer to any of these is yes, explain. (Attach additional sheets if necessary.): _____

_____

_____

_____

_____

Seller certifies that the information herein is true and correct to the best of the Seller's knowledge as of the date signed by the Seller.

Seller_____   Date _____

Seller_____   Date _____

Buyer's Initials (_____)(_____)
Seller's Initials (_____)(_____)

TDS REVISED 10/03 (PAGE 2 OF 3)

Reviewed by _____ Date _____

EQUAL HOUSING OPPORTUNITY

REAL ESTATE TRANSFER DISCLOSURE STATEMENT (TDS PAGE 2 OF 3)

FIGURE 4.4 *(Continued)*

Property Address: _____   Date: _____

III. AGENT'S INSPECTION DISCLOSURE
(To be completed only if the Seller is represented by an agent in this transaction.)

THE UNDERSIGNED, BASED ON THE ABOVE INQUIRY OF THE SELLER(S) AS TO THE CONDITION OF THE PROPERTY AND BASED ON A REASONABLY COMPETENT AND DILIGENT VISUAL INSPECTION OF THE ACCESSIBLE AREAS OF THE PROPERTY IN CONJUNCTION WITH THAT INQUIRY, STATES THE FOLLOWING:

☐ Agent notes no items for disclosure.

☐ Agent notes the following items: _____

_____

_____

_____

_____

Agent (Broker Representing Seller) _____ By _____ Date _____
　　　　　　　　　(Please Print)　　　　　　　　　(Associate Licensee or Broker Signature)

IV. AGENT'S INSPECTION DISCLOSURE
(To be completed only if the agent who has obtained the offer is other than the agent above.)

THE UNDERSIGNED, BASED ON A REASONABLY COMPETENT AND DILIGENT VISUAL INSPECTION OF THE ACCESSIBLE AREAS OF THE PROPERTY, STATES THE FOLLOWING:

☐ Agent notes no items for disclosure.

☐ Agent notes the following items: _____

_____

_____

_____

Agent (Broker Obtaining the Offer) _____ By _____ Date _____
　　　　　　　　　(Please Print)　　　　　　　　　(Associate Licensee or Broker Signature)

V. BUYER(S) AND SELLER(S) MAY WISH TO OBTAIN PROFESSIONAL ADVICE AND/OR INSPECTIONS OF THE PROPERTY AND TO PROVIDE FOR APPROPRIATE PROVISIONS IN A CONTRACT BETWEEN BUYER AND SELLER(S) WITH RESPECT TO ANY ADVICE/INSPECTIONS/DEFECTS.

I/WE ACKNOWLEDGE RECEIPT OF A COPY OF THIS STATEMENT.

Seller _____ Date _____   Buyer _____ Date _____

Seller _____ Date _____   Buyer _____ Date _____

Agent (Broker Representing Seller) _____ By _____ Date _____
　　　　　　　　　(Please Print)　　　　　　　　　(Associate Licensee or Broker Signature)

Agent (Broker Obtaining the Offer) _____ By _____ Date _____
　　　　　　　　　(Please Print)　　　　　　　　　(Associate Licensee or Broker Signature)

SECTION 1102.3 OF THE CIVIL CODE PROVIDES A BUYER WITH THE RIGHT TO RESCIND A PURCHASE CONTRACT FOR AT LEAST THREE DAYS AFTER THE DELIVERY OF THIS DISCLOSURE IF DELIVERY OCCURS AFTER THE SIGNING OF AN OFFER TO PURCHASE. IF YOU WISH TO RESCIND THE CONTRACT, YOU MUST ACT WITHIN THE PRESCRIBED PERIOD.

A REAL ESTATE BROKER IS QUALIFIED TO ADVISE ON REAL ESTATE. IF YOU DESIRE LEGAL ADVICE, CONSULT YOUR ATTORNEY.

SURE TRAC
The System for Success®

Published and Distributed by:
REAL ESTATE BUSINESS SERVICES, INC.
a subsidiary of the California Association of REALTORS®
525 South Virgil Avenue, Los Angeles, California 90020

EQUAL HOUSING OPPORTUNITY

Reviewed by _____ Date _____

TDS REVISED 10/03 (PAGE 3 OF 3)

REAL ESTATE TRANSFER DISCLOSURE STATEMENT (TDS PAGE 3 OF 3)

Source: Reprinted with permission of California Association of REALTORS®.

now codified in the CCC and begins with Section 2079; it became effective from January 1, 1986. It requires that all real estate licensees conduct a competent and diligent visual inspection of all accessible property areas in a real estate sale involving one to four residential units and disclose in writing to the prospective buyer all material facts affecting the value or desirability of the property. The statute of limitations for filing a lawsuit against a licensee who does not comply is two years after the escrow closes or, if fraudulent misrepresentation is found, ten years from the date of reasonable discover.

On page three of the C.A.R. TDS, Part III Agent's Inspection Disclosure, there are two boxes that may be checked. The first says, agent notes no items for disclosure. *The authors can think of few circumstances when a licensee would be justified in checking that box.* A check in the "Agent notes no items for disclosure" box is a blatant indication that said "agent" did not look. There are things to note on every property that may require further scrutiny by a professional. It's the licensee's job to find those things and disclose them to the buyer.

So, what do you look for during a "competent visual inspection"? Your obligation to the seller and buyer is to discover "red flags," that is, any condition that may signal to a reasonably observant person that a problem may exist. Your job is not to detect the actual problem but to look for any indication that a professional inspector should be brought in to make a more thorough inspection. Even though in a former occupation you may have been a contractor or other professional, you should not be diagnosing structural problems, unless you wish to be held to the standard of care required of a currently licensed professional in the field. It is your job to use the knowledge required to obtain a real estate license to make a visual inspection to determine if further inspection may be required.

Four primary factors may be a signal that further inspection should be recommended: insect infestation, water damage, material deterioration, and structural failure. Generally, if you find one of these factors, the odds are very high that one or more of the others may exist and further inspection by a professional should be recommended to the buyer.

Example: Broker Jim finds a half-inch separation of the front porch from the house and a diagonal crack in the foundation just below the doorway. This *may* indicate a structural failure of the foundation and *may* be a potential source of water penetration into the

structure (water damage) or a potential path for insects such as termites and wood-boring beetles to enter the structure. On observing these anomalies, a competent licensee should make a written recommendation that the buyer get a further inspection by a pest inspector, contractor, or home inspector. Under no circumstances should the licensee offer an opinion of potential consequences. Leave that to the pros. Should the buyer choose not to seek further inspection, the licensee should get a signed statement from the buyer that the licensee has recommended further inspection but that the buyer has declined. There may be very legitimate reasons for not pursuing such an inspection, e.g., the buyer may be a contractor himself, or the buyer may intend to rebuild that portion of the home anyway. In either case, the licensee should get a signed waiver of further inspection from the buyer.

Seller Disclosure Exemptions

The following transfers are exempt from disclosure:

- Transfers pursuant to a court order, that is, sales ordered by a probate or bankruptcy court.
- Transfers by a fiduciary representing trusts, guardianships, and conservatorships.
- Transfers between spouses or to a direct blood relative by the state controller.
- Transfers to or from any government entity, including exchanges requiring a public report (new construction).
- Transfers by foreclosure.
- Transfers from one co-owner to one or more co-owners.

Insect Infestation

Carpenter ants and subterranean termites cause the overwhelming majority of damage to real property. They are problematic, not only for their voracious appetites for cellulose fiber (primarily wood) but because their damage is primarily internal and can go undetected for long periods of time. If not found and treated, their damage can weaken the supporting wood members of a structure. Some signs to look for include:

- Subterranean termites leave earth/wood droppings that look like sawdust and/or mud tubes that look like gray sticks attached

to a property's foundation. Recommend further inspection by a licensed pest inspector.

- Drywood termites, which are all but impossible for you to detect, move more slowly than damp wood termites; however, they swarm each year and may enter a property through an attic vent and take up residence completely unnoticed. Recommend further inspection by a licensed pest inspector.

- Carpenter ants leave wood shavings near wood members. Recommend further inspection by a licensed pest inspector.

- Wood boring beetles leave a series of random small holes about ⅛th to ¼ of an inch in diameter. Recommend further inspection by a licensed pest inspector.

Water Damage

Water damage can be caused by several different issues, such as faulty plumbing, improper ventilation, condensation, seepage, improper drainage, or a high ground water level. The main indicators of water damage or problems are:

- Mold, mildew, and rust, especially in sinks, tubs, and exterior hose bibs and at the base of water heaters. Recommend further inspection by a licensed plumber. In the case of mold or mildew, recommend a professional mold inspection.

- Loose or warped wood flooring or other wood members. Recommend a professional home inspection.

- Loose or warped wood garage door trim. Recommend a professional home inspection.

- Water stains on ceilings indicating a leaky roof or a plumbing leak. In multistory condominiums, this may be from a plumbing leak in the unit above. (Note: If a home has "popcorn" ceilings and was built prior to 1978, any removal of stained ceiling material may contain asbestos and should be done only by a licensed professional.) Recommend a professional home inspection.

- Rotted wood. Recommend a professional home inspection.

- Cracked, chipped, loose, or curled tile. Recommend a professional home inspection.

- Roof defects such as loose or missing shingles, cracked roof tile, or holes in downspouts. Recommend a professional roof inspection by a licensed roof inspector.

- Peeling or flaking paint, which is especially important if the home was constructed prior to 1978 as it may contain lead. Recommend a professional home inspection.

Material Deterioration

One of the most severe types of material deterioration is wood rot, also known as damp rot, which is caused by an excessive moisture condition that leads to growth of a decaying fungus. Improper or substandard building materials or construction procedures can also produce material damage. A few things to look for when inspecting for material deterioration include:

- Decaying or warping of wood members such as decks, porches, and wood trim. Recommend a professional home inspection.

- Erosion or cracking of concrete or masonry such as driveways built without rebar or to an insufficient depth and retaining walls that lack sufficient drainage. Recommend a professional home inspection.

- Cracking, rotting, or warping of garage door trim that touches the ground, as well as door and window trim and wood patios. Recommend a professional home inspection.

Structural Failure

Structural failure can be caused by any of the above causes, plus poor design and environmental extremes. When inspecting for structural failure, licensees should be careful to look for the following:

- Bulging or "heaving" in floors and load-bearing walls. A roof ridgeline that sags or appears warped. Recommend a professional home inspection.

- Excessive deflection of joists or girders evidenced by an uneven or sloping floor, or one that creaks excessively. Recommend a professional home inspection.

- Cracks in structural columns, beams, and walls (interior and exterior), cracks in foundations (many if not most "hairline" cracks are often normal), a fireplace that appears to be separated from the structure, and any cracks around doors and windows that are V-shaped or diagonal as these may indicate soil instability of some sort, such as lateral movement or heaving. Minor hairline cracks in walls may be normal. Recommend a professional home inspection.

- Instability in any structural or load-bearing member. Recommend a professional home inspection.

The list of defects a property may have is far too extensive to mention here, but inspection techniques that have been developed by

licensees usually find some of the most common problems. For example:

- A licensee may carry a marble in her pocket for use in detecting an uneven floor that can be a sign of defective framing or expansive clay soil. Recommend a professional home inspection.

- Sticking doors or windows can be an indication of poor framing, expansive soil, poor workmanship, or warped lumber (usually because it was uncured [green] prior to installation). Recommend a professional home inspection.

- Doorjambs that have been reworked to make the door fit or doors that have been removed and recut to fit can be a sign of foundation settling or heaving. Recommend a professional home inspection.

- Ceiling stains often indicate some type of roof or plumbing problem and should always be thoroughly investigated by skilled professionals. Recommend a professional home and roof inspection.

- Leaning fence posts are often due to the existence of termites or a high water table that has eaten or rotted them out at the base. Recommend a professional home inspection.

These types of issues are commonly referred to as **red flag** warnings and should be noted in the Agent's Inspection Disclosure of the TDS. Keep in mind that the licensee is not expected to perform the duties of a home inspector, termite inspector, or other licensed professional; her legal responsibility is to conduct a visual inspection of reasonably accessible areas. In addition, the licensee must also conduct an oral interview and investigation with the sellers and disclose in her part of the TDS anything that might be a material fact or issue to a buyer. These types of issues may include such things as proximity to an airport, nearby train tracks, barking dogs, flood and earthquake zones, or a planned street widening.

Three of the most important things that licensees do to protect the interests of their principal(s) when selling or buying a home are:

- Recommend a professional home inspection. In today's litigious environment, this one item is probably the best single way to stay out of legal trouble. You should strongly recommend that the buyer get an inspection prior to becoming fully obligated to purchase a home. If a buyer elects not to get an inspection, have her acknowledge in writing that you, the licensee, have recommended further inspection but the buyer has declined the option. The seller may choose to arrange and pay for various inspections in advance, having a copy available for the buyer as soon as an offer is accepted. This is not only a great time saver but also makes

the seller aware of any significant defects in advance of detection by a buyer's inspection. This would be a significant seller advantage in any subsequent negotiations for repairs.

- Have the seller pay for a home protection plan (also called a home warranty plan) when the listing is taken. With some home warranty companies, this protects the seller for the covered items and systems during the "for sale" period as well as for a year after. If the seller declines to put a policy into effect during the sale period, have the buyer include a protection plan in her offer. It can be paid for by the buyer, by the seller, or half by each party—it's completely negotiable. This plan will cover all or most of the built-in appliances and systems such as plumbing, heating, and electrical for a one-year period after the close of escrow.

- Get a pest control inspection. Wise sellers get a pest control inspection and report prior to entering into a contract with a buyer. That way they know ahead of time exactly what the buyer may find in her pest inspection. This helps sellers make informed decisions regarding the terms they will sell on and allows them to use competent unlicensed repairmen for certain types of corrections.

The issuance of one or more of these types of reports does not relieve the licensee of her responsibility to conduct a thorough inspection of the reasonably accessible areas of a home. The licensees still retain liability for any undisclosed visible defects. Always recommend a professional home inspection.

In addition to any physical defects or problems to the property that the licensee notes, she must also disclose anything that might affect the buyer's decision to buy the property. These types of issues include, but are not limited to, flood and seismic hazard zones, barking dogs, nearby airports, and train tracks.

To assist the licensee in conducting a diligent visual inspection of the property and comply with mandatory disclosure requirements C.A.R. has developed an Agent Visual Inspection Disclosure (AVID) form, Statewide Buyer Seller Advisory (SBSA), Seller Property Questionnaire (SPQ) and Supplemental Statutory and Contractual Disclosures (SSD) that should be used with every listing. It should be noted that none of these advisory or disclosure forms are a substitute for local condition disclosures.

4.7 SELLER FINANCING DISCLOSURE

One of the first required disclosures for one to four residential units was the seller carryback financial disclosure. When financing became very hard to get and quite expensive in the early 1980s, the term

creative financing became popular, and it usually involved the seller carrying back financing in the form of a second, third, or fourth loan and the buyer taking title "subject to" the existing first loan. If the first loan had an attractive interest rate, the seller would often carry back a "wraparound or AITD, All Inclusive Trust Deed" loan or a contract of sale, thereby increasing the yield on her seller carryback portion of the new loan. The *Wellenkamp* decision had effectively made the due-on-sale clause in state-chartered savings and loan notes unenforceable and it was common for a buyer to take over such a loan and have the seller carry back what was often a very sizeable junior lien or one that was in as much as fifth place. Some real estate salespersons were not prudent in the representation of their sellers in these matters. When the buyer stopped making payments and the seller went to foreclose, she found that either she couldn't make the payments on all of the senior financing or the property was worth less that the total amount of loans that were senior to her, so her note was worthless.

This type of financing and the complaints made by the victims helped enact CCC Sections 2956 through 2967, which became law on July 1, 1983. These statutes require written disclosure of seller carryback financing on residential property of one to four residential units on the **Seller Financing Addendum and Disclosure (SFA)** form. The disclosure must be made to both the buyer and the seller, and there is no mandate that the units be owner-occupied for the statute to govern.

In mandating full disclosure, the California legislature began by defining *seller financing* and making the definition all-inclusive. The seller "extends credit" (carries back) whenever the buyer is given the right to defer payment of the purchase price, as long as a written agreement provides either for a finance charge or for payments to be made in more than four installments, which may be principal and interest or interest only, not including the down payment. This definition includes notes, trust deeds, mortgages, land contracts, installment contracts, leases with the option to purchase, security documents, and any other name that might be given to a financing agreement. For purposes of this section, we will use the term *seller* as the person who is carrying back the note, *buyer* as the one making or giving the note, and *note* as any of the above types of financing.

Because any type of seller financing *must be disclosed*, it is important to know who must disclose the terms of the financing. The disclosure requirements are imposed on the *arranger of credit* who is often a real estate licensee or an attorney who is a party to the transaction. Where more than one arranger of credit exists, the arranger who obtains the purchase contract (the selling licensee)

must make the disclosures unless someone else is designated in writing by the parties to the contract. Licensees acting for selling (buyer's) brokers should take care to remember that they are fully liable for the proper written disclosure of seller financing unless another person or licensee in the transaction agrees in writing to do it.

The timing of any disclosure is important. The financial disclosure must be made prior to the execution of any note and any notes signed prior to written disclosure must be contingent on the buyer's written approval of the disclosure before they are valid. The arranger, buyer, and seller must all sign the disclosure statements, and copies must be given to the buyer and seller. A copy must be retained in the arranger's file for three years.

A number of items and facts must be disclosed, including the following major items:

- The terms of the note, such as the original loan amount, interest rate, and term (number of payments).

- All other liens that are secured by the property, including the original loan amount, current balance, interest rate and any provisions for variations in the interest rate, term, any balloon payment, maturity date, and whether any payments are currently in default.

- A statement that the note, if not fully amortized, must be refinanced at maturity and that this might be difficult or impossible to accomplish in the current marketplace. In the event that a balloon payment is called for in any note, the seller or holder of the note must notify the buyer in writing at least 60 days and not more than 150 days prior to the due date of the note. The written notice must specify to whom the payment is due, the due date, and the exact amount due or a good-faith estimate, including the unpaid principal balance, interest, and any other allowable charges.

- That loans have or will have a negative amortization (payments do not equal interest due and result in the borrower owing more than the original loan amount) or that deferred interest ARMs (adjustable rate mortgages) could have negative amortization must be clearly disclosed and its potential effects clearly explained, as stated earlier.

- The name of the person liable for the payoff of the underlying loan in an all-inclusive trust deed (AITD) if the holder of the senior loan exercises a due-on-sale clause and accelerates the loan.

- The buyer's creditworthiness by way of a TRW or tri-merged credit report, job verification, financial statement review, and so on.

- A Request for Notice of Default filed and recorded on behalf of the seller to help protect the seller in the event of a default by the buyer on any senior loan.

- That a title insurance policy will be obtained and furnished to both the buyer and the seller.

- That a tax service has been arranged to notify the seller in the event that the property taxes are not paid on the property and who will be responsible for payment for the continued service of the tax service, and that arrangements have been made to notify the seller if the casualty insurance covering the property is terminated for any reason.

- That the deed of trust securing the seller's note will be recorded.

- The amount, source, and purpose of the funds, as well as when the buyer is to receive cash from the proceeds of the transaction.

Remember that this list is only a condensed version of what is required under the financing disclosure law. The total amount of information required by the CCC will be more fully understood by a careful review of the actual Seller Financing Addendum and Disclosure shown in Figure 4.5.

Addendum to the RPA-CA Seller Financing Addendum and Disclosure (SFA Revised 10/02)

At the top of page 1 of the form (Figure 4.5), you must indicate if the disclosure is an addendum to a residential purchase contract, counteroffer, or other contract showing the date of the other contract that is referenced. The property, the buyer, and the seller are identified. Each paragraph provides the following information:

- Paragraph 1 indicates the amount of the seller financing, the interest rate, payments, maturity date, and balloon payment if any.

- Paragraph 2 makes provision for the buyer to complete and provide the seller with a Uniform Residential Loan Application; the seller may cancel the sale if the buyer does not or will not provide the requested data within the time specified.

- Paragraph 3 provides for the type of document that will evidence the debt owed to the seller by the buyer.

- Paragraph 4 states that late charges (for a single-family residence) cannot exceed 6 percent of the payment and must have a ten-day grace period.

FIGURE 4.5 Seller Financing Addendum and Disclosure

CALIFORNIA ASSOCIATION OF REALTORS®

SELLER FINANCING ADDENDUM AND DISCLOSURE
(California Civil Code §§2956-2967)
(C.A.R. Form SFA, Revised 10/02)

This is an addendum to the ☐ Residential Purchase Agreement, ☐ Counter Offer, or ☐ Other _____
_____, ("Agreement"), dated _____,
On property known as _____ ("Property"),
between _____ ("Buyer"),
and _____ ("Seller").
Seller agrees to extend credit to Buyer as follows:

1.   **PRINCIPAL; INTEREST; PAYMENT; MATURITY TERMS:**   Principal amount $ _____, interest at _____%
per annum, payable at approximately $ _____ per ☐ month, ☐ year, or ☐ other _____,
remaining principal balance due in _____ years.

2.   **LOAN APPLICATION; CREDIT REPORT:** Within **5 (or _____) Days** After Acceptance: **(a)** Buyer shall provide Seller a completed
loan application on a form acceptable to Seller (such as a FNMA/FHLMC Uniform Residential Loan Application for residential one to four
unit properties); and **(b)** Buyer authorizes Seller and/or Agent to obtain, at Buyer's expense, a copy of Buyer's credit report. Buyer shall
provide any supporting documentation reasonably requested by Seller. Seller, after first giving Buyer a Notice to Buyer to Perform, may
cancel this Agreement in writing and authorize return of Buyer's deposit if Buyer fails to provide such documents within that time, or if
Seller disapproves any above item within **5 (or _____) Days** After receipt of each item.

3.   **CREDIT DOCUMENTS:** This extension of credit by Seller will be evidenced by: ☐ Note and deed of trust; ☐ All-inclusive
note and deed of trust; ☐ Installment land sale contract; ☐ Lease/option (when parties intend transfer of equitable title);
OR ☐ Other (specify) _____
**THE FOLLOWING TERMS APPLY ONLY IF CHECKED. SELLER IS ADVISED TO READ ALL TERMS, EVEN THOSE NOT
CHECKED, TO UNDERSTAND WHAT IS OR IS NOT INCLUDED, AND, IF NOT INCLUDED, THE CONSEQUENCES THEREOF.**

4. ☐   **LATE CHARGE:** If any payment is not made within _____ **Days** After it is due, a late charge of either $ _____,
or _____% of the installment due, may be charged to Buyer. **NOTE:** On single family residences that Buyer intends to occupy,
California Civil Code §2954.4(a) limits the late charge to no more than 6% of the total installment payment due and requires a
grace period of no less than 10 days.

5. ☐   **BALLOON PAYMENT:** The extension of credit will provide for a balloon payment, in the amount of $ _____,
plus any accrued interest, which is due on _____ (date).

6. ☐   **PREPAYMENT:** If all or part of this extension of credit is paid early, Seller may charge a prepayment penalty as follows (if
applicable): _____. Caution: California Civil Code
§2954.9 contains limitations on prepayment penalties for residential one-to-four unit properties.

7. ☐   **DUE ON SALE:** If any interest in the Property is sold or otherwise transferred, Seller has the option to require immediate
payment of the entire unpaid principal balance, plus any accrued interest.

8.* ☐ **REQUEST FOR COPY OF NOTICE OF DEFAULT:** A request for a copy of Notice of Default as defined in California Civil
Code §2924b will be recorded. **If Not**, Seller is advised to consider recording a Request for Notice of Default.

9.* ☐ **REQUEST FOR NOTICE OF DELINQUENCY:** A request for Notice of Delinquency, as defined in California Civil Code §2924e,
to be signed and paid for by Buyer, will be made to senior lienholders. **If not**, Seller is advised to consider making a Request for
Notice of Delinquency. Seller is advised to check with senior lienholders to verify whether they will honor this request.

10.* ☐ **TAX SERVICE:**
A. If property taxes on the Property become delinquent, tax service will be arranged to report to Seller. **If not**, Seller is
advised to consider retaining a tax service, or to otherwise determine that property taxes are paid.
B. ☐ Buyer, ☐ Seller, shall be responsible for the initial and continued retention of, and payment for, such tax service.

11. ☐ **TITLE INSURANCE:** Title insurance coverage will be provided to **both** Seller and Buyer, insuring their respective interests
in the Property. **If not,** Buyer and Seller are advised to consider securing such title insurance coverage.

12. ☐ **HAZARD INSURANCE:**
A. The parties' escrow holder or insurance carrier will be directed to include a loss payee endorsement, adding Seller to
the Property insurance policy. **If not**, Seller is advised to secure such an endorsement, or acquire a separate
insurance policy.
B. Property insurance **does not** include earthquake or flood insurance coverage, unless checked:
☐ Earthquake insurance will be obtained; ☐ Flood insurance will be obtained.

13. ☐ **PROCEEDS TO BUYER:** Buyer will receive cash proceeds at the close of the sale transaction. The amount received will be
approximately $_____, from _____ (indicate source of
proceeds). Buyer represents that the purpose of such disbursement is as follows: _____.

14. ☐ **NEGATIVE AMORTIZATION; DEFERRED INTEREST:** Negative amortization results when Buyer's periodic payments are
less than the amount of interest earned on the obligation. Deferred interest also results when the obligation does not
require periodic payments for a period of time. In either case, interest is not payable as it accrues. This accrued interest
will have to be paid by Buyer at a later time, and may result in Buyer owing more on the obligation than at its origination.
The credit being extended to Buyer by Seller will provide for negative amortization or deferred interest as indicated below.
(Check A, B, or C. CHECK ONE ONLY.)
☐ **A.** All negative amortization or deferred interest shall be added to the principal _____
(e.g., annually, monthly, etc.), and thereafter shall bear interest at the rate specified in the credit documents (compound interest);
OR ☐ **B.** All deferred interest shall be due and payable, along with principal, at maturity;
OR ☐ **C.** Other _____

*(For Paragraphs 8-10) In order to receive timely and continued notification, Seller is advised to record appropriate notices and/or to
notify appropriate parties of any change in Seller's address.

SFA REVISED 10/02 (PAGE 1 OF 3) Print Date

Buyer's Initials (_____)(_____)
Seller's Initials (_____)(_____)

Reviewed by _____ Date _____

EQUAL HOUSING OPPORTUNITY

SELLER FINANCING ADDENDUM AND DISCLOSURE (SFA PAGE 1 OF 3)

FIGURE 4.5 (*Continued*)

Property Address: _____   Date: _____

15. ☐ **ALL-INCLUSIVE DEED OF TRUST; INSTALLMENT LAND SALE CONTRACT:** This transaction involves the use of an all-inclusive (or wraparound) deed of trust or an installment land sale contract. That deed of trust or contract shall provide as follows:
    A. In the event of an acceleration of any senior encumbrance, the responsibility for payment, or for legal defense is: _____
    _____ ; OR ☐ **Is not** specified in the credit or security documents.
    B. In the event of the prepayment of a senior encumbrance, the responsibilities and rights of Buyer and Seller regarding refinancing, prepayment penalties, and any prepayment discounts are: _____ ;
    OR ☐ **Are not** specified in the documents evidencing credit.
    C. Buyer will make periodic payments to _____ (Seller, collection agent, or any neutral third party), who will be responsible for disbursing payments to the payee(s) on the senior encumbrance(s) and to Seller. **NOTE:** The Parties are advised to designate a neutral third party for these purposes.

16. ☐ **TAX IDENTIFICATION NUMBERS:** Buyer and Seller shall each provide to each other their Social Security Numbers or Taxpayer Identification Numbers.

17. ☐ **OTHER CREDIT TERMS** _____
    _____

18. ☐ **RECORDING:** The documents evidencing credit (paragraph 3) will be recorded with the county recorder where the Property is located. **If not**, Buyer and Seller are advised that their respective interests in the Property may be jeopardized by intervening liens, judgments, encumbrances, or subsequent transfers.

19. ☐ **JUNIOR FINANCING:** There will be additional financing, secured by the Property, junior to this Seller financing. Explain: ____

20. **SENIOR LOANS AND ENCUMBRANCES:** The following information is provided on loans and/or encumbrances that will be **senior** to Seller financing. **NOTE:** The following are estimates, unless otherwise marked with an asterisk (*). If checked: ☐ A separate sheet with information on additional senior loans/encumbrances is attached

	1st	2nd
A. Original Balance .... $	_____	$ _____
B. Current Balance .... $	_____	$ _____
C. Periodic Payment (e.g. $100/month): .... $	_____	$ _____ / _____
Including Impounds of: .... $	_____	$ _____ / _____
D. Interest Rate (per annum)	_____ %	_____ %
E. Fixed or Variable Rate:	_____	_____
If Variable Rate: Lifetime Cap (Ceiling) ..	_____	_____
Indicator (Underlying Index)	_____	_____
Margins	_____	_____
F. Maturity Date	_____	_____
G. Amount of Balloon Payment .... $	_____	$ _____
H. Date Balloon Payment Due	_____	_____
I. Potential for Negative Amortization? (Yes, No, or Unknown) ..	_____	_____
J. Due on Sale? (Yes, No, or Unknown)	_____	_____
K. Pre-payment penalty? (Yes, No, or Unknown)	_____	_____
L. Are payments current? (Yes, No, or Unknown)........	_____	_____

21. **BUYER'S CREDITWORTHINESS:** (CHECK EITHER A OR B. Do not check both.) In addition to the loan application, credit report and other information requested under paragraph 2:
    A. ☐ No other disclosure concerning Buyer's creditworthiness has been made to Seller;
OR **B.** ☐ The following representations concerning Buyer's creditworthiness are made by Buyer(s) to Seller:

Borrower _____	**Co-Borrower** _____
1. Occupation _____	1. Occupation _____
2. Employer _____	2. Employer _____
3. Length of Employment _____	3. Length of Employment _____
4. Monthly Gross Income _____	4. Monthly Gross Income _____
5. Other _____	5. Other _____

22. **ADDED, DELETED OR SUBSTITUTED BUYERS:** The addition, deletion or substitution of any person or entity under this Agreement or to title prior to close of escrow shall require Seller's written consent. Seller may grant or withhold consent in Seller's sole discretion. Any additional or substituted person or entity shall, if requested by Seller, submit to Seller the same documentation as required for the original named Buyer. Seller and/or Brokers may obtain a credit report, at Buyer's expense, on any such person or entity.

Buyer's Initials (_____)(_____)
Seller's Initials (_____)(_____)

SFA REVISED 10/02 (PAGE 2 OF 3)

Reviewed by _____ Date _____

SELLER FINANCING ADDENDUM AND DISCLOSURE (SFA PAGE 2 OF 3)

FIGURE 4.5 *(Continued)*

Property Address: _____   Date: _____

23. CAUTION:
  A. If the Seller financing requires a balloon payment, Seller shall give Buyer written notice, according to the terms of Civil Code §2966, at least 90 and not more than 150 days before the balloon payment is due if the transaction is for the purchase of a dwelling for not more than four families.
  B. If **any** obligation secured by the Property calls for a balloon payment, Seller and Buyer are aware that refinancing of the balloon payment at maturity may be difficult or impossible, depending on conditions in the conventional mortgage marketplace at that time. There are no assurances that new financing or a loan extension will be available when the balloon prepayment, or any prepayment, is due.
  C. If **any** of the existing or proposed loans or extensions of credit would require refinancing as a result of a lack of full amortization, such refinancing might be difficult or impossible in the conventional mortgage marketplace.
  D. In the event of default by Buyer: (1) Seller may have to reinstate and/or make monthly payments on any and all senior encumbrances (including real property taxes) in order to protect Seller's secured interest; (2) Seller's rights are generally limited to foreclosure on the Property, pursuant to California Code of Civil Procedure §580b; and (3) the Property may lack sufficient equity to protect Seller's interests if the Property decreases in value.

If this three-page Addendum and Disclosure is used in a transaction for the purchase of a dwelling for not more than four families, it shall be prepared by an Arranger of Credit as defined in California Civil Code §2957(a). (The Arranger of Credit is usually the agent who obtained the offer.)

_____
Arranger of Credit - (Print Firm Name)   By _____   Date _____

Address _____ City _____ State _____ Zip _____

Phone _____ Fax _____

> BUYER AND SELLER ACKNOWLEDGE AND AGREE THAT BROKERS: (A) WILL NOT PROVIDE LEGAL OR TAX ADVICE; (B) WILL NOT PROVIDE OTHER ADVICE OR INFORMATION THAT EXCEEDS THE KNOWLEDGE, EDUCATION AND EXPERIENCE REQUIRED TO OBTAIN A REAL ESTATE LICENSE; OR (C) HAVE NOT AND WILL NOT VERIFY ANY INFORMATION PROVIDED BY EITHER BUYER OR SELLER. BUYER AND SELLER AGREE THAT THEY WILL SEEK LEGAL, TAX AND OTHER DESIRED ASSISTANCE FROM APPROPRIATE PROFESSIONALS. BUYER AND SELLER ACKNOWLEDGE THAT THE INFORMATION EACH HAS PROVIDED TO THE ARRANGER OF CREDIT FOR INCLUSION IN THIS DISCLOSURE FORM IS ACCURATE. BUYER AND SELLER FURTHER ACKNOWLEDGE THAT EACH HAS RECEIVED A COMPLETED COPY OF THIS DISCLOSURE FORM.

Buyer _____   Date _____
                        (signature)

Address _____ City _____ State _____ Zip _____

Phone _____ Fax _____ E-mail _____

Buyer _____   Date _____
                        (signature)

Address _____ City _____ State _____ Zip _____

Phone _____ Fax _____ E-mail _____

Seller _____   Date _____
                        (signature)

Address _____ City _____ State _____ Zip _____

Phone _____ Fax _____ E-mail _____

Seller _____   Date _____
                        (signature)

Address _____ City _____ State _____ Zip _____

Phone _____ Fax _____ E-mail _____

SURE TRAC
The System for Success®

Published and Distributed by:
REAL ESTATE BUSINESS SERVICES, INC.
a subsidiary of the California Association of REALTORS®
525 South Virgil Avenue, Los Angeles, California 90020

Reviewed by _____ Date _____

SFA REVISED 10/02 (PAGE 3 OF 3)

SELLER FINANCING ADDENDUM AND DISCLOSURE (SFA PAGE 3 OF 3)

Source: Reprinted with permission of California Association of REALTORS®.

- Paragraph 5 indicates whether or not there will be a balloon payment, and if so, the dollar amount and the due date.
- Paragraph 6 sets forth any prepayment fees (often referred to as prepayment penalties).
- Paragraph 7, if checked, makes the loan due on sale or transfer of the property or any portion thereof (the seller's loan cannot be assumed or taken over by another party).
- Paragraph 8, if checked, makes provision for the seller to receive a copy of any notice of default that is recorded, indicating foreclosure of a prior (senior) lien.
- Paragraph 9, if checked, provides that the seller must receive a notice of delinquency if the trustor (buyer) is more than four months in default.
- Paragraph 10, if checked, shows that the parties have agreed to a tax service that will notify the seller if the buyer has failed to pay the property taxes.
- Paragraph 11, if checked, states that both the buyer and the seller will be covered by a policy of title insurance.
- Paragraph 12 provides a loss-payable clause that adds the seller to the buyer's casualty insurance policy and, if the parties so elect, provides for earthquake and flood insurance.
- Paragraph 13 provides that if the buyer will receive any cash from the transaction, the amount of cash he or she will receive must be shown.
- Paragraph 14 provides that if there is any negative amortization, it will be added to the principal and will bear interest or be due at maturity.
- Paragraph 15 points out dangers associated with AITDs or installment sale contracts regarding the acceleration of senior encumbrances as well as how the senior encumbrance is paid.
- Paragraph 16 covers the tax identification numbers (Social Security numbers for individuals) of the parties for tax reporting purposes.
- Paragraph 17 covers any additional credit terms.
- Paragraph 18 provides for recording of the documents.
- Paragraph 19 indicates whether or not there will be any junior financing.
- Paragraph 20 provides details of any senior liens with estimated amounts unless marked with asterisks.
- Paragraph 21 provides for details of the buyer's creditworthiness for verification purposes.

- Paragraph 22 states that the seller's consent is necessary to add or delete any person or entity prior to close of escrow.
- Paragraph 23 provides informational cautions about the effect of balloon payments as well as information about problems that may be encountered by the seller if the buyer is in default.

Both the buyer and the seller initial the bottom of page one of the Seller Financing Addendum and Disclosure (SFA-14) and fully execute or sign at the bottom of page two.

4.8 ENVIRONMENTAL HAZARDS DISCLOSURE

A home may contain any number of environmental hazards. The existence of hazards such as asbestos, formaldehyde, lead, and radon gas can pose serious health risks to humans. It is important to investigate and give written information about these issues to a potential home buyer. This is an area of disclosure where there is no substitute for the use of trained, licensed professionals.

Most new homes have very little in the way of these types of environmental hazards; however, compliance with the more stringent energy efficiency standards required in newer homes has made some of them more susceptible to elevated levels of radon and formaldehyde gas (see the *Combined Hazards Book* for a more complete discussion of these and other hazards).

Because of the nature of environmental issues and their potential effects on human life, allegations of failure to disclose an environmental hazard to a buyer can quickly become a highly emotional issue and can be the source of very large settlements or jury awards. The real estate practitioner is advised to maintain the highest degree of diligence when addressing these issues.

In California, sellers are required to disclose any known environmental hazards by legislative mandate (Chapter 969, Statutes of 1989, AB 983, Bane). This legislation was enacted to inform homeowners and prospective homeowners about environmental hazards located on and affecting residential property. The seller may not be aware of all environmental hazards on her property; thus, a statement that the seller is unaware of any environmental hazards is not a guarantee that the property is free of such hazards. It is in the interests of both parties in a real estate transaction to know what hazards are the most common, where they might be found, and what may be done about them. This legislation brought about the publication of a booklet called "Residential Environmental Hazards: A Guide for

Homeowners, Homebuyers, Landlords and Tenants" and is included in *The Combined Hazards Book*.

The Combined Hazards Book meets the requirements of AB 983. This book contains three sections entitled "Residential Environmental Hazards: A Guide for Homeowners, Homebuyers, Landlords and Tenants," "Protect Your Family from Lead in Your Home," and "The Homeowners Guide to Earthquake Safety" (including gas shutoff valve update). California requires that sellers disclose the presence of any known environmental hazard. Unless you are contractually required to provide the buyer with a copy of *The Combined Hazards Book*, you are not legally required to do so, but if a seller or licensee provides this book, the sellers are not obligated to provide additional information on these hazards.

Obviously, it is in the interest of all parties for the seller to provide *The Combined Hazards Book* and obtain a signed receipt of acknowledgment. Sellers should complete the Residential Earthquake Report contained in the book and provide a copy to the buyer for acknowledgment by signature. Buyers should also sign the tear-out receipt of *The Combined Hazards Book* located inside the back cover and give this receipt to their real estate licensee as proof of having received the book.

The first sixteen pages of *The Combined Hazards Book* are divided into seven sections (plus appendices) covering the following areas:

- Asbestos
- Formaldehyde
- Hazardous wastes
- Household hazardous wastes
- Lead
- Mold
- Radon

The appendices include a list of federal and state agencies and a glossary of terms.

All licensees should obtain a copy of this book and become completely familiar with the seven basic topics. As a licensee, you will constantly be asked questions about this subject by your buyers and sellers. You must be sure to have every buyer sign a receipt for a copy.

Hazardous Substances Released

Health and Safety Code Section 25359.7a requires **hazardous waste disclosure**. Owners of *nonresidential* property must give prior written notice to buyers or lessees if they know of the release of

hazardous substances on the property or if they have reasonable cause to believe hazardous substances are on or beneath the property.

Likewise, tenants are required to notify both residential and nonresidential landlords of hazardous substances they know have been released or believe to exist on or beneath the property. The failure to disclose is considered a default of the terms and conditions of the lease.

Lead-Based Paint

Purchasers of one to four residential units built prior to 1978 must be given a "Protect Your Family from Lead in Your Home" booklet published by the federal government (also present in *The Combined Hazards Book*). The buyer must be given a ten-day right to inspect the property. The known existence of lead-based paint must be fully disclosed in writing. (C.A.R.'s Lead-Based Paint and Lead-Based Paint Hazards Disclosure, Acknowledgement and Addendum, Standard Form FLD form satisfies this requirement.)

Mold

Mold is simply a microorganism that exists almost anywhere there is a source of water and food for the organism to ingest. Recognition of various molds is not a requirement of the real estate licensee. Usually the home inspector will detect its existence and make a notation on her report. Should the licensee discover suspicious fungal growth further inspection should be recommended. Molds can be highly toxic, and many people are susceptible to allergic reactions from mild to severe as a result of exposure to mold spores.

Radon

Trace amounts of decaying uranium can be found in most soils. The gas from this decomposition, if allowed to accumulate, can be a health hazard.

Military Ordnance Location

Military ordnance disclosure is part of the TDS law and is therefore required only where you are also required to provide a TDS. If a transferor has knowledge that a property is within one mile of a former **military ordnance location** (military training ground or ammunition storage area) that may contain explosives, the transferor must disclose in writing to the transferee that these former federal or state sites may contain potentially explosive ammunition. Upon receiving this notice, the buyer has the same three- or five-day rescission right she would have upon receiving a TDS.

4.9 NATURAL HAZARDS DISCLOSURE
Earthquake Safety

"The Homeowners Guide to Earthquake Safety" was created by the California Seismic Safety Commission and has since been incorporated in *The Combined Hazards Book.*

An **earthquake safety disclosure statement** must be completed and signed by every buyer and seller of a California home. This disclosure statement is called "Residential Earthquake Hazards Report" (Figure 4.6). The seller must answer nine questions that are explained in the text of the booklet.

1. Is the water heater braced, strapped, or anchored to resist falling during an earthquake? (page 12)
2. Is the house anchored or bolted to the foundation? (page 14)
3. If the house has cripple walls (page 16)
   - Are the exterior cripple walls braced?
   - If the exterior foundation consists of unconnected concrete piers and posts, have they been strengthened?
4. If the exterior foundation, or part of it, is made of unreinforced masonry, has it been strengthened? (page 20)
5. If the house is built on a hillside (page 22)
   - Are the exterior tall foundation walls braced?
   - Were the tall posts or columns either built to resist earthquakes or have they been strengthened?
6. If the exterior walls of the house, or part of them, are made of unreinforced masonry, have they been strengthened? (page 24)
7. If the house has a living area over the garage, was the wall around the garage door opening either built to resist earthquakes or has it been strengthened? (page 26)
8. Is the house outside an Alquist-Priolo Earthquake Fault Zone (zones immediately surrounding known earthquake faults)? (page 36)
9. Is the house outside a seismic hazard zone (zone identified as susceptible to liquefaction or landslide)? (page 36)

If these questions cannot be readily answered by a cursory visual inspection, the seller should probably seek the services of a licensed architect or engineer.

To complete the disclosure report, the seller must answer the questions to the best of her ability and knowledge. If the seller doesn't understand one or more of the questions, the licensee should be prepared to provide further explanation, within the scope of her

FIGURE 4.6   Residential Earthquake Hazards Report

Residential Earthquake Hazards Report

(See the back of this form for applicable government codes.)

NAME	ASSESSOR'S PARCEL NO.
STREET ADDRESS	YEAR BUILT
CITY AND COUNTY	ZIP CODE

Answer these questions to the best of your knowledge. If you do not have actual knowledge as to whether the weakness exists, answer "Don't Know." If your house does not have the feature, answer "Doesn't Apply." The page numbers in the right-hand column indicate where in this guide you can find information on each of these features.

	Yes	No	Doesn't Apply	Don't Know	See Page
1. Is the water heater braced, strapped, or anchored to resist falling during an earthquake?	☐	☐	☐	☐	3
2. Is the house anchored or bolted to the foundation?	☐	☐	☐	☐	4
3. If the house has cripple walls:					
• Are the exterior cripple walls braced?	☐	☐	☐	☐	5
• If the exterior foundation consists of unconnected concrete piers and posts, have they been strengthened?	☐	☐	☐	☐	6
4. If the exterior foundation, or part of it, is made of unreinforced masonry, has it been strengthened?	☐	☐	☐	☐	7
5. If the house is built on a hillside:					
• Are the exterior tall foundation walls braced?	☐	☐	☐	☐	8
• Were the tall posts or columns either built to resist earthquakes or have they been strengthened?	☐	☐	☐	☐	8
6. If the exterior walls of the house, or part of them, are made of unreinforced masonry, have they been strengthened?	☐	☐	☐	☐	9
7. If the house has a living area over the garage, was the wall around the garage door opening either built to resist earthquakes or has it been strengthened?	☐	☐	☐	☐	10
8. Is the house outside an Alquist-Priolo Earthquake Fault Zone (zones immediately surrounding known earthquake faults)?	☐	☐		☐	19
9. Is the house outside a Seismic Hazard Zone (zone identified as susceptible to liquefaction or landsliding)?	☐	☐		☐	19

If any of the questions are answered "No," the house is likely to have an earthquake weakness. Questions answered "Don't Know" may indicate a need for further evaluation. If you corrected one or more of these weaknesses, describe the work on a separate page.

As seller of the property described herein, I have answered the questions above to the best of my knowledge in an effort to disclose fully any potential earthquake weaknesses it may have.

EXECUTED BY

_____   _____   _____
(Seller)   (Seller)   Date

I acknowledge receipt of this form, completed and signed by the seller. I understand that if the seller has answered "No" to one or more questions, or if seller has indicated a lack of knowledge, there may be one or more earthquake weaknesses in this house.

_____   _____   _____
(Buyer)   (Buyer)   Date

This earthquake disclosure is made in addition to the standard real estate transfer disclosure statement also required by law.

The Homeowner's Guide to Earthquake Safety   29

Keep your copy of this form for future reference

"reasonable knowledge as a licensee." A licensee must take great care not to exceed the scope of her knowledge as a licensee by imparting information that requires specialized training or certification that she does not have. It is critical to know when to say, "I don't know the answer; you will have to get the advice of a licensed professional in that area."

The licensee must remember that even if a part of an answer is "No," the whole answer is "No." For example, assume that the home is on a hillside and has an in-law unit above the garage. You have verified that the area around the garage door has been reinforced, but the cripple wall area under the house has not. In this case, the seller's answer to the question regarding whether the house is reinforced against earthquake is "No." In addition to becoming knowledgeable about earthquake safety, licensees must be able to discover when a property was built as well as to deter-mine the Assessor's Parcel Number (APN) for the specific property in question.

Any work done by the seller to correct one or more of these structural deficiencies must be disclosed by the seller on an adden-dum to the report or on a separate sheet of paper.

To fulfill the legal disclosure requirements, the licensee must provide the buyer with both the disclosure statement and *The Combined Hazards Book*. Upon presentation of *The Combined Hazards Book* to the buyer, the licensee should have the buyer ac-knowledge receipt by signing the form at the back of the book (Figure 4.7).

In transactions requiring the seller to provide a TDS, the seller and/or the seller's licensee must also provide another disclosure statement called a Natural Hazards Disclosure Statement (C.A.R.'s NHD form satisfies this requirement). In some cases, this disclosure will be included in a professional disclosure report. Many professional providers offer this report at a nominal cost to the seller. Where a Natural Hazards Disclosure is required, the buyer also has the same three- or five-day right of rescission as with the TDS. *The Combined Hazards Book* includes the disclosures required for residential environmental hazards (discussed earlier) and earthquake safety but does not by itself meet the Natural Ha-zards Disclosure requirement, although this too is often included in the professionally prepared NHD for an additional charge.

At least six types of natural hazard zones have been specifically identified by California law as being of particular concern to home buyers. Two of these zones are concerned with fire, two with the

FIGURE 4.7   Residential Earthquake Hazards Report Receipt

To Whom It May Concern:

I have received a copy of **"The Homeowner's Guide to Earthquake Safety and Environmental Hazards"** which includes the Federal **"Protect Your Family from Lead"** booklet. In addition, per California Legislation in 2001, Chapter VII, Mold, has been included.

Property Address_____

Date _____   Time_____

Seller _____   _____
Print Name

Broker _____   _____
Print Name

Listing Agent _____   _____
Print Name

_____

Date _____

Selling Agent _____   _____
Print Name

Buyer _____   _____
Print Name

NOTE: This is a receipt for the combined "The Homeowner's Guide to Earthquake Safety and Environmental Hazards" which includes the Federal "Protect Your Family From Lead" booklet, and Chapter VII, Mold (added per SB 732, 2001). For applicable transactions, it is also necessary to complete C.A.R. Standard form FLD-14 (Lead-based paint and Lead-based paint Hazards Addendum, Disclosure, and Acknowledgement).

potential for flooding, and two discuss earthquake and seismic hazards:

1. *Wildland fire areas or state fire responsibility areas.* In these areas, the state not only sets fire protection requirements but also has primary firefighting responsibility. Seller must disclose.

2. *Very high fire hazard severity zones.* Owners are usually required to take special precautions to minimize fire danger. Seller must disclose.

3. *Inundation zones.* These areas are subject to possible inundation as a result of dam failure. Seller or seller's licensee must disclose.

4. *Special flood hazard areas.* The Federal Emergency Management Agency (FEMA) publishes maps that indicate known flood hazard areas. The seller's licensee must disclose this to a buyer if she has knowledge that the property is in such a zone or if a list of areas has been posted in the County Recorder's Office. Licensees are said to have "imputed" knowledge if such maps are available and they have access to them, so it is wise to check if you don't know for sure.

5. *Earthquake fault zones.* Locates areas designated by the State Geologist and specifies a certain distance from earthquake fault lines as areas of concern. Seller or seller's licensee must disclose.

6. *Seismic hazard zones.* These are areas subject to unusual ground movement during seismic activity such as earthquakes. Seller or seller's licensee must disclose.

This is not an exhaustive list of potential hazard zones. These are, however, the ones sellers and/or licensees have a duty to disclose. Of course, sellers are also required to disclose any potential hazard that they may be aware of at the time.

Special Study Zone

The Alquist-Priolo Special Study Zone Act requires that a licensee (or owner) disclose to any prospective purchaser that a property is located within a special study zone (geological hazard zone) if the property contains or eventually will contain a structure for human habitation (a residentially zoned parcel of land).

Special study zones are indicated on maps created by the California Division of Mines and Geology. Such zones cover an area 660 feet or one-eighth of a mile on each side of a fault line. Fault lines are a total of one-fourth of a mile in width.

The statutory form "Natural Hazards Disclosure Statement" is included as Figure 4.8.

FIGURE 4.8 Natural Hazards Disclosure Statement

CALIFORNIA
ASSOCIATION
OF REALTORS®

NATURAL HAZARD DISCLOSURE STATEMENT
(C.A.R. Form NHD, Revised 10/04)

This statement applies to the following property: _____

The transferor and his or her agent(s) or a third-party consultant disclose the following information with the knowledge that even though this is not a warranty, prospective transferees may rely on this information in deciding whether and on what terms to purchase the subject property. Transferor hereby authorizes any agent(s) representing any principal(s) in this action to provide a copy of this statement to any person or entity in connection with any actual or anticipated sale of the property.

The following are representations made by the transferor and his or her agent(s) based on their knowledge and maps drawn by the state and federal governments. This information is a disclosure and is not intended to be part of any contract between the transferee and transferor.

THIS REAL PROPERTY LIES WITHIN THE FOLLOWING HAZARDOUS AREA(S):

A SPECIAL FLOOD HAZARD AREA (Any type Zone "A" or "V") designated by the Federal Emergency Management Agency.

Yes _____   No _____   Do not know and information not available from local jurisdiction _____

AN AREA OF POTENTIAL FLOODING shown on a dam failure inundation map pursuant to Section 8589.5 of the Government Code.

Yes _____   No _____   Do not know and information not available from local jurisdiction _____

A VERY HIGH FIRE HAZARD SEVERITY ZONE pursuant to Section 51178 or 51179 of the Government Code. The owner of this property is subject to the maintenance requirements of Section 51182 of the Government Code.

Yes _____   No _____

A WILDLAND AREA THAT MAY CONTAIN SUBSTANTIAL FOREST FIRE RISKS AND HAZARDS pursuant to Section 4125 of the Public Resources Code. The owner of this property is subject to the maintenance requirements of Section 4291 of the Public Resources Code. Additionally, it is not the state's responsibility to provide fire protection services to any building or structure located within the wildlands unless the Department of Forestry and Fire Protection has entered into a cooperative agreement with a local agency for those purposes pursuant to Section 4142 of the Public Resources Code.

Yes _____   No _____

AN EARTHQUAKE FAULT ZONE pursuant to Section 2622 of the Public Resources Code.

Yes _____   No _____

A SEISMIC HAZARD ZONE pursuant to Section 2696 of the Public Resources Code.

Yes (Landslide Zone) _____   Yes (Liquefaction Zone) _____

No _____   Map not yet released by state _____

NHD REVISED 10/04 (PAGE 1 OF 2) Print Date Dec 04

Buyer's Initials (_____)(_____)
Seller's Initials (_____)(_____)

Reviewed by _____ Date _____

EQUAL HOUSING
OPPORTUNITY

MASTER COPY
NATURAL HAZARD DISCLOSURE STATEMENT (NHD PAGE 1 OF 2)

FIGURE 4.8 *(Continued)*

Property Address: _____   Date. _____

THESE HAZARDS MAY LIMIT YOUR ABILITY TO DEVELOP THE REAL PROPERTY, TO OBTAIN INSURANCE, OR TO RECEIVE ASSISTANCE AFTER A DISASTER.

THE MAPS ON WHICH THESE DISCLOSURES ARE BASED ESTIMATE WHERE NATURAL HAZARDS EXIST. THEY ARE NOT DEFINITIVE INDICATORS OF WHETHER OR NOT A PROPERTY WILL BE AFFECTED BY A NATURAL DISASTER. TRANSFEREE(S) AND TRANSFEROR(S) MAY WISH TO OBTAIN PROFESSIONAL ADVICE REGARDING THOSE HAZARDS AND OTHER HAZARDS THAT MAY AFFECT THE PROPERTY

Signature of Transferor(s) _____   Date _____

Signature of Transferor(s) _____   Date _____

Agent(s) _____   Date _____

Agent(s) _____   Date _____

Check only one of the following:

☐ Transferor(s) and their agent(s) represent that the information herein is true and correct to the best of their knowledge as of the date signed by the transferor(s) and agent(s).

☐ Transferor(s) and their agent(s) acknowledge that they have exercised good faith in the selection of a third-party report provider as required in Civil Code Section 1103.7, and that the representations made in this Natural Hazard Disclosure Statement are based upon information provided by the independent third-party disclosure provider as a substituted disclosure pursuant to Civil Code Section 1103.4. Neither transferor(s) nor their agent(s) (1) has independently verified the information contained in this statement and report or (2) is personally aware of any errors or inaccuracies in the information contained on the statement. This statement was prepared by the provider below:

Third-Party Disclosure Provider(s)_____   Date _____

Transferee represents that he or she has read and understands this document. Pursuant to Civil Code Section 1103.8, the representations made in this Natural Hazard Disclosure Statement do not constitute all of the transferor's or agent's disclosure obligations in this transaction.

Signature of Transferee(s) _____   Date _____

Signature of Transferee(s) _____   Date _____

Published and Distributed by:
REAL ESTATE BUSINESS SERVICES, INC.
a subsidiary of the California Association of REALTORS®
525 South Virgil Avenue, Los Angeles, California 90020

NHD REVISED 10/04 (PAGE 2 OF 2)

| Reviewed by _____ Date _____ |

MASTER COPY

NATURAL HAZARD DISCLOSURE STATEMENT (NHD PAGE 2 OF 2)

Source: Reprinted with permission of California Association of REALTORS®.

4.10 COMMON INTEREST SUBDIVISIONS

A **common interest subdivision** is a subdivision in which owners own or lease a separate lot or unit together with an undivided interest in the common areas of the project. These common areas are usually governed by a homeowner's association that may or may not have additional control over the subdivision by enactment and enforcement of rules and regulations and covenants, conditions, and restrictions (CC&R). These two documents can control everything from the color of exterior paint that may be used on a dwelling to how many pets an owner may have.

In addition and prior to transfer of title, owners of community apartment projects, condominiums, planned unit developments, and cooperatives must provide purchasers with a copy of the CC&R; bylaws; articles of incorporation; and an owner's association financial statement, including any delinquent assessments and costs. An owner's association may charge a reasonable fee for providing these documents and must furnish the owner with a copy of them within ten days after the owner requests them.

Nothing will give the buyer a clearer picture of the current financial and legal condition of the owner's association like requesting copies of the last one to two year's minutes of the association's meetings and a statement of any pending or contemplated litigation involving the association.

4.11 PRELIMINARY AND FINAL PUBLIC REPORTS (SUBDIVISIONS)

In the initial sale of a common interest subdivision, the purchaser must be given a brochure entitled *Common Interest Development General Information* as well as a copy of the Public Report. There are actually two **public reports**: the preliminary public report and the final public report. A developer may enter into "reservations to purchase" agreements with potential buyers prior to issuance of the final public report; however, these reservations are cancelable by either party at any time. The developer may enter into binding purchase contracts for a new subdivision only when the final public report is issued.

4.12 RIGHT OF RESCISSION

A number of real estate transactions have statutory **rescission rights**. The buyer, or borrower on a loan, must be informed in writing of her rights. Failure to fully disclose the following rights of rescission automatically extends these rights.

- *Mello-Roos Bond Disclosure*: Failure to disclose that a property is in a Mello-Roos district allows the transferee a three- to five-day right of rescission.

- *Time Share*: Purchasers of time-share properties now have a right of rescission period of three days after they sign the contract. This was a result of abusive sales tactics by time-share developers.

- *Truth-in-Lending Act*: When a loan, such as a home equity loan, a second loan, or a refinance of the existing first loan is placed on a property, the borrower has a rescission right until midnight of the third business day following the completion of the loan. This rescission period does not apply to a loan placed on a property for the initial purchase of that property.

- *Undivided Interest Subdivisions*: An undivided interest subdivision is one in which the owners are tenants in common with the other owners but do not have an exclusive possessor interest in a particular unit or space. A campground is a good example in that all owners have a right to use a space if one is available and there may be sales of more ownership spaces than actual spaces. Owners of these types of interests have a three-day right of rescission following the day the purchase contract is signed.

- *Interstate Land Sales Full Disclosure Act*: This is a federal act that mandates the issuance of a disclosure statement, known as a property report, for subdivisions of twenty-five or more unimproved residential properties of less than five acres each that are sold through interstate commerce. Purchasers have a seven-day right of rescission as well as the right to receive the required disclosures.

- *Home Equity Sales*: Fraud and unfair dealings by home equity purchasers led to enactment of this act, which allows a homeowner whose home is in foreclosure a right of rescission. The foreclosed homeowner has until midnight of the fifth day after signing of the sales agreement or 8:00 a.m. on the date of sale to rescind the agreement.

Other Required Disclosures

Megan's Law: Megan's Law provides for registration of sex offenders and public availability of knowledge regarding the location of these offenders. Every purchase contract or lease of one to four residential units must inform buyers or lessees of the public availability of this information.

Water Heater Bracing — Sellers of real property must certify to prospective buyers that the water heater has been properly braced.

Home Energy Ratings — When a home energy booklet is developed by the State of California, a copy of the booklet must be delivered to transferees of real property (including mobile homes).

Smoke Detector Notice — A buyer of a single-family home must receive a written statement indicating that the property is in compliance with current California law regarding the presence of smoke detectors.

Home Inspection Notice — For the sale of one to four residential units, including mobile homes, involving FHA financing, or U.S. Department of Housing and Urban Development (HUD)-owned property, the borrower must sign a notice entitled "The Importance of a Home Inspection." See Figure 4.9 on the next page.

4.13 CALIFORNIA ASSOCIATION OF REALTORS® DISCLOSURE CHART

For its members to better understand the scope and timing of the numerous disclosures real estate practitioners must be aware of, the C.A.R. prepares a California Real Estate Law Disclosure Chart. Many of these mandated disclosures are included in the C.A.R. Purchase Agreement.

SUMMARY

Fairness and informed consent are the purposes of disclosures required by the state of California and the federal government. They act as conduits for receipt of all of the facts before a person is required to make a decision and include detrimental facts that a licensee knows a buyer or seller would likely consider when making a decision. The fiduciary duty of a licensee requires full disclosure, which is inherent when an agency relationship is created. Licensees must carefully explain the various types of agency options that are available to a buyer or seller, mutually select their option, and confirm it in writing to avoid any misunderstandings. Disclose, elect, and confirm is the order of the disclosure process. A seller has disclosure obligations to a buyer. For one to four residential units, the seller must complete a Real Estate TDS and give it to a buyer within a prescribed time. Both the listing licensee and the selling licensee (if different from the listing licensee) must conduct a walk-through visual inspection of the reasonably accessible areas and disclose their findings to a prospective buyer in writing on the same form.

A natural death on the premises need not be disclosed and a death for any reason need not be disclosed after three years. A licensee need not disclose that a former resident was afflicted with or died of AIDS. Stigmatized property such as a death on the

FIGURE 4.9   HUD Notice to Purchasers; For Your Protection: Get a Home Inspection (HID)

CALIFORNIA
ASSOCIATION
OF REALTORS ®

FOR YOUR PROTECTION: GET A HOME INSPECTION
For FHA Transactions
(C.A.R. Form HID, Revised 4/08)

Name of Buyer(s) _____

Property Address _____

_____

WHY A BUYER NEEDS A HOME INSPECTION

A home inspection gives the buyer more detailed information about the overall condition of the home prior to purchase. In a home inspection, a qualified inspector takes an in-depth, unbiased look at your potential new home to:

- Evaluate the physical condition: structure, construction, and mechanical systems
- Identify items that need to be repaired or replaced
- Estimate the remaining useful life of the major systems, equipment, structure, and finishes

APPRAISALS ARE DIFFERENT FROM HOME INSPECTIONS

An appraisal is different from a home inspection. Appraisals are for lenders; home inspections are for buyers. An appraisal is required to:

- Estimate the market value of a house
- Make sure that the house meets FHA minimum property standards/requirements
- Make sure that the property is marketable

FHA DOES NOT GUARANTEE THE VALUE OR CONDITION OF YOUR POTENTIAL NEW HOME

If you find problems with your new home after closing, FHA cannot give or lend you money for repairs, and FHA can not buy the home back from you. That is why it is so important for you, the buyer, to get an independent home inspection. Ask a qualified home inspector to inspect your potential new home and give you the information you need to make a wise decision.

RADON GAS TESTING

The United States Environmental Protection Agency and the Surgeon General of the United States have recommended that all houses should be tested for radon. For more information on radon testing, call the toll-free National Radon Information Line at 1-800-SOS-Radon or 1-800-767-7236. As with a home inspection, if you decide to test for radon, you may do so before signing your contract, or you may do so after signing the contract as long as your contract states the sale of the home depends on your satisfaction with the results of the radon test.

BE AN INFORMED BUYER

It is your responsibility to be an informed buyer. Be sure that what you buy is satisfactory in every respect. You have the right to carefully examine your potential new home with a qualified home inspector. You may arrange to do so before signing your contract, or may do so after signing the contract as long as your contract states that the sale of the home depends on the inspection.

I/we understand the importance of getting an independent home inspection. I/we have considered this before signing a contract with the seller for a home. Furthermore, I/we have carefully read this notice and fully understand that FHA will not perform a home inspection nor guarantee the price or condition of the property.

☐ I/We choose to have a home inspection performed.

☐ I/We choose <u>not</u> to have a home inspection performed.

Buyer_____ Date _____

Buyer_____ Date _____

REBS INC.®

Published and Distributed by:
REAL ESTATE BUSINESS SERVICES, INC.
a subsidiary of the California Association of REALTORS®
525 South Virgil Avenue, Los Angeles, California 90020

HID REVISED 4/08 (PAGE 1 OF 1)   Print Date

Reviewed by _____ Date _____

EQUAL HOUSING
OPPORTUNITY

FOR YOUR PROTECTION: GET A HOME INSPECTION   (HID PAGE 1 OF 1)

Source: Reprinted with permission of California Association of REALTORS®.

property within the past three years and any history of methamphetamine contamination on the premises must be disclosed if a buyer reasonably wants to know about it.

When any type of seller financing is used, the terms must be fully spelled out and the buyer warned of any dangers requiring the use of a seller financing disclosure and addendum.

Earthquake weaknesses must be disclosed in the sale of one to four residential units built prior to January 1, 1960. *The Combined Hazards Book* containing the "Residential Earthquake Hazards Report" form is used for this purpose.

When the property is located in a special study zone (660 feet on either side of a designated earthquake fault) and the property contains or will eventually contain a structure for human habitation, the zone's location must be disclosed to the buyer. Flood hazard areas must be disclosed in a similar manner.

Purchasers must be given a "Watch Out for Lead-Based Paint" notice (also contained in *The Combined Hazards Book*) if they are purchasing a one to four residential unit property that was built prior to 1978.

Buyers must be informed about environmental hazards on or nearby the property that will affect the property. The broker has a duty to disclose all known environmental hazards. Buyers and lessees must also be informed about hazardous substances that have been released on or believed to be present on a property and tenants must inform landlords if they release hazardous substances on the property.

Buyers must be notified if a property is within a one-mile radius of a former military ordnance site where explosives might be located. Buyers and lessees should be told about the availability of information regarding registered sex offenders in the area.

Other required disclosures include the Mello-Roos Bond Disclosure information, home inspection notice, water heater bracing requirement, Public Report for California Subdivisions, common interest developments, home energy ratings, and disclosure of rescission rights for certain specified contracts.

CLASS DISCUSSION TOPICS

1. A home you listed is right around the corner from a fire station. You have shown the home to a couple who wishes to make an offer. Do you have a duty to disclose the existence of the fire station?

2. You represent a buyer in the purchase of a four-unit building in which she plans to live. The listing licensee has verbalized to you that one tenant is behind on his rent and that he is very belligerent. What, if anything, do you need to tell your buyer about this situation?

3. You are holding an Open House on a home in which the former occupant died of AIDS. A buyer, who appears very interested in the home, asks you if anyone has died of AIDS in the property. What should you do?

4. You sold a home to a family with two small children. During the escrow, the wife calls you and asks if any sex offenders live nearby. What action should you take?

5. You are the listing licensee of a condominium unit and an elderly lady with three cats wants to make an offer to purchase it through you. You know that the CC&R allow a maximum of two domestic animals, but you proceed with the offer anyway. Are you acting in a proper manner? What disclosure duties do you have and to whom do you owe them?

6. You have just received the Real Estate TDS from the listing agent. It states that an electrical transformer on the power pole in the yard burst and the liquid inside sprayed over the yard. It was properly cleaned up by the utility company. Your buyers ask you what you think; how should you respond?

7. Complete a Real Estate TDS as if you were the seller of the property in which you currently live.

8. The seller has stated in the Real Estate TDS that she replaced the roof "only about three years ago." You feel the roof is much older than that. What action should you take?

CHAPTER 4 QUIZ

1. Which of the following is not true regarding a licensee's duty in a real estate transaction?
   A. A listing licensee owes a duty of fairness only to her broker's client, not the buyer.
   B. A broker has a fiduciary duty to her client.
   C. Any material facts that the licensee becomes aware of must be disclosed to her client.
   D. All of the above.

2. Which of the following is not true regarding agency disclosure?
   A. A licensee need not provide the seller of a rental property with an agency disclosure.
   B. The agency disclosure must be signed by the buyer at least ten days prior to close of escrow.
   C. Neither a nor b.
   D. Both a and b.

3. Which of the following is true regarding agency disclosure?
   A. The listing licensee must confirm the agency prior to completing the listing agreement.
   B. The three steps to the disclosure process are disclose, elect, and confirm.
   C. The confirmation of agency must be in writing.
   D. All of the above.

4. The legislation resulting from *Easton v. Strassburger* limits the licensee's duty of inspection and disclosure to which of the following?
   A. A visual inspection only.
   B. Accessible and inaccessible areas.
   C. All types of property.
   D. None of the above.

5. Which of the following sellers must provide a Real Estate TDS?
   A. The seller of an owner-occupied triplex.
   B. The seller of a small office building.
   C. The seller of a residential lot.
   D. None of the above.

6. A special study zone refers to which of the following?
   A. An inner-city redevelopment area.
   B. An area of land that is steeply sloped.
   C. An area that is 1/8th of a mile on either side of a known earthquake fault line.
   D. Any area of undeveloped land.

7. Which of the following is the purpose of bracing a water heater?
   A. To make it last longer.
   B. To stabilize it in the event of an earthquake.
   C. To allow for better water flow.
   D. To install it in a location where a pressure-release valve can be installed.

8. Under the Truth-in-Lending Act (TILA), when a homeowner obtains a home equity loan on her home, the rescission period is

A. noon the following business day.

B. within five days after close of the purchase escrow.

C. there is no right of rescission period for a refinance.

D. midnight of the third business day following completion of the loan.

9. A "Watch Out for Lead-Based Paint" notice must be given to the buyer of any one to four residential unit built prior to which one of the following years?

A. 1960

B. 1930

C. 1978

D. None of the above

10. The California Real Estate Law Disclosure Chart was created by which of the following organizations?

A. California Association of Real Estate Boards

B. Mortgage Banker's Association

C. California State Bar Association

D. California Association of REALTORS®

Chapter

5

IMPORTANT PHRASES AND TERMS

Absentee owners

Center of influence

Contact management system

Do-not-call registry

Door knocking

For Sale by Owners

Geographic areas

Geographical farm

Lead generation

Networking

Niche marketing

Nongeographic area

Prospecting

Rental units

REOs

Social networking

Sphere of influence (SOI)

Lead Generation or Prospecting for Clients and Customers

Upon completion of this chapter, the student will be able to:

- Identify and select a personal lead generation plan.
- Compose and construct a personal business plan.
- Recognize "Do Not Call" limitations to lead generation.
- Assemble a personal "sphere of influence" list.
- Select and evaluate a personal prospect database.

5.1 WHAT IS LEAD GENERATION OR PROSPECTING?

Simply put, **lead generation** is the systematic process of locating buyers who are interested in buying property and sellers who are interested in selling property. In short, it is generating buyer and seller leads. The terms *lead generation* and **prospecting** as they relate to real estate are used synonymously.

Without listings, it is difficult to attract buyers. To attract buyers, you can send mailers to apartment complexes, take floor time at your office, hold Open Houses at other licensees' listings, and regularly **blog** on various websites such as Facebook, Twitter, ePro Agent, and MySpace. When you prospect for listings, hold them open, and advertise them, you will attract buyers as well as additional listings at the same time. Blogging will let thousands of Internet users to get to know you well enough to agree to list their property or buy a property from you or, if they are a licensee, to be confident enough in you to refer business to you.

A successful real estate professional is constantly engaged in generating leads to potential sellers and buyers. Successful prospecting is a continuing process of marketing the two services you have to offer: time and knowledge. New licensees tend to gravitate toward the side of the market that needs service the most. That will depend on what kind of market prevails at the time: seller's market or buyer's market. It's a supply/demand thing.

You may decide to focus on either buyers or sellers. Many licensees believe that the licensee with the most listings wins. There is a lot to be said for that belief because, if there were no listings at all, buyers would have to go door-to-door looking for someone willing to sell their home. The licensee with the most reasonably priced listings in the current market conditions will be the licensee who dominates the market in sales.

Attitude Is Everything

Prospecting alone is not enough though; you must have the right attitude. If you are cold-calling or doing some other form of direct contact with a "farm area" or a geographic **center of influence** and you are less than enthusiastic about the work at hand, it will show in your mannerisms and your speech. Your target audience will certainly notice it, often with a similar lack of enthusiasm.

The process of finding motivated buyers and sellers may expose a real estate professional to many different kinds of reactions from prospective buyers and sellers. It would be a mistake to perceive those reactions as a personal rejection. Unfortunately, this is what happens with too many new licensees and it is by far the biggest reason for the high attrition rate among newly licensed salespeople. Your answers to the following questions will help you evaluate your attitude toward lead generation and ultimately your future success.

- Do you recognize that without an adequate supply of ready, willing, and able clients and customers, you are essentially out of business? Even when you are working with several people, they often "cool off." You need a constant supply of new motivated clients to take their places.

- What is your attitude toward rejection? Generating leads can be a numbers game where you search for the few among the many. Far too many licensees get overly involved in busy work in order to justify not prospecting. Then, when the few prospects they do have disappoint them or cool off, they are totally out of business. This is a self-defeating style of conducting business and will certainly relegate any licensee caught up in such a cycle to a very

small income—or worse! Fear of rejection is probably the biggest single reason that otherwise very good licensees leave the real estate business. It's a simple formula: No prospecting or no leads generated means no listings, no sales, no income; all of which means the licensee will soon be seeking a new career in some other field and likely taking the same fear to a new endeavor.

- Is generating leads a major challenge for you? Today's highly competitive real estate market requires the practitioner to perform numerous types of duties every day just to keep up with the marketplace. As salespersons get busier and busier, locating new buyers and sellers is often the first thing to be eliminated. You must maintain an attitude that keeps lead generation (the creation of ever-needed new business) at the forefront of your daily activities.

- Do you have a well-organized business plan or **networking** system for locating those who need your services? Many different sources are available to you, some of which are far more productive than others. You need a system in place that allows you to measure the results obtained from your efforts, a plan for increased activities in the most productive sources and a plan to decrease or eliminate activity that has proven ineffective and unproductive. Good organization and daily planning are the key factors to success. An electronic **contact management system** will be very beneficial for you as it allows for easy updating, which is a necessity.

5.2 DO YOUR RESEARCH FIRST

No matter what type of lead generation you decide to do, you will need to do some detailed research first. For instance, if you focus on one or more **geographic areas**, you must research the neighborhoods in your area that have enough annual turnover to warrant the time and money it will take you to get known by the people who live there. You will also need to research the local Multiple Listing Service (MLS) system to see if one particular company and/or broker/agent is dominant in listings or sales in that area. This information will help to formulate an effective business plan.

If your idea is to focus on **For Sale by Owners** (FSBOs), you must research the local newspapers and, possibly, www.ForSaleBy Owner.com to see if there are enough FSBOs in your area to be a meaningful source for you. You will also need training on how to approach them and how to start and develop relationships that develop trust and confidence in you.

If you plan to develop an Internet site, and you should, you must decide who its primary visitors will be and the message you want to convey to them.

You will be developing a database that will include, among others, prospective buyers and sellers and licensees from around the country who will refer business to you, your **sphere of influence** (SOI) group. This is basically your holiday card list plus every local person you think might do business with you or refer someone to you, and perhaps some influential out-of-towners.

What are your goals and aspirations? Again, the questions—Who am I and what do I want?—continue to demand an answer. Do you want to break into the luxury home market? Do you want to specialize in rental home or vacation home listings? Would you like to specialize in the marketing of small apartment houses? These are examples of **niche marketing** groups that you will develop over time.

Door knocking, while still done in some areas, is rapidly becoming outdated unless it is done with a specific purpose in mind, such as announcing your company's involvement in a charitable event like "Toys for Tots." Our society has changed a lot in recent years, and, generally speaking, people do not like uninvited "guests" at their doors. In most cases, it is also unsafe for a licensee, especially women who are by themselves.

No matter what your decisions in this area may be, you must spend the time necessary gathering data about the following:

- The amount of business available from each source.
- The competition in your market area.
- The amount of support available from your broker.
- Your budget.

Several other possible areas are available for you to prospect in, but you must first think logically through each one to determine whether the "risk/reward" ratio is in your favor. Then set a budget for purchasing flyers, postcards, postage, and other materials necessary for monthly mailings. Keep in mind that **social networking** via the Internet is free and has become one of the preferred methods of acquiring new business.

5.3 FORMULATING A BUSINESS PLAN

Once you have thoroughly researched where and to whom you are going to offer your services, you must formulate a business plan that will keep you in touch with your target audiences on a regular basis. Let's face it, generating sales leads involves some degree of rejection

because some people just won't need the services of a real estate professional at that moment in time. So, you need a plan that will generate as many opportunities as possible to present what you offer to as many people as possible every day. Then, you need to work that plan with dedication until it produces the desired results.

Generating leads involves a great deal more than just blindly knocking on doors and/or mailing out hundreds of postcards. It first involves research as discussed earlier combined with a logical and thorough plan allowing you maximum exposure to your target audience with the least amount of expense and time commitment. It also requires a strong commitment on your part to "just do it," as the commercial says.

Unless you have unlimited funds, the best place to start is your annual budget. Cash is king to most new real estate licensees. How much of your cash can you reasonably commit to generating leads over the next twelve months? Once you determine this, divide the amount by twelve to get your monthly budget. Then look at all of the different lead-generating methods you have chosen and decide, in descending order, which ones will help you identify the greatest number of people who may need your help. Once you have your order established, decide how much of your monthly budget you are willing to commit to do these various activities on a regular monthly basis.

When you have completed your systematic analysis of all of the prospecting activities, put the most important ones into your daily planner. By committing them to writing where you must look at them each day, they take on greater credibility and become a regular appointment with a very important person—you!

Figure 5.1 is a sample of what might appear in the daily planner of a successful real estate professional.

Generating leads to prospective clients and customers is a very valuable activity; however, you must have some way to monitor how effective your activities are. The best way to do this is to carefully keep track of the following three things:

1. Where your most motivated leads are coming from. This will identify your most effective lead-generating activities.
2. *Conversion rate.* Quality is more important than quantity. This will show you what source is providing the most *effective* leads.
3. *Time spent.* Time is money in any service industry, and real estate is no different. An activity, such as holding an Open House, may be inexpensive, but if you find after a reasonable time that you are not generating motivated buyers and sellers from them, you may want to reschedule your time to more productive activities.

FIGURE 5.1 Sample Weekly Prospecting Plan

- MONDAY: Circle all FSBO ads from the Sunday paper. Send each one your introductory letter and "Forget-Me-Not." Make plans for a Sunday Open House. Create a Twitter Internet account.
- TUESDAY: Mail 100 postcards to the nearest neighbors of any new listings you've taken, advising them of your new listing.
- Call each FSBO you mailed a letter to on Monday to set up an appointment.
  (Note: Check the Do-Not-Call List before making any unsolicited calls.) Create an Internet Facebook account.
- WEDNESDAY: Call ten people in your sphere of influence list to see if they, or a friend, need real estate services. Create a LinkedIn Internet account.
- THURSDAY: Make thirty cold-calls into your farm area. Create a blog on at least two of your Internet sites. Send letters with return postcards to every rental property owner in your farm area.
- FRIDAY: Walk to 100 homes around your Sunday Open House location handing out written invitations. Call back all FSBOs who you were unable to reach earlier in the week. Blog for one hour.
- SATURDAY: Take "Forget-Me-Nots" to all of the FSBOs you are currently working with. Blog for at least one hour. Visit at least one past client to ask for referrals and drop off a token gift.
- SUNDAY: Hold an Open House.

Note: For more information on Forget-Me-Nots, see "For Sale by Owners" section later in this chapter.

You should constantly reevaluate your prospecting plan and activities. It is critical for you to give each activity sufficient time to work for you and not give up too soon; however, if an activity is not producing new leads for you after giving it sufficient time (usually three months or more at a minimum, depending on the activity), it is time to reevaluate whether or not you should continue, change, or eliminate the activity.

5.4 THE DO-NOT-CALL LIST

In 2004, the federal government passed legislation making it illegal to call a private party that had placed a telephone number on a newly created national **do-not-call (DNC) registry**. Quickly adopted at each state level, millions of people signed up immediately. As a real estate professional, you must be very careful to check each and every telephone number you call when you are soliciting business in any way. The DNC list may be accessed via the Internet and most real estate firms now have some way to access it from their office; if your broker doesn't have easy access to the directory, you need to bring it to her attention because a violation carries a fine of $10,000 and errors and omissions insurance carriers are not covering the violation.

The law is specific unless you have had an ongoing business relationship with someone, meaning you've done business with her within the eighteen months immediately preceding a call to her, you may not call and offer your services if that person is on the list.

Although this is problematic from an operational viewpoint, it has also created many opportunities. Many licensees who used to place cold calls regularly have quit because they consider it to be too cumbersome to look up every number. So if you are willing to do it, you will have much less competition.

5.5 FOR SALE BY OWNERS

FSBOs are probably one of the most effective prospecting sources available to real estate licensees. They are also the least understood. Too many licensees think that just making a telephone call or two to a FSBO will get them the listing, if the FSBO is going to list. Nothing could be farther from the truth. FSBOs are just like every other human being in that, if they decide to use a professional to represent them in the sale of their homes, they want relationships with the licensees and relationships take time to develop. The average FSBO will try to sell her house for seven to eleven weeks before seeking the help of a real estate professional.

Several steps, if carefully followed, will get you a steady supply of FSBO listings.

- Seek them out. Research contacts at www.ForSaleByOwner.com or in your local newspapers. If you see a sign while driving and it is a proper time of day (not at meal time), stop and ask if you can take a quick look at the home. If the FSBO declines, just say that you like to keep track of all homes on the market, whether it's a private or an MLS listing, because you sometimes have buyers whose needs you can't fill with the MLS property. If you had seen a FSBO's home and knew it was probably the right one, you might be able to work something out that both parties would be pleased with. This will usually get you an appointment.

- If you see a FSBO's ad on the Internet or in the newspaper, go to your county assessor's records or call your title company representative and get the FSBO's name.

- Write the FSBO a letter referencing the ad and saying you'll call in the evening in a couple of days to see if she will allow you to tour the property. Send them a "forget-me-not" with your letter as this will show you are truly helpful and a cut above the other licensees who may be calling. (A forget-me-not is a flyer regarding subjects such as "Ten things to look at *before* the home inspector arrives,"

"Six things to ask your buyer *before* you enter into a contract," "Top nine marketing and advertising tips to attract buyers," or any other helpful aids to sellers that you have created.) Experience shows that sending these types of helpful items on a continual basis helps to build trust in the licensee quickly.

- Two evenings later, check the DNC list and call the FSBO. If she is on the list, do not offer your services over the telephone, just ask if you may set an appointment to see the home. It is all right to call a FSBO and ask to view the home on behalf of a buyer who is working with you on a buyer/broker agreement, as the buyer will pay your commission if the seller doesn't.

- Prior to your first visit, gather the last six months of comparables in the FSBO's neighborhood and preview them via a drive-by prior to your meeting. This will help you to know the neighborhood and will add to the FSBO's confidence in you. Take the comparables with you when you look at the property.

- On your first visit, ask the FSBO to accompany you through the home if there is any indication she may not. Remember, at this point you are there to build a relationship, not to list the home. Take notes on a clipboard as you go through house and ask questions. (For example, if you see kids' toys or clothes, ask if the kids are excited about the move.) Ask if they are moving locally or out of town and if they've had any luck getting a buyer interested so far. Finally, don't forget to ask the all-important question: "What are you going to do if the property doesn't sell?"

- Stay in the house as long as reasonable. Before you leave, ask the FSBO if she has all of the forms required to write a contract with a buyer and to give a buyer the required written disclosure about the home. If the FSBO says no to either, offer a sample contract or disclosure statement, being sure to strike a line through each page and write "SAMPLE" on each page. If the FSBO already has the forms, go to step three. After you leave, send them a handwritten thank-you note the same day.

- Tell the FSBO you would like to stop by once a week to see how she is doing and to drop off one of your forget-me-nots. Ask if, in return, they will refer to you any buyers who aren't interested in their home. Today many FSBOs have a website specifically for their home. If you find this to be true, visit the site and give them honest and helpful feedback about how to enhance it.

- Simply repeat this process, called the "30-second visit," to drop off a forget-me-not each week, asking for the order as you go: "Have you folks thought of having someone like me handle the sale of your home professionally? I'd do a great job for you."

5.6 EXPIRED LISTINGS

Most listings expire because they are overpriced; however, such things as poor property condition, being difficult to show (no key-box, large dogs, or restricted hours), and an uncooperative tenant are also factors you may have to deal with.

In a "hot" seller's market, there are few expired listings to work on because demand is so high. In a normal or balanced market, there are more expired listings, and in a "slow" buyer's market, which has been the case recently, expired listings are more plentiful.

Working on expired listings requires you to check the MLS daily and search back twenty-four hours in the expired listing section. If you find one or more expired listings, ask yourself if you could service the property if you listed it. If the answer is no, because you aren't familiar with marketing that type of property or it is too far away from where you work, then pass it by.

Before you call the seller of an expired property, you should check the "active listing," "pending sale," and "sold" sections of the MLS to see if the property has been relisted and possibly sold right after the listing expired. If it doesn't show up there, check the DNC registry before calling the owner. If the owner is listed, you may not call her.

Print out the expired listing from the MLS and study it before you call the owner so you will be somewhat familiar with the property. When you call the owner, be prepared for what may be a hostile attitude, as her pride may be hurt and plans disrupted because nobody wanted the house. Owners don't like to blame themselves and will often try to transfer blame to real estate licensees in general.

When the owner answers the phone, identify yourself and ask if the listing has been extended but just wasn't entered in the MLS yet. State that the MLS is showing the home as "expired" and ask if they are still interested in selling their home. If the home has not been relisted and the owners are still interested in selling, ask if you may take just fifteen minutes of their time to compare your marketing plan to the previous broker's plan. If the owner asks why the property didn't sell, or any questions of that kind, always reply that you don't know, as you'd have to see the home first. Then ask for an appointment. They might ask why you are calling now given that they have never seen you or your business card in the home. If you know the property was overpriced, you could truly say you haven't had a client in that price range for that neighborhood. Then ask if you could take a look at the house.

The most effective style with most expired listing owners is to remain calm, even if they are upset. If they start to rant about the real

estate profession in general (and they often do!), say to them, "It sounds to me like you have had a bad experience with a real estate licensee; tell me about it." Do not disparage your competition. This is a very bad business practice, and if asked for your opinion about a competitor, you should refrain from saying anything nasty or negative about her.

Ask the owner why she feels the property didn't sell. This will get some very interesting conversations going. Do not argue with the owner over the phone. Your only goal at this point is to get an appointment to view the home and present your marketing plan.

If you do get an appointment, use the same techniques outlined in the "For Sale by Owners" section earlier in this chapter. However, there is one major difference between an expired listing owner and a FSBO: If the expired listing owner plans to relist, she will do it far sooner than most FSBOs. Therefore, there is a time constraint and any new licensee must meet the expired listing owner sooner and ask for the order sooner. Just remember that listings expire at 11:59 P.M. on the final day. Do not call earlier than the day following the expiration date.

After your meeting with an expired listing owner, be sure to send a handwritten thank-you note. This simple act will set you apart as a true professional and will help you get business.

If you do get an appointment to meet with an expired listing owner, do your homework before the appointment. Price will often be an issue and you will need as much data as you can find to make your case. Do not go to the appointment without being completely prepared.

5.7 YOUR SPHERE OF INFLUENCE

A SOI is a group of people you know or have some type of connection with that may cause them to do business with you or to refer someone to you. It is your local holiday card list of people, people you have previously worked with at other occupations, people from your old neighborhood, people who belong to the same civic organizations you belong to, such as Rotary, close friends and family, and any other group who knows you and thinks well of you. Once you start social networking on a regular basis, you will quickly grow an ever-larger group of real estate licensees from all over the country who will think of you when the opportunity arises to refer a client.

Some fortunate people enter the real estate field with a huge SOI. They may have lived locally for many years or their previous jobs have put them in contact with lots of people they were able to

form lasting relationships with. Or maybe they are "joiners" and know lots of people through their civic activities. In any event, a licensee with a huge SOI has a good head start when it comes to acquiring new clients and customers.

Everyone has some sort of SOI. As mentioned earlier in this text, everyone knows at least 250 to 300 people. Just sit down and think about it carefully. Consider your barber or stylist or your mail carrier, and the dry cleaners. Do you have a favorite checkout person at the grocery store? What about your pharmacist? See how thinking about all of the people you regularly come in contact with can build you a very workable SOI?

A new licensee should carefully gather this list and continue to build on it for the remainder of her career. Send out about ten to fifteen letters a day to the people on your SOI list telling about your recent change and new position and that you would appreciate the chance to help with any of their real estate needs, as well as the real estate needs of any of their friends or family, and that you would appreciate any referrals. Let them know you'll be following up to say hello and to be sure they received your letter.

Wait two days, then, after checking the DNC list, call every eligible person on your SOI list. If you get an answering machine, just leave a message. If someone answers, ask if they received your letter, then repeat what you said in the letter about wanting to help them and their friends. If you have a "meaningful" conversation with anyone, be sure to follow up with a personal, hand-addressed (no mailing label, no postage meter) thank-you note.

Stay in touch with this group on a regular basis. We will talk more about how to do this very effectively later in this chapter when we talk about building your database.

5.8 GEOGRAPHICAL FARM

A **geographical farm** is probably one of the most effective long-term types of prospecting available to a real estate licensee. Your first step in working a geographical farm is to drive the territory. By this I mean, you should get in your car, drive through different neighborhoods, and see how you feel about the prospect of working in one or more of them on a fairly constant basis.

Once you identify two or three neighborhoods that appeal to you, go to the MLS database and get at least a three-year history of each neighborhood. Check to see how many homes have sold in each neighborhood on an annual basis. The purpose of this is to find a neighborhood with a high enough turnover rate to justify

the time and money you will spend gaining market share there. The ideal area has between 250 and 500 homes and a turnover rate of about 7 to 10 percent a year.

Once you decide on a neighborhood, meet with your favorite title company representative to order a "geographic farm package." This is a complete list of the properties in that neighborhood including addresses, owner's names, mailing addresses (if different from the site address), and often mailing labels.

Caution: The mailing labels come from the county assessor's records, which are often several months out of date. If you are planning mass mailings to a specific area and have yet to verify who lives at each home, you may be better off addressing the mailings to "The Family at...," rather than to specific names. This way you avoid spending time and money trying to impress people that you are the "neighborhood specialist" who knows all about the neighborhood, but you are sending mailings to previous owners.

Try using an electronic database of some sort if at all possible. Microsoft Outlook, Top Producer, and Lead Commander are just a few of the more commonly used databases. Be sure your program has mail-merge capabilities.

Write a letter introducing yourself and mail fifteen to twenty letters each day. Tell the owners that you plan to specialize in marketing homes in the neighborhood, and state your reason. Let them know you will either call or drop by for a minute or two in the next few days just to say hello and to see if you can be of any help with a real estate question. Wait two days to be sure your letter was received, then check the DNC registry (so you don't get fined) and call the people who aren't on it or simply go door-to-door and introduce yourself. Plan to stay only a minute or so unless they keep you there with questions.

If you go door-to-door, do it during reasonable business hours, about 9:30 to 11:45 A.M. and 1:30 to 5:00 P.M. Never go after dark or during any meal time. Do not ring the doorbell as it scares people too much and may wake up a baby; just knock, take a couple of steps back from the door, and turn slightly away. If you are viewed from inside the property, this is seen as a nonthreatening gesture and will cause more people to open up to you. Women who are going door-to-door must be especially safety conscious about going into strangers' homes and should consider going in pairs or at least let someone know where you are and what time you will check in.

As you start to interface with people in your farm, you will confirm names. As you do this, replace "The Family at..." with the owner's actual name in your database.

Mail to your farm area monthly, as any less frequently will allow time for the owners to forget your name. If you have a farm that is larger than your budget allows you to mail to on a monthly basis, figure out how many homes you can afford to mail to and start with that, then build up to the entire area as your income allows. If you do this, start with a main street that gets a lot of traffic or with an intersection or intersections that everyone who lives in that neighborhood must use to get to and from their homes. By doing that, once you get a listing and put a sign on the property, it will be more visible to the entire neighborhood.

After mailing your introductory letter on your company stationery, switch to a quality newsletter that is written by someone else (not you) or start sending a series of postcards. You'll get the best results from postcards that are "sticky" or have shelf life. For example, baseball, football, or basketball schedules are put on refrigerators and not thrown away. You can enhance these results even further by alternative postcards with "Just Listed" or "Just Sold" postcards. As you start listing and selling properties, you should mail these kinds of postcards every other month to your geographic farm and to your SOI list. Noting a new sale or listing accomplishment on your Internet sites is also a good idea; however, do not post listings as it seems too commercial in nature. You are trying to build relationships on those sites, not sell property. Just mention what you listed or sold and include a brief comment about it. Postcard and Internet blog site recipients will get continual messages indicating that you are a "player" and really know what you are doing. They can be an effective image builder.

It usually takes several months or more of mailing to a geographic farm before you will start getting the resulting inquiries from the people who live there. So stay the course, mail, and contact owners regularly. Have faith that the process will work.

5.9 OPEN HOUSE

Hosting an Open House has a dual purpose: (1) it gives the licensee a chance to sell a house to an interested party who stops by and (2) it is a platform to meet new clients and customers. It is for the licensee to meet new potential buyers and sellers. If neighbors come, be very courteous because you have no way of knowing if they are thinking of moving soon and are "sizing up" licensees to see who they will ask to represent them. It could be said that this is passive prospecting at its best! Passive in that you are waiting for clients to come to you and not actively seeking them out, but active

in that your chances of having several families and neighbors stop by are usually quite good.

The location of your Open House is important. If you are holding one open that is in a somewhat remote location and a little hard to find, you may not get anyone to stop by. If you are holding a home open that is only a few blocks off of a main street, you will probably be quite busy and will have lots of visitors.

To get people to your Open House, you will need directional signs. Be sure to check with your local community about any restrictions for placing signs on public property. If you want them on private property, ask the owner's permission first. This makes you look much more professional and may even get you a new client now and then. Be sure that the directional arrows are facing in the right direction!

Do your neighborhood research early in the week, identifying all of the active listings in the neighborhood, sales from the past six months, and any pending sales out of the MLS. Then drive by the houses on your list to get familiar with them prior to the Open House. Doing so will help build your credibility if a prospective buyer asks you questions about neighborhood activity or if a neighbor is sizing you up as a future listing agent.

Whereas most people really do not like being forced to sign in at an Open House, many licensees regularly require it and do so quite effectively. A lot of salespersons use 3 × 5 index cards to make notes about visitors, such as the type of homes they are looking for. Then the licensee shows the card to the visitor and asks to call her if that exact home should come to the licensee's attention. Some people are reluctant to give their names and telephone numbers when they first meet a licensee but may be more comfortable giving their e-mail address for you to send them properties that are a close fit to their search criteria. They will often start a relationship with you in that way. Also, keeping a register of those people visiting an Open House automatically provides you with a list of the names of those people visiting your Open House, whose names must be given to the seller (within three days of expiration or cancellation) of the listing to protect your right to compensation should any of those people buy the home within the protection period.

Remember that you have an ethical duty to ask potential clients if they are working with another licensee under a Buyer/Broker Listing Agreement. The best way to do this is to ask them who is representing them. That way they can't say they are working with someone when they really aren't.

When you get to your Open House, don't allow anyone inside until you have done three things: (1) open as many curtains, blinds, or other window coverings as seems appropriate, (2) light for effect with electric lighting in areas such as dining rooms, bedrooms, and bathrooms, and (3) perform a security check, putting away any valuables you come across while setting up.

There is also the matter of your personal security. Although very rare, there have been instances of licensees being hurt or even killed at Open Houses. You should at least remember the following two safety items.

1. Keep yourself between the visitor and the door at all times. Never let your exit route get cut off.
2. Have a code and use it, especially when holding open a vacant home. Be sure that your spouse or someone in your office knows where you are and when you are due to return. They should expect a call from you at a predetermined time and should call you if they don't hear from you by that time. For instance, if everything is all right but people are there and there is a need to be cryptic just say, "It's over by the GREEN table." If you are uncomfortable, say, "It's over by the YELLOW table." If you feel threatened in any way, say "It's over by the RED table," which means get someone over here right away. Again, don't be overly concerned about this issue as these instances are very rare, but do use all necessary caution and good judgment.

Hosting an Open House also gives you the opportunity to go door-to-door in the immediate neighborhood handing out invitations to your Open House. This not only gets you more traffic to your Open House, it allows you to meet more people.

Internet Site

Reference your Internet site on your business cards and all of your marketing materials. The Internet is an excellent place to advertise yourself and all of your listings. Most of the major real estate firms offer websites to their licensees today, and while many offer it at no charge, some charge an annual maintenance or other small fee.

If you have to create your own website, this isn't the place to be cheap or skimp on cost. The old saying, "you only get one chance to create a good first impression," was never truer than when you are creating your personal website.

If your site has links to the MLS database and other city and county sites, it will attract people to it who are truly interested in buying or selling property and you will get some "hits" from them.

It is important that your site be "sticky," allowing visitors to use the various links you have available to navigate around to other websites, and when they exit those sites, they come right back to your site.

A website may contain all of a firm's listings, with multiple pictures and information about each home. Some sites include the licensee's picture on each listing. It is also fairly routine to have a firm's listings on many different sites at the same time. For example, major real estate franchises and affiliates have the capability of entering a listing into their local MLS and have it immediately downloaded to local, state, and national sites as well as www.realtor.com.

Many thousands of websites present properties for public viewing. Take a good look at your competitor's sites and build yours to meet or exceed theirs in presentation and ease of use, which will mean more business for you.

Absentee Owners

Two types of **absentee owners** are rental property owners and second-home owners. Both present an opportunity to obtain listings and buyers and both are excellent prospecting sources.

To farm rental property owners, have your favorite title company do a search for you of one or more subdivisions, finding all of the homes that show an owner's mailing address that is different from the property site address.

Once you have this list, you should regularly write to the owners to let them know how much the property in their neighborhood has either appreciated or depreciated. Explain that you would like to help them to sell the property or exchange it for a larger real estate investment or for one in a different neighborhood that is going up in value even faster. You may also suggest that the owners refinance their rentals and use the cash to acquire another one. When you send this type of letter, be sure to include all of your contact information. If the property is run down or shabby in appearance, take a picture of it and send it to the owner. That alone will sometimes motivate the owner to sell or exchange the property rather than fix it up. See Figure 5.2 for a sample letter to an absentee owner.

Check the *For Rent* section of the newspapers, including the smaller weekly papers, and call owners of **rental units** to ask if they have considered selling or exchanging their properties while they are vacant.

FIGURE 5.2   Sample Absentee Owner Letter

Date
Name
Mailing address
City, State, Zip

Dear [Name],
This letter could have significant financial importance to you.

I am a [broker/licensee] with [name of company] in [City] and I specialize in helping income property owners get the highest return available from their rental properties.

The county assessor's records show that you own a [home, apartment house, etc.] at [address]. I noticed that you have owned it for quite awhile. Property values here have really gone up (or down) lately which may have had an effect on your equity in this rental property.

That's the reason that I am writing; I am confident that I can help you to get a much higher return on that equity by doing one of the following:

- Refinance and use the proceeds to buy another rental in your area or here
- Exchange your rental for a larger one that generates more income and, maybe, a bigger tax shelter
- Exchange your rental for a rental near where you live
- Sell your rental and take advantage of the profits and the low capital gain rates that are currently available

If any of the above interests you, please call, write, or e-mail me at your earliest convenience. My contact information is on the enclosed business card for your convenience. You'll be glad you did, as it's a great time to make money in real estate!

Sincerely,

[Your name, DRE Lic #]
[Your address]
[Your city, state, zip]
[Your telephone]
[Your e-mail address]

Second homes or vacation homes can be a little more problematic to locate. In certain areas of the country, such as Tucson, Arizona, or many cities in Florida, it is often hard to tell if a home is a rental or a vacation home. The only effective way to find out is to write the owner at her mailing address and ask. If she is renting the home, then do as suggested earlier. If it *is* being used as a vacation home, then ask how often it is used, and if she would consider selling it and buying a smaller condominium or a home in a different area.

5.10 BUILDING YOUR DATABASE

Prospecting your entire database can be an expensive endeavor and you, as a businessperson, will want to get maximum return from it with minimum expense.

The most effective way to do this is to first build your database by including everyone that you can possibly think of that might do business with you or refer someone to you.

After you have completed the initial compilation of your database (it is never complete because you keep adding new clients and dropping some), sort it into categories using the A-B-C-D method.

- "A" clients are the "givers" of the world. These are people who really like helping other people, and when they are told by you that you value them as friends and you value their business and their referrals, they will go out of their way to do business with you and send you referrals. This category includes anyone who has already referred someone to you. Make contact with these people on a monthly basis.

- "B" clients are people in your database who have never referred anyone to you, but you think after they have heard from you several times that you value them as clients and value their referrals, they will start to refer people to you. Make contact with these people every two or three months and move them to your "A" or "C" list when you feel it is appropriate to do so.

- "C" clients are people who you know, but you are just not sure if they will ever do business with you or send you any referrals. You should probably make contact about every three or four months by mail or phone (check the DNC list first) and move them to the "B" list or delete them as time goes on.

- "D" stands for "delete." These are people who you know have a real estate licensee in the family or are just people that you really don't want to do business with. Delete them from your database immediately.

Another way to use your database to prospect effectively is to make e-mail lists. Place everyone in a general category and then segment them, using categories such as dog lovers, cat lovers, horse lovers, and golfers. This allows you to keep in touch in the following ways:

- Each time you see an interesting article about a dog or horse show, golf tournament, gardening event, or anything that a segment of your database would be interested in, send them an e-mail with details about it and direct them to your source.

They'll really appreciate it, and it is an excellent, inexpensive (free) way to keep in touch.

- Every time you get a new listing, e-mail it to yourself and blind copy (BCC) it to your whole database. Use a digital camera and take two or three good pictures of the home and attach them to your e-mail along with a good narrative description of the home. Ask if any of your clients would like to see the home or if they have a friend or family member who might. Your sellers will love the attention and effective advertising while you gain respect among your clients as an innovative marketer.

When you send e-mail to your clients, be sure to use proper e-mail protocol. For example, do not put their addresses in your "To" box. Enter your own address in this box instead and put the recipients' addresses as a "group" in your "BCC" box. This protects their privacy by keeping their addresses hidden. It shows that you respect their privacy and it gives them a greater sense of privacy. They will appreciate your effort and immediately come to know that an e-mail from you is something of value.

SUMMARY

Prospecting and lead generation is truly the lifeblood of the real estate business. Whether you are an old pro who makes regular contact with your very large, very loyal database, or a newcomer who is regularly seeing FSBOs, holding Open Houses, writing to absentee owners, blogging on several Internet sites, and all the rest, there is no doubt that continual prospecting of some sort must be a part of nearly every business day. Some licensees may choose lesser-known ways of generating leads, such as contacting lenders about **foreclosed properties (commonly known as REOs)**, checking the newspapers for individuals who have received business promotions, new businesses moving in or out of town, marriage and birth announcements, new building permits, and probates. Some licensees prefer to offer their service to a specific geographic or demographic area or work a particular segment of the market in an intense, systematic way, thus becoming well known as the areas real estate expert. It can be a geographic area such as a certain neighborhood, a certain price range such as starter homes or luxury homes; a **nongeographic area**, which is a certain property type, such as an apartment house or rental home; or a certain common interest group with which you have an affinity. A good lead generation plan calls for action and analysis. You must take regular action to meet people. You also need to periodically evaluate the effectiveness of your efforts so you don't waste any time or effort.

CLASS DISCUSSION TOPICS

1. Role-play a door-to-door prospecting situation or a telephone prospecting situation with another student.

2. Identify what you feel are the most effective lead-generating ideas and why.

3. Describe what steps you would take to actively offer your services to your SOI or to a group of divorce attorneys, medical doctors, or dentists.

4. Identify three "niche markets" that could be the most productive to you and why.

5. Prepare a business plan for the next thirty days and be prepared to share it with the class.

6. List your five best listing sources in order of effectiveness.

CHAPTER 5 QUIZ

1. When generating leads, which of the following can be the most effective?
   A. Ask clients if they want to make a profit.
   B. Ask clients if they want a quick sale and top dollar for their home.
   C. Ask clients if they will sell for a little less considering you have a very special family who wants to live in the neighborhood.
   D. Ask clients if they are willing to help you make a sale.

2. A reverse directory is used to do which of the following?
   A. Obtain legal descriptions of properties.
   B. Obtain names from the listed addresses.
   C. Obtain names that are not on the federal DNC registry.
   D. Obtain names of former owners (chain of title).

3. Which of the following is the most likely reason a listing expires and does not sell?
   A. The licensee failed to advertise sufficiently.
   B. The licensee didn't hold enough Open Houses.
   C. The tenant would allow the property to be shown only between 10:00 A.M. and 4:00 P.M.
   D. The property was not competitively priced to the current market.

4. When evaluating a geographic area for prospecting, which of the following is the most important factor to consider?
   A. The annual turnover rate.
   B. The total number of homes in the subdivision or neighborhood.
   C. The price range of the homes in the area.
   D. The amount of competition from other real estate licensees.

5. Legal notices provide good listing leads. Which of the following is not a legal notice?

    A. Foreclosure

    B. Vacancy

    C. Probate

    D. Eviction

6. Which of the following is the most important step to take in preparation for an initial visit with a FSBO?

    A. Take a picture of the house.

    B. Call to confirm that the owner is home.

    C. Research and become familiar with the current listings, pending sales, and six months of properties sold in the neighborhood.

    D. Dress in a business suit.

7. What should you do when hosting an Open House in a vacant home?

    A. Let someone know where you are and have them call you at a prescribed time.

    B. Check the home for lighting and security prior to letting anyone in.

    C. Ask prospective buyers about their housing requirements as they view the home.

    D. All of the above.

8. Which of the following should you always do when cold calling?

    A. Call during meal time to be sure someone is at home.

    B. Talk rapidly so you can make more calls.

    C. Hang up if someone gets too "long-winded."

    D. Check each number against the federal DNC list prior to making the call.

9. Which of the following is an important characteristic of your Internet site?

    A. It should be "sticky," meaning that people may navigate from your site to other sites and return to your site when finished browsing.

    B. It should be as short as possible because people don't read long sites.

    C. It should not host your listings because if viewers can see them, they won't have a reason to call you.

    D. It should have as few links as possible.

10. How often should you make contact with a SOI group or geographic farm?

    A. Annually

    B. Every six months

    C. Quarterly

    D. Monthly

Chapter

6

Working with Buyers

Upon completion of this chapter, the student will be able to:

- Compare and contrast buyer/seller sources.
- Design and implement a seller listing presentation.
- Evaluate buyer financial qualifications.
- Explain agency disclosure timing.
- Recognize buying signals.

6.1 SOURCES OF BUYERS

Sometimes several sources of buyers come to you when you least expect them. Therefore, it is imperative that you have an excellent, ongoing knowledge of the current listing inventory in your area.

Buyers may come from diverse sources such as Open House, repeat or referral clients, cold calling, your website or floor time. In the last chapter, we discussed the importance of accessing the latest listing and sales information from the Multiple Listing Service (MLS) and driving around the neighborhood prior to holding an Open House. You should do this to enhance your own knowledge and thereby earn the credibility that comes with being well prepared.

We have had many experiences over the years in which a couple comes to our Open House and, during our conversation, they ask about another house in the neighborhood. Because we took the time to know the inventory and the neighborhood, we were able

to tell them about the home and point out that there were others available as well. This helped us obtain many more showing appointments and sales over the years.

The same applies to floor time. Buyers rarely buy the home they first call about, but if you know the inventory, you can tell them about other, similar homes, which will greatly enhance your chances of getting an appointment with them.

Floor time, or opportunity time as it is sometimes referred to, can be a spotty but good source of new buyers if you are prepared. Several things must be done in preparation for floor time such as showing up at least ten minutes ahead of schedule to determine which properties are being advertised. Prior to starting your shift, go into the MLS database and search for switch properties. **Switch properties** are similar to the advertised properties in price and location, with not more than about a 15 percent difference in price up or down. Be prepared to field **ad calls** and **sign calls**.

Knowing about switch properties is helpful in that most buyers really don't know what they want when they start calling real estate offices. They have a general idea from their online ventures, but until they actually get in their cars and start to experience the actual interior of various homes, they are highly susceptible to change.

Again, only a very small percentage of buyers actually buy the home they initially call on. If you can't tell them about other homes—to entice them to come in the office and meet with you, you will not be very successful during floor time. It may also cost you and your company thousands of lost dollars. If you take what it costs to run an average size real estate office and divide that by the number of ad calls received in a month, you begin to see just what each call really represents.

What are the average buyers feeling when they call your office? They are experiencing some level of fear as they are about to talk to a salesperson. Their adrenaline is elevated and their hearts are beating a little faster than normal. The entire purpose of the call is usually to get as much information as possible and give as little information about themselves as possible. The more prepared you are to help in a calm, professional, relaxed manner, the more appointments you will get.

Let's look at a typical dialogue between a prospective buyer and a licensee. The receptionist announces an ad call and asks you to pick up the phone. (*Remember to smile when you talk on the phone. It makes a huge difference to the other person on the line; you can actually feel the difference.*)

"Hi, this is [your name]; how may I help you today?"

"Hi, I'm just calling to get a little information about the $800,000 home you have advertised in the local newspaper."

"I'm glad you called, that's one of our better listings. We are getting lots of interest. What would you like to know?"

"Well, I'd just like to get the address and drive by to see if it's something I like."

"I understand completely. By the way, my name is [your name], what's yours?"

"I really don't want to give you my name right now, I only want to get the address of that home and drive by."

"I can certainly understand. What is it about that home that prompted you to call?"

"Well, the ad says the house has four bedrooms, a pool, and a three-car garage, and it seems to be in my price range."

"That's great! In what price range are you preapproved by your lender?"

"Oh, we haven't been to a lender yet, but we think we qualify for about $800,000. Now, what's the address?"

"You know, it really makes me sad when I hear someone say they haven't been preapproved."

"Why?"

"Because I have seen too many people overestimate what they can afford. They end up very unhappy when they try to buy a particular home and lose it because they don't qualify for the loan. When you get preapproved, you essentially become a cash buyer and without the full purchase price onhand in cash or lender preapproval there's no chance of that happening. Being preapproved also means you can negotiate a little better with the seller. Would you like the names of a couple of really good lenders?"

"Well, yeah, I guess so. So what's the property address?"

"You know, as a general rule, we aren't supposed to give out addresses. The agreement we have with our sellers is that we will personally accompany each interested person to the property. Do you have time to see it this morning or would this afternoon be better?"

"Look, I just want to drive by it first. If I like it, I'll call you back and look at it with you."

"I really wish I could do that, but the listing is very specific in that we aren't to give out the address. By the way, there are

three other similar homes available in that neighborhood, one of which is an even lower price. Why don't we go look at all of them at once? I can promise you that I'm very easy to get along with and I can really help you."

"Well, I guess that will be all right."

"Great, you'll enjoy seeing the properties. Will you please spell your name for me and give me your phone number? I'll need to make appointments to see the properties and will call you to confirm. What time can you be at my office?"

"How about three o'clock this afternoon?"

"That works fine for me. Let me have your number and I'll set everything up and call you to confirm. By the way, have you signed a buyer/broker agreement with another broker?"

"No, I haven't. I'll wait for your call, and thanks!"

Not every caller will give you her phone number, which is perfectly normal. By being prepared and having a good current knowledge of the listing inventory, however, you will get many more appointments than if you were to "wing it."

You will also receive "sign calls" or calls from people who get your number from for-sale signs. They are usually already convinced about the neighborhood and are often okay with the architectural style of the home. Sometimes they are neighbors who are either just checking out local property values or thinking about selling as well. Treat them well because they may be sizing you up as a potential listing agent when they decide to sell.

Buyers who are referred to you by past clients or other sources are probably the easiest people to work with because you have been presold to them and have instant credibility. These people deserve a very high priority.

Today, websites account for a large majority of the initial property inquiry contacts received by licensees and real estate companies. The National Association of REALTORS® did a large survey that showed nearly 94 percent of buyers now use the Internet to start their search for a property or licensee to work with. The value of a personal website cannot be overstressed.

When an Internet buyer wants information, they will almost always request it from you by e-mail. You should have your cell phone set up to get e-mails as they are sent to you, and when you get an e-mail property information request, you should respond immediately if possible and certainly as quick as you can. Internet buyers are unique in that they want instant responses, and any delay

beyond a very short time may cost you a buyer. Many top performing licensees carry information about their personal listings with them wherever they go, so when they get an e-mail inquiry, they are fully prepared to answer the caller's questions.

6.2 THE FIRST APPOINTMENT

Safety first! There is nothing more important than your personal safety and, unfortunately, we live in a time when personal safety is an issue of concern. For first appointments, always meet the buyers at your office. If they are thinking of something other than real estate, they will not want to be seen with you in a public place. After the first appointment, it may be all right to meet the buyer elsewhere, but let someone know where you are going and who you are with. It is wise to have some sort of signal to use if necessary, such as calling your office and asking the receptionist about a "yellow file" if you are worried about who you are with or a "red file" if you are in trouble.

We cannot stress enough the importance of proper preparation, especially at your initial meetings with new buyers. Hopefully, you have directed them to a good lender for **preapproval** (a pending loan where all required documents have been checked by the lender and no issues have been found that might stop the loan from funding) of their financing before meeting with you. If not, prequalify them yourself when you meet to get a reasonable idea about the price range they can afford. Chapter 11 discusses financing and the importance of getting your buyers preapproved for the financing they will need to complete their purchase. It also talks about "front end" and "back end" loan-to-income ratios. If possible, use these ratios to **prequalify** them over the phone so you can have several homes to show them. You can always call and cancel if they turn out to be in the wrong price range. If you haven't qualified them over the phone, be sure to do it prior to viewing any properties.

When buyers arrive at your office, take them to a conference room or other room that affords privacy and no distractions and conduct a **buyer needs assessment**. Offer coffee or something to drink to make them comfortable. If you are not good with names, write their names where you can refer to them as needed. If you are uncertain how to pronounce a name, just ask and make a note of it. Use names frequently as people enjoy it.

Print out copies of the listings of homes you have tentatively scheduled to show and give the buyers copies of each of them. Most MLS systems have an "agent detail" and a "client detail" printout option. Be sure to provide the client with a detailed printout so

as to not distribute sellers' names, telephone numbers, and other confidential information. Printing confidential information in the remarks section of the listing could bring a severe fine from your MLS.

If possible, do not sit across from the buyers, as a desk or table can be perceived as a barrier, creating an "us versus you" feeling. If possible, sit to the side of the buyers just around the corner of the table.

Most of the talking you do should be in the form of questions. This shows that you are interested in the buyers and gets you important information. Go over their wants and needs again to see if anything new comes up. If they fail to restate something they mentioned on the phone, ask about it again. This will help you clarify their needs and reinforce the fact that you were really listening.

Many licensees use some type of qualification form to help them better understand each client and to remember things. Figure 6.1 is an example of a form you can use. Make copies of it or use it to enter information directly into your contact management system.

As a real estate professional, you will probably work with several buyers at once. Using this form will help you stay on top of the true needs of each buyer, which will allow you to better serve them. It also helps clarify their motivation.

As you are out showing homes to buyers, ask for their reactions to each home and note them on your form or in your database. This will give you a keener sense of the type of home they are really

FIGURE 6.1   Sample Client Information Sheet

Name(s) _____

Home phone _____ Cell phone _____ Fax _____

Address _____

Number of people in household _____

Own _____ Rent _____ How long at this address? _____

If own, must you sell before you buy? _____

Is your home for sale now? _____

If so, with whom and for how long? _____

What subdivisions are of special interest to you? _____

What interests you in a home? _____

Have you found a home you liked, but didn't buy? _____

If yes, why not? _____

What features must your new home have? _____

What prompted you to call our firm? (referral, ads, sign, etc.) _____

What are the best hours/days for you to look at property? _____

looking for, which can often be very different from what they told you at the start. Many buyers, if not most, do not make an offer on a home the first time out with you, but it does happen and you should be prepared for it.

6.3 PREAPPROVED FOR FINANCING

The loan qualification process is clearly the responsibility of lending professionals today. Hundreds of loan products are available, and helping buyers choose the right one is usually beyond the scope of what the real estate licensee does. However, there will be many times, such as weekend floor time or Open House, when you will meet people and want to show them some homes before they have a chance to meet with a loan officer. In this situation, you must know how to prequalify buyers so the homes you show them are at least close to the price range they will ultimately be approved for. See Figure 6.2 regarding the qualifying process.

Ask the buyer for her gross income (before deductions) and for the amount of long-term debt (credit cards, car payments in excess of ten months, and so on). Once you have this information, apply *front-end and back-end* qualifying ratios to the income.

The front-end ratio is usually around 28 to 30 percent of gross income. This means that the buyer's *total monthly payment* (loan payment, taxes, insurance, or HOA dues) is divided by gross monthly income, and the percentage may not exceed 28 to 30 percent.

$$\frac{\text{Total monthly payment (PITI)}}{\text{Gross monthly income}} = 28\% \text{ to } 30\%$$

FIGURE 6.2 Qualifying Process

The qualifying process has three parts.

1. Determine the needs and interests of the buyers.
2. Determine the buyers' motivations.
3. Determine the financial ability of the buyers regarding
   a. the source of their down payment and settlement costs.
   b. the amount of monthly payments that it is possible and comfortable for them to make.
   c. the amount of financing that they can obtain.

The back-end ratio may be from 36 percent to 40 percent. To get this number, add the buyers' long-term debt to their total monthly payment and divide by their gross monthly income. The resulting percentage should not exceed 36 to 40 percent. Lenders usually exclude car payments of ten months or less in duration.

$$\frac{\text{Total monthly credit obligations}}{\text{Gross monthly income}} = 36\% \text{ to } 40\%$$

Qualifying details are covered more fully in Chapter 11.

Down payment requirements vary by lender and by loan type. Loans vary from 80 percent or less loan-to-value (LTV) ratio to zero-down loans in which the buyer obtains an 80 percent first loan and 20 percent second loan from the same lender.

New first loans in excess of 80 percent LTV often require buyers to pay private mortgage insurance (PMI) until the first loan LTV ratio becomes less than 80 percent.

Buyers who are self-employed find it harder to qualify for loans. Except for "stated income" or "minimum documentation" loans, self-employed people are usually required to furnish the lender with at least the last two years of their federal income tax returns to verify their net income. You should caution self-employed buyers not to overstate their income on their loan applications because doing so is "lender fraud," which is a federal offense.

The total amount of financing buyers can qualify for plus their cash down payment equals the maximum home price they can afford. As a licensee, knowing this maximum loan amount allows you to be more accurate in the price range of the homes you show them. This also makes the overall home buying experience a more fulfilling one and prevents the buyer from making an offer she cannot afford, which could lead to embarrassment.

When you prequalify buyers, explore the cash they have available for the *earnest money deposit*. The size of the earnest money deposit should be commensurate with the value of the home they are offering to purchase. Explain carefully that the deposit check will be held uncashed until the offer is accepted and an escrow is opened. Also explain that the money will be held in escrow and not given to anyone, including the seller, until the escrow is closed; if the escrow is cancelled for a valid reason, the money will be returned to them.

Make it clear to the buyers that when they make an offer on a property, one of the following three things can happen:

1. *Rejection.* If an offer is rejected, the earnest money check is returned uncashed and the buyer is under no further obligation with regard to that property or seller.

2. *Acceptance.* If an offer has been accepted, the buyer has purchased a home. If for any reason the buyer cannot legitimately meet or waive a contingency, she may cancel the escrow and have the earnest money returned. The buyer should also be advised that if she willfully defaults or purposely fails to do something to carry out the terms of the contract and fails to close the escrow, the deposit will be at risk of forfeiture.

3. *Counteroffer.* If the sellers make a counteroffer, the buyers may accept the changes to the original contract and continue with the purchase process, they may reject it and look for another home, or they may counter the counteroffer. Prequalifying buyers not only includes the financing process, it includes taking a deeper look at what the buyers really want in a home, a full explanation of the agency disclosure form, your and the sellers' obligations regarding full disclosure of property condition issues, and such things as whether they have a home to sell first or not. When you take the time to prequalify your buyers and carefully explain why you are doing it, they will come to regard you as a caring professional and will be more inclined to use your services in the future and to refer you to others.

6.4 AGENCY DISCLOSURE

The law states that you must provide an Agency Disclosure form and obtain a signed acknowledgement of receipt at the earliest practicable moment prior to the execution of the buyer's offer to purchase. As stated in the form, anyone entering into a discussion with a real estate licensee regarding a real estate transaction should understand what type of agency relationship they wish to have with the licensee in the transaction. Give your buyers a copy of the Disclosure Regarding Real Estate Agency Relationships (AD) form and discuss the three representation models offered: seller's agent, buyer's agent, and agent representing both seller and buyer. You should point out that this form is NOT a contract and is simply a disclosure form that the California Civil Code requires licensees to provide buyers and sellers.

Their signature on this form merely acknowledges receipt of a copy and is not their agreement to elect any form of representation. There is nothing wrong with giving buyers the form to read while you are out looking at homes. They often seem more relaxed about it if it is presented in that way; however, should you find them a home they want to make an offer on the first day, make sure they sign acknowledging receipt of the form prior to signing a purchase contract.

The buyers should understand that the agency disclosure form refers to the agency relationship between them, the broker representing them, and that broker's licensees. This disclosure does not call for a decision at this point—it is only a disclosure of how licensees may represent buyers and sellers. A decision as to which form of representation will be elected cannot be made until the buyers have decided on the home they wish to purchase. Only then will you know whether dual agency will be necessary.

You are not yet finished making necessary agency disclosures. As stated in the Residential Purchase Agreement – California, Paragraph 2B, "Buyer and seller each acknowledge receipt of a disclosure of the possibility of multiple representation by the broker representing that principal. This disclosure may be part of a listing agreement, buyer broker agreement or separate document (C.A.R. Form DA)." You must provide this form that requires buyer consent, to be in compliance with the purchase contract. If they do not agree to dual agency, explain that you cannot show them any listings from your office, or, if you are a member of a multioffice firm, they cannot look at any listings from your entire company.

California law allows brokers to sell their own listings while representing both the buyers and the sellers, provided they have *prior informed consent* of all parties. If you have a buyer who wants to make an offer on one of your listings, for example, carefully explain your role as a dual agent.

6.5 BUYER/BROKER AGREEMENT

The prequalification meeting is also a good time to explain the buyer/broker agreement and the benefits of working under a buyer listing. Start by asking the buyers if they would like you to show them every home on the market that fits their needs or only the ones that are listed in the MLS. They will nearly always say that they want to see everything.

If so, explain that homes are available in which a seller has not listed with a broker or agreed to pay a commission and homes

exclusively listed with a broker who is not offering to cooperate with other brokers. In either instance, should you show one of these homes to your buyer, you have no guarantee of being paid for your efforts. If the buyer is working with you under a buyer-broker listing agreement, whereby she has agreed to pay you a commission if the seller doesn't, you can show the buyer everything that fits her needs. It helps to explain that buyers rarely have to pay the broker's fee as most sellers will pay the same amount the buyers have agreed to pay if they are presented with a good offer to purchase. A verbal commitment on your part that you will work very hard to find them the perfect home will also be well received and will help you to get the buyer/broker agreement signed more often.

6.6 TIPS ON SHOWING PROPERTY

If the buyer has a home that she must sell before making another purchase, talk about the benefits of having the home sold prior to any attempt to purchase another home. Point out that an offer contingent on the sale of an existing home is usually not well received by most sellers. Even if the sellers did accept a contingent offer, it would almost always involve a "contingency release clause" in which the sellers' home would stay on the market and the sellers may accept another offer subject to your buyers' rights. If the sellers do accept a subsequent offer, your buyers would usually have about three days to waive the contingency of selling their home; if they didn't, they would lose the new home and get a refund of their deposit. Trying to buy property in this manner is usually an exercise in futility. If this is the only way they will proceed, suggest to them that they are more likely to have their offer accepted if you also submit a copy of the fully executed listing on their home, along with comparable sales in their neighborhood that show how effectively their home is priced. This accomplishes two things: it gives reasonable assurance to the sellers that your buyers are serious and have priced their home accordingly, and it forces your buyers to price their home properly.

If the buyers are still afraid to sell their home because they would have no place to move, suggest they put a clause in the listing agreement saying, "This sale is contingent on the sellers purchasing a replacement property within X number of days after they accept an offer on their home." Although this will protect them from selling and having no place to go, it will probably scare off some potential buyers and licensees.

If you are aware that the buyers have special interests, do a search of the MLS with one or more of those interests as a search parameter. For instance, if the husband really wants a nice workshop or needs extra garage space for a vintage Corvette, include those specialty items along with the basics when you search for homes to show them.

A licensee once had a buyer who wanted a really nice workshop. She found one and showed the property to him and his family. The buyer never even looked at the rest of the house; he just stayed in the workshop the entire time they were at the property while the licensee and the wife viewed the rest of the property, then he proceeded to tell the licensee that he and his wife agreed it was the perfect property for them.

Do not let the poor condition of a property stop you from showing it to buyers. Instead, point out that the property has the features the buyers want and prepare them for the required "fix-up" work. This is a good reason for you to have some high-quality handymen and contractors on your "home sale team." You may find a "fixer upper" that meets much of the criteria of a buyer but may need cosmetic work such as paint, light carpentry, and yard work. If you know people who do these things, tell your buyer about the opportunity and that you know people who charge reasonable prices for making the needed repairs.

- Be fully prepared when you show property.
- Know every listing in the area that is in your buyer's price range. Be familiar with bus routes and schedules.
- Know the location of the area's shopping centers, recreational facilities, and places of worship.
- Have an accurate knowledge of school boundaries (be careful with this one as they sometimes change and can be a very important issue with many families). It is best to give them the phone number and/or Internet site of the local school system.
- Know your buyer's price range and do not show them properties they cannot afford.
- Map out your property tour in advance so you know where you are going.

Some licensees knowingly show unsuitable properties to buyers, just to make a certain property seem better than it really is by comparison. This is not ethical as it doesn't give the buyers a true picture of

property values in a given area. It is certainly all right to save the best for last as long as all the homes you've shown have been within the search criteria the buyers have given you.

Show and sell positive attributes of the neighborhood while being careful to disclose any material facts (positive or negative) that may influence a decision to buy. As you go from home to home, drive past as many amenities such as shopping centers, parks, golf courses, and other areas of interest as you can. Don't avoid anything you consider a negative influence in a neighborhood as this is concealment and may be grounds for action against you. You certainly should not violate the Civil Rights Act of 1968 by engaging in any kind of racial steering.

As you go through a neighborhood, point out any recent sales. This will help buyers get comfortable with current home values in a given area.

When you are going through each home, let the buyers go ahead of you. If you lead, you cannot see their reaction to the home and they will often focus on you instead of some of the home's best features.

Do not go into bedrooms with the buyers if possible. You help to fill up a room when you are in it and tend to make it feel smaller than it really is. With the exception of master bedrooms with large bathrooms, being in there serves no purpose. You can maintain visual and verbal contact from the door.

Ambiance is everything. Ask the sellers to be away during the showing to allow the buyers to feel at home and to ask you questions about the property. It also helps if the home's drapes and curtains are open, allowing in as much natural light as possible. Selective lighting with lamps and chandeliers is also very effective in creating a mood that will make the buyers feel at home.

Do not park your car uphill unless it is necessary. Getting in and out of the car is difficult when it is facing uphill and your buyers will tire sooner. Park across the street from the property whenever possible as this also gives the buyers a chance to take in the entire property as they walk toward it.

Always show professional courtesy to the property owners. If you pull up in front of a home and your buyers decide they hate it already and don't need to see it, tell them you need to either call or go to the door and cancel the showing. Don't leave the sellers in limbo, waiting for you to show up.

At times, you may be showing only two or three homes while other times, such as when you are with an out-of-town buyer, you may be looking for an entire day. Watch your buyers for signs of fatigue or hunger. If you even remotely feel they may need a rest or some food, ask if they would like to take a break at a restaurant. (Fast food places are all right for this, but not always the best choice, depending on the buyers.)

Be sure to give the buyers their space and, as appropriate, give them time in a room alone. It is a more intimate setting for them that way and they will experience a nicer feeling about the home. They may also need time to discuss personal issues.

If your buyer brings along a friend, instead of being resentful include the friend in any discussions and ask for her input. If the friend is clearly out of line, tactfully present current information about the home or neighborhood to refute what has been said and show that you know what you are talking about. If the friend gets even somewhat abusive, point it out and suggest that a respectful dialogue between everyone will go a lot further toward achieving the best results. See Figure 6.3 for more rules of professional conduct on showing a home.

6.7 BUYING SIGNALS

As you are looking through each home, watch for **buying signals**. These are usually in the form of questions or actions that indicate an interest in the property. Some buying signals include:

- Lingering for a long time in one room, either sitting down or walking about.
- Returning to a particular room several times and lingering for a time.
- Gently rubbing the kitchen cabinets or the countertop. Asking if certain pieces of personal property, such as the refrigerator, washer, or dryer, stay with the home.
- Inquiring about property taxes.
- Pacing off rooms or asking you for room dimensions.
- Verbally placing furniture in various rooms.
- Asking about the seller's motivation to sell.

All of these signals indicate an interest in the property. That's not to say the buyers will buy the particular property, but it shows they are clearly interested. When you experience these types of

FIGURE 6.3   Rules of Professional Conduct

- When showing a home, leave it exactly as you found it. Drapes and other window coverings, inside doors, and lights should all be left just the way you found them. Double-check all outside doors to see that they are locked. Secure pets as they were when you arrived and replace the key in the keybox.
- If someone else is showing the property when you arrive, wait in the car or an inconspicuous place until the other salesperson and her clients have left before you enter the property.
- If a listing specifies that it is shown by appointment only, never take a customer to the door unannounced. If you unexpectedly come upon a property that your client wants to see, call the listing agent from your cell phone or leave the client in your car while you go to the door, explain the situation to the homeowner, and ask for permission to see the property now or in a short time. If it is not convenient for the owner at that time, do not argue with them.
- Abide by any special showing instructions in the MLS printout of the listing, such as special showing hours or a certain number of hours advance notice prior to showing.
- Treat each home as you would want others to treat your listings. If you sense something is amiss, such as water leaks and doors open when you arrive, call the listing agent and report your findings.
- Leave your business card at each property and/or use the sign-in sheet that is provided at the property. This is a courtesy to both the homeowner and the listing agent. It is a good idea to write "previewing" or "showing" on your card.
- Never enter a home with a lit cigarette, pipe, or cigar and do not light one while you are in someone's home.
- Do not embarrass an owner or hurt her feelings by making uncomplimentary remarks about the property's price, its condition, or its furnishings. The owner may be within earshot.
- When you call another real estate firm for information about a listing, identify yourself and your company immediately.

behaviors, start to explore the depth of the buyers' interest by asking open-ended questions that require more than yes or no answers.

If you overhear the husband and wife mentioning that the dining room looks pretty big, ask them how they think their dining room set would look in that room. If you notice the children looking longingly at the swing set in the backyard, check to make sure there aren't any pets in the yard and ask them if they would like to check out the yard and try out the swing. If you notice the wife gently rubbing the countertop, ask if she can picture entertaining friends and family in the kitchen.

By asking these types of questions, you are selling the benefits of a home, not just its features. People notice features, but they

buy benefits. A home office is a feature, but a spouse who works long hours may see a real benefit in bringing some of that work home so she can be around the family while taking care of business. Bring it to their attention.

Stay keenly aware of the buyers' reaction to each home. Don't try to sell features you find impressive. Just point them out if the buyers have missed them and ask for their opinion. If what you say creates interest, then use the feature/benefit dialogue to enhance the value of the feature to the buyers.

It's also a good idea to involve children in the process. Ask their opinions about things that would seem to interest children of their ages, such as asking the teenage daughter if she would enjoy having her friends over for a swim party or which bedroom she would call her own and how she would decorate it.

You will sometimes see buying signals in more than one home. If you experience this, ask questions that make the buyers stop and compare one home to another such as:

- Do you think your dining room set would look better in this home or in the one on Elm Street?
- Which yard do you feel will better accommodate the pool you want, this home or the one on Bradshaw Street?
- I know you entertain quite a bit. Does this home have the best kitchen/family room/patio mix or is the Madison Avenue home better?

SUMMARY

Working with buyers often starts with an ad call, Internet inquiry via e-mail, or sign call to your office. You must know the inventory well and be prepared to talk about several properties with a potential buyer by having "switch properties" readily available. You must also reply to Internet inquiries almost immediately or you may lose the buyer.

Do your best to get the names and addresses of callers and ask them questions to assess their needs. Tell them about other properties that are also available in their price range to help create interest and get an appointment.

If possible, have each caller contact a lender for financing preapproval before your first meeting. If you are unable to do so, prequalify the caller yourself prior to showing any homes. Ask

about her needs and wants and have several properties ready to show. Have callers read and sign the agency disclosure form as early as possible and explain the benefits of working with you under a buyer/broker agreement.

Watch for buying signals. If you see them, ask open-ended questions to help the buyers see the benefit of proceeding with a purchase contract. Involve the entire family, including the children, in the decision-making process.

CLASS DISCUSSION TOPICS

1. Role-play an inquiry about one of your office listings with another student. Your goal is to get the caller's name, telephone number, basic needs, and a firm commitment to meet with you to look at property.

2. Role-play a first appointment with another student.

3. Role-play a property showing in which the buyers show interest in the remodeled kitchen, the bathrooms, and the swimming pool.

4. Role-play a situation in which you present the agency disclosure form and the buyer/broker agreement.

5. Role-play talking a buyer out of waiting to list her home until she has found a replacement.

CHAPTER 6 QUIZ

1. Someone calling about a newspaper ad
   A. already knows the area where the home is located.
   B. is very likely to buy that particular home.
   C. usually does not want to give their name and phone number.
   D. is satisfied with the home's architectural style.

2. Which of the following is the best source of new customers for a new licensee?
   A. Floor time
   B. Open House
   C. Referrals
   D. None of the above

3. Which of the following is the proper response to a caller inquiring if a property has a view?
   A. No, it doesn't.
   B. I'm not sure, let's go look at it.
   C. Is a view important to you?
   D. None of the above.

4. Which of the following is a good policy in handling a phone inquiry?
   A. Meet the caller at your office for the first appointment.
   B. Obtain the caller's name and telephone number.
   C. Give the caller only enough information to create interest in seeing the property.
   D. All of the above.

5. When is the best time to present the agency disclosure agreement to a new buyer?
   A. At the earliest opportunity after an ongoing relationship has been established.
   B. Just prior to filling out the purchase agreement.
   C. When escrow is opened.
   D. The very first time you meet them.

6. Which of the following is not a buying signal?
   A. Returning several times to or lingering in a room.
   B. Taking a cursory look through the property and leaving quickly.
   C. Running a hand over the countertop or along the cabinets several times.
   D. Asking if the refrigerator stays with the property.

7. What should you do when you are finished showing a home?
   A. Return the home to exactly the same condition as you found it.
   B. Let the cat outside to get some exercise.
   C. Flush your cigarette butt down the toilet after you are finished with it.
   D. Leave the door unlocked for the owners for when they get home.

8. What should you do when calling another real estate company about the availability of one of its listings?
   A. Pretend you are a buyer so you get more information.
   B. Identify yourself and the company you are with.
   C. Ask to speak to the listing agent only.
   D. Ask to speak to the branch manager about the property.

9. What should you do if you arrive at a home and another licensee is already showing it?
   A. Show the property but stay as far away from the other licensee as possible.
   B. Let the licensee know she needs to speed it up as you have your own timetable to meet.
   C. Wait in an inconspicuous place until the other licensee is through, then show the home.
   D. All of the above.

10. What should you do if the buyers bring their children along to see the property?
    A. Ask the children to be as quiet as possible.
    B. Ask the children's opinion about the properties.
    C. Involve the children in conversations about each home.
    D. Both b and c.

Chapter

7

IMPORTANT PHRASES AND TERMS

Alternate of choice close

Assumptive close

Closed-ended questions

Counseling

Counteroffer

Mirroring

Multiple counteroffer

Open-ended questions

Persuasion

Residential Purchase Agreement and Joint Escrow Instructions (RPA-CA)

Short sale

Trial closes

Writing and Presenting Effective Purchase Contracts

Upon completion of this chapter, the student will be able to:

- Create and employ an effective purchase contract.
- Distinguish effective counseling techniques.
- Compare and contrast various types of purchase contracts.
- Interpret and use the C.A.R. purchase contract.
- Compose and construct an offer to purchase.
- Demonstrate and appraise negotiating single and multiple offers when representing a buyer or seller.

7.1 SELLING OR COUNSELING

Although similar in nature, there is a difference between selling and counseling: Selling is using dialogue and questions to lead a customer to a predetermined end and **counseling** is using questions and dialogue to elicit a customer's true needs, wants, and desires. Truly professional real estate licensees use both selling and counseling while working with their customers.

Counseling almost always comes first. As discussed in the previous chapter, as a real estate licensee, you must take time with each customer or client, somewhere without distractions, and have a dialogue. Allow them to reveal what they truly want to accomplish; without this counseling session, you can end up showing them every home in town, which will soon lead to your mutual dissatisfaction. It is only through professional counseling that you get your customers to fully realize the issues that are truly important to them.

Selling, which is really professional **persuasion**, starts as you go through the process of showing property to customers. Watch for their reactions and ask for feedback about each property. By doing this, you can refine your property search each time you work with them.

It is important to remember that people do not make buying decisions based on features alone. They observe features and *make buying decisions* based on the benefits those features bring to them.

As you observe your customers' reactions, you will begin to see signs of potential interest in specific properties. At this point, you can feel them out by using **trial closes**. For instance, if you are showing a customer a home in which she lingers in the kitchen for some time and tells you she loves to entertain and really wants a large, modern kitchen, you might ask if she can see herself entertaining friends in this kitchen. If the answer is positive and enthusiastic, you should continue to ask questions to see if they are ready to make an offer.

Your customers may exhibit several buying signs in a particular home or they may reveal only one or two very intense ones. Acknowledge each one as you observe it and ask as many questions as needed to help your customers become emotionally involved in the property and create the desire to own it; this is best accomplished using both **open-ended** and **closed-ended questions**.

An open-ended question is one that requires more than a yes or no answer. For instance, if you observe a customer sitting alone by the pool of a particular home, walk over and ask, "How do you think your children would enjoy spending their summer days out here?" The answer will require a full response that will help you realize just how much she likes the setting. Having the customer verbalize her response further validates her feelings about the setting. Limiting the question to whether or not the kids would like the pool probably won't have the same emotional charge. Other examples of open-ended questions are:

- What types of projects do you see yourself doing in this workshop?
- How well do you think your furniture would fit in this family room?
- Where would you put your entertainment center?

At times, closed-ended questions are also appropriate and should be interspersed with the open-ended ones to avoid sounding trite or monotonous. Closed-ended questions can be answered with a simple yes or no, such as, "Do you like the way the dining room

chandelier lights the room?" Other closed-ended questions include:

- Do you like the landscaping?
- Are you as happy with what you see as I am?
- Isn't that three-car garage great?

Closed-ended questions are often more effective when used with tie-downs or words used at the end of closed-ended questions that ask for the client's validation of your question. Typical tie-downs include:

- Wouldn't it?
- Couldn't it?
- Can't it?
- Won't it?
- Shouldn't it?
- Don't you agree?

If we take the three examples cited earlier and use them with tie-downs, you can see how they can evoke a yes or no answer while emotionally involving the client.

- This landscaping is really beautiful, isn't it?
- This home has nearly everything you said you wanted, doesn't it?
- That three-car garage will give you plenty of parking, don't you agree?

When you see that the client has an elevated degree of interest in a property but still seems somewhat uncertain about making an offer, you may want to use an **alternate of choice close** to help solidify her decision to purchase the home. This offers the client two or more choices, both of which indicate a desire to make an offer. For example, if you saw strong interest in a property, but hesitation about the price, you could say, "It's a great home for you folks and I wouldn't want you to lose it. Would you consider offering full price or do you have something different in mind?"

Other alternate of choice closes include:

- Would you like to close the escrow and begin living here in thirty days or is forty-five days better for you?
- Do you want to put down 10 percent or is 20 percent better for you?

When you have explored the clients' motivations about a particular property—enough to determine real interest—but you still see a little hesitation, help them make a final decision by using an

assumptive close. An assumptive close is a statement you make that assumes the clients are going to make an offer on the property. For example, "Would you like the washer, dryer, and refrigerator to stay with the property?" If the answer is yes, you should proceed to the purchase contract. Other examples of assumptive closes include:

- If needed, I think we should offer to let the owners rent the property from you at your cost for up to fifteen days. Is that all right with you?
- Do you agree that a thirty-day escrow is the best timing for you?
- Do you want to split the cost of a home warranty with the owners?

7.2 WRITING THE RESIDENTIAL PURCHASE CONTRACT

It is paramount that you keep your customers' best interests in mind at all times and that they feel you do. So when you are in a selling or closing situation with a customer or client, you must be at your professional best. Your tone of voice, body language, and the way you handle objections and answer their questions will have a lot to do with whether or not they make an offer and get involved in a wonderful new home or become frightened or frustrated and decide not to buy from you.

Why do people buy homes? Ever since we came out of the caves and began to live in human-made dwellings, our human nature began showing in ever more complex ways. We wanted better, more comfortable, nicer-looking places in which to raise our families and to call our own. As a real estate professional, every buyer you work with has her own reasons for replacing one dwelling for another, and one or more of those reasons will play a part in every home you help someone acquire. Some common motives for buying include:

- **Security.** The desire for a safe, secure place to call home. This is one of the most basic of human needs, and every licensee should be aware of it. In addition to being the greatest asset most Americans have, it is a great leveler; that is, once your new fixed-rate loan is in place, if you are financing, your housing expense is stabilized for as long as you own the house. There is little that is more comforting for a retiree than a fully paid for home free of any mortgage payment.
- **Pride of ownership.** To the extent possible, most people purchase a home that is as nice as they can afford. What better way to make a statement to your friends and family about your

status as an individual, your financial station in life, or what a well-paying job you have, than to have them come and experience your beautiful new home!

- **Financial gain**. This is one of the strongest human motivations, so your clients will need and want to have a keen sense of property values in the area of any property they wish to acquire. Therefore, prepare a detailed comparative (also called a competitive market analysis) market analysis (CMA) of the neighborhood they are interested in to share with them, just as you would do for a seller if you were listing her property. Well located properties have shown a long-term tendency of appreciation in California and have been the first step in long-term financial prosperity for many thousands of people.

- **Tax benefits**. There are significant tax benefits in owning a home or second home. The interest homeowners pay on their primary or secondary residences and their property taxes are fully tax-deductible, up to certain limits. Other tax benefits include lower tax rates and the capital gain tax exclusion. Be sure to check periodically with your tax professional about current tax issues as they have significant importance in the buying decisions of most people.

- **Family**. How a home will help better the lives and lifestyles of family members is very often a major consideration in the buying process. Things such as proximity to shopping, better schools, parks and recreational activities, and quiet, safe neighborhoods all play a part in selecting a home. Some people will avoid certain developments with homeowners' associations that have restrictions in the number or size of pets, as many people view their pets as family.

- **Health issues**. Like the survival issue, health issues can be an important determining factor in where people choose to live. Issues such as neighborhood safety, water and air purity, noise levels, and proximity to medical facilities are all important issues of consideration.

Be aware of issues that may make people decide not to buy property. They are in the back of every prospective buyer's mind to some degree, and if you are aware of them, you will be better able to deal with them. With some buyers, homeownership means:

- **Restricted mobility**. Property ownership makes a person somewhat less mobile than if they rent; however, property in California is usually saleable, and it can almost always be rented, if necessary.

- **Greater responsibility**. Property owners have more responsibility than renters, such as maintaining the paint and landscaping; however, the benefits of stability, tax savings, and financial gain far outweigh the added responsibility.

- **Lack of liquidity**. Some people do not like to tie up their financial assets in what they perceive as an asset that takes too much time to convert to cash. Although a real estate investment is less liquid than a savings account, it may be used as collateral for loans when cash is needed and also has the ability to generate significant cash flows.

- **Large initial investment**. To some people, the thought of giving someone several thousand dollars of their savings is unpleasant. Veterans Admisistration (VA) and Federal Housing Administration (FHA) buyers can also buy with minimal down payments.

- **Increased carrying costs**. Whereas a fixed-rate mortgage will remain the same, other costs can increase. As a home ages, its maintenance costs increase and property taxes slowly increase. Adjustable-rate loans may increase in monthly payments. Buyers who bring up these issues should be reminded that they are paying much higher rent than they used to.

When you have seen what you think are enough signs to merit asking if the buyer is interested in making an offer on a house, just ask. You might say, for example, "Well, it looks like we have found you your new home." The response may be, "It's close, but not quite right," or "Yes, we sure have. Let's write up an offer."

Buyers may be a little tense at this moment for any or all of the reasons mentioned earlier. If this is so, you will find tremendous benefit in **mirroring** the buyer's body language. Mirroring is using posture and gestures that are the same as the person or people who you are with. Doing this with your clients may give them a sense of alliance with you and it makes for better communication with them.

As you sit down with your clients to discuss the price and terms of their offer, you can normally expect some objections. This is actually a good sign, so don't get defensive. Each time you encounter an objection, just ask yourself if it has any merit and handle it accordingly. Many objections are simply verbalized thoughts that the buyers make while they ponder what is happening; they don't really have any importance. If you try to counter these objections immediately, you give credibility to them and, instead of self-destructing, they may become a real stumbling block and get in the way. It is

best to ignore most objections the first time they are stated, unless they are about a real issue you feel merits a conversation.

As real objections arise, it is best to repeat them to the buyers for clarity. Then offer suggestions on how to best handle them. If, for example, the buyer says the rooms are too small, ask which room she is talking about. If she narrows it down and says that the dining room won't fit all of her furniture, tell her that one or two pieces could easily be put in the living room and would actually look good there. Some common objections include:

- The price is too high.
- The rooms are too small.
- The taxes are too high.
- I can't move in soon enough.
- The yard is too small.
- The property needs too much work.
- I have to sell my house first.

There is almost always a solution to each of these issues. Many times it involves making a concession about something when the "big picture" shows that the other features and benefits of the home clearly outnumber the issue in question. You will also be wise to use "pre-emptive" statements that will take care of anticipated objections that don't have any merit before they are even voiced. By doing so, you take away their importance before they are even brought up and they never become an issue. If you are about to write an offer on an older Spanish style home with signs of some termite infestation, for example, and the buyers have said they don't want a home with termites, you can put the issue to rest early in the conversation. You can say, "I think there may be some termites, but we should really ask the seller to have the property inspected, take care of any work that is found, and see to it that you have a warranty from the termite company, don't you agree?"

At some point you will find your clients the right home. You will know this from their answers to your questions, their body language, and their facial expressions, which can be subtle, but telling. You must now go to a convenient place, such as the client's home, your office, or a restaurant, to write the purchase contract on their behalf. Any place that affords a place to write with reasonable privacy is fine, although your office is the best.

After you are all seated in your conference room or wherever you are, call the listing salesperson in front of your buyers. If you know the licensee has a cell phone, call using that number. If your

call goes to voice mail, leave a message; many times, you will get a return call within a few minutes. If the licensee answers, relate that you are just sitting down to write a purchase agreement on her listing at [address] and ask if there is anything you need to know that will help you write a better contract.

As you begin to write the purchase agreement, give the buyers each page as you finish it and ask them to read it thoroughly. This helps keep them occupied while you are at work and has positive legal consequences.

When the agreement is complete and the buyers have signed it, call the listing salesperson again and ask her to set an appointment with the owners to present the offer. Have the listing salesperson call you back as soon as possible.

Once you have heard back from the other salesperson and established a time to present the offer, explain to them that the seller will either accept their offer or provide a counteroffer, and to complete the sale, you will need to deliver a copy of the signed offer to them or discuss any counteroffer with them. After you have presented the offer and it has either been accepted by the seller or you have received a counteroffer, immediately go to the buyers and give them a copy of the accepted offer or discuss the counteroffer with them. Do not call first as they will press you for details of any counteroffer, and you cannot properly handle the situation over the telephone.

7.3 UNDERSTANDING THE RESIDENTIAL PURCHASE AGREEMENT AND JOINT ESCROW INSTRUCTIONS (RPA-CA)

The **Residential Purchase Agreement and Joint Escrow Instructions (RPA-CA)** (which includes a *receipt* for the buyer's *deposit*) is the document used to create a contract between buyers and sellers for the purchase of real property.

The California Statute of Frauds stipulates that, except for leases of one year or less, all real estate contracts must be in writing. The obvious purpose for this is clarity by all parties to a contract as to what it says. Samuel Goldwyn, of Metro Goldwyn Mayer studios, (MGM), pointed out the essence of this when he said, "An oral contract is not worth the paper that it's written on."

When you draft a purchase agreement on behalf of a buyer, be sure the entire agreement is in writing in a clear and completely understandable manner. If you draft a contract that does not contain all of the provisions the buyer wanted, or write certain parts of the contract in

such a manner that your meaning is vague or can be interpreted in more than one way, you place yourself and the parties to the contract at risk of ending up in litigation. All parties to a purchase contract should carefully read and fully understand the contract before signing it.

Many different types of purchase contracts are available in California, and buyers and real estate practitioners may use any of them. In the past, however, the language used in each contract varied so much that there was a great deal of confusion among brokers. As a result, in 1985 the California Association of REALTORS®, in cooperation with the state bar and with the approval of the California Department of Real Estate, developed a model form: the Residential Purchase Agreement and Joint Escrow Instructions. This form (as with the many other forms published for professional REALTORS® by Real Estate Business Systems, Inc., a subsidiary of C.A.R.) is subject to review and amendment in April and October of each year. In order to adequately protect you, your client, and your broker, always make sure you are using the most current form (see Figure 7.1).

Content of the Form

The Residential Purchase Agreement and Joint Escrow Instructions form essentially acts as a checklist to ensure that a contract is complete in all respects and protects the rights of all parties. It clearly spells out the duties and responsibilities of each party to the contract. Any changes to the contract must be dated and initialed by the principals to the transaction; however, no changes of any kind are to be made by one party above the signature of the other party. Once the buyer signs the contract offer, any change by the seller must be made on a counteroffer form, and no change is to be made to the contract itself above the buyer's signature.

Understanding the C.A.R. RPA-CA Purchase Agreement Form Revised 4/10

Insert the name of the place (city, town, and so on) where the buyer actually signs the offer to purchase.

Paragraph 1: Offer

A. Insert the names of each person who will be a buyer, including the person who gave the deposit.
B. Describe the property, using a legal description, street address, and assessor's parcel number (APN).
C. Write down the purchase price in both words and numerals.
D. Write down the date the escrow is to close on.

FIGURE 7.1   California Residential Purchase Agreement

CALIFORNIA RESIDENTIAL PURCHASE AGREEMENT AND JOINT ESCROW INSTRUCTIONS
For Use With Single Family Residential Property — Attached or Detached
(C.A.R. Form RPA-CA, Revised 4/10)

Date _____

1. **OFFER:**
   A. **THIS IS AN OFFER FROM** _____ ("Buyer").
   B. **THE REAL PROPERTY TO BE ACQUIRED** is described as _____
      _____, Assessor's Parcel No. _____, situated in
      _____, County of _____, California ("Property").
   C. **THE PURCHASE PRICE** offered is _____
      _____ (Dollars $ _____).
   D. **CLOSE OF ESCROW** shall occur on _____ (date) (or ☐ _____ **Days** After Acceptance).
2. **AGENCY:**
   A. **DISCLOSURE:** Buyer and Seller each acknowledge prior receipt of a "Disclosure Regarding Real Estate Agency Relationships"
      (C.A.R. Form AD).
   B. **POTENTIALLY COMPETING BUYERS AND SELLERS:** Buyer and Seller each acknowledge receipt of a disclosure of the
      possibility of multiple representation by the Broker representing that principal. This disclosure may be part of a listing
      agreement, buyer representation agreement or separate document (C.A.R. Form DA). Buyer understands that Broker
      representing Buyer may also represent other potential buyers, who may consider, make offers on or ultimately acquire the
      Property. Seller understands that Broker representing Seller may also represent other sellers with competing properties of
      interest to this Buyer.
   C. **CONFIRMATION:** The following agency relationships are hereby confirmed for this transaction:
      Listing Agent _____ (Print Firm Name) is the agent of (check one):
      ☐ the Seller exclusively; or ☐ both the Buyer and Seller.
      Selling Agent _____ (Print Firm Name) (if not the same as the Listing
      Agent) is the agent of (check one): ☐ the Buyer exclusively; or ☐ the Seller exclusively; or ☐ both the Buyer and Seller. Real
      Estate Brokers are not parties to the Agreement between Buyer and Seller.
3. **FINANCE TERMS:** Buyer represents that funds will be good when deposited with Escrow Holder.
   A. **INITIAL DEPOSIT:** Deposit shall be in the amount of . . . . $ _____
      (1) Buyer shall deliver deposit directly to Escrow Holder by personal check, ☐ electronic funds transfer,
      ☐ Other _____ within 3 business days after acceptance
      (or ☐ Other_____);
      OR (2) (If checked) ☐ Buyer has given the deposit by personal check (or ☐_____)
      to the agent submitting the offer (or to ☐_____), made payable to
      _____. The deposit shall be held uncashed until Acceptance and
      then deposited with Escrow Holder (or ☐ into Broker's trust account) within **3** business days after
      Acceptance (or ☐ Other_____).
   B. **INCREASED DEPOSIT:** Buyer shall deposit with Escrow Holder an increased deposit in the amount of . . . .$ _____
      within _____ **Days** After Acceptance, or ☐ _____.
      If a liquidated damages clause is incorporated into this Agreement, Buyer and Seller shall sign a
      separate liquidated damages clause (C.A.R. Form RID) for any increased deposit at the time it is
      deposited.
   C. **LOAN(S):**
      (1) FIRST LOAN: in the amount of . . . .$ _____
      This loan will be conventional financing or, if checked, ☐ FHA, ☐ VA, ☐ Seller (C.A.R. Form SFA),
      ☐ assumed financing (C.A.R. Form PAA), ☐ Other _____. This loan shall be at a fixed
      rate not to exceed _____% or, ☐ an adjustable rate loan with initial rate not to exceed ____%.
      Regardless of the type of loan, Buyer shall pay points not to exceed ____% of the loan amount.
      (2) ☐ **SECOND LOAN** in the amount of . . . .$ _____
      This loan will be conventional financing or, if checked, ☐ Seller (C.A.R. Form SFA), ☐ assumed
      financing (C.A.R. Form PAA), ☐ Other _____. This loan shall be at a fixed rate not to
      exceed _____% or, ☐ an adjustable rate loan with initial rate not to exceed ____%. Regardless
      of the type of loan, Buyer shall pay points not to exceed ____% of the loan amount.
      (3) FHA/VA: For any FHA or VA loan specified above, Buyer has **17 (or ☐ _____) Days** After
      Acceptance to Deliver to Seller written notice (C.A.R. Form FVA) of any lender-required repairs or
      costs that Buyer requests Seller to pay for or repair. Seller has no obligation to pay for repairs or
      satisfy lender requirements unless otherwise agreed in writing.
   D. **ADDITIONAL FINANCING TERMS:** _____
      _____
   E. **BALANCE OF PURCHASE PRICE OR DOWN PAYMENT** in the amount of . . . .$ _____
      to be deposited with Escrow Holder within sufficient time to close escrow.
   F. **PURCHASE PRICE (TOTAL):** . . . .$ _____

Buyer's Initials (_____)(_____)   Seller's Initials (_____)(_____)

RPA-CA REVISED 4/10 (PAGE 1 OF 8) Print Date BD Apr 10

Reviewed by _____ Date _____

CALIFORNIA RESIDENTIAL PURCHASE AGREEMENT (RPA-CA PAGE 1 OF 8)

FIGURE 7.1 (*Continued*)

Property Address: _____ Date: _____

G. VERIFICATION OF DOWN PAYMENT AND CLOSING COSTS: Buyer (or Buyer's lender or loan broker pursuant to 3H(1)) shall, within **7 (or** ☐ _____) **Days** After Acceptance, Deliver to Seller written verification of Buyer's down payment and closing costs. (If checked, ☐ verification attached.)

H. LOAN TERMS:

    (1) LOAN APPLICATIONS: Within **7 (or** ☐ _____) **Days** After Acceptance, Buyer shall Deliver to Seller a letter from lender or loan broker stating that, based on a review of Buyer's written application and credit report, Buyer is prequalified or preapproved for any NEW loan specified in 3C above. (If checked, ☐ letter attached.)

    (2) LOAN CONTINGENCY: Buyer shall act diligently and in good faith to obtain the designated loan(s). Obtaining the loan(s) specified above **is a contingency** of this Agreement unless otherwise agreed in writing. Buyer's contractual obligations to obtain and provide deposit, balance of down payment and closing costs **are not contingencies** of this Agreement.

    (3) LOAN CONTINGENCY REMOVAL:

      (i) Within **17 (or** ☐ _____) **Days** After Acceptance, Buyer shall, as specified in paragraph 14, in writing remove the loan contingency or cancel this Agreement;

    OR (ii) (If checked) ☐ the loan contingency shall remain in effect until the designated loans are funded.

    (4) ☐ **NO LOAN CONTINGENCY** (If checked): Obtaining any loan specified above is NOT a contingency of this Agreement. If Buyer does not obtain the loan and as a result Buyer does not purchase the Property, Seller may be entitled to Buyer's deposit or other legal remedies.

I. APPRAISAL CONTINGENCY AND REMOVAL: This Agreement is (**or**, if checked, ☐ is NOT) contingent upon a written appraisal of the Property by a licensed or certified appraiser at no less than the specified purchase price. If there is a loan contingency, Buyer's removal of the loan contingency shall be deemed removal of this appraisal contingency (**or**, ☐ if checked, Buyer shall, as specified in paragraph 14B(3), in writing remove the appraisal contingency or cancel this Agreement within **17 (or** ____) **Days** After Acceptance). If there is no loan contingency, Buyer shall, as specified in paragraph 14B(3), in writing remove the appraisal contingency or cancel this Agreement within **17 (or** ☐ ____) **Days** After Acceptance.

J. ☐ **ALL CASH OFFER** (If checked): Buyer shall, within **7 (or** ☐ _____) **Days** After Acceptance, Deliver to Seller written verification of sufficient funds to close this transaction. (If checked, ☐ verification attached.)

K. BUYER STATED FINANCING: Seller has relied on Buyer's representation of the type of financing specified (including but not limited to, as applicable, amount of down payment, contingent or non contingent loan, or all cash). If Buyer seeks alternate financing, (i) Seller has no obligation to cooperate with Buyer's efforts to obtain such financing, and (ii) Buyer shall also pursue the financing method specified in this Agreement. Buyer's failure to secure alternate financing does not excuse Buyer from the obligation to purchase the Property and close escrow as specified in this Agreement.

4. ALLOCATION OF COSTS (If checked): Unless otherwise specified in writing, **this paragraph** only determines who is to pay for the inspection, test or service ("Report") mentioned; it **does not determine who is to pay for any work recommended or identified in the Report.**

  A. INSPECTIONS AND REPORTS:

    (1) ☐ Buyer ☐ Seller shall pay for an inspection and report for wood destroying pests and organisms ("Wood Pest Report") prepared by _____ a registered structural pest control company.

    (2) ☐ Buyer ☐ Seller shall pay to have septic or private sewage disposal systems inspected _____.

    (3) ☐ Buyer ☐ Seller shall pay to have domestic wells tested for water potability and productivity _____.

    (4) ☐ Buyer ☐ Seller shall pay for a natural hazard zone disclosure report prepared by _____.

    (5) ☐ Buyer ☐ Seller shall pay for the following inspection or report _____.

    (6) ☐ Buyer ☐ Seller shall pay for the following inspection or report _____.

  B. GOVERNMENT REQUIREMENTS AND RETROFIT:

    (1) ☐ Buyer ☐ Seller shall pay for smoke detector installation and/or water heater bracing, if required by Law. Prior to Close Of Escrow, Seller shall provide Buyer written statement(s) of compliance in accordance with state and local Law, unless exempt.

    (2) ☐ Buyer ☐ Seller shall pay the cost of compliance with any other minimum mandatory government retrofit standards, inspections and reports if required as a condition of closing escrow under any Law. _____.

  C. ESCROW AND TITLE:

    (1) ☐ Buyer ☐ Seller shall pay escrow fee _____

      Escrow Holder shall be _____.

    (2) ☐ Buyer ☐ Seller shall pay for **owner's** title insurance policy specified in paragraph 12E _____.

      Owner's title policy to be issued by _____.

      (Buyer shall pay for any title insurance policy insuring Buyer's **lender,** unless otherwise agreed in writing.)

  D. OTHER COSTS:

    (1) ☐ Buyer ☐ Seller shall pay County transfer tax or fee _____.

    (2) ☐ Buyer ☐ Seller shall pay City transfer tax or fee _____.

    (3) ☐ Buyer ☐ Seller shall pay Homeowners' Association ("HOA") transfer fee _____.

    (4) ☐ Buyer ☐ Seller shall pay HOA document preparation fees _____.

    (5) ☐ Buyer ☐ Seller shall pay for any private transfer fee _____.

    (6) ☐ Buyer ☐ Seller shall pay for the cost, not to exceed $ _____, of a one-year home warranty plan, issued by _____, with the following optional coverages:

      ☐ Air Conditioner ☐ Pool/Spa ☐ Code and Permit upgrade ☐ Other: _____.

      Buyer is informed that home warranty plans have many optional coverages in addition to those listed above. Buyer is advised to investigate these coverages to determine those that may be suitable for Buyer.

    (7) ☐ Buyer ☐ Seller shall pay for _____.

    (8) ☐ Buyer ☐ Seller shall pay for _____.

Buyer's Initials (_____)(_____)

RPA-CA REVISED 4/10 (PAGE 2 OF 8)

Seller's Initials (_____)(_____)

Reviewed by _____ Date _____

EQUAL HOUSING OPPORTUNITY

FIGURE 7.1 *(Continued)*

Property Address: _____   Date: _____

5. **CLOSING AND POSSESSION:**
    A. Buyer intends (or ☐ does not intend) to occupy the Property as Buyer's primary residence.
    B. **Seller-occupied or vacant property:** Possession shall be delivered to Buyer at 5 PM or (☐ _____ ☐ AM/☐ PM), on the date of Close Of Escrow; ☐ on _____; or ☐ no later than _____ **Days** After Close Of Escrow. If transfer of title and possession do not occur at the same time, Buyer and Seller are advised to: **(i)** enter into a written occupancy agreement (C.A.R. Form PAA, paragraph 2); and **(ii)** consult with their insurance and legal advisors.
    C. **Tenant-occupied property:**
        (i)   Property shall be vacant at least **5 (or** ☐ _____**) Days** Prior to Close Of Escrow, unless otherwise agreed in writing. **Note to Seller: If you are unable to deliver Property vacant in accordance with rent control and other applicable Law, you may be in breach of this Agreement.**
        OR (ii) (if checked) ☐ **Tenant to remain in possession.** (C.A.R. Form PAA, paragraph 3)
    D. At Close Of Escrow, **(i)** Seller assigns to Buyer any assignable warranty rights for items included in the sale, and **(ii)** Seller shall Deliver to Buyer available Copies of warranties. Brokers cannot and will not determine the assignability of any warranties.
    E. At Close Of Escrow, unless otherwise agreed in writing, Seller shall provide keys and/or means to operate all locks, mailboxes, security systems, alarms and garage door openers. If Property is a condominium or located in a common interest subdivision, Buyer may be required to pay a deposit to the Homeowners' Association ("HOA") to obtain keys to accessible HOA facilities.
6. **STATUTORY DISCLOSURES (INCLUDING LEAD-BASED PAINT HAZARD DISCLOSURES) AND CANCELLATION RIGHTS:**
    A. **(1)** Seller shall, within the time specified in paragraph 14A, Deliver to Buyer, if required by Law: **(i)** Federal Lead-Based Paint Disclosures (C.A.R. Form FLD) and pamphlet ("Lead Disclosures"); and **(ii)** disclosures or notices required by sections 1102 et. seq. and 1103 et. seq. of the Civil Code ("Statutory Disclosures"). Statutory Disclosures include, but are not limited to, a Real Estate Transfer Disclosure Statement ("TDS"), Natural Hazard Disclosure Statement ("NHD"), notice or actual knowledge of release of illegal controlled substance, notice of special tax and/or assessments (or, if allowed, substantially equivalent notice regarding the Mello-Roos Community Facilities Act and Improvement Bond Act of 1915) and, if Seller has actual knowledge, of industrial use and military ordnance location (C.A.R. Form SPQ or SSD).
        (2) Buyer shall, within the time specified in paragraph 14B(1), return Signed Copies of the Statutory and Lead Disclosures to Seller.
        (3) In the event Seller, prior to Close Of Escrow, becomes aware of adverse conditions materially affecting the Property, or any material inaccuracy in disclosures, information or representations previously provided to Buyer, Seller shall promptly provide a subsequent or amended disclosure or notice, in writing, covering those items. **However, a subsequent or amended disclosure shall not be required for conditions and material inaccuracies** of which Buyer is otherwise aware, or which are **disclosed in reports provided to or obtained by Buyer or ordered and paid for by Buyer.**
        (4) If any disclosure or notice specified in 6A(1), or subsequent or amended disclosure or notice is Delivered to Buyer after the offer is Signed, Buyer shall have the right to cancel this Agreement within **3 Days** After Delivery in person, or **5 Days** After Delivery by deposit in the mail, by giving written notice of cancellation to Seller or Seller's agent.
        (5) Note to Buyer and Seller: Waiver of Statutory and Lead Disclosures is prohibited by Law.
    B. **NATURAL AND ENVIRONMENTAL HAZARDS:** Within the time specified in paragraph 14A, Seller shall, if required by Law: **(i)** Deliver to Buyer earthquake guides (and questionnaire) and environmental hazards booklet; **(ii)** even if exempt from the obligation to provide a NHD, disclose if the Property is located in a Special Flood Hazard Area; Potential Flooding (Inundation) Area; Very High Fire Hazard Zone; State Fire Responsibility Area; Earthquake Fault Zone; Seismic Hazard Zone; and **(iii)** disclose any other zone as required by Law and provide any other information required for those zones.
    C. **WITHHOLDING TAXES:** Within the time specified in paragraph 14A, to avoid required withholding, Seller shall Deliver to Buyer or qualified substitute, an affidavit sufficient to comply with federal (FIRPTA) and California withholding Law (C.A.R. Form AS or QS).
    D. **MEGAN'S LAW DATABASE DISCLOSURE:** Notice: Pursuant to Section 290.46 of the Penal Code, information about specified registered sex offenders is made available to the public via an Internet Web site maintained by the Department of Justice at www.meganslaw.ca.gov. Depending on an offender's criminal history, this information will include either the address at which the offender resides or the community of residence and ZIP Code in which he or she resides. (Neither Seller nor Brokers are required to check this website. If Buyer wants further information, Broker recommends that Buyer obtain information from this website during Buyer's inspection contingency period. Brokers do not have expertise in this area.)
7. **CONDOMINIUM/PLANNED DEVELOPMENT DISCLOSURES:**
    A. **SELLER HAS: 7 (or** ☐ _____**) Days** After Acceptance to disclose to Buyer whether the Property is a condominium, or is located in a planned development or other common interest subdivision (C.A.R. Form SPQ or SSD).
    B. If the Property is a condominium or is located in a planned development or other common interest subdivision, Seller has **3 (or** ☐ _____**) Days** After Acceptance to request from the HOA (C.A.R. Form HOA): **(i)** Copies of any documents required by Law; **(ii)** disclosure of any pending or anticipated claim or litigation by or against the HOA; **(iii)** a statement containing the location and number of designated parking and storage spaces; **(iv)** Copies of the most recent 12 months of HOA minutes for regular and special meetings; and **(v)** the names and contact information of all HOAs governing the Property (collectively, "CI Disclosures"). Seller shall itemize and Deliver to Buyer all CI Disclosures received from the HOA and any CI Disclosures in Seller's possession. Buyer's approval of CI Disclosures is a contingency of this Agreement as specified in paragraph 14B(3).
8. **ITEMS INCLUDED IN AND EXCLUDED FROM PURCHASE PRICE:**
    A. **NOTE TO BUYER AND SELLER:** Items listed as included or excluded in the MLS, flyers or marketing materials are **not** included in the purchase price or excluded from the sale unless specified in 8B or C.
    B. **ITEMS INCLUDED IN SALE:**
        (1) All EXISTING fixtures and fittings that are attached to the Property;
        (2) EXISTING electrical, mechanical, lighting, plumbing and heating fixtures, ceiling fans, fireplace inserts, gas logs and grates, solar systems, built-in appliances, window and door screens, awnings, shutters, window coverings, attached floor coverings, television antennas, satellite dishes, private integrated telephone systems, air coolers/conditioners, pool/spa equipment, garage door openers/remote controls, mailbox, in-ground landscaping, trees/shrubs, water softeners, water purifiers, security systems/alarms; (If checked) ☐ stove(s), ☐ refrigerator(s); and
        (3) The following additional items:_____.
        (4) Seller represents that all items included in the purchase price, unless otherwise specified, are owned by Seller.
        (5) All items included shall be transferred free of liens and without Seller warranty.
    C. **ITEMS EXCLUDED FROM SALE:** Unless otherwise specified, audio and video components (such as flat screen TVs and speakers) are excluded if any such item is not itself attached to the Property, even if a bracket or other mechanism attached to the component is attached to the Property; and _____.

Buyer's Initials (_____)(_____)

RPA-CA REVISED 4/10 (PAGE 3 OF 8)

Seller's Initials (_____)(_____)

Reviewed by _____ Date _____

EQUAL HOUSING OPPORTUNITY

FIGURE 7.1 (*Continued*)

Property Address: _____ Date: _____

9. **CONDITION OF PROPERTY:** Unless otherwise agreed: **(i) the Property is sold (a) in its PRESENT physical ("as-is") condition as of the date of Acceptance and (b) subject to Buyer's Investigation rights; (ii)** the Property, including pool, spa, landscaping and grounds, is to be maintained in substantially the same condition as of the date of Acceptance; and **(iii)** all debris and personal property not included in the sale shall be removed by Seller by Close Of Escrow.
   A. Seller shall, within the time specified in paragraph 14A, DISCLOSE KNOWN MATERIAL FACTS AND DEFECTS affecting the Property, including known insurance claims within the past five years, and make any and all other disclosures required by law.
   B. Buyer has the right to inspect the Property and, as specified in paragraph 14B, based upon information discovered in those inspections: (i) cancel this Agreement; or (ii) request that Seller make Repairs or take other action.
   C. **Buyer is strongly advised to conduct investigations of the entire Property in order to determine its present condition. Seller may not be aware of all defects affecting the Property or other factors that Buyer considers important. Property improvements may not be built according to code, in compliance with current Law, or have had permits issued.**

10. **BUYER'S INVESTIGATION OF PROPERTY AND MATTERS AFFECTING PROPERTY:**
   A. Buyer's acceptance of the condition of, and any other matter affecting the Property, is a contingency of this Agreement as specified in this paragraph and paragraph 14B. Within the time specified in paragraph 14B(1), Buyer shall have the right, at Buyer's expense unless otherwise agreed, to conduct inspections, investigations, tests, surveys and other studies ("Buyer Investigations"), including, but not limited to, the right to: **(i)** inspect for lead-based paint and other lead-based paint hazards; **(ii)** inspect for wood destroying pests and organisms; **(iii)** review the registered sex offender database; **(iv)** confirm the insurability of Buyer and the Property; and **(v)** satisfy Buyer as to any matter specified in the attached Buyer's Inspection Advisory (C.A.R. Form BIA). Without Seller's prior written consent, Buyer shall neither make nor cause to be made: **(i)** invasive or destructive Buyer Investigations; or **(ii)** inspections by any governmental building or zoning inspector or government employee, unless required by Law.
   B. Seller shall make the Property available for all Buyer Investigations. Buyer shall **(i)** as specified in paragraph 14B, complete Buyer Investigations and, either remove the contingency or cancel this Agreement, and **(ii)** give Seller, at no cost, complete Copies of all Investigation reports obtained by Buyer, which obligation shall survive the termination of this Agreement.
   C. Seller shall have water, gas, electricity and all operable pilot lights on for Buyer's Investigations and through the date possession is made available to Buyer.
   D. **Buyer indemnity and Seller protection for entry upon property:** Buyer shall: **(i)** keep the Property free and clear of liens; **(ii)** repair all damage arising from Buyer Investigations; and **(iii)** indemnify and hold Seller harmless from all resulting liability, claims, demands, damages and costs of Buyer's Investigations. Buyer shall carry, or Buyer shall require anyone acting on Buyer's behalf to carry, policies of liability, workers' compensation and other applicable insurance, defending and protecting Seller from liability for any injuries to persons or property occurring during any Buyer Investigations or work done on the Property at Buyer's direction prior to Close Of Escrow. Seller is advised that certain protections may be afforded Seller by recording a "Notice of Non-responsibility" (C.A.R. Form NNR) for Buyer Investigations and work done on the Property at Buyer's direction. Buyer's obligations under this paragraph shall survive the termination or cancellation of this Agreement and Close Of Escrow.

11. **SELLER DISCLOSURES; ADDENDA; ADVISORIES; OTHER TERMS:**
   A. **Seller Disclosures (if checked):** Seller shall, within the time specified in paragraph 14A, complete and provide Buyer with a:
   ☐ Seller Property Questionnaire (C.A.R. Form SPQ) **OR** ☐ Supplemental Contractual and Statutory Disclosure (C.A.R. Form SSD)
   B. **Addenda (if checked):** ☐ Addendum # _____ (C.A.R. Form ADM)
   ☐ Wood Destroying Pest Inspection and Allocation of Cost Addendum (C.A.R. Form WPA)
   ☐ Purchase Agreement Addendum (C.A.R. Form PAA) ☐ Septic, Well and Property Monument Addendum (C.A.R. Form SWPI)
   ☐ Short Sale Addendum (C.A.R. Form SSA) ☐ Other
   C. **Advisories (If checked):** ☑ Buyer's Inspection Advisory (C.A.R. Form BIA)
   ☐ Probate Advisory (C.A.R. Form PAK) ☐ Statewide Buyer and Seller Advisory (C.A.R. Form SBSA)
   ☐ Trust Advisory (C.A.R. Form TA) ☐ REO Advisory (C.A.R. Form REO)
   D. **Other Terms:** _____

12. **TITLE AND VESTING:**
   A. Within the time specified in paragraph 14, Buyer shall be provided a current preliminary title report, which shall include a search of the General Index. Seller shall within 7 Days After Acceptance give Escrow Holder a completed Statement of Information. The preliminary report is only an offer by the title insurer to issue a policy of title insurance and may not contain every item affecting title. Buyer's review of the preliminary report and any other matters which may affect title are a contingency of this Agreement as specified in paragraph 14B.
   B. Title is taken in its present condition subject to all encumbrances, easements, covenants, conditions, restrictions, rights and other matters, whether of record or not, as of the date of Acceptance except: **(i)** monetary liens of record unless Buyer is assuming those obligations or taking the Property subject to those obligations; and **(ii)** those matters which Seller has agreed to remove in writing.
   C. Within the time specified in paragraph 14A, Seller has a duty to disclose to Buyer all matters known to Seller affecting title, whether of record or not.
   D. At Close Of Escrow, Buyer shall receive a grant deed conveying title (or, for stock cooperative or long-term lease, an assignment of stock certificate or of Seller's leasehold interest), including oil, mineral and water rights if currently owned by Seller. Title shall vest as designated in Buyer's supplemental escrow instructions. THE MANNER OF TAKING TITLE MAY HAVE SIGNIFICANT LEGAL AND TAX CONSEQUENCES. CONSULT AN APPROPRIATE PROFESSIONAL.
   E. Buyer shall receive a CLTA/ALTA Homeowner's Policy of Title Insurance. A title company, at Buyer's request, can provide information about the availability, desirability, coverage, survey requirements, and cost of various title insurance coverages and endorsements. If Buyer desires title coverage other than that required by this paragraph, Buyer shall instruct Escrow Holder in writing and pay any increase in cost.

13. **SALE OF BUYER'S PROPERTY:**
   A. This Agreement is NOT contingent upon the sale of any property owned by Buyer.
   OR B. ☐ (If checked): The attached addendum (C.A.R. Form COP) regarding the contingency for the sale of property owned by Buyer is incorporated into this Agreement.

Seller's Initials (_____)(_____)

Reviewed by _____ Date _____

RPA-CA REVISED 4/10 (PAGE 4 OF 8)

CALIFORNIA RESIDENTIAL PURCHASE AGREEMENT (RPA-CA PAGE 4 OF 8)

FIGURE 7.1 (Continued)

Property Address: _____ . Date: _____

14. **TIME PERIODS; REMOVAL OF CONTINGENCIES; CANCELLATION RIGHTS: The following time periods may only be extended, altered, modified or changed by mutual written agreement. Any removal of contingencies or cancellation under this paragraph by either Buyer or Seller must be exercised in good faith and in writing (C.A.R. Form CR or CC).**

   A. **SELLER HAS: 7 (or ☐ _____) Days** After Acceptance to Deliver to Buyer all Reports, disclosures and information for which Seller is responsible under paragraphs 4, 6A, B and C, 7A, 9A, 11A and B, and 12. Buyer may give Seller a Notice to Seller to Perform (C.A.R. Form NSP) if Seller has not Delivered the items within the time specified.

   B. **(1) BUYER HAS: 17 (or ☐ _____) Days** After Acceptance, unless otherwise agreed in writing, to:
      (i) complete all Buyer Investigations; approve all disclosures, reports and other applicable information, which Buyer receives from Seller; and approve all other matters affecting the Property; and
      (ii) Deliver to Seller Signed Copies of Statutory and Lead Disclosures Delivered by Seller in accordance with paragraph 6A.
    (2) Within the time specified in 14B(1), Buyer may request that Seller make repairs or take any other action regarding the Property (C.A.R. Form RR). Seller has no obligation to agree to or respond to Buyer's requests.
    (3) Within the time specified in 14B(1) (or as otherwise specified in this Agreement), Buyer shall Deliver to Seller either (i) a removal of the applicable contingency (C.A.R. Form CR), or (ii) a cancellation (C.A.R. Form CC) of this Agreement based upon a remaining contingency or Seller's failure to Deliver the specified items. However, if any report, disclosure or information for which Seller is responsible is not Delivered within the time specified in 14A, then Buyer has **5 (or ☐ _____) Days** After Delivery of any such items, or the time specified in 14B(1), whichever is later, to Deliver to Seller a removal of the applicable contingency or cancellation of this Agreement.
    (4) Continuation of Contingency: Even after the end of the time specified in 14B(1) and before Seller cancels this Agreement, if at all, pursuant to 14C, Buyer retains the right to either (i) in writing remove remaining contingencies, or (ii) cancel this Agreement based upon a remaining contingency or Seller's failure to Deliver the specified items. Once Buyer's written removal of all contingencies is Delivered to Seller, Seller may not cancel this Agreement pursuant to 14C(1).

   C. **SELLER RIGHT TO CANCEL:**
    (1) Seller right to Cancel; Buyer Contingencies: If, within time specified in this Agreement, Buyer does not, in writing, Deliver to Seller a removal of the applicable contingency or cancellation of this Agreement then Seller, after first Delivering to Buyer a Notice to Buyer to Perform (C.A.R. Form NBP) may cancel this Agreement. In such event, Seller shall authorize return of Buyer's deposit.
    (2) Seller right to Cancel; Buyer Contract Obligations: Seller, after first Delivering to Buyer a NBP may cancel this Agreement for any of the following reasons: **(i)** if Buyer fails to deposit funds as required by 3A or 3B; **(ii)** if the funds deposited pursuant to 3A or 3B are not good when deposited; **(iii)** if Buyer fails to Deliver a notice of FHA or VA costs or terms as required by 3C(3) (C.A.R. Form FVA); **(iv)** if Buyer fails to Deliver a letter as required by 3H; **(v)** if Buyer fails to Deliver verification as required by 3G or 3J; **(vi)** if Seller reasonably disapproves of the verification provided by 3G or 3J; **(vii)** if Buyer fails to return Statutory and Lead Disclosures as required by paragraph 6A(2); or **(viii)** if Buyer fails to sign or initial a separate liquidated damages form for an increased deposit as required by paragraphs 3B and 25. In such event, Seller shall authorize return of Buyer's deposit.
    (3) Notice To Buyer To Perform: The NBP shall: **(i)** be in writing; **(ii)** be signed by Seller; and **(iii)** give Buyer at least **2 (or ☐_____) Days** After Delivery (or until the time specified in the applicable paragraph, whichever occurs last) to take the applicable action. A NBP may not be Delivered any earlier than **2 Days** Prior to the expiration of the applicable time for Buyer to remove a contingency or cancel this Agreement or meet an obligation specified in 14C(2).

   D. **EFFECT OF BUYER'S REMOVAL OF CONTINGENCIES:** If Buyer removes, in writing, any contingency or cancellation rights, unless otherwise specified in a separate written agreement between Buyer and Seller, Buyer shall with regard to that contingency or cancellation right conclusively be deemed to have: **(i)** completed all Buyer Investigations, and review of reports and other applicable information and disclosures; **(ii)** elected to proceed with the transaction; and **(iii)** assumed all liability, responsibility and expense for Repairs or corrections or for inability to obtain financing.

   E. **CLOSE OF ESCROW:** Before Seller or Buyer may cancel this Agreement for failure of the other party to close escrow pursuant to this Agreement, Seller or Buyer must first Deliver to the other a demand to close escrow (C.A.R. Form DCE).

   F. **EFFECT OF CANCELLATION ON DEPOSITS:** If Buyer or Seller gives written notice of cancellation pursuant to rights duly exercised under the terms of this Agreement, Buyer and Seller agree to Sign mutual instructions to cancel the sale and escrow and release deposits, if any, to the party entitled to the funds, less fees and costs incurred by that party. Fees and costs may be payable to service providers and vendors for services and products provided during escrow. **Release of funds will require mutual Signed release instructions from Buyer and Seller, judicial decision or arbitration award. A Buyer or Seller may be subject to a civil penalty of up to $1,000 for refusal to sign such instructions if no good faith dispute exists as to who is entitled to the deposited funds (Civil Code §1057.3).**

15. **REPAIRS:** Repairs shall be completed prior to final verification of condition unless otherwise agreed in writing. Repairs to be performed at Seller's expense may be performed by Seller or through others, provided that the work complies with applicable Law, including governmental permit, inspection and approval requirements. Repairs shall be performed in a good, skillful manner with materials of quality and appearance comparable to existing materials. It is understood that exact restoration of appearance or cosmetic items following all Repairs may not be possible. Seller shall: **(i)** obtain receipts for Repairs performed by others; **(ii)** prepare a written statement indicating the Repairs performed by Seller and the date of such Repairs; and **(iii)** provide Copies of receipts and statements to Buyer prior to final verification of condition.

16. **FINAL VERIFICATION OF CONDITION:** Buyer shall have the right to make a final inspection of the Property within **5 (or _____) Days** Prior to Close Of Escrow, NOT AS A CONTINGENCY OF THE SALE, but solely to confirm: **(i)** the Property is maintained pursuant to paragraph 9; **(ii)** Repairs have been completed as agreed; and **(iii)** Seller has complied with Seller's other obligations under this Agreement (C.A.R. Form VP).

17. **PRORATIONS OF PROPERTY TAXES AND OTHER ITEMS:** Unless otherwise agreed in writing, the following items shall be PAID CURRENT and prorated between Buyer and Seller as of Close Of Escrow: real property taxes and assessments, interest, rents, HOA regular, special, and emergency dues and assessments imposed prior to Close Of Escrow, premiums on insurance assumed by Buyer, payments on bonds and assessments assumed by Buyer, and payments on Mello-Roos and other Special Assessment District bonds and assessments that are a current lien. The following items shall be assumed by Buyer WITHOUT CREDIT toward the purchase price: prorated payments on Mello-Roos and other Special Assessment District bonds and assessments and HOA special assessments that are a current lien but not yet due. Property will be reassessed upon change of ownership. Any supplemental tax bills shall be paid as follows: **(i)** for periods after Close Of Escrow, by Buyer; and **(ii)** for periods prior to Close Of Escrow, by Seller (see C.A.R. Form SPT or SBSA for further information). TAX BILLS ISSUED AFTER CLOSE OF ESCROW SHALL BE HANDLED DIRECTLY BETWEEN BUYER AND SELLER. Prorations shall be made based on a 30-day month.

Buyer's Initials (_____)(_____)   Seller's Initials (_____)(_____)

RPA-CA REVISED 4/10 (PAGE 5 OF 8)   Reviewed by _____ Date _____   EQUAL HOUSING OPPORTUNITY

CALIFORNIA RESIDENTIAL PURCHASE AGREEMENT (RPA-CA PAGE 5 OF 8)

FIGURE 7.1 *(Continued)*

Property Address: _____   Date: _____

18. **SELECTION OF SERVICE PROVIDERS:** Brokers do not guarantee the performance of any vendors, service or product providers ("Providers"), whether referred by Broker or selected by Buyer, Seller or other person. Buyer and Seller may select ANY Providers of their own choosing.

19. **MULTIPLE LISTING SERVICE ("MLS"):** Brokers are authorized to report to the MLS a pending sale and, upon Close Of Escrow, the sales price and other terms of this transaction shall be provided to the MLS to be published and disseminated to persons and entities authorized to use the information on terms approved by the MLS.

20. **EQUAL HOUSING OPPORTUNITY:** The Property is sold in compliance with federal, state and local anti-discrimination Laws.

21. **ATTORNEY FEES:** In any action, proceeding, or arbitration between Buyer and Seller arising out of this Agreement, the prevailing Buyer or Seller shall be entitled to reasonable attorney fees and costs from the non-prevailing Buyer or Seller, except as provided in paragraph 26A.

22. **DEFINITIONS:** As used in this Agreement:
    A. **"Acceptance"** means the time the offer or final counter offer is accepted in writing by a party and is delivered to and personally received by the other party or that party's authorized agent in accordance with the terms of this offer or a final counter offer.
    B. **"C.A.R. Form"** means the specific form referenced or another comparable form agreed to by the parties.
    C. **"Close Of Escrow"** means the date the grant deed, or other evidence of transfer of title, is recorded.
    D. **"Copy"** means copy by any means including photocopy, NCR, facsimile and electronic.
    E. **"Days"** means calendar days. However, after Acceptance, the last **Day** for performance of any act required by this Agreement (including Close Of Escrow) shall not include any Saturday, Sunday, or legal holiday and shall instead be the next Day.
    F. **"Days After"** means the specified number of calendar days after the occurrence of the event specified, not counting the calendar date on which the specified event occurs, and ending at 11:59 PM on the final day.
    G. **"Days Prior"** means the specified number of calendar days before the occurrence of the event specified, not counting the calendar date on which the specified event is scheduled to occur.
    H. **"Deliver", "Delivered"** or **"Delivery"**, regardless of the method used (i.e. messenger, mail, email, fax, other), means and shall be effective upon (i) personal receipt by Buyer or Seller or the individual Real Estate Licensee for that principal as specified in paragraph D of the section titled Real Estate Brokers on page 8;
    OR (ii) if checked, ☐ per the attached addendum (C.A.R. Form RDN).
    I. **"Electronic Copy"** or **"Electronic Signature"** means, as applicable, an electronic copy or signature complying with California Law. Buyer and Seller agree that electronic means will not be used by either party to modify or alter the content or integrity of this Agreement without the knowledge and consent of the other party.
    J. **"Law"** means any law, code, statute, ordinance, regulation, rule or order, which is adopted by a controlling city, county, state or federal legislative, judicial or executive body or agency.
    K. **"Repairs"** means any repairs (including pest control), alterations, replacements, modifications or retrofitting of the Property provided for under this Agreement.
    L. **"Signed"** means either a handwritten or electronic signature on an original document, Copy or any counterpart.

23. **BROKER COMPENSATION:** Seller or Buyer, or both, as applicable, agree(s) to pay compensation to Broker as specified in a separate written agreement between Broker and that Seller or Buyer. Compensation is payable upon Close Of Escrow, or if escrow does not close, as otherwise specified in the agreement between Broker and that Seller or Buyer.

24. **JOINT ESCROW INSTRUCTIONS TO ESCROW HOLDER:**
    A. **The following paragraphs, or applicable portions thereof, of this Agreement constitute the joint escrow instructions of Buyer and Seller to Escrow Holder,** which Escrow Holder is to use along with any related counter offers and addenda, and any additional mutual instructions to close the escrow: 1, 3, 4, 6C, 11B and D, 12, 13B, 14F, 17, 22, 23, 24, 28, 30, and paragraph D of the section titled Real Estate Brokers on page 8. If a Copy of the separate compensation agreement(s) provided for in paragraph 23, or paragraph D of the section titled Real Estate Brokers on page 8 is deposited with Escrow Holder by Broker, Escrow Holder shall accept such agreement(s) and pay out of Buyer's or Seller's funds, or both, as applicable, the respective Broker's compensation provided for in such agreement(s). The terms and conditions of this Agreement not specifically referenced above, in the specified paragraphs are additional matters for the information of Escrow Holder, but about which Escrow Holder need not be concerned. Buyer and Seller will receive Escrow Holder's general provisions directly from Escrow Holder and will execute such provisions upon Escrow Holder's request. To the extent the general provisions are inconsistent or conflict with this Agreement, the general provisions will control as to the duties and obligations of Escrow Holder only. Buyer and Seller will execute additional instructions, documents and forms provided by Escrow Holder that are reasonably necessary to close the escrow.
    B. A Copy of this Agreement shall be delivered to Escrow Holder within **3** business days after Acceptance (or ☐ _____). Escrow Holder shall provide Seller's Statement of Information to Title company when received from Seller. Buyer and Seller authorize Escrow Holder to accept and rely on Copies and Signatures as defined in this Agreement as originals, to open escrow and for other purposes of escrow. The validity of this Agreement as between Buyer and Seller is not affected by whether or when Escrow Holder Signs this Agreement.
    C. Brokers are a party to the escrow for the sole purpose of compensation pursuant to paragraph 23 and paragraph D of the section titled Real Estate Brokers on page 8. Buyer and Seller irrevocably assign to Brokers compensation specified in paragraph 23, respectively, and irrevocably instruct Escrow Holder to disburse those funds to Brokers at Close Of Escrow or pursuant to any other mutually executed cancellation agreement. Compensation instructions can be amended or revoked only with the written consent of Brokers. Buyer and Seller shall release and hold harmless Escrow Holder from any liability resulting from Escrow Holder's payment to Broker(s) of compensation pursuant to this Agreement. Escrow Holder shall immediately notify Brokers: **(i)** if Buyer's initial or any additional deposit is not made pursuant to this Agreement, or is not good at time of deposit with Escrow Holder; or **(ii)** if either Buyer or Seller instruct Escrow Holder to cancel escrow.
    D. A Copy of any amendment that affects any paragraph of this Agreement for which Escrow Holder is responsible shall be delivered to Escrow Holder within **2** business days after mutual execution of the amendment.

Buyer's Initials (_____)(_____)

Seller's Initials (_____)(_____)

RPA-CA REVISED 4/10 (PAGE 6 OF 8)

Reviewed by _____ Date _____

CALIFORNIA RESIDENTIAL PURCHASE AGREEMENT (RPA-CA PAGE 6 OF 8)

FIGURE 7.1   (*Continued*)

Property Address: _____   Date: _____

25. **LIQUIDATED DAMAGES:** If Buyer fails to complete this purchase because of Buyer's default, Seller shall retain, as liquidated damages, the deposit actually paid. If the Property is a dwelling with no more than four units, one of which Buyer intends to occupy, then the amount retained shall be no more than 3% of the purchase price. Any excess shall be returned to Buyer. Release of funds will require mutual, Signed release instructions from both Buyer and Seller, judicial decision or arbitration award. **AT TIME OF THE INCREASED DEPOSIT BUYER AND SELLER SHALL SIGN A SEPARATE LIQUIDATED DAMAGES PROVISION FOR ANY INCREASED DEPOSIT (C.A.R. FORM RID).**

Buyer's Initials _____ / _____	Seller's Initials _____ / _____

26. **DISPUTE RESOLUTION:**
   A. **MEDIATION:** Buyer and Seller agree to mediate any dispute or claim arising between them out of this Agreement, or any resulting transaction, before resorting to arbitration or court action. **Buyer and Seller also agree to mediate any disputes or claims with Broker(s) who, in writing, agree to such mediation prior to, or within a reasonable time after, the dispute or claim is presented to the Broker.** Mediation fees, if any, shall be divided equally among the parties involved. If, for any dispute or claim to which this paragraph applies, any party (i) commences an action without first attempting to resolve the matter through mediation, or (ii) before commencement of an action, refuses to mediate after a request has been made, then that party shall not be entitled to recover attorney fees, even if they would otherwise be available to that party in any such action. THIS MEDIATION PROVISION APPLIES WHETHER OR NOT THE ARBITRATION PROVISION IS INITIALED. **Exclusions from this mediation agreement are specified in paragraph 26C.**

   B. **ARBITRATION OF DISPUTES:**
   Buyer and Seller agree that any dispute or claim in Law or equity arising between them out of this Agreement or any resulting transaction, which is not settled through mediation, shall be decided by neutral, binding arbitration. Buyer and Seller also agree to arbitrate any disputes or claims with Broker(s) who, in writing, agree to such arbitration prior to, or within a reasonable time after, the dispute or claim is presented to the Broker. The arbitrator shall be a retired judge or justice, or an attorney with at least 5 years of residential real estate Law experience, unless the parties mutually agree to a different arbitrator. The parties shall have the right to discovery in accordance with Code of Civil Procedure §1283.05. In all other respects, the arbitration shall be conducted in accordance with Title 9 of Part 3 of the Code of Civil Procedure. Judgment upon the award of the arbitrator(s) may be entered into any court having jurisdiction. Enforcement of this agreement to arbitrate shall be governed by the Federal Arbitration Act. Exclusions from this arbitration agreement are specified in paragraph 26C.
   "NOTICE: BY INITIALING IN THE SPACE BELOW YOU ARE AGREEING TO HAVE ANY DISPUTE ARISING OUT OF THE MATTERS INCLUDED IN THE 'ARBITRATION OF DISPUTES' PROVISION DECIDED BY NEUTRAL ARBITRATION AS PROVIDED BY CALIFORNIA LAW AND YOU ARE GIVING UP ANY RIGHTS YOU MIGHT POSSESS TO HAVE THE DISPUTE LITIGATED IN A COURT OR JURY TRIAL. BY INITIALING IN THE SPACE BELOW YOU ARE GIVING UP YOUR JUDICIAL RIGHTS TO DISCOVERY AND APPEAL, UNLESS THOSE RIGHTS ARE SPECIFICALLY INCLUDED IN THE 'ARBITRATION OF DISPUTES' PROVISION. IF YOU REFUSE TO SUBMIT TO ARBITRATION AFTER AGREEING TO THIS PROVISION, YOU MAY BE COMPELLED TO ARBITRATE UNDER THE AUTHORITY OF THE CALIFORNIA CODE OF CIVIL PROCEDURE. YOUR AGREEMENT TO THIS ARBITRATION PROVISION IS VOLUNTARY."
   "WE HAVE READ AND UNDERSTAND THE FOREGOING AND AGREE TO SUBMIT DISPUTES ARISING OUT OF THE MATTERS INCLUDED IN THE 'ARBITRATION OF DISPUTES' PROVISION TO NEUTRAL ARBITRATION."

Buyer's Initials _____ / _____	Seller's Initials _____ / _____

   C. **ADDITIONAL MEDIATION AND ARBITRATION TERMS:**
      (1) EXCLUSIONS: The following matters shall be excluded from mediation and arbitration: (i) a judicial or non-judicial foreclosure or other action or proceeding to enforce a deed of trust, mortgage or installment land sale contract as defined in Civil Code §2985; (ii) an unlawful detainer action; (iii) the filing or enforcement of a mechanic's lien; and (iv) any matter that is within the jurisdiction of a probate, small claims or bankruptcy court. The filing of a court action to enable the recording of a notice of pending action, for order of attachment, receivership, injunction, or other provisional remedies, shall not constitute a waiver or violation of the mediation and arbitration provisions.
      (2) BROKERS: Brokers shall not be obligated or compelled to mediate or arbitrate unless they agree to do so in writing. Any Broker(s) participating in mediation or arbitration shall not be deemed a party to the Agreement.

27. **TERMS AND CONDITIONS OF OFFER:**
   This is an offer to purchase the Property on the above terms and conditions. The liquidated damages paragraph or the arbitration of disputes paragraph is incorporated in this Agreement if initialed by all parties or if incorporated by mutual agreement in a counter offer or addendum. If at least one but not all parties initial such paragraph(s), a counter offer is required until agreement is reached. Seller has the right to continue to offer the Property for sale and to accept any other offer at any time prior to notification of Acceptance. If this offer is accepted and Buyer subsequently defaults, Buyer may be responsible for payment of Brokers' compensation. This Agreement and any supplement, addendum or modification, including any Copy, may be Signed in two or more counterparts, all of which shall constitute one and the same writing.

28. **TIME OF ESSENCE; ENTIRE CONTRACT; CHANGES:** Time is of the essence. All understandings between the parties are incorporated in this Agreement. Its terms are intended by the parties as a final, complete and exclusive expression of their Agreement with respect to its subject matter, and may not be contradicted by evidence of any prior agreement or contemporaneous oral agreement. If any provision of this Agreement is held to be ineffective or invalid, the remaining provisions will nevertheless be given full force and effect. Except as otherwise specified, this Agreement shall be interpreted and disputes shall be resolved in accordance with the laws of the State of California. **Neither this Agreement nor any provision in it may be extended, amended, modified, altered or changed, except in writing Signed by Buyer and Seller.**

Buyer's Initials (_____)(_____)   Seller's Initials (_____)(_____)

RPA-CA REVISED 4/10 (PAGE 7 OF 8)

Reviewed by _____ Date _____

CALIFORNIA RESIDENTIAL PURCHASE AGREEMENT (RPA-CA PAGE 7 OF 8)

FIGURE 7.1 *(Continued)*

Property Address: _____ Date: _____

29. **EXPIRATION OF OFFER:** This offer shall be deemed revoked and the deposit shall be returned unless the offer is Signed by Seller and a Copy of the Signed offer is personally received by Buyer, or by _____, who is authorized to receive it, by 5:00 PM on the third Day after this offer is signed by Buyer (or, if checked,
☐ by _____ ☐AM/☐PM, on _____(date)).
Buyer has read and acknowledges receipt of a Copy of the offer and agrees to the above confirmation of agency relationships.

Date _____   Date _____
BUYER _____   BUYER _____

(Print name) _____   **(Print name)** _____

(Address) _____
☐ Additional Signature Addendum attached (C.A.R. Form ASA).

30. **ACCEPTANCE OF OFFER:** Seller warrants that Seller is the owner of the Property, or has the authority to execute this Agreement. Seller accepts the above offer, agrees to sell the Property on the above terms and conditions, and agrees to the above confirmation of agency relationships. Seller has read and acknowledges receipt of a Copy of this Agreement, and authorizes Broker to Deliver a Signed Copy to Buyer.
☐ (If checked) **SUBJECT TO ATTACHED COUNTER OFFER (C.A.R. Form CO) DATED:** _____.

Date _____   Date _____
SELLER _____   SELLER _____

(Print name) _____   **(Print name)** _____

(Address) _____
☐ Additional Signature Addendum attached (C.A.R. Form ASA).

(____/____) **CONFIRMATION OF ACCEPTANCE:** A Copy of Signed Acceptance was personally received by Buyer or Buyer's
(Initials) authorized agent on (date) _____ at _____ ☐AM/☐PM. **A binding Agreement is created when a Copy of Signed Acceptance is personally received by Buyer or Buyer's authorized agent whether or not confirmed in this document. Completion of this confirmation is not legally required in order to create a binding Agreement. It is solely intended to evidence the date that Confirmation of Acceptance has occurred.**

REAL ESTATE BROKERS:
A. Real Estate Brokers are not parties to the Agreement between Buyer and Seller.
B. Agency relationships are confirmed as stated in paragraph 2.
C. If specified in paragraph 3A(2), Agent who submitted the offer for Buyer acknowledges receipt of deposit.
D. **COOPERATING BROKER COMPENSATION:** Listing Broker agrees to pay Cooperating Broker **(Selling Firm)** and Cooperating Broker agrees to accept, out of Listing Broker's proceeds in escrow: **(i)** the amount specified in the MLS, provided Cooperating Broker is a Participant of the MLS in which the Property is offered for sale or a reciprocal MLS; or **(ii)** ☐ (if checked) the amount specified in a separate written agreement (C.A.R. Form CBC) between Listing Broker and Cooperating Broker. Declaration of License and Tax (C.A.R. Form DLT) may be used to document that tax reporting will be required or that an exemption exists.

Real Estate Broker (Selling Firm) _____ DRE Lic. #_____
By _____ DRE Lic. # _____ Date _____
Address _____ City _____ State _____ Zip _____
Telephone _____ Fax _____ E-mail _____
Real Estate Broker (Listing Firm) _____ DRE Lic. #_____
By _____ DRE Lic. # _____ Date _____
Address _____ City _____ State _____ Zip _____
Telephone _____ Fax _____ E-mail _____

ESCROW HOLDER ACKNOWLEDGMENT:
Escrow Holder acknowledges receipt of a Copy of this Agreement, (if checked, ☐ a deposit in the amount of $ _____),
counter offer numbered _____, ☐ Seller's Statement of Information and ☐ Other _____
_____, and agrees to act as Escrow Holder subject to paragraph 24 of this Agreement, any supplemental escrow instructions and the terms of Escrow Holder's general provisions if any.

Escrow Holder is advised that the date of Confirmation of Acceptance of the Agreement as between Buyer and Seller is _____.

Escrow Holder _____ Escrow # _____
By _____ Date _____
Address _____
Phone/Fax/E-mail _____
Escrow Holder is licensed by the California Department of ☐ Corporations, ☐ Insurance, ☐ Real Estate. License # _____

PRESENTATION OF OFFER: (_____) Listing Broker presented this offer to Seller on _____(date).
                                        Broker or Designee Initials

---

REJECTION OF OFFER: (_____)(_____) No counter offer is being made. This offer was rejected by Seller on_____(date).
                                Seller's Initials

THIS FORM HAS BEEN APPROVED BY THE CALIFORNIA ASSOCIATION OF REALTORS® (C.A.R.). NO REPRESENTATION IS MADE AS TO THE LEGAL VALIDITY OR ADEQUACY OF ANY PROVISION IN ANY SPECIFIC TRANSACTION. A REAL ESTATE BROKER IS THE PERSON QUALIFIED TO ADVISE ON REAL ESTATE TRANSACTIONS. IF YOU DESIRE LEGAL OR TAX ADVICE, CONSULT AN APPROPRIATE PROFESSIONAL.

This form is available for use by the entire real estate industry. It is not intended to identify the user as a REALTOR®. REALTOR® is a registered collective membership mark which may be used only by members of the NATIONAL ASSOCIATION OF REALTORS® who subscribe to its Code of Ethics.

R I	Published and Distributed by:
N	REAL ESTATE BUSINESS SERVICES, INC.
B S	*a subsidiary of the CALIFORNIA ASSOCIATION OF REALTORS®*
C	525 South Virgil Avenue, Los Angeles, California 90020

Reviewed by _____
Broker or Designee _____ Date _____

🏠 EQUAL HOUSING OPPORTUNITY

REVISION DATE 4/10

CALIFORNIA RESIDENTIAL PURCHASE AGREEMENT (RPA-CA PAGE 8 OF 8)

Source: Reprinted with permission of California Association of REALTORS®.

Paragraph 2: Agency

A. Both buyer and seller acknowledge receipt of C.A.R. form AD "Disclosure Regarding Real Estate Agency Relationships."

B. Buyer and seller acknowledge receipt of disclosure of possible multiple representations by the broker and notifies each party that her broker may be representing more than one buyer for the same type of property. This disclosure may be a part of a listing agreement, buyer representation agreement, or separate document (C.A.R. for DA).

C. This paragraph is where the final determination and election of the type of agency representation is confirmed and disclosed to all parties.

Paragraph 3: Finance Terms

Creates a financing contingency if the property is being financed. Real estate professionals have a duty to see that all financial obligations and commitments regarding real estate transactions are in writing and express the exact agreement of the parties. A copy of each contract must be furnished to each party immediately after signing the contract.

A. Write the amount of the initial deposit, also called the *earnest money deposit*. Be sure the amount is commensurate with the price of the property. A small deposit may make a buyer look insincere to the seller. Check the appropriate box and indicate in writing where the deposit is to be placed.

B. Provision is made for increasing the earnest money deposit (often to a total deposit equal to 3 percent of the purchase price). This is often done within ten days after final acceptance of the offer or immediately after the buyer waives the inspection contingency.

C. Fill in the amount of the new first loan, if any, and the terms that the buyer has either qualified for or hopes to obtain. Check the box indicating the type of loan the buyer wants. In the event that the buyer is unable to obtain the requested financing, she is relieved of any further obligation to purchase the home and is entitled to a return of her deposit. Consider setting the loan fee and interest rate slightly above current market rates so that a minor fluctuation will not relieve the buyer of her obligation to purchase the property, provided the buyer qualifies at the rate you set.

D. Fill in the amount of any secondary financing, including any seller carryback financing, complete the appropriate addendum, and present the addendum with the offer. This form also includes space for any special terms or conditions that are not on the addendums.

E. Provision is made for the balance of down payment or the purchase price to be deposited prior to escrow closing. If financing is involved, this line will contain the balance of the down payment; for a cash offer, this line will have the balance of the entire purchase price.

F. This paragraph shows the total purchase price. (Note: Be sure that lines A through E total the purchase price shown on line F.)

G. Provides that the buyer or buyer's lender shall deliver to seller written verification of the availability of the down payment and closing costs.

H. Provides that the buyer submit a prequalification or pre-approval letter to the seller from a lender, based on the loan application and credit report, within seven days or other designated time. This paragraph also provides that the loan contingency be removed within seventeen days or other specified time. There is a provision that [3H(4)], if the box is checked, there is no loan contingency. You must waive the loan contingency in writing.

I. Provides for Appraisal contingency and Removal. This paragraph states that the sale is contingent on the appraisal will be at least equal the purchase price. If the box is checked, the sale is NOT contingent on the appraisal meeting the purchase price; however, any reference in the contract creating an appraisal contingency must be waived in writing within seventeen days or upon waiver of the loan contingency.

J. This paragraph is checked only if the buyer is paying all cash for the property. It creates a duty on the buyer to give the seller written verification of the buyer's funds in sufficient amount to close the transaction.

K. The seller relies on buyers stated financing. Should buyer seek alternative financing seller is under no obligation to cooperate with buyer's efforts to obtain such financing.

Paragraph 4: Allocation of Costs

Paragraphs A through D of this section spell out who is responsible for payment of the fees for inspections or services mentioned.

A. **Inspections and Reports**. By checking either Buyer or Seller, the buyer may elect the person responsible for payment of the pest inspection and the name of the company that will perform the inspection. Paragraph 4A2,3,4 cover Septic/Sewage or other disposal systems, wells and water tests and natural hazard zone disclosure report provider. The report is limited to accessible

areas of the main building and any attached structures. The seller's consent must be obtained before performing water tests on upper-floor units. Other inspections and reports may be ordered by selecting the payee and inserting the information on lines 5 and 6.

B. **Government Requirements and Retrofit**. By checking the appropriate box, responsibility is allocated to the buyer or seller for smoke detector installation and water heater bracing, if necessary, and unless exempt, the seller must provide the buyer with a statement of compliance prior to close of escrow. By checking the second box, compliance with any other government mandated retrofit standards is allocated to the buyer or seller, if applicable.

C. **Escrow and Title**. By checking the boxes, the buyer states who shall be responsible for payment of the owner's title policy fee and the escrow fee. The agreement defaults to the buyer paying for her ALTA lender's title policy.

D. **Other Costs**. Various transfer taxes and/or fees as appropriate are allocated here, as well as the election of a home warranty including the company providing the warranty and the person who will pay for it.

Paragraph 5: Closing and Possession

A. This paragraph defaults to the buyer intending to occupy the premises as her primary residence. By checking the box, the buyer states that she will not be occupying the property. By not checking the box and declaring owner-occupancy when the buyer has no intention of doing so, it is considered lender fraud.

B. This paragraph specifies the time on the escrow closing date that the buyer will get possession of the property; or, if the seller is to remain in possession, the appropriate box is checked and the occupancy date is inserted. There is a recommendation to use an addendum to create the proper rental agreement after escrow closes and an advisory to consult with the buyer's legal or insurance advisor.

C. If property is tenant occupied, this paragraph advises the seller that she is to have the property vacated at least five days prior to close of escrow and that if the property cannot be vacated by the specified time, the seller could be in breach of contract. If the property is tenant occupied, the box is checked, making the sale subject to tenant's rights, and the C.A.R. form PAA is incorporated with this contract. There is also a box specifying that the contract be contingent on the parties reaching an

agreement, within a specified time, as to when the property will be vacated. It also states that the contract can be voided if the parties do not reach an occupancy agreement.

D. In this paragraph, all warranties on items included in the sale are assigned to the buyer, and the seller agrees to give the buyer available copies of any warranties. It also relieves the brokers of any responsibility for determining the assignability of warranties.

E. This paragraph states that the seller must provide the buyer with all keys or means of entry to the property, including mailboxes and garages. Also, if a homeowner's association requires a key deposit, the buyer agrees to pay it.

Paragraph 6: Statutory Disclosures (Including Lead-Based Paint Hazard Disclosures) and Cancellation Rights

A. (1) This paragraph mandates that the seller give the buyer all legally required disclosures required by law. These include, but are not limited to, the lead-based paint disclosure and pamphlet, Real Estate Transfer Disclosure Statement (TDS), Natural Hazard Disclosure Statement, release of illegal controlled substances, inclusion in a Mello-Roos Community Facilities Act, and C.A.R. form SSD or SPQ, which discloses an industrial use or military ordnance location.

(2) This paragraph mandates the buyer to sign and return the disclosures to the seller within the time prescribed in Paragraph 14B(1).

(3) This paragraph states that the seller has a duty to notify the buyer in writing if, during the escrow, she becomes aware of any adverse conditions or changes to the property or inaccuracies in any of the disclosures that would affect the buyer. No notification is required for any reports ordered by the buyer.

(4) This paragraph gives the buyer a right of rescission within a specified time after receiving disclosures from the seller. Lead disclosures sent by mail must be sent by certified mail or better, and the buyer and seller may not waive the lead disclosures, by law.

(5) Note to buyer that waiver of Statutory and Lead Disclosures is prohibited by law.

B. **Natural and Environmental Hazards**. This paragraph mandates that the seller provide the buyer with all pamphlets and guides relating to earthquake, fire, flood, and environmental issues within the time specified in Paragraph 14A.

C. **Withholding Taxes**. Seller shall provide buyer within the time specified an affidavit complying with Federal and State FIRPTA withholding requirements.

D. **Megan's Law Database Disclosure**. This paragraph discloses the existence of a sex offender's database maintained by the Dept. of Justice at www.meganslaw.ca.gov.

Paragraph 7: Condominium/Planned Unit Development Disclosures

A. Allows the seller seven days after acceptance (or more, as provided) to notify the buyer whether the property is a condominium or is in a PUD or common-interest subdivision. (C.A.R. form SSD.)

B. If the property is a condominium or is in a PUD or CIS, the seller has three days (or more, as provided) to order the following items from the HOA: copies of any documents required by law; any pending or anticipated litigation by or against the HOA; a statement containing the location of any parking and storage spaces; the most recent twelve months of HOA minutes for all meetings; the contact information of all HOAs governing the property (collectively, "CI Disclosures"). CI disclosures must be itemized and delivered to the buyer and the buyer's approval is a contingency of the contract as specified in Paragraph 14B(3).

Paragraph 8: Items Included and Excluded from the Purchase Price

A. **Note to Buyer and Seller**. This paragraph states that the buyer and seller are aware that the MLS sheet and any property flyers are not to be relied on for the inclusion of any items unless they are included in Paragraph 8B or C of the contract.

B. **Items Included in Sale**. This paragraph states that all fixtures currently attached to the property and any EXISTING items stated in this paragraph at the time of sale are included by reference. There is additional space for fixtures not mentioned earlier. The seller states that all items stated are owned by her and will be transferred free of liens and with no warranty.

C. **Items Excluded from Sale**. Excludes flat screen TVs and other audio equipment unless otherwise specified.

Paragraph 9: Conditions of Property

States that the property is sold in its present physical "as-is" condition as of the date of acceptance, subject to the buyer's inspection rights, shall be maintained in substantially the same condition as when the offer was accepted, and all debris and personal property shall be removed by COE.

A. Seller shall, in the time specified in 14A disclose known for the seller to disclose all material facts and defects, including insurance claims, and make other disclosures required by law.

B. Specifies buyer's right to inspect as per paragraph 14B, and based upon said inspection cancel this agreement, request seller make repairs, or take other action.

C. Advises the buyer to thoroughly investigate the property and not just rely on the seller's disclosure and advises that property may not be built to code, in compliance with current law or have permits issued.

Paragraph 10: Buyers Investigation of Property and Matters Affecting Property

A. Gives the buyer the right to conduct any and all inspections and investigations that she desires and to receive all disclosures that she is supposed to receive and makes the sale contingent on the buyer's approval of all of the above. It also states that the buyer cannot conduct invasive or destructive inspections nor have the property inspected by any building or zoning inspector unless required by law.

B. Requires the buyer to complete the inspections, waive the inspection contingency, or cancel the agreement per Paragraph 14 and give the seller copies of all reports obtained by the buyer, at no cost to the seller. The seller must have the utilities turned on for the buyer's inspectors and through the date possession is made available to the buyer.

C. Requires Seller to have utilities on for buyer's inspection and through the date possession is made to buyer.

D. **Buyer Indemnity and Seller Protection for Entry upon Property**. In this paragraph, the buyer agrees to keep the property free from mechanics' liens, repair any damage caused by her inspections, and hold the seller harmless from any claims caused by the buyer's actions or the actions of buyer's invitees onto the property. The seller is advised of protections offered by use of C.A.R. form Notice of Nonresponsibility (NNR).

Paragraph 11: Seller Disclosures: Addenda; Advisories; Other Terms

A. Provides for the inclusion of certain attached Seller Disclosures addenda, such as SPQ, SSD, or ADM advisories and supplements.

B. Addenda (if checked) Seller to provide CAR form WPA, PAA, SSA, SWPI, Seller Property Questionnaire.

C. Additional advisories such as PAK, TA, SBSA, or REO may be included if checked. Buyer's Inspection Advisory is pre-checked and must be included.

D. Other Terms and conditions may be listed here.

Paragraph 12: Title and Vesting

A. Creates the contingency of the buyer's approval of the preliminary title report.

B. Title to be taken in its present condition.

C. Per time stated in Paragraph 14A, the seller has a duty to disclose to the buyer all matters affecting the title whether recorded or not.

D. States the manner in which the buyer will receive title to the property from the seller. Advises the buyer that the manner of taking title may have legal and tax consequences. Consult a professional.

E. Advises the buyer that she will receive a CLTA/ALTA title insurance policy and that if the buyer desires different coverage, she should consult with a title company.

Paragraph 13: Sale of Buyer's Property

A. States that this agreement is not contingent upon the sale of any property owned by the buyer unless Paragraph B is checked.

B. If checked, states that CAR form COP regarding contingency sale is incorporated into this agreement.

Paragraph 14: Time Periods; Removal of Contingencies; Cancellation Rights

This paragraph states that the following time periods may only be altered by mutual written consent and any waiver of contingencies or cancellation hereunder must be in writing.

A. This paragraph gives the seller seven days (or more, as determined) after acceptance to deliver all reports that the seller is responsible for under Paragraphs 4, 6A, B and C, 7A, 9A, 11A and B, and 12A and advises that Buyer may give Seller a Notice to Seller to Perform (C.A.R. for NSP) if Seller has not delivered the items within the time specified.

B. (1) This paragraph gives the buyer seventeen days (or more, as determined) to complete all investigations and inspections, approve of all disclosures, reports, and other information and return copies of all reports to the seller.

(2) This paragraph requests repairs from the seller. Seller has no obligation to make repairs.

(3) By the time specified in Paragraph 14B(1) (or as otherwise specified in this agreement), the buyer must waive the applicable contingency or cancel the agreement. Additional time is given to the buyer for certain disclosures if the reports have not come in a timely manner.

(4) Additional time is given to the buyer for certain disclosures if the reports have not come in a timely manner. Once Buyer has delivered to Seller written removal of all contingencies Seller may not cancel this Agreement pursuant to 14C1.

C. (1) This paragraph allows the seller to cancel the sale after giving the buyer a Notice to Perform, if the buyer fails to waive any contingency as stated in the contract. It also states that failure to close escrow on time may be a breach of contract by either party.

(2) Seller right to cancel; Buyer contract obligations. Seller, after giving buyer an NBP, may cancel for a variety of reasons and return buyer deposit.

(3) The Notice to Buyer to Perform (C.A.R. form NBP) must be in writing, signed by the seller, and give the buyer at least twenty-four hours (or more, as agreed) or the time specified in the contract to perform. The notice may not be given earlier than two days prior to the expiration of the applicable time for the buyer to perform.

D. This paragraph states that if the buyer waives, in writing, any contingency or cancellation rights, she has essentially agreed that all inspections and investigations have been completed, that all reports and disclosures reviewed and, unless specified elsewhere, to proceed with the transaction and assume all liability for repairs to that cancellation right or for the inability to obtain financing.

E. **Close of Escrow.** Buyer or Seller may cancel for failure of the other party to close escrow after providing form DCE, Demand to Close Escrow.

F. If either party gives a written cancellation notice subject to rights held under the terms of the agreement, both parties agree to sign mutual cancellation instructions. All costs incurred must be paid and, if one party refuses to sign cancellation instructions without cause, she might be subject to a fine up to $1,000.

Paragraph 15: Repairs

When any repairs are necessary, the work done by the seller must be done per applicable law and in a skillful manner with like-kind

quality of materials. The seller must obtain receipts for repairs done by others, give the buyer a statement of repairs done by the seller, and provide all of the above to the buyer prior to final verification of condition.

Paragraph 16: Final Verification of Condition

The buyer has the right to make a final verification of the condition of the property within five days (or days specified) prior to close of escrow, but only to confirm repairs have been made, see that the property is in substantially the same condition as when purchased and to verify any other seller obligations. (CAR form VP).

Paragraph 17: Prorations of Property Taxes and Other Items

This paragraph spells out all of the items that the escrow agent must or may have to prorate on the escrow closing statement and states that, unless specified otherwise, all prorations will be as of the escrow closing date. It also states that tax bills issued after the close of escrow will be handled directly by the buyer and seller.

Paragraph 18: Selection of Service Providers

States that the parties may select any service provider they choose and, if brokers refer any service or product providers, they don't guarantee their performance.

Paragraph 19: Multiple Listing Service (MLS)

Authorizes the brokers to report a pending sale to the MLS and upon the close of escrow the sales price and other terms of the transaction shall be provided to the MLS. Author's Note: Without a specific Confidentiality and Non Disclosure Agreement (CND) between the buyer and seller there is no obligation to withhold this information before close of escrow.

Paragraph 20: Equal Housing Opportunity

This paragraph states that the property is sold in compliance with all federal, state, and local antidiscrimination laws.

Paragraph 21: Attorney Fees

This paragraph states that if any type of legal proceeding is initiated, the prevailing party shall be entitled to reimbursement of their attorney fees by the losing party, except as provided in Paragraph 28A.

Paragraph 22: Definitions

Subparagraphs A through L clearly state what various words, terms, and conditions mean.

Paragraph 23: Broker Compensation

Seller or buyer or both agree to pay compensation to broker as specified in a separate written agreement. Compensation to be paid upon close of escrow or as otherwise specified.

Paragraph 24: Joint Escrow Instructions to Escrow Holder

A. States the basis for the broker's compensation and acts as escrow instructions. States that in the event of a dispute between the signed escrow instructions and the purchase agreement, the escrow instructions prevail.

B. States that a copy of this agreement, which shall act as escrow instructions, shall be given to and signed for by the escrow holder.

C. Irrevocably assigns the broker's compensation from the seller's proceeds; states that the brokers are not a party to the contract except for payment of commission.

D. Gives a two-business day time limit for delivery of any contract amendments to the escrow holder.

Paragraph 25: Liquidated Damages

States that the seller is entitled to the buyer's deposit if the buyer defaults, but if the property is a one to four residential unit that the buyer intended to occupy, the damages are limited to 3 percent of the purchase price. The deposit can only be released with mutual written instructions. Buyer and seller shall sign a separate liquidated damage provision for any increased deposit. Agreement of the parties is required by initialing the box.

Paragraph 26: Dispute Resolution

A. **Mediation.** Both parties agree to mediate any disputes before resorting to arbitration. If legal action is initiated by any party without first attempting resolution through mediation, that party may be prevented from recovering attorney's fees. Parties must initial.

B. **Arbitration of Disputes.** If the parties initial this paragraph, they are agreeing to settle any dispute through binding arbitration, except for the exclusions in Paragraph 26C.

C. **Additional Mediation and Arbitration Terms:**
   (1) Exclusions are outlined
   (2) Brokers shall not be compelled to arbitrate unless they agree to do so in writing.

Paragraph 27: Terms and Conditions of Offer

This paragraph states in detail the basic terms and conditions of the agreement, allows the seller to continue to offer the property for sale and accept any offer anytime prior to notification of Acceptance. Also states that the buyer has read and received a copy of the purchase agreement. Also states that all copies of the agreement are considered originals and may be signed in counterpart.

Paragraph 28: Time of Essence; Entire Contract; Changes

States that time is of the essence; all terms and conditions of the agreement are in writing and cannot be contradicted by any oral understanding or agreement, and all changes or alterations to the contract must be in writing, signed, and agreed to by all parties.

Paragraph 29: Expiration of Offer

States that the offer will be deemed revoked unless signed by the seller and returned to the buyer or another named party (usually the broker) within a specified time. All buyers named on Page 1 must sign this paragraph, date it, and print their name(s).

Paragraph 30: Acceptance of Offer

By signing the agreement, the seller agrees to all of the terms and conditions of the offer, subject to any counteroffer if the box is checked. It confirms the agency relationships stated earlier in the contract and authorizes the broker to deliver a signed copy to the buyer. Confirmation of Acceptance: Provides a place to acknowledge personal receipt by Buyer or Buyer's authorized representative.

The box at the lower part of Page 8 should be filled in with the names of all brokers to the transaction and the escrow holder should sign for a copy as well. By signing it, the escrow holder is acknowledging receipt of the deposit that is stated in that section.

The licensee who represented the listing broker and presented the offer initials in the space provided. If the offer is rejected, the seller should initial and date in the space provided.

Short Sale

If the value of the property is less than the loan on the property, the lender might agree to a **short sale**. In a short sale, the lender agrees to accept the total proceeds of the sale as full satisfaction of

the seller's obligation, even though the proceeds will not pay off the loan, accrued interest, and penalties. This was quite prevalent in California from 1990 to 1994 and again from 2007 to 2010.

If you, as the buyer's representative, are aware that a property you are writing an offer for will be a short sale, you must include contract language that states, "This offer is contingent on the seller's lender giving the sellers and escrow company written confirmation by [date] that they will reduce their loan balance and accept a pay-off equal to the seller's net proceeds from the sale after payment of all seller-closing costs, seller-required corrective work and commissions, as payment in full." If you do not use this language in the purchase agreement and a short-sale situation exists, expect to get the above language in a counteroffer from the seller. *Caution:* If you are not familiar with the intricacies of handling a short sale, you should team up with a licensee who is. There are many areas of increased potential liability for licensees who are conducting short-sale escrows. Talk to your employing broker.

7.4 PREPARING TO PRESENT THE OFFER TO PURCHASE

Even when presented with solid facts and information, many owners are not completely convinced about the real market value of their properties when they're listed. To give your buyers the best possible representation when the sellers review their offers, you need to do some preparation.

You may have already researched and created a CMA for the buyer to assist in deciding an offer price; if not, you will need to do one now and have it with you when you present the offer or fax it to the listing licensee along with the offer if you will not be at the presentation. Also write the sellers a short, informal letter briefly describing the buyers (being careful not to violate any fair housing rules) and briefly explaining your offer, including how you arrived at the offered price, any seller concessions asked for by the buyers, and anything else that could be a major point of negotiation. Be sure to highlight all of the positive or strong points of the offer, such as a large down payment or a cash offer. If the MLS listing shows the seller's loan balance, you should also complete a seller's net proceeds sheet and take it with you or fax it in case the listing licensee hasn't done so.

Once you have called the listing licensee and established a time to present the offer to the sellers, notify your buyers and ask where they will be at that time. Tell them you will need to meet with

them right after you present the offer, as they will not be in contact until you have delivered a copy of the offer, signed by the sellers, to them; and if you get a counteroffer, you will need to go over it with them right away.

If you are presenting your offer in person, make enough copies of the purchase agreement, plus any addendums that are part of the agreement, and take them along so you, the listing seller's representative, and each of the sellers have a copy to use during the presentation.

7.5 NEGOTIATING THE OFFER WITH THE SELLERS AND LISTING LICENSEE

If possible, meet with the listing licensee before meeting with the sellers so she will be better prepared to present the offer properly.

When you meet with the sellers and their representative, it is usually best to make a little small talk before presenting the offer, allowing everyone to get comfortable with each other. Be careful not to overdo it, however, in case any type-A personalities present want to get right down to business. Before presenting the purchase agreement, you, as the selling licensee, are obligated to present a new C.A.R. form AD to the sellers for an acknowledging signature. You could say, "I know your licensee has already had a discussion of the types of agency that are available in California but as the representative of the buyer I am also required to disclose again because the sellers may not always be represented by a broker, as you are. Here is the required disclosure form. If you understand and are comfortable with this disclosure please sign this form acknowledging receipt of this copy."

Only after providing and getting the required acknowledging signature on the AD form may you then give a copy of the purchase agreement to the sellers and their representative. Ask the seller's representative to review the offer and make any notes she feels necessary. While they all review the offer, start to tell them about the buyers. Then move into small, easily negotiable parts of the offer such as the closing date, any personal property the buyers have asked for, the inclusion and benefit of a home warranty if one is requested by the buyers, the buyers' preapproval of any financing (if done), and the benefit of preapproval to the sellers. As the listing salesperson already has a relationship with the sellers, it is usually wise to let her present the price and any other major items to the sellers. If the salesperson is new or not well prepared, however, it may be best to proceed with the entire offer

presentation yourself while including the other salesperson as much as possible.

Have a legal pad with you for taking notes of any issues that evolve as the offer is presented. If the sellers make a comment like "we can't get out of the house that fast," make a note of it. It may be a great bargaining chip a little later. If you have written the offer with a well-justified purchase price and the sellers object to it, go over the comparable sales you have with you. Remember, you don't want to argue with them, so your comments should consist of comments like "I understand how you feel about your price, however, the current market data just doesn't support it. Perhaps we should take another look at the recent sales?" All references to price should come from "the market data" and not from you directly; it's much harder to argue with facts than a person.

Be aware of the sellers' and the listing licensee's body language and voice inflection. You will sometimes see and hear signs of stress (usually over price). When you experience this, it is often wise to deflect the issue for a time by bringing up an easier issue to consider, such as personal property or the closing date, and revisit the price issue a little later.

As you all go through the offer, both you and the seller's representative should be making notes about any changes to be made as well as any issues you wish to revisit before a counteroffer is made. When the discussion is nearing an end, quickly go over your notes and revisit any issues with the sellers you feel need further negotiation. Restate your buyer's case in each matter and ask the sellers if they can understand why the buyers feel as they do about each particular issue. If the sellers are about to provide a counteroffer on an issue that you know will be a deal-killer, advise the sellers and be prepared to offer suggestions that will find middle ground and keep the sale alive. As the buyer's representative, you have a duty to present the offer in as positive a manner as possible. You also have an ethical duty to recommend strongly that the owners accept the offer if you know it is in their best interests to do so.

7.6 SELLING YOUR OWN LISTING

Selling your own listing or being in a dual agency situation can be both rewarding and problematic. It can be rewarding because you receive twice the commission on a sale and the communication problems often encountered in many escrows are eliminated because you are not dealing with another licensee. You must,

however, be extra careful to keep both parties in the transaction happy while looking to both of their best interests.

Both the buyers and the owners must have informed prior consent to the dual agency situation before either of them makes any decisions. When some licensees write an offer on their own listing, they tell both the buyers and the owners that they will put up a firewall between them and ensure that both parties receive all of the information necessary to make good, informed decisions about whether to proceed with the transaction, but neither will receive any information about the other party that is damaging to their interests or inappropriate for the licensee to disclose.

Most judges are not in favor of one broker having a dual role in a transaction because of what they perceive as a conflict of interest. If you keep the Golden Rule and the code of ethics clearly in mind when you are in a dual agency situation, however, and put the clients' interests ahead of your own, you will find that your transactions will go smoothly.

7.7 HANDLING SINGLE AND MULTIPLE COUNTEROFFERS

A buyer can rescind her offer at any time prior to receiving a signed copy of the owner's acceptance of the offer, without any changes. If you get a seller's acceptance of an offer without any changes, immediately thank her, leave, and give a copy of the fully executed offer to your buyers and offer your congratulations. If you get a **counteroffer**, thank the seller and leave, but before visiting the buyer, take a few moments to decide how you will present the counteroffer. See Figure 7.2 for a sample counteroffer. Buyers can be as sensitive about receiving a counteroffer as the owners are about receiving an offer. Emotions can run high with both parties, and the better prepared you are to present an offer or any counteroffer in a calm, logical way, the more likely you will help consummate a sale. If the counteroffer contains multiple items, decide the importance of each item. When you meet with the buyers, start with the easiest issue and work up to the more emotional issues, such as price and occupancy.

If your buyers receive a counteroffer, they may (1) reject the offer and receive their earnest money deposit back, (2) accept the offer without change (in which case, you give them a signed copy and immediately return the signed counteroffer to the sellers or their licensee), or (3) counter the counteroffer.

FIGURE 7.2 Counteroffer

CALIFORNIA ASSOCIATION OF REALTORS®

COUNTER OFFER   No. _____
For use by Seller or Buyer. May be used for Multiple Counter Offer.
(C.A.R. Form CO, Revised 10/04)

Date _____, at _____, California.
This is a counter offer to the: ☐ California Residential Purchase Agreement, ☐ Counter Offer, or ☐ Other _____ ("Offer"),
dated _____, on property known as _____ ("Property"),
between _____ ("Buyer") and _____ ("Seller").

1. **TERMS:** The terms and conditions of the above referenced document are **accepted subject to the following:**
   A. **Paragraphs in the Offer that require initials by all parties, but are not initialed by all parties, are excluded from the final agreement unless specifically referenced for inclusion in paragraph 1C of this or another Counter Offer.**
   B. **Unless otherwise agreed in writing, down payment and loan amount(s) will be adjusted in the same proportion as in the original Offer.**
   C. _____
      _____
      _____
      _____
      _____
      _____
      _____
   D. **The following attached supplements are incorporated into this Counter Offer:** ☐ Addendum No. _____
      ☐ _____   ☐ _____

2. **RIGHT TO ACCEPT OTHER OFFERS:** Seller has the right to continue to offer the Property for sale or for other transaction, and to accept any other offer at any time prior to notification of acceptance, as described in paragraph 3. If this is a Seller Counter Offer, Seller's acceptance of another offer prior to Buyer's acceptance and communication of notification of this Counter Offer, shall revoke this Counter Offer.

3. **EXPIRATION:** This Counter Offer shall be deemed revoked and the deposits, if any, shall be returned unless this Counter Offer is signed by the Buyer or Seller to whom it is sent and a Copy of the signed Counter Offer is personally received by the person making this Counter Offer or _____, who is authorized to receive it, by 5:00PM on the third day after this Counter Offer is made or, (if checked) by ☐ _____ (date), at _____ AM/PM. This Counter Offer may be executed in counterparts.

4. ☐ **(If checked:) MULTIPLE COUNTER OFFER:** Seller is making a Counter Offer(s) to another prospective buyer(s) on terms that may or may not be the same as in this Counter Offer. Acceptance of this Counter Offer by Buyer shall **not** be binding unless and until it is subsequently re-Signed by Seller in paragraph 7 below and a Copy of the Counter Offer Signed in paragraph 7 is personally received by Buyer or by _____, who is authorized to receive it, by 5:00 PM on the third Day After this Counter Offer is made or, (if checked) by ☐ _____ (date), at _____ AM/PM. Prior to the completion of all of these events, Buyer and Seller shall have no duties or obligations for the purchase or sale of the Property.

5. **OFFER: BUYER OR SELLER MAKES THIS COUNTER OFFER ON THE TERMS ABOVE AND ACKNOWLEDGES RECEIPT OF A COPY.**
   _____ Date _____
   _____ Date _____

6. **ACCEPTANCE: I/WE** accept the above Counter Offer **(If checked ☐ SUBJECT TO THE ATTACHED COUNTER OFFER)** and acknowledge receipt of a Copy.
   _____ Date _____ Time _____ AM/PM
   _____ Date _____ Time _____ AM/PM

7. **MULTIPLE COUNTER OFFER SIGNATURE LINE: By signing below, Seller accepts this Multiple Counter Offer. NOTE TO SELLER: Do NOT sign in this box until after Buyer signs in paragraph 6. (Paragraph 7 applies only if paragraph 4 is checked.)**
   _____ Date _____ Time _____ AM/PM
   _____ Date _____ Time _____ AM/PM

8. (_____/_____) (Initials) **Confirmation of Acceptance:** A Copy of Signed Acceptance was personally received by the maker of the _____ Counter Offer, or that person's authorized agent as specified in paragraph 3 (or, if this is a Multiple Counter Offer, the Buyer or Buyer's authorized agent as specified in paragraph 4) on (date) _____, at _____ AM/PM. **A binding Agreement is created when a Copy of Signed Acceptance is personally received by the the maker of the Counter Offer, or that person's authorized agent (or, if this is a Multiple Counter Offer, the Buyer or Buyer's authorized agent) whether or not confirmed in this document. Completion of this confirmation is not legally required in order to create a binding Agreement; it is solely intended to evidence the date that Confirmation of Acceptance has occurred.**

SURE TRAC
The System for Success®

Published and Distributed by:
REAL ESTATE BUSINESS SERVICES, INC.
a subsidiary of the California Association of REALTORS®
525 South Virgil Avenue, Los Angeles, California 90020

Reviewed by _____ Date _____

EQUAL HOUSING OPPORTUNITY

CO REVISED 10/04 (PAGE 1 OF 1)   Print Date

COUNTER OFFER (CO PAGE 1 OF 1)

Source: Reprinted with permission of California Association of REALTORS®.

If the buyers decide to counter the counteroffer, they must sign acceptance of the original counteroffer and also check the box that states that an additional counteroffer is included. You then complete another counteroffer placing a number two next to the word "Counteroffer." Do this to keep each document in its proper sequence.

Complete the top of the new counteroffer and state succinctly the changes the buyers want. For example, the sellers counter to increase the purchase price to $820,000 and the escrow closing date to be thirty days instead of the forty-five that the buyers offered, and your buyers are in agreement with the new closing date, but only want to pay $810,000 for the property. You don't need to say anything about the change in the closing date as the buyers are in agreement, so you write, "The purchase price shall be $810,000. Down payment and loan are adjusted accordingly." Always finish each counteroffer you write with the phrase, "All other terms and conditions shall remain the same."

After you have the buyer's acceptance on the counteroffer or have written a counter to the counteroffer, immediately contact the seller's representative and either fax or personally deliver a signed copy to her. The contract is not binding until you have delivered the accepted counteroffer to the seller or their representative; deliverance is considered acceptance. In the event of a second counteroffer, immediately deliver the accepted counteroffer and counteroffer number two to the listing licensee and/or the sellers for review. This process continues until one party accepts the other's counteroffer without change.

There will be times when you represent buyers in one of several offers on the same property. The owners decide how to respond; they may wish to accept one of the offers if it is clearly better than the rest or, if all of the offers are rather similar, they may respond to all of the offers by issuing multiple counteroffers. This practice can be problematic if it is not handled properly and can even get the owners and the listing licensee in legal trouble if it isn't handled correctly.

Owners who use this method of dealing with multiple offers may risk having one or more buyers withdraw their offers because they do not wish to get involved in a bidding war.

Another way to deal with multiple offers is to counsel your sellers on which offer is the best, and counter that offer only, giving those buyers a fairly short time to respond. If they do not respond, or respond unfavorably, the owners can counter the next-best offer and so on until one party accepts their counteroffer.

7.8 BUYER'S ESTIMATED CLOSING COSTS

Some first-time buyers usually do not consider closing costs when they decide to buy a home. Instead they find out that they must come up with several thousand dollars at the last moment, which, if this information comes as a surprise, can create a difficult situation. So, while writing an offer on behalf of buyers, give them a written estimate of their closing costs. Many real estate firms and escrow companies have forms for this purpose. You are wise to obtain one and become familiar with it.

Your estimate should show all of the usual charges buyers customarily pay in your area, as well as the total down payment necessary to fulfill the terms of the purchase contract. Also calculate the buyer's monthly payment, including the loan payment and any tax or insurance impounds required by their lender. Costs for title and escrow services and lender fees vary from company to company so it is important for you to be as accurate as possible. It is a good practice to err slightly on the high side because news of having to bring more money than expected to the closing is not well received by buyers.

7.9 SETTING UP THE ESCROW TIMELINE

Once contract acceptance has been acknowledged by the buyer, open an escrow account as specified in the contract and deliver the buyer's check for the earnest money to the escrow company. Buyer's earnest money funds must be deposited with the chosen escrow company or the broker's trust account (whichever is specified in the contract) within three business days.

All of the parties to the purchase/sale of the property now have responsibilities to fulfill. If you create a timeline for everyone to work from, the escrow will go much smoother. Many escrow companies and real estate firms have preprinted forms specially made for this purpose. If one is not available, you must make your own, get a copy of it to your buyers and the seller's representative (who will hopefully give a copy to the sellers), and put one in your file.

The timeline should contain a checklist of every item or issue that needs to take place to obtain any necessary financing, conduct all necessary due diligence, provide all mandated disclosures, secure property and any other insurance required by buyers or lenders, and set a date to sign escrow instructions. The timeline should state the item, state a "to do by" date, and a completion date.

The issues that are necessary to close an escrow vary widely throughout California. Although this book does not include a detailed checklist, creating or obtaining one that is designed for your area will be a tremendous help to you and your buyers and will make for a much smoother transaction.

SUMMARY

Counseling is a prelude to selling. Selling is reading your customers and helping them decide to make a purchase.

Selling is about product knowledge, communication, discovery, knowing your customer, and persuasion. Your selling strategy should be based on the people you are with, their attitude toward the sales process, and their desire for a particular property.

Appealing to a buyer's motives, such as survival, pride of ownership, security, or a desire for comfort or convenience, is what closes a sale. Watching for buying signals and overcoming any sales resistance using closing techniques such as trial closes and alternate choice closes will help you determine when it is time to close. Sales are sometimes lost by real estate professionals because they talk when they should be listening, when they appear too eager for the sale, apply too much pressure, appear frightened, or do not possess enough knowledge to give competent advice. Being negative and arguing with the client are also reasons licensees lose sales. To represent someone properly in the purchase of a property, you must fully understand the Residential Purchase Agreement and Joint Escrow Instructions.

After writing an offer to purchase on behalf of a client, fully prepare for your presentation prior to meeting with the owners and their representative. Make sure your buyer's position is clearly stated.

In the event an offer to purchase is not acceptable to an owner, encourage the owner to issue a counteroffer to the buyers. If there are multiple offers on the same property, the owners may wish to use the **multiple counteroffer** paragraph to counter all of the offers at the same time; this is safe because the seller is not obligated to any of the buyers until she has countersigned one of the counteroffers and delivered it to the successful buyer.

Buyers entering into a purchase agreement should be told the approximate amount of their closing costs, including an itemized list of costs so everyone is assured that the buyers will have sufficient cash to close the purchase.

After you have an accepted contract, it is wise to create an escrow timeline for everyone involved so they can get things done within the time limits imposed by the contract.

CLASS DISCUSSION TOPICS

1. Use the following information to complete a Residential Purchase Agreement for the property where you currently live on behalf of Ralph and Mary Jenkins.

   - *Deposit*: $7,000 with an increase to 3 percent of the purchase price within fifteen days after final acceptance of the offer.
   - *Purchase price*: $500,000.
   - *Total down payment*: $100,000.
   - *Financing*: Contingent on obtaining a new first loan for $400,000 at an interest rate not to exceed 6 percent, with a loan fee not to exceed 1 percent of the loan amount. Loan qualification by the buyers shall be provided to the owners within five days after final acceptance of the offer.
   - *Appraisal contingency*: The offer is contingent on obtaining an appraisal for at least the purchase price.
   - *Escrow closing*: The escrow shall close within forty-five days after final acceptance of the offer.
   - *Occupancy*: This will be the buyer's primary residence.
   - *Home warranty*: The cost of a home warranty, which shall include the swimming pool and air conditioning, shall be split equally by the parties and shall not exceed a cost of $500.
   - *Personal property*: Refrigerator, washer, dryer, and pool equipment.
   - *Fees and costs*: The sellers shall pay the owner's title policy and any transfer fees. Catalina Escrow Company will conduct the escrow and the parties will split their fees. Sellers will pay for the required zone disclosure report. Sewer and well costs are not applicable and the sellers will pay to have smoke detectors installed and the water heater properly braced.
   - *Conditions*: The seller warrants the condition of the premises pursuant to Paragraph 9B(1) through (7), except for (5), which does not apply, and the time periods specified in Paragraph 16 are adequate.

2. Using another student as a buyer, role-play an assumptive close.

3. How would you overcome the following buyer objections?

   a. I don't want to sign the offer until my attorney looks it over.
   b. The price is way too high.
   c. We want to think about it overnight; we'll call you tomorrow.
   d. My rent is cheaper than the loan payment.

e. The HOA fees are really high.

f. I think I'll wait until interest rates drop a little more.

g. I'm not crazy about the location.

h. I don't want to sell until I find a house to buy.

i. I wanted an older home with charm; this is too new.

4. Describe the materials you would gather in preparing an offer presentation to a seller and listing licensee.

5. What action would you take if you are presenting an offer and the sellers tell you that they won't sell for that low price?

6. By role-playing with another student, explain your boundaries of conduct in selling your own listing.

7. Discuss what should be included in an escrow timeline.

CHAPTER 7 QUIZ

1. All of the following are buying signals except
   A. asking when they can leave to see the next house.
   B. measuring a room.
   C. rubbing the kitchen countertop.
   D. whispering with a spouse.

2. Which of the following describes a good salesperson?
   A. One who approaches every customer according to her personality type.
   B. One who uses terms the buyers can understand.
   C. One who listens carefully to the buyers' wants and needs and presents homes that meet their criteria.
   D. All of the above.

3. Which of the following should you do when writing a purchase agreement?
   A. Always ask the buyers to read it carefully before signing it.
   B. Check to see that initials and signatures are executed fully and properly.
   C. Be sure that any writing in Paragraph 28 is clear and concise.
   D. All of the above.

4. According to Paragraph 14B(1) of the purchase contract, how many days does the buyer have to complete a lead-based paint inspection?
   A. 7
   B. 17
   C. 10
   D. 5

5. Which of following is true regarding selling your own listing?
   A. It requires special care in disclosing your dual role to all parties.
   B. It is generally frowned upon by most attorneys.
   C. It is a great way to receive a full commission.
   D. All of the above.

6. What should you do before you present a counteroffer to your buyers?
   A. Call the buyers and tell them the terms of the counteroffer.
   B. Start with the price if it's been changed by the owners.
   C. Read the counteroffer to the buyers and immediately suggest another counter.
   D. See the buyers in person and go over each change made by the sellers, starting with the easiest one first.

7. Which of the following is not true about a multiple counteroffer?
   A. If there are multiple offers, the owners are obligated to counter all of the offers.
   B. The counteroffer is not fully accepted until it is signed by the buyers and countersigned by the sellers.
   C. Many buyers will walk away from a multiple counteroffer situation to avoid a bidding war.
   D. Using the multiple counteroffer section in Paragraph 2 of the counteroffer form will help avoid the possibility of selling a house to two or more people at the same time.

8. Which of the following refers to a short sale?
   A. An all-cash sale that is discounted because there is no financing contingency.
   B. A sale in which the appraisal contingency has been waived.
   C. A sale with a quick close of escrow.
   D. A sale in which the lender agrees to take the net proceeds from the sale as loan satisfaction.

9. Which of the following does not appear on an estimated buyers closing cost sheet?
   A. Loan origination fee
   B. Existing loan balance
   C. Prorated real property taxes
   D. Prorated HOA dues

10. Which of the following is a function of an escrow timeline?
   A. Acts as a reminder of important dates to all parties.
   B. Reminds all parties of the documents required to be given to whom.
   C. Reminds the licensees and principals when to be at inspections and escrow signing.
   D. All of the above.

Chapter

8

226

Preparing for the Listing Appointment

STUDENT LEARNING OUTCOMES

Upon completion of this chapter, the student will be able to:

- Plan and effect an MLS property search.
- Formulate and create a listing presentation manual including marketing plan and agenda.
- Organize and create a CMA.
- Calculate and compute an estimated seller's net proceeds from sale on a given property.

8.1 RESEARCH THOROUGHLY FIRST

When called on to give a listing presentation to the owners of a property, the worst mistake a licensee can make is to be unprepared. This happens all too often, and when it does, things almost always begin badly and get worse.

If you are unprepared, the owners often become uncomfortable. They perceive that you lack knowledge of their neighborhood. They may also feel they are in complete control and if they do list with you, they will do so at their price and their terms, which is often far too aggressive.

Take the following steps to ensure that you are in control during a listing presentation:

- Obtain comparable sales data
- Create a competitive (or comparative) market analysis (CMA)
- Create a marketing plan
- Prepare a detailed listing presentation manual

First, do a Multiple Listing Service (MLS) computer search of the property's neighborhood and obtain data on the past three to six months of activity in the following four areas: current listings, pending sales, sold (closed escrow) properties, and expired listings. Give priority to properties that have been sold in the past thirty days as most appraisers are required by lenders to give them the most credibility.

Once you have the data in hand, drive through the neighborhood and by each property you intend to include in your CMA. Make notes about each property on the MLS printouts. You may or may not have more properties than you need, so driving through the neighborhood ensures that you use the best ones in your analysis. Be sure to make an appointment and go in as many of the actively listed properties as possible to check on their condition firsthand.

8.2 COMPETITIVE (OR COMPARATIVE) MARKET ANALYSIS

CMA includes recent property sales in a target area as compared to a particular property. Usually three **comparable** properties or "comps" that have been sold and closed escrow are compared to the "subject property" (the one you hope to list), and adjustments are made for things such as lot size, property condition, location, and differing amenities such as granite countertops, two- versus three-car garage, and swimming pool versus none. The difference between the date of sale of the comp and the current date may make an additional price adjustment necessary because of current market and economic conditions.

The CMA should be limited only to residential properties and small apartment house sales. Other types of property such as land, large apartment complexes, and commercial property require a more in-depth analysis.

Once you have completed your research and driven through the neighborhood, select the closest or best comparables based on those with the most similarities to the subject property. Place the information on a computer-generated program for your analysis; once it is complete, you can transfer it to the appropriate place in the listing presentation manual.

The "active" category lists the prices current sellers are asking for their homes. As all homes in the neighborhood are essentially competing for the same general type of buyers, these homes

represent the seller's price competition and help set the general limitations of what the seller should ask for the home. Although the active list does not give any indication of what the property will actually sell for in the current market, it helps give the seller an idea of a possible sale price range and the number and type of homes that are competing for a similar buyer.

As a listing licensee, you must be careful not to price a property at a certain level based on what other owners are asking for their homes. Some of those properties may be overpriced, and you will risk overpricing the seller's property if you do this. Pricing homes in a way that allows the neighborhood homes to help sell a property is the mark of a true professional.

The "sold" section of the CMA is much more valuable than the current listing section because it shows an actual meeting of the minds between a buyer and seller where a sale actually occurred. Emphasis should be placed on the most recent sales because they reflect the most current market conditions. Market conditions can and do change over time. Appraisers are told to use comps within the past three months whenever possible. Adjusting older data for an increase or decrease in value because of current market conditions can be highly subjective. Take great care to do a thorough analysis of price trends in order to be as accurate as possible.

If some data on the sold property seems significantly higher or lower than the rest of the homes in the area, read its MLS listing carefully and call the listing licensee to find out why. Things such as a pending divorce, bankruptcy, sale in lieu of foreclosure, short sale or seller-paying-buyers' closing costs often indicate a sales price that did not reflect the true market value of the property.

If your MLS has a "sale pending" category, it will be worthwhile for you to check it and call the listing licensee of any comparable properties to determine how close to the asking price the owners received. Although many licensees think that a buyer's offered price must be kept confidential until after the close of escrow, such is not the case and never has been. In fact, unless there is a written agreement requiring confidentiality, the seller or seller's representative has no duty or obligation to keep any offer confidential. (NAR Code of Ethics Article #1, Standard of Practice 1–13) The shopping of offers has become much more prevalent with the increase of REO and foreclosure properties for sale.

The "expired" listings section of the CMA is the "losers list," or properties that did not sell. Generally, four variables can affect the value of a home: location, price, terms, and condition. Although improper pricing is the overwhelming reason a property does not

sell, these other factors may have been a contributing cause. The category of "condition" includes things such as poor curb appeal, deferred maintenance, or tenants—any one of these may have made showing the property difficult if not impossible. Conduct a reasonable investigation of expired listings you plan to include in your CMA so that any representations you make about why they did not sell are valid.

In a relatively stable market, the listing price of a property is usually slightly higher than the actual selling price; although market conditions have not reflected anything like stability for a number of years, this too will change. In any event, a careful review and discussion of recent asking price versus selling price trends with the selling owners will reveal an appropriate price range for the property. If the owners get too aggressive in their pricing strategies, review the expired listing section of your CMA and restate your case.

You will have done quite a bit of work to collect and analyze sufficient data to create an effective CMA and you need the owners to recognize that. Be sure to customize it as much as possible using supplemental information or other tools your company or MLS have for that purpose and include this additional data in your listing presentation manual. The first page should indicate that the CMA was prepared exclusively for this client (by name) by you and should include a picture of the property. The second page could describe the property in narrative form, stating all of its best features.

If any of the comparables selected have features that the home you want to list does not have, use a yellow highlighter to emphasize these features so the owners will be aware of them and appreciate the strength of the competition.

When owners decide to sell their property, they usually have some sort of timetable in mind. There is a direct relationship between the asking price of a property in relation to its actual value and the amount of time it will take to sell. By showing the owners a selling time chart, you will clearly demonstrate this fact and stand a better chance of properly pricing a listing.

8.3 THE LISTING PRESENTATION MANUAL

Once you have obtained all of the factual data regarding property values and have put it into the CMA, incorporate it into your **listing presentation manual**. The listing presentation manual is often assembled in a three-ring binder and incorporates all of the information you want to convey to the owners in a logical sequence. The order and makeup of each listing presentation manual or booklet is

largely a matter of individual taste. As this can be an important marketing tool and is subjective by nature, the look and appearance will vary with each licensee. If you are affiliated with a large multi-office or franchise company, they will no doubt have a CMA template to guide you. Keep in mind that the CMA represents your individual assessment of a particular listing and should not look identical to another licensees' interpretation of the same data.

Sections may be numbered or titled according to the creative sense of the licensee. For example, the first section could be headed "About Me" and could contain your personal resume along with copies of authorized certificates for any professional designations you have earned since obtaining your real estate license, including the benefits this additional education have to the seller. For instance, if you tell an owner that you are a Graduate of the REALTORS® Institute (GRI) and a Certified Residential Specialist (CRS), it is not likely to impress them unless they know or appreciate what those designations mean in terms of added value to their situation. If you present a feature (the designations), also present the benefit of that feature. For example, simply stating that you are a GRI and a CRS does almost nothing to make owners comfortable that you are the right person to represent them. Pointing out that as a GRI and a CRS you are better educated in real estate brokerage matters than 95 percent of the nation's real estate licensees and you are a highly skilled negotiator that will help the owners get top dollar for their home in a shorter time will get and hold the owners' attention. Whenever possible, tie a feature to a benefit.

The second section could be headed "What My Clients Say About Me" and could include copies of any complimentary letters or thank-you notes received from satisfied customers. This is probably the most powerful section in the manual because it is a direct third-party endorsement from people who have already experienced working with you and the benefit of your services. Every time you close an escrow, you should ask the clients if they would please send a short letter to your broker telling her about how they were treated. This can be a powerful marketing tool! Most sellers will stop everything to read these letters before proceeding. Often, a look of confidence on their faces will be plainly visible.

The third section could be "About My Company." Here is where you could put any features about your company you feel will be of benefit to a seller, such as your company's standing in the marketplace (if appropriate), listing volume, or listing conversion rate. This section should make the owners feel comfortable that your firm has the resources to represent them properly.

The fourth section could be your "Advertising and Marketing Plan" and should detail, both in graphics and in timeline form, exactly what you and your firm will do to advertise and market a property to attract potential buyers.

The fifth section could be headed "CMA." Title the last page of the CMA "Value Conclusions" and state what the market indicates the value range is (a low and a high), the probable sales price, and the recommended asking or list price.

Giving a range of value shows that no one person ever sets the value of a property. Instead it is set by a willing buyer and a willing seller through negotiation. Market conditions can also dictate variations in market value. The terms that a buyer offers, such as a cash offer with a quick close and few contingencies, can affect the market value. If you quote only one price, many, if not most, sellers become fixated on that price, when in reality an offer on good terms for slightly less may be just as valid.

Including the value conclusions at the end of the listing presentation manual allows you the time to get through the rest of the important features of the analysis before getting into pricing. It also allows the owners time to get comfortable with you and gain confidence in you before being presented with the pricing issue.

8.4 ESTIMATED SELLER'S PROCEEDS FORM

Every owner who puts their property on the market is usually interested in two important things:

1. How much money will I net from the sale of my property?
2. How soon will I get it?

For most owners, it is important to know how much money they will end up with after they sell their property because they usually need to reinvest all or most of the net proceeds into replacement property. Your ability to calculate an owner's net proceeds helps the seller better plan the next move and often takes focus away from trying to get an unobtainable price for the property. If you are conservative with your anticipated selling price and slightly liberal with your costs of sale, the owner will usually end up netting more money than you have estimated. Getting more than they expected will make this a more pleasant experience for the seller.

Many computer programs are available that will automatically estimate a seller's proceeds for you. For the times when you are at an owner's home or office without access to these programs, you should

know how to complete California Association of REALTORS® (C.A.R.) Estimated Seller's Proceeds form (see Figure 9.4). It is an excellent form that sellers find easy to understand. Most title and escrow companies are happy to provide this service as well.

Complete an Estimated Seller's Proceeds form at the list price when you list a property, and when an offer is presented at less than the list price, complete another form to restate the new proceeds that would be realized from a sale at the offered price.

SUMMARY

There is no substitute for complete and proper preparation when going on a listing appointment.

Pricing a property correctly entails doing a substantial amount of research including obtaining MLS information about similar properties in the same neighborhood, physically looking at properties and comparing them to the property you wish to list, making adjustments for any differences, and arriving at a value range. This is called CMA. When arriving at a value conclusion, the greatest weight should be given to sold properties as they represent actual sales in which a willing buyer and seller agreed to a property's value.

Sales that are significantly higher or lower than the rest of the comps should be investigated to see if there were special circumstances that affected the value of the property.

Use a form to show the sellers the economic trends in the local marketplace including the differences between listing and selling prices. Your CMA should become a part of your listing presentation manual. The manual should include a section about you, your company, your proposed marketing and advertising plan, the CMA, and a separate page with your value conclusions along with your recommended list price and selling price range.

Carefully calculate the owners' net sale proceeds using an easy-to-read Estimated Seller's Proceeds form.

CLASS DISCUSSION TOPICS

1. Prepare a CMA for the property where you currently live and present it to another student who is acting as the owner. Explain how you arrived at your recommended list price and market value range.

2. Prepare an Estimated Seller's Proceeds form for the property where you currently live or a fictitious one using the following information:
   - $500,000 sale price.
   - $220,000 existing loan at 6 percent interest per annum will be paid off.
   - Seller will carry back a new $50,000 second loan at 8 percent.
   - Seller will pay a 6 percent commission.

   (For this exercise, do not prorate taxes, insurance, HOA dues, or loan interest.)

3. Prepare the "About My Company" section of the listing presentation manual. Be prepared to role-play a discussion about it in class with another student acting as an owner.

CHAPTER 8 QUIZ

1. A CMA is best described in which one of the following ways?
   A. The comparative mortgage analysis.
   B. A formal appraisal.
   C. A reflection of the realities of the marketplace.
   D. A comparison of asking prices to selling prices.

2. A CMA should only be used to evaluate which of the following properties?
   A. Single family and one to four residential unit properties.
   B. Commercial and residential income property.
   C. Vacant land.
   D. All of the above.

3. Which of the following is the least accurate data on a CMA?
   A. The most recent data, as it is too new.
   B. The oldest data.
   C. Data that seem too high or too low for the area.
   D. Both b and c.

4. Which of the following is the most important factor to consider when deciding on a competitive asking price for a home?
   A. Selling prices of comparable properties that have been sold recently.
   B. List prices of properties that are currently for sale.
   C. List prices of properties that have expired within the past three months.
   D. None of the above.

5. Which of the following must an owner be made to realize?
   A. The higher the price of the home over market value, the sooner it will sell.
   B. The higher the price of the home over market value, the greater the chance it will sell quickly.
   C. Both a and b.
   D. Neither a nor b.

6. What should an owner do if she needs to sell a property quickly?
   A. Price the property just below fair market value.
   B. Paint, clean, and decorate so as to create as much curb appeal as possible.
   C. Place a keybox on the property for ease of showing by licensees.
   D. All of the above.

7. What does the check from the escrow company to the seller at the close of escrow include?
   A. The sales price minus the loan.
   B. The profit.
   C. The seller's proceeds.
   D. The net loan amount.

8. Your listing presentation book should
   A. be organized to follow your listing presentation.
   B. be used only in conjunction with your verbal presentation.
   C. help to build the owner's confidence in you and your company
   D. All of the above.

9. Which of the following sections of your listing presentation manual builds the owners' confidence in you the most?
   A. About Me.
   B. What My Clients Say About Me.
   C. About My Company.
   D. None of the above.

10. Which of the following should the "Value Conclusions" section of your CMA do?
    A. Give the owners a low and high value range.
    B. State the exact value.
    C. Overestimate the value to ensure you get the listing.
    D. Value the property a little low to ensure it will sell.

Chapter

9

IMPORTANT PHRASES AND TERMS

Alternative fee listing

Bilateral agreement

Exclusive authorization
and right to sell listing

Listing agreement

Market data
statistics

MLS access-only
listing

Net listing

Open listing

Option listing

Trial closes

The Listing Presentation

Upon completion of this chapter, the student will be able to:

- Use the Exclusive Authorization and Right to Sell California Residential Listing Agreement.
- Differentiate and use various Buyer Representation Agreements.
- Distinguish the defining characteristics of open, option, and net listings.
- Demonstrate the presentation of a marketing plan and competitive market analysis.

9.1 THE LISTING AGREEMENT

The two most important documents in the real estate industry are the *Residential Listing Agreement* (RLA) and the *Residential Purchase Agreement*. The RLA defines the broker's duties and rights and is a *bilateral* written employment agreement that grants a licensed real estate broker a fee for service.

Definition

A **listing agreement**, when executed (signed) by the parties, becomes a legally binding contract that authorizes a *broker to serve as licensee* and receive compensation from a principal in a real estate transaction. Listing contracts may be entered into for the purpose of representing a principal in the purchase, sale, rental, or lease of real property. The most common listing agreement is the exclusive right to sell residential listing, whereby a broker is authorized to find a ready, willing, and able purchaser for a property at a price

and terms established by the seller and within a specified time period. The agreement clearly states the mutual benefits to, and obligations of, the broker and the seller.

When a listing is signed, an agency relationship is created that requires the completion of a specified action, such as procuring a "ready, willing, and able" buyer for the purchase of the seller's property for compensation. Once the broker fulfills her part of the contract, she is legally entitled to receive the agreed to compensation from the seller. It should be noted here that the sale of the respective property is generally not required for the broker to earn the agreed to compensation; only that the broker find a potential buyer who is ready, willing, and able to purchase the property on the terms and conditions set forth by the seller.

Buyer/Broker or Buyer Representation Agreement listings, where the broker serves to meet the needs of a buyer, were practically unknown until the mid-1990s. Today, they are widely used by knowledgeable real estate professionals.

Elements

The listing (whether Buyer Representation Agreement [BRE] or Residential Listing Agreement [RLA]) is a service contract between a seller and a licensed California real estate broker. Because it is a contract, it must include all of the elements of a *contract*, including consideration, proper offer and consent (mutual consent), lawful object, and competency of the parties.

According to Civil Code 1624(5), listings must be in writing to be legally enforceable. Without a written listing contract, the broker has no legal protection whatsoever and she cannot force a seller to pay a commission if the seller refuses to do so.

A **bilateral agreement** is created in a listing when a broker agrees to use diligence in procuring a "ready, willing, and able" buyer, and the seller promises to pay compensation in return for the broker's successful effort. In the case of a Buyer Representation Agreement, the broker agrees to be diligent in locating a suitable property for a buyer and the buyer promises to pay the broker a fee for service when she successfully finds such a property. With regard to the buyer paying the broker's fee, these agreements normally state that "if anyone other than the Buyer compensates Broker for services covered by this agreement, that amount shall be credited toward the buyer's obligation to pay compensation." And, if the amount received by anyone other than the buyer exceeds the amount the buyer is obligated to pay, that amount shall be disclosed to the buyer and if allowed by law paid to the broker or credited to the buyer as dictated by the Buyer

Representation Agreement. The consideration that passes between the parties can be anything of value, including a promissory note.

9.2 TYPES OF LISTING AGREEMENTS

The basic listing agreement has many variations. Whereas some are general in nature, others are specific and are used for only one type of property. Despite the variation of the listing contract format, six basic listing types are exclusive authorization and right to sell listings, exclusive agency listings, open listings, exclusive authorization to acquire real property listings (Buyer Representation listings), option listings, and net listings. The main purpose of a listing agreement is to clearly define the duties and responsibilities of the broker and the seller (or buyer, in a buyer representation listing). Two kinds of listing categories are exclusive and nonexclusive. (In the case of Buyer Representation Agreement, three listing types are exclusive (CAR form BRE), nonexclusive (CAR form BNE), and nonexclusive/not for compensation (CAR form BRNN).) The chart in Figure 9.1 will help you to understand the variations.

Exclusive Authorization and Right to Sell Listing

An **exclusive authorization and right to sell listing** gives a broker the exclusive or sole right to compensation if, during the listing period, broker, seller, cooperating broker, or any other person procures a buyer who offers to purchase the property at the price and terms stipulated in the contract or any price and terms acceptable to the seller. With this type of listing, the listing broker is the sole

FIGURE 9.1   Broker Compensation Under Three Types of Listing Agreements

When a broker may receive a commission under three types of listings.

Type of listing	Broker paid a commission
Open listing	Only if a separate compensation agreement is signed by the seller. Broker is vulnerable.
Exclusive agency	Here the seller appoints the broker as her "exclusive agent," but the owner may sell the property herself with no compensation due broker, but must pay if broker procures a ready, willing, and able buyer. Broker is afforded some protection.
Exclusive authorization and right to sell	Under this contract, the broker is the seller's "exclusive agent" and is granted the right to compensation no matter who sells the property, including the owner. Best broker protection available.

agent and is entitled to the agreed to fee if the property is sold by anyone, even the owner, during the term of the listing.

By law, all exclusive listings must have a start date and a termination date. The termination date should be clear and specific. Language such as "until terminated" or "until the property is sold" should be avoided. California Real Estate Law Section 10176(f) makes it clear that a broker is subject to disciplinary action for "claiming, demanding or receiving a fee, compensation, or commission under any *exclusive* agreement authorizing or employing a broker to sell, buy, or exchange real estate for compensation or commission where such agreement does not contain a *definite, specified date* of final and complete termination."

A licensee is required to give the seller a copy of any listing at the time it is signed. It is a good business practice to give a client a copy of any document that they sign (as soon as they sign it) and licensees who become REALTORS® *must* give the seller a copy as soon as they sign it to be in compliance with the National Association of REALTORS® Code of Ethics.

Exclusive Agency Listing

There is only one major difference between the exclusive authorization and right to sell listing and the exclusive agency listing: if the buyer of the property is represented by a broker, then the listing agency earns a commission; however, the owner may sell the property directly to another person who is not represented by a broker and the owner will not pay a commission. The reasoning for this is that the exclusive agency listing refers to an "agency authorization" and not a "right to sell"; therefore, an owner, by not being a licensee, may sell directly without paying compensation.

Open Listing

An **open listing** is a written memorandum, often (but not necessarily) on real estate company letterhead, that when signed by the buyer or seller authorizes the broker to act as a licensee for the purchase or sale of real property. Any number of brokers could work on the listing, and the seller is not obligated to disclose that the property has been sold. The first broker to bring a buyer who is ready, willing, and able to purchase the property at the terms specified earns the commission. An open listing is a *unilateral* contract because there is only a promise to perform on one side. The contract is actually created only when the act is performed. Like a

newspaper ad offering a reward for the return of a lost item, everyone can look for the item but only the person who finds and returns it will be entitled to the reward.

This type of listing may be given by the owner to an unlimited number of brokers. According to the terms of an open listing, the first broker who finds a ready, willing, and able buyer acceptable to the seller (or an acceptable property for the buyer) is entitled to all of the compensation. Once an offer or property has been accepted, all other open listings are automatically cancelled and no commission is due any of the other brokers. Under an open listing, a buyer may buy a property herself or a seller may sell a property herself, with no commission due any broker. The seller or buyer is not required to notify the broker that the service has been completed.

It is rare that a real estate office will take an open listing because they feel that there is little likelihood that their office will procure a buyer and it is a disservice to the seller to allow them to feel that the firm is using diligence on their behalf. If you are turned down for an exclusive authorization listing because other brokers are willing to work on an open listing basis, hold fast to your standard and wait for a time until the owner is frustrated by the lack of effort and results of the "open listing" brokers and present her with a complete marketing plan and ask for an exclusive right to sell listing at that time.

Exclusive Authorization to Acquire Real Property (Buyer Representation Listings)

As recently as the late 1980s, all real estate licensees who wrote offers for buyers were actually representing the seller. Buyers had no representation. This was largely because, under Multiple Listing Service (MLS) rules at the time, if the cooperating broker accepted the compensation from the listing broker, the cooperating broker accepted the obligation to be a subagent of the seller along with it. This resulted in an untenable situation when the buyers realized that the licensee they believed was working exclusively in their interest was either not their licensee at all or was, in fact, a dual licensee. As a result, the California legislature recognized the problem by created and enacting Agency Disclosure legislation in 1988. Licensees are now required to disclose in writing to buyers and sellers the types of representation available to them (see California Civil Code Sections 2079.12 through 2079.24 or California Association of REALTORS® (C.A.R.) form Disclosure Regarding Real

Estate Agency Relationships [AD]). Brokers were allowed only three types of representation:

- Buyer exclusively
- Seller exclusively
- Both buyer and seller (dual agency)

This disclosure requirement applied to transactions involving the sale or purchase of one to four residential unit dwellings and to leases exceeding one year on like properties.

In 1989, as a result of this legislation, the C.A.R. changed their model MLS rules to allow listing offices to offer compensation to co-operating brokers without the obligation of subagency, thus creating the possibility for a "buyer exclusive licensee" or Buyer Broker: one who represents a buyer under a contract that allows the broker to be paid by the buyer. C.A.R. through its subsidiary Real Estate Business Systems (REBSs) publishes three forms to meet this need:

- Buyer Representation Agreement—Exclusive (BRE)
- Buyer Representation Agreement—Nonexclusive (BRNE)
- Buyer Representation Agreement—Nonexclusive/not for compensation (BRNN)

These forms are similar to the exclusive authorization and right to sell listing in many ways. They give the broker authority to act as the buyer's exclusive agent or not. The exclusive buyer's representative does not have a shared loyalty to the seller and looks at the transaction strictly from the buyer's side unless the buyer purchases a property that is listed with the buyer's broker's firm, then much care must be taken to obtain the written consent of both principals to dual agency prior to entering into a purchase agreement. The compensation is spelled out in the agreement in such a manner that it can be adjusted to the amount of services that the broker will render. It also allows, as indicated earlier, that any compensation received from a seller be credited toward the buyer's obligation to pay and is adjusted to comply with the terms agreed to in the Buyer Representation Agreement.

Under the Buyer Representation Agreement, the buyer's broker is held to the same fiduciary obligation in servicing the buyer as the listing broker owes to the seller. As with other contracts, the Buyer Representation Agreement must have a definite termination date. Although the third form (BRNN) grants the "nonexclusive and revocable" right to represent for one year or completion of a resulting transaction, whichever occurs first, the other agreements are not limited to one year.

The major advantage to the use of a Buyer Representation Agreement is that because the broker is compensated by the buyer, the broker (or broker's representative) can show the buyer all available properties that meet the buyer's needs, including but not limited to:

- For Sale by Owner properties
- Open listings
- Unlisted properties
- Foreclosure, short sales, and probate sales
- Any other available properties that meet the buyer's needs

The C.A.R. Buyer Representation Agreement form (BRE) shown in Figure 9.2 is a written contract between a buyer and a broker. Therefore, take great care to fill it out completely and correctly and have all necessary parties sign it. (Note: Other publishers have different versions of the form available. They will be organized differently and have clauses that vary from the C.A.R. form.)

Option Listing

An **option listing** agreement generally occurs when a broker has a contract to find a buyer and the owner grants the broker an option to purchase the property for herself. An option listing isn't really a listing at all; it is really a "contract to contract" that is sometimes used by some brokers.

A listing broker who has this type of option is forbidden by law to *profit at the expense of the owner*. According to California law, if the broker finds a buyer who is willing to pay more than the option price, and if the broker then exercises her option to buy to make a greater profit from the resale of the property, the broker must make a full disclosure to the owner as follows:

> *If a broker employed to sell property is also given an option to purchase the property herself, she occupies the dual status of agent and purchaser and she is not entitled to exercise her option except by divesting herself of her obligation as agent by making a full disclosure of any information in her possession as to the prospect of making a sale to another.*

In light of the potential for breach of fiduciary duties through the concealment of offers by brokers until they are able to exercise their option to buy, this type of listing should be avoided.

FIGURE 9.2 Buyer Representation Agreement-Exclusive

BUYER REPRESENTATION AGREEMENT - EXCLUSIVE
(C.A.R. Form BRE, Revised 4/07)

1. **EXCLUSIVE RIGHT TO REPRESENT:** _____ ("Buyer")
   grants _____ ("Broker")
   beginning on (date) _____ and ending at: **(i)** 11:59 P.M. on (date) _____, or **(ii)** completion of
   a resulting transaction, whichever occurs first ("Representation Period"), the exclusive and irrevocable right, on the terms specified in
   this Agreement, to represent Buyer in acquiring real property or a manufactured home. Broker agrees to exercise due diligence and
   reasonable efforts to fulfill the following authorizations and obligations. Broker will perform its obligations under this Agreement
   through the individual signing for Broker below, who is either Broker individually or an associate-licensee (an individual licensed as a
   real estate salesperson or broker who works under Broker's real estate license). Buyer agrees that Broker's duties are limited by the
   terms of this Agreement, including those limitations set forth in paragraphs 6 and 7.

2. **AGENCY RELATIONSHIPS:**
   A. **DISCLOSURE:** If the property described in paragraph 4 includes residential property with one to four dwelling units, Buyer
   acknowledges receipt of the "Disclosure Regarding Real Estate Agency Relationships" (C.A.R. Form AD) prior to entering into
   this Agreement.
   B. **BUYER REPRESENTATION:** Broker will represent, as described in this Agreement, Buyer in any resulting transaction.
   C. **(1) POSSIBLE DUAL AGENCY WITH SELLER:** (C(1) APPLIES UNLESS C(2)(i) or (ii) is checked below.)
   Depending on the circumstances, it may be necessary or appropriate for Broker to act as an agent for both Buyer and a seller,
   exchange party, or one or more additional parties ("Seller"). Broker shall, as soon as practicable, disclose to Buyer any election
   to act as a dual agent representing both Buyer and Seller. If Buyer is shown property listed with Broker, Buyer consents to
   Broker becoming a dual agent representing both Buyer and Seller with respect to those properties. In event of dual agency,
   Buyer agrees that: **(a)** Broker, without the prior written consent of Buyer, will not disclose to Seller that the Buyer is willing to pay
   a price greater than the price offered; **(b)** Broker, without the prior written consent of Seller, will not disclose to Buyer that Seller
   is willing to sell Property at a price less than the listing price; and **(c)** other than as set forth in (a) and (b) above, a dual agent
   is obligated to disclose known facts materially affecting the value or desirability of the property to both parties.
   OR (2) SINGLE AGENCY ONLY: (APPLIES ONLY IF (i) or (ii) is checked below.)
   ☐ **(i) Broker's firm lists properties for sale:** Buyer understands that this election will prevent Broker from showing Buyer those
   properties that are listed with Broker's firm or from representing Buyer in connection with those properties. Buyer's acquisition of
   a property listed with Broker's firm shall not affect Broker's right to be compensated under paragraph 3. In any resulting
   transaction in which Seller's property is not listed with Broker's firm, Broker will be the exclusive agent of Buyer and not a dual
   agent also representing Seller.
   OR ☐ **(ii) Broker's firm DOES NOT list property:** Entire brokerage firm only represents buyers and does not list property. In any
   resulting transaction, Broker will be the exclusive agent of Buyer and not a dual agent also representing Seller.
   D. **OTHER POTENTIAL BUYERS:** Buyer understands that other potential buyers may, through Broker, consider, make offers on or
   acquire the same or similar properties as those Buyer is seeking to acquire. Buyer consents to Broker's representation of such
   other potential buyers before, during and after the Representation Period, or any extension thereof.
   E. **NON CONFIDENTIALITY OF OFFERS:** Buyer is advised that Seller or Listing Agent may disclose the existence, terms, or
   conditions of Buyer's offer unless all parties and their agent have signed a written confidentiality agreement. Whether any such
   information is actually disclosed depends on many factors, such as current market conditions, the prevailing practice in the real
   estate community, the Listing Agent's marketing strategy and the instructions of the Seller.
   F. **CONFIRMATION:** If the Property (as defined below) includes residential property with one to four dwelling units, Broker shall
   confirm the agency relationship described above, or as modified, in writing, prior to or coincident with Buyer's execution of a
   Property Contract (as defined below).

3. **COMPENSATION TO BROKER:**
   **NOTICE: The amount or rate of real estate commissions is not fixed by law. They are set by each Broker
   individually and may be negotiable between Buyer and Broker (real estate commissions include all
   compensation and fees to Broker).**
   Buyer agrees to pay to Broker, irrespective of agency relationship(s), as follows:
   A. **AMOUNT OF COMPENSATION: (Check (1), (2) or (3). Check only one.)**
   ☐ **(1)** _____ percent of the acquisition price AND (if checked ☐) $ _____,
   OR ☐ **(2)** $ _____,
   OR ☐ **(3)** Pursuant to the compensation schedule attached as an addendum _____.
   B. **BROKER RIGHT TO COMPENSATION:** Broker shall be entitled to the compensation provided for in paragraph 3A:
   (1) If during the Representation Period, or any extension thereof, Buyer enters into an agreement to acquire property described
   in paragraph 4, on those terms or any other terms acceptable to Buyer. (Broker shall be entitled to compensation whether any
   escrow resulting from such agreement closes during or after the expiration of the Representation Period.)
   (2) If, within ___ **calendar days** after expiration of the Representation Period or any extension thereof, Buyer enters into an
   agreement to acquire property described in paragraph 4, which property Broker introduced to Buyer, or for which Broker acted
   on Buyer's behalf. The obligation to pay compensation pursuant to this paragraph shall arise only if, prior to or within **3 (or** ☐
   _____) **calendar days** after expiration of this Agreement or any extension thereof, Broker gives Buyer a written notice of those
   properties which Broker introduced to Buyer, or for which Broker acted on Buyer's behalf.

Buyer and Broker acknowledge receipt of a copy of this page.
Buyer's Initials (_____)(_____)
Broker's Initials (_____)(_____)

BRE REVISED 4/07 (PAGE 1 OF 4) Print Date

Reviewed by _____ Date _____

EQUAL HOUSING OPPORTUNITY

BUYER REPRESENTATION AGREEMENT – EXCLUSIVE (BRE PAGE 1 OF 4)

FIGURE 9.2 (*Continued*)

Property Address: _____ Date: _____

C. **PAYMENT OF COMPENSATION:** Compensation is payable:
   (1) Upon completion of any resulting transaction, and if an escrow is used, through escrow.
   (2) If acquisition is prevented by default of Buyer, upon Buyer's default.
   (3) If acquisition is prevented by a party to the transaction other than Buyer, when Buyer collects damages by suit, settlement or otherwise. Compensation shall equal one-half of the damages recovered, not to exceed the compensation provided for in paragraph 3A, after first deducting the unreimbursed expenses of collection, if any.
D. **BUYER OBLIGATION TO PAY COMPENSATION:** Buyer is responsible for payment of compensation provided for in this Agreement. **However, if anyone other than Buyer compensates Broker for services covered by this Agreement, that amount shall be credited toward Buyer's obligation to pay compensation.** If the amount of compensation Broker receives from anyone other than Buyer exceeds Buyer's obligation, the excess amount shall be disclosed to Buyer and if allowed by law paid to Broker, or (if checked) ☐ credited to Buyer, or ☐ other _____.
E. Buyer hereby irrevocably assigns to Broker the compensation provided for in paragraph 3A from Buyer's funds and proceeds in escrow. Buyer agrees to submit to escrow any funds needed to compensate Broker under this Agreement. Broker may submit this Agreement, as instructions to compensate Broker, to any escrow regarding property involving Buyer and a seller or other transferor.
F. **"BUYER"** includes any person or entity, other than Broker, related to Buyer or who in any manner acts on Buyer's behalf to acquire property described in paragraph 4.
G. (1) Buyer has not previously entered into a representation agreement with another broker regarding property described in paragraph 4, unless specified as follows (name other broker here):_____
   _____
   (2) Buyer warrants that Buyer has no obligation to pay compensation to any other broker regarding property described in paragraph 4, unless Buyer acquires the following property(ies):_____.
   (3) If Buyer acquires a property specified in G(2) above during the time Buyer is obligated to compensate another broker, Broker is neither **(i)** entitled to compensation under this Agreement, nor **(ii)** obligated to represent Buyer in such transaction.
4. **PROPERTY TO BE ACQUIRED:** Any purchase, lease or other acquisition of any real property or manufactured home described as follows:_____
   _____
   Price range: $_____ to $ _____
5. **INTERNET ADVERTISING:** Buyer acknowledges and agrees that: **(i)** properties presented to them may have been marketed through a "virtual tour" on the Internet, permitting potential buyers to view properties over the Internet; **(ii)** neither the service provider nor Broker has control over who will obtain access to the service or what action such persons might take; and **(iii)** Broker has no control over how long the information concerning the properties will be available on the Internet.
6. **BROKER AUTHORIZATIONS AND OBLIGATIONS:**
   A. Buyer authorizes Broker to: **(i)** locate and present selected properties to Buyer, present offers authorized by Buyer, and assist Buyer in negotiating for acceptance of such offers; **(ii)** assist Buyer with the financing process, including obtaining loan pre-qualification; **(iii)** upon request, provide Buyer with a list of professionals or vendors who perform the services described in the attached Buyer's Inspection Advisory; **(iv)** order reports, and schedule and attend meetings and appointments with professionals chosen by Buyer; **(v)** provide guidance to help Buyer with the acquisition of property; and **(vi)** obtain a credit report on Buyer.
   B. For property transactions of which Broker is aware and not precluded from participating in by Buyer, Broker shall provide and review forms to create a property contract ("Property Contract") for the acquisition of a specific property ("Property"). With respect to such Property, Broker shall: **(i)** if the Property contains residential property with one to four dwelling units, conduct a reasonably competent and diligent on-site visual inspection of the accessible areas of the Property (excluding any common areas), and disclose to Buyer all facts materially affecting the value or desirability of such Property that are revealed by this inspection; **(ii)** deliver or communicate to Buyer any disclosures, materials or information received by, in the personal possession of or personally known to the individual signing for Broker below during the Representation Period; and **(iii)** facilitate the escrow process, including assisting Buyer in negotiating with Seller. Unless otherwise specified in writing, any information provided through Broker in the course of representing Buyer has not been and will not be verified by Broker. Broker's services are performed in compliance with federal, state and local anti-discrimination laws.
7. **SCOPE OF BROKER DUTY:**
   A. While Broker will perform the duties described in paragraph 6B, Broker recommends that Buyer select other professionals, as described in the attached Buyer's Inspection Advisory, to investigate the Property through inspections, investigations, tests, surveys, reports, studies and other available information ("Inspections") during the transaction. Buyer agrees that these Inspections, to the extent they exceed the obligations described in paragraph 6B, are not within the scope of Broker's agency duties. Broker informs Buyer that it is in Buyer's best interest to obtain such Inspections.
   B. Buyer acknowledges and agrees that Broker: **(i)** does not decide what price Buyer should pay or Seller should accept; **(ii)** does not guarantee the condition of the Property; **(iii)** does not guarantee the performance, adequacy or completeness of inspections, services, products or repairs provided or made by Seller or others; **(iv)** does not have an obligation to conduct an inspection of common areas or offsite areas of the Property; **(v)** shall not be responsible for identifying defects on the Property, in common areas or offsite unless such defects are visually observable by an inspection of reasonably accessible areas of the Property or are known to Broker; **(vi)** shall not be responsible for inspecting public records or permits concerning the title or use of the Property; **(vii)** shall not be responsible for identifying the location of boundary lines or other items affecting title; **(viii)** shall not be responsible for verifying square footage, representations of others or information contained in Investigation reports, Multiple Listing Service, advertisements, flyers or other promotional material; **(ix)** shall not be responsible for providing legal or tax advice regarding any aspect of a transaction entered into by Buyer or Seller; and **(x)** shall not be responsible for providing other advice or information that exceeds the knowledge, education and experience required to perform real estate licensed activity. Buyer agrees to seek legal, tax, insurance, title and other desired assistance from appropriate professionals.

Buyer and Broker acknowledge receipt of a copy of this page.
Buyer's Initials (_____)(_____)
Broker's Initials (_____)(_____)

BRE REVISED 4/07 (PAGE 2 OF 4)

Reviewed by _____ Date _____

EQUAL HOUSING OPPORTUNITY

BUYER REPRESENTATION AGREEMENT – EXCLUSIVE (BRE PAGE 2 OF 4)

FIGURE 9.2 (Continued)

Property Address: _____ Date: _____

C. Broker owes no duty to inspect for common environmental hazards, earthquake weaknesses, or geologic and seismic hazards. If Buyer receives the booklets titled "Environmental Hazards: A Guide for Homeowners, Buyers, Landlords and Tenants," "The Homeowner's Guide to Earthquake Safety," or "The Commercial Property Owner's Guide to Earthquake Safety," the booklets are deemed adequate to inform Buyer regarding the information contained in the booklets and, other than as specified in 6B above, Broker is not required to provide Buyer with additional information about the matters described in the booklets.

8. **BUYER OBLIGATIONS:**
   A. Buyer agrees to timely view and consider properties selected by Broker and to negotiate in good faith to acquire a property. Buyer further agrees to act in good faith toward the completion of any Property Contract entered into in furtherance of this Agreement. Within **5 (or** ☐ **) calendar days** from the execution of this Agreement, Buyer shall provide relevant personal and financial information to Broker to assure Buyer's ability to acquire property described in paragraph 4. If Buyer fails to provide such information, or if Buyer does not qualify financially to acquire property described in paragraph 4, then Broker may cancel this Agreement in writing. Buyer has an affirmative duty to take steps to protect him/herself, including discovery of the legal, practical and technical implications of discovered or disclosed facts, and investigation of information and facts which are known to Buyer or are within the diligent attention and observation of Buyer. Buyer is obligated, and agrees, to read all documents provided to Buyer. Buyer agrees to seek desired assistance from appropriate professionals, selected by Buyer, such as those referenced in the attached Buyer's Inspection Advisory.
   B. Buyer shall notify Broker in writing (C.A.R. Form BMI) of any material issue to Buyer, such as, but not limited to, Buyer requests for information on, or concerns regarding, any particular area of interest or importance to Buyer ("Material Issues").
   C. **Buyer agrees to: (i) indemnify, defend and hold Broker harmless from all claims, disputes, litigation, judgments, costs and attorney's fees arising from any incorrect information supplied by Buyer, or from any Material Issues that Buyer fails to disclose in writing to Broker; and (ii) pay for reports, Inspections and meetings arranged by Broker on Buyer's behalf.**
   D. Buyer is advised to read the attached Buyer's Inspection Advisory for a list of items and other concerns that typically warrant Inspections or investigation by Buyer or other professionals.

9. **DISPUTE RESOLUTION:**
   A. **MEDIATION:** Buyer and Broker agree to mediate any dispute or claim arising between them out of this Agreement, or any resulting transaction, before resorting to arbitration or court action, subject to paragraph 9B(2) below. Paragraph 9B(2) below applies whether or not the arbitration provision is initialed. Mediation fees, if any, shall be divided equally among the parties involved. If, for any dispute or claim to which this paragraph applies, any party commences an action without first attempting to resolve the matter through mediation, or refuses to mediate after a request has been made, then that party shall not be entitled to recover attorney's fees, even if they would otherwise be available to that party in any such action. THIS MEDIATION PROVISION APPLIES WHETHER OR NOT THE ARBITRATION PROVISION IS INITIALED.
   B. **ARBITRATION OF DISPUTES: (1) Buyer and Broker agree that any dispute or claim in Law or equity arising between them regarding the obligation to pay compensation under this Agreement, which is not settled through mediation, shall be decided by neutral, binding arbitration, including and subject to paragraph 9B(2) below. The arbitrator shall be a retired judge or justice, or an attorney with at least five years of residential real estate law experience, unless the parties mutually agree to a different arbitrator, who shall render an award in accordance with substantive California law. The parties shall have the right to discovery in accordance with California Code of Civil Procedure §1283.05. In all other respects, the arbitration shall be conducted in accordance with Title 9 of Part III, of the California Code of Civil Procedure. Judgment upon the award of the arbitrator(s) may be entered in any court having jurisdiction. Interpretation of this Agreement to arbitrate shall be governed by the Federal Arbitration Act.**
   (2) EXCLUSIONS FROM MEDIATION AND ARBITRATION: The following matters are excluded from mediation and arbitration: (i) a judicial or non-judicial foreclosure or other action or proceeding to enforce a deed of trust, mortgage or installment land sale contract as defined in California Civil Code §2985; (ii) an unlawful detainer action; (iii) the filing or enforcement of a mechanic's lien; and (iv) any matter that is within the jurisdiction of a probate, small claims or bankruptcy court. The filing of a court action to enable the recording of a notice of pending action, for order of attachment, receivership, injunction, or other provisional remedies, shall not constitute a waiver of the mediation and arbitration provisions.
   "NOTICE: BY INITIALING IN THE SPACE BELOW YOU ARE AGREEING TO HAVE ANY DISPUTE ARISING OUT OF THE MATTERS INCLUDED IN THE 'ARBITRATION OF DISPUTES' PROVISION DECIDED BY NEUTRAL ARBITRATION AS PROVIDED BY CALIFORNIA LAW. YOU ARE GIVING UP ANY RIGHTS YOU MIGHT POSSESS TO HAVE THE DISPUTE LITIGATED IN A COURT OR JURY TRIAL. BY INITIALING IN THE SPACE BELOW YOU ARE GIVING UP YOUR JUDICIAL RIGHTS TO DISCOVERY AND APPEAL, UNLESS THOSE RIGHTS ARE SPECIFICALLY INCLUDED IN THE 'ARBITRATION OF DISPUTES' PROVISION. IF YOU REFUSE TO SUBMIT TO ARBITRATION AFTER AGREEING TO THIS PROVISION, YOU MAY BE COMPELLED TO ARBITRATE UNDER THE AUTHORITY OF THE CALIFORNIA CODE OF CIVIL PROCEDURE. YOUR AGREEMENT TO THIS ARBITRATION PROVISION IS VOLUNTARY."
   "WE HAVE READ AND UNDERSTAND THE FOREGOING AND AGREE TO SUBMIT DISPUTES ARISING OUT OF THE MATTERS INCLUDED IN THE 'ARBITRATION OF DISPUTES' PROVISION TO NEUTRAL ARBITRATION."

Buyer's Initials _____ / _____	Broker's Initials _____ / _____

Buyer and Broker acknowledge receipt of a copy of this page.
Buyer's Initials (_____)(_____)
Broker's Initials (_____)(_____)

BRE REVISED 4/07 (PAGE 3 OF 4)

Reviewed by _____ Date _____

EQUAL HOUSING OPPORTUNITY

BUYER REPRESENTATION AGREEMENT – EXCLUSIVE (BRE PAGE 3 OF 4)

FIGURE 9.2 (*Continued*)

Property Address: _____ Date: _____

10. **TIME TO BRING LEGAL ACTION:** Legal action for breach of this Agreement, or any obligation arising therefrom, shall be brought no more than two years from the expiration of the Representation Period or from the date such cause of action may arise, whichever occurs first.

11. **OTHER TERMS AND CONDITIONS:** The following disclosures or addenda are attached:
    A. ☑ Buyer's Inspection Advisory (C.A.R. Form BIA) _____
    B. ☐ Statewide Buyer and Seller Advisory (C.A.R. Form SBSA) _____
    C. ☐ _____
    D. ☐ _____

12. **ATTORNEY FEES:** In any action, proceeding or arbitration between Buyer and Broker regarding the obligation to pay compensation under this Agreement, the prevailing Buyer or Broker shall be entitled to reasonable attorney fees and costs, except as provided in paragraph 9A.

13. **ENTIRE AGREEMENT:** All understandings between the parties are incorporated in this Agreement. Its terms are intended by the parties as a final, complete and exclusive expression of their agreement with respect to its subject matter, and may not be contradicted by evidence of any prior agreement or contemporaneous oral agreement. This Agreement may not be extended, amended, modified, altered or changed, except in writing signed by Buyer and Broker. In the event that any provision of this Agreement is held to be ineffective or invalid, the remaining provisions will nevertheless be given full force and effect. This Agreement and any supplement, addendum or modification, including any copy, whether by copier, facsimile, NCR or electronic, may be signed in two or more counterparts, all of which shall constitute one and the same writing.

Buyer acknowledges that Buyer has read, understands, received a copy of and agrees to the terms of this Agreement.

Buyer _____ Date _____
Address _____ City _____ State _____ Zip _____
Telephone _____ Fax_____ E-mail _____

Buyer _____ Date _____
Address _____ City _____ State _____ Zip _____
Telephone _____ Fax_____ E-mail _____

Real Estate Broker (Firm) _____ DRE License # _____
By (Agent) _____ DRE License # _____ Date _____
Address _____ City _____ State _____ Zip _____
Telephone _____ Fax_____ E-mail _____

BRE REVISED 4/07 (PAGE 4 OF 4)   Reviewed by _____ Date _____

BUYER REPRESENTATION AGREEMENT – EXCLUSIVE (BRE PAGE 4 OF 4)

Source: Reprinted with permission of California Association of REALTORS®.

Net Listing

A **net listing** is an employment contract in which the broker's compensation is all monies received over and above the net amount specified by the seller. The danger for unethical, illegal, or outright criminal practice makes the net listing one to avoid.

The broker's compensation is not a fixed fee but rather the difference between the net amount the seller wishes to realize and the amount the broker may be able to receive from the sale of the property. In real estate, as well as in most other areas where fees for service are not spelled out in advance, the opportunity for fraud or misrepresentation is more than most consumers realize. Net listings are illegal in a number of states and *you are strongly advised not to use them.*

Alternative Fee Listing (Limited Agency Broker)

Better known as a *Fee for Services*, or *menu-type listing*, this type of listing is where the broker charges a flat fee for her counseling and guidance services and then allows the seller to choose from and pay separately for other services on the broker's *menu of services*. In short, this is an unbundling of services allowing the client or customer to pay only for the services received. These services could include:

* Entry of the listing on the MLS
* Signs
* Negotiation service
* Flyers/property brochures
* Additional website inclusion such as www.realtor.com
* Open House
* Property staging services (suggestions and/or furniture rental)

MLS Access-Only Listing

With this type of listing, the broker agrees to list the property only for the purpose of giving the seller access to the MLS. All negotiations with a buyer or buyer's representative will be conducted directly with the seller. The "listing" broker usually charges an up-front flat fee for this type of limited agency listing.

9.3 THE EXCLUSIVE AUTHORIZATION AND RIGHT TO SELL LISTING FORM

The RLA is a written service contract between the owner or owners of a piece of residential real property and a licensed California real estate broker. It must be filled out correctly and signed by all parties.

Certain types of property and the details of each transaction will cause the exact wording of a listing to vary; however, certain provisions are a basic part of every listing contract. Figure 9.3 shows a sample of the C.A.R. RLA exclusive authorization and right to sell listing form. The following is a detailed examination of this form. (Note: All C.A.R. forms are reviewed twice a year and subject to modification. Always make sure you are using the most current form.)

Paragraph 1: Exclusive Agency Right to Sell

In this paragraph you will enter the name(s) of the owner(s) and the name of the listing broker. (Before completing the listing contract, it is important to check the public records for the specific property. This can be done through a property profile obtained from your title company or by an online records check. If the seller is not listed as the owner of record, or as the only owner of record, taking the listing may be a waste of your time.) If the listing is being taken by a licensee (salesperson or broker associate), it is on behalf of the broker and the employing broker's name is written here. The licensee who completes the form should sign at the bottom of the last page as the "licensee" of the broker. (Remember, the seller is entering into this contract with the real estate broker, not the salesperson.) The words *exclusive and irrevocable agency right* in this paragraph are what make this an exclusive authorization and right to sell.

After the broker's name, enter the starting and ending dates of the listing. While three- to six-month listings are common, market conditions, advertising deadlines, property preparation, or repair times must be considered when deciding on the length of the listing period.

Next, enter the location of the property by city and county as well as by an unmistakable street address. In some instances, you will not have an address and you would need to use a legal description such as the county assessor's parcel number or a lot and block description. If an address is too lengthy to place in the space provided, insert the words "see addendum" and put the address or description on an addendum and have the sellers sign it. Sellers have been known to sell the wrong property as a result of inaccurate address, parcel, or unit numbers. Attention to detail is definitely part of the job description for a real estate licensee.

Paragraph 2: Items Excluded and Included

Indicates that all fixtures are included and all personal property is excluded, unless stated otherwise. Provides space for items included and excluded to be noted. Caution: If the seller has excluded certain

FIGURE 9.3 C.A.R. RLA Exclusive Authorization and Right to Sell Listing Form

---

CALIFORNIA ASSOCIATION OF REALTORS®

RESIDENTIAL LISTING AGREEMENT
(Exclusive Authorization and Right to Sell)
(C.A.R. Form RLA, Revised 2/09)

1. **EXCLUSIVE RIGHT TO SELL:** _____ ("Seller")
hereby employs and grants _____ ("Broker")
beginning (date) _____ and ending at 11:59 P.M. on (date) _____ ("Listing Period")
the exclusive and irrevocable right to sell or exchange the real property in the City of _____,
County of_____, Assessor's Parcel No. _____
California, described as:_____ ("Property").

2. **ITEMS EXCLUDED AND INCLUDED:** Unless otherwise specified in a real estate purchase agreement, all fixtures and fittings that are attached to the Property are included, and personal property items are excluded, from the purchase price.
ADDITIONAL ITEMS EXCLUDED: _____.
ADDITIONAL ITEMS INCLUDED: _____.
Seller intends that the above items be excluded or included in offering the Property for sale, but understands that: **(i)** the purchase agreement supersedes any intention expressed above and will ultimately determine which items are excluded and included in the sale; and **(ii)** Broker is not responsible for and does not guarantee that the above exclusions and/or inclusions will be in the purchase agreement.

3. **LISTING PRICE AND TERMS:**
   A. The listing price shall be: _____
   _____ Dollars ($ _____).
   B. Additional Terms: _____
   _____

4. **COMPENSATION TO BROKER:**
   Notice: The amount or rate of real estate commissions is not fixed by law. They are set by each Broker individually and may be negotiable between Seller and Broker (real estate commissions include all compensation and fees to Broker).
   A. Seller agrees to pay to Broker as compensation for services irrespective of agency relationship(s), either ☐ _____ percent of the listing price (or if a purchase agreement is entered into, of the purchase price), or ☐ $ _____,
   AND _____, as follows:
      (1) If during the Listing Period, or any extension, Broker, Seller, cooperating broker, or any other person procures a buyer(s) who offers to purchase the Property on the above price and terms, or on any price and terms acceptable to Seller. (Broker is entitled to compensation whether any escrow resulting from such offer closes during or after the expiration of the Listing Period.)
   OR (2) If within _____ calendar days **(a)** after the end of the Listing Period or any extension; or **(b)** after any cancellation of this Agreement, unless otherwise agreed, Seller enters into a contract to sell, convey, lease or otherwise transfer the Property to anyone ("Prospective Buyer") or that person's related entity: **(i)** who physically entered and was shown the Property during the Listing Period or any extension by Broker or a cooperating broker; or **(ii)** for whom Broker or any cooperating broker submitted to Seller a signed, written offer to acquire, lease, exchange or obtain an option on the Property. Seller, however, shall have no obligation to Broker under paragraph 4A(2) unless, not later than **3 calendar days** after the end of the Listing Period or any extension or cancellation, Broker has given Seller a written notice of the names of such Prospective Buyers.
   OR (3) If, without Broker's prior written consent, the Property is withdrawn from sale, conveyed, leased, rented, otherwise transferred, or made unmarketable by a voluntary act of Seller during the Listing Period, or any extension.
   B. If completion of the sale is prevented by a party to the transaction other than Seller, then compensation due under paragraph 4A shall be payable only if and when Seller collects damages by suit, arbitration, settlement or otherwise, and then in an amount equal to the lesser of one-half of the damages recovered or the above compensation, after first deducting title and escrow expenses and the expenses of collection, if any.
   C. In addition, Seller agrees to pay Broker: _____.
   D. Seller has been advised of Broker's policy regarding cooperation with, and the amount of compensation offered to, other brokers.
      (1) Broker is authorized to cooperate with and compensate brokers participating through the multiple listing service(s) ("MLS") by offering MLS brokers either ☐ _____ percent of the purchase price, or ☐ $ _____.
      (2) Broker is authorized to cooperate with and compensate brokers operating outside the MLS as per Broker's policy.
   E. Seller hereby irrevocably assigns to Broker the above compensation from Seller's funds and proceeds in escrow. Broker may submit this Agreement, as instructions to compensate Broker pursuant to paragraph 4A, to any escrow regarding the Property involving Seller and a buyer, Prospective Buyer or other transferee.
   F. **(1)** Seller represents that Seller has not previously entered into a listing agreement with another broker regarding the Property, unless specified as follows: _____.
      (2) Seller warrants that Seller has no obligation to pay compensation to any other broker regarding the Property unless the Property is transferred to any of the following individuals or entities: _____
      _____
      (3) If the Property is sold to anyone listed above during the time Seller is obligated to compensate another broker: **(i)** Broker is not entitled to compensation under this Agreement; and **(ii)** Broker is not obligated to represent Seller in such transaction.

RLA REVISED 2/09 (PAGE 1 OF 3) Print Date

Seller acknowledges receipt of a copy of this page.
Seller's Initials (_____)(_____)

Reviewed by _____ Date _____

RESIDENTIAL LISTING AGREEMENT - EXCLUSIVE (RLA PAGE 1 OF 3)

FIGURE 9.3 (*Continued*)

Property Address: _____ Date: _____

5. **OWNERSHIP, TITLE AND AUTHORITY:** Seller warrants that: **(i)** Seller is the owner of the Property; **(ii)** no other persons or entities have title to the Property; and **(iii)** Seller has the authority to both execute this Agreement and sell the Property. Exceptions to ownership, title and authority are as follows: _____.

6. **MULTIPLE LISTING SERVICE:** All terms of the transaction, including financing, if applicable, will be provided to the selected MLS for publication, dissemination and use by persons and entities on terms approved by the MLS. Seller authorizes Broker to comply with all applicable MLS rules. MLS rules allow MLS data about the Property to be made available by the MLS to additional Internet sites unless Seller gives Broker instructions to the contrary. MLS rules generally provide that residential real property and vacant lot listings be submitted to the MLS within 48 hours or some other period of time after all necessary signatures have been obtained on the listing agreement. However, Broker will not have to submit this listing to the MLS or can prohibit this listing or certain information from or about it from appearing on certain internet sites if, Broker submits to the MLS such an instruction signed by Seller (C.A.R. Form SEL or the locally required form). Information about this listing will be provided to the MLS of Broker's selection unless a form instructing Broker to the contrary is attached to this listing Agreement.

7. **SELLER REPRESENTATIONS:** Seller represents that, unless otherwise specified in writing, Seller is unaware of: **(i)** any Notice of Default recorded against the Property; **(ii)** any delinquent amounts due under any loan secured by, or other obligation affecting, the Property; **(iii)** any bankruptcy, insolvency or similar proceeding affecting the Property; **(iv)** any litigation, arbitration, administrative action, government investigation or other pending or threatened action that affects or may affect the Property or Seller's ability to transfer it; and **(v)** any current, pending or proposed special assessments affecting the Property. Seller shall promptly notify Broker in writing if Seller becomes aware of any of these items during the Listing Period or any extension thereof.

8. **BROKER'S AND SELLER'S DUTIES:** Broker agrees to exercise reasonable effort and due diligence to achieve the purposes of this Agreement. Unless Seller gives Broker written instructions to the contrary, Broker is authorized to order reports and disclosures as appropriate or necessary and advertise and market the Property by any method and in any medium selected by Broker, including MLS and the Internet, and, to the extent permitted by these media, control the dissemination of the information submitted to any medium. Seller agrees to consider offers presented by Broker, and to act in good faith to accomplish the sale of the Property by, among other things, making the Property available for showing at reasonable times and referring to Broker all inquiries of any party interested in the Property. Seller is responsible for determining at what price to list and sell the Property. **Seller further agrees to indemnify, defend and hold Broker harmless from all claims, disputes, litigation, judgments and attorney fees arising from any incorrect information supplied by Seller, or from any material facts that Seller knows but fails to disclose.**

9. **DEPOSIT:** Broker is authorized to accept and hold on Seller's behalf any deposits to be applied toward the purchase price.

10. **AGENCY RELATIONSHIPS:**
    A. **Disclosure:** If the Property includes residential property with one-to-four dwelling units, Seller shall receive a "Disclosure Regarding Agency Relationships" form prior to entering into this Agreement.
    B. **Seller Representation:** Broker shall represent Seller in any resulting transaction, except as specified in paragraph 4F.
    C. **Possible Dual Agency With Buyer:** Depending upon the circumstances, it may be necessary or appropriate for Broker to act as an agent for both Seller and buyer, exchange party, or one or more additional parties ("Buyer"). Broker shall, as soon as practicable, disclose to Seller any election to act as a dual agent representing both Seller and Buyer. If a Buyer is procured directly by Broker or an associate-licensee in Broker's firm, Seller hereby consents to Broker acting as a dual agent for Seller and such Buyer. In the event of an exchange, Seller hereby consents to Broker collecting compensation from additional parties for services rendered, provided there is disclosure to all parties of such agency and compensation. Seller understands and agrees that: **(i)** Broker, without the prior written consent of Seller, will not disclose to Buyer that Seller is willing to sell the Property at a price less than the listing price; **(ii)** Broker, without the prior written consent of Buyer, will not disclose to Seller that Buyer is willing to pay a price greater than the offered price; and **(iii)** except for (i) and (ii) above, a dual agent is obligated to disclose known facts materially affecting the value or desirability of the Property to both parties.
    D. **Other Sellers:** Seller understands that Broker may have or obtain listings on other properties, and that potential buyers may consider, make offers on, or purchase through Broker, property the same as or similar to Seller's Property. Seller consents to Broker's representation of sellers and buyers of other properties before, during and after the end of this Agreement.
    E. **Confirmation:** If the Property includes residential property with one-to-four dwelling units, Broker shall confirm the agency relationship described above, or as modified, in writing, prior to or concurrent with Seller's execution of a purchase agreement.

11. **SECURITY AND INSURANCE:** Broker is not responsible for loss of or damage to personal or real property, or person, whether attributable to use of a keysafe/lockbox, a showing of the Property, or otherwise. Third parties, including, but not limited to, appraisers, inspectors, brokers and prospective buyers, may have access to, and take videos and photographs of, the interior of the Property. Seller agrees: **(i)** to take reasonable precautions to safeguard and protect valuables that might be accessible during showings of the Property; and **(ii)** to obtain insurance to protect against these risks. Broker does not maintain insurance to protect Seller.

12. **KEYSAFE/LOCKBOX:** A keysafe/lockbox is designed to hold a key to the Property to permit access to the Property by Broker, cooperating brokers, MLS participants, their authorized licensees and representatives, authorized inspectors, and accompanied prospective buyers. Broker, cooperating brokers, MLS and Associations/Boards of REALTORS® are **not** insurers against injury, theft, loss, vandalism or damage attributed to the use of a keysafe/lockbox. Seller does (or if checked ☐ does not) authorize Broker to install a keysafe/lockbox. If Seller does not occupy the Property, Seller shall be responsible for obtaining occupant(s)' written permission for use of a keysafe/lockbox.

13. **SIGN:** Seller does (or if checked ☐ does not) authorize Broker to install a FOR SALE/SOLD sign on the Property.

14. **EQUAL HOUSING OPPORTUNITY:** The Property is offered in compliance with federal, state and local anti-discrimination laws.

15. **ATTORNEY FEES:** In any action, proceeding or arbitration between Seller and Broker regarding the obligation to pay compensation under this Agreement, the prevailing Seller or Broker shall be entitled to reasonable attorney fees and costs from the non-prevailing Seller or Broker, except as provided in paragraph 19A.

16. **ADDITIONAL TERMS:** _____
_____
_____

Seller acknowledges receipt of a copy of this page.
Seller's Initials (_____)(_____)

RLA REVISED 2/09 (PAGE 2 OF 3)

Reviewed by _____ Date _____

EQUAL HOUSING
OPPORTUNITY

RESIDENTIAL LISTING AGREEMENT - EXCLUSIVE (RLA PAGE 2 OF 3)

FIGURE 9.3 (*Continued*)

Property Address: _____ Date: _____

17. **MANAGEMENT APPROVAL:** If an associate-licensee in Broker's office (salesperson or broker-associate) enters into this Agreement on Broker's behalf, and Broker or Manager does not approve of its terms, Broker or Manager has the right to cancel this Agreement, in writing, within **5 Days** After its execution.

18. **SUCCESSORS AND ASSIGNS:** This Agreement shall be binding upon Seller and Seller's successors and assigns.

19. **DISPUTE RESOLUTION:**
   A. **MEDIATION:** Seller and Broker agree to mediate any dispute or claim arising between them out of this Agreement, or any resulting transaction, before resorting to arbitration or court action, subject to paragraph 19B(2) below. Paragraph 19B(2) below applies whether or not the arbitration provision is initialed. Mediation fees, if any, shall be divided equally among the parties involved. If, for any dispute or claim to which this paragraph applies, any party commences an action without first attempting to resolve the matter through mediation, or refuses to mediate after a request has been made, then that party shall not be entitled to recover attorney fees, even if they would otherwise be available to that party in any such action. THIS MEDIATION PROVISION APPLIES WHETHER OR NOT THE ARBITRATION PROVISION IS INITIALED.
   B. **ARBITRATION OF DISPUTES: (1) Seller and Broker agree that any dispute or claim in law or equity arising between them regarding the obligation to pay compensation under this Agreement, which is not settled through mediation, shall be decided by neutral, binding arbitration, including and subject to paragraph 19B(2) below. The arbitrator shall be a retired judge or justice, or an attorney with at least 5 years of residential real estate law experience, unless the parties mutually agree to a different arbitrator, who shall render an award in accordance with substantive California law. The parties shall have the right to discovery in accordance with California Code of Civil Procedure §1283.05. In all other respects, the arbitration shall be conducted in accordance with Title 9 of Part III of the California Code of Civil Procedure. Judgment upon the award of the arbitrator(s) may be entered in any court having jurisdiction. Interpretation of this agreement to arbitrate shall be governed by the Federal Arbitration Act.**
   (2) EXCLUSIONS FROM MEDIATION AND ARBITRATION: The following matters are excluded from mediation and arbitration: (i) a judicial or non-judicial foreclosure or other action or proceeding to enforce a deed of trust, mortgage, or installment land sale contract as defined in California Civil Code §2985; (ii) an unlawful detainer action; (iii) the filing or enforcement of a mechanic's lien; and (iv) any matter that is within the jurisdiction of a probate, small claims, or bankruptcy court. The filing of a court action to enable the recording of a notice of pending action, for order of attachment, receivership, injunction, or other provisional remedies, shall not constitute a waiver of the mediation and arbitration provisions.
   "NOTICE: BY INITIALING IN THE SPACE BELOW YOU ARE AGREEING TO HAVE ANY DISPUTE ARISING OUT OF THE MATTERS INCLUDED IN THE 'ARBITRATION OF DISPUTES' PROVISION DECIDED BY NEUTRAL ARBITRATION AS PROVIDED BY CALIFORNIA LAW AND YOU ARE GIVING UP ANY RIGHTS YOU MIGHT POSSESS TO HAVE THE DISPUTE LITIGATED IN A COURT OR JURY TRIAL. BY INITIALING IN THE SPACE BELOW YOU ARE GIVING UP YOUR JUDICIAL RIGHTS TO DISCOVERY AND APPEAL, UNLESS THOSE RIGHTS ARE SPECIFICALLY INCLUDED IN THE 'ARBITRATION OF DISPUTES' PROVISION. IF YOU REFUSE TO SUBMIT TO ARBITRATION AFTER AGREEING TO THIS PROVISION, YOU MAY BE COMPELLED TO ARBITRATE UNDER THE AUTHORITY OF THE CALIFORNIA CODE OF CIVIL PROCEDURE. YOUR AGREEMENT TO THIS ARBITRATION PROVISION IS VOLUNTARY."
   "WE HAVE READ AND UNDERSTAND THE FOREGOING AND AGREE TO SUBMIT DISPUTES ARISING OUT OF THE MATTERS INCLUDED IN THE 'ARBITRATION OF DISPUTES' PROVISION TO NEUTRAL ARBITRATION."

   | Seller's Initials _____ / _____ | Broker's Initials _____ / _____ |

20. **ENTIRE AGREEMENT:** All prior discussions, negotiations and agreements between the parties concerning the subject matter of this Agreement are superseded by this Agreement, which constitutes the entire contract and a complete and exclusive expression of their agreement, and may not be contradicted by evidence of any prior agreement or contemporaneous oral agreement. If any provision of this Agreement is held to be ineffective or invalid, the remaining provisions will nevertheless be given full force and effect. This Agreement and any supplement, addendum or modification, including any photocopy or facsimile, may be executed in counterparts.

By signing below, Seller acknowledges that Seller has read, understands, received a copy of and agrees to the terms of this Agreement.

Seller _____ Date _____
Address _____ City _____ State ____ Zip _____
Telephone _____ Fax _____ E-mail _____

Seller _____ Date _____
Address _____ City _____ State ____ Zip _____
Telephone _____ Fax _____ E-mail _____

Real Estate Broker (Firm) _____ DRE Lic. # _____
By (Agent) _____ DRE Lic. # _____ Date _____
Address _____ City _____ State ____ Zip _____
Telephone _____ Fax _____ E-mail _____

THIS FORM HAS BEEN APPROVED BY THE CALIFORNIA ASSOCIATION OF REALTORS® (C.A.R.). NO REPRESENTATION IS MADE AS TO THE LEGAL VALIDITY OR ADEQUACY OF ANY PROVISION IN ANY SPECIFIC TRANSACTION. A REAL ESTATE BROKER IS THE PERSON QUALIFIED TO ADVISE ON REAL ESTATE TRANSACTIONS. IF YOU DESIRE LEGAL OR TAX ADVICE, CONSULT AN APPROPRIATE PROFESSIONAL.
This form is available for use by the entire real estate industry. It is not intended to identify the user as a REALTOR®. REALTOR® is a registered collective membership mark which may be used only by members of the NATIONAL ASSOCIATION OF REALTORS® who subscribe to its Code of Ethics.

Published and Distributed by:
REAL ESTATE BUSINESS SERVICES, INC.
a subsidiary of the California Association of REALTORS®
525 South Virgil Avenue, Los Angeles, California 90020

| Reviewed by _____ Date _____ |

RLA REVISED 2/09 (PAGE 3 OF 3)

RESIDENTIAL LISTING AGREEMENT - EXCLUSIVE (RLA PAGE 3 OF 3)

Source: Reprinted with permission of California Association of REALTORS®.

fixtures in the listing, the buyer's representative must also exclude them in the purchase agreement or they will stay with the property. Also, if the seller has included certain personal property in the listing (such as washer, dryer, and microwave), these items must be included in the purchase agreement or they may not be included in the sale. It is not always obvious whether an item is a fixture or personal property. Where there may be a question, as with custom-made drapes, be sure to clarify your understanding in the listing.

Paragraph 3: Listing Price and Terms

The terms of sale include:

a. The price at which the property is being offered. This will be the price at which the seller is willing to sell and the price which, if accepted by the seller, will determine the broker's right to compensation.

b. Be sure to write out the complete price in words and numbers separately.

c. Spell out any additional terms such as any financing options that the seller is willing to accept, or not accept, such as VA and FHA, or any financing that the seller is willing to carry. If additional terms are specified, the broker (or the broker's representative licensee) must bring a buyer who is ready, willing, and able to meet these additional terms for the broker to earn the agreed to compensation.

Paragraph 4: Compensation to Broker

Boldface type calls attention to the fact that commissions are negotiable and not set by law. This statement is required in listings of one to four residential units. Space is provided for the amount of compensation to be paid and the broker's protection (Safe Harbor Provision) period is entered. There have been occasions when sellers, in order to avoid paying the broker's fee, have been tempted to reject an offer only to sell to the same buyer after the listing period has ended. This provision helps minimize the potential for this kind of abuse. However, two limiting factors are, first, this clause applies only to persons who physically entered and were shown the property. Second, the listing broker must provide a written list of the names of these prospective buyers within three calendar days after the end of the listing period. This is one good reason for requiring all visitors to your Open House to sign the register. The Open House register is kept by licensees primarily not to provide the names of potential prospects (although it does do that) but to provide protection from the possibility of losing a fee to someone who was shown the home but delayed purchase until after the listing expired.

Paragraph 5: Ownership, Title, and Authority

In this paragraph, the seller warrants that the seller is the owner of the property, no other entity has ownership, and the seller has the authority to sell the property. Space is provided for exceptions.

Paragraph 6: Multiple Listing Service

A statement is made that the property will be submitted to the local MLS for dissemination to the other participants. The listing must be submitted within forty-eight hours after the seller signs it unless the seller makes a written instruction to the listing licensee to exclude it. You must submit the signed exclusion to the MLS within forty-eight hours. Check your local MLS for any variations in the listing requirement.

Paragraph 7: Seller Representations

In this paragraph, the seller represents that the property is not in default; no bankruptcy or other such proceedings are going on; there is no known government or other proceedings going on, such as eminent domain proceedings, that would affect title to the property; and no pending or proposed special assessments.

Paragraph 8: Broker's and Seller's Duties

The broker agrees to be diligent in her efforts to achieve the purpose of the agreement. The seller agrees to consider offers received in good faith and to hold the broker harmless from any claims that result from incorrect information supplied to the broker by the seller or for failure to disclose material facts to the broker.

Paragraph 9: Deposit

Broker is authorized to accept and hold on seller's behalf any deposit from a buyer to be applied toward the purchase price.

Paragraph 10: Agency Relationships

This paragraph states that the Seller shall receive a "Disclosure Regarding Agency Relationships" form prior to entering into this agreement. It outlines the possibility for Dual Agency with a buyer and that the broker may have or obtain other listings similar to seller's property. Paragraph "C" makes a disclosure similar to the Disclosure and Consent for Representation of More Than One Buyer or Seller (C.A.R. for DA) signed by the buyer. Paragraph "E" states that Confirmation of Agency Relationships will be made before or concurrent with Seller's execution of a purchase agreement.

Paragraph 11: Security and Insurance

This paragraph states that the broker is not responsible for loss or damage to the property in connection with the use of a keybox or the showing of the property. It also states that others, such as appraisers, may have access to the property and may take pictures. The seller is advised to take reasonable precautions regarding valuables.

Paragraph 12: Keysafe/Lockbox

This section authorizes the broker to install a lockbox on the premises. The lockbox, often called a *keysafe* or *keybox*, allows for easier entry to the property by other MLS brokers and affiliates. If there is any loss or damage as a result of having the lockbox on the property, it is covered by the owner's property insurance and the broker has no responsibility. If the owner does not want a lockbox, she may elect not to have one by checking the box and the property would then be shown by the buyer's representative picking up a key from the listing broker's office or by appointment.

Paragraph 13: Sign

A for-sale sign in front of the property enhances the fact that it is for sale and allows interested buyers to call about the property; however, the licensee must obtain the owner's written authorization before having a for-sale sign installed. This authorization is provided by Paragraph 13 if the seller does not check the box withholding consent.

Paragraph 14: Equal Housing Opportunity

This paragraph states that the property is being offered in compliance with antidiscrimination laws. The seller cannot discriminate against a person from a protected class.

Paragraph 15: Attorney Fees

This paragraph states that in any action, proceeding, or arbitration between the seller and broker attempting to settle any dispute regarding the obligation to pay compensation under this agreement, the prevailing party shall be entitled to reasonable attorney fees from the losing party, except as provided in Paragraph 19A. The exception denies attorney fees if any party commences an action without first attempting to resolve the matter through mediation or if either party refuses to mediate after a request has been made.

Paragraph 16: Additional Terms

All additional terms involving the sale of the property should be entered in Paragraph 3B. Additional terms involving the listing should be entered here.

Paragraph 17: Management Approval

If the listing was taken by an associate licensee, this paragraph allows the broker to cancel the listing in writing, within five days of execution, if she disapproves of its terms. Obviously, this makes it essential for the licensee to get the listing agreement to the broker/manager for approval as soon as possible.

Paragraph 18: Successors and Assigns

The listing agreement is enforceable on the seller and the seller's successors and assigns. If the seller transfers the property without the broker's consent, the broker may decide to act as the listing licensee for the transferee rather than sue for the agreed to fee. This provision could be used to convince the transferee to allow the listing to continue.

Paragraph 19: Dispute Resolution

A. Mediation. Requires nonbinding mediation of any disputes between broker and seller prior to binding arbitration. If either party fails to attempt to resolve the matter before filing an action, they will not be entitled to recover attorney fees if they prevail in a further action. Great care must be taken in any discussion of either mediation or arbitration as licensees may cross the line of "practicing law without a license." The C.A.R. website has two Question & Answer (Q&A) briefs available to its members called *Mediation for the Consumer* and *Arbitration for the Consumer*. These memos have been written by C.A.R. attorneys and can be provided to sellers and buyers as an adequate explanation of mediation and arbitration without fear of practicing law without a license.

B. Arbitration of Disputes. Except for exempt issues stated in paragraph 19B(2) of the contract, any disputes regarding payment of compensation that are not settled through mediation will be settled through binding arbitration. This paragraph requires agreement of the parties (broker and seller) to be indicated by their initials. If neither party (or only one party) initials this paragraph, it is not binding. If the seller initials the arbitration paragraph, the broker must initial (the listing licensee initials on the broker's behalf) or there is no agreement. Licensees may provide the Q&A on *Arbitration for the Consumer* as a further explanation of arbitration as mentioned earlier.

Paragraph 20: Entire Agreement

By their signatures, the parties stipulate that this agreement is the *entire agreement* and all prior statements or representations are

either incorporated in this agreement or superseded by it, and no verbal statements are being relied on by the seller or the broker. It also states that the agreement may be signed in counterparts, thereby making each one the same as an original.

Signatures

The sellers acknowledge that they have read the contract, that they understand it, and that they agree to its terms and have received a copy. The sellers and the licensee (on broker's behalf) sign the document.

9.4 PRESENTING THE COMPETITIVE MARKET ANALYSIS AND YOUR MARKETING PLAN

You have carefully researched the market data for the neighborhood and put together your marketing plan for the owners. You are now ready to meet with the owners. Note: It is wise to have your laptop with you each time you are with the sellers so, when the need arises, you can access all of the websites in which their listing may be listed. This is especially true at your listing presentation appointment.

It is always best to do a two-stage listing presentation if possible; however, it is not always practical. In a two-stage listing presentation, you will meet the sellers at the property to ascertain their motivation for selling and to view the property in preparation for your market analysis. You will be looking for things such as the overall condition of the property, its amenities (such as granite countertops, slate or tile roofs, and remodeling), its location, as compared to other recent sales in the area, the lot size and utility (a large, steeply sloped lot may not be worth as much as a smaller one that is level and completely use-able), and the date of sale of each sold property (in an appreciating or depreciating market, you must make allowances for any increase or decrease in value of sales that are several months old).

If you can do an MLS property search while at the property and you can get a sense for the price range of comparable properties in the area, you may want to proceed with your listing presentation at that time. If not, simply gather your information, set the next appointment, thank them, and leave.

Do a thorough review of all of the **market data statistics**, come to conclusions as to a range of value for the specific property, and assemble your entire listing presentation.

When you arrive for the second listing appointment, ask the sellers for another quick walk-through of the property so that you can double-check your notes. This shows true interest and quickly

gains the sellers' favorable attention while relieving some of the sellers' tension at the same time. If you haven't yet determined the sellers' reason for selling, ask them at this time. You really do need to know, as their timing may be critical to your pricing strategy for the sale of their home.

Ask if you can put your things down at the kitchen table as this is the most comfortable place to conduct your presentation and fill out any paperwork. Try to sit around the corner of the table from them. Do not sit across from them, if possible, as this is often seen as confrontational. Do not sit between the sellers as it is hard to maintain eye contact with two people on either side of you. Make enough small talk to ease any tension, but be aware of their body language and voice inflections and move along as you feel appropriate.

Your listing presentation should start with you. You should include copies of any additional professional education such as the Certified Residential Specialist (CRS) or Graduate of the REALTORS® Institute (GRI) designations and a copy of any diplomas you think may be appropriate. (A PhD in astrophysics may or may not be appropriate to mention; a Juris Doctor [JD] may not be appropriate to mention unless you are comfortable being held to the standard of care expected of a professionally current attorney.) Note: Real estate professional designations are features and mean little by themselves, so be prepared to explain what the benefit may be to the sellers.

The second part of your listing should include as much information about your company as you need to present it as positively as possible. If market data statistics about your company are impressive, be sure to share them with the sellers. The theme of these first two sections should be "we are excellent at getting homes sold at great prices for people in a reasonably short time, with few, if any problems." Keep it simple.

The third part of your presentation notebook should be letters or notes from satisfied clients. These are probably the most powerful items in your notebook, and you can expect the sellers to pause to read some of the letters. There is nothing more powerful than third-party support from satisfied sellers and buyers.

The fourth section should contain your marketing plan for the property. It should include examples of magazine and newspaper ads as well as copies of how their property might be shown on your company's website and links to any other sites in which the property will appear, such as Google, YAHOO! and Facebook. Mention the power of the MLS exposure and the fact that your company's policy

is to fully cooperate with all brokerage firms in the MLS to maximize the exposure of the owner's property.

This is the time to fully explain to the owners that there is a direct correlation between the number of buyers who actually view the property and the number of offers received. Explain that your main goal is to maximize exposure of their property to as many potential buyers as possible. Tell the owners that you hope to create a competitive demand for their home sufficient to generate multiple offers.

Your marketing plan should have a section in it that talks about "staging" the property. Staging means doing whatever is necessary to present the property as favorably as possible. Staging a property also suggests that both you and the owners walk through the property looking for any defects or anything a buyer might perceive as a defect. You would need to be careful about the owners' feelings when you do this because talking about some things, such as strong pet odors, can offend or embarrass them. Keep your comments general and avoid specifics; there will be time for that *after* you have the listing. We will discuss staging a property in more detail in Chapter 10.

The last section of your listing presentation should contain your competitive market analysis (CMA) and your estimate of value. In Chapter 10, we will be talking about whether you are conducting an appraisal or an estimate of value when you do a CMA. The important thing is to do a detailed and complete job of analyzing and providing market data information with your analysis and give an honest, well-researched, and well-thought-out opinion of the market value of the owners' property.

As you are presenting your information to the owners, carefully watch for signals that they are getting bored or are angry or offended at any of the information that you are presenting. If you are presenting pages in your listing presentation about your company and you notice one of the owners tapping their fingers, this is a clear signal to speed it up a bit. If you present facts, such as average days on market, or recommend a price range, and you see one of the owners turn away and cross their arms over their chest, that is a sure sign that they are not happy with what they just heard. You should be constantly aware of facial expressions, body language, and other nonverbal communications; obviously, smiles are good and frowns are not.

Normally you will go through the information about you and your company first and then go over your proposed marketing and advertising program for their home. You would want to know how

you are doing at some point, and there are **trial closes** that you can use to "test the water" along the way. When you present your advertising plan and you show the owners a copy of an ad that your company has placed in the local newspaper or on the Internet, you can say, "How would you feel about seeing your home in an ad like this in a couple of days?" If they give a positive response, it is a sign that they are pleased with your presentation so far; if they say that they aren't sure about it, then you still have some convincing to do.

After you have presented the information about you and your company, you should then present them with copies of letters from any satisfied clients. If you have the clients' permission, tell the sellers you are meeting with that they should feel free to contact any of the clients that you have presented personally and ask them about how you work and the kind of results that you get. As a new licensee, you won't have any letters like this, but strive for them because they build the best credibility.

Competitive Market Analysis

When you present your CMA, take your time. Remember, you are familiar with the process and with the research that you have done, the owners are not. Present the owners with the worksheet that you used when you compared their property to three active, expired, and sold listings in the neighborhood and explain how you did your analysis by comparing those three "sold" homes to theirs and made upward or downward adjustments in value as you compared each of them to the subject home. By showing them your worksheet, you make a strong statement that your indication of value was arrived at by a written analysis of factual data and not by guesswork.

Show them the active listings that are available and point out that because they are the owners' competition they set the upper limit of what the owners can ask for their home. Be sure to discuss any expired listings to show how their list price compared to the competition at the time and why they expired without selling.

When you present your analysis of the owners' property value, you may sense some element of discomfort. If you do, question them about what is bothering them. If they have had other brokers over for a listing presentation, someone may have stated that they can get the owners a higher price than the price range you have suggested. If you experience this, ask to see the other broker's CMA so that you can compare the comparable sold properties to the ones used in your market analysis. Chances are there won't be one. But if there is one and the comparables justify a different price, you would

need to adjust your recommended selling range. If not, tell them that you have a duty to be completely honest with them about the value of their property and that you have carefully analyzed the market value before presenting it to them and that the market data that you have shown them just doesn't support the other broker's statements about their property's value. You should remind them that buyers, not sellers, set the market value of a property by making an informed offer to purchase it; without that, there is no sale.

You might want to say, "Mr. and Mrs. [seller], if I list your home, I take on several different jobs: analyst, marketer, negotiator, and escrow technician. The first and most important one is that of an analyst. I have already shown you what happens when you list a home too high; it's just a frustrating waste of your time and all you would have accomplished would be to help sell your neighbors' homes by comparison. At the same time, if you list your home too low, you would create a bargain for someone else at your expense. That's why I take the time to do a complete job of researching current data and then use my skills to analyze what those facts mean to you so that you are priced to your maximum advantage. I never do that on a hunch because hunches cost you money."

The next phase of your presentation will be to present the listing agreement and go over it with the owners. Some owners will not want to go over the complete agreement in detail, so again, watch for body language or other verbal or nonverbal signals that you should give the "condensed" version. The listing agreement has two paragraphs in it that are also good trial closes. When you come to the paragraph about placing a for-sale sign on the property, you can remind them that a large percentage of buyers find their new home by driving through neighborhoods and writing down phone numbers from for-sale signs and calling real estate offices for more information. A trial close would be to ask "Where do you think I should place the sign for maximum exposure?" Many times they will give you direction, and this often says that they have decided to list with you.

Another place for a trial close is the paragraph that gives permission for a keybox. You would start by explaining that in order to get the maximum number of buyer showings, they should allow a keybox to be placed on the property (it is an advantage to have one with you and show them how it works). After you explain the benefit, ask them if they have a spare key for the keybox. You will be surprised at how often they get you a spare key right then. If they still haven't decided to list with you at that point, they will just tell you.

There will be times when it is not prudent to place a keybox on the property. If there are pets, especially dogs, in the property, which may

bite someone, you should first ask if they can be maintained somewhere else when the seller is not home until the property is sold; if not, then you should consider not using a keybox. Other reasons might include children at home alone after school, tenants (especially uncooperative ones), and the presence of extensive valuables or weapons in the property. You will then need to work "by appointment only."

Ask for the order. Sometimes, you will complete your entire presentation and you still will not know if the owners are ready to list with you or not. When this happens, you would need to simply ask for the business. You may want to simply say, "Well, I am ready to go to work for the two of you right now; how do you feel about it?" or you may wish to use some other way of asking. The important thing is to enthusiastically ask for the business!

9.5 ESTIMATED SELLER'S PROCEEDS

After you have completed the listing agreement and given the owners a signed copy, you should move right to the Estimated Seller's Proceeds (ESP) form (Figure 9.4). You would, of course, need some information from the owners, such as their loan balance, if any; the interest rate on their loan, the property taxes, the amount of any homeowners association (HOA) dues, and any special assessments that apply to the property. You would need to use a hypothetical closing date for purposes of prorating loans, real estate taxes, and HOA dues.

Fill out the form carefully *at list price* and give the owners a copy. The amount of net proceeds that the owners receive from the sale of their property is of vital importance to them, so it is wise to be a little liberal with your estimated expenses so that you slightly understate their net sale proceeds. If your calculations show a higher net than they actually receive, they will not be happy with you, but if they receive more than you estimate, you are a saint and they will be likely to do business with you again and to refer their friends. See ESP form in Figure 9.4.

Many computer programs will calculate the seller's proceeds for you; however, you will not always have a computer available when you take a listing, so it is wise to become skilled at calculating a seller's net proceeds manually. The C.A.R. ESP form is a good one to use as it is clear and easy to understand, and because it is so complete, you are likely to be quite accurate as to the owners' actual expenses and net proceeds.

Each time you present an offer to the sellers, you should fill out an ESP form at the offered price for the sellers as their net proceeds may vary from the one that you did when you listed the property.

FIGURE 9.4   Estimated Seller's Proceeds Form

CALIFORNIA
ASSOCIATION
OF REALTORS®

ESTIMATED SELLER PROCEEDS
(C.A.R. Form ESP, Revised 4/06)

SELLER: _____   DATE: _____
PROPERTY ADDRESS: _____
This estimate is based on costs associated with_____type of financing.
PROJECTED CLOSING DATE: _____   PROPOSED SALE PRICE: $ _____
Current Annual Property Taxes: $ _____ Rate: _____ % Monthly Homeowners Dues, if any: $ _____

CHARGES BY EXISTING LIEN HOLDERS
Interest to payoff date (first loan)	# Days _____	$ _____
Interest (secondary financing)	# Days _____	$ _____
Interest on lines of credit or other financing		$ _____
Prepayment penalty		$ _____
Demand and Reconveyance fees		$ _____
Other lender fees (wire transfers, courier, etc.)		$ _____

ENCUMBRANCES (EXISTING LIENS)
First Loan	Rate: _____%	$ _____
Secondary Financing	Rate: _____%	$ _____
Secured Lines of Credit		$ _____
Bonds, Liens, etc.		$ _____
Other_____		$ _____
TOTAL ENCUMBRANCES		$ _____

ESCROW AND TITLE CHARGES
Escrow Fee ☐ including any Exchange Fees	$ _____
Title Insurance Policy	$ _____
Drawing, Notary and Recording Fees	$ _____

GROSS EQUITY $ _____
(Expected sale price less encumbrances)

ESTIMATED CREDITS
Prorated Property Taxes	# Days _____	$ _____
Prorated Homeowners Dues	# Days _____	$ _____
Other_____		$ _____
Other_____		$ _____
TOTAL ESTIMATED CREDITS		$ _____

OTHER EXPENSES & PRORATIONS
Brokerage Fee - Listing Amount	$_____ or _____%	$ _____
- Selling Amount	$_____ or _____%	$ _____
Transfer Tax - County	Rate per $1,000 $ _____	$ _____
- City	Rate per $1,000 $ _____	$ _____
Property Taxes	# Days _____	$ _____
Homeowners Dues	# Days _____	$ _____
Buyer's Closing Costs		$ _____
Natural Hazard Disclosure and/or other Reports		$ _____
Wood Destroying Pest and/or other Inspection Fees		$ _____
Corrective Work and/or other Repairs		$ _____
Home Warranty Program		$ _____
Rents and Security Deposits		$ _____
VA/FHA Discount Points and Fees		$ _____
HOA Transfer and/or Move-Out Fees		$ _____
Other _____		$ _____
		$ _____
		$ _____

TOTAL ESTIMATED EXPENSES $ _____

PROCEEDS RECAP
Expected Sale Price	$ _____
LESS Total Encumbrances	- _____
LESS Total Estimated Expenses	- _____
PLUS Total Estimated Credits	+ _____
ESTIMATED TOTAL SELLER PROCEEDS	$ _____
LESS any Note Carried by Seller	- _____
LESS any Federal/State Withholding	- _____
ESTIMATED SELLER CASH PROCEEDS	$ _____

This estimate, based upon the above sale price, type of financing and projected closing date, has been prepared to assist Seller in estimating costs and proceeds. Amounts will vary depending upon differences between actual and estimated repairs that may occur in the transaction, unpaid loan balances, assessments, liens, impound accounts, charges by lenders, escrow companies, title insurers and other service providers and other items. Not all liens may yet have been identified. Neither Broker nor Agent guarantee these figures represent the actual, or only, amounts and charges.
By signing below Seller acknowledges that Seller has read, understands and received a copy of this Estimated Seller Proceeds.

Seller _____   Date _____
Seller _____   Date _____

Real Estate Broker (Firm) _____   DRE Lic. # _____
By (Agent) _____ DRE Lic. # _____   Date _____
Address _____ City _____   State ____ Zip _____
Telephone _____ Fax _____   E-mail _____

SURE TRAC
The System for Success

Published and Distributed by:
REAL ESTATE BUSINESS SERVICES, INC.
a subsidiary of the California Association of REALTORS®
525 South Virgil Avenue, Los Angeles, California 90020

ESP REVISED 4/06 (PAGE 1 OF 1) Print Date

Reviewed by _____ Date _____

EQUAL HOUSING OPPORTUNITY

ESTIMATED SELLER PROCEEDS (ESP PAGE 1 OF 1)

Source: Reprinted with permission of California Association of REALTORS®.

9.6 COMMON SELLER OBJECTIONS AND HOW TO HANDLE THEM

Whenever you give a listing presentation, you will almost certainly receive some objections from the owners. Many of these occur over and over again, and knowing them in advance and being prepared for them will result in you obtaining more listings. The most common seller objections are:

- *"We don't see many of your company's signs around here."* Your answer to this needs to be truthful, but there are several ways to make a case for listing with you. You might say, "Well, it's true that we don't get a lot of listings in this area, but we always sell the ones that we do get, and for excellent prices too." Also, more signs mean more unsold listings.

- *"Bill over at XYZ Realty said that he would sell my house for [x] percent commission. Will you match that?"* "You know, Mr. Smith, it makes me feel bad when I hear people say that, because in reality, a reduced commission costs you money in the end; let me explain. Your highest sales price will come from our efforts to generate as much buyer traffic to your house as possible, hopefully to obtain multiple offers. It costs money to advertise and market a home properly. The money has to come from somewhere and my firm and I spend it to do just that, knowing that we will receive a large enough fee from the sale to reimburse us. Firms that work for reduced fees know they will only get a small fee, so they can't afford to advertise and market like we do. They usually generate less buyer traffic to your home, creating less competition, and you often don't get as high a price, which can cost you way more than the so-called commission savings. I'd hate to see you do that to yourself."

- *"We don't want a lockbox; you'll have to show it by appointment only."* "Tell me what your concerns are." *"We don't want anyone in our home unless you're there to watch them, and we don't want people walking in on us."* "I understand completely. Let me show you how the keysafe works." (Have one with you and demonstrate it for the sellers.) "Not only are these made of case-hardened steel that can't be sawn off, they are electronic and record the licensees that have shown the property. Every buyer that is shown the property will be accompanied by their representative, who is trained to keep an eye on them." "Salespeople will not just show up and come in; they will call first, per the showing instructions in the MLS listing. If no one is home, they will leave a message as to when they are coming by so that you won't be

surprised. Does that sound safe enough?" "Mr. Smith, it is very important that we make it easy for licensees to show your home so that we can get the maximum exposure to potential buyers. If you were a salesperson with six homes to show to a buyer and five were on keysafe but one (yours) was by appointment only, which one do you think might not get shown?"

- *"We don't want our neighbors to know that we're selling, so we don't want a for-sale sign."* "I understand how you feel, but, believe me, your neighbors will know that you are selling. I don't want your neighbors to get the wrong idea about what you are doing here. Imagine what they will think you are doing if they see an expensive car drive up with a few people who go in your house and come out a few minutes later, then another expensive car drives up and the same thing happens again and again. What do you think they think you are doing? Besides, after they get familiar with neighborhoods that they like, 56 percent of buyers make their first contact with a home by calling us from a for-sale sign; I don't want to lose that many buyers, do you?"

- *"We want our home advertised every week in the newspaper."* "Let me explain how we handle that. First, less than 10 percent of today's buyers look for homes in the newspapers; they use the Internet; that's why we have put most of our advertising resources there. We have many homes for sale and we couldn't advertise all of them every week. What we do is advertise by price range to attract calls. Then we show all of the homes in that price range to each prospective buyer. There's just as good a chance that your home will be shown from a call on another home as on your home. You'll be pleased with the results."

- *"We want you to hold Open House every week until the property is sold."* "It would be nice if I could do that, but I often have more than one listing to service at the same time. Let me assure you that I will hold the home open as often as possible, and when I can't do it, I'll make every effort to have one of our best salespersons do it for me; how does that sound?" It may also interest you to know that Open House traffic has dwindled to a trickle because buyers can see many properties by virtual tours from their own home."

- *"We want to sell as-is."* "Would you please tell me why you feel that way?" *"We don't want to get stuck with a bunch of costly repairs."* "That's understandable. The problem with putting that in the listing is that it will scare away potential buyers because they will think that you have a lot of repairs to do. Remember, you can limit your liability for repairs through

negotiation when an offer is presented to you. Structuring that is part of my job. If you are really concerned, then I recommend that we get a presale home inspection and termite inspection, so that we know exactly what potential repairs might be required."

- *"We aren't taking a penny less than the asking price."* "The price that you accept for your home is entirely up to you. I have shown you what your home is worth today and I will update you as we go along. When you get an offer that is less than the list price, but is at market value based on what I have shown you, you very much risk losing a good sale on your home by counteroffering too high; it could even result in your getting less than market value later on because if your home is on the market for a long time, agents and buyers will begin to wonder what's wrong with it because it's not selling. You need to be very careful about that."

- *"We need that much money to be able to pay off some bills and still buy our next home."* "That's what we call 'need-based pricing,' and it doesn't work. You see, a buyer doesn't care at all about what you need or want to do with your sales proceeds; he only cares about paying market value for your home, so if you over-price it to meet your personal needs, the buyer will buy another home and yours won't sell."

- *"We don't want to list until we have found our next home."* "It would be nice if we could do that, but you would have to make your offer to purchase the next home contingent on the sale of this one and, many if not most sellers are reluctant to accept a contingent offer, usually because they feel they have lost control; it would be a frustrating experience for you. If you are really concerned about that, then let's make the sale of this home contingent on you purchasing a replacement home within thirty days after yours is sold. That would fully protect you. How does that sound?"

- *"We don't want to sell to any minorities."* Sometimes the sellers won't be quite that blunt. They may be more subtle with statements such as "We want the buyer to be like us." Or "We want to sell to someone who shares our values." Or "Our property should appeal to a fairly narrow range of buyer." If you detect this type of discrimination, simply tell the sellers, "I'm very sorry, but if that's how you feel, I can't do business with you. A major part of my job is to do whatever I can to protect you from any liability that could result in litigation. What you are expressing to me would be a violation of the Fair Housing laws and could cause us both to be sued."

Note: You should pack up and leave at that time, and you have a duty to report the people to your broker and the local Department of Housing and Urban Development (HUD) office.

SUMMARY

In this chapter you learned the essentials of a listing agreement. You learned about the different types of listings that can exist between a broker and a seller and the strengths and weaknesses of each one.

You learned about the protection offered when working with buyers via a Buyer Representation Agreement listing, often called a Buyer-Broker agreement, and you learned through a paragraph-by-paragraph analysis of the RLA exclusive authorization and right to sell listing form, what a listing is, the protections it affords the broker and the sellers, and how to properly present it to property owners at a listing appointment.

You learned how to prepare a marketing plan for the sale of a property, the logical sequence of how to present it to the owners along with a detailed CMA that shows owners within a narrow range what their home is worth, how to market it in a fashion that is acceptable in the current market conditions, and the importance of providing an ESP form so that they have a reasonable indication of the cash and proceeds they will receive from a sale.

You learned what many of the most common seller objections are and a suggested response to each one.

CLASS DISCUSSION TOPICS

1. Be prepared to explain the difference between a Broker Representation Agreement listing and an exclusive agency listing.

2. Prepare the "About Me" and "About My Company" sections of your listing presentation manual and be prepared to present them to another student in class.

3. Prepare a CMA for the property that you currently live in or for one of your office listings, if you are an active licensee. Present the analysis to two other students who will act as the owners.

4. Prepare an ESP form for a home, using the following: $400,000 sale price; $237,000 loan with a 6.5 percent interest rate; HOA monthly dues of $120, with the current month not paid; real estate taxes of $3,600 per year, with the first installment paid; a 6 percent brokerage fee paid by the sellers; and a December first closing date. Use normal title and escrow fees for your area.

5. Acting as the licensee, handle the following objection: *"We want a discount on the commission."*

CHAPTER 9 QUIZ

1. The exclusive authorization and right to sell listing is
   A. a unilateral agreement.
   B. an exclusive contract to find property for a buyer.
   C. a service contract between an owner and a broker.
   D. None of the above.

2. When a listing agreement is signed
   A. an agency relationship is formed.
   B. a fiduciary relationship is formed.
   C. the broker agrees to use diligence in procuring a purchaser for the property.
   D. All of the above.

3. An open listing
   A. may be verbal.
   B. is not enforceable if it is verbal.
   C. does not guarantee the broker payment of a commission.
   D. All of the above.

4. A CMA is best described as
   A. a comparative mortgage analysis that compares loans for a buyer.
   B. a formal appraisal.
   C. a full accounting of all current listings in a particular city.
   D. an estimate of value that reflects the realities of the current marketplace.

5. A seller that needs to sell very quickly should
   A. list somewhat above the value indicated in the CMA.
   B. list at the value indicated in the CMA.
   C. list somewhat below the value indicated in the CMA.
   D. None of the above.

6. Seller's proceeds best describes
   A. the seller's net profit.
   B. the net sale price.
   C. the gross sale price.
   D. the money received from the escrow or title company at escrow closing.

7. Your listing presentation manual should
   A. be organized to follow your verbal presentation.
   B. help you explain the value to an owner of using a licensee to market the property, and you and your firm in particular.
   C. include forms for presenting the CMA and your marketing plan.
   D. All of the above.

8. If you are with a small office, which of the following statements shows the advantages of listing with your firm?
   A. All we need is one buyer, and even we can do that.
   B. We can use the business.
   C. The competition is fierce, so we try harder than the big guys.
   D. We specialize in a small number of select properties in your area.

9. If an owner says that she doesn't want to list until she has found her new home, you should
   A. take a post-dated listing.
   B. postpone listing her home and start showing her property.
   C. explain that an offer that is contingent on the sale of her current home is definitely not in her best interest.
   D. list her home contingent on the sale of her home.

10. Need-based pricing is when
   A. an owner tells you that she has to get a certain price because she has other financial obligations.
   B. her family needs her to relocate to take care of her aging parents.
   C. an owner prices her property to the needs of the buyers.
   D. an owner is selling her home to a shelter for the needy.

Chapter

10

IMPORTANT PHRASES AND TERMS

Advertising policy

Latent defect

Listing toolkit

Marketing binder

Marketing plan

NAR Membership
  Marks Manual

Red flag inspection

Rider strips

Staging a home

Unique visitors

Servicing the Listing

Upon completion of this chapter, the student will be able to:

- Use information boxes, property brochures, MLS, and the Internet to market a seller's property.
- Create effective residential advertising.
- Construct effective pricing strategies.
- Compose a weekly activity report.
- Demonstrate buyer offer presentation to seller.
- Present multiple offers to seller.
- Create an escrow timeline.

10.1 YOUR MARKETING PLAN

A good marketing plan (bold) is most often in checklist format and should include all activities you will do to market and advertise the sellers' home. Figure 10.1 is an example of a marketing plan.

As the California Association of REALTORS® (C.A.R.) Residential Listing Agreement (RLA) gives the broker or manager the right to cancel within five days of execution if the broker/manager does not agree with its terms, licensees must submit all executed contracts for broker/manager approval as soon as possible. When you turn in the listing, make arrangements to install a for-sale sign and enter the listing into the Multiple Listing Service (MLS) if appropriate. Some companies have the administrative staff do this, but you need to know how to do it because staff may not always be available and you will be the one who pays any MLS fine for a wrongful data entry.

FIGURE 10.1 Marketing Plan

For the property at 123 Main Street, Hillsborough, California		
Event	Scheduled	Completed
1. Give copy of signed Agency Disclosure and Listing Agreement to seller	_____	_____
2. Give blank TDS to seller to complete	_____	_____
3. Take pictures of the property	_____	_____
4. Submit listing to office	_____	_____
5. Order for-sale sign	_____	_____
6. Presale staging walk-through	_____	_____
7. Make two extra keys	_____	_____
8. Meet with sellers to go over repair/ staging list	_____	_____
9. Create and print marketing brochure	_____	_____
10. Place the listing on the Internet	_____	_____
11. Assist with scheduling repairs	_____	_____
12. Create and assemble marketing binder	_____	_____
13. Test keys in lock and place in keybox	_____	_____
14. Install keybox on property	_____	_____
15. Insert brochures in bin on for-sale sign	_____	_____
16. Enter listing into MLS	_____	_____
17. Schedule Open House advertising	_____	_____
18. Execute "Top 100" mailing	_____	_____
19. Present listing at office meeting	_____	_____
20. Schedule property for MLS property tour (broker Open House)	_____	_____
21. Schedule regular advertising	_____	_____
22. Hold Open House	_____	_____
23. Pick up cards/sign-in sheets weekly	_____	_____
24. Call back or e-mail buyers' licensee for feedback	_____	_____
25. Weekly meeting with sellers	_____	_____
26. Price evaluation meeting	_____	_____

Note: Steps 16 through 25 are repeated as needed until the property is sold.

Next Meeting

At your second meeting with the owners, which is often the following day, install the keybox if one is being used. Note: Do not put the key that the sellers gave you in the keybox; keep it as a master and make at least two copies. Test the copies in the appropriate door lock to see that they work and place one key

in the keybox. Then, if a licensee inadvertently walks off with the key, you have others. As the keybox will record the users, check to see who entered the home last and call to ask whether they have returned the key. Sellers do not like to hear that the key to their home is missing, even if the key is in the pocket of some forgetful licensee. It is also wise to have the lock shop mark the keys to be used in the keybox: "Do Not Duplicate."

At this meeting, go through the home again with the sellers and give them your homeowner instructions. Explain that you both need to view the home from the perspective of a potential buyer. Make a list of things that need correcting and that may prompt a buyer to reduce their offering price. This is called **staging a home** and can include things such as painting one or more rooms or the exterior of the house, removing furniture to give a room a bigger feel, storing clutter that may distract a potential buyer, and doing some much-needed yard work. When you and the sellers are finished, sit down and compare lists. Discuss the importance of each item on both lists and make a combined list, then number each item in order of importance. Ask the sellers if they would like your assistance in getting any of the repairs scheduled or if they would like any contractor or handyman referrals. When providing contractor referrals, always provide three or more names of contractors that have performed successfully for you or other licensees and allow the seller to choose.

When you turn in the new listing, make arrangements to have a for-sale sign installed and have the listing entered into as many Internet sites as your company will allow, including your **personal webpage** and the MLS, if appropriate. Whether or not your company is large enough to have sufficient support staff to handle these administrative functions, you should know how to do all of these things yourself.

At times you will take a "delayed-input listing," where you complete the RLA, but on written instructions from the sellers, you delay inputting it into the MLS for a time to allow for making repairs, painting, removing furniture, and so on. If your MLS requires submission of all listings, you will need a C.A.R. Seller Instruction to Exclude Listing (SEL) from the MLS or other "authorization to exclude" signed by the seller for submission to the MLS. Either the C.A.R. form or one from your MLS should suffice.

Have your digital camera with you and take several pictures of the interior and exterior of the home for the MLS and your various websites. Upload your pictures into the MLS (and any appropriate websites) as soon as possible following the expiration of

the "authorization to exclude." This is especially important in a fast-paced market where you will probably get instant showing requests.

While you are at the property for the second visit, it is a good idea to conduct your **Agent's Inspection Disclosure**, also known as a walk-through **"red flag" inspection**. The observations you make here will be put into Part III of the Real Estate Transfer Disclosure Statement (TDS) before giving it to a buyer's licensee.

Start at the curb and work your way around and through the entire home, noting anything about the property's condition you see that may be of interest to a prospective buyer. Note things such as buckled sidewalks that may be a trip hazard; leaning fences (which often indicate dry-rotted posts); stains on carpets, ceilings, or walls; sticking doors; uneven floors; and any visible "smoky" wall sockets that may indicate an electrical problem. If you are listing an older home with an obviously remodeled kitchen, you have a duty to ask about the existence of building permits and if they were signed off by the building inspector. Keep in mind that you do not have a duty to disclose "latent defects"; as the listing licensee, you do have a duty to ask if the sellers know of any. If they tell you about any defects, you must disclose them.

In the event the sellers are having any presale inspections, such as a home inspection, pool inspection, or termite inspection, ask if they would like you to order them. If so, schedule them and meet the inspectors at the property to accompany them as they do the inspection. You can't beat firsthand knowledge about a property's condition as seen through the eyes of a qualified professional. This is especially true if the home is an older one that the sellers have lived in for a long time as there may be significant property condition issues to deal with.

For-Sale Sign

Turn in your listing to your office as soon as possible and either have the staff order a for-sale sign or install one yourself. If the staff does it, tell the sellers when to expect to see the sign installed. If necessary, give instructions to the sign company for exactly where you want the sign placed for maximum exposure. Also be aware that some homeowner associations (HOAs) either restrict the size and placement of for-sale signs or do not allow them at all. If you list a home in a development with an HOA, be sure to ask the sellers about any sign restrictions. If they do not know, ask to see their covenants, conditions, and restrictions (CC&R) and/or rules and regulations.

Rider Strips

Rider strips are narrow strips of metal or plastic with your name and contact telephone number on them. They are usually placed immediately under the for-sale sign or are anchored to the horizontal support bar that holds the for-sale sign. They may also contain special features of the home, such as a swimming pool or remodeled kitchen. It is probably best to have your cell phone number and e-mail address on the rider so you can take calls from prospective buyers anywhere, anytime. Note: If you are selling your own personal property, you must put an "owner/licensee" rider on any for-sale sign you use for your property. A for-sale sign is considered advertising by the Department of Real Estate and you *must* disclose your owner/licensee status in all advertising.

Talking Signs

A talking sign is a radio transmitter that sends out a short message about a home's features. Although it can be either AM or FM, FM models have a greater range (about 250 feet). If you use talking signs, prepare your message as soon as possible and install the broadcasting machine at the seller's home within a couple of days of taking the listing. Be as careful about the content of your radio ad as you would be about printed advertising because, although the talking sign machine is usually yours, your broker is liable for representations you make to the public as well as compliance with fair housing issues.

Lockbox Installation

Bring a lockbox, or keybox as they are often called, to the listing appointment with you to show to the sellers. Keyboxes are electronic, and many use infrared light to activate the opener after a licensee enters her code.

Many MLS forms now come with a preprinted disclaimer warning sellers that any action that allows other people access to their homes when they, or you, as the listing licensee, are not there presents a security risk. This warning is incorporated in the C.A.R. Listing Agreement under security and insurance Paragraph 11.

You should suggest that the sellers contact their insurance agents and make sure their policies cover them in the event something is damaged or stolen or missing. Suggest they put expensive items away in a safe place. Many insurance policies also state that the policy is void if the property has been vacant for longer than thirty consecutive days. If this is going to be an issue, have your sellers discuss it with their insurance agent as well.

Information Boxes

Most real estate associations carry information boxes, also called *flyer boxes*, as well as tubes that can be attached to your for-sale sign or hung below the sign. These low-cost containers include information about the property and are the source of many calls to real estate licensees, so get in the habit of using them regularly.

Property Brochures

Depending on the value of the property you are marketing, you may have two different qualities of property brochures. Both brochures may include the same information—the ones you place in a stand inside the property can be four-color on a high-quality paper, whereas the copies you put in the outdoor information box may be black and white.

Explaining that you need to work as a team, have the sellers keep the information box full of brochures. They should let you know when they are running low so that you can get more made if necessary.

Multiple Listing Service

Most areas of the United States have some sort of MLS. The MLS is an organization formed by a group of brokers to share their listings with each other in an orderly, controlled fashion. Most MLS organizations allow only exclusive authorization to sell listings placed into their databases with some exceptions. Many organizations are "mandatory" services whereby each subscribing broker agrees that all of her listings MUST be placed into the MLS database unless otherwise limited by the seller in writing. As a result of a 2008 settlement agreement between the National Association of REALTORS® and the Justice Department, real estate licensees may voluntarily share access to each others' listings via an IDX (Internet Data Exchange) or a VOW (Virtual Office Website). Strict rules and regulations concern access to MLS listings, so be sure to attend an antitrust seminar as soon as possible and consult your broker or legal counsel if you have any questions about the proper use of the MLS or either of these Internet tools.

When a member takes a listing, it is sent to a central facility that makes it available to all of the subscribing members. All members and those associations with reciprocal agreements have the right to sell the listing and participate in a portion of the commission. No one may advertise the listing except the listing broker, unless she has the broker's permission; however, many companies have websites that download the entire MLS database every day (twice a day

in many instances) and make the properties available to the public in a limited format.

In the event that the property is sold by a "cooperating broker" who represents the buyers in the transaction, the commission is paid according to the published offering in the MLS.

When a property is sold by a cooperating broker, called the "selling agent," there is normally a four-way split of the commission. For example, if the seller negotiated a 6 percent commission to the listing broker and the listing broker has offered 3 percent to the cooperating broker via the MLS, then 3 percent would go to the "listing" office and 3 percent would go to the "selling office." Each broker would, in turn, split whatever compensation was paid with the listing or selling licensee according to company policy. The selling broker then pays her licensee as agreed in the broker/salesperson agreement.

It should be noted here that if the listing brokers' offer of compensation is deemed unacceptable to the cooperating or selling licensee, that licensee may call the listing broker/licensee and, if possible, negotiate more favorable compensation. The selling licensee must never use the contract in an attempt to negotiate a higher commission. Proper procedure requires that the cooperating licensee call the listing broker/licensee before submitting an offer to attempt to negotiate any change in the compensation offered in the MLS.

In addition, compensation offered in the MLS is for members of that MLS or members of other multiple listing associations having reciprocal agreements to share listings or compensation. Compensation published through an MLS listing is not an offer to compensate nonmember licensees. Nonmember brokers/licensees are free to negotiate their own compensation with the listing broker prior to submitting an offer (see Figure 10.2).

The Internet

The Internet is a venue of choice by an overwhelming majority of home-buying consumers and is still expanding in popularity at a record pace. As a real estate professional, you are doing your clients a real disservice if you are not fully using the Internet to market their properties.

A large number of real estate associations and their MLSs have local sites for consumer access. Your MLS membership normally means that each listing you enter will automatically be available for public viewing in a limited format—one that omits the owners' names, telephone numbers, and any other personal or confidential information. The National Association of REALTORS® is a

FIGURE 10.2   Dividing an MLS Listing Commission

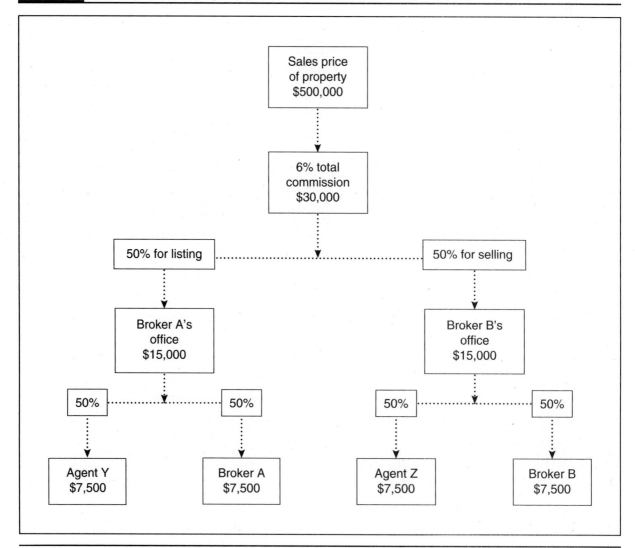

minority owner of www.realtor.com, which consumers can also access. Many real estate firms across the country have agreements with this site to display their listings nationally. As an individual, you can subscribe to www.realtor.com and have much of your personal information shown as well; this allows people to contact you directly from www.realtor.com. Note: The Internet address is the only place where you could see the word REALTOR® used without being in all capital letters. The term REALTOR® is a trademarked word and its preferred form is all capitals with the circle ® except when accessing Internet addresses. For additional information on the use of logos and NAR marks please see the **NAR Membership Marks Manual** available online at www.REALTOR.org or www.realtor.org.

Almost every real estate company has a website today. Consumers readily use it as a means of starting a property search in the nonthreatening environment of their own home or office. If you or your company have a personal website, be sure your web address is included on all business cards, stationery, envelopes, and all other forms of printed materials. Many licensees are opting for e-mail addresses and websites with their names in them (for example, Bob@BobSellsSanFrancisco.com or http://BobSells LosAngeles.com).

Upload the digital pictures you took of your listing as soon as it is placed on the Internet. People will see it almost instantly, and if there are no pictures almost everyone will eliminate it from their search results right away.

Virtual Tours

Owing to advanced technology, a buyer can now walk through an entire house and often the surrounding neighborhood without ever leaving her computer monitor. These virtual tours are available on the Internet and are easy to use. Besides being a potential source of buyers and other listings, virtual tours are an impressive tool to show prospective sellers when you are at a listing consultation. New home builders are embracing this technology at a rapid pace as well. Today's digital cameras have a movie function that makes virtual tours easy to take and upload to the Internet. You should have a digital camera as part of your **listing toolkit**.

Advertising

Take the time to prepare at least three ads for you and your company to use right after you have taken a listing so the property's best features are still vivid in your mind. Be sure to keep fair housing issues in mind and describe the property, not the potential buyers. Use the following **AIDA** (Attention, Interest, Desire, Action) formula so your ads get the maximum response.

Attention. You need a "header" in your ad in large or bold print that gets the reader to stop scanning the paper and read your ad.

Interest. The first few words of your ad need to create interest in reading more. Paint word pictures here.

Desire. The body of your ad should convey further information or an emotional feeling that creates a desire to see the property in the reader's mind.

Action. The end of your ad should contain a "call to action" such as "Priced for quick sale. See it today!"

Using the AIDA formula and prewriting at least three ads (and rewriting until they are just right) will increase their effectiveness, generate more calls to you, and keep you from having to write a mediocre ad just to meet a deadline.

Be sure to send copies of your advertising to your sellers so they know how their ads appear.

Open House

In 2009 the National Association of REALTORS® released a survey showing that less than 4 percent of homebuyers now use Open Houses to start their home search or to meet a real estate licensee. Given this fact, not every home is a good candidate for an Open House. Some are too remote and hard to get to, others have house pets that the sellers won't take away or someone home with an illness, and so on. If your sellers want an Open House and you feel it will be productive, make arrangements to list it on the MLS and your company's Internet Open House site. Place an ad with the proper paper and be sure to tell the owners they must be away from the property while you are working, as potential buyers will be uneasy about asking questions or showing interest with the owners.

Directional signs placed at key intersections are helpful in creating more traffic to your Open House; however, many public agencies do not allow the placement of these signs on public property. Therefore, be careful to check your local sign ordnances before you install directional signs to an Open House. Do not place a sign on someone's private property without asking permission first. You will be pleasantly surprised at how pleased the owners are that you are professional enough to ask first.

Office Tour

Also called *caravan* because of the long line of licensees' cars that go from house-to-house, most real estate companies have a weekly office tour or caravan of their new listings. Ask all licensees that view your listing on the office tour to leave a business card as it is very impressive to sellers when they come home and find a large number of licensee business cards on their kitchen counters. Many licensees provide refreshments or drawings for the licensees that view their listing to entice more people to visit.

Many real estate companies provide a sheet for the tour that contains property information, directions to the property, and space to

evaluate the price and condition of the property and to make suggestions about improvements to make the property more saleable.

Multiple Listing Service Tour

Most MLS organizations have weekly property tours or caravans. Large MLSs often break the tour down into smaller areas and alternate them each week so the licensees have time to see more of the available listings. Licensees usually like to see the homes that they have potential buyers for, but every licensee should be familiar with all active listings in a specific price range and/or neighborhood.

Be sure to give the owners as much advance notice as possible as to when their homes will be inspected by MLS members. Ask them to "shine the apple" for you on the tour day and, if possible, set the mood with some low, soft music. Some other general rules for the property tour are:

- The owners should not be at home. Licensees tend to hurry through a home where the owners are present.

- If possible, you or your assistant should be at the home during the entire tour.

- Place property flyers for each licensee in a spot where they will be sure to pick one up. They will see many homes that day and you want them to remember yours.

- On cold days, ask the owners to start a fire in the fireplace. Be sure to stay until it has died down to embers and make sure it is protected by a fireplace screen. Pressed logs are best for this purpose. If the home has air-conditioning, on hot days, ask the owners to turn the air-conditioning down an extra two or three degrees.

- Depending on the weather, have nonalcoholic hot or cold drinks in disposable cups available. Licensees who take the time to stop for a cup of lemonade or coffee will remember the home more than those who come and go quickly. You will attract more licensees if you offer food, but if you do, be sure it is bite-sized to minimize crumbs on the floors.

Just Listed Postcard

Once the property is listed, have at least 100 Just Listed postcards made and send them to the homes around your new listing. Include a picture and the address of the property on a postcard, along with a small picture of you. Also include a brief statement about the property noting that you will be in contact soon to see if they know someone who may be interested in living in the neighborhood. This is an excellent prospecting tool as well.

Your E-mail Database

One powerful marketing strategy you can use is to e-mail your entire database with news about your new listing. Start your e-mail by introducing the new listing including where it is located, its physical features, and the price. Attach at least two pictures of the home and ask if anyone is interested in seeing it or knows someone who might be. Your sellers will love this type of advertising, and it's free! Be sure to e-mail yourself and BCC your group.

Social Networking

Many Internet sites are available where you may market your listings by uploading pictures and information to the site's main webpage along with a brief description of the property and an MLS number. These search sites and portals such as Facebook, Twitter, Yahoo!, and Google are frequented by huge numbers of buyers and real estate licensees; your buyer may only be a click away.

10.2 GOOD COMMUNICATION

Good communication starts when the listing is signed, and it should not stop until the property is sold and the sellers have moved to their new home. A good listing licensee gets the listing signed and makes an appointment with the sellers for a couple of days later to go over her marketing plan in detail. Note: After the listing is signed and before you leave the seller's home, explain what will be happening over the next couple of days. Also give the sellers a copy of the transfer disclosure statement and ask them to fill it out and have it ready for you to pick up when you see them the following day. Sellers do not like completing these forms and will often procrastinate unless you give it some urgency. Tell them that you need it for the **marketing binder** for the house.

When a listing is signed, the owner and licensee go through two different periods together: the marketing period, which occurs before the sellers receive an offer to purchase, and the escrow period, which occurs after the sellers accept an offer to purchase. Both periods require excellent communication between the sellers and the licensee for things to go smoothly.

Most owners who have been unhappy with the sale process cite poor communication with their licensee as the number one issue. Though the practice is unethical, some licensees have been known to make unrealistic representations to get the listing and are then unable to produce the desired result so a sale is slow in coming, if

at all. The lack of activity can upset sellers, but the lack of communication will lead the seller to conclude that the licensee is doing nothing; an unhappy seller and a lost listing is ensured. Often, when communication has broken down, the licensee makes matters much worse by avoiding contact with the sellers and will fail to call them to try to renew the listing.

Weekly Activity Report

A written marketing activity report can be a critical tool in the communication process. Explain carefully to the sellers what you have done so far to sell their home and what they can expect over the next several days. Your weekly written report should recap the scheduled Open House activities, Open House results, and any other activities that took place that week. Don't make the mistake of sending monthly reports to give the impression that there has been more activity; owners do not like to wait that long to be updated on what has been taking place.

Get in the habit of preparing your weekly activity reports at the same time every week. It will become routine for you and will give you a chance to review the activity weekly yourself, to see if any other action such as a price adjustment is needed.

When you send your activity reports to the sellers, reference any ads that have run in any newspapers, and after the property is on any Internet sites, send the sellers a note with the website address listed so they can see it for themselves. Keep the sellers advised regularly as to how many **unique visitors** (first-time visitors) have looked at the site.

Broker Letter

Your broker should send the sellers a letter thanking them for listing the property with the firm. She should state what a good choice they made in choosing you, the licensee, as their representative, and if you cannot be reached, they should feel free to call her. If you took the listing at a price you thought was too aggressive, and after a time you need to adjust it, ask your broker to send the sellers a letter stating that she has some concerns regarding the home's sales activity and recommends that they meet with you to discuss a repositioning of their listing in the MLS.

Showings

Explain to the sellers that although licensees will always try their best to abide by the showing instructions in the MLS listing, there

will be times when they may need to "bend the rules" a little. Sometimes a licensee will show a home in a certain neighborhood, for example, and based on the buyer's reaction, the licensee will sense that your listing could be the perfect home for them. In cases like this, the licensee should still call first and ask for permission to show the home with very little or even no notice. Your sellers should be as flexible as possible in this type of situation. Licensees refer to these types of situations as *crashing gently*.

The opposite can also happen. Many licensees have personally experienced arriving at a home that they had planned to show only to have the buyers say: "Forget it, I'm not even going in." If this happens, you should either go to the door or call and cancel the appointment. Your sellers must be as tolerant as possible in this situation as well.

Most sellers are very proud of their homes and may want to personally show it off to prospective buyers. Explain that almost all buyers are reluctant to ask questions about the home or show any type of positive emotion about it when the sellers are around. Sellers should leave just prior to the scheduled showing time, if at all possible, so the buyers will feel completely at home and free to ask questions and become emotionally involved with the home. All information the sellers want to convey to the buyers should be given to you ahead of time and incorporated into your marketing brochure.

If the sellers must stay at home, it is best for them to go outside while the buyers look at the inside and come indoors when the buyers go outside. During inclement weather, the sellers should stay as far from the buyers as possible.

Explain Your Advertising Policy

Make sure your sellers understand your company's **advertising policy** and philosophy as well as the different media you use. Carefully explain about the very low percentage of buyers who use the newspaper to look for homes and that neither you nor your company advertise every home every day as this would be prohibitively expensive and would not generate any more calls than advertising by price range. Let them know that you advertise enough homes so that all price ranges are represented. The purpose of advertising is to get people to call so that either the listing licensee or the duty licensee can tell them about all of the homes your company has listed in that price range or neighborhood and ask for an appointment to show the caller all of them, including your listing. Since

the start of the new millennium, there has been a major shift by brokerage firms away from newspaper hard copy and toward the Internet, and for good reason. Over 90 percent of buyers start their home and licensee search on the Internet, whereas newspaper classified readership has dropped to an all-time low.

Prepare the Owners for an Offer

The second time you meet with the sellers, give them a blank copy of the purchase agreement that will be used to make an offer on their home. Ask them to read it and ask you any questions at your next meeting. Explain that if the home is priced competitively, they may get an offer very quickly, and although it may not be exactly what they want, most of the time the best offers come first. Also explain that when an offer comes in, the sellers have four choices: to *accept* the offer, without change, which then binds the buyers to the contract, contingencies notwithstanding; to *reject* the offer or simply *not reply* to it, which is never a good practice; or to provide a *counteroffer*, stating to the buyers their bottom line acceptable price and terms.

Pricing Strategy

We talked earlier about creating and presenting the competitive market analysis (CMA). It is a worthy enough subject to review the importance of good communication about this issue here. If you have listed the property effectively for the current market conditions, you should experience a good amount of showings and receive an offer reasonably soon. If the price is too aggressive, however, in your second meeting with the sellers, repeat what you told them earlier about competitive pricing and remind them that if they do not have several showings, and at least one offer within the first thirty days, you will expect them to make the price adjustment necessary to become competitive. Note: Do not talk about "lowering" the price. The human mind hears "lowering" as a loss or lessening of something. In reality, the sellers never had the inflated value of the property to lose in the first place, but they will still consider it a loss if you refer to it that way. Use "price adjustment" or "repositioning in the MLS" when talking about any change in price.

If the price is too high, remind the sellers that by comparison they are really helping to sell their neighbors' homes, because when buyers look at all the available homes in the neighborhood, the other homes look like very good buys.

The last thing that you want is to carry the burden of an overpriced listing for a long time; doing so can hurt your reputation in

the brokerage community. It can also get you down emotionally and cost you a lot of money in wasted advertising and time that could have been spent on more meaningful opportunities. It might also help to explain to the owners that by taking an improperly priced listing for a long period of time, you hurt them and your other sellers. Let them know that all of the licensees who participate in the MLS readily show and sell your listings because you have a reputation for properly pricing your listings. If you take a listing that is priced too high for an extended period of time, your reputation will suffer and your sellers' homes won't be shown as readily. Tell them that you will be willing to take the listing at their price for thirty days and if they have not received a good offer or sold the property in that time, you will be back with a change form, with the listed price adjusted to slightly above the demonstrated market value so people will finally become interested. You will also bring a listing cancellation form. Tell them that they are free to sign either form and you will accept their decision but that one of the forms must be signed. As listing agreements are bilateral in nature and cannot be cancelled by only one party, you must put your option as stated here in writing in the "additional terms" section of the listing. You will be amazed how often the owners suddenly get serious and really start to listen to you about proper pricing at the listing consultation when you are this assertive about the importance of effective pricing.

Market Conditions

Market conditions are subject to constant changes. These changes can make a good listing look like a bad one and make a seemingly overpriced listing look like a good buy. Everything from the rise and fall of interest rates to what's said by the news media can affect the market conditions in which a home is sold. One of your most important jobs as a listing licensee is to keep your sellers well-informed about the current market conditions and to give them suggestions for using that information to their best advantage.

An excellent example is the chaos of the marketplace created by the overwhelming number of short sales and foreclosures currently taking place. A short sale is a sale where the seller has insufficient funds to bring to escrow closing to effect the sale of her home and the lender agrees to accept the net proceeds of a sale, after all selling expenses including commissions and costs are paid, as full payment of their existing loan. In other words, part of their loan is written off as a loss by them. A foreclosure sale, or REO sale, is a sale by a lender that has taken a property back through the foreclosure process; she now owns the home and acts as the seller.

10.3 MODIFYING OR EXTENDING THE LISTING CONTRACT

At times the licensee who took the listing moves to a different real estate company or leaves the business. When this happens, it is important to remember that all listings are taken in the name of the broker and are not the property of a single licensee. It is up to each individual broker how she wishes to handle this. Some will release the listing to the licensee's new company and take a referral fee. Others will keep the listing and reassign it to another salesperson within the office. Remember, it is not only unethical for the licensee to contact the sellers and ask them to cancel their listing, it is also a violation of the salesperson/broker contract.

There is usually a rather close relationship between the licensee and their seller, so timely and effective communication with the seller is important. The broker must first determine whether or not she wishes to retain the listing and immediately contact the sellers.

If the broker retains the listing, she should have a replacement licensee ready to take over. The sellers may or may not be happy with the broker's decision, so good, clear, effective communication by the broker and the replacement licensee is of paramount importance. The new licensee should call and introduce herself and make an appointment to meet with the sellers as soon as possible. Depending on how much time is left on the listing, the newly assigned licensee may request an extension of the listing.

If you have a listing that is within three to four weeks away from its expiration date, you should contact the sellers and ask for a meeting to go over your marketing efforts to date. Discuss your pricing strategy and any other nonmonetary issues that may be hindering a sale and then ask for an extension of the listing if you want one.

At any time during the course of the listing, if any change is made, whether it is a change of listing licensee, price, or terms, it should be made on a modification form called the Modification of Terms Authorization and Right to Sell Acquire or Rent, C.A.R. form MT (see Figure 10.3).

10.4 PRESENTING OFFERS TO YOUR SELLERS

At some point during the course of your marketing efforts, you will receive a phone call from another licensee that she has taken an offer on one of your listings. You may also write an offer on one of your listings on behalf of buyers you have been working with. Depending on current market conditions, you may even receive

FIGURE 10.3 Modification of Terms Authorization and Right to Sell (Form MT)

CALIFORNIA
ASSOCIATION
OF REALTORS ®

**MODIFICATION OF TERMS
AUTHORIZATION AND RIGHT TO SELL,
ACQUIRE OR RENT**
(C.A.R. Form MT, Revised 4/08)

The Listing Agreement (or, if checked, ☐ Buyer Representation Agreement,) dated_____,

between _____ ("Broker") and

_____ ("Principal"), regarding the real property,

manufactured home or business described as_____

_____

is modified as follows:

PRICE: The listing price, price range, lease or rental amount shall be changed to:

_____

_____ Dollars ($ _____)

EXPIRATION DATE: The expiration date is changed to: _____.

OTHER: _____

_____

_____

_____

_____

_____

All other terms of the Listing Agreement or Buyer Representation Agreement, as applicable, remain in full force and effect, except as modified herein.

I acknowledge that I have read, understand and have received a copy of this Modification of Terms.

Date_____ at_____, California

_____   _____
Principal   Principal

Broker _____   By _____ Date_____
         (Firm)   (Agent)

Published and Distributed by:
REAL ESTATE BUSINESS SERVICES, INC.
a subsidiary of the California Association of REALTORS®
525 South Virgil Avenue, Los Angeles, California 90020

MT REVISED 4/08 (PAGE 1 OF 1) Print Date

Reviewed by _____ Date _____

EQUAL HOUSING
OPPORTUNITY

MODIFICATION OF TERMS AUTHORIZATION AND RIGHT TO SELL, ACQUIRE OR RENT (MT PAGE 1 OF 1)

Source: Reprinted with permission of California Association of REALTORS®.

more than one offer on your listing at almost the same time. Any of these scenarios will require contacting your sellers to let them know you have a purchase contract on their home you would like to review with them.

The sellers will almost always ask you the dollar amount of the offer. It is best to avoid giving specific details ahead of time as they will tend to worry unnecessarily and may even become hostile if the price is lower than they were expecting. Even if you have the offer in hand, just tell them that you will go over it in detail when you meet. Set the appointment and get off the phone as quickly as you can.

If the offer is written by another licensee, either from your office or company or from another brokerage firm, ask if the salesperson would like to accompany you to present her offer in person. If they say yes, call and set the appointment with the sellers and call the licensee back to confirm the time and place. If they prefer to fax or e-mail the offer to you and have you present it, call the sellers and let them know that you will be receiving an offer shortly and set an appointment with them to present it. It is always an advantage for a buyer's licensee to personally present the offer to the seller whenever possible. The buyer's licensee knows the details of the offer much better than the listing licensee and is in a position to quickly contact the buyer if a counteroffer is made.

Sometimes you would have already received an offer on one of your listings from a licensee and set an appointment to present it before receiving a call from another licensee with a second offer. The proper thing to do is to let the second licensee know you already have one offer and ask her to attend your meeting with the owners. If this happens, immediately inform the first licensee about the second offer. If you receive more calls from licensees with additional offers, repeat the process with everyone each time. Remember, you have a fiduciary duty to your sellers to get them the highest price on the best terms possible. Notifying each licensee about multiple offers will help them to get their buyers to make their best offer up front, usually producing a higher price for the sellers.

If you write an offer on your own listing, it is best to call the sellers and tell them that you will be meeting shortly with some people to write an offer on their home and you wanted to set a time to see them later that day or evening. Even if the offer is already written, make an appointment to present it in person. A competent explanation of an eight page dual agent contract requires a personal presentation by the licensee. If, prior to presenting your offer, you receive a call or calls from other licensees with offers, just follow the earlier example.

Presenting Your Buyer's Offer

If you have an offer on your own listing, make copies for each of the owners to review as you review the details. Write down the main points of interest (price, financing, closing, occupancy dates, and so on) and have them in front of you when you present the offer. This allows you to present the important issues in a controlled and timely method and helps you to cover all important issues.

When you meet with the owners, sit in a comfortable place, usually at the kitchen table where you took the listing. Make a little small talk first, being careful not to overdo it, especially with type-A personalities. This will bring down the owners' adrenaline and make them easier to communicate with.

If, and only if, the offer being presented is from a cooperating licensee at another firm, it will be necessary to disclose agency to the seller before presenting the offer even though the seller may have already received such a disclosure from the listing licensee (see Chapter 4 on agency disclosure).

It is sometimes best to start with some of the easier and more negotiable issues. Talk about the escrow closing date, occupancy date, whether or not the buyers are preapproved for any required financing, and any personal property being requested in the purchase contract. After discussing these issues, hand each owner a copy of the purchase contract and review the price. Be sure you have all relevant and recent comparable neighborhood sales statistics with you. If you get into a discussion about the price offered by the buyers, you can refer to the sales statistics for clarity regarding the current market value.

If you have a written offer with a fair price, don't be bashful about saying so; you owe it to the buyers and sellers to see that they are treated fairly. If the price offered is low, you, as the listing licensee and sellers' representative, have a duty to say so. Remember, when you write an offer on a property listed with your company, your broker is a dual agent and must be fair and honest with all parties. Openly state the truth and give whatever reasonable guidance is necessary to each party to help them make well-informed decisions. Again, your prime directive as a fiduciary is not to make the sale but to provide information and guidance so the parties have the information necessary to make an informed decision without any input from you on price or terms. If the parties are reasonable, with your advice and guidance they will make good, sound decisions and if appropriate the sale will take place as a result.

We always hope for an accepted offer without any counteroffer, and that advice should always be given to the owners if it is truly in their best interests. If there is a true need to provide a counteroffer

in order to change a condition of the purchase contract to better meet the sellers' needs, it should be recommended.

Sellers sometimes ask you to reduce your commission because they know that in a dual agency transaction you will be getting a larger fee. If this happens, explain that doing so would be a real disincentive for you. If you sold your buyer any other home, you would get the full compensation offered through the MLS and you would still get the listing side of the commission from the sale of their home when someone else sells it. It doesn't make sense for you to take less of a fee for doubling the liability by combining both jobs into one property.

Presenting Co-op Offers

The purchase agreement package should start with a cover letter from the buyer to the seller with a brief biography on the buyers, what they like about the home, and their reasoning for the price offered, if appropriate. Next in the packet is the Disclosure Regarding Real Estate Agency Relationships (AD) form and then the contract. Whether the listing licensee or the licensee representing the buyer presents the offer, California Civil Code 2079 requires the buyer's representative to disclose agency before presenting the offer. This is accomplished by having the sellers sign an AD form. The dialogue could go something like this—"Mr. Seller, I know your representative may have already explained how licensees work"—or if the offer is being presented by the sellers own licensee, "I know we have already gone over the subject of agency before I listed your property … but I am required by law to make this disclosure for the buyer's licensee before I present their offer. If you feel as though you have an understanding of agency representation I would ask that you simply sign this form acknowledging receipt of a copy. If you have any questions I'd be happy to answer them now."

If this disclosure is done properly, the listing licensee will have just one AD form in the file and the buyer's licensee may have two AD forms in her file: one from the buyer and one from the seller or one AD form signed by both buyer and seller. This additional step is required for two reasons: (1) because it's the law and (2) because there may not always be a listing licensee, as in the case of a For Sale by Owner. If, in assessing the competence of the other party's representative, you sense a lack of confidence or some degree of inexperience, you might ask if the licensee would prefer that you make the presentation. If the licensee is experienced and you know her, ask that copies of the offer be given to everyone and that she present the offer. You can stop her as necessary to ask questions or

clarify issues. As the buyer's representative knows the buyers, she may be in a better position to present their offer and provide additional information about the buyers.

Your job as the seller's representative is to carefully and thoroughly review the offer and make notes about all of the major points of the contract as well as any issues you know should be brought to the owners' attention. After the buyer's representative is finished with her presentation, go over the notes you made with the owners. In many cases you or they will want to discuss the offer in private. Ask the other licensee to wait in another room or step outside while you discuss the offer with the owners and decide whether to accept or provide a counteroffer.

After you review all of the issues, have the owners sign the offer, and ask the buyer's representative to return and give her the signed original, keeping one copy for you and one for the owners. If you are issuing a counteroffer, write it first and have the owners sign the offer (subject to the counteroffer) and the counteroffer. Then explain the reasoning behind each item in the counteroffer to the buyer's licensee. This will help the licensee gain approval from the buyers.

If you issue a counteroffer, ask the buyer's representative when she will be meeting with the buyers. If immediately, tell them how to reach you and how they can get you a signed copy of the counteroffer.

Presenting Multiple Offers

At times the California real estate market goes into hyper speed and receiving multiple offers is the norm on almost every listing. In the event you have more than one offer on your listing, it may be best to have everyone meet at your office rather than at the seller's home. Having a large group of strangers sitting in their living room may be daunting for many owners.

Depending on how many offers you have, you may want all of the buyer's licensees to show up at one time or stagger the times by twenty minutes or so to avoid a crowd.

Have the buyer's representatives wait in the lobby or living room and bring them in one at a time to present their offers while you review each offer and take notes. When dealing with multiple offers, it is a good idea to draw a line or lines vertically on a legal pad and put the facts of each offer side-by-side. This makes a comparative discussion with the owners much easier.

After all the offers have been presented, review them privately with the owners to determine if one is acceptable without change. If so, simply complete the "Rejection of Offer" section at the bottom

of the Residential Purchase Agreement – California (RPA-CA) on the other offers and return them to the respective licensees and keep a copy for you and the sellers.

10.5 HANDLING SINGLE OR MULTIPLE COUNTEROFFERS

If none of the offers are acceptable, your sellers have two choices: (1) they can issue a counteroffer for the offer that seems to be the best overall, giving a fairly short time for the buyers' acceptance, and go on to the next offer if the first buyers do not respond; or (2) they can check the box in the second paragraph of the counteroffer, stating that the buyers are aware of the multiple counteroffers, and even if they sign and return a counteroffer, they will not be considered to be "in contract" unless and until the buyers or sellers countersign the accepted counteroffer in Paragraph 6 of the counteroffer (see Figure 10.4) and confirmation of acceptance is acknowledged and personally received by the maker of the counter offer or her authorized representative.

Never counteroffer more than one offer at a time unless you check the multiple counteroffer box on the counteroffer form. Otherwise you may end up selling the home to two buyers, creating potential legal problems and very bad relations with your owners.

If your sellers have multiple offers and choose to counter only one offer at a time, prioritize the offers so you know which one to counteroffer next if the first buyers do not accept the seller's counter. Tell each licensee where they are in line and retain their offers until such time as you have an accepted counteroffer. If any of the offers are clearly unacceptable, explain why to the respective licensees.

Good communication is essential when dealing with multiple offers. Multiple licensees and their buyers are waiting to hear if their offer has been accepted. All parties should be treated with respect. Until you have an accepted offer, you don't know which buyer will ultimately be the new owner of your listing.

A word of caution: Whenever you have multiple offers, always give extra credibility to cash offers or fully preapproved buyers who are financing versus buyers who are financing but not preapproved. There is little joy in having six offers on your listing, accepting the highest price offered, only to be told ten days later that the sale is being cancelled because the buyers didn't qualify for their loan. In the meantime, you lost all of the other five offers. Believe me, this will not be welcome news to your seller.

FIGURE 10.4 Counteroffer

CALIFORNIA ASSOCIATION OF REALTORS®

COUNTER OFFER No. _____

For use by Seller or Buyer. May be used for Multiple Counter Offer.

(C.A.R. Form CO, Revised 10/04)

Date _____, at _____, California.
This is a counter offer to the: ☐ California Residential Purchase Agreement, ☐ Counter Offer, or ☐ Other _____ ("Offer"),
dated _____, on property known as _____ ("Property"),
between _____ ("Buyer") and _____ ("Seller").

1. **TERMS:** The terms and conditions of the above referenced document are **accepted subject to the following:**
   A. Paragraphs in the Offer that require initials by all parties, but are not initialed by all parties, are excluded from the final agreement unless specifically referenced for inclusion in paragraph 1C of this or another Counter Offer.
   B. Unless otherwise agreed in writing, down payment and loan amount(s) will be adjusted in the same proportion as in the original Offer.
   C. _____
      _____
      _____
      _____
      _____
      _____
   D. The following attached supplements are incorporated into this Counter Offer: ☐ Addendum No. _____
      ☐ _____   ☐ _____

2. **RIGHT TO ACCEPT OTHER OFFERS:** Seller has the right to continue to offer the Property for sale or for other transaction, and to accept any other offer at any time prior to notification of acceptance, as described in paragraph 3. If this is a Seller Counter Offer, Seller's acceptance of another offer prior to Buyer's acceptance and communication of notification of this Counter Offer, shall revoke this Counter Offer.

3. **EXPIRATION:** This Counter Offer shall be deemed revoked and the deposits, if any, shall be returned unless this Counter Offer is signed by the Buyer or Seller to whom it is sent and a Copy of the signed Counter Offer is personally received by the person making this Counter Offer or _____,
   who is authorized to receive it, by 5:00PM on the third day after this Counter Offer is made or, (if checked)
   by ☐ _____ (date), at _____ AM/PM. This Counter Offer may be executed in counterparts.

4. ☐ **(If checked:) MULTIPLE COUNTER OFFER:** Seller is making a Counter Offer(s) to another prospective buyer(s) on terms that may or may not be the same as in this Counter Offer. Acceptance of this Counter Offer by Buyer shall **not** be binding unless and until it is subsequently re-Signed by Seller in paragraph 7 below and a Copy of the Counter Offer Signed in paragraph 7 is personally received by Buyer or by _____, who is authorized to receive it, by 5:00 PM on the third Day After this Counter Offer is made or, (if checked) by ☐ _____ (date), at _____ AM/PM. Prior to the completion of all of these events, Buyer and Seller shall have no duties or obligations for the purchase or sale of the Property.

5. **OFFER: BUYER OR SELLER MAKES THIS COUNTER OFFER ON THE TERMS ABOVE AND ACKNOWLEDGES RECEIPT OF A COPY.**
   _____ Date _____
   _____ Date _____

6. **ACCEPTANCE: I/WE** accept the above Counter Offer (If checked ☐ **SUBJECT TO THE ATTACHED COUNTER OFFER**) and acknowledge receipt of a Copy.
   _____ Date _____ Time _____ AM/PM
   _____ Date _____ Time _____ AM/PM

7. **MULTIPLE COUNTER OFFER SIGNATURE LINE:** By signing below, Seller accepts this Multiple Counter Offer. NOTE TO SELLER: Do NOT sign in this box until after Buyer signs in paragraph 6. (Paragraph 7 applies only if paragraph 4 is checked.)
   _____ Date _____ Time _____ AM/PM
   _____ Date _____ Time _____ AM/PM

8. (_____/_____) (Initials) **Confirmation of Acceptance:** A Copy of Signed Acceptance was personally received by the maker of the _____ Counter Offer, or that person's authorized agent as specified in paragraph 3 (or, if this is a Multiple Counter Offer, the Buyer or Buyer's authorized agent as specified in paragraph 4) on (date) _____, at _____ AM/PM. **A binding Agreement is created when a Copy of Signed Acceptance is personally received by the the maker of the Counter Offer, or that person's authorized agent (or, if this is a Multiple Counter Offer, the Buyer or Buyer's authorized agent) whether or not confirmed in this document. Completion of this confirmation is not legally required in order to create a binding Agreement; it is solely intended to evidence the date that Confirmation of Acceptance has occurred.**

Published and Distributed by:
REAL ESTATE BUSINESS SERVICES, INC.
a subsidiary of the California Association of REALTORS®
525 South Virgil Avenue, Los Angeles, California 90020

SURE TRAC The System for Success®

Reviewed by _____ Date _____

EQUAL HOUSING OPPORTUNITY

CO REVISED 10/04 (PAGE 1 OF 1) Print Date

COUNTER OFFER (CO PAGE 1 OF 1)

Source: Reprinted with permission of California Association of REALTORS®.

A set of dos and don'ts is included here for you to use as a checklist when drafting a counteroffer.

Dos

- Start by checking the appropriate box on the last page of the original offer that indicates that the offer is accepted subject to a counteroffer. If the contract you are working with does not have such a box and/or statement, handwrite one just above the signature line but before the sellers sign the agreement.
- Be sure the counteroffer is completely filled out at the top, identifying the property, the buyers and sellers, and the date of the purchase contract of the counteroffer.
- Number each item in the counteroffer and separate each one with a blank line for clarity. Refer to the corresponding contract paragraph whenever possible.

Refer to the checklist that you made while reviewing the offer so you do not miss any important items in your counteroffer. Be especially careful about personal property included, escrow closing dates, the occupancy date, the price, and tightening up any time limits for waiving contingencies.

Be sure the sellers sign and initial where required both the purchase contract and the counteroffer. Retain copies for the sellers and for your file, giving the original and any remaining copies back to the buyer's licensee.

If you fax the counteroffer to the buyer's representative, you must fax both sides of the agency disclosure signed and initialed by the sellers, the entire contract, and the counteroffer. Call the buyer's licensee and let her know you sent the fax. Caution: Do not assume your fax went through. Wait for the fax machine to print the transmittal page. Confirm the number of pages you have sent. If it is "0" or a number less than you thought you sent, resend it. You should also confirm that your company's fax-machine is set to the correct time and date so that all time- and date-stamped documents accurately reflect the time of transmission.

Don'ts

If you are writing the counteroffer with the buyer's licensee present, don't let a dispute about contract language interfere with making the sale happen.

- Don't make partial changes in contract paragraphs on the counteroffer. Instead rewrite the entire paragraph for clarity and state that the new paragraph replaces the old one by reference.

- Don't restate items or issues that are already agreed to in the purchase contract. Doing so is redundant and can lead to confusion. Don't make a change just for the sake of change; if a clause, paragraph, or statement is clear and agreeable to all parties, leave it alone.

- Don't use unnecessary words or flowery sentences. Make a clear and complete statement about each issue addressed in the counteroffer in language that is understandable and not interpretable in more than one way.

- Don't let the buyer's licensee badger your sellers to put something in the counteroffer that they really don't want to.

- Don't write long or detailed paragraphs directly on the counteroffer form. Write them out separately first, then reread the paragraphs for clarity. If and when they accurately reflect the conditions agreed to by the parties to the contract, put them on the counteroffer form.

10.6 RELEASE OF CONTRACT

Not every sale closes escrow successfully. Many things can cause it to fail, such as the buyer's financing falls through, estimates for dealing with termites and property repairs are higher than the sellers want to pay, the buyers get "buyer's remorse," or the buyer's home doesn't sell.

When escrow fails to close, you will need to get a Cancellation of Contract, Release of Deposit and Joint Escrow Instructions form signed by all parties to the escrow (see Figure 10.5). This form identifies the type of document it is releasing and the property being released. It also names and instructs the escrow company to cancel the escrow, identified by the escrow number, and gives instructions for the release of any deposits held. This form must be signed by all of the principals and all brokers involved in the sale.

SUMMARY

This chapter covers the importance of constant and open communication with owners whom you represent, as well as how to present a CMA. You learned how to create and implement an effective marketing plan and what it takes to properly service a listing through to a successful escrow closing.

You learned how to properly represent a seller in negotiating an offer and how to present offers and counteroffers. You learned how creating an escrow timeline helps keep everyone involved in an escrow on track.

FIGURE 10.5   Release of Contract

CALIFORNIA ASSOCIATION OF REALTORS®

CANCELLATION OF CONTRACT, RELEASE OF DEPOSIT AND JOINT ESCROW INSTRUCTIONS
(C.A.R. Form CC, Revised 4/06)

In accordance with the terms and conditions of the: ☐ California Residential Purchase Agreement; or ☐ Other _____ ("Agreement"), dated _____, including all amendments and related documents, on property known as _____ ("Property"), between _____ ("Buyer") and _____ ("Seller").

Paragraphs 1 and 2 below constitute escrow instructions to Escrow Holder. Release of funds (pursuant to paragraph 2) requires mutual Signed release instructions from Buyer and Seller, judicial decision or arbitration award. A party may be subject to a civil penalty of up to $1,000 for refusal to sign such instructions if no good faith dispute exists as to who is entitled to the deposited funds (Civil Code §1057.3).

1. **CANCELLATION OF CONTRACT:** ☐ Buyer or ☐ Seller or ☐ both Buyer and Seller cancel(s) the Agreement and ☐ (if applicable), escrow # _____ with _____, Escrow Holder, for the following reason:
   A. ☐ Seller has failed to take the following applicable contractual action as required by the Agreement: _____
   _____.
   OR B. ☐ Seller has failed to remove the applicable contingency after being given a Notice to Seller to Perform (C.A.R. Form NSP).
   OR C. ☐ Buyer has failed to remove the applicable contingency after being given a Notice to Buyer to Perform (C.A.R. Form NBP).
   OR D. ☐ Buyer has failed to take the applicable contractual action after being given a Notice to Buyer to Perform (C.A.R. Form NBP).
   OR E. ☐ As otherwise permitted by paragraph _____ of the Agreement.
   OR F. ☐ Per mutual agreement.

   _____   _____
   Buyer's or Seller's Signature (party cancelling the contract)   Date

   _____   _____
   Buyer's or Seller's Signature (party cancelling the contract)   Date

2. **RELEASE OF DEPOSIT**
   A. ☐ Seller authorizes release of deposit, less Buyer's fees and costs, to Buyer.

   OR B. ☐ Buyer authorizes release of deposit, less Seller's fees and costs, to Seller. (☐ A liquidated damages clause was properly included as part of the Agreement, and the Property contains no more than four residential units, one of which the Buyer intended to occupy. Buyer's authorization of release of deposit to Seller is limited to no more than 3% of the purchase price. Any additional deposit to be returned to Buyer.)

   OR C. ☐ Both Buyer and Seller acknowledge mutual cancellation of the Agreement and authorize Escrow Holder to continue to hold the deposit until receiving subsequent mutual instructions, judicial decision or arbitration award.

   OR D. ☐ Other: _____.

Unless otherwise specified above, Buyer and Seller (i) mutually release each other from all obligation to buy, sell or exchange the Property under the Agreement, and from all claims, actions and demands that each may have against the other(s) by reason of the Agreement; and (ii) intend that all rights and obligations arising out of the Agreement are null and void.

Date _____   Date _____
Buyer _____   Seller _____
Buyer _____   Seller _____

Published and Distributed by:
REAL ESTATE BUSINESS SERVICES, INC.
a subsidiary of the California Association of REALTORS®
525 South Virgil Avenue, Los Angeles, California 90020

CC REVISED 4/06 (PAGE 1 OF 1) Print Date

Reviewed by _____ Date _____

EQUAL HOUSING OPPORTUNITY

CANCELLATION OF CONTRACT, RELEASE OF DEPOSIT AND JOINT ESCROW INSTRUCTIONS (CC PAGE 1 OF 1)

Source: Reprinted with permission of California Association of REALTORS®.

CLASS DISCUSSION TOPICS

1. Prepare a marketing plan for the home in which you currently live or for a home of your choice. Be prepared to discuss it in class.

2. Discuss the various things that a licensee should be looking for when conducting a **"red flag" inspection** of a new listing and the differences between known and **latent defects**. List some types of latent defects.

3. Prepare two ads for the home in which you currently live or a hypothetical one. Be prepared to read them to the class for discussion.

4. Role-play your company's advertising policy to another student, who will play the seller.

5. Discuss what most of the major topics of a counteroffer are and why.

CHAPTER 10 QUIZ

1. Which of the following is not considered good communication with the owner of a property?
   A. Weekly status report.
   B. Telling the owner that the market is so hot that she will get over full price.
   C. Weekly visit to the property to pick up business cards and call back licensees who showed the property for feedback.
   D. None of the above.

2. Which of the following should not be included in the homeowner instructions?
   A. Be at home every time the property is shown.
   B. Keep lawns and bushes neatly trimmed.
   C. Use fresh paint anywhere that looks tired.
   D. All of the above.

3. Your marketing binder should include
   A. a plat map of the property.
   B. a copy of a new roof invoice from a year ago.
   C. a copy of the Real Estate TDS.
   D. All of the above.

4. Prior to holding an Open House, you should
   A. take 100 Open House flyers door-to-door in the neighborhood and invite the neighbors.
   B. confirm the Open House date and time with the owners.
   C. place an Open House ad in the local paper and on your company Internet site.
   D. All of the above.

5. When should the owners complete the TDS?

  A. By the end of the second day after the home is listed.

  B. Within a week after the home is listed.

  C. Within ten days after the home is listed.

  D. When the owners accept an offer for the property.

6. Prior to installing a for-sale sign, you should

  A. check with the city or county to see if there are any sign restrictions.

  B. check with the owners to see if there are any CC&Rs that restrict the use of a for-sale sign.

  C. locate the spot where the sign will be most visible.

  D. Both b and c.

7. The AIDA formula used in advertising stands for

  A. Attention, investment, deployment, and call to action.

  B. Attitude, in-depth ad, development, and area.

  C. Attention, interest, desire, and (call to) action.

  D. None of the above.

8. When writing a counteroffer, you should

  A. completely rewrite lengthy paragraphs that you want to change, not just change some words.

  B. number each item in the counteroffer.

  C. use a line space between each item in the counteroffer for clarity.

  D. All of the above.

9. When Paragraph 2 of the counteroffer is used

  A. a sale is made as soon as the buyers sign and return the counteroffer.

  B. the counteroffer is given to only one buyer at a time.

  C. all counteroffers made must be the same.

  D. None of the above.

10. Which of the following is not a valid reason for an escrow to fail to close?

  A. The sellers set a $1,000 limit on the termite damage repairs and the report came in with $2,000 in repairs and neither party will pay the difference.

  B. The buyers' parents said they paid too much and have "buyer's remorse."

  C. The buyers failed to qualify for the financing required in the purchase contract.

  D. The sale was contingent on the sale and closing of the buyers' home and it did not sell.

Chapter

11

IMPORTANT PHRASES AND TERMS

Adjustable-rate mortgage (ARM)

Adjustment period

Back-end ratio

Blanket trust deed

Bridge loan

Cal Vet loans

Certificate of reasonable value (CRV)

Commercial banks

Computerized loan origination (CLO)

Conforming loans

Controlled business arrangement (CBA)

Conventional loan

Convertible ARM

Cosigner

Credit unions

Direct endorsement

Fair Credit Reporting Act

Fannie Mae

Federal Agricultural Mortgage Corporation

FHA-insured loans

Fixed-rate loans

Freddie Mac

Front-end ratio

Ginnie Mae

Index

Institutional lenders

Jumbo loans

Life insurance companies

Margin

Mortgage bankers

Mortgage companies

Mortgage loan broker

Nonconforming loans

Noninstitutional lenders

Open-end trust deed

Payment shock

Pension funds

Piggyback loan

Portfolio loans

Private mortgage insurance (PMI)

Qualify borrowers

REIT

RESPA

Release clause

Renegotiable-rate mortgages

Reverse mortgage

Savings and loan associations

Secondary financing

Secondary mortgage market

Seller carryback financing

VA-guaranteed loans

Wraparound trust deed

Real Estate Financing

Upon completion of this chapter, the student will be able to:

- Describe and demonstrate methods of borrower loan prequalification.
- Identify and differentiate institutional and conventional lenders.
- Compare and contrast sources of real estate financing.
- Recognize and describe types of mortgages and trust deeds.
- Describe the purpose of secondary financing.
- Demonstrate an understanding of real estate financing regulations.

11.1 AN APPRAISAL OR AN ESTIMATE OF VALUE?

Until the mid-1980s, real estate licensees who analyzed property values routinely called their analyses *appraisals*. After the savings and loan meltdown in that decade, however, the federal and state governments mandated major changes in the lending industry and legislated that appraisers be certified by taking a number of state-approved courses. One change was that people who were not certified and licensed as appraisers could not use the term *appraisal* to define their value estimates. As a result, they may use only terms such as *estimate of value* or *market analysis*.

11.2 FINANCING SOURCES

Americans on average spend more than 20 percent of their income on renting or purchasing real estate; in California, because of its relatively high prices, most people spend much more. Because very few people can pay cash for their real estate, most real estate transactions depend on funds from the various lending sources when the transaction takes place.

Understanding where the money actually comes from will help you to better understand how it is used. Money to finance real estate transactions is made available through two primary money market areas: (1) indirectly from lending institutions that loan money that is deposited into escrow and (2) directly from someone who has saved the money. To best serve your customers and clients, you must be constantly aware of the status of the money markets on national, regional, and local levels. Get to know as many of the lenders in your area as you can and become aware of their policies concerning interest rates, discount points, loan origination fees (often called *points*), and other lending costs.

11.3 PRIMARY AND SECONDARY FINANCING

The date of recording at the county recorder's office is the sole determining factor as to the "position" of a trust deed. The one first recorded is considered in first or primary position; all others are considered to be *junior liens* and are subordinate to it. Because there is a direct relationship between the order of recording and the element of risk to the lender, primary financing generally has lower interest rates than junior loans. They are the first ones to be repaid if the borrowers default.

Any junior trust deed is considered **secondary financing**. The holder of a second trust deed bears a greater risk than the holder of a first trust deed. Therefore, second trust deeds customarily bear higher rates of interest. In the event of a default on the first trust deed, the holder of the second trust deed must either cure the default by making up all of the delinquent payments, plus interest and late charges, and then foreclose on the second or wait until the foreclosure sale and bid cash for the property. If the holder of the second trust deed fails to do either, she may lose part or all of the money.

Whereas primary financing refers to first trust deeds, the *primary mortgage market* refers to loans being made directly to borrowers that are secured by either first or second trust deeds. This is called the *retail market*. The **secondary mortgage market** refers to the sale of existing mortgages and trust deeds to various types of investors.

Three agencies, **Fannie Mae**, **Ginnie Mae**, and **Freddie Mac**, are responsible for creating and establishing a viable secondary mortgage market. Their operations have created a national securities market for the sale of real estate debt instruments by the originators to secondary institutional buyers. Selling the loans frees up capital to create more real estate loans. The secondary mortgage market also minimizes the effects of regional cycles and redistributes the funds from wealthy areas to cash-poor areas of the country.

Fannie Mae

Fannie Mae, formerly the Federal National Mortgage Association (FNMA), was established to stimulate the secondary mortgage market by buying Veterans Affairs (VA)-guaranteed loans and Federal Housing Administration (FHA)-insured loans made by private lenders. Fannie Mae evolved into a private, profit-oriented corporation that markets its own securities and handles a variety of real estate loans. These loans are usually purchased at a discount and are resold to other private lenders or investors. Having this ready source of money available to purchase their loans helps to stabilize the market and gives the lenders a sense of security, encouraging them to make more loans.

Ginnie Mae

The Government National Mortgage Association (GNMA) is now a government-owned agency, but privatization is currently being considered. Ginnie Mae deals in higher-risk, but important, programs, such as low-income housing, urban renewal projects, and other special purpose government-backed programs. Ginnie Mae participates in the secondary mortgage market through its mortgage-backed securities programs whereby qualified mortgage lenders and approved dealers obtain additional capital to make new loans by pooling a group of similar existing loans and pledging them as collateral. Ginnie Mae's role is to guarantee that the holders of these securities will pay the loan payments from these securities in a timely manner.

Freddie Mac

Freddie Mac, formerly the Federal Home Loan Mortgage Corporation (FHLMC), was founded with money provided by twelve Federal Home Loan Banks when new mortgage loans could not be made because money was flowing out of the **savings and loan (S&L) associations**. Freddie Mac created needed funds by offering its own securities, backed by Ginnie Mae and its pool of mortgages. This gave the S&L associations a secondary mortgage market for selling their conventional loans. Freddie Mac, now a

profit-oriented corporation, buys loans that have been closed within one year at specified discount rates.

In 2008, as adjustable rate loans began to trigger from the start rate to the much higher long term interest rate, foreclosures of U.S. homes skyrocketed due to the deepening recession. As homes were foreclosed and portfolio losses mounted, all major buyers of loan portfolios backed by U.S. mortgages stopped buying them and Fannie Mae and Freddie Mac stepped in to keep the money supply flowing; however, the extent of the foreclosure problem became so large that both agencies were soon out of money and in very poor financial shape. The Federal Government stepped in and took over both agencies and put hundreds of millions of dollars into each agency, thereby allowing them to continue operating.

Federal Agricultural Mortgage Corporation

The **Federal Agricultural Mortgage Corporation**, or Farmer Mac, was government chartered, but it is now a private corporation that provides a secondary mortgage market for farm and rural housing.

11.4 CONFORMING VERSUS NONCONFORMING LOANS

A lender who makes a loan either keeps the loan in its portfolio or sells it in the secondary mortgage market. Loans that are kept by the lender are called **portfolio loans**. Loans that are sold are called *non-portfolio loans*. **Conforming loans** are conventional loans that meet the underwriting standards for purchase by Fannie Mae or Freddie Mac. These are either fifteen-year or thirty-year loans and are not assumable. They have strict guidelines regarding down payments and maximum loan amounts. Because the conforming loan limits are adjusted annually, and as a result of the American Recovery and Reinvestment Act of 2009, conforming loan limits in California now vary between $417,000 and $729,750 for a single family residential loan. Check with your loan broker for current rates. Because there is a ready market for the sale of these loans, lenders are willing to make them and to purchase them on the secondary mortgage market. Because of the strict underwriting requirements they must meet, the interest rates for conforming loans are generally less than rates charged for **nonconforming loans**.

Any loans with an initial principal balance in excess of the current conforming limits are considered nonconforming or **jumbo loans**. Another reason jumbo loans usually carry a higher interest rate is that they must be held or warehoused until the lender has accumulated a

multimillion dollar portfolio of them. In past years such portfolios have been sold as a block to entities such as the California Teachers Association Pension Fund or other large private investors.

11.5 TYPES OF LENDERS

The two groups of lenders are institutional and noninstitutional.

Institutional Lenders

Institutional lenders are commercial banks, savings associations, life insurance companies, credit unions, or any lending institution whose activities are regulated by law.

Commercial Banks

In California, **commercial banks** are either state chartered or federally chartered and are regulated by state or federal laws, respectively. They tend to favor short-term loans, such as consumer loans and auto loans, and follow relatively conservative lending practices. Their real estate loans are generally for 80 percent of the appraised value of the property or less, and borrowers with less than 20 percent down payment are usually required to buy **private mortgage insurance (PMI)**. The homeowner may request to cancel the PMI when she can produce an appraisal showing that the loan balance is less than 75–80 percent of the property's value, there has not been a late payment in the prior year, and PMI is past a minimum of 24 months. Banks seldom allow any secondary financing when making a new-purchase money loan but are active in the hard-money second loan and equity line markets.

Commercial banks make a variety of loans, including equity lines of credit, auto loans, and loans to their business customers. They have a strong preference to make loans to their own customers because this creates a banking relationship and helps create more depositors. They also have a strong preference to sell their real estate loans and retain the servicing of the loan for a fee.

Savings Associations

With the passage of the Financial Services Modernization Act of 1999 *savings associations* became savings banks and were then merged into large financial holding companies. Originally, these institutions were intended to promote thrift through savings and thereby promote home ownership. Interest paid on savings was usually somewhat higher than that paid by commercial banks. The deposits were invested primarily in residential mortgage loans, home repairs, and construction loans.

Savings associations were chartered either by the federal government or the state of incorporation and were regulated on a national level by the Office of Thrift Supervision (OTS). Savings banks remain a principle source of mortgage funds in California.

Life Insurance Companies

The lending policies of **life insurance companies** are governed by the laws of the state in which the company is chartered and originated, the availability of loan funds, and the policies of the company's management.

Insurance companies supply most of the large loans that are necessary for commercial properties, industrial properties, hotels, and shopping centers. In California, they make loans for up to 75 percent of a property's value. Their commercial real estate loans are generally for twenty-five to thirty years.

Although insurance company loans are often assumable (do not contain a due-on-sale clause) and often have a lower interest rate than the commercial banks or savings associations would charge, the insurance companies often require an equity position as a limited partner as a condition of making the loan. In the mid-1980s, the lending practices of insurance companies were a major factor to the overbuilding of office buildings and shopping centers that took place in many areas of the country.

Noninstitutional Lenders

Noninstitutional lenders who make real estate loans include pension funds, credit unions, and real estate investment trusts (REITs).

Mortgage Bankers

Mortgage bankers, also called **mortgage companies**, can be licensed in California by either the Department of Corporations or the Department of Real Estate.

Mortgage bankers make loans using their own funds and usually resell the loans to institutional lenders on the secondary mortgage market. They are currently the largest single source of new residential loans made in California.

Mortgage bankers generally resell the loans they make and rely primarily on loan origination fees and loan servicing fees as their main sources of income. If they believe mortgage rates are about to drop, they often hold loans and resell them later at a premium above face value.

Most mortgage bankers only make a nonconforming loan when they have a ready buyer for such a loan.

Real Estate Investment Trusts

Created in 1960, the **REIT** encourages small investors to pool their resources with others to raise venture capital for real estate transactions. To qualify as a REIT, the trust must have a minimum of 100 investors and 95 percent of the trust's income must be distributed to its investors annually.

Most REITs are mortgage trusts that invest all of their money in mortgages. In addition, there are many equity trusts that invest solely in real property ownership and hybrid trusts invest in both mortgages and property ownership.

Credit Unions

While limiting their lending to members only, **credit unions** are a good source of secondary financing and equity lines of credit. Some offer first and second trust deed loans as well.

Pension Funds

Although **pension funds** are used to invest primarily in stocks, they are becoming a more important factor in the mortgage market. They are a major purchaser of home loans originated by mortgage bankers, but they mostly lend on large projects. They also make direct loans but work through a third-party loan originator.

Seller Carryback Financing

When conventional financing is too costly for a buyer or is simply not available, an owner can often be persuaded to carry back a first or second trust deed on a property to facilitate a sale. If the seller does not need the money and the buyer will pay an attractive rate of interest, the seller is a likely candidate for carryback financing. During the early 1980s, seller carryback financing was often the only source of financing available.

Generally, **seller carryback financing** is structured to meet the needs of both the buyers and the sellers. Such loans are generally fixed-rate loans with payments amortized over a thirty-year period, but with a due date from five to seven years for first loans and interest-only loans and from three to five years for second loans. Most owners are not interested in tying up their money for longer periods than that; however, when their loan matures, if prevailing certificate of deposit rates and other investments are yielding a lower return than the note that they carried back, they are often open to rewriting the loan for a shorter time period. Care must be taken to **always** recommend in writing that the sellers seek legal counsel before committing to a seller carryback.

Real Estate Brokers

According to the *Mortgage Loan Brokerage Law*, a **mortgage loan broker** is a person who acts for compensation in negotiating a new loan and who must be licensed as a real estate broker or salesperson. Real estate brokers who negotiate mortgage loans under the Mortgage Loan Brokerage Law are limited in the amount that they may charge as a commission for arranging the loan and for costs and expenses of making the loan. First trust deed loans of $30,000 or more and second trust deeds of $20,000 or more are not covered under the scope of the law, but commissions and expenses are negotiable between the broker and the buyer.

Maximum commissions allowed under the Mortgage Loan Brokerage Law are as follows:

- First trust deeds of less than $30,000—5 percent of the principal if less than three years; 10 percent if three or more years

- Second trust deeds of less than $20,000—5 percent of the principal if less than two years; 10 percent if at least two years but less than three years; 15 percent if three or more years

If the loan falls within the scope of the law, the expenses of making the loan that can be charged to the borrower, such as appraisal fees, title and escrow fees, recording and notary fees, and credit reporting fees, cannot exceed 5 percent of the principal loan amount; however, if 5 percent of the loan is less than $390, the broker may charge up to that amount. Regardless of the size of the loan, the borrower cannot be charged more than $750 for costs and expenses. In no event may the $750 maximum be charged if it exceeds the actual costs and expenses incurred.

As most loans arranged by mortgage brokers are well above the limits established by the law, these limitations on loan costs and commissions seldom become an issue and the lender can negotiate whatever the market will bear in the way of costs and commissions, provided that the loans exceed the $30,000 and $20,000 thresholds, respectively.

Mortgage brokers generally do not service the loans they arrange, and because they are essentially middlemen, they must be careful to see that the security for the loans satisfies the lender's criteria.

Real Estate Brokers—Scope of Lending Activity

Real estate brokers can engage in three distinct areas of lending activity.

1. *Hard money makers and arrangers.* Articles V and VII of the real estate law deal primarily with hard money loans in which

the mortgage broker acts as an intermediary who brings lenders and borrowers together. This activity is commonly known as *mortgage brokerage* and the real estate licensee is acting as a *mortgage broker*.

The loans are made not in the broker's name but in the name of the lender. Most hard money loans are equity loans rather than purchase loans, and therefore the borrowers are not protected under the anti-deficiency ordinance. In the event of a foreclosure in which the sale proceeds do not satisfy the loan amount, the lender may look to the borrowers' other assets.

2. *Third-party originators.* Third-party originators prepare loan applications for borrowers, which they submit to lenders. They may be dual licensees or the licensee of either the borrower or the lender. Trusts, pension plans, and out-of-state lenders who wish to invest directly in California loans frequently use third-party originators. Thus, lenders who are not prepared to take loan applications in California can be direct lenders rather than having to purchase loans that others originated in the secondary mortgage market. They deal primarily in purchase money loans.

3. *Mortgage bankers.* Not all mortgage bankers are real estate brokers. Some mortgage bankers are licensed under the *California Residential Mortgage Lending Act,* administered by the Department of Corporations. A mortgage banker must elect which license to operate under. Thus, California has two state agencies, the Department of Corporations and the Department of Real Estate, regulating the same type of activity, depending on which license the mortgage banker has opted for.

On July 30, 2008, Congress passed the Housing and Economic Recovery Act (HERA), a major new housing law. A key component of this legislation is the SAFE Act or Secure and Fair Enforcement Mortgage Licensing Act. Its purpose is to establish a nationwide mortgage licensing system. The deadline (July 31, 2010) for implementation has provisions for further extensions with the U.S. Department of Housing and Urban Development's (HUD) approval.

11.6 TYPES OF LOANS

Real estate financing used to be simple. The loan officers would drop off loan applications at the real estate offices and when an agent sold a property, she met with the buyers and completed the

loan "app" and took it, along with the purchase contract and the preliminary title report, to the loan officer. A couple of days later the loan was approved. All of that has changed drastically in the past several years, and although the majority of one to four family dwelling units are still financed by conventional loans, the choice of a loan is no longer an easy one. Both buyers and sellers must be aware of the types of loans currently available, including the loan that best suits their particular needs and even where to go or who to see for financing. Many real estate firms are jumping on the "one-stop shopping" bandwagon and affiliating with lenders and title companies, so the "lending landscape" is changing at a rapid pace.

Conventional Loan

A **conventional loan** is any loan not backed by the government. The advantages of conventional over government-backed loans are that conventional loans usually have a shorter processing time and involve less red tape. Because of the more stringent underwriting standards applied to government-backed loans, they do not have the flexibility of conventional loans and borrowers can usually get a higher loan amount with conventional financing. More loan products are also available to borrowers using conventional financing than to those using government-backed loans.

In past years, many lenders made conventional loans with zero down payment, an 80 percent first loan, and a 20 percent second loan. The first loan was amortized over thirty years and the second loan, usually made by the same lender, was amortized over fifteen years. The advantage of this type of financing is that the borrower obtained both loans with little or no loan fee at an attractive interest rate with no PMI (because the first loan is only 80 percent of the value, it is not required) and often with no prepayment penalty. As might be expected, current economic conditions have severely curtailed this type of loan.

Borrowers should compare loans and lenders on the following basis:
- Interest rate offered (variable or fixed)
- Loan costs and fees charged
- The existence of any prepayment penalties
- Length of the loan (longer-term loans have lower payments)
- Loan-to-value (LTV) ratio or the percentage of the appraised value the lender will lend. This determines what the down payment must be.

Government Participation Loans

Three types of government-backed loans are **VA-guaranteed loans**, **Cal Vet loans**, and **FHA-insured loans**. A comparison of these types of loans appears in Figure 11.1.

FIGURE 11.1   Government Home Loan Programs

	GI (VA)	Cal Vet	FHA
Who is eligible?	U.S. Veterans	California residents who meet the veteran requirements	Anyone who qualifies
Type of loan	Guaranteed	Contract of sale	Insure (initial premium may be financed)
Points and fees	Negotiable loan fees plus a funding fee from 1% to 2%	Up to 1% origination fee plus possible mortgage insurance	Loan fee 1%
Who makes the loans?	Approved lending institutions	Calif. Dept. of Veterans Affairs (mortgage brokers can originate loans)	Approved lending institutions
Interest rates	Negotiable	Rates May Vary*	Negotiable
Term	Maximum 30 years	40 years, but usually 30	Usually 30 years
Maximum you can pay for a home	Loan cannot exceed the appraisal	Cannot exceed the Cal Vet appraisal (certificate of reasonable value [CRV])	No limit
Maximum loan	No money down, maximum $417,000; loan can't exceed CRV	Single family, maximum $250,000	1 unit = $172,632 1 unit = $312,895 for high-cost counties
Down payment	None required	2%	Approximately 3% (see FHA section for special programs)
Secondary financing	Generally not allowed at purchase, but can be placed later	Yes, but the 1st and 2nd cannot exceed 90% of the CRV	Not allowed at purchase, but can be placed later
Prepayment fees	None	6 months' interest on original loan amount during first 5 years	None
Assumability	Loans before 3/1/88 are assumable; subsequent loans require buyer to qualify	Assumable with prior Cal Vet approval	Loans before 12/15/89 are assumable; subsequent loans are assumable with FHA approval

*Check the Cal Vet web site at http://www.calvetpurchase.com/calvet_rates.htm

Department of Veterans Affairs

The Servicemen's Readjustment Act of 1944, commonly referred to as the GI Bill, was intended to assist veterans who were returning from overseas after World War II to make the necessary readjustment to civilian life, particularly through the acquisition of homes. The VA does not make loans; it guarantees a portion of the loan made by a lender. On most VA loans made in California, the VA guarantees 25 percent of the loan, up to the maximum loan amount; however, there is a sliding scale that the VA will guarantee that goes as high as 40 percent of the loan for lesser-priced properties. As these limits change from time to time, real estate professionals that use this program to help their buyers obtain financing should periodically check with a lender that makes VA loans to stay current on the guarantee limits.

The largest VA loan that does not require a down payment in California varies between $417,000 and $962,500, depending on the county. Department of VA loans can be used:

- to refinance existing mortgage loans for dwellings owned and occupied by veterans.
- to buy or build a home or business property.
- to purchase a farm or farm equipment.
- to alter, repair, or improve real estate.
- to purchase a mobile home.

To qualify for a VA-guaranteed loan, an individual must have had at least 181 consecutive days of active duty service in the military. A VA-approved appraiser evaluates the property.

Although the amount of the loan is not regulated, the amount of the guarantee is. The loan cannot exceed the appraisal, which is commonly known as the **certificate of reasonable value (CRV)**.

It once took an act of Congress to adjust the VA loan interest rate. This was very cumbersome and lenders would regularly charge "discount points" to make up for interest they lost on VA loans that were made at less than prevailing conventional rates. The buyer was not allowed to pay these discount points, so the seller had to pay them. The VA interest rate can now freely move with market conditions, and although discount points are still with us, they are not often charged.

A veteran may reuse her VA loan, once it has been repaid in full or formally assumed by another veteran; however, the VA funding fee is increased by an additional 1 percent. Veterans with service-related disabilities are exempt from paying funding fees.

Cal Vet Loans

The California Farm and Home Purchase Program, or Cal Vet loan program, allows California veterans to acquire suitable farm or home property with low-cost financing. The state of California actually lends the money rather than guaranteeing or insuring payments. The property is acquired by the state, which then sells the property to the California veteran under a land contract or contract of sale. The state retains title to the property until the land contract is paid in full. Some features of Cal Vet loans are the following:

- The state raises the funds for Cal Vet loans by issuing tax-exempt bonds.
- Cal Vet loans have an adjustable interest rate that cannot exceed 7.5 percent.
- Cal Vet loans can be arranged through lenders that have been approved to make them.
- Mortgage brokers who originate and process Cal Vet loans receive a 1 percent loan origination fee and a $350 processing fee.
- A Cal Vet loan requires a 2 percent down payment. The interest rate is pegged at a given interest rate for a home and 1 percent higher for a mobile home in a rental park. There is a special program for lower-income, first-time homeowner veterans at a lower interest rate. As the "pegged" interest rate and maximum loan amount is adjusted from time to time, you will need to verify what the current rate and maximum loan amount is before working with a California veteran who uses this program.
- Cal Vet loans are processed under VA guidelines. The loans are available to peacetime as well as wartime veterans and active duty military personnel.

Federal Housing Administration

The purposes of the FHA are clearly stated in its preamble to "encourage improvement in housing standards and conditions, to provide a system of mutual mortgage insurance and for other purposes."

To further these purposes, two divisions were formed: Title I and Title II. In general, the following types of loans are available:

- Title I loans for modernization, repairs, or alterations on existing homes.
- Title II loans for purchase or construction of residential housing. Section 203(b) of Title II accounts for most loans for one to four family residences.

FHA loans provide high LTV ratios based on appraisal, which can go as high as 98.75 percent.

The maximum FHA loan varies by region, which for 2010 is from $271,050 to $729,750 in California, but the purchaser must have a minimum down payment of 3 percent of the purchase price.

The mortgage insurance premium (MIP) must be paid at the time of loan origination. Based on the down payment, an MIP is also added to the monthly payments for the duration of the loan.

Lenders may be authorized to make the underwriting decision that a particular loan qualifies for FHA insurance. This is known as a **direct endorsement** and it serves to reduce the loan processing time.

Other Types of Mortgages and Trust Deeds

Blanket Trust Deed

With a **blanket trust deed** the borrower uses more than one parcel of property as security for the loan. This type of document should contain a **release clause** that allows the reconveyance or release of part of the encumbered property on repayment of a predetermined portion of the loan. Builders and developers regularly use these types of trust deeds with new subdivisions.

Open-End Trust Deed

An **open-end trust deed** allows the borrower to receive additional loan money up to a preapproved amount using the same mortgage or trust deed as security. Someone who is doing an extensive remodel of a structure would be a likely user of this type of loan. The advantage is that the borrower only needs to draw necessary funds and does not have to pay interest on the entire loan while not using all of the loan proceeds.

Wraparound Trust Deed

A **wraparound trust deed**, also called an *all-inclusive trust deed* (AITD), is used when it is impossible or impractical to obtain new financing or to refinance an existing loan on a property. With a wraparound loan, the existing financing is left in place and the seller continues to pay on the existing loans while giving the borrower a new, larger loan, usually at a higher interest rate. The new loan is for the principal balances on the existing loans, plus the amount of equity carried back by the seller.

For example, assume a property is being sold for $600,000 with $200,000 down. There is an existing loan in place for $400,000

at 6 percent interest. New financing would be at 9 percent, but the seller is willing to carry a wraparound loan for $400,000 at 8 percent, which would include the underlying financing.

$400,000 loan	6%	}	$400,000
		}	wraparound loan
$200,000	8%	}	at 8%

In this scenario the seller receives 8 percent on her equity plus a 2 percent difference or "spread" on the existing loan. If the $16,000 interest received by the seller on her equity loan is added to the $8,000 "spread" that the seller receives on the lender's loan, the seller receives a total of $24,000 return on her $200,000 loan. This creates a yield of 12 percent on the seller's $200,000 equity loan (divide $24,000 by $200,000). By maintaining the payments on the existing loan, the seller knows that the payments are being made and gets to take advantage of the use of the lender's money. If the buyer had assumed the existing loan, the buyer (not the seller) would get the benefit of the lower interest rate.

If the existing loan or loans have an acceleration clause or due-on-sale clause, a wraparound loan would be risky. This is because the underlying lender could demand immediate payment in full of their loan if they learned that the property had been partially or fully sold to another party without consent. As an agent, be careful using this type of financing. Always give full written disclosure of the inherent risks involved if there is an acceleration clause and be sure to state in the purchase contract who is responsible for the costs of refinancing and paying any prepayment penalties and other fees if the loan is called due by the lender.

If the property is not a candidate for new conventional financing because of its condition, type, or location, the risk of using wraparound financing with an underlying loan containing a due-on-sale clause becomes even greater. If the lender calls the loan on the new buyer and she is unable to get new financing to pay the loan off, the buyer can lose the property to foreclosure and the lender will almost surely come looking for you, so do not do it!

Bridge Loan

A **bridge loan**, or *gap loan*, is an interim loan acquired by a buyer to have the funds necessary to close escrow on her new property prior to closing escrow on the property she is selling. This can sometimes occur when buying a new home and the buyer's existing home is not sold or is sold and in escrow but hasn't closed escrow yet. It essentially means that the buyer is carrying

at least three loans (the old property loan, the new property loan, and the bridge loan) until her existing home closes escrow. Many lenders are reluctant to make bridge loans unless the customer's existing home is already sold and most or all contingencies have been waived or unless the customer is strong financially. These types of loans usually have short terms and a much higher interest rate because of the inherent risk involved.

Renegotiable-Rate Mortgages

Renegotiable-rate mortgages, also known as *rollover loans*, usually have payments based on a thirty-year amortization and a fixed rate of interest for the first five or seven years, at which time they become due and payable in full. Only part of the principal balance is repaid during the life of the loan. The lender will usually rewrite the loan at the then prevailing interest rate or the borrower can refinance with another lender. There is a risk to the borrower inherent in this type of loan. For example, if the existing lender decided not to renew the loan and money was very tight or the borrower had a bad payment history with the lender and the borrower could not get financing elsewhere, the borrower may not be able to pay off the lender and could stand to lose the property or be forced to sell it.

Reverse Mortgage (Reverse Annuity Mortgage)

Not used for home purchases, a **reverse mortgage** is a loan whereby the equity the borrower has in the home is converted into an annuity and the lender makes monthly payments to the borrower based on the amount of equity in the home and the borrower's age. The loan increases with each monthly payment made to the borrower and is not repaid until the borrower dies or the property is sold.

A standard loan charges simple interest, that is, the interest for the previous month is paid with each payment and is charged on the principal balance only. A reverse mortgage, however, has *compound interest* whereby interest is charged on interest. Each month, when the lender makes a payment to the borrower, the loan balance increases by the amount of the payment and the interest due thereon. The next month's interest will be based on the new larger balance created by each advance.

Piggyback Loan

A **piggyback loan** is sometimes shared by two lenders, where one takes the first position (greater security) and the second lender takes the higher risk with the secondary position. It is really a first

and second trust deed in one instrument. In residential lending, this type of lending activity has routinely been replaced by the same lender committing to both a first and a second trust deed loan at the same time or a first trust deed loan and an equity line of credit at the same time.

Fixed-Rate Loans

Lenders were badly hurt by making long-term **fixed-rate loans** in the past and have a strong preference for making adjustable-rate loans instead as they are a safer loan to make. The public has a strong preference for low-cost, fixed-rate loans, however, so the lenders readily make these loans to meet the demand of the consumers.

In the late 1970s and early 1980s, the United States was experiencing very high inflation and interest rates increased to record levels. Many lenders, especially the S&L associations, had their capital invested in long-term fixed-rate loans. Lenders had to pay much higher interest rates on their savings accounts to attract funds, and in many cases, the average yield from their portfolios of loans was less than the average rate they were paying depositors for funds. While this only lasted a few years, lenders lost millions of dollars and most still worry that history will repeat itself.

Lenders offer adjustable-rate loans at lower interest rates than fixed-rate loans and usually offer lower borrowing costs.

Fifteen-Year Versus Thirty-Year Fixed-Rate Loans

A buyer who is able to pay the higher payment associated with a fifteen-year fixed-rate loan will benefit from significant savings on the total amount of interest that she will pay over the life of the loan as compared with a thirty-year fixed-rate loan.

For example, at 6.5 percent interest the monthly payment on a $200,000 loan for fifteen years is $1,742.21. The same loan amortized over thirty years has a monthly payment of $1,264.14. Total payments for the fifteen-year loan are $313,598.65, whereas total payments for the thirty-year loan are $455,088.98. The borrower would save more than $141,490.33 by financing with a fifteen-year versus a thirty-year loan. The actual savings would be even more since lenders charge a lower rate of interest on fifteen-year loans than they do on thirty-year loans as shorter loans are considered safer.

Adjustable-Rate Mortgage

Although a fixed-rate loan's interest rate does not change, the interest rate in an **adjustable-rate mortgage (ARM)** changes periodically in relation to some sort of index, and its payments

increase or decrease accordingly. Lenders usually charge lower initial interest rates for ARMs than for fixed-rate loans because the initial rate will last only a relatively short period of time. This makes the ARM less expensive for the borrower and makes it easier to qualify for compared to a fixed-rate loan of the same amount. For those lenders who qualify the borrower on the initial interest rate, it also allows the borrower to acquire a larger loan. This generally means that a buyer can purchase a more expensive property than she can with a fixed-rate loan. As long as interest rates stay the same or drop, the ARM will continue to be a less expensive way to finance a home purchase.

Another advantage of ARM loans is that they generally do not have prepayment fees or penalties. This makes them particularly attractive to people who know they will be reselling within a relatively short period of time. The absence of a prepayment fee can save the buyer a significant amount of money.

Against these advantages the borrower needs to weigh the risk that any increase in interest rates will lead to higher monthly payments and possibly negative amortization in the future. Negative amortization occurs when an ARM has a limit on the amount that the payment can increase in any given time period and the interest rate increases to a point where the "capped" monthly payment does not fully pay all of the interest due. The amount of "excess" interest charged each month, over what the payment will allow, is added to the principal balance and the loan can actually grow.

There is a tradeoff with an ARM whereby the borrower obtains a lower interest rate in return for assuming some risk of higher payments in the future. When considering an ARM, the buyer should carefully evaluate whether or not she can make the payments if she were charged the maximum interest rate allowed in the loan.

Nearly 200 different ARM loan products are being offered by financial institutions today. The borrower and her real estate licensee must ask the following questions to compare loans:

- Will I be taking on any other significant debts, such as school tuition, a new baby, or a new car in the near future?
- Will my payments increase even if interest rates in general do not increase?
- Is my income likely to increase enough to cover higher loan payments if interest rates rise?
- Can I afford the potentially higher payments with my current income?

- How long do I plan to own this home? (The longer I own the home, the greater the chances of a rise in interest rates.)

If the buyer's answers to all of these questions are satisfactory, an ARM may be the right choice; however, the buyer must still decide which ARM is best for her circumstances. This requires answers to even more questions.

ARMs have certain terms and clauses that are not found in fixed-rate loans, and the real estate professional must fully understand and be ready to explain them to a buyer. These terms include *adjustment period, index, margin, interest rate cap, overall cap, payment cap, negative amortization,* and *conversion clause.* The remainder of this section defines these terms and explains the calculations that will enable a borrower to choose the proper ARM for her circumstances.

Adjustment Period The **adjustment period** of an ARM loan is the time span between changes, if any, in the interest rate and monthly loan payment. Note: Some ARMs have only a rate change, whereas others have both a rate and a payment change. If the rate changes, but not the payment, the loan may become a negative amortized loan. Each ARM loan is unique and adjustments may occur monthly, every six months, annually, or every three, five, or seven years. Loans that adjust once a year or more are called one-year, three-year, five-year, or seven-year ARMs. Adjustment periods vary from lender to lender, and any given lender may offer several different ARM loans, each with a different adjustment period. The borrower and her agent are well-advised to ask as many questions of the loan officer as necessary to become fully informed of the terms of any ARM loan as possible. The buyer should take the time to read the loan documents carefully at escrow closing to be sure the terms of the actual loan documents concur with what was offered at loan application.

The three-, five-, and seven-year ARMs have become popular in recent years as they allow buyers to obtain financing at lower interest rates than thirty-year fixed-rate loans, while providing the borrower with a reasonable and predictable time period to own her property without worrying about a sudden rise in monthly payments. This is especially valuable to buyers who are subject to corporate transfers on a fairly regular and predictable basis. Many of these loans include prepayment fees, so the borrower must assess the anticipated time period before any transfer will likely take place and allow for a margin of error. These fees are often six-month's interest on 80 percent of the unpaid principal balance of the loan and can be costly. Planning is important.

Index and Margin Rate changes in ARM loans are tied to some sort of **index** rate. The only requirements a lender must meet in selecting an index rate are the index control must not be the lender and the index must be readily available to and verifiable by the public.

These indexes usually fluctuate with the general interest rate movement. If the index moves down, interest rates usually follow and the borrower usually sees a decrease in monthly payments. If the index rate goes up, interest rates follow and so the buyer's monthly payment increases.

Lenders base ARM rates on a variety of indexes. Lenders often offer a variety of ARM loan products, and each one has a different index and margin. The most common indexes are six-month, three-year, or five-year treasury securities (T-bills); national or regional cost-of-funds indexes (in California, the eleventh district cost of funds index of the Federal Home Loan Bank Board (FHLBB) is the most prevalent); and the London Inter-Bank Offering Rate (LIBOR) that has historically been the most volatile of the margins. A borrower should ask the lender for the source of the margin that will be used in the loan that is selected so it may be tracked to see how it moved up or down historically.

To determine the borrower's interest rate on an ARM loan, lenders add a few percentage points to the index rate (usually two or three). This increase is called the **margin**, although it is often referred to as the spread or differential.

index rate + margin = ARM interest rate

The amount of the margin may differ from one lender to another, but it is always constant over the life of any given loan. Loans with higher origination costs usually have lower margins. Lenders may choose to adjust the ARM interest rate upward, but downward adjustments are mandated. Any adjustments to the interest rate of an ARM loan can only be made on a predetermined time schedule (*the adjustment period*) as stated previously. Each loan will contain all of the terms that the borrower has agreed to, such as initial interest rate (start rate), index, margin, caps, interest rate change frequency, and any payment change frequency, in the note that accompanies the deed of trust.

When comparing ARM loans, look at both the margin and the index for each loan. Indexes that have higher average values are usually coupled with lower margins. Be sure your buyer discusses margins with the lender and understands them fully.

In calculating an ARM payment, the initial period is calculated the same as a fixed-rate loan payment. After the first-period

adjustment, it is as if the borrower were starting a new loan each time. Calculations must be made to figure the loan balance and the number of payments left, and the new interest rate must be taken into account. The agent can only accurately predict the initial loan payment period because she cannot predict future interest rates.

ARM Discounts

ARM loans are safer for lenders. To make them attractive to borrowers, lenders will offer ARM loans with initial interest rates that are lower than the combined index and margin. Such rates are called *teaser rates*, *discounted rates*, *tickler rates*, or *introductory rates* and are usually combined with loan fees and higher interest rates after the discount period expires. These rates may expire after the first adjustment period of one month, three months, six months, or a year, for example. When the discount rate period ends, the ARM rate automatically increases to the contract rate (predetermined index plus margin). This can mean a substantial and maybe dangerous increase in the borrower's interest rate and monthly payment. In many cases, the borrower's interest rate and payment will increase even if current interest rates have decreased.

Many lenders use the initial payment as the basis for qualifying a borrower for a loan. If a lender approves a borrower for a loan based on a low introductory rate, the borrower must take great care to see that she will be able to afford the monthly payments later, when the discount expires and the rate is adjusted. Any savings a borrower makes during the initial period of a discounted ARM loan may be offset during the life of the loan if interest rates increase beyond what the borrower could have obtained a fixed-rate loan for. The large increases in interest rates and monthly payments that are often associated with these types of loans at the end of the discounted period can subject the borrower to **payment shock**.

Any time the lender's qualifying interest rate is less than the lender's current ARM index rate plus margin, a below-market rate is being offered. Assume that the current index rate is 4.5 percent and the margin is 1.5 percent. That makes the ARM rate 6 percent. If the lender's qualifying introductory rate is 4.5 percent, the introductory rate is 1.5 percent below the market rate and is a discounted rate.

The annual percentage rate (APR) gives a more accurate picture of the true cost of a loan and must be disclosed by law. The APR represents an interest rate based on a buyer's net loan proceeds, the loan amount less the cost of credit (loan fees, or *points*, and other processing fees). This is outlined in the Real Estate Settlement Procedures

Act (RESPA) letter and lender's good-faith estimate of settlement charges that is sent within three days of application for a loan. Lenders who offer below-market rates must account for the higher index rate that will be charged when they disclose the APR to the borrower.

Because so many loan products are available and so many possible local variations in licensed appraisers, the real estate professional needs to be thoroughly knowledgeable in the area of real estate finance in order to properly advise and protect the interests of a first-time buyer. It is always advisable, when recommending lenders, to offer the buyer a list of three or more lenders or loan brokers whose services you or another licensee in your office have experienced in the past. Licensee involvement in choosing specific financing for a buyer without proper background is an ethical violation and goes beyond the duty required of a California licensee. Now, with national mortgage licensing on the horizon, any involvement should be kept to a minimum. Licensees who chose specific lenders or financing for buyers who are in foreclosure or short sales now wish they hadn't. Let the buyer make her own lender selection. That being said, a borrower who selects an ARM solely on the basis of a low initial rate may end up in trouble later. Licensees can help a borrower avoid this by looking at mortgages that offer certain protections described in the next section.

Convertible ARMs A **convertible ARM** loan contains a conversion clause that allows a borrower to convert her adjustable-rate loan to a fixed-rate loan at predesignated times. The new fixed interest rate is generally set at the current market rate plus a 0.375 percent servicing fee. This type of loan is advantageous for a borrower who experiences a change in employment or other circumstances where she desires the safety of a fixed-rate loan.

Assumable ARMs

Most ARMs are assumable; however, most lenders place conditions on the assumption of the loan. The lender usually requires the new borrower to submit an application to assume the loan, submit credit information, and meet the lender's customary credit standards. Most lenders also charge a loan assumption fee of some sort.

Some lenders restrict the assumption of an ARM to only one time; others allow multiple assumptions but adjust the loan cap or the margin to reflect current market conditions, and others allow multiple assumptions with the original cap still in place. Any request by a borrower to assume an ARM should include a careful review of the existing loan documents to have a thorough knowledge of what that particular loan's terms and conditions are.

Caps on an ARM Most ARMs have caps or limits that protect borrowers from increases in monthly payments or interest rates that are beyond an amount specified in the promissory note. If interest rates rise, loans with no caps on interest rates or payments expose borrowers to unlimited upward adjustments of monthly payments. Because payment caps limit only the amount of payment increases and not interest rate increases, a situation can occur in some ARMs where the payments do not cover all of the interest owed on a loan. This is called negative amortization and can lead to an increase in the loan's principal balance as the excess interest is added to the loan. The licensee should be sure that the buyer understands the provisions for this "deferred interest" in any ARM that contains a payment cap.

Some loans prohibit negative amortization, whereas others allow it but cap the overall amount of negative amortization that can be added to the loan's principal balance. In these cases, any excess interest over the cap is forgiven and not added to the loan amount.

Caps vary from lender to lender. The borrower needs to determine the cap rates in any loan being considered. Two types of interest rate caps are:

- A *lifetime cap,* or *overall cap,* limits the interest rate increase over the life of the loan. If, for instance, the introductory rate is 4 percent, which is below the current market rate, and at the first adjustment the rate becomes 6 percent, the overall cap rate will attach to the 6 percent, thus a 6 percent cap could mean an interest rate as high as 12 percent.

- A *periodic cap* limits the interest rate increase or decrease from one adjustment period to the next. These caps are usually 7.5 percent of the previous period's payment amount or one or two percentage points. For instance, if an ARM has a monthly payment of $2,000 and the payment cap is 7.5 percent, the payment cannot rise more than $150 in the next adjustment period.

An ARM usually has both a periodic and an overall interest rate cap. A drop in the index does not always mean a drop in the monthly payments. With some ARMs that have interest rate caps, the monthly payment may increase even though the index has stayed the same or declined. This may happen after an interest rate cap has been holding the interest rate below the sum of the index plus margin. When the next adjustment period comes along and the interest rate stays the same or declines, previous obligations are in arrears and must be paid; thus, the monthly payment will increase. This is referred to as a *hidden ledger*.

Some ARMs have a stated cap, such as 12 percent, whereas others are stated as a percentage over the initial interest rate, such as an overall rate cap of 5 percent. Caps can vary from lender to lender and from loan to loan, so the real estate professional needs to be sure to point this out to her clients.

Figure 11.2 contains a list of questions a borrower who is seeking an ARM should pose to any lender she is talking to.

Interest-Only Loans

California's real estate market prices have continued to rise at a rapid pace for quite some time. Buyers are seeing their ability to qualify for most standard loan products eroding more with each passing day as their salary increases are not keeping pace with the rapid rise in home prices. Lenders are scrambling to find ways to offer loan products that will allow buyers to continue buying homes.

Many lenders have recently started offering interest-only loans. These are loans that do not have any provision for repayment of the principal amount in the monthly payment. Some of these loans are for a full thirty years, whereas some have varying but shorter durations before they are either due in full or convertible to a standard thirty-year, fixed-rate loan. Although the borrower does not realize any benefit in loan reduction from the monthly payment, this type of loan allows her to acquire a larger loan than any type of amortized loan, and the lenders security for the loan quickly becomes safer as time passes and the property continues to rise in value.

The potential problem with an interest-only loan is that if a buyer uses this type of financing to acquire a property and the market slows or even declines, as it recently has in California, and the buyer must sell the property after only a short time, she may experience a loss after paying all of the related sales costs. The real estate licensee should be sure that her client is aware of all of these factors prior to using an interest-only loan.

Loan Costs

When comparing loans, you must also compare loan costs. Lenders break down loan costs so consumers can understand exactly what they are paying for. No matter what the cost or fee is called, the important factor is the total of all loan costs, which for many loans can be added to the loan amount and financed. Loan costs can include:

- An initial application fee
- Loan fees (often called *points*)

FIGURE 11.2 ARM Checklist

- What is the initial (or qualifying) interest rate on the ARM?
- How long is this initial rate in effect? When is the first rate and/or payment adjustment?
- To what index is the ARM's interest rate tied? What is the current level of this index?
- What margin above the index is used to calculate the actual ARM interest rate?
- How are the index and margin used to calculate the initial margin rate and the rates at the adjustment periods?
- What happens to the interest rate at the first adjustment, assuming the index rate stays the same?
- What is the APR of the loan and how does it compare with the APR of other ARM loans and the APR of a fixed-rate loan?
- How often does the interest rate change?
- Does an interest rate change automatically mean a payment change?
- Does the ARM have an interest rate cap? If so, what is the limit on the increase at each adjustment period? If the index rate increases more than the loan limit, can the unused change in the index be carried over to the next adjustment period (this may result in what is called a hidden ledger)? Does the periodic interest rate cap apply to the first adjustment, and does it apply to rate decreases as well as increases?
- Does the ARM have an overall cap rate? If so, what are the minimum and maximum rates?
- Does the ARM have a payment cap? If so, what is the maximum amount that the monthly payment can increase to at each adjustment? Does the payment cap apply to the first adjustment?
- If negative amortization is possible for this ARM, how often is the loan "recast" to pay off the increase in principal balance? When the loan is recast, is there a limit on how much the payment can increase?
- Does negative amortization result if the interest rate increase requires a higher payment than the payment cap allows? Does the payment cap apply to any increases in payments that result from a recasting of the loan due to negative amortization?
- Is this loan assumable? How many times can this loan be assumed? What are the qualification features? Will there be a new cap if the loan is assumed or will the original cap stay in place?
- Can the borrower convert this loan to a fixed-rate loan at any time? Does this loan have an open-end credit feature?
- If this loan has a loan-to-value greater than 80 percent, is private mortgage insurance required?
- Does this loan have a prepayment fee? If so, how is it structured and for how long?
- What other features does this loan have?

- A flat fee in addition to loan fees or points
- Loan escrow costs (if not a purchase-money loan)
- Title insurance
- PMI
- Notary and recording fees

A number of charges are developed by lenders, such as processing fees, document preparation fees, and other fees, commonly referred to as *garbage fees,* for miscellaneous lender services.

Choosing the Right Loan

Lenders offer a wide variety of loans to suit nearly every consumer need. Buyers who are shopping for real estate financing should approach choosing the right loan with the same care that they would take with any other large purchase.

Whereas borrowers who believe they will be in a home for only a short time are probably good prospects for an adjustable rate loan with minimal or no prepayment fees, borrowers who feel they will be long-term residents in a home are wise to consider a fixed-rate loan.

Borrowers who feel that interest rates are stable or about to rise are wise to obtain a fixed-rate loan. Borrowers who feel that interest rates are on the decline may wish to obtain financing that has no prepayment fee so that they can refinance at a later date without penalty.

Borrowers who are financially challenged to meet standard lender qualifying ratios will be interested in VA-guaranteed, FHA-insured, interest-only, or adjustable-rate loans. ARM and interest-only loans allow a borrower to qualify for a larger loan and buy a better lifestyle for their family, but they must be aware of the inherent risks.

Real estate licensees must have a good working knowledge of the financing process and be able to communicate that process to their clients. The more aware the licensee and client are that they must work as a team to obtain the best financing, the smoother the home-buying process will be.

Real estate lenders essentially rent money, and if they are to stay in business, they must rent it at a profit. That profit comes from points, reasonable lender fees, and interest. If lenders reduce or waive interest, fees, or other charges in one area, they will raise it in another. For instance, if a lender offers a borrower a reduced interest rate on a particular loan product, it will usually make up for the loss by charging a higher loan fee.

11.7 GETTING THE BUYERS PREAPPROVED (THE FINANCING PROCESS)

Five basic steps to the financing process are:

1. Qualifying the borrower.
2. Qualifying the property.
3. Approving and processing the loan.
4. Closing the loan.
5. Servicing the loan.

Buyers are really not concerned with Step 5 (servicing the loan), as long as they know where to mail their monthly payments; however, the real estate professional should have a good working knowledge about what happens to a loan once it has closed.

California almost always has strong consumer demand for housing, which creates a "sellers' market." Multiple offers are not uncommon on many homes, and for a buyer who is financing her home purchase to be competitive in her attempt to acquire a property, she should go beyond being prequalified and get "preapproved."

Qualifying the Borrower

It is essential that you, as the real estate professional, know how and why lenders **qualify borrowers** in the manner they do. Earlier in this book we discussed how lenders do not usually keep the loans they make but sell them in the secondary-money market. Fannie Mae and Freddie Mac, the two main buyers of home loans, have strict underwriting guidelines that each loan must meet or they will not buy the loan. So, unless a lender wants to hold onto a loan for a time, it must be careful to approve each borrower so that they, as well as the property, meet these strict underwriting guidelines. Figure 11.3 introduces a standard loan application form, which nearly every buyer is asked to complete, usually with the help of a loan originator.

When processing a new loan, most lenders use the "three Cs"— *character*, *capacity*, and *collateral*—as their minimum standard in determining if a borrower meets or exceeds the qualifications set by the lender.

Character Regarding a borrower's *character*, lenders look at her overall attitude toward paying financial obligations on time as evidenced by a *tri-merged credit report*. This report shows the buyer's ontime payment history as well as her proper use or abuse of credit.

FIGURE 11.3 Uniform Residential Loan Application

Uniform Residential Loan Application

This application is designed to be completed by the applicant(s) with the Lender's assistance. Applicants should complete this form as "Borrower" or "Co-Borrower," as applicable. Co-Borrower information must also be provided (and the appropriate box checked) when ☐ the income or assets of a person other than the Borrower (including the Borrower's spouse) will be used as a basis for loan qualification or ☐ the income or assets of the Borrower's spouse or other person who has community property rights pursuant to state law will not be used as a basis for loan qualification, but his or her liabilities must be considered because the spouse or other person has community property rights pursuant to applicable law and Borrower resides in a community property state, the security property is located in a community property state, or the Borrower is relying on other property located in a community property state as a basis for repayment of the loan.

If this is an application for joint credit, Borrower and Co-Borrower each agree that we intend to apply for joint credit (sign below):

Borrower _____ Co-Borrower _____

I. TYPE OF MORTGAGE AND TERMS OF LOAN

Mortgage Applied for:	☐ VA ☐ FHA	☐ Conventional ☐ USDA/Rural Housing Service	☐ Other (explain):	Agency Case Number	Lender Case Number

Amount $	Interest Rate ___ %	No. of Months	Amortization Type:	☐ Fixed Rate ☐ GPM	☐ Other (explain): ☐ ARM (type):

II. PROPERTY INFORMATION AND PURPOSE OF LOAN

Subject Property Address (street, city, state & ZIP)	No. of Units

Legal Description of Subject Property (attach description if necessary)	Year Built

Purpose of Loan	☐ Purchase ☐ Construction ☐ Other (explain): ☐ Refinance ☐ Construction-Permanent	Property will be: ☐ Primary Residence ☐ Secondary Residence ☐ Investment

Complete this line if construction or construction-permanent loan.

Year Lot Acquired	Original Cost $	Amount Existing Liens $	(a) Present Value of Lot	(b) Cost of Improvements $	Total (a + b) $

Complete this line if this is a refinance loan.

Year Acquired	Original Cost $	Amount Existing Liens $	Purpose of Refinance	Describe Improvements ☐ made ☐ to be made Cost: $

Title will be held in what Name(s)	Manner in which Title will be held	Estate will be held in: ☐ Fee Simple ☐ Leasehold (show expiration date)

Source of Down Payment, Settlement Charges, and/or Subordinate Financing (explain)

III. BORROWER INFORMATION

Borrower	Co-Borrower

Borrower's Name (include Jr. or Sr. if applicable)	Co-Borrower's Name (include Jr. or Sr. if applicable)

Social Security Number	Home Phone (incl. area code)	DOB (mm/dd/yyyy)	Yrs. School	Social Security Number	Home Phone (incl. area code)	DOB (mm/dd/yyyy)	Yrs. School

☐ Married ☐ Unmarried (include single, divorced, widowed) ☐ Separated	Dependents (not listed by Co-Borrower) no. / ages	☐ Married ☐ Unmarried (include single, divorced, widowed) ☐ Separated	Dependents (not listed by Borrower) no. / ages

Present Address (street, city, state, ZIP) ☐ Own ☐ Rent ___ No. Yrs.	Present Address (street, city, state, ZIP) ☐ Own ☐ Rent ___ No. Yrs.

Mailing Address, if different from Present Address	Mailing Address, if different from Present Address

If residing at present address for less than two years, complete the following:

Former Address (street, city, state, ZIP) ☐ Own ☐ Rent ___ No. Yrs.	Former Address (street, city, state, ZIP) ☐ Own ☐ Rent ___ No. Yrs.

IV. EMPLOYMENT INFORMATION

Borrower	Co-Borrower

Name & Address of Employer	☐ Self Employed	Yrs. on this job	Name & Address of Employer	☐ Self Employed	Yrs. on this job
		Yrs. employed in this line of work/profession			Yrs. employed in this line of work/profession

Position/Title/Type of Business	Business Phone (incl. area code)	Position/Title/Type of Business	Business Phone (incl. area code)

If employed in current position for less than two years or if currently employed in more than one position, complete the following:

FIGURE 11.3 (Continued)

Borrower		IV. EMPLOYMENT INFORMATION (cont'd)		Co-Borrower	
Name & Address of Employer	☐ Self Employed	Dates (from – to)	Name & Address of Employer	☐ Self Employed	Dates (from – to)
		Monthly Income $			Monthly Income $
Position/Title/Type of Business	Business Phone (incl. area code)		Position/Title/Type of Business	Business Phone (incl. area code)	
Name & Address of Employer	☐ Self Employed	Dates (from – to)	Name & Address of Employer	☐ Self Employed	Dates (from – to)
		Monthly Income $			Monthly Income $
Position/Title/Type of Business	Business Phone (incl. area code)		Position/Title/Type of Business	Business Phone (incl. area code)	

V. MONTHLY INCOME AND COMBINED HOUSING EXPENSE INFORMATION

Gross Monthly Income	Borrower	Co-Borrower	Total	Combined Monthly Housing Expense	Present	Proposed
Base Empl. Income*	$	$		Rent	$	
Overtime				First Mortgage (P&I)		$
Bonuses				Other Financing (P&I)		
Commissions				Hazard Insurance		
Dividends/Interest				Real Estate Taxes		
Net Rental Income				Mortgage Insurance		
Other (before completing, see the notice in "describe other income," below)				Homeowner Assn. Dues		
				Other:		
Total	$	$	$	Total	$	$

*   Self Employed Borrower(s) may be required to provide additional documentation such as tax returns and financial statements.

Describe Other Income   *Notice:* Alimony, child support, or separate maintenance income need not be revealed if the Borrower (or Co-Borrower) does not choose to have it considered for repaying this loan.

B/C		Monthly Amount
		$

VI. ASSETS AND LIABILITIES

This Statement and any applicable supporting schedules may be completed jointly by both married and unmarried Co-Borrowers if their assets and liabilities are sufficiently joined so that the Statement can be meaningfully and fairly presented on a combined basis; otherwise, separate Statements and Schedules are required. If the Co-Borrower section was completed about a non-applicant spouse or other person, this Statement and supporting schedules must be completed about that spouse or other person also.   Completed ☐ Jointly ☐ Not Jointly

ASSETS Description	Cash or Market Value	Liabilities and Pledged Assets. List the creditor's name, address, and account number for all outstanding debts, including automobile loans, revolving charge accounts, real estate loans, alimony, child support, stock pledges, etc. Use continuation sheet, if necessary. Indicate by (*) those liabilities, which will be satisfied upon sale of real estate owned or upon refinancing of the subject property.		
Cash deposit toward purchase held by:	$			
List checking and savings accounts below		**LIABILITIES**	Monthly Payment & Months Left to Pay	Unpaid Balance
Name and address of Bank, S&L, or Credit Union		Name and address of Company	$ Payment/Months	$
Acct. no.	$	Acct. no.		
Name and address of Bank, S&L, or Credit Union		Name and address of Company	$ Payment/Months	$
Acct. no.	$	Acct. no.		
Name and address of Bank, S&L, or Credit Union		Name and address of Company	$ Payment/Months	$

FIGURE 11.3 *(Continued)*

VI. ASSETS AND LIABILITIES (cont'd)				
Name and address of Bank, S&L, or Credit Union		Name and address of Company	$ Payment/Months	$
Acct. no.	$	Acct. no.		
Stocks & Bonds (Company name/ number & description)	$	Name and address of Company	$ Payment/Months	$
		Acct. no.		
Life insurance net cash value	$	Name and address of Company	$ Payment/Months	$
Face amount: $				
Subtotal Liquid Assets	$			
Real estate owned (enter market value from schedule of real estate owned)	$			
Vested interest in retirement fund				
Net worth of business(es) owned (attach financial statement)	$			
Automobiles owned (make and year)	$	Alimony/Child Support/Separate Maintenance Payments Owed to:	$	
Other Assets (itemize)	$	Job-Related Expense (child care, union dues, etc.)	$	
		Total Monthly Payments	$	
Total Assets a.	$	Net Worth (a minus b) ►	$	**Total Liabilities b.**	$

Schedule of Real Estate Owned (If additional properties are owned, use continuation sheet.)

Property Address (enter S if sold, PS if pending sale or R if rental being held for income) ▼	Type of Property	Present Market Value	Amount of Mortgages & Liens	Gross Rental Income	Mortgage Payments	Insurance, Maintenance, Taxes & Misc.	Net Rental Income
		$	$				
Totals		$	$	$	$	$	$

List any additional names under which credit has previously been received and indicate appropriate creditor name(s) and account number(s):

Alternate Name	Creditor Name	Account Number

VII. DETAILS OF TRANSACTION		VIII. DECLARATIONS

	VII. DETAILS OF TRANSACTION	
a.	Purchase price	$
b.	Alterations, improvements, repairs	
c.	Land (if acquired separately)	
d.	Refinance (incl. debts to be paid off)	
e.	Estimated prepaid items	
f.	Estimated closing costs	
g.	PMI, MIP, Funding Fee	
h.	Discount (if Borrower will pay)	
i.	Total costs (add items a through h)	

VIII. DECLARATIONS

If you answer "Yes" to any questions a through i, please use continuation sheet for explanation.

	Borrower		Co-Borrower	
	Yes	No	Yes	No
a. Are there any outstanding judgments against you?	☐	☐	☐	☐
b. Have you been declared bankrupt within the past 7 years?	☐	☐	☐	☐
c. Have you had property foreclosed upon or given title or deed in lieu thereof in the last 7 years?	☐	☐	☐	☐
d. Are you a party to a lawsuit?	☐	☐	☐	☐
e. Have you directly or indirectly been obligated on any loan which resulted in foreclosure, transfer of title in lieu of foreclosure, or judgment?	☐	☐	☐	☐

(This would include such loans as home mortgage loans, SBA loans, home improvement loans, educational loans, manufactured (mobile) home loans, any mortgage, financial obligation, bond, or loan guarantee. If "Yes," provide details, including date, name, and address of Lender, FHA or VA case number, if any, and reasons for the action.)

FIGURE 11.3 (Continued)

VII. DETAILS OF TRANSACTION		VIII. DECLARATIONS				
			Borrower		Co-Borrower	
		If you answer "Yes" to any question a through I, please use continuation sheet for explanation.	Yes	No	Yes	No
j. Subordinate financing		f. Are you presently delinquent or in default on any Federal debt or any other loan, mortgage, financial obligation, bond, or loan guarantee?	☐	☐	☐	☐
k. Borrower's closing costs paid by Seller		g. Are you obligated to pay alimony, child support, or separate maintenance?	☐	☐	☐	☐
l. Other Credits (explain)		h. Is any part of the down payment borrowed?	☐	☐	☐	☐
		i. Are you a co-maker or endorser on a note?	☐	☐	☐	☐
m. Loan amount (exclude MIP, Funding Fee financed)						
		j. Are you a U.S. citizen?	☐	☐	☐	☐
n. PMI, MIP, Funding Fee financed		k. Are you a permanent resident alien?	☐	☐	☐	☐
o. Loan amount (add m & n)		l. Do you intend to occupy the property as your primary	☐	☐	☐	☐
		If "Yes" complete question m below.				
p. Cash from/to Borrower (subtract j, k, l & o from i)		m. Have you had an ownership interest in a property in the last years?	☐	☐	☐	☐
		(1) What type of property did you own—principal residence (PR), second home (SH), or investment property (IP)?				
		(2) How did you hold title to the home— by yourself (S), jointly with your spouse, or jointly with another person (O)?				

X. ACKNOWLEDGMENT AND AGREEMENT

Each of the undersigned specifically represents to Lender and to Lender's actual or potential agents, brokers, processors, attorneys, insurers, servicers, successors and assigns and agrees and acknowledges that: (1) the information provided in this application is true and correct as of the date set forth opposite my signature and that any intentional or negligent misrepresentation of this information contained in this application may result in civil liability, including monetary damages, to any person who may suffer any loss due to reliance upon any misrepresentation that I have made on this application, and/or in criminal penalties including, but not limited to, fine or imprisonment or both under the provisions of Title 18, United States Code, Sec. 1001, et seq.; (2) the loan requested pursuant to this application (the "Loan") will be secured by a mortgage or deed of trust on the property described in this application; (3) the property will not be used for any illegal or prohibited purpose or use; (4) all statements made in this application are made for the purpose of obtaining a residential mortgage loan; (5) the property will be occupied as indicated in this application; (6) the Lender, its servicers, successors or assigns may retain the original and/or an electronic record of this application, whether or not the Loan is approved; (7) the Lender and its agents, brokers, insurers, servicers, successors, and assigns may continuously rely on the information contained in the application, and I am obligated to amend and/or supplement the information provided in this application if any of the material facts that I have represented herein should change prior to closing of the Loan; (8) in the event that my payments on the Loan become delinquent, the Lender, its servicers, successors or assigns may, in addition to any other rights and remedies that it may have relating to such delinquency, report my name and account information to one or more consumer reporting agencies; (9) ownership of the Loan and/or administration of the Loan account may be transferred with such notice as may be required by law; (10) neither Lender nor its agents, brokers, insurers, servicers, successors or assigns has made any representation or warranty, express or implied, to me regarding the property or the condition or value of the property; and (11) my transmission of this application as an "electronic record" containing my "electronic signature," as those terms are defined in applicable federal and/or state laws (excluding audio and video recordings), or my facsimile transmission of this application containing a facsimile of my signature, shall be as effective, enforceable and valid as if a paper version of this application were delivered containing my original written signature.

Acknowledgement. Each of the undersigned hereby acknowledges that any owner of the Loan, its servicers, successors and assigns, may verify or reverify any information contained in this application or obtain any information or data relating to the Loan, for any legitimate business purpose through any source, including a source named in this application or a consumer reporting agency.

Borrower's Signature X	Date	Co-Borrower's Signature X	Date

X. INFORMATION FOR GOVERNMENT MONITORING PURPOSES

The following information is requested by the Federal Government for certain types of loans related to a dwelling in order to monitor the lender's compliance with equal credit opportunity, fair housing and home mortgage disclosure laws. You are not required to furnish this information, but are encouraged to do so. The law provides that a lender may not discriminate either on the basis of this information, or on whether you choose to furnish it. If you furnish the information, please provide both ethnicity and race. For race, you may check more than one designation. If you do not furnish ethnicity, race, or sex, under Federal regulations, this lender is required to note the information on the basis of visual observation and surname if you have made this application in person. If you do not wish to furnish the information, please check the box below. (Lender must review the above material to assure that the disclosures satisfy all requirements to which the lender is subject under applicable state law for the particular type of loan applied for.)

BORROWER ☐ I do not wish to furnish this information		CO-BORROWER ☐ I do not wish to furnish this information	
Ethnicity: ☐ Hispanic or Latino ☐ Not Hispanic or Latino		**Ethnicity:** ☐ Hispanic or Latino ☐ Not Hispanic or Latino	
Race: ☐ American Indian or Alaska Native ☐ Asian ☐ Black or African American		**Race:** ☐ American Indian or Alaska Native ☐ Asian ☐ Black or African American	
☐ Native Hawaiian or Other Pacific Islander ☐ White		☐ Native Hawaiian or Other Pacific Islander ☐ White	
Sex: ☐ Female ☐ Male		**Sex:** ☐ Female ☐ Male	

To be Completed by Loan Originator:
This information was provided:
☐ In a face-to-face interview
☐ In a telephone interview
☐ By the applicant and submitted by fax or mail
☐ By the applicant and submitted via e-mail or the Internet

Loan Originator's Signature X		Date
Loan Originator's Name (print or type)	Loan Originator Identifier	Loan Originator's Phone Number (including area code)
Loan Origination Company's Name	Loan Origination Company Identifier	Loan Origination Company's Address

FIGURE 11.3   *(Continued)*

CONTINUATION SHEET/RESIDENTIAL LOAN APPLICATION		
Use this continuation sheet if you need more space to complete the Residential Loan Application. Mark **B** f or Borrower or **C** for Co-Borrower.	Borrower:	Agency Case Number:
	Co-Borrower:	Lender Case Number:

I/We fully understand that it is a Federal crime punishable by fine or imprisonment, or both, to knowingly make any false statements concerning any of the above facts as applicable under the provisions of Title 18, United States Code, Section 1001, et seq.

Borrower's Signature	Date	Co-Borrower's Signature	Date
X		X	

Freddie Mac Form 65   6/09   **Page 5 of 5**   **Fannie Mae Form 1003**   6/09

Source: www.eFannieMae.com.

A borrower may have more than enough verifiable income to make a loan payment, but a credit report showing several late payments may be an indication that the borrower doesn't see the importance of paying obligations on time. Late payments cost the lender money because it does not have the money to relend to others if the borrower is late in paying it to them. This affects the lender's overall yield on its loan portfolio. Therefore, the lender may reject the borrower's loan application or require a higher interest rate or loan fee.

Capacity When a lender considers a borrower's *capacity*, it is assessing whether or not the borrower has the ability to meet the financial obligation on a regular and sustained basis. The lender looks at the borrower's source of income and her total amount of other financial obligations. If a borrower's main source of income is from a job she only recently started or is seasonal in nature, the lender will not be as ready to make the loan as if she showed long-term employment and few financial obligations. If the borrower has a sustained, verifiable history of a second job or overtime, the lender will usually take the income from that source into consideration when analyzing the borrower's capacity to pay.

Lenders usually take a spouse's income into consideration when computing a family's gross income for qualifying purposes, even if only one spouse is applying for the loan. Occasionally, a lender will determine that a borrower is only marginally qualified or not quite qualified for a loan and it will require a **cosigner**—a person with additional capital or sustained income who agrees to share liability for the repayment of the loan—to strengthen the borrower's application. Some lenders reduce the down payment requirement based on the cosigner's financial strength.

When analyzing a new loan application, the lender is evaluating whether it is safe to make the requested loan to the borrower. The obvious questions are:

- Can the borrower afford the payments?
- Will the borrower make the payments in a timely fashion?
- Are the borrower's earnings sufficient to make the payments on a sustained basis?
- What is the amount of the borrower's down payment and its source?

Prior to approving the loan, with the buyer's written permission, the lender will obtain a tri-merged credit report (three credit reports

from three companies that are "merged" for an overall rating), written verifications about the borrower's employment history (at least the last two years), and current employment. The lender will then verify the source and amount of the borrower's down payment, if any. All of this information is shown on the loan application (see Figure 11.3).

Once the lender knows the purchase price, loan amount, and down payment, they can calculate the borrower's total loan payment (*principal*, *interest*, *taxes*, and *insurance*). When the monthly payment is determined, the lender can apply the *qualifying ratios* to assess whether or not it meets their underwriting guidelines. The borrower's income is examined using two different percentages. The **front-end ratio** is the total payment (PITI) divided by the borrower's gross income. Conforming loans require that the front-end ratio be approximately 28 percent or less. This number is not inflexible; the lender will allow a higher ratio for a well-qualified buyer or one with a large down payment.

The second number is the **back-end ratio**, or *total obligation ratio*. This ratio should be approximately 36 percent or less to qualify for a conforming loan. Nonconforming loans may have different values for these ratios, some as high as 50 percent. The preceding ratios are for LTV ratios of 80 percent or less that do not require PMI.

For example, your clients, Bill and Dee, have a combined monthly income of $7,000 and want to buy a home for $400,000. They have $100,000 in the bank, plus enough for their closing costs and a reserve. If they put $80,000 down, they will have a $320,000 loan. A fixed rate, thirty-year loan with no PMI at 5.75 percent would be $1,894 per month; the monthly property taxes would be about 1/12 of 1.25 percent of the purchase price and the insurance would be about $65 per month.

Loan payment	$1,894
Taxes	$417
Insurance	$65
TOTAL PAYMENT	$2,376 (PITI)/$7,000 (combined gross income) = 34 percent.

Their front-end ration is 34 percent.

If Bill and Dee also have a car payment of $450 per month and credit card debt that they can't pay off with combined monthly payments of $230, their back-end ratio would be:

PITI	$2,376
Car loan	$450*
Credit cards	$230
TOTAL	$3,056* / $7,000 = 44 percent.

---

*Most lenders will not consider a car payment a liability if the borrower has ten or fewer payments left.

As you can see, Bill and Dee's ratios of 34/44 are too high to qualify for the fixed-rate financing; however, if they switch to an interest-only loan at 5.5 percent interest, their payment decreases to $1,467 per month.

	Front-end ratio
PITI	$1,949 / $7,000 = 28 percent.
	Back-end ratio
PITI	$1,949
Car loan	$450
Credit cards	$230
TOTAL	$2,629 / $7,000 = 38 percent.

By switching to an interest-only loan, Bill and Dee have brought their ratios reasonably in line with the lender's standards and will probably be able to buy the home you have shown them. Keep in mind that an interest-only loan in a declining market may be a sure formula for a future short sale.

Qualifying the Property

The underlying security, or *collateral*, for the loan is ultimately the property itself. This is why lenders require a careful, analytical assessment of the property's value by a licensed appraiser prior to making the loan. The appraiser will take into account things such as the age, condition, lot size, and location of the property as well as its amenities, such as granite counters and swimming pools. The date of sale will also be assessed so that any sales that took place several months prior are evaluated in "today's dollars." The appraiser will then pick the three properties that are closest in overall amenities to the "subject property" (the home being appraised) and will make positive or negative adjustments in value to the subject property for features that are better or worse than the "comps" used in the appraisal.

Different lenders have different underwriting standards, and the licensee should be aware of these differences so the borrower is matched with a lender that is most appropriate for her and the property being purchased.

Once the credit report, employment, income verifications, and appraisal are in the lender's possession, along with any other required supporting documents, such as the last two years of 1040 federal income tax returns for self-employed people, the loan officer will take the loan to a loan committee whose job is to evaluate the entire package and approve or disapprove the loan.

If the loan is disapproved, the borrower is notified and starts the process all over again with other terms and conditions or another lender. Once the loan is approved, the loan documents are drawn and sent, along with the required disclosures and other loan documents, to the escrow company, where they are added to the documents that the escrow and title companies require to be signed. One of the last documents drawn by the escrow company is the HUD-1 Settlement Statement. This form is a detailed accounting of all charges and credits to the buyer, including any deposits held by the escrow company, and shows the amount of money the buyer must bring to the escrow company in certified funds or by wire transfer prior to escrow closing.

The various fees and costs can be confusing to first-time buyers. The knowledgeable licensee plays a vital role in making the closing go smoothly by arriving at the escrow company early enough to review all of the closing and loan papers and "check the math" carefully.

Computerized Loan Origination

The Internet has now made **computerized loan origination (CLO)** a reality. Various sites provide detailed information on interest rates, fees, points, and APRs for many types of loans. A borrower can even apply online or print out an application, fill it out, and mail it to the lender. Some lenders are equipped to evaluate a borrower and give a conditional loan approval in a matter of minutes. This type of approval is subject to conditions, such as an acceptable appraisal and title report.

There are a number of national lenders you may want to check out as well as a number of competitive internet lenders. Most urban areas have a wide variety of websites for major lenders operating local offices.

Some loan originator sites require users to pay a fee prior to using their site. When a borrower is charged a fee for using a site for a CLO, a disclosure must be provided to the borrower in a RESPA-specified format.

A borrower can evaluate all aspects of many different types of loans to make an informed decision, complete and submit the loan

application, and be qualified by the lender, all on the Internet. The resulting competition often lowers loan costs to the borrower.

At this time, the major drawback to obtaining online financing is that the lenders universally do a poor job of communicating with the borrower's real estate licensee and often with the escrow company. As a result, as a licensee, you should become familiar with the Internet lending sites and how they work. As a real estate professional, you should have a thorough knowledge of available local lenders.

11.8 REAL ESTATE FINANCING REGULATIONS

Because an in-depth understanding of real estate finance is critical to consumer protection and an important part of preparation for a California real estate licensee, a more in-depth study of this subject is recommended. What follows is a survey of the principle federal regulations every licensee should know. For a detailed accounting of real estate financing laws and regulations, consult a book on real estate finance.

Fair Credit Reporting Act

The **Fair Credit Reporting Act** affects credit reporting agencies and users of credit information. If a loan is rejected by a lender because of information disclosed in a credit report, the borrower must be notified. The borrower is entitled to know all information the agency has in its file, as well as the sources and the names of all creditors who received reports within the past six months.

Mortgage Loan Originator (MLO)

January 1, 2011 is the deadline for licensees who perform residential mortgage loan originator activities to obtain an MLO license endorsement. Licensees must complete the National and California State specific examination. This National component is currently available for all applicants. An MLO license endorsement application to the California DRE is required as well as a set of fingerprints to the National Mortgage Licensing System and Registry (NMLS&R). See www.dre.ca.gov/lic_safe.html for further information.

Truth-in-Lending Act (TILA)

The Truth-in-Lending Act (Regulation Z) is a key part of the federal Consumer Credit Protection Act passed in 1969. The Truth-in-Lending Act applies to banks, savings banks, credit unions, residential mortgage brokers, and consumer finance companies.

This disclosure act requires that lenders reveal to customers exactly how much they are being charged for credit in terms of an annual percentage rate (APR). This allows customers to make informed cost-of-credit comparisons among various credit sources.

Individuals seeking credit are given a right of rescission period under the act. This means that an individual has until midnight of the third day after signing a credit contract to cancel it without penalty. This right of rescission applies to loans that place any type of lien on a borrower's residence. The rescission rights do not apply to purchase money loans obtained by a buyer when making the initial purchase of their home. They do apply to refinance loans, equity loans, and consumer loans made after the initial acquisition of the buyer's home.

Real Estate Settlement Procedures Act

The regulations contained in the **RESPA** apply only to first loans on one to four residential unit properties. This disclosure act requires that within three days after the date of the loan application, a lender must furnish the buyer with an itemized list of all closing costs that will be encountered in escrow. This must be a good-faith estimate provided to every person requesting credit and must list each charge for each settlement service the buyer is likely to incur, expressed as a dollar amount or range. The lender must also provide a copy of an informational booklet prepared by the secretary of HUD. It must be delivered or placed in the mail to the applicant no later than three business days after the application is received. For current information on GFE requirements and other RESPA guidelines, go to www .RESPAnews.com <http://www.RESPAnews.com>

Controlled Business Arrangement

A **controlled business arrangement (CBA)** is a situation in which a broker offers "one-stop shopping" for a number of broker-controlled services, such as home inspection, title insurance, mortgage services, and escrow services. RESPA permits such CBAs as long as the consumer is clearly informed in writing of the relationship between the broker and the service providers and is made aware that other providers are also available. Referral fees may not be exchanged between the companies. A broker-controlled mortgage company must have its own employees and cannot contract out its services. Doing so would violate RESPA provisions that prohibit kickbacks for referral services.

SUMMARY

Primary financing refers to first trust deeds and secondary financing refers to junior liens. The primary mortgage market refers to lenders making loans directly to borrowers (the retail market) and the secondary mortgage market refers to the sale of existing loans.

A secondary mortgage market is created by Freddie Mac and Fannie Mae buying VA, FHA, and conforming conventional loans. Conforming loans meet the standards established by Fannie Mae.

Institutional lenders such as savings associations, banks, and insurance companies are the major source of primary real estate financing. Noninstitutional lenders include mortgage companies, which originate most real estate loans today. Mortgage companies (mortgage bankers) generally sell their loans in the secondary market or act as loan correspondents for other lenders and service their loans for them.

Mortgage loan brokers are real estate brokers who serve as middlemen for loans. These loans may have a high loan cost and bear a higher interest rate than do loans from institutional lenders. Other noninstitutional lenders include pension funds, credit unions, and REITs.

Seller carryback financing is also another source of funds for real estate loans.

Government loans provide for lower down payment requirements and include VA, FHA, and Cal Vet loans. Conventional "no-down" loans became prevalent in recent years in the form of an 80 percent first loan combined with a 20 percent second loan or equity loan from the same lender at the initial purchase of the property but fell into disfavor during the deep housing recession that started in 2006 and are no longer offered.

Buyers have many loan types to choose from, including fixed-rate loans, adjustable-rate loans, reverse mortgages, and renegotiable-rate mortgages. Lenders vary in the features they offer for each loan type. A buyer must carefully analyze their own needs and the importance of factors such as interest rate, down payment requirement, assumability, loan costs and fees, loan term, qualifying rate of interest, and other issues that pertain to those needs.

The Internet provides a convenient and often efficient way to shop for and compare loans and fees and a way to complete and submit a loan application. Many Internet lenders do not communicate well with brokers or escrow companies so the borrower should be careful to research each one carefully.

The financing process involves using front-end and back-end ratios for qualifying the buyer, qualifying the property through a certified appraisal, approving and processing the loan, closing the loan through the escrow company, and servicing the loan.

Lending is strictly governed by several consumer protection acts such as RESPA, Fair Credit Reporting Act, the National Mortgage Licensing System and Registry (NMLS&R), and the Truth-in-Lending Act.

CLASS DISCUSSION TOPICS

1. Assume you are a borrower with only a 5 percent down payment and so-so credit. You are also a veteran. Obtain information from two different lenders about conventional 95 percent financing and VA financing and analyze both to see which one is the better loan for you.

2. Using a front-end ratio of 35 percent and a back-end ratio of 40 percent, qualify a buyer who earns $100,000 per year for a thirty-year loan of $450,000 at 6.25 percent interest. Assume taxes of $5,000 per year and insurance at $850 per year. The buyer has a $525 monthly car payment with eighteen payments left and pays a minimum of $320 a month on credit cards.

3. Explain the process in which primary lenders make loans, then get the money back from them to re-loan.

4. Explain the differences between Cal Vet loans, VA loans, and FHA loans. What security documents are used for each and what function does each agency play in the loan process?

5. What issues does an appraiser analyze when making a value judgment of a subject property against three comparables? How could each issue, such as location and condition, affect the value of the subject property?

CHAPTER 11 QUIZ

1. A reverse mortgage refers to what type of loan?
   A. A loan that gets smaller with each payment.
   B. A mortgage that has simple interest.
   C. A loan that pays like an annuity and has compound interest.
   D. None of the above.

2. An adjustable-rate loan index is 5 percent at the time the loan is made. The margin for the loan is 2 percent. With a 5 percent lifetime cap, what is the highest the interest rate could go?
   A. 6 percent
   B. 7 percent
   C. 7.5 percent
   D. 12 percent

3. A lender who believes interest rates will soon be rising significantly will be most interested in what type of loan?
   A. Thirty-year fixed-rate loan
   B. Adjustable-rate loan
   C. Fifteen-year fixed-rate loan
   D. Renegotiable-rate mortgage

4. What kind of loan covers more than one property?
   A. Subordinated loan
   B. Adjustable-rate loan
   C. Blanket loan
   D. Land loan

5. A convertible ARM is a loan that can be changed to
   A. another qualified borrower.
   B. a different property.
   C. a fixed-rate loan.
   D. None of the above.

6. What is the underlying security for a loan?
   A. Property
   B. Borrower's character
   C. Borrower's capacity
   D. Borrower's capital

7. What is the lender's margin under an ARM?
   A. The difference between the index interest rate and the rate charged by the lender.
   B. The difference between the points paid by the borrower and the points paid by the lender when it sells the loan to FNMA.
   C. The spread created by FRMC.
   D. None of the above.

8. A buyer who works for a large corporation says she will be transferred in two years. What is the best loan for her?
   A. An assumable loan.
   B. A loan with low initial loan costs.
   C. A loan with no prepayment fee.
   D. All of the above.

9. Which loan type is most likely to meet all the criteria of Question 8?
   A. Reverse mortgage
   B. Fixed-rate mortgage
   C. VA-guaranteed loan
   D. Adjustable-rate mortgage

10. Under a CBA, a broker would need to disclose in writing to a client her ownership in
   A. a mortgage brokerage firm.
   B. a title insurance company.
   C. a property insurance company.
   D. All of the above.

IMPORTANT PHRASES AND TERMS

ALTA policy

Beneficiary
statement

Closing costs

CLTA policy

Credits

Debits

Deed of
reconveyance

Escrow

Escrow instruction
amendments

Escrow instructions

Extended policy

Good funds

Impound account

Marketable title

Preliminary title
report

Proration

Rebate law

Recurring costs

Special title
insurance policies

Standard policy

Title insurance

Escrow and Title Insurance

Upon completion of this chapter, the student will be able to:

- Define and explain the purpose of a property escrow.
- Identify the parties to the escrow.
- Compare and contrast the responsibilities of the parties to the escrow and the real estate licensee.
- Indicate the advantages of an escrow to each party.
- Identify escrow documents.
- Compare and contrast a mortgage versus a deed of trust.
- Explain the differences between an ALTA and a CLTA title insurance policy.

12.1 ESCROW

In France, when an owner of real property agreed to sell it to another party, she executed an *escroue*, or roll of writing or deed. This was given to a third party to hold until all of the terms and conditions of the sale were met and all monies were paid as agreed. The English term became escrow, meaning "a bond, a deed, money, or real property held in trust by a third party, with mutually agreed on instructions that the item(s) held in escrow be delivered to the grantee upon fulfillment of all conditions."

Escrow is the last phase of a property transaction and is defined by the California Financial Code as follows:

> *Escrow means any transaction wherein one person for the purpose of effecting the sale, transfer, encumbering or leasing*

of real or personal property to another person, delivers any written instrument, money, evidence of title to real or personal property or other things of value to a third person to be held by such third person until the happening of a specified event. The performance is then to be delivered by such third person to a grantee, grantor, promisee, promisor, obligee, obligor, bailee, or bailer or any agent or employee or any of the latter.

Over the years this definition has changed somewhat and the activities of an escrow agent have expanded considerably. An escrow agent is now considered to be an impartial third party who receives and disburses documents, money, and papers from every party involved in a transaction, such as the sale of real property. The escrow operates in a limited dual agency capacity.

Escrow Requirements

When a buyer offers a seller a sum of money on certain terms and conditions, and the seller accepts the amount of money and the terms and conditions, a binding contract is formed. This is generally the first requirement for an escrow. Escrow is created on the conditional delivery of monies and transfer instruments to a third party.

Although not generally required by California law, escrows have overwhelmingly become the method of choice in this state to protect the interests of the parties involved in real property sales and exchanges, leases, loans, mobile home sales, sale or encumbrance of personal property, sale of a promissory note secured by a trust deed, or the pledging and sale of securities. The transfer of money and other items of value for title to real property is handled differently in various parts of the country. Some states allow the listing real estate brokerage firm to act as the escrow agent, whereas in much of the eastern part of the United States an attorney is used for real estate closings. Some communities allow the local lender to handle escrow closings, but in California closings are handled through an escrow. There are significant differences between northern and southern California in the way escrow instructions are delivered.

Escrow Responsibility

The duty of an escrow agent is to hold all money and documents during the transaction. When all conditions agreed on by the buyer and seller are met, the deed and the monies involved are concurrently disbursed to the appropriate parties (see Figure 12.1). Funds paid at or just prior to closing must be **good funds** before they can be disbursed. Good funds are readily available funds such as personal checks that have cleared, cashier's checks, wire transfers,

FIGURE 12.1   Escrow Responsibilities

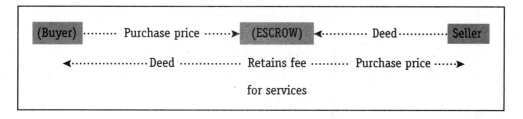

and cash. Funds tendered to escrow that do not meet the "Good Funds" requirement must be tendered at least ten days prior to escrow closing in order to have time to clear the depository from which they came. Failure to submit these types of funds in time to clear may result in a delayed escrow closing or even in a cancellation of the escrow.

Broker Responsibility

Once signed, the escrow instructions require the escrow to act as a dual agent to carry out the instructions of the buyer and the seller. However, this does not relieve the broker/licensee of her agency duties as agreed to in the purchase contract.

The broker and her licensee have a duty to track the escrow to see that the escrow officer is sending and receiving what is required, when it is required. Once a property is in escrow, the main function of the broker is to monitor the escrow for smooth functioning; if any problems arise, the broker should immediately notify the parties and attempt to resolve the issues. If the property is being financed, the broker should also monitor the loan approval process to see that the lender is progressing in a timely manner.

Parties to an Escrow

Buyers

When the buyers have performed their obligations in full by paying the entire purchase price and waiving all contingencies, they are entitled to receive a deed from the sellers, transferring title to them, subject only to encumbrances agreed on by both parties. Buyers do not want to pay sellers until the buyers are certain of receiving title to the property as agreed.

Sellers

An escrow is opened only when a buyer/seller agreement has been made; however, sellers do not want to relinquish the title to their

property until they are sure that they will get their money as agreed to in the contract. While the escrow is open, the sellers retain legal title to the property until they have received their money, at which time they will simultaneously transfer their title to the buyer by a grant deed. Once all contingencies are waived and a "firm sale" is made, the transfer of title will be binding on the sellers and their heirs. In the event of the death of a seller while a property is in escrow, the heirs could be required to complete the sale and would receive the net proceeds of the sale. If a buyer dies during an escrow, the heirs may be required to proceed with the purchase; however, if the buyer was financing the purchase, the lender would probably not make the loan and the sale may not take place.

Lenders

When making loans to buyers to complete real estate purchases, lenders, like buyers, do not want to commit their funds until they are assured that the title to property they are lending on has free and clear title. Therefore, they rely on neutral third parties (escrow agents in California) to hold the loan proceeds, other monies, and documents and not disburse them until clear title is confirmed. The lender is protected through the issuance of an American Land Title Association Lender's Title Insurance Policy (ALTA lender's policy). Once clear title is confirmed and all other terms and conditions of the contract are fulfilled, it is the responsibility of the escrow officer to properly disburse all deeds, papers, and monies to the proper parties.

Brokers

Real estate broker/licensees are not parties to the escrow unless they act as principals (selling their own property). While a broker/licensee is not a party to the escrow, she should understand escrow procedures in order to act more efficiently as a guide to clients regarding escrow matters and better monitor the escrow as it proceeds. Once an escrow is opened, a broker/licensee has no authority to change the escrow instructions without written authorization by the proper parties to the escrow. If the escrow instructions state that a commission is to be paid to a broker upon successful closing, there is usually a statement included that the seller has made an irrevocable assignment of the commission to the broker. This statement is included in the California Association of REALTORS® (C.A.R.) Purchase Agreement signed by both seller and buyer. This prevents the seller from closing the escrow without paying the broker. Some brokers give written authorization for an escrow officer to pay their salesperson their share of an earned commission directly from escrow.

Escrow Agents

In California, all escrow companies must be corporations and, as such, be licensed by the California Commissioner of Corporations. Individuals cannot be licensed under the escrow law, but certain individuals and organizations are permitted to act as escrow agents without being licensed. These include:

- Brokers
- Savings and loan companies
- Banks
- Title and trust companies
- Attorneys, provided they have a prior client relationship with a party to the escrow

In northern California, the majority of escrow transactions are handled by title insurance companies, which usually issue the title insurance policy or policies and act as the escrow officer. In southern California, the majority of escrows are handled by escrow companies and a title insurance company issues the title policy or policies separately. Another marked difference is that in northern California the escrow instructions are not signed until immediately prior to escrow closing, whereas in southern California escrow instructions are signed when the escrow is opened. Escrow instructions are a part of the RPA-CA purchase contract but may or may not be used by the escrow company.

Broker as Escrow

The only time that the broker exemption from licensing as an escrow applies is when the broker represents either the buyer or the seller in the transaction or is acting as a principal in the transaction. Many larger real estate firms have escrow services as separate profit centers for their operations and the broker may charge a fee for her escrow services. A number of computerized escrow programs are available to brokers who wish to engage in escrow services.

The broker cannot use a fictitious business name that contains the word escrow and cannot advertise that she provides escrow services without specifying that such services are only in connection with the broker's real estate brokerage activities. Although acting as an escrow, a broker must dispense with agency relationships as well as any special interests and adopt the position of a neutral depository, the same as any other escrow agency.

Any money held by a broker in connection with an escrow must be placed in a special trust account that is subject to periodic

inspection by the Commissioner of Corporations and is subject to an annual audit at the broker's own expense.

A broker can be licensed separately as an escrow company and operate the escrow business as a controlled business arrangement.

Escrow Licensure Requirements

Any corporation that makes application for an escrow license under the escrow act must:

- Be financially solvent.
- Furnish a surety bond for $10,000.
- Set up a trust fund for all monies deposited in escrow.
- Arrange for bonding of responsible employees.
- Submit to an annual independent audit at its own expense.
- Keep accurate records, subject to audit at any time by the Commissioner of Corporations and the Department of Real Estate.

Laws Governing Escrow

No escrow officer may:

- Solicit or accept escrow instructions or amended or supplemental instructions containing any blanks to be filled in after the instructions are signed.
- Pay referral fees to anyone except a regular employee of its own escrow company.
- Disseminate misleading or deceptive statements referring to its supervision by the state of California.
- Permit any person to make additions to, deletions from, or alterations of an escrow instruction unless it is signed or initialed by all signers of the original instructions.
- Describe either orally or in writing any transaction that is not included under the definition of escrow in the California Financial Code. Figure 12.2 summarizes the legal requirements pertaining to the actions of escrow officers.

Advantages of an Escrow

Although the purchase of a personal computer or some other type of consumer goods entails simply giving the clerk your credit or debit card or writing a check, the purchase and sale of real estate is far more complex.

The buyer could pay the purchase price to the seller in return for a deed to the property without any further action; however,

FIGURE 12.2 Legal Requirements for Escrow Officers

Officers must:

- Act only according to issued written instructions.
- Hold monies deposited by parties until disbursed.
- Act as a neutral party at all times.
- Give to parties only that information that concerns them.
- Follow escrow instructions in every detail unless the instructions are in violation of the law.
- Ensure the escrow does not close with unverified funds.

Officers may not:

- Negotiate with the parties separately.
- Make a transaction for another officer.
- Suggest that terms or provisions be inserted in the escrow.
- Notify parties that they have not ordered a certain document that may be necessary to close an escrow.
- Act as collection agencies to persuade a client to furnish funds.

neither party should agree to such an arrangement for the following reasons:

- An accurate description of the property is necessary for legal purposes and to ensure that the correct property is being conveyed.
- The title to the property may be encumbered. The buyer needs someone to conduct a search of the title so title insurance can be issued for the buyer's protection.
- The buyer and seller need an experienced person to prepare the necessary paperwork, including the grant deed or other conveyance instrument for their signatures.
- The buyer and seller need assurance that their instructions have been carried out and that the deeds will be delivered and any monies transferred only when all of the contract's terms and conditions have been met.

There are also distinct advantages to escrow and the use of a neutral third party in a real estate purchase and sale transaction. These include:

- Professional handling of the accounting and other details of the transaction.
- The validity of a binding contract between the parties.
- A neutral custodian or keeper of the funds, papers, documents, and written instructions until the transaction is closed.

- Assurance that the sellers' monies have been paid as agreed to and all other terms and conditions of the contract have been met prior to relinquishing title to the property.
- Assurance that the buyers' monies will not be transferred until the title is subject only to what was disclosed to and approved by them and to the specifications of the contract between them and the sellers.

Escrow Procedures

To fulfill the requirements of an escrow, certain procedures must be followed. When the broker opens an escrow, she must provide certain information to the escrow officer. All parties to the escrow must be aware of their respective responsibilities for it to close in a timely manner and to everyone's satisfaction.

Figure 12.3 details the many duties and responsibilities that must be properly handled in an escrow.

Opening the Escrow

The steps to open an escrow vary somewhat between northern and southern California; however, in either case the following is generally the order:

- The broker or licensee usually opens the escrow after obtaining a fully executed purchase agreement signed by all parties.
- The real estate broker or licensee may prepare the escrow instructions but generally requests the escrow officer to do so. The broker will usually give a copy of the purchase agreement, which also acts as escrow instructions, to the escrow officer.
- Prepared escrow instructions are signed by all parties to the contract. In southern California, a single set of instructions called *bilateral escrow instructions* is generally signed by the buyer and seller when the escrow is opened. In northern California, both bilateral and unilateral, or separate escrow instructions, are used and are generally signed at the title company just prior to closing.
- The escrow officer orders a title search from a title company, which sends its report to escrow. (In northern California, the escrow officer is likely an employee of the title company that will do the search.)
- The escrow officer prepares the grant deed.
- Buyers' and sellers' escrow instructions and the deed are signed and held in escrow in preparation for closing.

FIGURE 12.3   The Life of an Escrow

- Prepare escrow instructions and pertinent documents.
- Obtain signatures.
- Order **preliminary title report**.
- If a new loan, forward required documents to the lender.
- Receive and review preliminary title report.
- If a loan assumption, request **beneficiary statement**.
- If a new loan, verify lender has the necessary documentation for loan submission.
- Request loan payoff demands, if any.
- Request clarification of other liens, such as judgments, if any.
- Review real property taxes stated on preliminary title report.
- If a loan assumption, review beneficiary statement for terms and conditions of transfer and current payment status. (For example, is prior approval necessary to record?)
- If a new loan, obtain loan approval and determine that terms are correct.
- Receive and review loan payoff demands and place in the file, if any.
- If a new loan, request loan documents.
- Review the file to determine if all conditions have been met and all documents are accurate and available for signature. Some conditions may include: termite inspection, contingencies waived in writing, fire insurance ordered, and additional documents prepared or received, such as grant deed and deeds of trust.
- Prepare buyer's and seller's estimated closing cost sheets and other escrow closing papers.
- Meet with buyers and sellers to sign papers.
- If a new loan, return loan documents to lender.
- Forward documents to the title company.
- If a new loan, request loan funds.
- If a new loan, receive loan funds and order recording.
- Close escrow file, including preparing closing statements and disbursing funds.
- Complete closing, including forwarding final documents to all parties (buyers, sellers, lenders, and brokers).

Escrow Instructions

Escrow instructions are the road map of an escrow. They are the instrument that principals to the escrow use to give written direction to the neutral third party, the escrow agent, to carry out the agreement that was reached by the principals. All principals in the escrow (buyers/borrowers, lenders, and sellers) sign identical or conforming instructions that fully set out the agreements between the parties to the transactions within the escrow. Such instructions are included

in the C.A.R. Purchase Agreement (Paragraph 28) and delivered to the escrow holder within three business days after acceptance. If another contract is used, separate escrow instructions may be required. When the escrow instructions are fully executed (signed by all parties), they are delivered to the escrow agent. In northern California, if not done via the purchase agreement, it is done just prior to escrow closing and the escrow instructions are usually signed along with the new loan papers, if any, and the other closing documents. In southern California, this is done very soon after an escrow is opened and the loan documents, other closing documents, and any amended escrow instructions are signed prior to closing.

Some title and escrow companies usually use preprinted forms for their escrow instructions. When a C.A.R. contract containing escrow instructions has not been used, however, lenders and other authorized institutions may issue their instructions in the form of a letter.

When licensees of the principals to the escrow meet with the escrow officer to open the escrow, they give the escrow officer mutually agreed-on instructions that are recorded on a worksheet.

It should be carefully noted that, if separate escrow instructions are used, once signed by all parties, the escrow instructions may take precedence over the terms of the purchase contract. The real estate licensees and the escrow officers must take special care to see that all of the agreed upon terms and conditions of the purchase agreement are carefully and fully incorporated into the escrow instructions and reviewed prior to obtaining signatures of the principals. In the event there is no purchase contract, the escrow instructions prevail. It is not unusual for the escrow officer to take escrow instructions from the real estate licensees or the principals over the telephone.

As a real estate licensee, when you give escrow instructions to the escrow officer, you may forward a copy of the Residential Purchase Agreement—California (RPA-CA) purchase agreement or, at a minimum, provide the following information:

1. Buyer and seller information, including full names, addresses, ZIP codes, all telephone numbers (home, cellular, and business), and the marital status of each party.
2. Information about all brokers and salespeople involved in the transaction, including names, addresses, ZIP codes, telephone numbers, and e-mail addresses.
3. Current loan information on the property, including:
   * Names and complete addresses of all lenders involved.
   * Approximate loan balances, if they are to be paid off.

- Verifiable, accurate loan balances of any loans that are to be assumed or taken "subject to" by the buyers, including account or loan numbers.

4. Existing fire insurance policy information including the name of the insurance licensee or agency, phone number, account number, and remaining balance if it is to be assumed by the buyers.

5. Termite report, including any supplemental reports, if any.

6. Personal property included in the sale, if any.

7. Escrow closing date.

8. Current tax bills. This is not as important as it once was because of tax records being readily available on the Internet, but it still speeds up the process for the escrow officer.

9. If an income-producing property is being sold, more information is needed, including the following:

   - Estoppel certificate. This is a written statement from the tenant that verifies who she is, her complete name(s), addresses, contact information, the amount of rent she is currently paying, the amount of any security deposits or last month's rent being held and by whom, and a statement confirming that any rent due to untenable property condition issues is not being withheld.

   - A tenant roll, including names, addresses, and telephone numbers.

   - The amount of cleaning or security deposits held by the owner or property manager.

   - Any service contracts for coin-operated washer/dryers, monthly pest control service, property management contracts, and so, if any.

   - Copies of all rental agreements and/or leases.

   - A list of current rents and rental due dates. This is sometimes given in lieu of an estoppel certificate with smaller rental units, but an estoppel certificate is highly recommended.

Once signed by all parties to the escrow, the escrow instructions can be amended only by mutual written consent, known as **escrow instruction amendments**. Neither the buyer nor the seller can unilaterally alter the escrow instructions once they are signed.

Closing the Escrow

The escrow arrangements are complete when all of the instructions from the buyer, seller, and lender have been fulfilled by the escrow agent; the balance of the purchase price has been paid into escrow,

either by the buyer or by the buyer and lender; and a deed has been signed. The basic steps in closing escrow include:

- After the escrow agent receives all funds, documents, and written instructions necessary to close the escrow, she makes any adjustments and **prorations** on a settlement sheet.

- A statement showing the current status of any indebtedness and the unpaid balance of any loan secured by the property is requested from the lender. By law the beneficiary must respond within twenty-one days after receipt of the request.

- All documents used in connection with the transfer of the property are sent to the title insurance company for recording. In northern California, the title company already has them as they are usually doing the escrow. Timing becomes important at this step. The title search runs right up to the last minute of the escrow recording to ensure that nothing has been recorded subsequent to the title search that was conducted when the escrow was opened. If the last-minute search shows no changes, the deed(s) and other documents are scheduled for recording, usually the following morning. A title policy can then be issued with the assurance that there were no intervening documents recorded against the property since the last search.

- On the day the deed is recorded, the escrow officer disburses funds to each party according to the written instructions signed earlier. These payments can include:
  a. The seller's lender (all principal and any prorated interest due through closing)
  b. Sales commissions to all real estate agencies involved
  c. Escrow and title companies
  d. Contractors, which may include termite inspectors, repair contractors, roofing companies, home inspectors, and repair technicians (furnace, plumbing, electrical, and so on)

- After recording, the escrow officer sends escrow closing statements to all appropriate parties.

- The title insurance company issues a title insurance policy as soon as possible, usually within a few days at the most.

- After the deed is recorded at the county recorder's office, it is mailed to the new owners.

Not every escrow closes successfully. Low appraisals, high termite reports, irreconcilable issues on the title report, and other conditions or contingencies that cannot be met can cause an escrow to fail. If an escrow fails, the parties must agree to release the buyer's

deposit (less any fees or costs). Per Civil Code 1057.3(b), if a party to the escrow refuses to release the funds in bad faith, that party can be liable for treble damages of not less than $100 or more than $1,000.

Common Escrow Documents

Grant Deed

A grant deed is a conveyance instrument. It is commonly used to convey title of real estate from a buyer to a seller. It has two specific warranties that accompany its use whether specifically stated on the grant deed or not. The grant deed warrants that the grantor has not conveyed title to anyone else and has not caused any encumbrance to attach to the property other than those disclosed (see Figure 12.4).

Quitclaim Deed

A quitclaim deed is often used when one owner of a property wishes to give up any ownership she has or may have in a property (see Figure 12.5). Quitclaim deeds are often used with divorcing spouses. By recording a quitclaim deed, a party is stating that if they ever had any interest in a property, they are deeding it to the grantee named in the deed, but they are not stating that they ever did have title to the property. If a spouse quitclaims her interest in a property to the other spouse and the couple remains married for some time, a new quitclaim deed will probably need to be filed if the "grantee spouse" wishes to sell or convey the property to a third party. The reason is that California is a community property state. As there is a chance that community funds were used to pay loans, real estate taxes, or repairs on the property after the original quitclaim deed was filed, a new community property interest would have been created after the original quitclaim deed was filed. The title would not be insurable without the "grantor spouse" quitclaiming her interest to the other spouse once again, just prior to the sale.

Deed of Trust and Assignment of Rents

Unlike the grant deed, which is a conveyance instrument, a deed of trust is a security instrument used to tie the promissory note that the buyer signed when she obtained a loan to the property being used as security for the loan. There may be several deeds of trust recorded against a property and the order or timing of recording is the determining factor as to the position of each note and deed of trust, that is, the earliest deed of trust recorded is considered a first trust deed, and so on.

FIGURE 12.4 Grant Deed

RECORDING REQUESTED BY

ORDER #

APN

WHEN RECORDED MAIL TO

Name

Street Address

City State Zip

SPACE ABOVE THIS LINE FOR RECORDER'S USE

Grant Deed

The undersigned grantor(s) declare(s):
Documentary transfer tax is $________
( ) computed on full value of property conveyed, or
( ) computed on full value less value of liens and encumbrances remaining at time of sale.
( ) Unincorporated area: ( ) City of ________
( ) Realty not sold.
FOR A VALUABLE CONSIDERATION, receipt of which is hereby acknowledged,

hereby GRANT(S) to

that property in

Mail Tax Statements to ________________

Date ________________

STATE OF CALIFORNIA

COUNTY OF________________

On ________________ **before me, the undersigned, a Notary Public in and for said State, personally appeared**

____

personally known to me (or proved to me on the basis of satisfactory evidence) to be the person(s) whose name(s) is/are subscribed to the within instrumentand acknowledged to me that he/she/they executed the same in his/her/theirauthorized capacity(ies), and that by his/her/theirsignature(s)on the instrumentthe person(s), or the entity upon behalf of which the person(s) acted, executed the instrument.

WITNESS my hand and official seal.

Signature________________

Name ________________
(typed or printed)

FTGIS-140 8/94

(This area for official notarial seal)

MAIL TAX STATEMENTS AS DIRECTED ABOVE

Source: Used with the permission of Old Republic Title Co. Not to be used or reproduced for any other purpose.

FIGURE 12.5 Quitclaim Deed

RECORDING REQUESTED BY

ORDER #

APN

WHEN RECORDED MAIL TO

Name

Street
Address

City
State
Zip

SPACE ABOVE THIS LINE FOR RECORDER'S USE

Quitclaim Deed

The undersigned grantor(s) declare(s):
Documentary transfer tax is $ _____
(   ) computed on full value of property conveyed, or
(   ) computed on full value less value of liens and encumbrances remaining at time of sale.
(   ) Unincorporated area: (   ) City of _____
(   ) Realty not sold.
FOR A VALUABLE CONSIDERATION, receipt of which is hereby acknowledged,

hereby REMISE(S), RELEASE(S) AND FOREVER QUITCLAIM(S) to

that property in

Mail Tax Statements to _____

Date _____

STATE OF CALIFORNIA

COUNTY OF_____

On _____   before me, the
undersigned, a Notary Public in and for said State, personally appeared
_____

personally known to me (or proved to me on the basis of satisfactory
evidence) to be the person(s) whose name(s) is/are subscribed to the within
instrument and acknowledged to me that he/she/they executed the same in
his/her/their authorized capacity(ies), and that by his/her/their signature(s) on
the instrument the person(s), or the entity upon behalf of which the person(s)
acted, executed the instrument.

WITNESS my hand and official seal.

Signature _____

Name _____
        (typed or printed)

FTGIS-100 8/94

(This area for official notarial seal)

MAIL TAX STATEMENTS AS DIRECTED ABOVE

A deed of trust will also contain an assignment of rents. This clause is used so that in the event the borrower defaults on her payments and the lender must foreclose on the property, the lender is given the legal right to collect any rental income if the property is rented (see Figure 12.6).

Assignment of Deed of Trust

It is not unusual for the beneficiary of a note secured by a deed of trust to want to sell or convey that note and deed to another party. This is accomplished by recording an assignment of deed of trust, which gives public notice, via the recording, that the beneficial interest in the note and deed of trust has been assigned to another party (see Figure 12.7).

Confidential Statement of Information

When an escrow is opened, the title company searches the county records, looking for any documents recorded against both the buyer and the seller. As a licensee, it is not uncommon to get the "prelim," or Preliminary Title Search, on a property, only to find various liens and encumbrances recorded against the seller that may or may not be hers. When you encounter this situation, the title company will require your seller to fill out a Confidential Statement of Information. This document lists the seller's social security number, mother's maiden name, addresses and occupations for the past ten years, and former marriages. By obtaining this information and comparing it to the recorded encumbrances, the title company can clear the parties of any liability for the issues that are not the seller's and proceed to issue a policy of title insurance.

Common Escrow Transaction Terms

Reconveyance

If the seller has a loan that is not being assumed by the buyer, the loan must be paid to clear the title. The seller instructs the escrow officer to pay the loan, and when it is done, the seller, who may also be referred to as the trustor, mortgagor, or borrower, receives a **deed of reconveyance**. The seller is charged a reconveyance fee for this service. The estimated loan balance is entered into the seller's escrow instructions and the actual total due the lender will not be known until the escrow agent receives a written **beneficiary statement** from the lender prior to closing. This provides detailed information about the actual loan balance and the daily interest charge through the day of closing.

FIGURE 12.6   Deed of Trust and Assignment of Rents

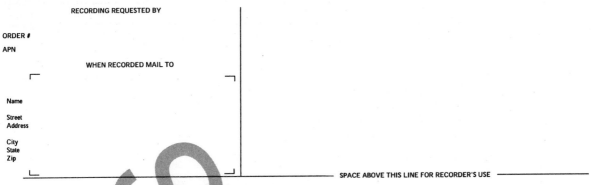

RECORDING REQUESTED BY

ORDER #
APN

WHEN RECORDED MAIL TO

Name

Street
Address

City
State
Zip

——— SPACE ABOVE THIS LINE FOR RECORDER'S USE ———

Deed of Trust and Assignment of Rents

This Deed of Trust, made this   day of   , between

, herein called TRUSTOR,

whose address is

herein called TRUSTEE, and

, herein called BENEFICIARY,

Witnesseth: That Trustor IRREVOCABLY GRANTS, TRANSFERS AND ASSIGNS to TRUSTEE IN TRUST, WITH POWER OF SALE, that property in California, described as:

Together With the rents, issues and profits thereof, SUBJECT, HOWEVER, to the right, power and authority hereinafter given to and conferred upon Beneficiary to collect and apply such rents, issues and profits.

For the Purpose of Securing:
1. Performance of each agreement of Trustor herein contained. 2. Payment of the indebtedness evidenced by one promissory note of even date herewith, and any extension or renewal thereof, in the principal sum of $_____ executed by Trustor in favor of Beneficiary or order. 3. Payment of such further sums as the then record owner of said property hereafter may borrow from Beneficiary, when evidenced by another note (or notes) reciting it is so secured.

To Protect the Security of This Deed of Trust, Trustor Agrees:
(1) To keep said property in good condition and repair; not to remove or demolish any building thereon; to complete or restore promptly and in good and workmanlike manner any building which may be constructed, damaged or destroyed thereon and to pay when due all claims for labor performed and materials furnished therefor; to comply with all laws affecting said property or requiring any alterations or improvements to be made thereon; not to commit or permit waste thereof; not to commit, suffer or permit any act upon said property in violation of law; to cultivate, irrigate, fertilize, fumigate, prune and do all other acts which from the character or use of said property may be reasonably necessary, the specific enumerations herein not excluding the general.

Deed of Trust and Assignment of Rents, Page 1 of 3

FIGURE 12.6   (Continued)

(2) To provide, maintain and deliver to Beneficiary fire insurance satisfactory to and with loss payable to Beneficiary. The amount collected under any fire or other insurance policy may be applied by Beneficiary upon any indebtedness secured hereby and in such order as Beneficiary may determine, or at option of Beneficiary the entire amount so collected or any part thereof may be released to Trustor. Such application or release shall not cure or waive any default or notice of default hereunder or invalidate any act done pursuant to such notice.

(3) To appear in and defend any action or proceeding purporting to affect the security hereof or the rights or powers of Beneficiary or Trustee; and to pay all costs and expenses, including cost of evidence of title and attorney's fees in a reasonable sum, in any such action or proceeding in which Beneficiary or Trustee may appear, and in any suit brought by Beneficiary to foreclose this Deed.

(4) To pay: at least ten days before delinquency all taxes and assessments affecting said property, including assessments on appurtenant water stock; when due, all incumbrances, charges and liens, with interest, on said property or any part thereof, which appear to be prior or superior hereto; all costs, fees and expenses of this Trust.

Should Trustor fail to make any payment or to do any act as herein provided, then Beneficiary or Trustee, but without obligation so to do and without notice to or demand upon Trustor and without releasing Trustor from any obligation hereof, may: make or do the same in such manner and to such extent as either may deem necessary to protect the security hereof, Beneficiary or Trustee being authorized to enter upon said property for such purposes; appear in and defend any action or proceeding purporting to affect the security hereof or the rights or powers of Beneficiary or Trustee; pay, purchase, contest or compromise any incumbrance, charge or lien which in the judgment of either appears to be prior or superior hereto; and, in exercising any such powers, pay necessary expenses, employ counsel and pay his reasonable fees.

(5) To pay immediately and without demand all sums so expended by Beneficiary or Trustee, with interest from date of expenditure at the amount allowed by law in effect at the date hereof, and to pay for any statement provided for by law in effect at the date hereof regarding the obligation secured hereby any amount demanded by the Beneficiary not to exceed the maximum allowed by law at the time when said statement is demanded.

(6) That any award of damages in connection with any condemnation for public use of or injury to said property or any part thereof is hereby assigned and shall be paid to Beneficiary who may apply or release such moneys received by him in the same manner and with the same effect as above provided for disposition of proceeds of fire or other insurance.

(7) That by accepting payment of any sum secured hereby after its due date, Beneficiary does not waive his right either to require prompt payment when due of all other sums so secured or to declare default for failure so to pay.

(8) That at any time or from time to time, without liability therefor and without notice, upon written request of Beneficiary and presentation of this Deed and said note for endorsement, and without affecting the personal liability of any person for payment of the indebtedness secured hereby, Trustee may: reconvey any part of said property; consent to the making of any map or plat thereof; join in granting any easement thereon; or join in any extension agreement or any agreement subordinating the lien or charge hereof.

(9) That upon written request of Beneficiary stating that all sums secured hereby have been paid, and upon surrender of this Deed and said note to Trustee for cancellation and retention and upon payment of its fees, Trustee shall reconvey, without warranty, the property then held hereunder. The recitals in such reconveyance of any matters or facts shall be conclusive proof of the truthfulness thereof. The grantee in such reconveyance may be described as "the person or persons legally entitled thereto". Five years after issuance of such full reconveyance, Trustee may destroy said note and this Deed (unless directed in such request to retain them).

(10) That as additional security, Trustor hereby gives to and confers upon Beneficiary the right, power and authority, during the continuance of these Trusts, to collect the rents, issues and profits of said property, reserving unto Trustor the right, prior to any default by Trustor in payment of any indebtedness secured hereby or in performance of any agreement hereunder, to collect and retain such rents, issues and profits as they become due and payable. Upon any such default, Beneficiary may at any time without notice, either in person, by agent, or by a receiver to be appointed by a court, and without regard to the adequacy of any security for the indebtedness hereby secured, enter upon and take possession of said property or any part thereof, in his own name sue for or otherwise collect such rents, issues and profits, including those past due and unpaid, and apply the same, less costs and expenses of operation and collection, including reasonable attorney's fees, upon any indebtedness secured hereby, and in such order as Beneficiary may determine. The entering upon and taking possession of said property, the collection of such rents, issues and profits and the application thereof as aforesaid, shall not cure or waive any default or notice of default hereunder or invalidate any act done pursuant to such notice.

(11) That upon default by Trustor in payment of any indebtedness secured hereby or in performance of any agreement hereunder, Beneficiary may declare all sums secured hereby immediately due and payable by delivery to Trustee of written declaration of default and demand for sale and of written notice of default and of election to cause to be sold said property, which notice Trustee shall cause to be filed for record. Beneficiary also shall deposit with Trustee this Deed, said note and all documents evidencing expenditures secured hereby.

After the lapse of such time as may then be required by law following the recordation of said notice of default, and notice of sale having been given as then required by law, Trustee, without demand on Trustor, shall sell said property at the time and place fixed by it in said notice of sale, either as a whole or in separate parcels, and in such order as it may determine, at public auction to the highest bidder for cash in lawful money of the United States, payable at time of sale. Trustee may postpone sale of all or any portion of said property by public announcement at such time and place of sale, and from time to time thereafter may postpone such sale by public announcement at the time fixed by the preceding postponement. Trustee shall deliver to such purchaser its deed conveying the property so sold, but without any covenant or warranty, express or implied. The recitals in such deed of any matters or facts shall be conclusive proof of the truthfulness thereof. Any person, including Trustor, Trustee, or Beneficiary as hereinafter defined, may purchase at such sale.

After deducting all costs, fees and expenses of Trustee and of this Trust, including cost of evidence of title in connection with sale, Trustee shall apply the proceeds of sale to payment of: all sums expended under the terms hereof, not then repaid, with accrued interest at the amount allowed by law in effect at the date hereof; all other sums then secured hereby; and the remainder, if any, to the person or persons legally entitled thereto.

(12) Beneficiary, or any successor in ownership of any indebtedness secured hereby, may from time to time, by instrument in writing, substitute a successor or successors to any Trustee named herein or acting hereunder, which instrument, executed by the Beneficiary and duly acknowledged and recorded in the office of the recorder of the county or counties where said property is situated, shall be conclusive proof of proper substitution of such successor Trustee or Trustees, who shall, without conveyance from the Trustee predecessor, succeed to all its title, estate, rights, powers and duties. Said instrument must contain the name of the original Trustor, Trustee and Beneficiary hereunder, the book and page where this Deed is recorded and the name and address of the new Trustee.

- Deed of Trust and Assignment of Rents, Page 2 of 3

FIGURE 12.6 (*Continued*)

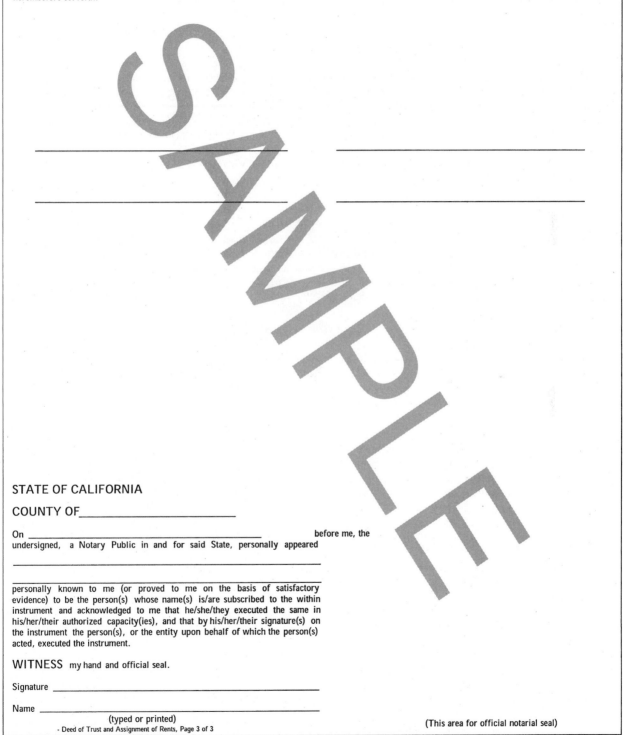

(13) That this Deed applies to, inures to the benefit of, and binds all parties hereto, their heirs, legatees, devisees, administrators, executors, successors and assigns. The term Beneficiary shall mean the owner and holder, including pledgees, of the note secured hereby, whether or not named as Beneficiary herein. In this Deed, whenever the context so requires, the masculine gender includes the feminine and/or neuter, and the singular number includes the plural.

(14) That Trustee accepts this Trust when this Deed, duly executed and acknowledged, is made a public record as provided by law. Trustee is not obligated to notify any party hereto of pending sale under any other Deed of Trust or of any action or proceeding in which Trustor, Beneficiary or Trustee shall be a party unless brought by Trustee.

The undersigned Trustor requests that a copy of any Notice of Default and of any Notice of Sale hereunder be mailed to him at his address hereinbefore set forth.

STATE OF CALIFORNIA

COUNTY OF_____

On _____ before me, the undersigned, a Notary Public in and for said State, personally appeared

_____

_____

personally known to me (or proved to me on the basis of satisfactory evidence) to be the person(s) whose name(s) is/are subscribed to the within instrument and acknowledged to me that he/she/they executed the same in his/her/their authorized capacity(ies), and that by his/her/their signature(s) on the instrument the person(s), or the entity upon behalf of which the person(s) acted, executed the instrument.

WITNESS my hand and official seal.

Signature _____

Name _____
        (typed or printed)
- Deed of Trust and Assignment of Rents, Page 3 of 3

(This area for official notarial seal)

FIGURE 12.7 Assignment of Deed of Trust

RECORDING REQUESTED BY

ORDER #
AP

WHEN RECORDED MAIL TO

Name
Street Address
City State Zip

SPACE ABOVE THIS LINE FOR RECORDER'S USE

NOTE - This Assignment should be kept with the Note and Deed of Trust hereby assigned.

ASSIGNMENT OF DEED OF TRUST

FOR VALUABLE CONSIDERATION, the undersigned hereby grants, assigns, and transfers to

all beneficial interest under that certain Deed of Trust dated
by

to
as Trustee, and recorded on ______________, in Book/Reel ________, at Page/Image ________, Series Number ________ of Official Records of ______________ County, California, together with the Promissory Note secured by said Deed of Trust and also all rights accrued or to accrue under said Deed of Trust. The property covered by said Deed of Trust is briefly described as follows:

Date ______________

______________ ______________

______________ ______________

STATE OF CALIFORNIA

COUNTY OF ______________

On ______________ before me, the undersigned, a Notary Public in and for said State, personally appeared

____

personally known to me (or proved to me on the basis of satisfactory evidence) to be the person(s) whose name(s) is/are subscribed to the within instrument and acknowledged to me that he/she/they executed the same in his/her/their authorized capacity(ies), and that by his/her/their signature(s) on the instrument the person(s), or the entity upon behalf of which the person(s) acted, executed the instrument.

WITNESS my hand and official seal.

Signature ______________

Name ______________
(typed or printed)

(This area for official notarial seal)

Source: Used with the permission of Old Republic Title Co. Not to be used or reproduced for any other purpose.

Closing Costs

The total amount of fees and charges the seller and buyer must pay above the purchase/sales price are called **closing costs**. These costs can include the seller's loan balance and interest due, the California Land Title Association Owner's Title Insurance Policy (CLTA owner's policy), and the ALTA lender's policy, document recording fees, transfer taxes, escrow services, loan reconveyance fees, property inspection fees, and other charges. Amounts will vary by area and the price of the property being sold. Who is charged what fees can vary by area as well. Different title and escrow companies' fees also vary but are usually not very different. As a real estate professional, you should get a new title and escrow fee schedule from at least two different escrow and title companies every year and keep them with you for ready reference.

Closing costs generally fall into three categories: legal, financial, and buyer/seller adjustments. The buyer can also have a reserve account as an additional closing cost, depending on her financing. Figure 12.8 lists the **closing costs** customarily paid by each party.

Beneficiary Statement

If the buyer is assuming an existing loan, the escrow officer will obtain a beneficiary statement from the one holding the note and trust deed, showing the exact loan balance and the date to which the loan is currently paid. This will ensure that the buyer receives the proper amount of credit on her escrow statement.

Impounds

When a lender makes a new first loan, especially one in excess of 80 percent of the purchase price, it will generally require the borrower to set up an impound account. This is a separate account the buyer pays into with each loan payment. These funds are used by the lender to pay the buyer's property taxes and fire insurance when they become due. The lender often requires about five months of taxes and two months of insurance to set up the initial account and then adjust the payment each year for the actual amount necessary. If the amount of money in a buyer's impounds gets too high, the lender is required by law to refund the overage in a prescribed time and manner. When the property sells, any funds in the account are returned to the buyer within a reasonable time.

Recurring Costs

Impound account funds are referred to as **recurring costs**.

FIGURE 12.8   Buyer's and Seller's Closing Costs

Seller's Costs

Legal closing fees:

- Owner's title insurance policy (will vary by county)
- Escrow services
- Drawing deed
- Obtaining deed of reconveyance
- Recording reconveyance
- Notary fees
- Documentary transfer tax, if applicable. The county tax is usually $.55 per $500 or fractional part thereof; city transfer tax may or may not apply, so become familiar with the cities in your local area.
- Other agreed-on charges

Financial closing fees:

- Loan discount fees (discount points)
- Appraisal charge for advance commitment
- Structural pest control and any other inspection reports and any agreed-on repairs; seller is obligated to pay for the report only on VA loans; the buyer usually pays when conventional financing is used
- Beneficiary statement showing the balance of any existing loan
- Loan payoff (all trust deeds, if more than one)
- Interest on existing loan(s) from date of last payment through the closing date
- Any prepayment fees on existing loan(s)
- Other agreed-on charges and fees

Buyer/seller adjustments:

- Any improvement assessments in arrears (may have to pay in full)
- Any real property taxes in arrears
- Real estate broker's commission
- Any recorded liens or judgments necessary to clear the title
- Occupancy adjustments
- Reimburse buyer for any prepaid rents and security/cleaning deposits held by the seller, pay prorated share of property taxes, and insurance and loan interest through the closing date

Buyer's Costs

Legal closing fees:

- ALTA lender's policy (if financing)
- CLTA owner's policy (will vary by county as to who pays)
- Escrow fees
- Notary fees
- Drawing junior loan note and trust deed, if used
- Recording deed
- Other agreed-on charges and fees

FIGURE 12.8 *(Continued)*

Financial closing fees:

- Loan origination fee
- Appraisal fee often paid in advance to lender
- Credit report
- Notary fees
- Drawing any junior loan notes and trust deeds, if applicable
- Termite inspection fee, unless VA loan
- Tax agency fee
- Property inspection fees
- Assumption fee, if existing loan is assumed
- Interest on new loan from the day the lender forwards the loan proceeds to escrow to the day of the first payment date
- New one-year fire insurance premium. This is not required for cash purchases but is highly recommended
- Mortgage insurance premium (if a new FHA loan)

Buyer/seller adjustments:

- Prepaid insurance (reimburse seller if policy is assumed)
- Prepaid real estate taxes (reimburse seller)
- Prepaid impounds (reimburse seller if buyer is assuming the seller's loan)
- Prepaid improvement assessments (reimburse seller)
- Other occupancy adjustments such as rent if seller is to remain in possession of the property for a time after closing.

Reserves (impounds)

On first loans greater than 80 percent LTV, many lenders require that the property taxes and often the insurance be paid with the monthly payment. These funds go into an **impound account**. The charge is usually about five months of taxes and two months of insurance reserve to start.

Variations

Some buyers negotiate a condition of sale with the seller whereby the seller pays all or a portion of the buyer's **closing costs**. This is perfectly legal as long as it is in writing and fully disclosed to the buyer's lender. Most lenders set a limit on the amount of money the seller can credit the buyer at 3 percent of the purchase price.

Prorations

The adjustment and distribution of costs to be shared by the buyer and seller is called proration. Costs typically prorated include loan interest, property taxes, insurance, and, in the event that income property is involved, prepaid rents. Costs are prorated by the escrow officer as of the escrow closing date or a date that the buyer and seller have agreed to. Who is responsible for costs on the day of closing varies by local custom and can be changed by mutual agreement. Proration is usually based on a 30-day month and a 360-day year.

Loan Interest

If the buyer is taking over the seller's loan, interest will be prorated between the buyer and seller. Because interest is normally paid in

arrears, if a closing is set for the twentieth day of the month, the loan payment is due on the first day of the month, and the payment was paid by the seller, the seller owes the buyer twenty days' interest for the twenty-day period that the seller occupied the property but has not paid for yet.

Insurance

Fire insurance policies are normally paid one year in advance. If the buyer assumes the seller's policy prior to its renewal date, the seller is entitled to a prorated refund of the unused portion of the policy.

Property Taxes

Property taxes are levied annually (July 1 through June 30 of the following year) and are paid in two installments. Taxes usually require proration. If, for example, the seller had paid the first installment of the taxes (July 1 through December 31) and escrow closed on February 28 of the following year, the seller owes the buyer two months of property taxes. The buyer must pay the entire second installment when due (seller owes for January and February; buyer owes for March through June). A supplemental tax bill will be sent covering the difference between the sellers' tax rate and the buyers' tax rate based on the new assessment. Be sure to advise buyers to expect this supplemental bill from the tax assessor when appropriate.

Rents

Prepaid rents are prorated in cases involving income-producing property. If, for example, in the sale of a four-unit apartment building with a monthly rental income of $4,000 and escrow closed on the fifteenth day of the month, the seller receives the $4,000 rent and owes the buyer $2,000 in prorated rent.

Closing Statements

A separate closing statement is issued for each party and they will seldom, if ever, match. Each settlement statement includes **credits** (entitled receipt of monies) and **debits** (amounts owed). In contrast to usual accounting procedures, on the seller's settlement statement, all credits to the seller such as the selling price and prorations are totaled, then all debits owed by the seller such as loans, interest, taxes, and commissions are deducted from the credits. The difference is usually entered as a cash credit to the seller in the form of a check for this amount from the escrow account at the close. From time to time in California, there have been instances where sellers had to bring a check to the escrow company to close the escrow

because the total charges to close the escrow exceeded the purchase/sale price and selling expenses of the property being sold.

On the buyer's statement, the buyer is charged (debited) with the purchase price of the property. Any financing obtained by the buyer is credited to her, as are any cash deposits held in escrow. Prorations may be either a credit or a debit while escrow fees and related costs are debited. The total of new or assumed loans, deposits, and prorated credits usually do not equal the total of the purchase price plus **closing costs**, hence, the buyer is required to bring in the amount of money necessary to balance the buyer's account. These funds must be in the form of a certified check or wired funds to close the escrow without delay. Escrow officers are not allowed to accept cash. Both the buyer's and the seller's accounts must balance; however, because each has their own set of costs, the actual monetary amounts will seldom if ever be alike for both parties. Figure 12.9 will help you to understand the debits and credits of closing statements.

Escrow officers are extremely busy and sometimes make mistakes. One of your final duties as a licensee involved in an escrow is to arrive at the escrow signing appointment early enough to look over the paperwork and check the math on the closing statement. If there is financing, check the terms and interest rate on the loan documents as well. Sit in on the signing and help explain to your clients anything that they are unsure of.

After both parties to the escrow have signed all necessary documents, the escrow officer will send the grant deed and any trust deeds to the county recorder's office for recording, thus assuring the buyer and any lender that their interests are protected. The final escrow statements are completed and sent to each party, including the brokers, and the actual title insurance policy is sent to the buyer. When these items are done, the escrow is complete.

Escrow could be held liable for its negligence or breach of duty; however, escrow companies do not have a duty to warn a party of possible fraud or other detrimental factors in a transaction. If a broker conducted the escrow, however, she has these disclosure obligations.

12.2 TITLE INSURANCE

In a number of states **marketable title** is shown by an abstract of title. An abstract of title is a recorded history of a property and includes a summary of every recorded document concerning the property. An attorney reads the abstract and gives a written opinion of title based on what the abstract of title reveals. An inherent

FIGURE 12.9   Escrow Closing Statement

Prepared for: Jim Prothero

Prepared on: 10/10/2009
Prepared by: Jim Prothero
Representing: self

Property: 255 Shoreline Drive, Suite 150, Redwood City, San Mateo County, CA
Type: 1-4 Family Residential

Escrow Location: San Mateo County CA

Closing Date: 12/15/2009
Services: Title & Escrow

Seller's Preliminary Estimated Statement		
Item	**Debits**	**Credits**
Sales Price		$611,500.00
Loan Payoff [1st mortgage]		
Current Balance	$452,500.00	
Interest adjustment 12/1 to 12/17, 16 day(s) @ $92.39	$1,478.17	
Statement/Demand Fee	$60.00	
Reconveyance Fee	$45.00	
Prepayment Penalty	$16,500.00	
Loan Payoff [2nd mortgage]		
Current Balance	$87,592.00	
Interest adjustment 12/1 to 12/17, 16 day(s) @ $14.89	$238.25	
Statement/Demand Fee	$60.00	
Reconveyance Fee	$45.00	
Prepayment Penalty	$0.00	
Sum of other loans	$0.00	
Broker's Commission	$36,690.00	
Home Warranty Premium	$165.00	
Prop. Taxes, 12/10 to 12/15	$69.89	
Prop. Taxes Next Installment Due	$0.00	
Homeowners Assoc. Dues, 11/1 to 12/15		$0.00
Homeowner's Dues Transfer Fee		$0.00
Standard Owners Policy (3/22/2009)	$0.00	
Escrow Fees (9/4/2008)	$0.00	
Notary Fee*	$30.00	
Additional Charges		
Courier Fees*	$30.00	
Overnight Delivery (Payoff Check)*	$0.00	
Drawing Fees*	$50.00	
Recording Fees*	$0.00	
Wire Transfer Fee*	$25.00	
City Transfer Tax	$0.00	
County Transfer Tax	$672.65	
Credit To Buyer	$3,500.00	
Miscellaneous Fees*	$0.00	
Subtotals	$599,750.96	$611,500.00
Due to Seller (ESTIMATED)		**$11,749.04**
Totals		**$611,500.00**

These are ESTIMATED fees, actual fees will vary from state to state, county to county and office to office.

The figures reflected in this Preliminary Estimated Statement are PRELIMINARY ESTIMATED FEES based upon information you have entered. Actual fees may vary for each transaction depending upon loan type and terms, any applicable discount rates, local governmental charges and any additional services required for your transaction. A more accurate statement will be made in the "Estimated Closing Statement" furnished by our escrow officer after we have received the loan documents. The exact total of all fees and costs will be reflected in the final closing statement.

Title and Escrow Fees Provided Compliments of:		
http://www.ortc.com	**Old Republic Title Company**	1-866-TITLE-HELP

problem with verifying title by abstracts is that recorded records do not reveal title defects such as unknown spousal interest, an illegal contract, failure of delivery, forged documents in the chain of title, or the incapacity of a grantor. Title insurance covers these risks and more, which explains why the use of title insurance has been growing in popularity and use.

Title insurance insures the ownership of real property, which includes the land, the buildings, permanent improvements on the land (known as appurtenances), and mineral rights unless the mineral rights have been reserved for other parties by a previous deed restriction or other recorded action. Encumbrances and other actions that may cloud the title are also insured. Buyers are assured that a thorough search of all public records that affect the property being purchased has been made and that they have a marketable title that will stand against any claims by a third party.

Title insurance is paid only once, at the time title passes from one owner to another, and it remains in effect until the property is sold or conveyed again, at which time title passes to the new owner.

A buyer who does not purchase title insurance is not covered, even though the previous owner had title insurance.

If the property is financed, both the buyer and the lender purchase title insurance, the buyer to protect her investment and ownership rights, and the lender to insure its interest in the property.

The two basic types of title insurance are standard coverage and extended coverage. Generally, these are the CLTA owner's policy and the ALTA lender's policy. The title insurance industry, in recent years, begun to offer a new homeowner's policy that offers the standard coverage plus many of the benefits offered in the **extended policy**, such as encroachments and unrecorded easements. There is a nominal additional charge for the homeowner's policy.

CLTA Policy

Also called a **standard policy**, the California Land Title Association **(CLTA) policy** is usually the one used by the buyer or new owner of a property. (See the sample CLTA policy in Figure 12.10 for its coverage.)

The **CLTA policy** of title insurance covers matters of record, if not specifically excluded from coverage (such as mineral or water rights), as well as unrecorded specified risks, such as:

- Forgery.
- Lack of capacity of a grantor.
- Failure of delivery of a prior deed.

FIGURE 12.10 Sample California Land Title Association Policy

OLD REPUBLIC TITLE COMPANY

ORDER NO. PROTHERO

OFFICE NOTE

1. Verify policy approval with the title department at least five days prior to close of escrow (in excess of $ 250,000.00 and/or any unusual risk).

SAMPLE

Page___1__of___1__Pages

ORT 3157-E

FIGURE 12.10 (*Continued*)

OLD REPUBLIC TITLE COMPANY

601 ALLERTON STREET • REDWOOD CITY, CA • 94063 • (650) 365-8080 • Fax: (650) 365-9524

PRELIMINARY REPORT

Issued for the sole use of:

    The Beverly Hills Realty Service
    10000 Rodeo Drive
    Beverly Hills, California 90000

    Attention: R. Royce

Our Order No. PROTHERO

Reference

When Replying Please Contact:

    Will Closeyourdeal

Property Address: 1030 Cement Pond Way, Menlo Park, CA   90000

In response to the above referenced application for a policy of title insurance, OLD REPUBLIC TITLE COMPANY hereby reports that it is prepared to issue, or cause to be issued, as of the date hereof, a Policy or Policies of Title Insurance describing the land and the estate or interest therein hereinafter set forth, insuring against loss which may be sustained by reason of any defect, lien or encumbrance not shown or referred to as an Exception below or not excluded from coverage pursuant to the printed Schedules, Conditions and Stipulations of said policy forms.

The printed Exceptions and Exclusions from the coverage of said Policy or Policies may be set forth in Exhibit A attached. Copies of the Policy forms should be read. They are available from the office which issued this report.

Please read the exceptions shown or referred to below and the exceptions and exclusions set forth in Exhibit A of this report carefully. The exceptions and exclusions are meant to provide you with notice of matters which are not covered under the terms of the title insurance policy and should be carefully considered.
It is important to note that this preliminary report is not a written representation as to the condition of title and may not list all liens, defects, and encumbrances affecting title to the land.

This report (and any supplements or amendments hereto) is issued solely for the purpose of facilitating the issuance of a policy of title insurance and no liability is assumed hereby. If it is desired that liability be assumed prior to the issuance of a policy of title insurance, a Binder or Commitment should be requested.

Dated as of _____ April 15th _____ ,2009 , at 7:30 A.M.

                    OLD REPUBLIC TITLE COMPANY

For Exceptions Shown or Referred to, See Attached

Page____1__of____7___Pages

ORT 3157-A (Rev. 5/1/00)

FIGURE 12.10 *(Continued)*

OLD REPUBLIC TITLE COMPANY
ORDER NO. PROTHERO

The form of policy of title insurance contemplated by this report is:

A Homeowner's Policy of Title Insurance (1998); AND an ALTA Loan Policy - 1970 (Rev. 1992) with ALTA Endorsement Form 1 Coverage, OR, an ALTA Loan Policy - 1992 with ALTA Endorsement Form 1 Coverage. A specific request should be made if another form or additional coverage is desired.

The estate or interest in the land hereinafter described or referred to covered by this Report is:

a FEE as to Parcel and an EASEMENT as to Parcel.

Title to said estate or interest at the date hereof is vested in:

The heirs or devisees of Granny Clampett, Deceased, subject to the administration of the Estate of said decedent.

Page **2** of **7** Pages

ORT 3157-A1 (Rev 1-1-95)

FIGURE 12.10 *(Continued)*

OLD REPUBLIC TITLE COMPANY
ORDER NO. PROTHERO

The land referred to in this Report is situated in the County of <u>San Mateo , in the unincorporated area,</u>
State of California, and is described as follows:

    PARCEL ONE:

    Lot 86, as shown on that certain map entitled, "TEXAS TEA ESTATES UNIT NO. 2,
    SAN MATEO COUNTY RECORDS", filed in the Office of the Recorder of San Mateo
    County on May 2, 1986 in Book 46 of Maps , at Page 58.

    Certificate of Correction for Subdivisions recorded December 3, 1986 in Book
    1986 Page 145331 Official Records at Instrument No. 70636.

    PARCEL TWO:

    A non-exclusive easement for ingress and egress to and from "THE STILL" as shown
    on that certain map entitled, "TEXAS TEA ESTATES UNIT NO. 2, SAN MATEO COUNTY
    RECORDS", filed in the Offcie of the Recorder of San Mateo County on May 2, 1986
    in Book 46 of Maps, at Page 58.

    A.P.N. 000-090-090   J.P.N. 000-009-090-090

At the date hereof exceptions to coverage in addition to the Exceptions and Exclusions in said policy form would be as
follows:
    1. Taxes and assessments, general and special, for the fiscal year 2009-2010 a
    lien, but not yet due or payable.

    Assessor's Parcel No. : 000-090-090

    2. Taxes and assessments, general and special, for the fiscal year 2009-2010 as
    follows:

    Assessor's Parcel No. : 000-090-090
    Code No.   : 01-111
    1st Installment   : $ 15,000.00   Marked Paid
    2nd Installment   : $ 15,000.00   NOT Marked Paid
    Land   : $ 3,264,500.00
    Imp. Value   : $ 3,264,500.00
    P.P. Value   : $ 0.00
    Exemption   : $ 7,000.00   - Householder

Page___3__of __7__Pages

ORT 3157-B

FIGURE 12.10 *(Continued)*

3. Said property having been declared tax defaulted for non-payment of delinquent taxes for the fiscal year 2006-2007, and subsequent delinquencies

Amount to Redeem by April 30th, 2009, for the above stated year (and subsequent years, if any) is $46,582.36

Assessor's Parcel No. : 000-090-090

4. Supplemental taxes, for the fiscal year 2006-2007 and any additional amount which may be assessed pursuant to the provisions of Section 75, et seq., of the Revenue and Taxation Code of the State of California;

Amounts due under Tax Bill dated: July 31st, 2006

Assessor's Parcel No.   : 000-090-090-01

Total Supplemental Value : $ 560,000.00

1st Installment   : $ 12,366.00   Marked Paid

2nd Installment   : $ 12,366.00   NOT Marked Paid

          Delinquent on   : December 10th, 2002

5. An easement affecting that portion of said land and for the purposes stated herein and incidental purposes as shown on the filed Map.

For   : Public utitlites
Affects : the Northerly 5 feet

6. Building set-back line as shown on the filed Map.

Affects   : Easterly 25 feet

7. Covenants, Conditions and Restrictions, but omitting any covenants or restrictions if any, based upon race, color, religion, sex, handicap, familial status, or national origin unless and only to the extent that said covenant (a) is exempt under Title 42, Section 3607 of the United States Code or (b) relates to handicap but does not discriminate against handicapped persons, as provided in an instrument

Entitled   : Declaration
Executed by: Ellie Mae and Company
Dated   : April 28th, 1986
Recorded   : May 28th, 1986 in Official Records under Recorder's Serial Number
              86015668

Page____4__of____7__Pages

FIGURE 12.10 *(Continued)*

NOTE: Section 12956.1 of the Government Code provides the following: "If this document contains any restriction based on race, color, religion, sex, familial status, marital status, disability, national origin, or ancestry, that restriction violates state and federal fair housing laws and is void. Any person holding an interest in this property may request that the county recorder remove the restrictive covenant language pursuant to subdivision (c) of Section 12956.1 of the Government Code."

8. Deed of Trust to secure an indebtedness of the amount stated below and any other amounts payable under the terms thereof,

```
Amount             :  $4,500,000.00
Trustor/Borrower   :  Granny Clampett
Trustee            :  Old Republic Title Company
Beneficiary/Lender :  First Franklin Financial Corporation
Dated              :  September 12th, 2005
Recorded           :  September 18th, 2005 in Official Records under Recorder's
                      Serial Number 98000146
Loan No.           :  $$$$$$
Returned to Address:  2150 North First Street San Jose, CA 95131
```

The record beneficial interest under said Deed of Trust as a result of the last recorded assignment thereof is,

```
Vested In          :  Beverly Hills Bank and Trust Company
By Assignment From :  First Franklin Financial Corporation
Recorded           :  October 1st, 2005 in Official Records under Recorder's
                      Serial Number 2005-105666
Loan No.           :  $$$$$
```

Notice of Default under the terms of said Deed of Trust,

```
Executed by        :  Cal-Western Reconveyance Corporation
Dated              :  December 6th, 2008
Recorded           :  December 7th, 2008 in Official Records, under Recorder's
                      Serial Number 2008-240337
Trustee's No.      :  1072462-08
Returned to           Cal-Western Reconveyance Corp. P.O. Box 22004 525 East Main
                      Street El Cajon, CA 92022-9004
```

Page___5__of___7__Pages

ORT 3157-E

FIGURE 12.10 (*Continued*)

OLD REPUBLIC TITLE COMPANY

ORDER NO. PROTHERO

Notice of Trustee's Sale under said Deed of Trust,

Executed by	:	Cal-Western Reconveyance Corporation
Dated	:	March 8th, 2009
Recorded	:	March 9th, 2009 in Official Records, under Recorder's Serial Number 2009-037390
Trustee's No.	:	1072462-08
Sale Date	:	April 6th, 2009
Returned to Address	:	525 East Main Street P.O. Box 22004 El Cajon, CA 92022-9004

9. Proceedings pending in the Superior Court, as follows:

County	:	San Mateo
Estate of	:	Granny Clampett, Decedent
Case No.	:	11111111 Probate

10. Any facts, rights, interests or claims which a correct survey would show.

11. Any facts, rights of interest or claims which are not shown by the Public Record, but could be ascertained by making inquiry of the parties in possession of the herein described real property.

12. Any interest of the spouse/domestic partner of Granny Clampett on August 15th, 1998.

------------------- Informational Notes --------------------
1. NOTE: According to the public records, there have been no deeds conveying the property described in this report recorded within a period of two years prior to the date hereof except as follows:

A Grant Deed executed by Daisey Mae to Granny Clampett, dated August 10, 1994 ans recorded August 15, 1998, in Official Records as San Mateo County Recorders Serial Number 98000145.

2. Short term rate may apply to orders placed within 60 months from September 18th, 2001 (unless specifically excluded by application of our Schedule of Fees and Charges).

3. Information shown by the public records and/or The San Mateo County Tax Rolls indicates the mailing address of the vestee(s) herein to be: 1030 Cement Pond Way, Redwood City, Ca 94061 .

Page____6__of____7__Pages

ORT 3157-E

FIGURE 12.10 (*Continued*)

```
JP/jp

CC:   1      The Beverly Hills Realty Service, 10000 Rodeo Drive, Beverly
             Hills, CA 90000, Attn: R. Royce
      2      Old Republic Title Company, 796 A El Camino Real, San Carlos, CA
             94070, Attn: Helen Ferretti
      3 + 1, BANK of Millions, P.O. Box 00000, City of Industry, CA 91896,
             Attn: Jane Hathaway/Jethro Bodine
```

Page ___**7**__ of ___**7**__ Pages

ORT 3157-E

- Deeds of a corporation or Limited Liability Company (LLC) whose charter has expired.
- Undisclosed spousal interests, that is, a grantor who claimed to be single previously owned the property with a wife who had a community property interest that she had not deeded away.
- Deeds of a licensee whose legal capacity has terminated, that is, a person named in corporate minutes as the signatory for the corporation signed a deed after she was removed from that position.
- Federal estate tax liens.

A CLTA policy of title insurance excludes coverage for the following:

- Title defects known by the insured and not disclosed to the title insurance company.
- Taxes and assessments that are not yet liens.
- Reservations in government patents.
- Zoning (although a special endorsement is possible that current zoning authorizes a current use).
- Water rights.
- Mining claims filed in mining districts only; legal descriptions are not required.
- Matters that would be revealed by a correct survey.
- Unrecorded easements and liens, such as a mechanic's lien, equestrian easement, or prescriptive easements.
- Unrecorded matters that a visual inspection of the property would disclose, such as an encroachment.
- Rights of parties in possession such as unrecorded leases or deeds and options to purchase.

ALTA Policy

An American Land Title Association **(ALTA) policy**, also called an *extended policy*, is almost always purchased for the lender's benefit. The buyer pays for the lender's protection and the policy insures that the lender has a valid and enforceable lien subject only to the exclusions noted in the "exception to title" schedule (commonly known as *Schedule B*) of the ALTA policy. It insures the lender for the amount of the loan only and not the entire purchase price of the property. There are three basic ALTA policies: one deals with construction loans only; one deals with homes described by lot, block, and tract; and one deals with homes described by either metes and bounds or government survey.

The ALTA extended coverage policy protects the lender only from the covered risks. Buyers who desire extended ALTA protection may pay for that extra protection or opt for the homeowner's coverage policy. This homeowner's policy costs about 10 percent more than the standard coverage.

In addition to the coverage offered by the standard policy (CLTA), the extended policy (ALTA) of title insurance includes the following:

- Lack of access
- Unrecorded liens
- Rights of parties in physical possession
- Unrecorded easements
- Mining claims
- Rights and claims that would be disclosed by a physical inspection or correct survey
- Water rights

A survey is generally required by title insurers before they will issue an extended coverage policy of title insurance because of the greater potential exposure to claims.

An extended coverage policy of title insurance does not cover the following:

- Liens placed by the insured
- Violations of the May Act
- Government regulations such as zoning
- Eminent domain proceedings
- Matters known to the insured that were not conveyed to the insurer of the title

The following list shows the limitations of coverage in a standard and extended coverage policy, as well as what is not covered.

Standard coverage:

- Defects found in public records
- Improperly delivered deeds
- Forged documents
- Incorrect marital statements
- Incompetent grantors

Extended coverage:

- Standard coverage, plus defects discoverable through unrecorded liens not known about by the insured; property inspection, including unrecorded rights of persons in possession; and examination of a survey.

Not covered by either title policy:

- Defects known to the buyer.
- Defects and liens listed in the policy of title insurance.
- Changes in land use brought about by changes in zoning ordinances.

Preliminary Title Report

The actual title insurance policy is not usually delivered to the buyer until the escrow closes; however, usually within two to three days after the escrow is opened, a preliminary title report is issued by the insurer.

The purpose of this report is to give an interim response to an application for title insurance and is also intended to notify the parties of what type of policy or policies will be issued. The preliminary title report, or *prelim*, as it is commonly called, identifies the title to the estate or interest in the property to be acquired. In Schedule B, it also lists the liens, encumbrances, restrictions, and defects that would be excluded from coverage if the requested policy were to be issued as of the date of the report.

Your role as a licensee is to obtain a copy of the prelim as soon as possible, read it thoroughly, and discuss its contents with your clients. The report provides the prospective buyer and the lender an opportunity to discover unacceptable items in the title report and an opportunity to seek their removal. Any objections to the title report must usually be made to the seller and the title company within a time limit specified in the purchase contract.

One recent change in prelim reports is that the printed exclusions and encumbrances are fully set forth in the report and are not merely incorporated by reference. The result is now a more complete form of communicating the exact terms of the offer of title insurance to a prospective buyer.

The title insurance industry is constantly upgrading its standards by constant collection and maintenance of title records, how they search the records, and higher underwriting standards. Between 1980 and the late 1990s, the California title insurance industry paid out more than $162 million in insured losses.

A preliminary title report, sometimes erroneously referred to as a preliminary insurance policy, is not an insurance policy at all; it is an offer to insure the title to a property, subject to listed exceptions and on certain terms and conditions. It also shows the current vested owners of the property.

The title insurer always makes a last-minute check of the county records to ensure there are no new recordings concerning a property's title before issuing its title insurance policy.

Special Policies

There are several types of **special title insurance policies**, such as construction lender policies, policies insuring leasehold interests, policies for mineral rights such as oil and gas interests in a property, and policies for vendees (purchasers under real property sales contracts). Special coverage policy amendments can also be purchased.

In the event that a policy contains ambiguous language that fails to meet the "reasonable person" test commonly used by the California courts, any ruling would almost always be in favor of the insured, but a professional licensee will always get any ambiguous language explained by the title company rather than risk being the exception to the rule.

Rebates

It is a violation of the Real Estate Settlement Procedures Act (RESPA) for a title company to provide any type of rebate or other financial inducement to a real estate broker for the referral of business. Brokers must be charged the same fees as any other customers without offset of any kind. The **rebate law** applies equally to the title insurance and the escrow industry. Besides being grounds for disciplinary action by the California Department of Real Estate, a licensee or broker who receives a rebate from a title insurer or escrow company may be found guilty of commercial bribery and be subject to a $10,000 fine and up to one year in jail for each transaction. RESPA violations are prosecuted through the Justice Department.

SUMMARY

An escrow is a third-party "stakeholder" who acts as a neutral depository for the receipt and disbursement of documents and funds in a real estate transaction. The escrow has agency duties to all parties, including any lender involved, and cannot be completed until all conditions are met. The broker is not a party to the escrow, except for payment of any commission or fee due, and the escrow officer has no duty to obey instructions of the broker after the escrow instructions as signed.

A broker can act as an escrow without a license if the broker is a principal to the transaction or represented either the buyer or the seller. An escrow must be a corporation and meet strict licensing requirements unless acting under the broker, lender, or attorney exemptions.

In southern California, an escrow is opened with the parties signing escrow instructions. In northern California, escrow instructions are usually contained within the RPA-CA or else not signed until just before escrow closing. For a valid escrow, a signed agreement and conditional delivery of transfer documents must exist. The delivery is generally conditioned on the buyers fully meeting their contractual obligations. Brokers may correspond with and supply information to the escrow by telephone or in person. Once the escrow instructions have been signed by the buyers and sellers, they are binding on both parties and any changes must be in writing and signed by both parties; signed escrow instructions may supersede the terms of the purchase agreement.

The escrow is considered closed when the escrow records the deed and disburses funds and documents. A closing statement is then issued showing the credits and debits to each party in the transaction, which can consist of fixed charges and fees as well as prorations of loan interest, property taxes, insurance, rents, and homeowners association (HOA) dues and assessments. Prorations are based on a 30-day month and a 360-day year. Although it is customary for the escrow officer to carefully go over the closing statement with buyers and sellers to be sure they fully understand the documents they are signing, the licensee should be in attendance with the complete file to answer any questions that may arise.

Escrow companies are liable for their negligence, but they are not liable for failure to warn a party of possible fraud or to point out a risk or detrimental fact in a transaction. This is the responsibility of the real estate licensee.

An abstract of title only shows the recorded history of a property and a title opinion on an abstract, which must come from an attorney; it does not reveal title defects such as lack of legal capacity, forgery, and unknown spousal interest. These and many other risks are covered by a standard policy of title insurance that covers risks of record. Lenders can be covered from risk by an ALTA extended coverage policy. If buyers want this extra coverage, they must pay an additional premium for it.

The prelim title report is an offer to insure the title to a property on certain terms and conditions and affords the buyer no protections unless a title insurance policy is purchased. There are special title insurance policies for the specific needs of builders, people who are buying property under a contract for sale, and other special needs. The rebate law prohibits title insurance and escrow companies from rebating fees or items of value for referrals and carries fines and imprisonment for violators.

CLASS DISCUSSION TOPICS

1. Who customarily pays for the CLTA policy in your area?

2. Obtain a fee schedule from your local title and escrow company and be prepared to tell the class what the escrow fee would be for a $400,000 sale. What would the ALTA lender's policy be for a $300,000 loan on the same property?

3. If an escrow fails, do title companies in your area customarily charge the buyer a fee for the preliminary title report?

4. If the property taxes for a home are $3,000 per year, the seller had paid the first installment, and escrow closed on November 30, would the seller receive a credit or a debit as a proration on the escrow closing statement? If so, how much?

5. What sort of rebate or item of value can a broker receive from an escrow company for referring business? Why?

6. If a wife quitclaimed her interest in a property to her husband and several years later they divorced, would the title company require a new quitclaim deed? Why?

7. Why must the escrow remain neutral to all parties?

CHAPTER 12 QUIZ

1. No escrow company may
   A. disseminate misleading or deceptive statements referring to its supervision by the state of California.
   B. describe either orally or in writing any transaction that is not included under the definition of escrow in the California Financial Code.
   C. pay referral fees to anyone except a regular employee of its own escrow company.
   D. All of the above.

2. What are escrow officers legally required to do?
   A. Act according to issued written instructions.
   B. Act on behalf of one party only.
   C. Follow escrow instructions in every detail even if the instructions are in violation of the law.
   D. Give each party all information they have about the other party.

3. What is/are the major advantage(s) of using an escrow?
   A. An escrow provides a custodian of papers, instructions, funds, and documents until the transaction is closed.
   B. An escrow makes possible the handling of accounting details in a professional manner.
   C. An escrow assures sellers that the funds have been paid and all other terms and conditions have been met prior to recording the deed.
   D. All of the above.

4. Escrow instructions
   A. are the written directions from the principals to the impartial third party to do all the necessary acts to carry out the escrow agreement of the principals.
   B. are not binding until they are signed by at least one of the principals.
   C. may be altered by either principal within ten days after opening of the escrow.
   D. may not be prepared by a real estate broker if she represents the buyer or seller.

5. Which of the following recurring costs can be included in an escrow?
   A. Property taxes.
   B. Impound account.
   C. Prorated interest on any new financing.
   D. All of the above.

6. What is an abstract of title?
   A. It gives the buyer more protection than title insurance.
   B. It is an attorney's opinion of the condition of the title to a property.
   C. It reveals title defects such as forged instruments and failure of delivery.
   D. It is a summary of most of the recorded documents concerning a property.

7. A CLTA or standard policy covers all of the following non-recorded items except
   A. lack of capacity of a grantor.
   B. federal estate tax liens.
   C. water rights.
   D. deeds of a corporation whose charter has expired.

8. An ALTA policy is also known as what?
   A. A plain coverage policy.
   B. A limited exclusion policy.
   C. A CLTA policy.
   D. An extended policy.

9. Which one of the following is true of a preliminary title report?

   A. It is a commitment of title insurance.

   B. It is binding on the title company as soon as it is received by the principals.

   C. It lists the defects, liens, restrictions, and encumbrances that would be excluded from coverage if the requested title insurance policy was issued on the day of the report.

   D. It must be issued within three calendar days after requested by the escrow officer.

10. Which one of the following is not true of a preliminary title report?

   A. It is an offer to insure title.

   B. It is an abstract of title reporting a complete chain of title.

   C. It is a statement of the terms and conditions of the offer to issue a title policy.

   D. None of the above.

Chapter

13

The Life of an Escrow

Upon completion of this chapter, the student will be able to:

- Explain the progress of the life of an escrow.
- Identify the separate concerns of seller and buyer in an escrow.
- Schedule property inspections.
- Arrange insurance for buyers.
- Demonstrate sign-off procedure from a licensee perspective.
- Negotiate repair requests with sellers and buyers.

13.1 OPEN ESCROW

Once a buyer and seller have reached an agreement for the sale and purchase of a property, the next step is to open an escrow. The Business and Professions Code (10145) and the Regulations of the Real Estate Commissioner (2832.a) state that to be in compliance with BPC 10145 "... the broker place funds accepted on behalf of another into the hands of the owner of the funds, into a neutral escrow depository or into a trust fund account in the name of the broker, or in a fictitious name if the broker is the holder of a license bearing such fictitious name, as trustee at a bank or other financial institution no later than three business days following receipt of the funds by the broker or by the broker's salesperson. (2832c) A check received from the offeror may be held uncashed by the broker until acceptance of the offer if (1) the check by its terms is not negotiable by the broker or if the offeror has given written instructions that the check shall not be deposited nor cashed until acceptance of the offer and (2) the offeree is informed that the check is being held before or at the

time the offer is presented for acceptance." The Residential Purchase Agreement – California (RPA-CA) offers this as an option.

The licensee responsible for opening the escrow should always ask the client to choose an escrow company (title and Escrow Company in northern California). Although you may have a favorite title or escrow officer, it is customary for the buyer to choose the title and escrow company because it may be a violation of Real Estate Settlement Procedures Act (RESPA) for the seller to require the buyer to use a particular title insurance company as a condition of the sale. Now, as a result of the passage of AB957 Buyer's Choice Act passed as emergency legislation on October 11, 2009, "... a mortgagee or beneficiary under a deed of trust who acquired title to residential real property improved by 1-4 dwelling units at a foreclosure sale (or trustee's sale) [are prevented] from, requiring, directly or indirectly, as a condition of selling the property, that the buyer purchase title insurance or escrow services in connection with the sale from a particular title insurer or escrow agent. The law does not prohibit a buyer from agreeing to accept a title insurer or an escrow agent recommended by the seller if written notice of the right to make an independent selection is first provided by the seller to the buyer." (CAR legal)

In some counties it is customary for buyer and seller to split escrow and title fees but no matter who pays the title insurance fee the choice of Title Company may be the buyer's choice. If you have any question check with your broker. In almost every case the client will allow you to pick the escrow or title company. However, by providing at least three recommendations and allowing the buyer to choose the title and escrow company you won't run the risk of having an angry client because they didn't get along with the escrow agent or the fees for the escrow or a **policy of title insurance** were slightly higher than someone else's.

Escrow may be opened by telephone, fax, email, or in person. If you open the escrow by telephone, you must give all of the transaction details to the escrow officer so that she can prepare escrow instructions. To be complete in your instructions and to save time, have a copy of the RPA-CA or write down all of the details of the transaction on a notepad and have it in front of you when you talk to the escrow officer. The escrow officer will need at least the following information:

- Complete names, addresses, and telephone number(s) of all principals.
- Address or sufficient description of the property being sold. It is always wise to give the escrow licensee the Assessor's Parcel Number (APN).

- Names, addresses, and telephone numbers, including fax numbers, of any brokers involved and the sales licensees who are representing them.

- Any commission that is payable and how it is split, if there is more than one broker.

- Escrow closing date.

- The lender's name, address, and telephone numbers, including fax numbers, and the name of the loan licensee if applicable.

- Any credits from one party to another.

- Any rent to be paid by one party to the other. [This should be negotiated during the offer presentation. The offer should be accompanied by a **prepossession agreement** if the buyer needs to occupy the property before close of escrow, or the counteroffer should be accompanied by a **postpossession agreement** if the seller needs to rent the property back after close of escrow. The benefit of using these forms is that they clearly spell out any rent to be paid, when it is to be paid, any insurance issues, or deposits (performance deposits required by a seller if the buyer moves in prior to close of escrow or pre-possession; or if the seller retains possession after escrow closing or post-possession). They also contain a mandated date that the property must be vacated by if the seller is retaining possession after the escrow closes.]

- Any special homeowners' assessments that exist and how they are to be handled (prorated and assumed by the buyer or paid in full by the seller).

- **Holdbacks.** Holdbacks are monies deducted from the seller's proceeds and held in escrow, pending the completion of any **negotiated repairs**, or any other issue that requires the seller to pay for something that will occur after the escrow has closed.

- Where and to whom you want to send **preliminary** title reports.

- Any other special instructions stipulated in the purchase contract.

In southern California, buyers must meet with the escrow company to sign the escrow instructions as soon as possible after the escrow is opened; in northern California, they do not, as **escrow instructions** are a part of the purchase contract and are not signed until just before closing. In any event, the escrow officer must have a copy of the purchase agreement, any counteroffers and/or addendums, and the above-referenced information at the onset of escrow.

If you have opened escrow by telephone, you can ask the escrow licensee to send someone to your office to pick up a copy of the required documents and the earnest money **deposit** check. Be sure they are picked up within the state-mandated time limit.

Once you have opened an escrow, call the other broker, if there is one, with the name and telephone number of the escrow or title company, the escrow officer's name, and the escrow number. Ask the escrow officer to fax a copy of the receipt for the buyer's deposit to the listing licensee. Always get a receipt from the title/escrow company showing receipt of the buyer's earnest money or other deposit. It doesn't happen often, but title/escrow companies have lost deposit checks.

13.2 ORDER INSPECTIONS

Once the escrow is opened, you must order any inspections required by the buyer. This is essentially your "due diligence" period. Even if you are selling a parcel of land, many issues must be addressed and verified, such as current or potential zoning, location of utilities, flood plains, and special study zones. If you are selling a one to four owner-occupied home unit, you have many other issues to contend with. Always recommend that the buyer get as many inspections as she wishes; to do less is to put you, the buyer, and your broker at risk.

Home Inspector

It is good business practice to suggest that the buyer obtain a written report by a **home inspector**. The role of the **home inspector** is to check the entire property for visible defects, or any conditions that could lead to defects, and to make any necessary repair recommendations. The inspector will check the major systems of the home, such as the plumbing, electrical, furnace, and air-conditioning for safety and soundness. She will also check for any faulty grade level where the ground immediately surrounding the home is sloping toward the home instead of away from it. **Home inspectors** are usually not licensed roof inspectors but will give the roof a cursory visual inspection. If there is a crawl space, the inspector will crawl under the main structure and look for any signs of water leakage or penetration, damaged HVAC (heating, ventilation, and air-conditioning) pipes, standing water, and other indications of potential or actual deterioration. She will observe the fences for deterioration of the fence posts or missing or damaged slats. If the home inspector sees what may be damage or potential damage to operating systems that she is not fully schooled on, she will make a written recommendation to the buyer that another specialized inspection and report be obtained, such as a **pool inspection** or a report from a licensed roofing

contractor. Give the buyer the names of at least three home inspection companies that you have had consistently good experiences with and let the buyer pick which one she wants to use.

Pest Inspector

Another report routinely ordered by licensees on behalf of buyers is a pest inspection. The report name can be somewhat misleading because the **pest inspector** is actually looking for several things when performing an inspection. These include:

- Termites. The inspector looks all around the inside (if accessible) and the outside of the foundation, as well as the baseboard area and walls of the property, in an attempt to find any subterranean termite tubes. If she sees any, the inspector will break one or more of them to determine if they are old or new and will make corrective recommendations if applicable. The inspection also includes opening the access area to the attic and going as far in as possible with a flashlight looking for drywood termites. Drywood termites have wings; each spring they swarm and start new colonies in new locations. They often get into the attic of a home where they can go undetected for years. Fortunately, drywood termites are slow eaters, but if detected, it often means "tenting" or fumigating the home.
- Wood-boring beetle infestation. This is best noticed by a series of random holes in wood members that are about 1/16th of an inch in diameter, often accompanied by sawdust-looking droppings at the base of the wood member.
- Wood rot, often called *dry rot*. This is caused by a condition of excessive moisture on untreated wood and can structurally undermine decks, walls, and other areas of a home.

Pool Inspector

If the property has a swimming pool and/or spa, the home inspector will look it over for obvious leaks or other noticeable problems. If anything looks suspicious, she will probably recommend that the buyer contact a pool company skilled in the maintenance and operation of pools and pool equipment to conduct a complete inspection.

Licensed Roofer

As a licensee, you may sell a house with obvious roof defects. If so, you have a duty to point it out to the buyer verbally and in your part of the Transfer Disclosure Statement (TDS). If the

home inspector sees what she thinks is a roofing problem, she will note it as well. If the problem is visible, the fact that it is in her report does not relieve you of your duty to disclose what you see in your visual inspection. In either instance a recommendation should be made for a licensed roofing contractor to conduct an inspection and make a report. A roof can be one of the biggest repairs that a new homeowner can face, and extra care must be taken here. The following are some signs of roof deterioration:

- Curled or missing asphalt shingles.
- Mission tile roofs with obvious cracks in any of the tiles or missing or dislocated tiles.
- Tar and gravel roofs with areas where the gravel is missing and black blisters are visible.
- Wood shingle roofs where obvious damp rot is visible, nails or brads are popped out and protruding, or broken or missing shingles.

Mandated Disclosures

Depending on the type and age of the property being purchased and where it is located, any number of **mandated disclosures** may be required. These may include:

- *Geologic Special Study Zones.* Any home within a one-mile radius of a known active earthquake fault must be disclosed to a potential buyer. As a licensee you must be familiar with these areas if any are even remotely near where you list and sell property. Failure to disclose that a property is within one of these areas is grounds for rescission of the purchase contract and disciplinary action against you and your broker.

- *Transfer Disclosure Statement (TDS).* Every seller of a one to four owner-occupied home unit is required to give the buyer a written report of the home's condition and its surroundings. Most real estate licensees routinely use the form supplied by the California Association of REALTORS® for this purpose. The seller must complete her part and the listing licensee must conduct a verbal investigation with the owners and a walk-through "red flag" visual inspection of all accessible areas of the premises. When the home is sold, the buyer's licensee must also conduct a walk-through "red flag" visual inspection. Whether you represent the buyer or the seller, the California Department of Real Estate holds you to a higher standard than a nonlicensee—your duty is to be observant.

13.2 Order Inspections   393

Start your inspection at the front curb and slowly walk through the entire grounds of the property, looking for things such as:

Exterior

- Cracked or lifted sidewalks.
- Leaks in sprinkler systems, as evidenced by wet areas in otherwise dry ground, or standing water.
- Rotted fence posts that are leaning at an angle.
- Barking dogs near the property.
- Cracks, sinking, or buckling of the walkway or driveway (hairline cracks are common and are generally acceptable but should be noted).
- Settling or separation of the front or rear porch or deck from the house.
- Cracks in the exterior finish of the house (stucco may have hairline cracks).
- Obvious roof problems requiring a licensed roof inspection.
- Dried out areas of landscaping, which may indicate areas where the sprinkler system has failed and may require further inspection.
- Chipping or peeling paint, which may indicate poor maintenance or an excessive moisture condition requiring further inspection.
- Missing window screens.
- Broken, rotted, or rusted-through gutters.
- A leaning chimney that may require further inspection.
- A garage door with a gap at one side of the bottom, which may indicate the foundation is settling, or poorly aligned door runners on a sectional door that may require further inspection.

Interior

- Doors that close by themselves, which may indicate foundation or support problems requiring further inspection.
- Diagonal cracks at the corners of windows or interior doors.
- Old tile flooring that may contain asbestos backing.
- "Popcorn" ceilings that may have asbestos if installed before 1978.
- Uneven floors.
- Sagging or stained ceilings, which could mean water penetration.
- Any random dark splotches on interior walls, ceilings, or floors, especially adjacent to "water areas," which may indicate mold.
- Burns or dark, smoky smudges on electric wall plates.

- Stains on hardwood floors or carpeted areas may indicate animal urine stains and damaged wood.
- Doors that stick when closed.
- Black "sticky stuff" behind the refrigerator that may require a mold inspection.
- Noticeable odors such as pet odors.
- Obvious room additions or remodeling. (You will need to read the seller's and listing licensee's parts of the TDS to see what is disclosed. If nothing is disclosed, ask about your observations and contact the appropriate building department to investigate and notify the buyer of your findings.) Note: The purchase contract states that you may not bring building inspectors or other government officials onto the property without the seller's written permission.
- Musty smells, which may need to be investigated by trained professionals. (This may be an expensive mold problem.)
- Anything that doesn't look or feel right.

Obviously, the process of investigating the physical condition of the property itself is a job that should never be taken lightly. Undetected problems can cost your buyer (and maybe you) a lot of money and time. Take your time with this and do a thorough job.

Besides the physical condition of the property, several other mandated disclosures that you may need to address can include:

- *Mello-Roos Areas.* These areas qualify for special funding through taxation for improvements to the area's infrastructure. This information should be included on the Natural Hazard Disclosure Statement, but it pays dividends to become aware of the areas in your market that are affected by them.
- *Flood or Extreme Fire Hazard Zones.* You must be familiar with any flood zones or extreme fire hazard areas in your market as homeowners in these areas must often pay substantial sums of money for extra insurance and cannot get financing without it.
- *Asbestos.* If the property was built before 1978, you must be certain that the buyers are notified in writing of the possibility of the existence of asbestos so they have a chance to test for its presence during the inspection period.
- *Lead-Based Paint.* Homes built before 1978 probably have at least some lead-based paint. Be sure your buyers receive, review, and sign for the seller's lead-based paint addendum before signing the offer to purchase. Stiff fines are imposed on real

estate licensees for not properly disclosing the existence of lead-based paint. Details on this and other disclosure issues are noted in Chapter 4. You will benefit greatly by reading that chapter again.

The items listed above are some but not all of the mandated disclosures or inspections to obtain when you represent a buyer or seller in the purchase of a home.

13.3 FINANCING

If you are representing the buyers, you should have had them pre-approved by a **lender** before showing them any property. If you haven't done so, do it now. Provide the names of at least three good loan licensees that you have worked with and request that they start the process of getting fully preapproved for any financing they require. If your buyer says they have their own lender, get that person's full contact information.

If your buyers are preapproved, you must contact the loan licensee to ensure that she gets all of the necessary information about the sale, including:

- The residential purchase agreement and receipt for deposit.
- Any counteroffers and/or addendums to the purchase agreement.
- A preliminary title report as soon as it is available.
- The contact information regarding the escrow and title officers, including their names, addresses, companies, telephone and fax numbers, and the escrow number.
- If they are self-employed, the buyers' federal income tax returns from the previous two years.
- If they are self-employed, a current profit and loss (P&L) statement on their business.

Once the lender has all of this information, she will obtain a tri-merged credit report and, if not already done, obtain employment and savings verifications, order the appraisal, and send the buyers a **good-faith estimate** of closing costs.

Once the loan licensee has all of the required documentation, including the appraisal, she will prepare the "loan package" for submission to the loan committee. The loan committee will review the package and determine if the loan is a safe one to make. If the committee agrees to make the loan, the loan documents will be drawn and faxed, messengered, emailed, or sent to the escrow or title company. If the loan is rejected because of new or existing

credit issues or a low appraisal, you and the buyers will be notified. If this happens, talk to your broker about your options.

13.4 REVIEW REPORTS

As your career progresses, you will gain an ever-increasing knowledge about home inspections and other disclosure-related issues. It is important that you always remember that you are the originator of the disclosures and reports and not the interpreter of them. If you give opinions about what is noted in the various reports, you could be liable if the buyers rely on your opinions and are subsequently harmed by any inaccurate statement you made regarding a report or disclosure. Your job is to read the reports and note anything that you see as a *potential or actual problem*. For instance, if the roof report shows that the roof is at the end of its useful life and the buyers ask what you think they should do, or how long you think the roof may last, refer them to a **licensed roofing contractor** for advice. If you tell them "It looks like it may last another winter or two," and it develops a major leak with ceiling and furniture damage due to water penetration at the first rainfall, *you and your broker may have a problem* and will probably be buying a roof!

Similarly, a buyer may ask, "Well, the ceiling contains asbestos, but that really shouldn't be a problem, should it?" If you give an opinion, you are acting like an environmental specialist, not a real estate professional. You could be held liable if the buyer moves in and suddenly develops respiratory problems, even if the problems are not asbestos related. Just refer her to the professionals who did the reports. The best advice for you is to "be the source of the source, not the source."

Some major reports you will need to assist your client in interpreting and negotiating are the following:

- *TDS.* Within five days after the sale is made, as the buyer's licensee, you will receive the TDS. Carefully review it yourself and then with the buyers. If anything is disclosed that you feel should be repaired or replaced, or any issue that would affect your clients' rights or enjoyment of the property, bring it to their attention in writing so they can make good, sound decisions as to what inspections to obtain, what other professionals, such as an attorney or structural engineer, should be engaged, and so on.

- *Preliminary Title Report (Prelim).* An often overlooked report is the prelim, or preliminary title report. As the real estate

licensee you will usually get the prelim within three to four days after escrow has been opened. The following are two areas of particular importance that you should review:

- **Title Vesting.** The prelim states the current vested owners of the property. Compare the names shown in the prelim to the names on the purchase agreement to see that they match. (The authors have been involved in many situations over the years in which they represented buyers in the purchase of a home and the preliminary title report included two more owners on title in addition to the husband and wife that signed the purchase agreement. In almost every case it was one set of parents who cosigned for the buyers and were included on title to the property. As they never filed a quitclaim deed to release their interest, the parents were still legal owners of the property. We had to scramble to get them removed from the title before closing.)

As a listing licensee, you can avoid this problem by obtaining a "property profile" or listing package from your favorite title company before taking the listing. These packages of information always show the current vesting and will alert you to this type of problem in advance, allowing you plenty of time to make corrections. Because of current federal regulations, you may have to pay for this profile report.

- **Schedule B.** Schedule B of the preliminary title report shows the exceptions to title, or what the title insurer will not insure against, including things such as the current property taxes, easements of record, recorded liens (such as judgments and tax liens), and loans.

As the listing licensee, you will usually get the same information in the property profile that is contained in the prelim. Total all of the liens to see that there is sufficient equity to allow a sale at market value and have enough money left to pay all of the seller's expenses before you take the listing.

The listing license should total all of the liens as soon as they get the prelim to recheck that the sellers have sufficient equity to complete the transaction.

The prelim will also show things such as bankruptcy proceedings, foreclosure notices, and the filing of any *lis pendis*, or legal proceeding recorded against the property. Just imagine getting a buyer into escrow, not checking the prelim, and discovering three weeks later that the property is overencumbered, and then comes

the subject of bankruptcy proceedings and your buyers have no possibility of buying the home; they won't like you, for sure!

- *Homeowners' Association (HOA) Documents.* When you sell a property that is subject to an HOA, you must get a complete set of HOA documents and review them with the buyers. These documents have the effect of limiting the rights of the buyers, and it is critical they become fully aware of any restrictions or other matters of interest during the inspection period or within the time limit prescribed. For example, you sell a condominium to an elderly lady with three cats that she adores. You get the HOA documents and learn that all owners are limited to two domestic pets. If you failed to disclose this to the lady and she missed it when she read the covenants, conditions, and restrictions (CC&Rs) and closed the escrow on the property, you could find yourself in an uncomfortable position of telling her that she must get rid of one of her cats.

  You must obtain and review the following HOA documents:
  - CC&Rs
  - Articles of incorporation (filed with the state, not recorded in each county)
  - Bylaws
  - Rules and regulations
  - Current budget, including reserve accounts and notation of any special reserves for major expenditures
  - Any pending or current litigation filed by the HOA against another party or parties

  Most HOAs are run by professional management companies and getting the mandated documents from them is not usually a problem. If the development has forty-nine or fewer units, however, the associations are often difficult to obtain documents from and are often very slow to respond to requests. Be prepared to be as persistent as necessary in order to affect a timely delivery of the required documents.

- *Public Report.* If you represent a developer in the sale of a new subdivision, California law prescribes that if the development has five or more units you must give the potential buyer a copy of the Final Public Report issued by the California Department of Real Estate. Developments with four or less units are exempt.

  As a licensee representing a buyer in the purchase of a qualifying subdivision home, you should see that the buyer is given

the public report in a timely manner and allowed sufficient time to read it and ask questions. The purchase agreements used by some developers state that the buyers have received a copy of the Final Public Report and have read and approved it. If this happens with buyers you are representing, point this out and recommend that paragraph be stricken from the contract and replaced with language giving them adequate time to read the report.

13.5 NEGOTIATE REPAIRS

After the buyers have ordered, received, and reviewed any reports with you, they must notify the sellers in writing of any repairs they want the sellers to make. This must be done within the time limit specified in the purchase agreement. For example, rotted fence posts are negotiable; the buyers can request the seller to fix them as a part of the negotiations. The seller has no obligation to fix such items unless she agrees to do so in writing. When you draft a request for repairs on behalf of the buyers, be sure to separate these *requests* from any *mandated repairs*.

If it is clear that agreed-upon repairs cannot be completed by close of escrow, the buyers and sellers should agree to a holdback of sufficient funds from the seller's proceeds in escrow so there is no issue of the contractors being paid. Lenders that allow holdbacks often require one-and-one-half times the amount of the repairs held in escrow until the repairs are made. Some lenders do not allow holdbacks, so if the repairs are large or costly in nature, be sure to get the lender's approval well in advance of closing. If the lender does not approve the holdbacks, the buyers and sellers can agree to an extension of the escrow closing date.

The ability of the buyers and their licensee to negotiate repairs is often subject to current market conditions. In an overheated, strong seller's market, it is much more difficult to get the sellers to agree to negotiable repair requests than it is when the market is slow with lots of listings competing for few buyers. Your knowledge of the "temperature" of the market will help the buyers choose which repairs, if any, they should negotiate for with the sellers. In the seller's market, for example, cosmetic issues, such as worn paint, loose tile, or other low-cost, nonstructural items that may need attention, may receive a lower priority than structural or safety items such as roof repairs or replacement or electrical fuse boxes. Your guidance and knowledge of the marketplace will

be invaluable to the buyers in helping them to prioritize what, if anything, they should ask for in the way of repairs.

Although many repairs can be done by a competent handyman, always take the conservative approach and recommend the use of a **licensed contractor** for most repairs. There are state-mandated limitations on what non-licensed, **handyman**-type repair people can do and you and your broker are at risk by recommending a *handyman* that exceeds those limitations. A *handyman* should never be used for any repair that requires a building permit or that exceeds a total dollar amount than that set by the state, which changes from time to time.

13.6 PROPERTY INSURANCE

There are two insurance issues your buyers must address when obtaining property insurance. As homeowners, they must verify that they are insurable and that the property is insurable. To do so they should contact their **insurance broker** within a day or two after escrow is opened and request insurance on the home that they are buying. The insurance broker will obtain a Comprehensive Loss Underwriting Exchange (CLUE) report. As the buyer's real estate representative, you should obtain a CLUE report or loss-history report from the seller's insurance agent, allowing the buyer's insurance company to determine if the property being purchased is insurable as well. Both of these issues must be addressed during the inspection period so that if either the buyers or the property is not insurable or the only insurance available is too expensive, the buyers can cancel the escrow and have their deposit returned.

In recent years, the insurance industry has taken large losses due to damage claims for water penetration, mold, and mildew issues. To better control their losses, they developed a national database known as the CLUE. Virtually all large insurance companies and many of the smaller ones are members. Each time an insurance agent is contacted by a policyholder regarding *any* inquiry or claim or potential claim, it is noted on the exchange. Buyers who have made two or more inquiries or claims during the previous three years may not be insurable with any of the major insurance companies and will have to go to a smaller company and pay a much higher premium—if they can get insurance at all. The same process applies to the property being purchased. If the sellers have filed two or more claims or made two or more inquiries, the major

insurance companies may not be willing to insure the property and the buyers must look to the smaller and often more expensive companies.

An "inquiry" is any call to the insurance licensee about an actual or potential loss that would be covered by a homeowners' policy, including everything from a bicycle stolen from the premises to a water heater leak that caused major structural damage and mold in the walls of the property.

13.7 THE FINAL WALK-THROUGH INSPECTION

The final walk-through inspection is conducted for two reasons: (1) to see that the property is substantially in the same condition as it was when the buyers made the offer to purchase it and (2) to see that any agreed-upon repairs have been made properly.

The final walk-through inspection should be conducted three to four days before closing the escrow. It may be necessary to conduct more than one inspection if the sellers are still occupying the home when the first inspection is made and their furnishings and belongings make it difficult or impossible to really look over the property. For example, a licensee who conducted a final walk-through inspection with her clients when the home was empty noted one closet that was so full of "stuff" she was barely able to open the door. On her advice, the buyers signed off on the inspection, with the exception of the closet, and stated that they would not close the escrow until they had an opportunity to check it. Sure enough, when the licensee went back to inspect the closet, the back wall and floor were covered with mold that the seller was trying to hide. The water heater was against the other side of the closet wall and it had failed in the recent past, causing a huge amount of mold to grow inside and outside of the adjacent wall. The escrow closed after repair estimates were obtained and money was withheld from the seller's escrow proceeds.

When you conduct the final walk-through inspection, you should use the same system that you used during your "red flag" inspection required by the TDS. Start at the curb and work your way in and around the property until you have covered the entire premises, comparing notes with your first inspection as you go along.

It is not uncommon for a seller to offer the buyer a monetary credit in escrow for the reasonable amount of agreed-upon repairs in return for a written release from any further liability in connection with the repairs. If your client agrees to this, be sure the agreement is limited only to the agreed-upon repairs and not a general release of all property condition issues. Sometimes lenders will mandate repairs as a condition of making the new loan; if this happens, the buyer and seller cannot do a credit for these specific repairs, and they must be negotiated by the buyer and seller and completed before loan funding and escrow closing.

13.8 THE CLOSING

It is important to remember that you do not get paid if the escrow does not close, so be diligent about seeing to your client's best interests up to and through the **closing appointment**. In a properly supervised escrow, many different functions must be conducted by many different people. It is your job to "hold the baton," or, in essence, become the orchestra leader and see that each duty is carried out in a timely and proper manner.

Good communication is the key to making things happen the way they should, when they should, and to keep small problems small and everything moving according to the predetermined schedule. Your repeat and referral business will grow as a direct result of how effectively you communicate with your client and everyone else during the course of an escrow.

In preparing for the escrow closing, you should do the following:

- Call the escrow officer to insure she has all of the client's information necessary to draw any required documents.
- Make sure all applicable disclosures have been made and signed for by the appropriate parties.
- Make certain all agreed-upon inspections, such as the home inspection or pest control inspections, have been made and signed for by the appropriate parties.
- If you are the listing licensee, be sure you have made arrangements for the transfer of all property keys, including the mailbox key, garage door openers, and recreation/exercise rooms..
- If you are the buyer's licensee, provide the website addresses and/or telephone numbers of all of the utility companies that must be notified to change ownership as well as all appliance manuals and warranties.

- As the buyer's representative, set an appointment with the escrow officer to sign any remaining escrow, loan, or transfer documents. Remind the buyers that their closing funds must be in the form of certified funds or a wire transfer.

On the day you are to meet with either buyer or seller and the escrow officer, remind them that they must bring a photo identity card of some sort (driver's license, passport, and so on) for the notary. Plan to arrive at the escrow office about fifteen minutes ahead and ask to review the closing papers. Bring your calculator with you and review the **prorations** (proration of taxes, prepaid interest on any new loans or HOA dues) for accuracy, check the spelling of your clients' names, and generally look over the paperwork for any errors. If you are representing the buyers, check the interest rate on their promissory note to see that it is what the lender said it would be.

When the buyers or sellers arrive, introduce them to the escrow agent if they have not already met. Tell them that you arrived early to double-check the closing papers and will sit with them as the escrow agent goes over each one. It is not uncommon for the clients to have questions, and it is imperative that you be there to help answer them. If the escrow is a short sale and you are the seller's representative, be sure to look for any promissory note the seller's lender is requiring them to sign for the amount of the "escrow shortfall." If such a note exists, ask the seller if she was aware of it.

After signing any remaining paperwork, thank your clients for the opportunity to be of service to them and tell them how much you enjoyed working with them. Ask if they have any friends or family whose real estate needs you can help with. You'll be pleasantly surprised at how often this leads to another listing or sale.

SUMMARY

In this chapter you learned the step-by-step process of guiding a buyer or seller through an escrow. You learned that any deposit received must be placed in a neutral depository by the end of the third business day after an offer is accepted, and the importance of contacting any cooperating broker involved in the transaction to let them know the escrow information. You learned about the critical timing of ordering and conducting inspections, issuing mandated disclosures, reviewing all inspection reports with buyer or seller as appropriate, and the art of negotiating repair requests with the sellers. You also learned the

importance of ordering insurance for the buyers and conducting walk-through inspections early enough to allow for the "what-if" factor (for example, what if the agreed-upon repairs aren't done as promised). You learned the importance of arriving at the escrow **closing appointment** early to check the closing papers and how to thank your client for their business and ask for referrals.

CLASS DISCUSSION TOPICS

1. Name at least three of the information items you must give the escrow licensee about your buyer, and explain why they are important.

2. In southern California, **escrow instructions** are signed shortly after the escrow is opened, whereas they are not signed until just before closing in northern California. Discuss which system, if either, is better and why.

3. Is it best to have your buyers with you when you do your TDS walk-through inspection? Why or why not?

4. Discuss the importance of a thorough review of all of the HOA documents.

5. Discuss the difference between requested and mandated repairs.

6. Why is it important to arrive early for the escrow signing-off appointment?

CHAPTER 13 QUIZ

1. When must the buyer's earnest money deposit be placed with a neutral depository or broker's trust account?
   A. Within three business days after acceptance of the offer.
   B. The same business day that the offer is accepted.
   C. Within one day after receipt of the deposit.
   D. None of the above.

2. What should you always do before opening an escrow on behalf of a buyer?
   A. Tell them which escrow agency you intend to use.
   B. Tell them to use the Yellow Pages and select an escrow agency.
   C. Ask if they have a preferred company. If they do not, give them the names of at least three companies that have performed well for you and ask them if they have any preference.
   D. Any of the above, as long as you place the deposit with the escrow company within three business days.

3. Which of the following should you do when conducting various property inspections?

A. Suggest that the buyers get the seller's permission to be at the property with you.

B. Be sure the buyers are not at the property unless they have been invited by the sellers.

C. Recommend buyers be present whenever possible for any inspections.

D. None of the above.

4. A home inspector states it is her opinion that the roof is at the end of its useful life, but it doesn't appear to be leaking. She recommends that a licensed roofing contractor be consulted. Your buyers say they do not want to pay for a roof inspection. What should you do?

A. Do and say nothing further since the buyers have made a decision.

B. Give them the names of two reputable roofing contractors, in case they change their minds.

C. Explain the benefits of getting a written report from a licensed professional to get a better understanding of the true condition of the roof and to use in negotiations with the sellers. If they still don't agree, make good notes of your conversation in your escrow communication log and, if possible, e-mail that information to the buyers and CC yourself for your escrow file.

D. Order the roof report anyway to protect all parties.

5. When you show up for an inspection that your buyers couldn't attend, you notice that a large dog is continually barking through the fence. The dog wasn't there when you showed the property to your buyers. What action should you take?

A. Do nothing because it is not a physical problem with the structural part of the property.

B. Report it in writing on your portion of the real estate TDS. If you have already completed your report and given it to the buyers, give them a written addendum to the report and copy the seller's licensee.

C. Call the Humane Society and complain.

D. Call the buyers and tell them about the dog.

6. What information must the loan officer have to process your buyer's loan?

A. Purchase agreement, any counteroffers, any addendums, a preliminary title report, the title and escrow contact information.

B. Purchase agreement and escrow information.

C. Title and escrow information only.

D. The name of the listing licensee only, as the loan licensee will get all documentation from her.

7. What additional documentation must the buyers have if they are self-employed?

    A. Title report on the home they are selling.

    B. A current financial statement on their business.

    C. Federal income tax returns from the previous two years and a P&L statement on their business.

    D. Both b and c.

8. In reviewing inspection reports with your buyers, you should

    A. tell them which items require repairs.

    B. review all repair items and help the buyers prioritize them based on the market conditions.

    C. suggest that they do not "rock the boat" by making any repair requests.

    D. None of the above.

9. A CLUE report discloses which of the following?

    A. The extent of any water damage to a property.

    B. The total dollar amount of all claims paid against a property in the past five years.

    C. The total number of inquiries and/or claims made on a property in the past five years or the total amount of time the sellers have owned it, whichever is shorter.

    D. All of the above.

10. Which one of the following is the most important thing you can do in preparation for an escrow closing appointment?

    A. Call your clients to coordinate the signing appointment.

    B. Remind the buyers that their closing funds must be in the form of a certified check or wire transfer.

    C. Remind your clients to bring a picture identification.

    D. All of the above.

Chapter

14

IMPORTANT PHRASES AND TERMS

1031 exchange

Acquisition indebtedness

Ad valorem taxes

Basis

Boot

Deferred gain

Depreciation

Entity rule

Equal-or-up-rule

Equity indebtedness

Excluded gain

Foreign Investment in Real Property Tax Act (FIRPTA)

Foreign person

Home improvements

Homeowner's exemption

Installment sale

Intermediary

Investment property rule

Like-kind rule

No-choice rule

No-loss rule

Original basis

Primary personal residence

Proposition 13

Proposition 58

Proposition 60

Proposition 90

Realized gain

Recognized gain

Short-term capital gains

Special assessments

Supplemental tax bill

Tax-deferred exchange

Triple net lease

Veteran's exemption

Real Estate Taxation Issues

Upon completion of this chapter, the student will be able to:

- Describe the **basis** of real estate tax assessments.
- Identify various property tax exemptions.
- Recognize a need for reassessment.
- Calculate depreciation.
- Illustrate the benefits of an installment sale.
- Calculate cost **basis** for primary residence.
- Estimate tax benefits of home ownership.
- Illustrate the benefits of the Taxpayer Relief Act of 1997.

14.1 REAL PROPERTY TAXES

The word *ad valorem* means "according to value." Real property taxes are *ad valorem* **taxes** and are calculated as a percentage of a property's "full cash value." Throughout history, landowners have almost always been taxed on the **basis** of their real estate holdings. There is no way to evade taxation on one's real estate holdings, which makes it a favorite with governments. If a taxpayer fails to pay taxes, the levying body can file and foreclose on a tax lien to satisfy any unpaid tax obligations. In the United States property taxes are deductible on a homeowner's income tax return; however, special improvement assessments are not tax deductible.

The degree of taxation on real estate has a profound effect on the real estate market. High taxes may cause potential property buyers to hesitate involving themselves with taking on the added

expense of property ownership. Real estate tax revenues are a major source of income on the county and local levels and enable county and city governments to provide for the health, safety, education, and welfare of the citizens.

The Tax Bill

To have a better understanding of real estate taxes in California, the real estate licensee should know the chronological order in which real property taxes are processed. Figure 14.1 shows the order in which real property taxes become due, then delinquent, as well as when filing for exemptions must be done.

If the owner pays the taxes, the original tax bill is sent directly to the owner. If the lender pays the taxes for the owner through an impound account, the tax bill is sent to the lender and a copy of it is sent to the owner stating that it is for information only. Special assessments are included in the tax bill. Taxes that are not paid on time become delinquent and are subject to penalties even if the

---

FIGURE 14.1   Real Property Taxation Calendar

JANUARY

1: Taxes for the next year become a lien on real property.

FEBRUARY

1: Second installment of taxes due.

APRIL

10: Second installment of taxes becomes delinquent at 5:00 p.m.

15: Homeowner's exemption must be filed.

JUNE

8: Tax delinquency list is published.

30: "Book sale" is held. Tax year ends.

JULY

1: Tax year begins.

SEPTEMBER

1: Tax rates are determined.

NOVEMBER

1: First installment of taxes due.

DECEMBER

10: First installment of taxes becomes delinquent at 5:00 p.m.

---

taxpayer never received the tax bill. It is the taxpayer's responsibility to see that the taxes are paid on time.

The typical tax bill includes:

- An identifying parcel number with reference to the map page and property number or other description.
- The full cash value as of March 1, 1975, for property purchased prior to that date or as of the date of a subsequent reassessment.
- A breakdown between land assessments and improvement assessments (may be important if the property is subject to any depreciation allowance as it sets the land-to-improvements ratio that many accountants use in determining the amount of depreciation available to the taxpayer).
- A breakdown of the bonded indebtedness or special assessments and the full amount of the tax.
- Itemized separate payment cards with the full tax equally divided into first and second installments.

Supplemental Tax Bill

At some time in your career a recent homebuyer will call and tell you that she just received a tax bill for her property that isn't hers; she may be frustrated and even angry. You can avoid this type of unpleasant encounter by explaining to buyers that some time after escrow closes, they will get at least one **supplemental tax bill** in the mail.

Property taxes are billed and paid for the fiscal year of July 1 through June 30 of the following calendar year. When a buyer purchases an existing home or construction is completed on a new home, it takes time to notify the tax collector's office of the sale and for the tax collector's office to issue the new property tax bill based on the new assessed value. If the newly assessed value is higher than the previous one, the tax assessment is higher and the difference in the tax owed is assessed dating back to the sale or completion date. This "added" tax is billed to the new owner via a supplemental tax bill.

For example, a home was purchased on April 1 of this year for $400,000. Assuming that local taxes and bond issues added another 0.25 percent to the basic levy of 1 percent, the total tax rate is 1.25 percent of the purchase price.

The new tax is $5,000 (1.25 percent of $400,000). The old assessment was 1.25 percent of $200,000 so the tax due is $2,500 for the year from July 1 to June 30 of the following year.

When the home was purchased, the property tax owed by the new buyers was for the last three months of the tax year, or $625 ($2,500 divided by 12 and then multiplied by 3 = $625); however, the assessor will assess the new buyers for the increase in value for the same three months as follows: New tax assessment = $5,000 ÷ 12 = $416.67 per month, or $1,250 for the months of April through June. The new buyers would have already paid the original $625 through escrow, but they would get a supplemental tax bill for the difference in the old and new assessment of $625.

Special Assessments

Special taxes may be imposed on cities, counties, and special districts by a two-thirds vote of the electorate of the district. These **special assessments** are levied to pay for improvements such as flood control, special lighting, sewers, streets, irrigation, and drainage. This is a bond indebtedness that varies from county to county and within each jurisdiction. For assessment purposes, the land and building(s) are usually appraised separately. The value of the building is usually determined by comparable sales verified by appraisers working for the county assessor's office, by using a residence cost handbook, or rules covering unit-cost prices and rates of depreciation.

Proposition 13

Also known as the *Jarvis/Gann Initiative* after the two legislators who sponsored the bill, **Proposition 13** was enacted in 1978. It basically states that newly acquired real estate or new construction will be assessed according to the fair market value (FMV) at time of purchase and taxed at a maximum rate of 1 percent, which is also called the basic levy. Additionally, properties acquired before 1978 are reduced to the amount shown on the 1975 tax roll. Because bond issues vary within a county, additional taxes may be levied, up to an additional 1 percent and added to the basic levy, causing overall tax rates to vary within a county from 1 percent to 2 percent.

Another aspect of Proposition 13 is that the tax may be increased by up to 2 percent per year as long as the increase does not exceed the Consumer Price Index (CPI) increase. This 2 percent is the maximum the county assessor may increase the property's value in any tax year. As revenue-starved as California has been for many years, the 2 percent increase is pretty much guaranteed.

For example, a home was purchased for $400,000 one year ago and the taxes were assessed at 1.2 percent of value, or $4,800. The real value of the home may be $475,000 or higher, but for property tax purposes the new assessment of the property can only go

as high as 102 percent of last year's assessment, or $408,000. Assuming the overall tax rate was still 1.2 percent, this would only allow a tax increase of $96 to a total tax of $4,896.

One objective of Proposition 13 is to keep property taxes low. Under Proposition 13, certain transfers of title, such as the creation of revocable living trusts, cosigners for loan qualification purposes, and transfers between married couples (such as changing from joint tenancy to community property), are exempt from reassessment. Other transfers, such as a sale, cause a reassessment of the property and, in most cases, probably increase the taxes.

Proposition 58

Proposition 58 provides that transfers of real property between spouses and transfers of the principal residence and the first $1,000,000 of other real property between parent and child are exempt from reassessment. A child is defined by the code as a natural child, born of the parents, and stepchild or spouse of that stepchild when the relationship of stepparent and stepchild exists, a son-in-law or daughter-in-law of the parent(s), or a child who was adopted by the age of eighteen. Proposition 193 subsequently extended exemption from reassessment to persons who inherit property from a grandparent. A grandchild can keep her grandparents' assessed value for tax purposes.

A claim must be filed with the county assessor to receive this exclusion. The transferee must certify in writing, and under penalty of perjury, that she is a parent or child of the transferor. A statement must also be made as to whether or not the property is the transferor's principal residence. If the property is not the transferor's principal residence and the full cash value of the real estate transferred (the taxable value on the tax roll immediately prior to the transfer date) exceeds the allowable $1,000,000 exclusion, the eligible transferee must specify the amount and allocation of the exclusion on the claim.

Proposition 60

Proposition 60 provides that qualified homeowners aged fifty-five or over and taxpayers who are severely and permanently disabled may transfer the current base year value of their present principal residence to a replacement residence (sell their current home and buy another one) with the following conditions:

- Both properties must be in the same county.
- The transferor must be at least fifty-five years old as of the date of transfer (closing date of the sale). If married, only one spouse

must be fifty-five or older and must reside in the property; if co-owners, only one co-owner must be fifty-five or older and must reside in the property.

- The original residence must be eligible for a homeowner's exemption at the time of sale; however, if the replacement dwelling is acquired first, then the original resident of the replacement dwelling must be eligible for the homeowner's exemption after the purchase as a result of the claimant's occupancy as her principal residence.

- The replacement property must be purchased or newly constructed on or after November 6, 1986, and within two years of the sale of the original residence.

- If the replacement dwelling is purchased prior to the sale of the original property, the purchase price of the replacement residence must be equal to or less than the value of the original dwelling. If the replacement dwelling is purchased within the first year after the sale of the original dwelling, the value of the replacement dwelling may be 105 percent of that of the original dwelling. If the replacement dwelling is purchased within the second year, the replacement dwelling's purchase price may be 110 percent of the original dwelling's sales price.

For example, the preceding rule can be divided into two scenarios. In Scenario 1, the new home is bought first by the homeowner. In Scenario 2, the homeowner sells the old home first and then buys the new one.

Scenario 1	Buy replacement home at price equal to or less than that of old home.	Sell old home within two-year period.	
Scenario 2	*After sale*	*Year 1*	*Year 2*
	On the sale of old home, the two-year period starts.	Purchase can be 1.05 percent of sale price of old home.	Purchase can be 1.10 percent of sale price of old home.

- The claimant or claimant's spouse or any co-owner must not have been previously granted property tax relief as provided by this provision of law.

- Property tax relief under this section includes but is not limited to mobile homes, single family residences, condominiums, projects, community apartment projects, cooperative housing corporation units or lots, and owner's living units that are a portion of a large structure.

The following examples are actual scenarios that indicate a valid and an invalid transfer, for tax purposes, under Proposition 60.

Example 1. Replacement home acquired prior to sale.

- A replacement home was acquired on March 1, 2005, for $375,000.

  The old home was sold on November 12, 2005, for $325,000. *This sale did not qualify for the Proposition 60 exemption as the replacement home exceeded the 105 percent increase allowed. The maximum allowed acquisition price of the new home would only have been $341,250.*

  Example 2. Replacement home acquired after sale.

- The old home was sold on October 1, 2003, for $500,000. The replacement home was acquired on July 1, 2005, for $550,000. *This sale qualifies because the replacement home was purchased within the second year after sale of the old home and did not exceed the 110 percent rule.*

Proposition 90

Proposition 90 is an extension of Proposition 60. Proposition 60 limits the purchase of the replacement home to the same county, whereas Proposition 90 allows the purchase of the replacement home in a different California county, if the recipient county has adopted Proposition 90. Some counties that have adopted Proposition 90 are Los Angeles, Riverside, Orange, San Diego, and Kern. If the recipient county has not adopted Proposition 90, the homeowner is not eligible for the exemption, even if she met all of the requirements of Proposition 60.

Change-in-Ownership Statement

Any person acquiring an interest in property subject to local taxation must notify the county recorder or assessor by filing a *change in ownership statement* within forty-five days after the date of recording or, if the transfer is not recorded, within forty-five days after the date of transfer. Failure to do so will result in a penalty.

Exemptions

Many of the properties that are assessed are partially or wholly tax exempt. For example, many churches, all government and several nonprofit educational institutions, charitable organizations, and

nonprofit charitable organizations are entirely exempt. Relief is also available in various forms to veterans, senior citizens, homeowners, and renters.

Homeowner's Exemption

Each residential property that is owner-occupied on the lien date of March 1 receives an annual tax **homeowner's exemption** of $7,000 from the "full cash value" of the property. The homeowner need apply only once for the exemption as long as there is no change in ownership or residency of the property for which the claim is being made. The property must be owner-occupied on or before March 1 to claim the exemption for the upcoming tax year beginning on July 1. A homeowner is only allowed one tax exemption at a time; once this exemption has been filed, it remains in effect until terminated. An assessment plus a 25 percent penalty may be assessed if the assessor is not notified of a termination of an exemption.

Veteran's Exemption

California war veterans may receive a $4,000 exemption on the full cash value assessment of their homes. However, a person can take only one exemption at a time so she would not file for the lower **veteran's exemption** if she qualifies for the higher homeowner's exemption. A totally disabled veteran may be eligible for an exemption of the first $100,000 of value of her residence.

Senior Citizen Property Tax Postponement Act

The Senior Citizen Property Tax Postponement Act gives relief to homeowners that are at least sixty-two years of age as of January 1. The state of California pays all or part of the taxpayer's property taxes for them. People who are blind or totally disabled and meet the income requirements are also eligible. The taxes are postponed and are not repaid until the property is sold or the homeowner sells the property. Taxes become a lien against the property and the homeowner pays 5 percent interest on the loan. However, on February 20, 2009, the Governor signed Senate Bill X3 8 (Chapter 4, Statutes of 2009), which immediately suspended the Senior Citizens Property Tax Deferral Program. This legislation prohibits the filing of claims for property tax postponement and prohibits the controller from accepting claims filed after February 20, 2009. Check with the State Comptrollers Office for possible reinstatement.

14.2 INCOME TAXES

Our legislators often use the tax laws to affect public policy, therefore, the tax laws are always changing. As real estate professionals we must stay up-to-date on any changes that occur as they can have a profound effect on our clients. This section discusses income taxes as they relate to personal residences as well as business or investment property ownership.

Caution: As a real estate professional, you are licensed to assist clients in the purchase and sale of real estate. Unless you are also licensed as a tax professional and are willing to be held to that standard of care, you must be careful about the nature and extent of tax advice you give your clients. Overstepping the boundaries in this area can subject your client to huge tax penalties and financial losses and subject you to costly civil litigation.

Any advice you give must be immediately followed by a written statement, signed by the client, stating that she has not relied on any tax or legal advice that you have given and the transaction that she is involved in with you is contingent on the written approval of her tax and/or legal counsel.

Capital Gain Tax

The capital gain tax rates have changed rather drastically in the past several years. The Internal Revenue Code (IRC) states that the tax treatment of capital gains and losses depends on whether the gains and losses are long term or short term and on whether or not the taxpayer is a corporation. For noncorporate taxpayers, the maximum tax rate on "net" long-term capital gains is lower than the top rate on ordinary income.

The main features of the income tax treatment of capital gains and losses are:

- **Short-term capital gains** and losses are netted, long-term capital gains and losses are netted, and then long- and short-term gains and losses are netted against each other (2602 et seq.). Further netting may be necessary if a noncorporate taxpayer has capital losses as well as long-term capital gain subject to differing maximum tax rates.
- Adjusted net capital gain is taxed at a maximum rate of 15 percent. Starting in 2008, taxpayers in the 15 percent or less tax brackets pay no long-term capital gain tax. If the adjusted net capital gain would otherwise be taxed at a rate below 25 percent if it were ordinary income, it is taxed at a rate of 5 percent (at a 0 percent rate for tax years beginning after 2007).

- Gain realized through depreciation recapture is taxed at a maximum rate of 25 percent. Depreciation is not allowed on a primary residence and reduces sharply for taxpayers with an adjusted gross income of $100,000 or more. These figures change periodically so always tell your clients to consult their tax professional.

As most readers of this book will be involved primarily in the brokerage of residential homes, let's first take a look at the tax implications of owning a primary and/or a secondary home.

Primary Personal Residence

Special tax treatment is available for property that is considered to be a homeowner's **primary personal residence**, or the residence that the taxpayer lives in and occupies most of the time. A taxpayer may have only one personal residence, also referred to as her *principal residence*, at a time, and it may be a

- Single-family house
- Condominium
- Mobile home
- Cooperative housing
- Motor home
- Houseboat
- Trailer

If you live in one unit of a multiunit dwelling that you own, that unit is considered your principal residence. Tax benefits for that property are divided proportionately between those available as your principal residence and those available as income or investment property owned by you.

Secondary Residence

A dwelling owned by a taxpayer that she occupies exclusively, but is not the dwelling that she occupies most of the time, is considered a *secondary residence.* One secondary residence receives favorable income tax treatment, but unlike a primary residence, a secondary residence does not qualify for universal exclusion treatment.

Land

Vacant land cannot be considered a personal residence. A principal residence that is located on a large parcel of land gives rise to the question of how much of the land is used in conjunction with the principal residence and how much is used for other purposes. Any

court-related tests have always looked to the intent of the taxpayer and the "reasonable man" rule, rather than on the amount of land involved.

Universal Exclusion for Gain on Sale of Principal Residence

A seller of a personal residence, regardless of age, who has owned and used the home as a principal residence for at least two of the five years immediately before the sale can exclude from taxation up to $250,000 of gain ($500,000 for married couples and other joint filers who meet certain conditions). The exclusion can be used only once every twenty-four months.

Married couples filing jointly in the year of sale may exclude up to $500,000 of the gain, provided one of the spouses owned the home for at least two of the previous five years; however, both spouses must have used the home as a principal residence for at least two of the previous five years. Failure to meet this second test results in a maximum of $250,000 gain being excluded from taxation.

The two-year occupancy requirement need not be continuous. As long as the total time the owners occupied the property as their principal residence during the past five years met or exceeded twenty-four months, they qualify for the exemption, even if they rented the property for a time during that period.

The federal universal exclusion of $250,000/$500,000 has also been adopted by California, so if the gain from a sale meets the federal criteria for exclusion from taxation, it is also excluded from California taxation.

Deductible Versus Nondeductible Home Buying Expenses

When someone buys a home, she usually pays about 2 percent of the purchase price in closing costs (less for cash buyers, because they do not pay loan fees or American Land Title Association [ALTA] lender's title policy expenses). These expenses fall into one of the following three categories:

- Itemized deductions (deductible in the year of purchase)
- Expenses added to the property's **basis**
- Nondeductible expenses

Itemized deductions include things such as prorated interest on a new loan, prorated property taxes paid at settlement, and loan

origination fees (points). These are tax deductible and are shown on Schedule A of the buyer's tax return.

Expenses that add to the property's basis are usually nonrecurring closing costs such as escrow and professional fees, pest control, home inspection fees, title insurance, appraisal fees, and notary and recording fees.

Certain closing costs are neither a tax write-off nor a buying expense. Items such as Veterans Affairs (VA) or Federal Housing Administration (FHA) discount points, tax and/or insurance impound accounts, and homeowner's insurance. One major difference between VA/FHA and conventional loans is that fees for VA/FHA loans are considered to be a form of service charge by the Internal Revenue Service (IRS) and are not an itemized deduction (Rev. Rul. 67297; Rev. Rul. 6865).

Building a Home

For taxpayers who build their own homes, the **original basis** is all of the related costs to acquire the land and build the structure, including but not limited to land cost, permits, architectural and legal fees, building materials, and so forth. If the owners provide labor to help build the structure or other improvements, but do not actually pay themselves a fee for doing so, their labor is not tax deductible.

Buying an Existing Home

People who buy existing homes have an original basis equal to the purchase price plus allowable costs. A taxpayer who is selling one home and buying another will end up with an adjusted basis. If asked, you should refer this person to a tax professional to make the calculation of the new adjusted basis.

Inheriting a Home

A taxpayer who inherits a home receives it with a "stepped-up" basis equal to the Fair Market Value (FMV) at the time of the decedent's death. An "alternative valuation date" can also be used and the licensee should refer the client to a qualified tax preparer for further information on this subject.

Business and Investment Property

In this section you will see that property held for investment or production of income is treated differently with regard to taxation than one's personal residence. A distinct difference is the concept of depreciation.

Depreciation

All business and investment property has the ability to produce an income for the owner. Expenses are also associated with the ownership of such property. With the exception of land, which doesn't waste or depreciate, improved real estate held for business or investment does wear out. The government has made a special expense allowance available to owners of business and investment properties that makes an allowance for the replacement of the worn out or out-of-date improvements. This is called **depreciation**, although now we often use the term *cost recovery system*.

For purposed of depreciation, business and investment real estate can be divided into two distinct types:

1. Residential property. Residential property is essentially housing; it's where we live and it includes every type of housing such as single-family homes, condominiums, duplexes, triplexes, and small and large apartment complexes.
2. Nonresidential property. Nonresidential property is any property that does not provide housing for people and includes mini-storage complexes, office buildings, industrial plants, hotels, motels, and more. Raw land is also primarily commercial in nature until it is developed.

Since January 1, 1987, all investment or business property must use the straight-line method of depreciation, which is generally twenty-seven-and-a-half years for residential property and thirty-nine years for nonresidential property. Either residential or nonresidential property owners have the option of using a forty-year depreciation schedule.

Property Basis

To fully understand the tax implications of investment properties, the licensee must understand the concept of **basis**. The three types of basis are *original basis*, *depreciable basis*, and *adjusted basis*. As a licensee, you should have a good understanding of how to compute a client's basis; however, be reminded of the caveat stated earlier in this chapter about exceeding your ability in this matter and referring the client to a Certified Professional Accountant CPA or tax advisor.

The *original basis* is used to determine the depreciable basis and adjusted basis correctly. The *depreciable basis* is used to determine the amount of depreciation available to the taxpayer, if any. The *adjusted basis*, which changes over time, is required to calculate the gain or loss on a property when it is sold.

Original Basis

The *original basis* of a property is the sum total of its purchase price and the expenses associated with its purchase. When a client purchases an investment property, several things are included on the escrow closing statement and generally fall into the following four categories:

- Purchase price
- Operating expenses
- Acquisition expenses (nonrecurring closing costs)
- Nondeductible items, such as inspections

Purchase Price

Usually noted on the escrow statement as the *total consideration*, the purchase price is the amount actually paid for the property, exclusive of all other costs associated with the acquisition of the property. If the property is financed, the loan does not affect the basis.

Operating Expenses

Operating expenses are usually recurring costs associated with running the property and include things such as painting, landscape maintenance, interest, insurance, and property taxes. Loan origination fees are nonrecurring fees written off over the life of the loan, as compared to purchase-money loan fees for an owner-occupied residence, which is considered an advance interest payment and is deductible in the year of purchase. Loan origination fees are never added to the basis of a property except when refinancing.

Acquisition Expenses

Acquisition expenses are nonrecurring escrow costs, excluding loan acquisition fees that are incurred when acquiring a property. They are added to the purchase price to make up the original basis of the property being acquired. The formula for determining original basis is stated as:

Original basis = purchase price + acquisition expenses

Depreciable Basis

The *depreciable basis* is defined as the original basis multiplied by the percentage of improvements to land. The two formulas for determining the depreciable basis are stated as:

Depreciable basis = original basis − land value

and

Depreciable basis $=$ original basis $\times$ percentage of improvements to land

Investment real estate is composed of two values, land value and improvement value, or the value of the structure(s). Because the land is not depreciable, its value must be deducted from the total original basis to arrive at the depreciable basis (the improvements). The three methods of determining the percentage of improvements to land are contract method, appraisal method, and assessed value method.

Contract Method

With this method the buyer and seller decide on the value of the land and improvements and state those values in the purchase contract or escrow instructions. The determination of value must be "arm's length" and meet the "reasonable person" test or it may be disallowed. It is advisable for a licensee to suggest that the owner seek professional help with this method prior to entering into a purchase agreement.

Appraisal Method

When using the appraisal method, the property owner hires a professional appraiser to appraise the property, breaking out the separate values of the land and improvements. This method may assign a higher or lower value to the improvements than the owner desires, so it is suggested that this method be combined with the assessed value method to determine which one provides the taxpayer with the higher original improvements basis for depreciation purposes.

The adjusted basis is used as a basis for calculating net capital gain tax on the sale of all real estate, so it is important that homeowners and investors fully understand the relationship between the adjusted basis and the final sales price of a home or investment property. Calculation of the basis is affected by how the property was originally acquired. There are three different ways to acquire a property, and each presents the new owner with a different set of tax consequences.

1. *Basis by purchase* is the price paid for the property, as described earlier.
2. *Basis by gift* is the gift giver's (donor's) adjusted basis plus the gift tax paid, not to exceed the Fair Market Value (FMV) of the property at the time it was gifted.
3. *Basis by inheritance* is generally the FMV of the property at the time of the owner's demise.

Computing Capital Gain

The basis of a property is the beginning point for computing the net capital gain or loss on the final sale. Numerous adjustments to the basis are made during the ownership period; some, such as capital improvements, appraisal and legal fees at acquisition, title insurance, and sales costs on disposition, increase the basis, whereas accrued depreciation reduces it. The net result is the adjusted basis and the net capital gain or loss is the difference between the adjusted basis and the net sales price.

For example,

$1,000,000	Purchase price
+ 20,000	Acquisition expenses
+ 30,000	Capital improvements (roof, three water heaters)
$1,050,000	
− 102,000	Accumulated depreciation
$ 948,000	Adjusted cost basis
$1,500,000	Sales price
− 75,000	Sales costs
− 948,000	Adjusted cost basis
$ 477,000	Total capital gain

Depreciation Calculation

The following six steps are used to calculate the depreciation:

1. Compute the original basis.
2. Determine the allocation of land to improvements.
3. Compute the depreciable basis.
4. Determine whether the property is residential or nonresidential. Use twenty-seven-and-a-half years for residential and thirty-nine years for nonresidential.
5. Using the federal tax table shown in Figure 14.2, find the month the property was put into service by the taxpayer. In this example the property was put into service in September so you would go to Column 9 and the first year (Row 1) to find the percentage figure of 1.061 percent (0.0161).
6. Compute the depreciation by multiplying the depreciable basis by the appropriate percentage found in Figure 14.2.

For example, your client purchased an apartment house in September of this year for $1,000,000. She paid $20,000 in nonrecurring

FIGURE 14.2   Federal Tax Table for Depreciation of Real Property (%)

General Depreciation System					Method: Straight line				Recovery period: 27.5 years		
The month in the 1st recovery year the property is placed in service:											
Year	1	2	3	4	5	6	7	8	9	10	11	12
1	3.485	3.182	2.879	2.576	2.273	1.970	1.667	1.364	1.061	0.758	0.455	0.152
2–8	3.636	3.636	3.636	3.636	3.636	3.636	3.636	3.636	3.636	3.636	3.636	3.636

General Depreciation System					Method: Straight line				Recovery period: 39 years		
The month in the 1st recovery year the property is placed into service:											
1	2.461	2.247	2.033	1.819	1.605	1.391	1.177	0.963	0.749	0.535	0.321	0.107
2–39	2.564	2.564	2.564	2.564	2.564	2.564	2.564	2.564	2.564	2.564	2.564	2.564

closing costs. The land is valued at $320,000. She asks you what her depreciation will be this year.

- Compute the original basis.
  Purchase price + nonrecurring costs.
  Original basis = $1,000,000 + 20,000 = $1,020,000
- Determine the allocation between land and improvements. Land value is given at $320,000.
- Compute the depreciable basis.
  Depreciable basis = $1,020,000 – $320,000 = $700,000.
- Determine the type of property (residential is twenty-seven-and-a-half-year schedule).
- Find the month the property was put into service. This property was put into service *by this taxpayer* in September, so go to Column 9 of the first year (Row 1) to find the percentage figure of 1.061 percent (0.0161).
- Multiply the depreciable basis by the percentage found in Step 5. Depreciation = depreciable basis ($700,000) × percent (1.061) = $7,427.

The client is allowed a tax deduction for depreciation of $7,427 in the first year of ownership.

Depreciation Recapture and Capital Gains Tax

Capital gains depreciation recapture is now taxed at 25 percent per Section 1250 of the IRC.

Tax-Deferred Exchanges

IRC Section 1031, which is a part of the federal tax code, allows a taxpayer who owns *qualifying* real estate to exchange that real

estate for other qualifying real estate and defer some or all of the capital gains tax due until later if certain conditions are met. This act is correctly known as a **tax-deferred exchange**, or **1031 exchange**, as it is referred to by real estate practitioners. California has a similar code section. IRC Section 1031 also allows for tax-deferred exchange of qualifying personal property that is used in business or trade. The actual code section is rather small and consists of only a few paragraphs; however, there is a huge volume of case law, such as the *Mercantile Trust Decision* and the *Biggs Decision* that have further defined its implications. If you plan to be involved in the marketing and sale of business and investment property, you are well advised to study this code section and the case law that defines it in greater depth. See Chapter 16 for a detailed look at what being a commercial broker is all about.

California property has a long history of rapid appreciation or increase in value. Many owners wish to dispose of current property and obtain other property without paying the high taxes associated with doing so. The *1031 exchange* allows those individuals to do so and defer the tax until a later date. This is really equivalent to a tax-deferred loan from the government and gives the owner more money to invest in other property. Many owners who have refinanced one or more times find themselves in the position of having insufficient equity to pay the tax liability if they sell their property; however, they can still effect an exchange because they avoid the taxation issue.

A taxpayer who wishes to become involved in a 1031 exchange must first answer the following two questions:

1. Does the transaction qualify under IRC Section 1031?
2. Do the "numbers" (mathematics) of the transaction qualify in whole or in part?
   - Do the equities balance?
   - Is any "boot" given or received?
   - What is the taxpayer's basis in the new property?

Exchange Mechanics

In the past, exchanges involved three people or entities: the exchanger (the person who wanted to trade her property for another property on a tax-deferred basis), the seller (the owner of the property wanted by the exchanger), and the buyer (the person who wanted to buy the exchanger's property). Once the exchanger found a property she wished to acquire and a buyer was found for her property, the rest was "paperwork" done at the escrow company.

In the late 1990s, the IRS issued a *Revenue Ruling* stating that an **intermediary** must be used to effect a tax-deferred exchange or it would be disallowed. An intermediary is a neutral third party that acts as a custodian and depository of all documents and monies relating to a tax-deferred exchange. Note: The intermediary must maintain control over and receipt of any money received on behalf of the taxpayer during the holding period or the taxpayer will be considered to have actual or "constructive" receipt of it and it will become taxable.

Although an intermediary acts much like an escrow, it is not necessarily an escrow. The following example demonstrates how an intermediary works.

A wants to exchange her property for another property owned by B. A lists her property for sale with a broker, subject to a 1031 tax-deferred exchange. C wants to buy A's property. A contracts to sell to C through an intermediary and contracts to buy from B through the same intermediary. C gives her money to the intermediary and gets a deed to A's property from the intermediary. B deeds her property to the intermediary and gets money from the intermediary. A deeds her property to the intermediary and gets a deed to B's property from the intermediary. Figure 14.3 shows a diagram of how the money and deeds pass through an intermediary in a tax-deferred exchange.

The Equal-or-Up-Rule

For all capital gains taxes to be deferred in an exchange, the taxpayer may not receive any **boot** through the exchange escrow (boot, which is personal property of any kind, including cash, is taxable). The only way to accomplish this is to trade equal or up in property value and loans. This is called the **equal-or-up-rule**.

If a taxpayer trades equal in value, but puts in cash and obtains a lower loan, she receives mortgage relief by receiving a smaller loan than the one she gave up, which is taxable if it is done through the exchange escrow. If the taxpayer trades down in value, but puts less cash (equity) into the new property and keeps the loan the same size as the one she gave up, then *cash boot* is received, which is taxable if received through the exchange escrow. A taxpayer who trades down and gets a smaller loan on the new property receives both mortgage relief and cash boot and is taxed on both.

The Entity Rule

Property may be held by four separate entities: individuals, partnerships, corporations, and Limited Liability Companies (LLCs). The

FIGURE 14.3 Use of an Intermediary in a Tax-Deferred Exchange

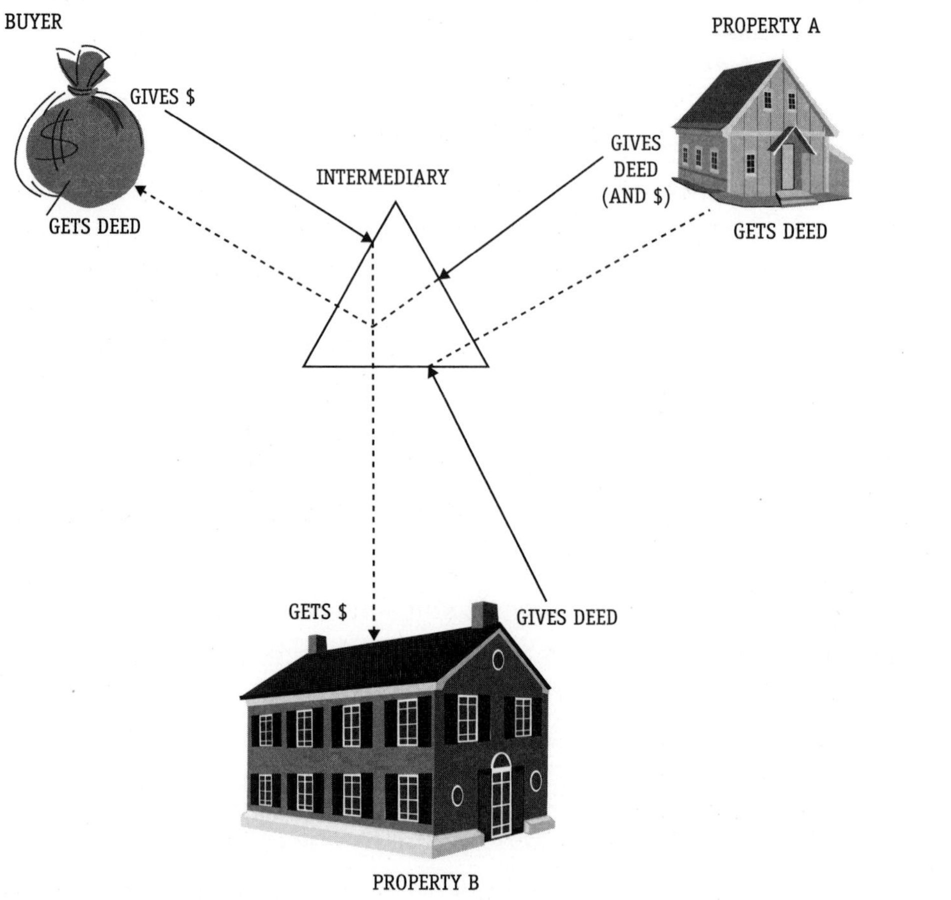

entity rule essentially states that the way a party holds title to property going into an exchange is the way the party must hold property coming out of an exchange.

The entity rule is not addressed in IRC Section 1031; it is one of the many revenue rulings made by the courts and is most used to interpret whether or not a tax-deferred exchange is really a *step transaction*. A step transaction is one in which the entity effecting the exchange is really attempting to end up with the "received" exchange property held by a different entity than the one that entered into the exchange.

For example, A and B decide to form a corporation and run a business. Each of them owns a small building and they decide they would like their new corporation to reside in a larger building where they will conduct their business. A and B sell their properties subject to a tax-deferred exchange and they acquire a large building in the name of their corporation through the exchange. Because they sold as individuals and acquired as a corporation, the

IRS disallows the exchange as a step transaction. If they acquired the new building as individual co-owners, the transaction would be a valid exchange.

The Investment Property Rule

The **investment property rule** comes from IRC Section 1031(a)(1) and states in general that no gain or loss shall be recognized on the exchange of property held for productive use in a trade or business or for investment if such property is exchanged solely for property of like kind that is to be held either for productive use in a trade or business or for investment. This precludes tax deferment for the trade of a personal residence for business or investment property as they do not meet the like-kind rule.

IRC Section 1031(a)(2) lists the following nonqualifying exceptions to this rule:

- Certificates of trust or beneficial interests.
- Stock in trade or other property held primarily for sale.
- Contractual rights.
- Partnership interests.
- Stocks, bonds, or notes.
- Other securities or evidence of indebtedness or interest.

Taxpayers and the IRS are constantly battling over how an investment is classified. The only test the courts seem to give any credibility to is the *intent and actions* of the taxpayer. If a taxpayer turns over several properties a year for profit, the IRS will likely deem her a dealer and the properties will probably be deemed inventory. To meet the investment property rule, a property must be held for about two to three years to show the intent of investing.

Note that in any exchange where the "up-leg" property owner is not reinvesting, the exchange can be valid for one party and not for the other.

Like-Kind Rule

Exchanges of property must observe the **like-kind rule**. Property is categorized as either *real* or *personal* property and neither is considered like kind for tax-deferred exchange taxation purposes.

The like-kind nature of personal property is sometimes difficult to determine as it must have the exact same nature or character. For example, Reg. 1.1031(1)-1(c0)(1) states that no gain or loss is recognized if a taxpayer exchanges property held for productive

use in her trade or business, together with cash, for other property of like kind for the same use, such as an automobile to be used for a like purpose.

Overall, the definition or test of like-kind status is much more narrowly defined for personal property than it is for real property. For real property, like-kind property is any piece of qualifying real property exchanged for any other piece of qualifying real property. IRC Section 1032(a) states clearly that like-kind refers only to the nature or character of the property and not its grade or quality and includes improved and unimproved land.

It should be noted that vacant land; improved real estate, such as office buildings, apartment houses, farms, and orchards; and leases with thirty or more years remaining at the time of the exchange (including all options) and mineral and rights (if considered real property by the state) are all considered qualifying real property.

The No-Choice Rule

If an exchange qualifies as an exchange, it must be treated as an exchange. Any gain must be deferred if the transaction was structured as an exchange. Simply stated, the **no-choice rule** says an exchanger who qualifies for a 1031 tax-deferred exchange cannot recognize the gain or loss.

The No-Loss Rule

The **no-loss rule**, which comes from IRC Section 1031(a)(1), is used in conjunction with the no-choice rule and states that if a real estate transaction qualifies as a tax-deferred exchange, a loss *cannot be recognized and losses* must be deferred along with gains.

The Delayed Exchange

IRC Section 1031(a)(3) allows a "delayed exchange" as long as the following criteria are met: "Requirement that the property be identified within 45 days after the relinquished property closes escrow and that the exchange be completed not more than 180 days after transfer of exchanged property—for purposes of this subsection, any property received by the taxpayer shall be treated as property which is not like-kind property if:

(A) Such property is not identified as property to be received in the exchange on or before the day which is 45 days after the date on which the taxpayer transfers the property relinquished in the exchange.

- Installation or removal of partitions
- Replacing or moving electrical wiring
- New roof
- Room additions
- Patios and/or pools
- Fencing and landscaping
- Plastering or strengthening walls
- Installation of or adding to a sprinkler system

Maintenance items are not home improvements and do not add to a property's basis. Some examples are:

- Replacement of built-in appliances
- Painting
- Carpeting
- Papering
- Drapes
- Furniture

Note: These items are considered operating expenses if the property is a rental property and may be expensed in the year paid.

Relief for "Forced" Sales

Taxpayers who fail to meet the once-every-two-years rule may find that a relief provision applies to them if certain conditions apply. If a taxpayer's failure to meet the provision is a result of the home being sold due to a change of the place of employment, health status, or other unforeseen circumstances, to the extent provided by the regulations, the taxpayer may be entitled to a partial exclusion. Under these circumstances, the excludable portion of the gain that would have been tax free had the requirements been met is based on the relationship that (a) the aggregate periods of ownership and use of the home by the taxpayer as a principal residence during the five years ending on the sale date or (b) the period of time after the last sale to which the exclusion applied and before the date of the current sale. Whichever is shorter, bears to (c) two years.

The law does not specify whether the computation should use days or months.

For example, if someone has lived in a home for eighteen months and, because of health reasons must be moved to a rest

home, she fails to meet the two-year test. However, because the move is health related, the homeowner is probably entitled to a prorated amount of exclusion based on the formula stated earlier. Eighteen months is 75 percent of the twenty-four months required so the homeowner is allowed to exclude 75 percent of her gain, up to the $250,000 limitation for a single person.

Other Tax Shelter Issues

Depreciation is shown as an expense for income tax purposes and can therefore somewhat reduce the tax liability of a real estate investor and could result in a "paper loss" even though the property has an actual positive cash flow.

Taxpayers can use real estate operating losses (passive losses) to offset real estate income without limit. Real estate losses can also be used, with limitations, to offset active income such as wages.

Taxpayers with an adjusted gross income of less than $100,000 can use real estate losses (which are considered passive losses) to shelter up to $25,000 of their active income. Taxpayers will see their eligibility for passive losses rapidly decrease as their adjusted gross income exceeds $100,000. As the passive loss rules change from time to time, always refer your clients to a competent tax advisor for any passive loss calculations.

Real estate professionals can use passive losses from investment property to offset other income without any limitations if they meet specific criteria, which include devoting at least 750 hours during the tax year to property management activities.

If investors do not actively manage their properties (active management includes hiring a property manager), they are precluded from sheltering active income. Because investors have no management responsibilities in investments such as limited partnerships and **triple net leased** properties (where the lessee pays the stipulated rent plus insurance, taxes, and all property expenses), the investor cannot use such losses to shelter active income.

14.4 FOREIGN INVESTMENT IN REAL PROPERTY TAX ACT (FIRPTA)

Before 1985, a "foreigner," or **foreign person** (a person who is neither a U.S. citizen nor a U.S. resident alien is in the United States on a temporary visa and does not pay income tax), could

purchase property in the United States, later sell it for a profit, then move out of the country without paying any income tax on the profit made from the sale. It is almost impossible to collect taxes from such an individual, so in January 1985, the U.S. Congress passed the **Foreign Investment in Real Property Tax Act (FIRPTA)**. California passed a similar law, which we will refer to as CAL-FIRPTA.

Federal Withholding

FIRPTA generally requires that a buyer withhold estimated taxes equal to 10 percent of the sale price in transactions involving real property in the United States that is sold or exchanged by a foreign person. In addition, CAL-FIRPTA requires that a buyer withhold estimated taxes equal to one-third of the amount required to be held under FIRPTA, or 3⅓ percent of the sales price. The 10 percent estimated withholding must be reported and paid to the IRS within ten days after the close of escrow. If the buyer fails to withhold the estimated taxes and the seller fails to pay taxes on the sale, the buyer is subject to the lesser of a penalty equal to 10 percent of the purchase price or the seller's actual tax penalty plus interest and penalties.

For personal residences, FIRPTA applies only to sales prices of $300,000 or more. When a buyer signs an affidavit (see Figure 14.4) stating that she plans to use the property as a personal residence and the purchase price is less than $300,000, the buyer is relieved of any duty to withhold estimated taxes.

All other property of any type requires withholding when a foreign person sells the property (see Figure 14.5). If, for instance, a foreign person owns a neighborhood retail center and sells it for $3,000,000, then $300,000 must be held for the federal government and an additional $100,000 for the state of California.

There are times when a foreign person owns property with one or more U.S. citizens. In this instance the amount of withholding must be prorated to reflect the amount of capital invested by each person. If, for instance, a foreigner and two other people who are U.S. citizens sell a property, withholding is prorated at 33⅓ percent. In this example, this would require FIRPTA withholding of $100,000 and CAL-FIRPTA withholding of $33,333.

"Withholding under Section 1.1445(a) may be reduced or eliminated pursuant to a withholding certificate issued by the IRS

FIGURE 14.4 Buyer's Affidavit

BUYER'S AFFIDAVIT

**That Buyer is acquiring property for use as a residence
and that sales price does not exceed $300,000.**
(FOREIGN INVESTMENT IN REAL PROPERTY TAX ACT)
(C.A.R. Form AB, 2/91)

CALIFORNIA ASSOCIATION OF REALTORS®

1. I am the transferee (buyer) of real property located at _____
_____.

2. The sales price (total of all consideration in the sale) does not exceed $300,000.

3. I am acquiring the real property for use as a residence. I have definite plans that I or a member of my family will reside in it for at least 50 percent of the number of days it will be in use during each of the first two 12 month periods following the transfer of the property to me. I understand that the members of my family that are included in the last sentence are my brothers, sisters, ancestors, descendents, or spouse.

4. I am making this affidavit in order to establish an exemption from withholding a portion of the sales price of the property under Internal Revenue Code §1445.

5. I understand that if the information in this affidavit is not correct, I may be liable to the Internal Revenue Service for up to 10 percent of the sales price of the property, plus interest and penalties.

Under penalties of perjury, I declare that the statements above are true, correct and complete.

Date _____ Signature _____

Typed or Printed Name _____

Date _____ Signature _____

Typed or Printed Name _____

IMPORTANT NOTICE: An affidavit should be signed by each individual transferee to whom it applies. Before you sign, any questions relating to the legal sufficiency of this form, or to whether it applies to a particular transaction, or to the definition of any of the terms used, should be referred to an attorney, certified public accountant, other professional tax advisor, or the Internal Revenue Service.

SURE TRAC
The System for Success®

Published and Distributed by:
REAL ESTATE BUSINESS SERVICES, INC.
a subsidiary of the California Association of REALTORS®
525 South Virgil Avenue, Los Angeles, California 90020

Reviewed by _____ Date _____

EQUAL HOUSING OPPORTUNITY

FORM AB REVISED 2/91 (PAGE 1 OF 1) **Print Date**

BUYER'S AFFIDAVIT (AB PAGE 1 OF 1)

Source: Reprinted with permission of California Association of REALTORS®.

FIGURE 14.5 Seller's Affidavit of Nonforeign Status

**SELLER'S AFFIDAVIT OF NONFOREIGN STATUS
AND/OR CALIFORNIA WITHHOLDING EXEMPTION**
FOREIGN INVESTMENT IN REAL PROPERTY TAX ACT (FIRPTA)
AND CALIFORNIA WITHHOLDING LAW
(Use a separate form for each Transferor)
(C.A.R. Form AS, Revised 11/06)

Internal Revenue Code ("IRC") Section 1445 provides that a transferee of a U.S. real property interest must withhold tax if the transferor is a "foreign person." California Revenue and Taxation Code Section 18662 provides that a transferee of a California real property interest must withhold tax unless an exemption applies.

I understand that this affidavit may be disclosed to the Internal Revenue Service and to the California Franchise Tax Board by the transferee, and that any false statement I have made herein may result in a fine, imprisonment or both.

1. **PROPERTY ADDRESS** (property being transferred): _____ ("Property")
2. **TRANSFEROR'S INFORMATION:**
   Full Name _____ ("Transferor")
   Telephone Number _____
   Address _____
   (Use HOME address for individual transferors. Use OFFICE address for an "Entity" i.e.: corporations, partnerships, limited liability companies, trusts and estates.)
   Social Security No., Federal Employer Identification No. or California Corporation No. _____
   Note: In order to avoid withholding, IRC Section 1445 (b) requires that the Seller (a) provides this affidavit to the Buyer with the Seller's taxpayer identification number ("TIN"), or (b) provides this affidavit, including Seller's TIN, to a "qualified substitute" who furnishes a statement to the Buyer under penalty of perjury that the qualified substitute has such affidavit in their possession. A qualified substitute may be (i) an attorney, title company, or escrow company (but not the Seller's agent) responsible for closing the transaction, or (ii) the Buyer's agent.
3. **AUTHORITY TO SIGN:** If this document is signed on behalf of an Entity Transferor, THE UNDERSIGNED INDIVIDUAL DECLARES THAT HE/SHE HAS AUTHORITY TO SIGN THIS DOCUMENT ON BEHALF OF THE TRANSFEROR.
4. **FEDERAL LAW:** I, the undersigned, declare under penalty of perjury that, for the reason checked below, if any, I am exempt (or if signed on behalf of an Entity Transferor, the Entity is exempt) from the federal withholding law (FIRPTA):
   ☐ (For individual Transferors) I am not a nonresident alien for purposes of U.S. income taxation.
   ☐ (For corporation, partnership, limited liability company, trust and estate Transferors) The Transferor is not a foreign corporation, foreign partnership, foreign limited liability company, foreign trust or foreign estate, as those terms are defined in the Internal Revenue Code and Income Tax Regulations.
5. **CALIFORNIA LAW:** I, the undersigned, declare under penalty of perjury that, for the reason checked below, if any, I am exempt (or if signed on behalf of an Entity Transferor, the Entity is exempt) from the California withholding law.
   Certifications which fully exempt the sale from withholding:
   ☐ The total sales price for the Property is $100,000 or less.
   ☐ The Property qualifies as my principal residence (or the decedent's, if being sold by the decedent's estate) within the meaning of IRC Section 121 (owned and occupied as such for two of the last five years).
   ☐ The Property was last used as my principal residence (or the decedent's, if being sold by the decedent's estate) within the meaning of IRC Section 121 without regard to the two-year time period.
   ☐ The transaction will result in a loss or zero gain for California income tax purposes. (Complete FTB Form 593-E.)
   ☐ The Property has been compulsorily or involuntarily converted (within the meaning of IRC Section 1033) and Transferor intends to acquire property similar or related in service or use to be eligible for non-recognition of gain for California income tax purposes under IRC Section 1033.
   ☐ Transferor is a corporation (or an LLC classified as a corporation) that is either qualified through the California Secretary of State or has a permanent place of business in California.
   ☐ Transferor is a partnership (or an LLC that is not a disregarded single member LLC, classified as a partnership) and recorded title to the Property is in the name of the partnership or LLC. If so, the partnership or LLC must withhold from nonresident partners or members as required.
   ☐ Transferor is exempt from tax under California or federal law.
   ☐ Transferor is an insurance company, qualified pension/profit sharing plan, IRA or charitable remainder trust.
   Certifications which may partially or fully exempt the sale from withholding:
   ☐ The Property is being, or will be, exchanged for property of like kind within the meaning of IRC Section 1031.
   ☐ Payments for the Property are being made in installments, the transferor is a non-resident seller and withholding will be applied to each principal payment.
   ☐ As a result of the sale of the Property, Seller's tax liability, calculated at the maximum tax rate regardless of Seller's actual rate, will be less than the 3 1/3% withholding otherwise required. Seller will be required to sign a certification, under penalty of perjury, specifying the amount to be withheld. **(Not to be used for sales closing prior to January 1, 2007)**

By_____ Date _____
(Transferor's Signature) (Indicate if you are signing as the grantor of a revocable/grantor trust.)

_____   _____
Typed or printed name   Title (If signed on behalf of Entity Transferor)

Buyer's unauthorized use or disclosure of Seller's TIN could result in civil or criminal liability.

Buyer_____ Date _____
(Buyer acknowledges receipt of a Copy of this Seller's Affidavit)

Buyer_____ Date _____
(Buyer acknowledges receipt of a Copy of this Seller's Affidavit)

Published and Distributed by:
REAL ESTATE BUSINESS SERVICES, INC.
a subsidiary of the California Association of REALTORS®
525 South Virgil Avenue, Los Angeles, California 90020

Reviewed by _____ Date _____

AS 11/06 (PAGE 1 OF 2)

SELLER'S AFFIDAVIT OF NONFOREIGN STATUS AND/OR CALIFORNIA WITHHOLDING EXEMPTION (AS PAGE 1 OF 2)

FIGURE 14.5 *(Continued)*

IMPORTANT NOTICE: An Affidavit should be signed by each individual or entity Transferor to whom or to which it applies. Before you sign, any questions relating to the legal sufficiency of this form, or to whether it applies to you or to a particular transaction, or about the definition of any of the terms used, should be referred to an attorney, certified public accountant, or other professional tax advisor, the Internal Revenue Service, or the California Franchise Tax Board. For further information on federal guidelines, see C.A.R. Legal Q & A *"Federal Withholding: The Foreign Investment in Real Property Tax Act,"* and/or IRS Publication 515 or 519. For further information on state guidelines, see C.A.R. Legal Q & A *"California Nonresident Withholding,"* and/or California FTB Pub. 1016.

FEDERAL GUIDELINES

FOREIGN PERSONS DEFINED. The following general information is provided to assist sellers in determining whether they are "foreign persons" for purposes of the Foreign Investment in Real Property Tax Act (FIRPTA), IRC §1445. FIRPTA requires a buyer to withhold and send to the Internal Revenue Service 10% of the gross sales price of a United States (U.S.) real property interest if the seller is a foreign person. No withholding is required for a seller who is a U.S. person (that is, not a foreign person). In order for an individual to be a U.S. person, he/she must be either a U.S. citizen or a U.S. resident alien. The test must be applied separately to each seller in transactions involving more than one seller. Even if the seller is a foreign person, withholding will not be required in every circumstance.

NONRESIDENT ALIEN INDIVIDUAL. An individual whose residence is not within the U.S. **and** who is not a U.S. citizen is a nonresident alien. The term includes a nonresident alien fiduciary. An alien actually present in the U.S. who is not just staying temporarily (i.e., not a mere transient or sojourner), is a U.S. resident for income tax purposes. An alien is considered a U.S. resident and not subject to withholding under FIRPTA if the alien meets either the **green card test** or the **substantial presence test** for the calendar year.

GREEN CARD TEST. An alien is a U.S. resident if the individual was a lawful permanent resident of the U.S. at any time during the calendar year. This is known as the "green card test."

SUBSTANTIAL PRESENCE TEST. An alien is considered a U.S. resident if the individual meets the substantial presence test for the calendar year. Under this test, the individual must be physically present in the U.S. on at least: (1) 31 days during the current calendar year; and (2) 183 days during the current year and the two preceding years, counting all the days of physical presence in the current year but only 1/3 the number of days present in the first preceding year, and 1/6 the number of days present in the second preceding year.

DAYS OF PRESENCE IN THE U.S. TEST. Generally, a person is treated as physically present in the country at any time during the day. However, if a person regularly commutes to work in the U.S. from a residence in Canada or Mexico, or is in transit between two points outside the U.S. and is physically present in the country for less than 24 hours, he/she is not treated as present in the U.S. on any day during the transit or commute. In addition, the individual is not treated as present in the U.S. on any day during which he/she is unable to leave the U.S. because of a medical condition which arose while in the U.S.

EXEMPT INDIVIDUAL. For the substantial presence test, do not count days for which a person is an exempt individual. An exempt individual is anyone in the following categories:
(1) An individual temporarily present in the U.S. because of (a) full-time diplomatic or consular status, (b) full-time employment with an international organization or (c) an immediate family member of a person described in (a) or (b).
(2) A teacher or trainee temporarily present in the U.S. under a "J" visa (other than as a student) who substantially complies with the requirements of the visa. An individual will not be exempt under this category for a calendar year if he/she was exempt as a teacher or trainee or as a student for any two calendar years during the preceding six calendar years.
(3) A student temporarily present in the U.S. under an "F" or "J" visa who substantially complies with the requirements of the visa. Generally, a person will not be exempt as a student for any calendar year after the fifth calendar year for which he/she was exempt as a student, teacher or trainee. However, the individual may continue to be exempt as a student beyond the fifth year if he/she is in compliance with the terms of the student visa and does not intend to permanently reside in the U.S.

CLOSER CONNECTION TO A FOREIGN COUNTRY. Even if an individual would otherwise meet the substantial presence test, that person is not treated as meeting the test for the current calendar year if he/she:
(1) Is present in the U.S. on fewer than 183 days during the current year, and
(2) Has a tax home in a foreign country and has a closer connection to that country than to the U.S.

SPECIAL RULES. It is possible to be both a nonresident alien and a resident alien during the same tax year. Usually this occurs for the year a person arrives in or departs from the U.S. Other special provisions apply to individuals who were U.S. residents for at least three years, cease to be U.S. residents, and then become U.S. residents again.

NONRESIDENT ALIEN INDIVIDUALS MARRIED TO U.S. CITIZENS OR RESIDENT ALIENS may choose to be treated as resident aliens for most income tax purposes. However, these individuals are considered **nonresidents** for purposes of withholding taxes.

A FOREIGN PERSON OR PARTNERSHIP is one that does not fit the definition of a domestic corporation or partnership. A domestic corporation or partnership is one that was created or organized in the U.S., or under the laws of the U.S., or of any U.S. state or territory.

GUAM AND U.S. VIRGIN ISLANDS CORPORATIONS. A corporation created or organized in or under the laws of Guam or the U.S. Virgin Islands is not considered a foreign corporation for the purpose of withholding tax for the tax year if:
(1) at all times during the tax year, less than 25% in value of the corporation's stock is owned, directly or indirectly, by foreign persons, and
(2) at least 20% of the corporation's gross income is derived from sources within Guam or at least 65% of the corporation's income is effectively connected with the conduct of a trade or business in the U.S. Virgin Islands or the U.S. for the 3-year period ending with the close of the preceding tax year of the corporation, or the period the corporation has been in existence if less.

A NONRESIDENT ALIEN TRUSTEE, ADMINISTRATOR OR EXECUTOR of a trust or an estate is treated as a nonresident alien, even though all the beneficiaries of the trust or estate are citizens or residents of the U.S.

Copyright © 1988-2008, CALIFORNIA ASSOCIATION OF REALTORS®, INC.
AS REVISED 11/06 (PAGE 2 OF 2)

Buyer's Initials (_____)(_____)
Seller's Initials (_____)(_____)

Reviewed by _____ Date _____

SELLER'S AFFIDAVIT OF NONFOREIGN STATUS AND/OR CALIFORNIA WITHHOLDING EXEMPTION (AS PAGE 2 OF 2)

Source: Reprinted with permission of California Association of REALTORS®.

in accordance with the rules of this section." Your "foreign" seller must allow six to eight weeks to receive the IRS certificate, so plan carefully. Even if a foreign person is selling within the scope and acceptable limits of the two-out-of-five-year rule, which would make the transaction exempt from taxation, she must still get an IRS withholding statement to avoid having funds withheld. The burden of knowing whether or not the seller is a foreign person falls on the buyer; however, a few measures will relieve the buyer of the obligation to withhold. One way is to have the seller provide the buyer with an affidavit of nonforeign status. The seller must also provide a U.S. taxpayer identification number (usually a Social Security number) to the escrow agent and state, under penalty of perjury, that she is not a foreign person.

California Withholding

As previously stated, California has adopted its own law, known as CAL-FIRPTA, which covers real property sales by foreign persons who are neither U.S. citizens nor U.S. resident aliens. Since January 1, 1991, when California real property is sold, if the seller's last known street address is located outside of California (except for partnerships), the buyer must withhold 3⅓ percent of the selling price if certain conditions are not met. An exemption from withholding exists if any of the following conditions are present:

- The sales price of the California property is $100,000 or less
- The seller is a bank acting as a trustee of a deed of trust
- The buyer does not have written instructions from the real estate person
- The seller receives a homeowner's property tax exemption in the taxable year in which the transfer of title occurs
- The seller is a partnership
- The property is being acquired in foreclosure by a corporation

Both the buyer who fails to withhold and the escrow officer who fails to provide written notice of the withholding requirements are subject to penalties of $500 or 10 percent of the amount required to be withheld, whichever is greater.

The buyer is the one who is required to withhold; however, the seller can request a waiver from withholding or a reduced amount of withholding by submitting a written request on California Form 597-A, the Application for Withholding Certificate for Disposition

by Nonresidents of California Real Property Interests, to the Franchise Tax Board (FTB). The form must be filled out completely and must include the seller's full name(s), Social Security number or California corporation number, and all pertinent facts to support no withholding or withholding at a rate less than 3⅓ percent. The FTB will usually not allow a waiver or reduction unless there appears to be little or no taxable gain on the transaction.

On a tax-deferred exchange of California real property by a nonresident, withholding is required unless a waiver is granted or the seller signs a statement that she will file a California tax return at year-end to report the transaction. If boot is received by the seller in a 1031 exchange, withholding is required at the rate of 7 percent.

If a nonresident sells a property using the installment method, the FTB will allow periodic payments of withholding in accordance with the terms of the installment sale agreement provided the buyer and seller request special arrangements by requesting a waiver on Form 597-A.

SUMMARY

Real estate taxes are *ad valorem*, or "according to value," taxes. Property is reassessed when sold and a supplemental tax bill is sent to the new owner. Property is taxed for the basic levy at a maximum rate of 1 percent of its FMV. The assessed tax cannot increase more than 2 percent per year. Additional special assessments can be added up to 1 percent of the property's FMV. The homeowner's exemption is $7,000 from the assessed valuation. There is also a veteran's exemption of the first $100,000 for totally disabled veterans.

Property transfers between family members may be exempt from reassessment if certain conditions are met. Taxpayers over fifty-five years of age may sell their primary residence and buy a replacement in the same county with certain restrictions and keep the assessed valuation of their old property (105 percent/110 percent rule). This can be extended to other counties if the recipient county has agreed to it (Proposition 90).

Some low income and disabled senior citizens may have their property taxes postponed until they pass away or no longer occupy the property. Depreciation is a noncash expense for tax purposes that applies to the improvements of income, business, and

investment property and is considered a return *of* the investment, whereas cash flow is considered a return *on* the investment. Any gain on sale is taxed on the difference between the net sales price after deducting selling expenses and the adjusted basis. Depreciation schedules are twenty-seven-and-a-half years for residential property and thirty-nine years for nonresidential property. A taxpayer may elect a forty-year cost recovery period.

A taxpayer can defer gains on the sale of business or investment property by use of a 1031 tax-deferred exchange. The property must meet the like-for-like rule and the taxpayer would be taxed on any **boot** (personal property or debt relief) received through the exchange. A delayed tax-deferred exchange is possible if the taxpayer identifies the "new" property within 45 days after transferring the "old" property and closes escrow on the new one within 180 days of the transfer or by the end of the next tax accounting period.

Installment sales allow a taxpayer to spread any gain over more than one tax year, which could result in a lower tax bracket for the investor when each installment of the gain is reported and paid.

A sale-leaseback allows a seller to gain the use of 100 percent of the capital that was tied up as equity, whereas the new lease payments would be fully deductible as a business expense.

Residential property owners may deduct the acquisition indebtedness interest on a first loan of up to $1,000,000 for primary and secondary residences (combined), as well as the interest on secondary financing equity indebtedness loans up to $100,000. The capital gain on an owner-occupied residence is determined by deducting the adjusted cost basis (cost plus qualifying improvements) and the selling expenses from the sales price. Many changes have been made to the tax laws as they apply to real estate in recent years. One of the most significant changes is the once-every-twenty-four-month exclusion of up to $250,000 for single taxpayers and $500,000 for married homeowners filing jointly, from taxation for gain on the sale of a principal residence. To qualify, the property must have been the principal residence for two of the last five years (not necessarily sequentially).

Capital gains have a tax rate of 15 percent for long term (over one year), whereas capital gains on property sold within a year after acquisition are taxed at ordinary income rates. Depreciation recapture is generally taxed at 25 percent.

The buyer is responsible for withholding 10 percent of the sales price of a property purchased from a foreign national to meet the federal FIRPTA requirements and 3⅓ percent to meet California requirements unless the transaction is exempt from such withholding.

CLASS DISCUSSION TOPICS

1. Diagram a three-party exchange using an intermediary.

2. Compute the adjusted basis when the original basis was $580,000, qualifying improvements to the property totaled $46,000, and depreciation taken was $44,290.

3. You just closed escrow on a rental home that you now own. Escrow closed on March 1. The first installment of the property taxes ($2,800) was paid by the sellers in December and you were credited with two months of taxes in escrow. How much property tax will you have to pay by the April deadline and why?
   If the old assessment was $325,000 and you paid $600,000 for the property, how much will your supplemental tax bill be?

4. Your clients, a married couple, are selling their home and buying another through you. They paid $250,000 for the home and have put $25,000 in qualified improvements into it. They have lived there for five years. If they sell the home for $700,000, what, if any, capital gains tax will they be liable for?

CHAPTER 14 QUIZ

1. What did Proposition 90 provide for?
   A. Property tax assessment set at a maximum of 2 percent of FMV.
   B. Old property assessed valuation moved to new house in the same county for people over fifty-five years old.
   C. Old property assessed valuation moved to new property in a different county for people over fifty-five years old.
   D. Property tax of old home moved to new home if over forty-five years old.

2. What did Proposition 13 provide for?
   A. It set assessments for property acquired before 1978 back to the value shown on the 1975 tax roll.
   B. It set a maximum tax rate.
   C. The tax can be increased a maximum of 3 percent a year.
   D. Both a and b.

3. Depreciation for a commercial property uses which of the following?
   A. Twenty-seven-and-a-half-year table
   B. Thirty-nine-year table
   C. Straight-line method
   D. Both b and c

4. Which of the following is required to have a valid delayed tax-deferred exchange?
   A. The exchange property must be identified in writing within forty-five days after the taxpayer relinquishes her property.
   B. The sale must be completed within 180 days after the taxpayer relinquishes her property or by the end of the next tax reporting period.
   C. An intermediary must be used.
   D. All of the above.

5. The advantage of a sale-leaseback to a business owner is
   A. the property continues to appreciate.
   B. the property taxes are a tax deduction.
   C. the loan interest payments are fully tax deductible.
   D. 100 percent of the equity is freed up to use for business expansion or whatever the owner/seller wants and the new lease payments are 100 percent deductible as a business expense.

6. Which of the following is not considered "boot" received in a tax-deferred exchange?
   A. Cash received.
   B. Cash given.
   C. Assuming a smaller loan than the one you are giving up.
   D. Both b and c.

7. A homeowner has a first loan of $300,000 at 6 percent interest and a second loan taken out after she acquired the property of $130,000 at 7.5 percent interest. What is the total amount of interest that can be written off on her income tax in a tax year?
   A. $27,750
   B. $25,500
   C. $25,800
   D. None of the above

8. Bill bought an apartment house for $1,000,000. He had $25,000 in acquisition costs that added to his basis. The tax bill shows the land at 35 percent of value. What is his original basis?
   A. $666,250
   B. $1,000,025
   C. $1,000,000
   D. Not enough information to compute

9. A foreign person is selling her home and does not have a withholding certificate. The sales price is $560,000. Her loan is $387,000. She is in the 15 percent tax bracket. How much of her sale proceeds does the buyer need to hold in escrow?
   A. $38,700
   B. $67,500
   C. $56,000
   D. None of the above

10. A homeowner paid $200,000 for her home and paid $6,000 in nonrecurring acquisition costs. Over the years she has installed an outside wall ($3,000), replaced the roof ($5,000), added a bath ($12,000), and installed new carpets and drapes ($3,500). What is her current basis in her home?

A. $226,000

B. $206,000

C. $212,000

D. $229,500

Chapter

15

IMPORTANT PHRASES AND TERMS

Annual percentage rate (APR)

Bait-and-switch advertising

Blind ads

Business card

Car signs

Company dollar

Display advertising

E-mail advertising

Fair housing violation

Institutional advertising

Internet

Media

Name tag

Niche markets

Outdoor advertising

Specialty gifts

Specific advertising

Sphere of influence

Truth-in-Lending Act

Advertising and Marketing

Upon completion of this chapter, the student will be able to:

- Design a seller advertising program.
- Compare and contrast advertising and marketing plans.
- Practice AIDA approach to advertising and marketing.
- Locate and identify client and customer sources.
- Evaluate Internet and e-mail as a venue for advertising.
- Define and recognize false and misleading advertising.
- Recognize violations of Regulation Z.
- Describe and identify violations of Article 12 of NAR Code of Ethics.

15.1 ADVERTISING AND MARKETING

Advertising is the process of calling attention to something to arouse a desire to buy the product or service being promoted. Marketing is the process of creating a favorable or positive image of a particular product or service. Although the two disciplines are close in nature and more often than not go hand-in-hand to win the customer, they are also different.

Advertising

Although the real estate industry could not exist without advertising, the venues available to real estate brokers to promote properties, their companies, and licensees are rapidly changing. Real estate advertising is generally divided into two major types: specific

advertising and institutional advertising. Institutional advertising and marketing are quite similar in nature.

Specific advertising is concerned with immediate results. It describes a particular property or subdivision and suggests to the customer that she must see it immediately. This type of advertising usually lists several key features of the property to create a desire for more knowledge in the consumer's mind.

Institutional advertising attempts to create a favorable image of the real estate company and its licensees. Like marketing, it keeps the company's name in the public eye and aims to inspire trust, confidence, and goodwill. Brokers in a community sometimes get together and share in a large institutional ad aimed at bettering their collective reputations in the community.

The AIDA Approach

Most advertising is done with one purpose in mind: to bring customers to a real estate office, a website, or an Open House. Having plenty of saleable listings is wonderful, but you need customers. A well-thought-out advertising strategy greatly enhances the number of potential customers an office or licensee may serve.

People seldom buy a home for shelter alone. Most people are also looking for other things, such as social status, ego satisfaction, safety, good schools, a shorter commute, or more room. Advertising communicates these benefits by stating the property's features, such as its price, size, and location.

Most buyers do not read ads, they skim them. You increase your chances of getting a buyer interested in one of your ads if you use the AIDA (Attention, Interest, Desire, Action) approach:

- <u>A</u>ttention – Because readers scan ads, you must do something to cause them to pause at your ad long enough to become interested in it. The best way to accomplish this is to use a headline that grabs their attention. Bold print, large print, and "catchy" words or short phrases will help accomplish this. Use of color or "white space" will help the headline to stand out. Don't be afraid to use humor as well. Words like SWIM INTO SUMMER would certainly make a reader who is looking for a home with a pool stop and read further.

- <u>I</u>nterest – The first few words of your ad should maintain the reader's interest and create a desire for more information. These words should arouse the reader's curiosity or cause the reader to envision enjoying the benefits offered. Words like "watch

the stars from the bubbling spa" help place the reader at the scene.

- **D**esire – Once you have the reader's attention and interest, appeal to her senses and emotions. Be concise and inspire a desire to know more about the property. Build enjoyable mental images for the reader. Choose words like large private yard, beautifully maintained four-bedroom home, and gourmet kitchens are yours when you own this Brentwood beauty! This will allow the reader to see herself in the home and will create a strong desire to see the property.

- **A**ction – The last part of the ad should move the reader to take action—to see the property and to obtain more information. The action desired by a real estate advertisement is either a phone call to your office or, more importantly, your cell phone or a personal visit to your office, Open House, or building site. Include a "call to action," such as "Don't miss this fine home, call Tom at XYZ Realty today!"

Because readers respond to emotional appeals more often than rational ones, use adjectives in your advertising that paint pictures. Saying a house has "3 BR, 2 BA, Family Room, 3-car gar," for example, does nothing to place the reader in the property, enjoying its benefits. An ad structured like the one about the bubbling spa allows readers to become emotionally involved with the property by "being there" due to your description. They can "feel" the warm water of the pool and spa and they can "see" the stars.

Personal Advertising

- One of the most effective and least expensive means of personal advertising is a **name tag** identifying you as a real estate professional. Be sure your name and your company's name and/or logo are clearly visible from a short distance away. If you are a REALTOR®, your name tag should say so, along with any professional designations you have achieved.

- Your personal advertising should also include your **business card**. Design it to stand out among a group of cards and include a recent picture. This will help immensely. Also list on the card all of your professional designations and all of your contact information, including your name; DRE salesperson or broker license number, company name and logo if available; office address; office, cell, and fax numbers; and any special skills you use in your business, such as a foreign language. Be careful to avoid a "busy" looking card containing so much information the reader becomes confused. It may help to use a foldout or tent-style card.

- A set of magnetic **car signs** is a low-cost advertising tool. Include at least your name, your firm's name and logo, REALTOR®, if applicable, and your direct telephone or cell number.
- Invest in your personal **Internet** site. If you are with a large firm that has an attractive, well-read site, create a link from it to your personal site. You will get more "hits" on your site from people who started at the company site. This is a highly effective way to market yourself and your skills while advertising your own listings.

Classified Advertising

Newspaper advertising is the oldest form of advertising used by the real estate industry. (The first ad appeared in the early 1700s in Boston.) Newspaper advertising has dwindled in recent years as advertisers have followed the customer base to the Internet, which has become the overwhelming choice of consumers. Today, nearly 90 percent of consumers start their real estate "hunt" for licensees to work with or homes to see on the Internet.

Although newspaper ads have a short effective life span, they have an extensive coverage and a great degree of selectivity. An ad can be placed in a newspaper's entire market area or region, which often results in more calls on a specific property for less money.

Newspaper ads are divided into classified and display advertisements. We will have more to say on display advertising, which is more institutional in nature, later in the marketing section.

All ads must display the name of the real estate company and its telephone number. Ads that do not identify the advertiser as a broker or licensee are called **blind ads**; they are illegal in California and a violation of the code of ethics.

Unlike many other products, it is possible to advertise real estate effectively by stating its negative features. An ad with a headline that says, "Bring Your Toolbox and Save!" will usually generate many calls from prospective do-it-yourselfers. (Author's note: I once listed a six-bedroom home but couldn't get any calls off of a normal ad. I ran an ad that said, "Burlingame Hotel? Well, not quite, but this home sure has plenty of room." I received several calls in only a few days and sold the home to someone looking for a home for the elderly. I did not advertise for that type of person in the ad, which would have been a **fair housing violation**.)

It is wise to include your Internet address on all of your print advertising. Less than 1 percent of people who call on an ad actually buy the home they called about. Written ads are limited to the number of

properties you have placed in the ad; however, if a reader is directed to your Internet site, she can view all of your and your company's listings and contact you about any of them. It will greatly increase your chances of receiving customer contacts from your print ads.

Print advertising is expensive, and care must be taken to monitor the source of the leads. This can be done in two ways:

1. If your company has a "floor" or "up" desk, a control sheet should be easily accessible to the licensee on duty for tracking the advertising medium of all incoming advertising calls. These forms should be submitted to the managing broker each day to identify the source of the most productive advertising media.

2. Use a source code in each ad or a different phone number or extension for each **media** medium used. The code system can make tracking each individual ad easy.

E-Mail Advertising

E-mail advertising has become one of the most powerful forms of direct advertising. Whereas the effectiveness of newspaper advertising is decreasing, the number of consumers viewing online real estate advertising is increasing.

As you build your client base, be sure to get the e-mail address of each client and add it to your database. The California Association of REALTORS® (C.A.R.) Consent for Communication (CFC) form would be appropriate because various state and federal "Do-Not-Call" regulations prohibit unsolicited phone, e-mail, and fax. Always get the client's written permission to communicate whenever possible. The two highly effective things you can do with your client e-mail list are:

- Separate your **sphere of influence** (SOI) database into special interest or activity groups, such as dog lovers, cat lovers, golfers, hikers, and horse lovers. Once these lists are readily available on your computer, watch all of the different media (newspapers, television, radio, and so on) for articles and events that may interest your clients. For instance, an article about a women's golf tournament in town soon with several "name" players may interest one of your groups. Simply call up that group on your e-mail account. Insert your name in the "TO" box and the group name of your golfers in the "BCC" (*B*lind *C*arbon *C*opy) box. Write a heading in the subject line and send them a note regarding the tournament and where you saw the information.

Note: When sending e-mail to a list, never include all of your clients' e-mail addresses in the "TO" box. Most people don't like

their addresses floating around out there. They will come to respect you for maintaining their privacy and will know that e-mail in their inbox with your name on it will have something special for them and they will always open it.

- Send an e-mail every time you get a new listing. Open a new e-mail message, insert your name in the "TO" box, insert your entire database in the "BCC" box, and the words "New Listing" in the subject box. Write a short, descriptive paragraph about your new listing, insert a couple of digital pictures of the property, and write a brief "call to action" paragraph. For example, "If you would like to see this wonderful new listing or have a friend or family member that might, please contact me at your earliest convenience. We'll beat the crowd!" Be sure to include your sellers on the list; they will love it, guaranteed!

The Internet

The Internet is probably the future of real estate advertising. Its use is skyrocketing, whereas print advertising is dwindling. You are well advised to have a presence on the Internet. Most medium-to-large real estate companies have their own Internet websites. They usually have one or more ways of viewing their listings as well as the Multiple Listing Service (MLS) listings and include one or more ways to contact a specific licensee. If you have a personal website, it should be linked to the company's website so anyone who visits can be easily directed to your site.

All of your listings should be included on both the company's and your own website as quickly as possible. Upload as many pictures as possible with each listing. Many MLS now require at least one photograph of the property. Recent studies show that listings with six pictures are visited 300 percent more than listings with only one picture.

As soon as each new listing is posted on the Internet, forward it to your sellers to show them what you are doing for them. Many websites have a method of keeping track of how many "hits" are received on each property. If this is available to you, use it. It is an excellent way to verify the "overpriced listing" issue and get the price adjustment you are seeking, if you can show that there have been 300 "hits" on the property in the past month with no further inquiries to you.

Call-Capture "800" Telephone Numbers

In the last several years, call-capture 800 telephone numbers have grown in popularity and ease of use. Although somewhat expensive to operate, the cost for this type of 800 number is now around

$30 per month. This involves the licensee obtaining an 800 (or 888) number that "captures" the telephone number of the person who calls in for information. The licensee puts an ad in the paper or in a "Homes for Sale" type of magazine offering information on various real estate subjects, such as How to Get Top Dollar for Your Home or Seven Things Every Seller Should Know Before Listing, that will entice people to call. When someone calls the 800 number, she is asked to "queue in" a code from the ad, according to the information she requests. She is then asked to leave her name and address on the recording for mailing the brochure. The licensee then takes this information, mails the requested brochure, and follows up in a day or two asking if she may be of any help with the caller's real estate needs. Compliance with the federal and state Do-Not-Call lists should be a concern when using this type of marketing tool.

Direct Mail

Target marketing is an effective use of direct mail. With every new listing, ask yourself who are the likely buyers of the property. Once you have established your target market (such as a neighborhood of homes that are in a price range where the owners would be likely candidates to sell their current home and "move up" to the home you have listed), get the names and addresses of as many homes in the neighborhood as your budget will allow and send the owners a flyer or brochure about your listing along with a cover letter asking if they are considering making a change. Also ask them to contact you for a private showing and let them know you have many other fine homes in the same price range available through the MLS. Your letter should also contain a statement that if their home is currently listed with a broker, your letter is not intended as a solicitation of that broker's listing.

Real Estate Magazines

Many real estate magazines are available to the consumer. They generally have a decent track record of calls for the price paid; however, far too many licensees use them ineffectively by putting several pictures of homes in them with quickly written ad copy providing a number of features without relating the benefits. To obtain the maximum number of calls from your written advertising, all of your copy should state *features tied to benefits to the consumer.*

If your ad says that you are "No. 1" at something, it means nothing to the reader, except that you may be prone to exaggeration, and certainly will not prompt her to call you. However, you will probably receive inquiries if your ad says you are the

top-selling residential licensee in the town of Hillsborough because your negotiating skills always get your buyers the best price possible. Just be sure you are the "top-selling residential licensee" based on MLS or other corroborating evidence. You also need to understand that if you hold yourself out as a "specialist" or "expert" in a given area of expertise, you will be held to that standard in the event of any litigation you may become involved in.

Marketing

The goal of marketing is to create an image of something or someone or to create curiosity in the consumer's mind about a person, product, or service. It is repetitive in nature and is not a one-time event as advertising usually is. Marketing uses several different media that would not necessarily be effective for home advertising because of the cost involved.

Display Advertisements

Display advertising, like some magazine advertising, can be either personal or institutional in nature and can include advertising specific listings as well. Display advertisements are usually limited to the slick, upscale magazines found in most market places. You will almost never see display advertising in homebuyer magazines.

Because of their cost, display ads are primarily used to sell subdivisions rather than single-family homes. However, almost every upscale area has one or more real estate licensees who specialize in luxury home sales. They tend to purchase half-page to whole-page display ads promoting themselves and advertising their listings as well. Advertising their listings in conjunction with the upscale personal promotion or marketing serves the dual purpose of advertising for buyers as well as validating them as effective listing licensees to the property owners in that area.

Radio and Television

Television provides three types of real estate advertising or marketing:

1. Showing still pictures or video tours of homes in an area along with the broker's name and number. This program entices buyers to call about the properties shown.
2. A public television program sponsored by a real estate firm. The firm runs institutional ads during the show.
3. Standard institutional-style commercials aired during normal programs.

Almost all of the public and paid program advertising are run by very large national real estate companies, large franchise companies, or developers because of the cost involved.

Radio commercials are almost always institutional in nature and are usually run by mid-to-large real estate companies. Occasionally individual licensees run radio or television ads, but because of the high cost, it is rare. When placing radio advertising and marketing spots, the advertiser must be careful to match the demographics of the average listener at any given radio station to the type of property being marketed. Expensive homes and hip-hop stations, for example, are not usually a good match.

Direct Mail

Direct mail is often used to promote a real estate company in a local metropolitan area. Not to be confused with SOI direct mailings, which are individually initiated and personal in nature, direct mail is institutional in nature and is designed to build the image of a real estate firm in a community. This type of mailing often involves sending pamphlets, postcards, brochures, or letters to several thousand homes at a time. It is more effective when a return-response card is enclosed. Licensees can use direct mail effectively as well. They can regularly mail to a set target group, such as a specific neighborhood they want to become well known in or a group of apartment owners. This type of mailing does not necessarily involve advertising a specific listing; it can be of a personal or professional promotion nature that shows the licensee's expertise to the target audience in that area.

Newsletters

Newsletters can be excellent company or personal promotion vehicles. Some companies and/or licensees mail many thousands of real estate newsletters a month to their local community. Each newsletter includes information of interest to the local community such as school events and town meetings. It can also position a firm or an individual licensee as the most effective one in the city and explain why. An easy-to-read contact number and a mail-back card should be attached for people interested in real estate services (selling or buying). This type of marketing program can be successful if you or your company are the first to launch it and if you are reliably consistent.

Telephone Directories

Most real estate firms are listed in some form of the Yellow Pages. Although this may be expensive, you or your firm can increase the

cost effectiveness of these publications by placing your ad in large, bold print and including your Internet address.

Press Releases

Press releases are really free advertisements. In fact, most of the articles in the real estate section of any given paper are press releases. Topics may include a licensee who received a certification or professional designation from National Association of REALTORS® (NAR) or C.A.R., an office grand opening, the opening of a new residential subdivision or condominium development that a real estate firm is marketing, office promotions, and the sale of a historic property. Press releases are submitted to newspapers in a double-spaced format in twelve-point type. They should be newsworthy and well written—ready for publication.

Be sure to include a glossy 5-by-7 photo of the person or the property with the identity of the person or property printed on the backside of the photograph.

Specialty Gifts

Many real estate firms budget for **specialty gifts** such as free local maps and directories in their advertising and marketing. Although the diminishing profit margins of many residential real estate operations in recent years has curtailed much of this type of promotion, they are still used extensively.

Many companies make various types of marketing items available to licensees "at cost." Other common items are calendars, notepads, and to-do list pads. These usually display the company name and/or logo, the licensee's name, and contact numbers and sometimes include the licensee's picture.

When ordering promotional items, be sure that any notepads or to-do list pads you order for mailing to clients or customers have "sticky" or magnetic backing. It helps if the item being sent is something worth keeping, preferably worth keeping within their field of vision where they can see it often, like on the refrigerator. Magnetic or countertop calendars, for example, are better than wall calendars because they are placed on the refrigerator or on the countertop. The wall calendar may be placed in a drawer with the good intention of putting it up sometime later. This seldom happens. Order event calendars with team sports information, such as game dates and names of opposing teams as well as "to-do" lists with magnetic backings for use on metallic refrigerator doors. Think about it. Of all the unsolicited mail you receive, how much do you keep and why? If you wouldn't keep it, don't send it to a client.

Outdoor Advertising

Outdoor advertising venues such as billboards, electric message boards at airports, window displays, and movie screens are all forms of advertising and marketing that have notable effect on public awareness. These venues are quite costly and are used almost exclusively by the large, multibranch real estate firms.

15.2 A BUDGET FOR YOUR BUSINESS PLAN

Two of the three largest expenditures a successful real estate company must budget for are advertising and marketing. Obtaining listings does a company little good without buyers. Advertising is one of the most important tools available to any broker/licensee involved in the process of attracting *attention*, developing *interest*, creating *desire*, and motivating *action*.

This also applies to the individual sales associates. A certain amount of money must be budgeted for advertising, marketing, and personal promotion. Many top sales associates set aside 12 to 20 percent of their commissions for advertising and marketing. Most successful real estate companies budget a similar amount from the company's share of commissions earned (the **company dollar**) for these same costs, including company promotion. Market conditions and the type of community in which the office is located often dictate how much money is budgeted.

There is an old saying: "You can't spend your way out of a bad market." The only time that a real estate firm or sales associate may want to increase advertising expenses beyond what is budgeted is when a bad market starts to get better or when they are trying to gain market share in a particular area.

15.3 THE ADVANTAGES OF NICHE MARKETING

Niche marketing is essentially a specialty market. Top performing licensees and successful real estate firms have found that once they have established a strong presence in a community they can take their market share even higher by focusing on one particular segment of the market and using a large portion of their advertising and marketing dollars to reach it.

The saturation effect of spending budgeted dollars in a more concentrated area or segment of the market tends to increase consumer awareness considerably. The name and reputation of the

sales associate or company grows fast because of increased visibility to the members of the targeted niche.

Some examples of **niche markets** are:

- Luxury home market: This market is usually heavily guarded "turf" and it will normally take a very concentrated effort over an extended period of time to successfully gain market share. It can happen if the licensee or company is totally committed and has enough revenue to sustain itself for what may be a two- to three-year campaign.
- Small apartment houses.
- Land or subdivision lots.
- Rental homes.
- Neighborhood subdivisions (specific geographic areas).
- First-time homebuyers.

15.4 COMPLIANCE WITH DEPARTMENT OF REAL ESTATE AND STATE AND FEDERAL STATUTES

Advertising and marketing of real property is regulated by California Real Estate Law, the Real Estate Commissioner's Regulations, and the Federal Consumer Protection Act (Truth-in-Lending Act). The following code sections, articles, and other information are placed here as a ready reference for you to use each time you write or place any ads or create any marketing materials.

California Real Estate Law (from the Business and Professions Code)

Code Section 10139 – "Penalties for Unlicensed Person"

Any unlicensed person acting as a licensee who advertises using words indicating that she is a real estate broker is subject to a fine not to exceed $20,000 and/or imprisonment in the county jail for a term not to exceed six months, or by both fine and imprisonment; or if a corporation, be punished by a fine not exceeding $60,000.

Code Section 10140 – "False Advertising"

Every officer or employee who knowingly advertises a false statement concerning any land or subdivision is subject to a fine of $1,000 and/or one year's imprisonment, or both. In addition, the licensee may have her license suspended or revoked.

Code Section 10140.5 – "Disclosure of Name"

Each advertisement published by a licensee that offers to assist in filing applications for the purchase or lease of government land must indicate the name of the broker for whom it is published and state that she is licensed as a real estate broker by the State of California.

Code Section 10140.6 – "Disclosure of Licensed Status"

(a) A licensee may not publish in any newspaper or periodical or by mail an ad for any activity for which a real estate license is required that does not contain a designation disclosure that she is performing acts for which a license is required.

(b)(1) (effective July 1, 2009) A real estate licensee shall disclose her license identification number on all solicitation materials intended to be the first point of contact with consumers and on real property purchase agreements when acting as a licensee in those transactions.

(2) For purposes of this section, "solicitation materials intended to be the first point of contact with consumers" include business cards, stationery, advertising fliers, and other materials designed to solicit the creation of a professional relationship between the licensee and a consumer and exclude an advertisement in print or electronic media and "for-sale" signs.

Code Section 10235 – "Misleading Advertisement"

A licensee may not advertise, print, display, publish, distribute, televise, or broadcast false or misleading statements regarding rates and terms or conditions for making, purchasing, or negotiating loans or real property sales contracts, nor may a licensee permit others to do so.

Code Section 10236.1 – "Inducements"

A licensee may not advertise to offer a prospective purchaser, borrower, or lender any gift as an inducement for making a loan or purchasing a promissory note secured directly by a lien on real property or a real property sales contract.

Code Section 10131.7 – "Mobile Home Advertising"

A licensee is prohibited from engaging in the following activities:

- Advertising a mobile home that is not in an established mobile home park or is not being sold with the land.
- Failing to withdraw an advertisement of a mobile home within forty-eight hours after removal from the market.

- Advertising or representing a used mobile home as a new one.
- Making a false statement that a mobile home is capable of traveling on California highways.
- Falsely advertising that no down payment is required on the sale of a mobile home when in fact one is required.

Real Estate Commissioner's Regulations

The real estate commissioner can adopt regulations that have the same force and intent as law.

Article 9, Section 2770 – "Advertising"

A salesperson may not advertise any service for which a license is required without identifying the name of her employing broker.

Article 9, Section 2770.1 – "Advertising License Designation"

Abbreviation such as "bro," or other similar term or abbreviation referring to "broker," is deemed sufficient identification in ads to comply with the Business and Professions Code.

Except where quoted these code sections and commissioner's rules are condensations of the actual regulations, and the reader is urged to read the code sections and rules in their entirety.

Article 9, Section 2773

This "new Commissioner's Regulation clarifies the materials which require disclosure of the license number. In addition to business cards and stationery, the regulation also requires the license number to be included on (i) websites owned, controlled, and/or maintained by the soliciting real estate licensee, and (ii) promotional and advertising fliers, brochures, email and regular mail, leaflets, and any marketing or promotional materials designed to solicit the creation of a professional relationship between the licensee and a consumer, or which is intended to incentivise, induce or entice a consumer to contact the licensee about any service for which a license is required."

NAR Code of Ethics

Although NAR code of ethics is not law, it imposes a standard of conduct on its entire REALTOR® membership. Abiding by the tenets of the code of ethics serves to keep real estate practitioners well within the proper boundaries of ethical and legal procedures and business practices.

Article 12 of the code of ethics deals with advertising and states in part:

REALTORS® shall be honest and truthful in their real estate communications and shall present a true picture in their advertising, marketing, and other representations. REALTORS® shall ensure that their status as real estate professionals [broker, salesperson, appraiser, property manager, and so on] is readily apparent in their advertising, marketing, and other representations, and that the recipients of all real estate communications are, or have been notified that those communications are from a real estate professional.

(Author's note: It should be made clear that the following Standards of Practice are examples only. One violates the specific article, not the "standard of practice." See "NAR Code of Ethics" in Chapter 3.)

12-4. REALTORS® shall not offer for sale or lease or advertise property without authority.

12-5. REALTORS® shall not advertise or permit any person employed by or affiliated with them to advertise listed property without disclosing the name of the firm.

12-6. REALTORS®, when advertising unlisted real property for sale/lease in which they have an ownership interest, shall disclose their status as both owners/landlords and REALTORS® or real estate licensees.

Truth-in-Lending Act

The **Truth-in-Lending Act**, or *Regulation Z* as it is commonly known, is a part of the federal Consumers Credit Protection Act of 1968. It requires disclosure of credit costs as a percentage of the loan as well as total finance charges. It is enforced by the Federal Trade Commission.

Truth-in-lending applies to credit extended with a finance charge or credit cost payable in more than four installments. If the amount or percentage of down payment, the number of payments or repayment period, or the amount of payment or amount of finance charges (called trigger terms) is included in any advertisement, the ad must include three elements:

1. The amount or percentage of down payment.
2. The terms of repayment.
3. The **annual percentage rate (APR)**, which is the "true" interest rate when points and other loan costs are included. The "nominal" or actual interest rate is stated on the promissory note.

These disclosures will not be triggered by advertising the APR only.

If creditors extend credit secured by a dwelling more than five times in a year, they must furnish the purchaser a truth-in-lending disclosure statement showing all loan facts. For first mortgages or loans used to purchase real property, the total amount of finance charges for the term of the loan need not be shown. Tax and insurance impounds are not loan costs and need not be listed on the disclosure statement.

The Truth-in-Lending Act makes **bait-and-switch advertising** a federal offense. Bait-and-switch advertising occurs when brokers/licensees advertise a property that is not really intended for sale or is "not available" in order to attract buyers for other property.

Rescission Rights

If the loan is for consumer credit secured by the borrower's residence, the borrower has the right to cancel the loan until midnight of the third business day following loan completion (signing of the loan documents). The rescission right does not apply to loans acquired during the initial purchase of a home (often called *purchase money loans*).

Exemptions

Several types of loans are exempt from all truth-in-lending disclosure requirements. Personal property loans over $25,000, interest-free loans with four or fewer installments, business loans, construction loans, and agricultural loans do not require the borrower to receive a truth-in-lending disclosure. Carryback loans for sellers (not exceeding five per year) and loans on nonowner-occupied properties, which are considered a business, are also exempt from any disclosures.

SUMMARY

Advertising is the process of attracting someone's attention to a product or service. Its main focus is on obtaining a sale. Marketing is the process of building or enhancing the reputation or image of a person, company, or large project.

People generally don't read ads, they skim them. Advertising is more effective when the AIDA formula is used as it attracts more interested customers.

Personal advertising should include the use of a name tag, picture business cards, magnetic car signs, use of the company's website and a personal website, classified advertising (for both buyers and sellers), e-mail advertising to your SOI database, the Internet, call-capture 800 telephone numbers, direct mail, and real estate magazines.

You learned that placing blind ads is illegal and you were reminded not to violate the fair housing laws when writing ads (describe the property, not the buyers), and you learned to create advertising that tied features to benefits that would create desire in the reader.

You learned how radio, television, direct mail, newsletters, telephone directories, and press releases are effective marketing techniques and how the use of "sticky" specialty gifts will keep you and your company in front of people all the time. You also learned about the requirement to include your real estate license number on all first-contact materials: business cards, fliers, company and personal stationery, and so on.

You learned the percentages of income successful licensees and companies budget for advertising and marketing, when to increase your advertising and marketing budget to take advantage of market conditions, and the powerful impact that niche marketing can have on the growth of your business.

Finally, you learned about many state laws and commissioner's rules and regulations that pertain to advertising and marketing in brokerage and lending practices.

CLASS DISCUSSION TOPICS

1. Prepare two classified ads for the home in which you live. One should have an attention-getting heading and the other should have a feature heading. Read both to the class and discuss which one is the better ad.

2. Check the websites of three local brokers. Print out the main page of each site and bring them to class for a discussion as to which one is the best and why.

3. Research as many media forms as you can and obtain all the ways a real estate company in your area advertises. Discuss the effectiveness of the program as a whole.

4. Describe what you think your favorite niche market is and why.

CHAPTER 15 QUIZ

1. The AIDA approach to ad writing includes
   A. action.
   B. intent.
   C. desire.
   D. Both a and c.

2. Which of the following are included in personal advertising?
   A. Name tags
   B. Business cards
   C. Personal website
   D. All of the above

3. Which of the following places is best for marketing a parcel of heavy industrial land?
   A. The local weekly newspaper
   B. The Internet
   C. A trade magazine
   D. An upscale monthly magazine

4. Direct mail gets a better response if you
   A. include a return response card.
   B. mail to more people than you intended.
   C. mail early in the month when there is less mail.
   D. use first-class postage instead of bulk mail.

5. A licensee with a limited advertising budget would probably use all of the following advertising media except
   A. the Internet.
   B. area magazines.
   C. television.
   D. magnetic car signs.

6. A blind ad is an ad that fails to include which of the following?
   A. The broker's identification
   B. The price of the property
   C. The property address
   D. None of the above

7. A system of tracking ad calls
   A. needs close follow-up by the broker.
   B. should be very simple to use.
   C. may include a different phone number for each advertised property.
   D. All of the above.

8. Which of the following regulates advertising and marketing?
   A. California Real Estate Law
   B. Real Estate Commissioner's Rules and Regulations
   C. NAR code of ethics
   D. All of the above

9. Which of the following is not a violation of the Truth-in-Lending Act?
   A. Advertising a property the licensee does not intend to sell.
   B. Advertising the APR only.
   C. Stating the amount of down payment required and failing to state the terms of repayment and the APR.
   D. All of the above.

10. Internet advertising of property listings is most effective when
   A. multiple pictures are included.
   B. a virtual tour is available for viewing.
   C. a link is available for the viewer to contact the listing licensee.
   D. All of the above.

Chapter

16

IMPORTANT PHRASES AND TERMS

Accredited Management Organization (AMO)

Bonuses

Buyer's representative

Certified Commercial Investment Member (CCIM)

Certified Property Manager (CPM)

Communication

Condominium association management

Escrow coordinator

Exculpatory clause

Gross lease

Husband/wife team

Industrial property

Institute of Real Estate Management (IREM)

Land brokerage

Licensed assistants

Management agreement

Net lease

Office buildings

Percentage lease

Real Estate Professional Assistant (REPA)

REALTORS® Land Institute (RLI)

Rent survey

Residential income property

Retail shopping centers

Self-storage facilities

Seventy-hour syndrome

Specialization

Standard of care

Sublease

Thirty-day notice

Three-day notice

Unlawful detainer action

Alternate Real Estate Careers

STUDENT LEARNING OUTCOMES

Upon completion of this chapter, the student will be able to:

- Compare and contrast the different responsibilities of commercial and residential licensees.
- Recognize various real estate advanced designations.
- Compare and evaluate duties of a property manager.
- Compare and contrast characteristics of gross versus net leases.
- Distinguish tenant and landlord responsibilities.
- Explain the legal process of eviction.
- Compare and contrast the advantages and disadvantages of a licensed versus an unlicensed assistant.

16.1 COMMERCIAL REAL ESTATE BROKERAGE

Although residential and commercial real estate brokerage share many of the same traits, there is a vast difference in what is required to function at a high level of proficiency in each field. The value of residential real estate is determined primarily by using "comps" or recent sales statistics, whereas commercial real estate is valued based on its highest and best use and the income that is or can be produced from that use. To assess the accurate value of a parcel of commercial real estate, the commercial practitioner must first determine the property's highest and best use, which may sometimes be different than its current use.

A **rent survey** must then be conducted to determine the property's income and how close it compares to current market rental

rates in the area at that time. The property's value is then determined by applying one or more methods of measuring its financial return to an investor. For instance, if an apartment house was being evaluated for its current market value and the rent survey found that its rental income was substantially below the current market, this would factor in to its current value. A buyer would not pay the going capitalization rate for apartment houses in the area based on the "pro forma" rents (the current "optimal" rents that could be charged) because she would have to increase the rents over time. The real value of that building on that day would be somewhere between the capitalization rate of the pro forma rents and the current rents. Failure to do a rent survey can result in substantially overvaluing or undervaluing a commercial property.

Education and Specialization

The National Association of REALTORS® has many courses that may be taken to becoming certified in commercial real estate, including the **Certified Commercial Investment Member (CCIM)** designation offered through the REALTORS® National Marketing Institute. Its course content covers the broad spectrum of analysis and tax issues concerning commercial real estate. The CCIM is one of the most comprehensive series of courses for someone serious about becoming a well-informed commercial practitioner.

Many real estate practitioners wish to specialize in only one type of commercial brokerage. If the geographic area you practice in is large enough to warrant this, it is highly recommended as the in-depth knowledge obtained through **specialization** in one area earns the practitioner far more credibility in the eyes of her clients.

Other specialized areas with graduate certifications include, but are not limited to, the **CPM** or **Certified Property Manager** offered through the **Institute of Real Estate Management** for licensees who wish to specialize in property management, and the **RLI** designation offered through the **REALTORS® Land Institute** for licensees who wish to specialize in **land brokerage** and development.

A licensee who decides to specialize in commercial real estate is well advised to affiliate with a company that has excellent training. It is also advisable to have a considerable cash reserve, as it can often take a year or longer before the first commission check arrives. Although the sales commissions for commercial brokers are usually larger than most residential sales, they are fewer and often more sporadic than residential brokerage fees.

Commercial brokers work on a variety of income properties, including the following:

- **Industrial property** is highly specialized and includes light-to-heavy manufacturing plants, assembly plants, chemical plants, and others; the majority of these are owner/user properties and are seldom sold as investments.

- **Self-storage facilities** are the rows of little "garages" you see as you drive most interstate highways.

- **Office buildings** will vary in size from a small building of only about 2,000 square feet to multistory buildings with a million or more square feet. In large urban areas, it is not uncommon to see a multistory building with a "mixed use" that includes retail shops on the ground floor, office space on the next several floors, and apartments or condominiums above that.

- **Residential income property** may include everything from a small duplex to a large apartment complex of several hundred units.

- **Retail shopping centers** include small strip centers, neighborhood centers, power centers, discount centers, specialty centers such as medical or dental buildings, and regional malls.

Each type of commercial property has its own unique issues that the commercial licensees must know to give competent investor representation. For instance, office buildings can be in great demand at one point in time, only to experience a glut on the market with high vacancies at a later date because of overbuilding or a weak economy, which can stifle demand for office space. Apartment complexes experience high and low vacancy rates because of a rise or fall in employment in an area. High or low long-term interest rates also have an effect on apartment vacancies: If rates are low, more people can afford to buy homes so vacancies rise; when rates are high, fewer people can afford to buy so vacancies are lower. Retail shopping centers can be vulnerable to extended vacancies in a depressed economy. Retail sales decline, forcing tenants out of business.

All income-producing property is sensitive to interest rates. When an income-producing property is offered for sale, any increase in interest rates takes net operating income, and value, right off the property's bottom line.

The two ways to enter commercial real estate are:

1. Work for a large commercial real estate firm. The advantage here is in the training you will receive and the credibility you will have with the commercial property owners you will come in

contact with. The disadvantage is that it may be a long time before you collect a commission check, quite often a year or more.

2. Work as a residential licensee while taking courses, learning the commercial business, and starting to make regular contact with commercial property owners. As you increase your knowledge of the commercial market in your area and start to build a clientele, you will spend less time on residential activities, eventually making a complete switch to commercial real estate over a set period of time. The disadvantage of this method is that the residential firm you are with may not have credibility as a commercial firm to the local commercial property owners. You may lose business because of it. A carefully built marketing strategy will often overcome this objection.

If your market is large enough to allow it, specialize in the purchase, sale, or leasing of a specific type of commercial property. Your enhanced knowledge and expertise will benefit the commercial owners you contact, resulting in greater credibility and more business.

16.2 PROPERTY MANAGEMENT AND LEASING

Property management has become a specialized field, with some firms specializing in residential income properties and others only managing retail shopping centers, office buildings, or some other type of commercial property.

Most investors do not want to be involved in the day-to-day management of their commercial real estate investments; instead, they employ the services of a professional firm to oversee them. This is often advisable from a legal standpoint as well as an operational one. Many laws must be adhered to, such as the Americans with Disabilities Act (ADA) and fair housing issues, which were covered earlier in this book. Serious commercial property owners usually want the added benefit of a professional manager handling compliance with these issues.

An **Accredited Management Organization (AMO)** designation is given by IREM to a company that meets the following standards:

- At least one CPM in charge
- Annual accreditation renewal
- Adherence to minimum standards and the rules set by IREM
- Property management as a primary activity

Many property management firms specialize only in **condominium association management**. These firms collect homeowners' association dues, send newsletters, hold the required annual meetings, enforce sanctions against homeowners who violate rules, provide landscape and common area maintenance and management, prepare tax returns, and handle worker's compensation and insurance claims. Virtually all property management firms work under a **management agreement**, whereby the firm is empowered with specific duties and obligations on behalf of the property owner. The three types of property managers include:

- Licensed Property Manager. This person is a real estate licensee employed by a real estate firm that manages property or an individual broker who manages property for others for a fee. Persons working under the direct supervision of a licensed broker specializing in property management need not be licensed.

- Individual Property Manager. This person manages a single property for an owner and may or may not be a real estate licensee. This is usually a salaried position and may or may not include free or reduced rent in one of the building's units.

- Resident Manager. A resident manager lives on the premises and may be employed by the owner or a property management firm. This person usually has special training or previous experience and the type of personality that lends itself to dealing well with tenants. Some necessary traits include:
  - Sales skills necessary to "show and sell" the rental units.
  - Computer and data analysis skills.
  - The ability to identify problematic maintenance issues and ensure the proper and timely care of the property.
  - A "take-charge" attitude and a high degree of confidence.
  - Accuracy in handling bookkeeping duties, money, and bank deposits.
  - A keen sense of what is happening on the premises and in the area.
  - The ability to select residents based on credit reports and personal references.
  - Ability to make timely and accurate reports.

State-Defined Responsibilities

A property manager is responsible to refrain from personal profit without the principal's full knowledge and consent; show good faith and loyalty to her principal; fully disclose all pertinent facts;

perform her duties with skill, care, and due diligence; and avoid commingling funds.

In addition, the California Department of Real Estate (DRE) provides a list of specific duties that each property manager is charged with. These include:

- Paying insurance premiums and taxes and recommending tax appeals when warranted.
- Establishing the rental schedule that will bring the highest yield consistent with good economics.
- Keeping abreast of economic and competitive market conditions.
- Merchandising the space and collecting the rents.
- Frequently inspecting vacant space.
- Creating and supervising maintenance schedules and repairs.
- Planning alterations and modernizing programs.
- Supervising all purchasing.
- Advertising and publicizing vacancies through selected media and broker lists.
- Developing a policy for tenant resident relations.
- Auditing and paying bills.
- Maintaining proper records and making regular reports to the owner.
- Hiring, instructing, and maintaining satisfactory personnel to staff the building(s).
- Qualifying and investigating prospective tenants' credit.
- Preparing and decorating specifications and secure estimates.
- Preparing and executing leases.

Specific Duties

Under a property management agreement, the manager assumes all executive functions of the owner and is fully in charge of the details connected with the operation and physical upkeep of the property (see Figure 16.1).

A conscientious manager is responsible for the following:

- Handle residents' questions promptly and properly.
- Never deny a resident's request without clearly stating why.
- Advise renters what is expected of them and what they can expect from the owner (this should be in writing as a matter of policy).
- Treat residents fairly and sympathetically.
- Use care to protect the tenants' and prospective tenants' legal rights with regard to fair housing and ADA issues and so on.

FIGURE 16.1   Property Management Agreement

PROPERTY MANAGEMENT AGREEMENT
(C.A.R. Form PMA, Revised 4/09)

CALIFORNIA
ASSOCIATION
OF REALTORS®

_____ ("Owner"), and
_____ ("Broker"), agree as follows:

1. **APPOINTMENT OF BROKER:** Owner hereby appoints and grants Broker the exclusive right to rent, lease, operate and manage the property(ies) known as _____
_____ and any additional property that may later be added to this Agreement ("Property"), upon the terms below, for the period beginning (date) _____ and ending (date) _____, at 11:59 PM.
(If checked:) ☐ Either party may terminate this Property Management Agreement ("Agreement") on at least 30 days written notice _____ months after the original commencement date of this Agreement. After the exclusive term expires, this Agreement shall continue as a non-exclusive agreement that either party may terminate by giving at least 30 days written notice to the other.

2. **BROKER ACCEPTANCE:** Broker accepts the appointment and grant, and agrees to:
   A. Use due diligence in the performance of this Agreement.
   B. Furnish the services of its firm for the rental, leasing, operation and management of the Property.

3. **AUTHORITY AND POWERS:** Owner grants Broker the authority and power, at Owner's expense, to:
   A. ADVERTISING: Display FOR RENT/LEASE and similar signs on the Property and advertise the availability of the Property, or any part thereof, for rental or lease.
   B. RENTAL;LEASING: Initiate, sign, renew, modify or cancel rental agreements and leases for the Property, or any part thereof; collect and give receipts for rents, other fees, charges and security deposits. Any lease or rental agreement executed by Broker for Owner shall not exceed _____ year(s) or ☐ shall be month-to-month. Unless Owner authorizes a lower amount, rent shall be: ☐ at market rate; OR ☐ a minimum of $ _____ per _____; OR ☐ see attachment.
   C. TENANCY TERMINATION: Sign and serve in Owner's name notices that are required or appropriate; commence and prosecute actions to evict tenants; recover possession of the Property in Owner's name; recover rents and other sums due; and, when expedient, settle, compromise and release claims, actions and suits and/or reinstate tenancies.
   D. REPAIR;MAINTENANCE: Make, cause to be made, and/or supervise repairs, improvements, alterations and decorations to the Property; purchase, and pay bills for, services and supplies. Broker shall obtain prior approval of Owner for all expenditures over $ _____ for any one item. Prior approval shall not be required for monthly or recurring operating charges or, if in Broker's opinion, emergency expenditures over the maximum are needed to protect the Property or other property(ies) from damage, prevent injury to persons, avoid suspension of necessary services, avoid penalties or fines, or suspension of services to tenants required by a lease or rental agreement or by law, including, but not limited to, maintaining the Property in a condition fit for human habitation as required by Civil Code §§ 1941 and 1941.1 and Health and Safety Code §§ 17920.3 and 17920.10.
   E. REPORTS, NOTICES AND SIGNS: Comply with federal, state or local law requiring delivery of reports or notices and/or posting of signs or notices.
   F. CONTRACTS;SERVICES: Contract, hire, supervise and/or discharge firms and persons, including utilities, required for the operation and maintenance of the Property. Broker may perform any of Broker's duties through attorneys, agents, employees, or independent contractors and, except for persons working in Broker's firm, shall not be responsible for their acts, omissions, defaults, negligence and/or costs of same.
   G. EXPENSE PAYMENTS: Pay expenses and costs for the Property from Owner's funds held by Broker, unless otherwise directed by Owner. Expenses and costs may include, but are not limited to, property management compensation, fees and charges, expenses for goods and services, property taxes and other taxes, Owner's Association dues, assessments, loan payments and insurance premiums.
   H. SECURITY DEPOSITS: Receive security deposits from tenants, which deposits shall be ☐ given to Owner, or ☐ placed in Broker's trust account and, if held in Broker's trust account, pay from Owner's funds all interest on tenants' security deposits if required by local law or ordinance. Owner shall be responsible to tenants for return of security deposits and all interest due on security deposits held by Owner.
   I. TRUST FUNDS: Deposit all receipts collected for Owner, less any sums properly deducted or disbursed, in a financial institution whose deposits are insured by an agency of the United States government. The funds shall be held in a trust account separate from Broker's personal accounts. Broker shall not be liable in event of bankruptcy or failure of a financial institution.
   J. RESERVES: Maintain a reserve in Broker's trust account of $ _____.
   K. DISBURSEMENTS: Disburse Owner's funds held in Broker's trust account in the following order:
      (1) Compensation due Broker under paragraph 6.
      (2) All other operating expenses, costs and disbursements payable from Owner's funds held by Broker.
      (3) Reserves and security deposits held by Broker.
      (4) Balance to Owner.
   L. OWNER DISTRIBUTION: Remit funds, if any are available, monthly (or ☐ _____), to Owner.
   M. OWNER STATEMENTS: Render monthly (or ☐ _____), statements of receipts, expenses and charges for each Property.
   N. BROKER FUNDS: Broker shall not advance Broker's own funds in connection with the Property or this Agreement.
   O. KEYSAFE/LOCKBOX: ☐ (If checked) Owner authorizes the use of a keysafe/lockbox to allow entry into the Property and agrees to sign a keysafe/ lockbox addendum (C.A.R. Form KLA).

Owner's Initials (_____)(_____)
Broker's Initials (_____)(_____)

Reviewed by _____ Date _____

EQUAL HOUSING OPPORTUNITY

PROPERTY MANAGEMENT AGREEMENT (PMA PAGE 1 OF 3)

FIGURE 16.1   (*Continued*)

Owner Name: _____   Date: _____

4. OWNER RESPONSIBILITIES: Owner shall:

    A. Provide all documentation, records and disclosures as required by law or required by Broker to manage and operate the Property, and immediately notify Broker if Owner becomes aware of any change in such documentation, records or disclosures, or any matter affecting the habitability of the Property.

    B. Indemnify, defend and hold harmless Broker, and all persons in Broker's firm, regardless of responsibility, from all costs, expenses, suits, liabilities, damages, attorney fees and claims of every type, including but not limited to those arising out of injury or death of any person, or damage to any real or personal property of any person, including Owner, for: **(i)** any repairs performed by Owner or by others hired directly by Owner; or **(ii)** those relating to the management, leasing, rental, security deposits, or operation of the Property by Broker, or any person in Broker's firm, or the performance or exercise of any of the duties, powers or authorities granted to Broker.

    C. Maintain the Property in a condition fit for human habitation as required by Civil Code §§ 1941 and 1941.1 and Health and Safety Code §§ 17920.3 and 17920.10 and other applicable law.

    D. Pay all interest on tenants' security deposits if required by local law or ordinance.

    E. Carry and pay for: **(i)** public and premises liability insurance in an amount of no less than $1,000,000; and **(ii)** property damage and worker's compensation insurance adequate to protect the interests of Owner and Broker. Broker shall be, and Owner authorizes Broker to be, named as an additional insured party on Owner's policies.

    F. Pay any late charges, penalties and/or interest imposed by lenders or other parties for failure to make payment to those parties, if the failure is due to insufficient funds in Broker's trust account available for such payment.

    G. Immediately replace any funds required if there are insufficient funds in Broker's trust account to cover Owner's responsibilities.

5. DISCLOSURE:

    A. LEAD-BASED PAINT

      (1) ☐   The Property was constructed on or after January 1, 1978.

    OR (2) ☐   The Property was constructed prior to 1978.

        (i)   Owner has no knowledge of lead-based paint or lead-based paint hazards in the housing except:_____
_____.

        (ii) Owner has no reports or records pertaining to lead-based paint or lead-based paint hazards in the housing, except the following, which Owner shall provide to Broker: _____.

    B. POOL/SPA DRAIN

    Any pool or spa on the property does (or, ☐ does not) have an approved anti-entrapment drain cover, device or system.

6. COMPENSATION:

    A. Owner agrees to pay Broker fees in the amounts indicated below for:

      (1) Management: _____.

      (2) Renting or Leasing: _____.

      (3) Evictions: _____.

      (4) Preparing Property for rental or lease: _____.

      (5) Managing Property during extended periods of vacancy: _____.

      (6) An overhead and service fee added to the cost of all work performed by, or at the direction of, Broker: _____.

      (7) Other: _____.

    B. This Agreement does not include providing on-site management services, property sales, refinancing, preparing Property for sale or refinancing, modernization, fire or major damage restoration, rehabilitation, obtaining income tax, accounting or legal advice, representation before public agencies, advising on proposed new construction, debt collection, counseling, attending Owner's Association meetings or _____
_____.

    If Owner requests Broker to perform services not included in this Agreement, a fee shall be agreed upon before these services are performed.

    C. Broker may divide compensation, fees and charges due under this Agreement in any manner acceptable to Broker.

    D. Owner further agrees that:

      (1) Broker may receive and keep fees and charges from tenants for: **(i)** requesting an assignment of lease or sublease of the Property; **(ii)** processing credit applications; **(iii)** any returned checks and/or (☐ if checked) late payments; and **(iv)** any other services that are not in conflict with this Agreement.

      (2) Broker may perform any of Broker's duties, and obtain necessary products and services, through affiliated companies or organizations in which Broker may own an interest. Broker may receive fees, commissions and/or profits from these affiliated companies or organizations. Broker has an ownership interest in the following affiliated companies or organizations: _____
_____.

      Broker shall disclose to Owner any other such relationships as they occur. Broker shall not receive any fees, commissions or profits from unaffiliated companies or organizations in the performance of this Agreement, without prior disclosure to Owner.

      (3) Other: _____

7. AGENCY RELATIONSHIPS: Broker shall act, and Owner hereby consents to Broker acting, as dual agent for Owner and tenant(s) in any resulting transaction. If the Property includes residential property with one-to-four dwelling units and this Agreement permits a tenancy in excess of one year, Owner acknowledges receipt of the "Disclosure Regarding Agency Relationships" (C.A.R. Form AD). Owner understands that Broker may have or obtain property management agreements on other property, and that potential tenants may consider, make offers on, or lease through Broker, property the same as or similar to Owner's Property. Owner consents to Broker's representation of other owners' properties before, during and after the expiration of this Agreement.

8. NOTICES: Any written notice to Owner or Broker required under this Agreement shall be served by sending such notice by first class mail or other agreed-to delivery method to that party at the address below, or at any different address the parties may later designate for this purpose. Notice shall be deemed received three (3) calendar days after deposit into the United States mail OR ☐ _____

Owner's Initials (_____)(_____)
Broker's Initials (_____)(_____)

Reviewed by _____ Date _____

PROPERTY MANAGEMENT AGREEMENT (PMA PAGE 2 OF 3)

FIGURE 16.1 *(Continued)*

Owner Name: _____   Date: _____

9. **DISPUTE RESOLUTION**

   A. **MEDIATION:** Owner and Broker agree to mediate any dispute or claim arising between them out of this Agreement, or any resulting transaction before resorting to arbitration or court action, subject to paragraph 9B(2) below. Paragraph 9B(2) below applies whether or not the arbitration provision is initialed. Mediation fees, if any, shall be divided equally among the parties involved. If, for any dispute or claim to which this paragraph applies, any party commences an action based on a dispute or claim to which this paragraph applies, without first attempting to resolve the matter through mediation, or refuses to mediate after a request has been made, then that party shall not be entitled to recover attorney fees, even if they would otherwise be available to that party in any such action. THIS MEDIATION PROVISION APPLIES WHETHER OR NOT THE ARBITRATION PROVISION IS INITIALED.

   B. **ARBITRATION OF DISPUTES:** (1) Owner and Broker agree that any dispute or claim in law or equity arising between them regarding the obligation to pay compensation under this agreement, which is not settled through mediation, shall be decided by neutral, binding arbitration, including and subject to paragraph 9B(2) below. The arbitrator shall be a retired judge or justice, or an attorney with at least 5 years of residential real estate law experience, unless the parties mutually agree to a different arbitrator, who shall render an award in accordance with substantive California Law. The parties shall have the right to discovery in accordance with Code of Civil Procedure § 1283.05. In all other respects, the arbitration shall be conducted in accordance with Title 9 of Part III of the California Code of Civil Procedure. Judgment upon the award of the arbitrator(s) may be entered in any court having jurisdiction. Interpretation of this agreement to arbitrate shall be governed by the Federal Arbitration Act.
   (2) EXCLUSIONS FROM MEDIATION AND ARBITRATION: The following matters are excluded from mediation and arbitration hereunder: **(i)** a judicial or non-judicial foreclosure or other action or proceeding to enforce a deed of trust, mortgage, or installment land sale contract as defined in Civil Code § 2985; **(ii)** an unlawful detainer action; **(iii)** the filing or enforcement of a mechanic's lien; and **(iv)** any matter that is within the jurisdiction of a probate, small claims, or bankruptcy court. The filing of a court action to enable the recording of a notice of pending action, for order of attachment, receivership, injunction, or other provisional remedies, shall not constitute a waiver of the mediation and arbitration provisions.
   "NOTICE: BY INITIALING IN THE SPACE BELOW YOU ARE AGREEING TO HAVE ANY DISPUTE ARISING OUT OF THE MATTERS INCLUDED IN THE 'ARBITRATION OF DISPUTES' PROVISION DECIDED BY NEUTRAL ARBITRATION AS PROVIDED BY CALIFORNIA LAW AND YOU ARE GIVING UP ANY RIGHTS YOU MIGHT POSSESS TO HAVE THE DISPUTE LITIGATED IN A COURT OR JURY TRIAL. BY INITIALING IN THE SPACE BELOW YOU ARE GIVING UP YOUR JUDICIAL RIGHTS TO DISCOVERY AND APPEAL, UNLESS THOSE RIGHTS ARE SPECIFICALLY INCLUDED IN THE 'ARBITRATION OF DISPUTES' PROVISION. IF YOU REFUSE TO SUBMIT TO ARBITRATION AFTER AGREEING TO THIS PROVISION, YOU MAY BE COMPELLED TO ARBITRATE UNDER THE AUTHORITY OF THE CALIFORNIA CODE OF CIVIL PROCEDURE. YOUR AGREEMENT TO THIS ARBITRATION PROVISION IS VOLUNTARY."
   "WE HAVE READ AND UNDERSTAND THE FOREGOING AND AGREE TO SUBMIT DISPUTES ARISING OUT OF THE MATTERS INCLUDED IN THE 'ARBITRATION OF DISPUTES' PROVISION TO NEUTRAL ARBITRATION."

   Owner's Initials _____ / _____   Broker's Initials _____ / _____

10. **EQUAL HOUSING OPPORTUNITY:** The Property is offered in compliance with federal, state and local anti-discrimination laws.

11. **ATTORNEY FEES:** In any action, proceeding or arbitration between Owner and Broker regarding the obligation to pay compensation under this Agreement, the prevailing Owner or Broker shall be entitled to reasonable attorney fees and costs from the non-prevailing Owner or Broker, except as provided in paragraph 9A.

12. **ADDITIONAL TERMS:** ☐ Keysafe/Lockbox Addendum (C.A.R. Form KLA); ☐ Lead-Based Paint and Lead-Based Paint Hazards Disclosure (C.A.R. Form FLD) _____

13. **TIME OF ESSENCE; ENTIRE CONTRACT; CHANGES:** Time is of the essence. All understandings between the parties are incorporated in this Agreement. Its terms are intended by the parties as a final, complete and exclusive expression of their Agreement with respect to its subject matter, and may not be contradicted by evidence of any prior agreement or contemporaneous oral agreement. If any provision of this Agreement is held to be ineffective or invalid, the remaining provisions will nevertheless be given full force and effect. Neither this Agreement nor any provision in it may be extended, amended, modified, altered or changed except in writing. This Agreement and any supplement, addendum or modification, including any copy, may be signed in two or more counterparts, all of which shall constitute one and the same writing.

Owner warrants that Owner is the owner of the Property or has the authority to execute this contract. Owner acknowledges Owner has read, understands, accepts and has received a copy of the Agreement.

Owner _____   Date _____
Owner _____
    Print Name   Social Security/Tax ID # (for tax reporting purposes)
Address _____ City _____   State _____ Zip _____
Telephone _____ Fax _____   E-mail _____

Owner _____   Date _____
Owner _____
    Print Name   Social Security/Tax ID # (for tax reporting purposes)
Address _____ City _____   State _____ Zip _____
Telephone _____ Fax _____   E-mail _____

Real Estate Broker (Firm) _____   Date _____
By (Agent) _____   DRE Lic. #: _____
Address _____ City _____   State _____ Zip _____
Telephone _____ Fax _____   E-mail _____

THIS FORM HAS BEEN APPROVED BY THE CALIFORNIA ASSOCIATION OF REALTORS® (C.A.R.). NO REPRESENTATION IS MADE AS TO THE LEGAL VALIDITY OR ADEQUACY OF ANY PROVISION IN ANY SPECIFIC TRANSACTION. A REAL ESTATE BROKER IS THE PERSON QUALIFIED TO ADVISE ON REAL ESTATE TRANSACTIONS. IF YOU DESIRE LEGAL OR TAX ADVICE, CONSULT AN APPROPRIATE PROFESSIONAL.
This form is available for use by the entire real estate industry. It is not intended to identify the user as a REALTOR®. REALTOR® is a registered collective membership mark which may be used only by members of the NATIONAL ASSOCIATION OF REALTORS® who subscribe to its Code of Ethics.

R E B S
I N C

Published and Distributed by:
REAL ESTATE BUSINESS SERVICES, INC.
a subsidiary of the California Association of REALTORS®
525 South Virgil Avenue, Los Angeles, California 90020

Reviewed by _____ Date _____   EQUAL HOUSING OPPORTUNITY

PMA REVISED 4/09 (PAGE 3 OF 3)

PROPERTY MANAGEMENT AGREEMENT (PMA PAGE 3 OF 3)

Source: Reprinted with permission of California Association of REALTORS®.

Establishing Rent Schedules

The law of supply and demand in an area dictates the amount set for level rents. To set proper rent schedules, the manager must make a thorough analysis of the neighborhood and immediate area. The analysis should include, but is not limited to:

- Current area vacancy factors.
- Availability of transportation, recreation, churches, and schools, and proximity to shopping.
- Trends in population growth and occupants per unit.
- The character, age, and condition of the immediate neighborhood.
- The financial ability and size of families in the immediate area.
- Directional growth of the community and the economic health of local businesses.
- The condition of the housing market versus population growth trends.

The objective of good property management is to achieve a level of rent and vacancy that provides the highest net return to the property owner. Conducting regular rental surveys and establishing competitive rent schedules is primary to this objective. Bad tenants who use and often abuse a property while not paying rent are worse than having a vacant unit. The only competition a vacant unit has is other vacant units, not rented units.

Accounting Records

Although the number of bookkeeping records needed depends on the type of property managed and the volume of business involved, the selection and maintenance of an adequate trust account system is essential in property management because of the fiduciary nature of the business. The property management broker is charged with the responsibility of trust fund recordkeeping. An annual audit by an outside accounting firm is highly recommended.

The following are reasons for keeping accounting records:

- The law states that a separate record must be kept for each managed property.
- They provide the broker with a source of information when problems arise or an inquiry is made.
- Income tax purposes.

- They serve as controls in analyzing costs, preparing budgets, and evaluating income and expenses.
- Contractual relations and the Business and Professions Code mandate a complete and accurate accounting of all funds.
- For full disclosure and accounting to third parties with interest in the property.
- The fiduciary relationship between the owner and the manager dictates a full disclosure.

Trust Account Ledger

Section 2831 of the commissioner's regulations (and BPC §10145) requires that a trust account ledger for all property management accounts be established. Rents are posted to the account as they come in and any money paid out on behalf of the owner is recorded as each payment is made. These payments can include loans, property taxes, utilities, management fees and/or commissions, repairs, and other costs of operation. The manager sends a statement to the owner at the end of each month, along with any net rental proceeds, if so directed. Today, this is often done by computer.

Leasing

A primary responsibility of a property manager is leasing property or acting as a consultant in the drafting of a lease. When a lease is created, the owner is the *lessor* and the tenant is the *lessee*. A leasehold estate arises when an owner or a property manager acting as the owner's representative grants a tenant the right to occupy the owner's property for a specified period of time for a valuable consideration.

The four basic types of leasehold estates are the estate for years, the estate from period to period, the estate at sufferance, and the estate at will.

Estate for years is an estate that continues for a definite fixed period of time. The duration of the lease may be for any time period from days to years.

Estate from period to period is commonly called a *periodic tenancy*. The lease continues from period to period, year to year, month to month, or week to week, as designated in the lease agreement. The most common periodic tenancy is month to month.

Estate at sufferance is created when a tenant obtains possession of a property legally but remains on the property without the owner's consent after the expiration of the tenant's leasehold interest. A tenant at sufferance can be removed like a trespasser unless rent is paid to and accepted by the owner or licensee. The estate then becomes a periodic tenancy based on the period for which the rent is paid.

Estate at will has no set time limit. Possession is given with permission, but no agreement is made with respect to rent. For example, a tenant takes possession before the lease terms are agreed to. In California, such an estate may only be terminated by either party giving a **thirty-day notice (CCC §789)**.

Types of Leases

Property managers usually work with three basic types of leases: gross lease, net lease, and percentage lease.

Gross lease

Under a **gross lease** the tenant pays a fixed amount of rent and the owner pays all other operating expenses of the property. Most residential leases and small commercial leases are gross leases.

To keep a tenant from holding over at the end of the lease term, the lease might include a holdover clause, which materially raises the rental rate. This encourages the tenant to either vacate the premises or sign a new lease.

Net Lease

Under the terms of a **net lease** or triple-net lease, the tenant must pay all or part of the operating costs of the property, except for loan payments, also called *debt servicing*. In a triple-net or NNN lease, the utilities, real estate taxes, repairs and maintenance, and other special assessments are the tenant's responsibility. In a double-net or NN lease, the tenant and owner each pay certain operating expenses. For instance, Starbuck's drive-through properties usually require the owner to pay for exterior paint, parking lot, and roof maintenance.

Net leases are common in commercial leases for properties such as office buildings and fast food restaurants and are usually long term. Because of the longer term of the lease, it usually contains an escalator clause that provides for annual rental increases to keep the initial rent even with the cost of living index as it rises over time. The increases are usually tied to the *Consumer Price Index*.

Percentage Lease

A **percentage lease** generally provides for a stated percentage of the gross receipts of a business to be paid as rent. The percentage lease is usually tied in with a minimum rent and a covenant to remain in business and often includes minimum hours of operation and a covenant by the lessee not to conduct any off-site sales activity. Percentage leases are typically used in restaurants and shopping centers and often contain a requirement that each tenant spend a certain percentage of its gross income on cooperative advertising in conjunction with the other tenants in the center.

Many percentage leases contain a *recapture clause*, which provides that, if a tenant does not attain a desired gross, the lessor has the right to terminate the lease.

Many retail shopping centers have an anchor tenant or a shadow anchor tenant. An anchor tenant is a business—a large chain supermarket such as Safeway or a Walgreen's Drug Store located in or immediately adjacent to a retail center that draws a large number of customers to the center. Commonly, leases in these types of centers have a clause that states that if the anchor tenant or shadow anchor tenant in a retail center immediately adjacent to a center vacates, the other tenants in or immediately adjacent to the "vacated" center are or, under certain conditions, may be entitled to a rent abatement until the anchor tenant is replaced.

Different businesses are charged different percentages of their gross income as rent, and the greater the tenant's markup, the higher the percentage on the lease. For example, a supermarket may pay 1–2 percent of its gross receipts as rent, whereas a parking garage may pay as high as 40–50 percent of its gross receipts as rent.

Various professional associations publish average percentages currently being charged for different types of businesses. The owner's or property manager's job is to charge the maximum amount possible while allowing the business to remain a viable entity.

Legal Capacity

It is common for business owners to want their corporation or Limited Liability Company (LLC) to be the tenant in the lease. This is most often not a good practice unless you have a written personal guarantee of payment of the rent and associated costs by the individual or individuals who are the owners of the corporation or LLC. It is not hard for someone to transfer all assets out of a corporation or LLC they own and then have the corporation or LLC declare bankruptcy, thus allowing the real owners to effectively

cancel the lease and all liability connected therewith, without any personal liability.

Requirements of a Valid Lease

To be valid, a lease must:

- Contain the names of the lessor and lessee and be signed by both parties.
- Be in writing if for longer than one year (statute of frauds). Leases for one year or less need not be in writing.
- Show the amount of rent and manner of payment.
- State the duration of time the lease is to be in force.
- Contain an adequate description of the demised property.
- Be between parties who are capable of contracting.
- Show any automatic renewal provisions in boldface type.

Residential Leasing

A tenant who ruins the property and does not pay the rent is worse than no tenant at all. Great care must be taken by property managers in the tenant selection process.

Rigid antidiscrimination issues must be dealt with properly; however, a leasing licensee can discriminate against a tenant for other reasons such as bad credit, late rent payments at a prior rental, noted property damage, and poor credit. Leasing licensees are under no obligation to accept a bad tenant; it is easier to turn these people down than it is to evict them. Leasing licensees may charge a nonrefundable screening fee of up to $30 per applicant. This fee is to cover the cost of gathering information about a prospective tenant to make a decision about renting to her.

Note: The method of screening tenants must be uniform in nature to avoid being charged with discriminatory rental screening practices. Review the fair housing issues stated in Chapter 3.

Lease Provisions

Even if leasing licensees enter into a lease for less than a year, it is still wise to use a written lease so all of the agreed-upon terms are clearly stated for mutual protection. If leasing a property that is subject to rules and regulations, attach them as a rider to the lease and have the tenant sign for them.

Don't try to draft a lease or use a "cut-and-paste" method of assembling a lease as this may create errors and omissions that would probably be considered the unlawful practice of law. Use the *Residential Lease or Month-to-Month Rental Agreement (C.A.R. Form LR, Revised 10/04)* referenced in Figure 16.2 for

FIGURE 16.2 Residential Lease Agreement (C.A.R. Form Revised 11/08)

CALIFORNIA ASSOCIATION OF REALTORS ®

RESIDENTIAL LEASE OR MONTH-TO-MONTH RENTAL AGREEMENT
(C.A.R. Form LR, Revised 11/08)

Date _____, _____ ("Landlord") and
_____ ("Tenant") agree as follows:

1. PROPERTY:
  A. Landlord rents to Tenant and Tenant rents from Landlord, the real property and improvements described as: _____
     _____ ("Premises").
  B. The Premises are for the sole use as a personal residence by the following named person(s) **only:** _____
     _____.
  C. The following personal property, maintained pursuant to paragraph 11, is included: _____
     _____ or ☐ (if checked) the personal property on the attached addendum.

2. TERM: The term begins on (date) _____ ("Commencement Date"), **(Check A or B):**
  ☐ **A. Month-to-Month:** and continues as a month-to-month tenancy. Tenant may terminate the tenancy by giving written notice
       at least 30 days prior to the intended termination date. Landlord may terminate the tenancy by giving written notice as
       provided by law. Such notices may be given on any date.
  ☐ **B. Lease:** and shall terminate on (date) _____ at _____ ☐ AM/☐ PM.
       Tenant shall vacate the Premises upon termination of the Agreement, unless: **(i)** Landlord and Tenant have extended this
       agreement in writing or signed a new agreement; **(ii)** mandated by local rent control law; or **(iii)** Landlord accepts Rent from
       Tenant (other than past due Rent), in which case a month-to-month tenancy shall be created which either party may
       terminate as specified in paragraph 2A. Rent shall be at a rate agreed to by Landlord and Tenant, or as allowed by law. All
       other terms and conditions of this Agreement shall remain in full force and effect.

3. RENT: "Rent" shall mean all monetary obligations of Tenant to Landlord under the terms of the Agreement, except security deposit.
  A. Tenant agrees to pay $ _____ per month for the term of the Agreement.
  B. Rent is payable in advance on the **1st (or** ☐ _____**) day** of each calendar month, and is delinquent on the next day.
  C. If Commencement Date falls on any day other than the day Rent is payable under paragraph 3B, and Tenant has paid one full
     month's Rent in advance of Commencement Date, Rent for the second calendar month shall be prorated based on a 30-day
     period.
  D. PAYMENT: Rent shall be paid by ☐ personal check, ☐ money order, ☐ cashier's check, or ☐ other _____,
     to (name) _____ (phone) _____ at (address)
     _____, (or at any other location
     subsequently specified by Landlord in writing to Tenant) (and ☐ if checked, rent may be paid personally, between the hours of
     _____ and _____ on the following days_____). If any payment is
     returned for non-sufficient funds ("NSF") or because tenant stops payment, then, after that: (i) Landlord may, in writing, require
     Tenant to pay Rent in cash for three months and (ii) all future Rent shall be paid by ☐ money order, or ☐ cashier's check.

4. SECURITY DEPOSIT:
  A. Tenant agrees to pay $ _____ as a security deposit. Security deposit will be
     ☐ transferred to and held by the Owner of the Premises, or ☐ held in Owner's Broker's trust account.
  B. All or any portion of the security deposit may be used, as reasonably necessary, to: **(i)** cure Tenant's default in payment of Rent (which
     includes Late Charges, NSF fees or other sums due); **(ii)** repair damage, excluding ordinary wear and tear, caused by Tenant or by a
     guest or licensee of Tenant; **(iii)** clean Premises, if necessary, upon termination of the tenancy; and **(iv)** replace or return personal
     property or appurtenances. **SECURITY DEPOSIT SHALL NOT BE USED BY TENANT IN LIEU OF PAYMENT OF LAST
     MONTH'S RENT.** If all or any portion of the security deposit is used during the tenancy, Tenant agrees to reinstate the total security
     deposit within five days after written notice is delivered to Tenant. Within 21 days after Tenant vacates the Premises, Landlord shall:
     (1) furnish Tenant an itemized statement indicating the amount of any security deposit received and the basis for its
     disposition and supporting documentation as required by California Civil Code § 1950.5(g); and **(2)** return any remaining
     portion of the security deposit to Tenant.
  C. **Security deposit will not be returned until all Tenants have vacated the Premises and all keys returned. Any security
     deposit returned by check shall be made out to all Tenants named on this Agreement, or as subsequently modified.**
  D. No interest will be paid on security deposit unless required by local law.
  E. If the security deposit is held by Owner, Tenant agrees not to hold Broker responsible for its return. If the security deposit is held
     in Owner's Broker's trust account, **and** Broker's authority is terminated before expiration of this Agreement, **and** security deposit
     is released to someone other than Tenant, **then** Broker shall notify Tenant, in writing, where and to whom security deposit has
     been released. Once Tenant has been provided such notice, Tenant agrees not to hold Broker responsible for the security
     deposit.

5. MOVE-IN COSTS RECEIVED/DUE: Move-in funds made payable to _____
   shall be paid by ☐ personal check, ☐ money order, or ☐ cashier's check.

Category	Total Due	Payment Received	...nce ...	Date Due
Rent from _____ to _____ (date)				
*Security Deposit				
Other _____				
Other _____				
Total				

*The maximum amount Landlord may receive as security deposit, however designated, cannot exceed two months' Rent for
unfurnished premises, or three months' Rent for furnished premises.

LR REVISED 11/08 (PAGE 1 OF 6) Print Date

Tenant's Initials (_____)(_____)
Landlord's Initials (_____)(_____)

Reviewed by _____ Date _____

EQUAL HOUSING OPPORTUNITY

RESIDENTIAL LEASE OR MONTH-TO-MONTH RENTAL AGREEMENT (LR PAGE 1 OF 6)

FIGURE 16.2 *(Continued)*

Premises: _____ Date: _____

6. LATE CHARGE; RETURNED CHECKS:

   A. Tenant acknowledges either late payment of Rent or issuance of a returned check may cause Landlord to incur costs and expenses, the exact amounts of which are extremely difficult and impractical to determine. These costs may include, but are not limited to, processing, enforcement and accounting expenses, and late charges imposed on Landlord. If any installment of Rent due from Tenant is not received by Landlord within **5 (or ☐ _____) calendar days** after the date due, or if a check is returned, Tenant shall pay to Landlord, respectively, an additional sum of $ _____ or _____% of the Rent due as a Late Charge and $25.00 as a NSF fee for the first returned check and $35.00 as a NSF fee for each additional returned check, either or both of which shall be deemed additional Rent.

   B. Landlord and Tenant agree that these charges represent a fair and reasonable estimate of the costs Landlord may incur by reason of Tenant's late or NSF payment. Any Late Charge or NSF fee due shall be paid with the current installment of Rent. Landlord's acceptance of any Late Charge or NSF fee shall not constitute a waiver as to any default of Tenant. Landlord's right to collect a Late Charge or NSF fee shall not be deemed an extension of the date Rent is due under paragraph 3 or prevent Landlord from exercising any other rights and remedies under this Agreement and as provided by law.

7. PARKING: (Check A or B)

   ☐ **A.** Parking is permitted as follows: _____

         The right to parking ☐ is ☐ is not included in the Rent charged pursuant to paragraph 3. If not included in the Rent, the parking rental fee shall be an additional $ _____ per month. Parking space(s) are to be used for parking properly licensed and operable motor vehicles, except for trailers, boats, campers, buses or trucks (other than pick-up trucks). Tenant shall park in assigned space(s) only. Parking space(s) are to be kept clean. Vehicles leaking oil, gas or other motor vehicle fluids shall not be parked on the Premises. Mechanical work or storage of inoperable vehicles is not permitted in parking space(s) or elsewhere on the Premises.

   OR ☐ **B.** Parking is not permitted on the Premises.

8. STORAGE: (Check A or B)

   ☐ **A.** Storage is permitted as follows: _____

         The right to storage space ☐ is, ☐ is not, included in the Rent charged pursuant to paragraph 3. If not included in the Rent, storage space fee shall be an additional $ _____ per month. Tenant shall store only personal property Tenant owns, and shall not store property claimed by another or in which another has any right, title or interest. Tenant shall not store any improperly packaged food or perishable goods, flammable materials, explosives, hazardous waste or other inherently dangerous material, or illegal substances.

   OR ☐ **B.** Storage is not permitted on the Premises.

9. UTILITIES: Tenant agrees to pay for all utilities and services, and the following charges: _____ except _____, which shall be paid for by Landlord. If any utilities are not separately metered, Tenant shall pay Tenant's proportional share, as reasonably determined and directed by Landlord. If utilities are separately metered, Tenant shall place utilities in Tenant's name as of the Commencement Date. Landlord is only responsible for installing and maintaining one usable telephone jack and one telephone line to the Premises. Tenant shall pay any cost for conversion from existing utilities service provider.

10. CONDITION OF PREMISES: Tenant has examined Premises and, if any, all furniture, furnishings, appliances, landscaping and fixtures, including smoke detector(s).

   (Check all that apply:)

   ☐ **A.** Tenant acknowledges these items are clean and in operable condition, with the following exceptions: _____ _____.

   ☐ **B.** Tenant's acknowledgment of the condition of these items is contained in an attached statement of condition (C.A.R. Form MIMO).

   ☐ **C.** Tenant will provide Landlord a list of items that are damaged or not in operable condition within **3 (or ☐ _____) days** after Commencement Date, not as a contingency of this Agreement but rather as an acknowledgment of the condition of the Premises.

   ☐ **D.** Other:_____.

11. MAINTENANCE:

   A. Tenant shall properly use, operate and safeguard Premises, including if applicable, any landscaping, furniture, furnishings and appliances, and all mechanical, electrical, gas and plumbing fixtures, and keep them and the Premises clean, sanitary and well ventilated. Tenant shall be responsible for checking and maintaining all smoke detectors and any additional phone lines beyond the one line and jack that Landlord shall provide and maintain. Tenant shall immediately notify Landlord, in writing, of any problem, malfunction or damage. Tenant shall be charged for all repairs or replacements caused by Tenant, pets, guests or licensees of Tenant, excluding ordinary wear and tear. Tenant shall be charged for all damage to Premises as a result of failure to report a problem in a timely manner. Tenant shall be charged for repair of drain blockages or stoppages, unless caused by defective plumbing parts or tree roots invading sewer lines.

   B. ☐ Landlord ☐ Tenant shall water the garden, landscaping, trees and shrubs, except:_____ _____.

   C. ☐ Landlord ☐ Tenant shall maintain the garden, landscaping, trees and shrubs, except:_____ _____.

   D. ☐ Landlord ☐ Tenant shall maintain _____

   E. Tenant's failure to maintain any item for which Tenant is responsible shall give Landlord the right to hire someone to perform such maintenance and charge Tenant to cover the cost of such maintenance.

   F. The following items of personal property are included in the Premises without warranty and Landlord will not maintain, repair or replace them: _____.

Tenant's Initials (_____)(_____)
Landlord's Initials (_____)(_____)

Reviewed by _____ Date _____

RESIDENTIAL LEASE OR MONTH-TO-MONTH RENTAL AGREEMENT (LR PAGE 2 OF 6)

FIGURE 16.2 (*Continued*)

Premises: _____ Date: _____

12. **NEIGHBORHOOD CONDITIONS:** Tenant is advised to satisfy him or herself as to neighborhood or area conditions, including schools, proximity and adequacy of law enforcement, crime statistics, proximity of registered felons or offenders, fire protection, other governmental services, availability, adequacy and cost of any wired, wireless internet connections or other telecommunications or other technology services and installations, proximity to commercial, industrial or agricultural activities, existing and proposed transportation, construction and development that may affect noise, view, or traffic, airport noise, noise or odor from any source, wild and domestic animals, other nuisances, hazards, or circumstances, cemeteries, facilities and condition of common areas, conditions and influences of significance to certain cultures and/or religions, and personal needs, requirements and preferences of Tenant.

13. **PETS:** Unless otherwise provided in California Civil Code § 54.2, no animal or pet shall be kept on or about the Premises without Landlord's prior written consent, except: _____

14. ☐ **(If checked) NO SMOKING:** No smoking is allowed on the Premises. If smoking does occur on the Premises, **(i)** Tenant is responsible for all damage caused by the smoking including, but not limited to, stains, burns, odors and removal of debris; **(ii)** Tenant is in breach of this Agreement; **(iii)** Tenant, Authorized Guests, and all others may be required to leave the Premises; and **(iv)** Tenant acknowledges that in order to remove odor caused by smoking, Landlord may need to replace carpet and drapes and paint entire premises regardless of when these items were last cleaned or replaced. Such actions and other necessary steps will impact the return of any security deposit.

15. **RULES/REGULATIONS:**
    A. Tenant agrees to comply with all Landlord rules and regulations that are at any time posted on the Premises or delivered to Tenant. Tenant shall not, and shall ensure that guests and licensees of Tenant shall not, disturb, annoy, endanger or interfere with other tenants of the building or neighbors, or use the Premises for any unlawful purposes, including, but not limited to, using, manufacturing, selling, storing or transporting illicit drugs or other contraband, or violate any law or ordinance, or commit a waste or nuisance on or about the Premises.
    B. **(If applicable, check one)**
       ☐ **1.** Landlord shall provide Tenant with a copy of the rules and regulations within _____ days or _____.
       OR ☐ **2.** Tenant has been provided with, and acknowledges receipt of, a copy of the rules and regulations.

16. ☐ **(If checked) CONDOMINIUM;PLANNED UNIT DEVELOPMENT:**
    A. The Premises is a unit in a condominium, planned unit development, common interest subdivision or other development governed by a homeowners' association ("HOA"). The name of the HOA is _____. Tenant agrees to comply with all HOA covenants, conditions and restrictions, bylaws, rules and regulations and decisions. Landlord shall provide Tenant copies of rules and regulations, if any. Tenant shall reimburse Landlord for any fines or charges imposed by HOA or other authorities, due to any violation by Tenant, or the guests or licensees of Tenant.
    B. **(Check one)**
       ☐ **1.** Landlord shall provide Tenant with a copy of the HOA rules and regulations within _____ days or _____.
       OR ☐ **2.** Tenant has been provided with, and acknowledges receipt of, a copy of the HOA rules and regulations.

17. **ALTERATIONS; REPAIRS:** Unless otherwise specified by law or paragraph 29C, without Landlord's prior written consent, **(i)** Tenant shall not make any repairs, alterations or improvements in or about the Premises including: painting, wallpapering, adding or changing locks, installing antenna or satellite dish(es), placing signs, displays or exhibits, or using screws, fastening devices, large nails or adhesive materials; **(ii)** Landlord shall not be responsible for the costs of alterations or repairs made by Tenant; **(iii)** Tenant shall not deduct from Rent the costs of any repairs, alterations or improvements; and **(iv)** any deduction made by Tenant shall be considered unpaid Rent.

18. **KEYS; LOCKS:**
    A. Tenant acknowledges receipt of (or Tenant will receive ☐ prior to the Commencement Date, or ☐ _____):
       ☐ _____ key(s) to Premises,   ☐ _____ remote control device(s) for garage door/gate opener(s),
       ☐ _____ key(s) to mailbox,   ☐ _____,
       ☐ _____ key(s) to common area(s),   ☐ _____.
    B. Tenant acknowledges that locks to the Premises ☐ have, ☐ have not, been re-keyed.
    C. If Tenant re-keys existing locks or opening devices, Tenant shall immediately deliver copies of all keys to Landlord. Tenant shall pay all costs and charges related to loss of any keys or opening devices. Tenant may not remove locks, even if installed by Tenant.

19. **ENTRY:**
    A. Tenant shall make Premises available to Landlord or Landlord's representative for the purpose of entering to make necessary or agreed repairs, decorations, alterations, or improvements, or to supply necessary or agreed services, or to show Premises to prospective or actual purchasers, tenants, mortgagees, lenders, appraisers, or contractors.
    B. Landlord and Tenant agree that 24-hour written notice shall be reasonable and sufficient notice, except as follows. 48-hour written notice is required to conduct an inspection of the Premises prior to the Tenant moving out, unless the Tenant waives the right to such notice. Notice may be given orally to show the Premises to actual or prospective purchasers provided Tenant has been notified in writing within 120 days preceding the oral notice that the Premises are for sale and that oral notice may be given to show the Premises. No notice is required: **(i)** to enter in case of an emergency; **(ii)** if the Tenant is present and consents at the time of entry or **(iii)** if the Tenant has abandoned or surrendered the Premises. No written notice is required if Landlord and Tenant orally agree to an entry for agreed services or repairs if the date and time of entry are within one week of the oral agreement.
    C. ☐ **(If checked)** Tenant authorizes the use of a keysafe/lockbox to allow entry into the Premises and agrees to sign a keysafe/lockbox addendum (C.A.R. Form KLA).

20. **SIGNS:** Tenant authorizes Landlord to place FOR SALE/LEASE signs on the Premises.

21. **ASSIGNMENT; SUBLETTING:** Tenant shall not sublet all or any part of Premises, or assign or transfer this Agreement or any interest in it, without Landlord's prior written consent. Unless such consent is obtained, any assignment, transfer or subletting of Premises or this Agreement or tenancy, by voluntary act of Tenant, operation of law or otherwise, shall, at the option of Landlord,

Tenant's Initials (_____)(_____)
Landlord's Initials (_____)(_____)

LR REVISED 11/08 (PAGE 3 OF 6)

Reviewed by _____ Date _____

EQUAL HOUSING OPPORTUNITY

RESIDENTIAL LEASE OR MONTH-TO-MONTH RENTAL AGREEMENT (LR PAGE 3 OF 6)

FIGURE 16.2 (*Continued*)

Premises: _____ Date: _____

terminate this Agreement. Any proposed assignee, transferee or sublessee shall submit to Landlord an application and credit information for Landlord's approval and, if approved, sign a separate written agreement with Landlord and Tenant. Landlord's consent to any one assignment, transfer or sublease, shall not be construed as consent to any subsequent assignment, transfer or sublease and does not release Tenant of Tenant's obligations under this Agreement.

22. **JOINT AND INDIVIDUAL OBLIGATIONS:** If there is more than one Tenant, each one shall be individually and completely responsible for the performance of all obligations of Tenant under this Agreement, jointly with every other Tenant, and individually, whether or not in possession.

23. ☐ **LEAD-BASED PAINT (If checked):** Premises was constructed prior to 1978. In accordance with federal law, Landlord gives and Tenant acknowledges receipt of the disclosures on the attached form (C.A.R. Form FLD) and a federally approved lead pamphlet.

24. ☐ **MILITARY ORDNANCE DISCLOSURE:** (If applicable and known to Landlord) Premises is located within one mile of an area once used for military training, and may contain potentially explosive munitions.

25. ☐ **PERIODIC PEST CONTROL:** Landlord has entered into a contract for periodic pest control treatment of the Premises and shall give Tenant a copy of the notice originally given to Landlord by the pest control company.

26. ☐ **METHAMPHETAMINE CONTAMINATION:** Prior to signing this Agreement, Landlord has given Tenant a notice that a health official has issued an order prohibiting occupancy of the property because of methamphetamine contamination. A copy of the notice and order are attached.

27. **MEGAN'S LAW DATABASE DISCLOSURE:** Notice: Pursuant to Section 290.46 of the Penal Code, information about specified registered sex offenders is made available to the public via an Internet Web site maintained by the Department of Justice at www.meganslaw.ca.gov. Depending on an offender's criminal history, this information will include either the address at which the offender resides or the community of residence and ZIP Code in which he or she resides. (Neither Landlord nor Brokers, if any, are required to check this website. If Tenant wants further information, Tenant should obtain information directly from this website.)

28. **POSSESSION:**
   A. Tenant is not in possession of the premises. If Landlord is unable to deliver possession of Premises on Commencement Date, such Date shall be extended to the date on which possession is made available to Tenant. If Landlord is unable to deliver possession within **5 (or ☐ _____) calendar days** after agreed Commencement Date, Tenant may terminate this Agreement by giving written notice to Landlord, and shall be refunded all Rent and security deposit paid. Possession is deemed terminated when Tenant has returned all keys to the Premises to Landlord.
   B. ☐ Tenant is already in possession of the Premises.

29. **TENANT'S OBLIGATIONS UPON VACATING PREMISES:**
   A. Upon termination of this Agreement, Tenant shall: **(i)** give Landlord all copies of all keys or opening devices to Premises, including any common areas; **(ii)** vacate and surrender Premises to Landlord, empty of all persons; **(iii)** vacate any/all parking and/or storage space; **(iv)** clean and deliver Premises, as specified in paragraph C below, to Landlord in the same condition as referenced in paragraph 10; **(v)** remove all debris; **(vi)** give written notice to Landlord of Tenant's forwarding address; and **(vii)** _____ .
   B. All alterations/improvements made by or caused to be made by Tenant, with or without Landlord's consent, become the property of Landlord upon termination. Landlord may charge Tenant for restoration of the Premises to the condition it was in prior to any alterations/improvements.
   C. **Right to Pre-Move-Out Inspection and Repairs: (i)** After giving or receiving notice of termination of a tenancy (C.A.R. Form NTT), or before the end of a lease, Tenant has the right to request that an inspection of the Premises take place prior to termination of the lease or rental (C.A.R. Form NRI). If Tenant requests such an inspection, Tenant shall be given an opportunity to remedy identified deficiencies prior to termination, consistent with the terms of this Agreement. **(ii)** Any repairs or alterations made to the Premises as a result of this inspection (collectively, "Repairs") shall be made at Tenant's expense. Repairs may be performed by Tenant or through others, who have adequate insurance and licenses and are approved by Landlord. The work shall comply with applicable law, including governmental permit, inspection and approval requirements. Repairs shall be performed in a good, skillful manner with materials of quality and appearance comparable to existing materials. It is understood that exact restoration of appearance or cosmetic items following all Repairs may not be possible. **(iii)** Tenant shall: **(a)** obtain receipts for Repairs performed by others; **(b)** prepare a written statement indicating the Repairs performed by Tenant and the date of such Repairs; and **(c)** provide copies of receipts and statements to Landlord prior to termination. Paragraph 29C does not apply when the tenancy is terminated pursuant to California Code of Civil Procedure § 1161(2), (3) or (4).

30. **BREACH OF CONTRACT; EARLY TERMINATION:** In addition to any obligations established by paragraph 29, in the event of termination by Tenant prior to completion of the original term of the Agreement, Tenant shall also be responsible for lost Rent, rental commissions, advertising expenses and painting costs necessary to ready Premises for re-rental. Landlord may withhold any such amounts from Tenant's security deposit.

31. **TEMPORARY RELOCATION:** Subject to local law, Tenant agrees, upon demand of Landlord, to temporarily vacate Premises for a reasonable period, to allow for fumigation (or other methods) to control wood destroying pests or organisms, or other repairs to Premises. Tenant agrees to comply with all instructions and requirements necessary to prepare Premises to accommodate pest control, fumigation or other work, including bagging or storage of food and medicine, and removal of perishables and valuables. Tenant shall only be entitled to a credit of Rent equal to the per diem Rent for the period of time Tenant is required to vacate Premises.

32. **DAMAGE TO PREMISES:** If, by no fault of Tenant, Premises are totally or partially damaged or destroyed by fire, earthquake, accident or other casualty that render Premises totally or partially uninhabitable, either Landlord or Tenant may terminate this Agreement by giving the other written notice. Rent shall be abated as of the date Premises become totally or partially uninhabitable. The abated amount shall be the current monthly Rent prorated on a 30-day period. If the Agreement is not terminated, Landlord shall promptly repair the damage, and Rent shall be reduced based on the extent to which the damage interferes with Tenant's reasonable use of Premises. If damage occurs as a result of an act of Tenant or Tenant's guests, only Landlord shall have the right of termination, and no reduction in Rent shall be made.

33. **INSURANCE:** Tenant's or guest's personal property and vehicles are not insured by Landlord, manager or, if applicable, HOA, against loss or damage due to fire, theft, vandalism, rain, water, criminal or negligent acts of others, or any other cause. **Tenant**

LR REVISED 11/08 (PAGE 4 OF 6)

Tenant's Initials (_____)(_____)
Landlord's Initials (_____)(_____)

| Reviewed by _____ Date _____ |

EQUAL HOUSING OPPORTUNITY

RESIDENTIAL LEASE OR MONTH-TO-MONTH RENTAL AGREEMENT (LR PAGE 4 OF 6)

FIGURE 16.2 (*Continued*)

Premises: _____ Date: _____

is advised to carry Tenant's own insurance (renter's insurance) to protect Tenant from any such loss or damage. Tenant shall comply with any requirement imposed on Tenant by Landlord's insurer to avoid: **(i)** an increase in Landlord's insurance premium (or Tenant shall pay for the increase in premium); or **(ii)** loss of insurance.

34. **WATERBEDS:** Tenant shall not use or have waterbeds on the Premises unless: **(i)** Tenant obtains a valid waterbed insurance policy; **(ii)** Tenant increases the security deposit in an amount equal to one-half of one month's Rent; and **(iii)** the bed conforms to the floor load capacity of Premises.

35. **WAIVER:** The waiver of any breach shall not be construed as a continuing waiver of the same or any subsequent breach.

36. **NOTICE:** Notices may be served at the following address, or at any other location subsequently designated:
    Landlord: _____ Tenant: _____
    _____ _____
    _____ _____

37. **TENANT ESTOPPEL CERTIFICATE:** Tenant shall execute and return a tenant estoppel certificate delivered to Tenant by Landlord or Landlord's agent within 3 days after its receipt. Failure to comply with this requirement shall be deemed Tenant's acknowledgment that the tenant estoppel certificate is true and correct, and may be relied upon by a lender or purchaser.

38. **TENANT REPRESENTATIONS; CREDIT:** Tenant warrants that all statements in Tenant's rental application are accurate. Tenant authorizes Landlord and Broker(s) to obtain Tenant's credit report periodically during the tenancy in connection with the modification or enforcement of this Agreement. Landlord may cancel this Agreement: **(i)** before occupancy begins; **(ii)** upon disapproval of the credit report(s); or **(iii)** at any time, upon discovering that information in Tenant's application is false. A negative credit report reflecting on Tenant's record may be submitted to a credit reporting agency if Tenant fails to fulfill the terms of payment and other obligations under this Agreement.

39. **MEDIATION:**
    A. Consistent with paragraphs B and C below, Landlord and Tenant agree to mediate any dispute or claim arising between them out of this Agreement, or any resulting transaction, before resorting to court action. Mediation fees, if any, shall be divided equally among the parties involved. If, for any dispute or claim to which this paragraph applies, any party commences an action without first attempting to resolve the matter through mediation, or refuses to mediate after a request has been made, then that party shall not be entitled to recover attorney fees, even if they would otherwise be available to that party in any such action.
    B. The following matters are excluded from mediation: **(i)** an unlawful detainer action; **(ii)** the filing or enforcement of a mechanic's lien; and **(iii)** any matter within the jurisdiction of a probate, small claims or bankruptcy court. The filing of a court action to enable the recording of a notice of pending action, for order of attachment, receivership, injunction, or other provisional remedies, shall not constitute a waiver of the mediation provision.
    C. Landlord and Tenant agree to mediate disputes or claims involving Listing Agent, Leasing Agent or property manager ("Broker"), provided Broker shall have agreed to such mediation prior to, or within a reasonable time after, the dispute or claim is presented to such Broker. Any election by Broker to participate in mediation shall not result in Broker being deemed a party to this Agreement.

40. **ATTORNEY FEES:** In any action or proceeding arising out of this Agreement, the prevailing party between Landlord and Tenant shall be entitled to reasonable attorney fees and costs, except as provided in paragraph 39A.

41. **C.A.R. FORM:** C.A.R. Form means the specific form referenced or another comparable from agreed to by the parties.

42. **OTHER TERMS AND CONDITIONS;SUPPLEMENTS:** ☐ Interpreter/Translator Agreement (C.A.R. Form ITA);
    ☐ Keysafe/Lockbox Addendum (C.A.R. Form KLA); ☐ Lead-Based Paint and Lead-Based Paint Hazards Disclosure (C.A.R. Form FLD) _____
    _____
    _____

    The following ATTACHED supplements are incorporated in this Agreement: _____
    _____
    _____

43. **TIME OF ESSENCE; ENTIRE CONTRACT; CHANGES:** Time is of the essence. All understandings between the parties are incorporated in this Agreement. Its terms are intended by the parties as a final, complete and exclusive expression of their Agreement with respect to its subject matter, and may not be contradicted by evidence of any prior agreement or contemporaneous oral agreement. If any provision of this Agreement is held to be ineffective or invalid, the remaining provisions will nevertheless be given full force and effect. Neither this Agreement nor any provision in it may be extended, amended, modified, altered or changed except in writing. This Agreement is subject to California landlord-tenant law and shall incorporate all changes required by amendment or successors to such law. This Agreement and any supplement, addendum or modification, including any copy, may be signed in two or more counterparts, all of which shall constitute one and the same writing.

44. **AGENCY:**
    A. **CONFIRMATION:** The following agency relationship(s) are hereby confirmed for this transaction:
       Listing Agent: (Print firm name) _____ is the agent of
       (check one): ☐ the Landlord exclusively; or ☐ both the Landlord and Tenant.
       Leasing Agent: (Print firm name) _____ (if not same as Listing
       Agent) is the agent of (check one): ☐ the Tenant exclusively; or ☐ the Landlord exclusively; or ☐ both the Tenant and Landlord.
    B. **DISCLOSURE:** ☐ (If checked): The term of this lease exceeds one year. A disclosure regarding real estate agency relationships (C.A.R. Form AD) has been provided to Landlord and Tenant, who each acknowledge its receipt.

45. ☐ **TENANT COMPENSATION TO BROKER:** Upon execution of this Agreement, Tenant agrees to pay compensation to Broker as specified in a separate written agreement between Tenant and Broker.

Tenant's Initials (_____)(_____)
Landlord's Initials (_____)(_____)

LR REVISED 11/08 (PAGE 5 OF 6)

Reviewed by _____ Date _____

EQUAL HOUSING OPPORTUNITY

RESIDENTIAL LEASE OR MONTH-TO-MONTH RENTAL AGREEMENT (LR PAGE 5 OF 6)

FIGURE 16.2 (*Continued*)

Premises: _____ Date: _____

46. ☐ **INTERPRETER/TRANSLATOR:** The terms of this Agreement have been interpreted for Tenant into the following language: _____. Landlord and Tenant acknowledge receipt of the attached interpretor/translator agreement (C.A.R. Form ITA).

47. **FOREIGN LANGUAGE NEGOTIATION:** If this Agreement has been negotiated by Landlord and Tenant primarily in Spanish, Chinese, Tagalog, Korean or Vietnamese, pursuant to the California Civil Code, Tenant shall be provided a translation of this Agreement in the language used for the negotiation.

48. **OWNER COMPENSATION TO BROKER:** Upon execution of this Agreement, Owner agrees to pay compensation to Broker as specified in a separate written agreement between Owner and Broker (C.A.R. Form LCA).

49. **RECEIPT:** If specified in paragraph 5, Landlord or Broker, acknowledges receipt of move-in funds.

> Landlord and Tenant acknowledge and agree Brokers: **(a)** do not guarantee the condition of the Premises; **(b)** cannot verify representations made by others; **(c)** cannot provide legal or tax advice; **(d)** will not provide other advice or information that exceeds the knowledge, education or experience required to obtain a real estate license. Furthermore, if Brokers are not also acting as Landlord in this Agreement, Brokers: **(e)** do not decide what rental rate a Tenant should pay or Landlord should accept; and **(f)** do not decide upon the length or other terms of tenancy. Landlord and Tenant agree that they will seek legal, tax, insurance and other desired assistance from appropriate professionals.

Tenant agrees to rent the Premises on the above terms and conditions.

Tenant _____ Date _____
Address _____ City _____ State _____ Zip _____
Telephone _____ Fax _____ E-mail _____
Tenant _____ Date _____
Address _____ City _____ State _____ Zip _____
Telephone _____ Fax _____ E-mail _____

☐ **GUARANTEE:** In consideration of the execution of this Agreement by and between Landlord and Tenant and for valuable consideration, receipt of which is hereby acknowledged, the undersigned ("Guarantor") does hereby: **(i)** guarantee unconditionally to Landlord and Landlord's agents, successors and assigns, the prompt payment of Rent or other sums that become due pursuant to this Agreement, including any and all court costs and attorney fees included in enforcing the Agreement; **(ii)** consent to any changes, modifications or alterations of any term in this Agreement agreed to by Landlord and Tenant; and **(iii)** waive any right to require Landlord and/or Landlord's agents to proceed against Tenant for any default occurring under this Agreement before seeking to enforce this Guarantee.

Guarantor (Print Name) _____
Guarantor _____ Date _____
Address _____ City _____ State _____ Zip _____
Telephone _____ Fax _____ E-mail _____

Landlord agrees to rent the Premises on the above terms and conditions.

Landlord _____ Landlord _____
Address _____
Telephone _____ Fax _____ E-mail _____

> **REAL ESTATE BROKERS:**
> **A.** Real estate brokers who are not also Landlord under this Agreement are not parties to the Agreement between Landlord and Tenant.
> **B.** Agency relationships are confirmed in paragraph 44.
> **C.** **COOPERATING BROKER COMPENSATION:** Listing Broker agrees to pay Cooperating Broker (Leasing Firm) and Cooperating Broker agrees to accept: **(i)** the amount specified in the MLS, provided Cooperating Broker is a Participant of the MLS in which the Property is offered for sale or a reciprocal MLS; or **(ii)** ☐ (if checked) the amount specified in a separate written agreement between Listing Broker and Cooperating Broker.

Real Estate Broker (Listing Firm) _____ DRE Lic. # _____
By (Agent) _____ DRE Lic. # _____ Date _____
Address _____ City _____ State _____ Zip _____
Telephone _____ Fax _____ E-mail _____

Real Estate Broker (Leasing Firm) _____ DRE Lic. # _____
By (Agent) _____ DRE Lic. # _____ Date _____
Address _____ City _____ State _____ Zip _____
Telephone _____ Fax _____ E-mail _____

THIS FORM HAS BEEN APPROVED BY THE CALIFORNIA ASSOCIATION OF REALTORS® (C.A.R.). NO REPRESENTATION IS MADE AS TO THE LEGAL VALIDITY OR ADEQUACY OF ANY PROVISION IN ANY SPECIFIC TRANSACTION. A REAL ESTATE BROKER IS THE PERSON QUALIFIED TO ADVISE ON REAL ESTATE TRANSACTIONS. IF YOU DESIRE LEGAL OR TAX ADVICE, CONSULT AN APPROPRIATE PROFESSIONAL.

This form is available for use by the entire real estate industry. It is not intended to identify the user as a REALTOR®. REALTOR® is a registered collective membership mark which may be used only by members of the NATIONAL ASSOCIATION OF REALTORS® who subscribe to its Code of Ethics.

Published and Distributed by:
REAL ESTATE BUSINESS SERVICES, INC.
a subsidiary of the California Association of REALTORS®
525 South Virgil Avenue, Los Angeles, California 90020

Reviewed by _____ Date _____

LR REVISED 11/08 (PAGE 6 OF 6)

RESIDENTIAL LEASE OR MONTH-TO-MONTH RENTAL AGREEMENT (LR PAGE 6 OF 6)

Source: Reprinted with permission of California Association of REALTORS®.

simple leases and obtain the services of a real estate attorney for more complex leases, especially those of a commercial nature.

Name of Parties

A lease must contain the full names of all parties. A lease to a party who is under the age of eighteen requires a cosigner unless the underage party is an emancipated minor by reason of marriage or court order. The parties must sign the lease "jointly and severally," so that each party to the lease is liable for the entire rent and you can look to one or all of the tenants for payment.

Dates

The lease must have a beginning and an ending date.

Description of the Premises

The demised premises must be described in such a way that there is no ambiguity. If a storage room, garage, or parking space is included, it should be clearly stated in writing.

Rent and Late Charge

The amount of rent and where and when it is due must be clearly stated. A provision must be made for a late charge if the rent is not received by a specified time on or after its due date. The late charge should not exceed 6 percent of the rent due to avoid having it deemed too high by a court and declared an unenforceable penalty.

Waterbeds

Common waterbed agreements require the tenant to pay for a policy of waterbed insurance and use a waterbed liner. Pet agreements are common in residential leases. They usually restrict the size and/or number of pets.

Inspection of the premises

Some leases provide for pretenancy and end-of-tenancy walk-through inspections. Deficiencies must be noted on a form provided for this purpose, which must be signed by the tenant and landlord (see Figure 16.3).

Cleaning and Security Deposits

A security deposit functions as an insurance policy for the landlord in the event the premises are left damaged or dirty or if rent is owed. Although nonrefundable *cleaning deposits* are not allowed, a landlord may charge a security deposit equal to two months'

FIGURE 16.3 Move In/Move Out Inspection (C.A.R. Form MIMO, Revised 11/07)

CALIFORNIA
ASSOCIATION
OF REALTORS ®

MOVE IN / MOVE OUT INSPECTION
(C.A.R. Form MIMO, Revised 11/07)

Property Address _____ Unit No. _____

Inspection: Move In _____ (Date) Move Out _____ (Date)

Tenant(s) _____

> When completing this form, check the Premises carefully and be specific in all items noted. Check the appropriate box:
> **N - NEW   S - SATISFACTORY/CLEAN   O - OTHER   D - DEPOSIT DEDUCTION**

	MOVE IN N S O	Comments	MOVE OUT S O D	Comments
Front Yard/Exterior				
Landscaping	☐ ☐ ☐		☐ ☐ ☐	
Fences/Gates	☐ ☐ ☐		☐ ☐ ☐	
Sprinklers/Timers	☐ ☐ ☐		☐ ☐ ☐	
Walks/Driveway	☐ ☐ ☐		☐ ☐ ☐	
Porches/Stairs	☐ ☐ ☐		☐ ☐ ☐	
Mailbox	☐ ☐ ☐		☐ ☐ ☐	
Light Fixtures	☐ ☐ ☐		☐ ☐ ☐	
Building Exterior	☐ ☐ ☐		☐ ☐ ☐	
Entry				
Security/Screen Doors	☐ ☐ ☐		☐ ☐ ☐	
Doors/Knobs/Locks	☐ ☐ ☐		☐ ☐ ☐	
Flooring/Baseboards	☐ ☐ ☐		☐ ☐ ☐	
Walls/Ceilings	☐ ☐ ☐		☐ ☐ ☐	
Light Fixtures/Fans	☐ ☐ ☐		☐ ☐ ☐	
Switches/Outlets	☐ ☐ ☐		☐ ☐ ☐	
Living Room				
Doors/Knobs/Locks	☐ ☐ ☐		☐ ☐ ☐	
Flooring/Baseboards	☐ ☐ ☐		☐ ☐ ☐	
Walls/Ceilings	☐ ☐ ☐		☐ ☐ ☐	
Window Coverings	☐ ☐ ☐		☐ ☐ ☐	
Windows/Locks/Screens	☐ ☐ ☐		☐ ☐ ☐	
Light Fixtures/Fans	☐ ☐ ☐		☐ ☐ ☐	
Switches/Outlets	☐ ☐ ☐		☐ ☐ ☐	
Fireplace/Equipment	☐ ☐ ☐		☐ ☐ ☐	
Dining Room				
Flooring/Baseboards	☐ ☐ ☐		☐ ☐ ☐	
Walls/Ceilings	☐ ☐ ☐		☐ ☐ ☐	
Window Coverings	☐ ☐ ☐		☐ ☐ ☐	
Windows/Locks/Screens	☐ ☐ ☐		☐ ☐ ☐	
Light Fixtures/Fans	☐ ☐ ☐		☐ ☐ ☐	
Switches/Outlets	☐ ☐ ☐		☐ ☐ ☐	

Tenant's Initials   (_____)(_____)   Tenant's Initials   (_____)(_____)

Landlord's Initials (_____)(_____)   Landlord's Initials (_____)(_____)

MIMO REVISED 11/07 (PAGE 1 OF 5) Print Date

Reviewed by _____ Date _____

EQUAL HOUSING
OPPORTUNITY

MOVE IN / MOVE OUT INSPECTION (MIMO PAGE 1 OF 5)

FIGURE 16.3   (*Continued*)

Property Address: _____   Date: _____

	MOVE IN				MOVE OUT			
	N	S	O	Comments	S	O	D	Comments

Other Room _____
Doors/Knobs/Locks	☐	☐	☐	_____	☐	☐	☐	_____
Flooring/Baseboards	☐	☐	☐	_____	☐	☐	☐	_____
Walls/Ceilings	☐	☐	☐	_____	☐	☐	☐	_____
Window Coverings	☐	☐	☐	_____	☐	☐	☐	_____
Windows/Locks/Screens	☐	☐	☐	_____	☐	☐	☐	_____
Light Fixtures/Fans	☐	☐	☐	_____	☐	☐	☐	_____
Switches/Outlets	☐	☐	☐	_____	☐	☐	☐	_____

Bedroom # _____
Doors/Knobs/Locks	☐	☐	☐	_____	☐	☐	☐	_____
Flooring/Baseboards	☐	☐	☐	_____	☐	☐	☐	_____
Walls/Ceilings	☐	☐	☐	_____	☐	☐	☐	_____
Window Coverings	☐	☐	☐	_____	☐	☐	☐	_____
Windows/Locks/Screens	☐	☐	☐	_____	☐	☐	☐	_____
Light Fixtures/Fans	☐	☐	☐	_____	☐	☐	☐	_____
Switches/Outlets	☐	☐	☐	_____	☐	☐	☐	_____
Closets/Doors/Tracks	☐	☐	☐	_____	☐	☐	☐	_____

Bedroom # _____
Doors/Knobs/Locks	☐	☐	☐	_____	☐	☐	☐	_____
Flooring/Baseboards	☐	☐	☐	_____	☐	☐	☐	_____
Walls/Ceilings	☐	☐	☐	_____	☐	☐	☐	_____
Window Coverings	☐	☐	☐	_____	☐	☐	☐	_____
Windows/Locks/Screens	☐	☐	☐	_____	☐	☐	☐	_____
Light Fixtures/Fans	☐	☐	☐	_____	☐	☐	☐	_____
Switches/Outlets	☐	☐	☐	_____	☐	☐	☐	_____
Closets/Doors/Tracks	☐	☐	☐	_____	☐	☐	☐	_____

Bedroom # _____
Doors/Knobs/Locks	☐	☐	☐	_____	☐	☐	☐	_____
Flooring/Baseboards	☐	☐	☐	_____	☐	☐	☐	_____
Walls/Ceilings	☐	☐	☐	_____	☐	☐	☐	_____
Window Coverings	☐	☐	☐	_____	☐	☐	☐	_____
Windows/Locks/Screens	☐	☐	☐	_____	☐	☐	☐	_____
Light Fixtures/Fans	☐	☐	☐	_____	☐	☐	☐	_____
Switches/Outlets	☐	☐	☐	_____	☐	☐	☐	_____
Closets/Doors/Tracks	☐	☐	☐	_____	☐	☐	☐	_____

Bedroom # _____
Doors/Knobs/Locks	☐	☐	☐	_____	☐	☐	☐	_____
Flooring/Baseboards	☐	☐	☐	_____	☐	☐	☐	_____
Walls/Ceilings	☐	☐	☐	_____	☐	☐	☐	_____
Window Coverings	☐	☐	☐	_____	☐	☐	☐	_____
Windows/Locks/Screens	☐	☐	☐	_____	☐	☐	☐	_____
Light Fixtures/Fans	☐	☐	☐	_____	☐	☐	☐	_____
Switches/Outlets	☐	☐	☐	_____	☐	☐	☐	_____
Closets/Doors/Tracks	☐	☐	☐	_____	☐	☐	☐	_____

Tenant's Initials   (_____)(_____)   Tenant's Initials   (_____)(_____)

Landlord's Initials   (_____)(_____)   Landlord's Initials   (_____)(_____)

MIMO REVISED 11/07 (PAGE 2 OF 5)

Reviewed by _____ Date _____

EQUAL HOUSING OPPORTUNITY

MOVE IN / MOVE OUT INSPECTION   (MIMO PAGE 2 OF 5)

FIGURE 16.3 (*Continued*)

Property Address: _____   Date: _____

	MOVE IN				MOVE OUT			
	N	S	O	Comments	S	O	D	Comments
Bath #_____								
Doors/Knobs/Locks	☐	☐	☐	_____	☐	☐	☐	_____
Flooring/Baseboards	☐	☐	☐	_____	☐	☐	☐	_____
Walls/Ceilings	☐	☐	☐	_____	☐	☐	☐	_____
Window Coverings	☐	☐	☐	_____	☐	☐	☐	_____
Windows/Locks/Screens	☐	☐	☐	_____	☐	☐	☐	_____
Light Fixtures	☐	☐	☐	_____	☐	☐	☐	_____
Switches/Outlets	☐	☐	☐	_____	☐	☐	☐	_____
Toilet	☐	☐	☐	_____	☐	☐	☐	_____
Tub/Shower	☐	☐	☐	_____	☐	☐	☐	_____
Shower Door/Rail/Curtain	☐	☐	☐	_____	☐	☐	☐	_____
Sink/Faucets	☐	☐	☐	_____	☐	☐	☐	_____
Plumbing/Drains	☐	☐	☐	_____	☐	☐	☐	_____
Exhaust Fan	☐	☐	☐	_____	☐	☐	☐	_____
Towel Rack(s)	☐	☐	☐	_____	☐	☐	☐	_____
Toilet Paper Holder	☐	☐	☐	_____	☐	☐	☐	_____
Cabinets/Counters	☐	☐	☐	_____	☐	☐	☐	_____

	N	S	O	Comments	S	O	D	Comments
Bath #_____								
Doors/Knobs/Locks	☐	☐	☐	_____	☐	☐	☐	_____
Flooring/Baseboards	☐	☐	☐	_____	☐	☐	☐	_____
Walls/Ceilings	☐	☐	☐	_____	☐	☐	☐	_____
Window Coverings	☐	☐	☐	_____	☐	☐	☐	_____
Windows/Locks/Screens	☐	☐	☐	_____	☐	☐	☐	_____
Light Fixtures	☐	☐	☐	_____	☐	☐	☐	_____
Switches/Outlets	☐	☐	☐	_____	☐	☐	☐	_____
Toilet	☐	☐	☐	_____	☐	☐	☐	_____
Tub/Shower	☐	☐	☐	_____	☐	☐	☐	_____
Shower Door/Rail/Curtain	☐	☐	☐	_____	☐	☐	☐	_____
Sink/Faucets	☐	☐	☐	_____	☐	☐	☐	_____
Plumbing/Drains	☐	☐	☐	_____	☐	☐	☐	_____
Exhaust Fan	☐	☐	☐	_____	☐	☐	☐	_____
Towel Rack(s)	☐	☐	☐	_____	☐	☐	☐	_____
Toilet Paper Holder	☐	☐	☐	_____	☐	☐	☐	_____
Cabinets/Counters	☐	☐	☐	_____	☐	☐	☐	_____

	N	S	O	Comments	S	O	D	Comments
Bath #_____								
Doors/Knobs/Locks	☐	☐	☐	_____	☐	☐	☐	_____
Flooring/Baseboards	☐	☐	☐	_____	☐	☐	☐	_____
Walls/Ceilings	☐	☐	☐	_____	☐	☐	☐	_____
Window Coverings	☐	☐	☐	_____	☐	☐	☐	_____
Windows/Locks/Screens	☐	☐	☐	_____	☐	☐	☐	_____
Light Fixtures	☐	☐	☐	_____	☐	☐	☐	_____
Switches/Outlets	☐	☐	☐	_____	☐	☐	☐	_____
Toilet	☐	☐	☐	_____	☐	☐	☐	_____
Tub/Shower	☐	☐	☐	_____	☐	☐	☐	_____
Shower Door/Rail/Curtain	☐	☐	☐	_____	☐	☐	☐	_____
Sink/Faucets	☐	☐	☐	_____	☐	☐	☐	_____
Plumbing/Drains	☐	☐	☐	_____	☐	☐	☐	_____
Exhaust Fan	☐	☐	☐	_____	☐	☐	☐	_____
Towel Rack(s)	☐	☐	☐	_____	☐	☐	☐	_____
Toilet Paper Holder	☐	☐	☐	_____	☐	☐	☐	_____
Cabinets/Counters	☐	☐	☐	_____	☐	☐	☐	_____

Tenant's Initials   (_____)(_____)   Tenant's Initials   (_____)(_____)

Landlord's Initials   (_____)(_____)   Landlord's Initials   (_____)(_____)

MIMO REVISED 11/07 (PAGE 3 OF 5)

Reviewed by _____ Date _____

EQUAL HOUSING OPPORTUNITY

MOVE IN / MOVE OUT INSPECTION (MIMO PAGE 3 OF 5)

FIGURE 16.3 *(Continued)*

Property Address: _____   Date: _____

	MOVE IN				**MOVE OUT**			
	N	**S**	**O**	**Comments**	**S**	**O**	**D**	**Comments**
Kitchen								
Flooring/Baseboards	☐	☐	☐	_____	☐	☐	☐	_____
Walls/Ceilings	☐	☐	☐	_____	☐	☐	☐	_____
Window Coverings	☐	☐	☐	_____	☐	☐	☐	_____
Windows/Locks/Screens	☐	☐	☐	_____	☐	☐	☐	_____
Light Fixtures	☐	☐	☐	_____	☐	☐	☐	_____
Switches/Outlets	☐	☐	☐	_____	☐	☐	☐	_____
Range/Fan/Hood	☐	☐	☐	_____	☐	☐	☐	_____
Oven(s)/Microwave	☐	☐	☐	_____	☐	☐	☐	_____
Refrigerator	☐	☐	☐	_____	☐	☐	☐	_____
Dishwasher	☐	☐	☐	_____	☐	☐	☐	_____
Sink/Disposal	☐	☐	☐	_____	☐	☐	☐	_____
Faucet(s)/Plumbing	☐	☐	☐	_____	☐	☐	☐	_____
Cabinets	☐	☐	☐	_____	☐	☐	☐	_____
Counters	☐	☐	☐	_____	☐	☐	☐	_____

_____
_____

Hall/Stairs								
Flooring/Baseboards	☐	☐	☐		☐	☐	☐	
Walls/Ceilings	☐	☐	☐		☐	☐	☐	
Light Fixtures	☐	☐	☐		☐	☐	☐	
Switches/Outlets	☐	☐	☐		☐	☐	☐	
Closets/Cabinets	☐	☐	☐		☐	☐	☐	
Railings/Banisters	☐	☐	☐		☐	☐	☐	

_____
_____

Laundry _____

	N	**S**	**O**		**S**	**O**	**D**	
Faucets/Valves	☐	☐	☐	_____	☐	☐	☐	_____
Plumbing/Drains	☐	☐	☐	_____	☐	☐	☐	_____
Cabinets/Counters	☐	☐	☐	_____	☐	☐	☐	_____

_____
_____

Systems								
Furnace/Thermostat	☐	☐	☐	_____	☐	☐	☐	_____
Air Conditioning	☐	☐	☐	_____	☐	☐	☐	_____
Water Heater	☐	☐	☐	_____	☐	☐	☐	_____
Water Softener	☐	☐	☐	_____	☐	☐	☐	_____

Other _____
_____
_____
_____
_____
_____
_____
_____
_____

Tenant's Initials   (_____)(_____)   Tenant's Initials   (_____)(_____)

Landlord's Initials (_____)(_____)   Landlord's Initials (_____)(_____)

MIMO REVISED 11/07 (PAGE 4 OF 5)

Reviewed by _____ Date _____

EQUAL HOUSING OPPORTUNITY

MOVE IN / MOVE OUT INSPECTION (MIMO PAGE 4 OF 5)

FIGURE 16.3 (*Continued*)

Property Address: _____ Date: _____

	MOVE IN				MOVE OUT			
	N	S	O	Comments	S	O	D	Comments
Garage/Parking								
Garage Door	☐	☐	☐	_____	☐	☐	☐	_____
Other Door(s)	☐	☐	☐	_____	☐	☐	☐	_____
Driveway/Floor	☐	☐	☐	_____	☐	☐	☐	_____
Cabinets/Counters	☐	☐	☐	_____	☐	☐	☐	_____
Light Fixtures	☐	☐	☐	_____	☐	☐	☐	_____
Switches/Outlets	☐	☐	☐	_____	☐	☐	☐	_____
Electrical/Exposed Wiring	☐	☐	☐	_____	☐	☐	☐	_____
Window(s)	☐	☐	☐	_____	☐	☐	☐	_____
Other Storage/Shelving	☐	☐	☐	_____	☐	☐	☐	_____
Back/Side/Yard								
Patio/Deck/Balcony	☐	☐	☐	_____	☐	☐	☐	_____
Patio Cover(s)	☐	☐	☐	_____	☐	☐	☐	_____
Landscaping	☐	☐	☐	_____	☐	☐	☐	_____
Sprinklers/Timers	☐	☐	☐	_____	☐	☐	☐	_____
Pool/Heater/Equipment	☐	☐	☐	_____	☐	☐	☐	_____
Spa/Cover/Equipment	☐	☐	☐	_____	☐	☐	☐	_____
Fences/Gates	☐	☐	☐	_____	☐	☐	☐	_____
Safety/Security								
Smoke/CO Detector(s)	☐	☐	☐	_____	☐	☐	☐	_____
Security System	☐	☐	☐	_____	☐	☐	☐	_____
Security Window Bars	☐	☐	☐	_____	☐	☐	☐	_____

Personal Property
_____
_____

Keys/Remotes/Devices
Keys   _____
Remotes/Devices   _____

☐ **Attached Supplement(s)** _____

THIS SECTION TO BE COMPLETED AT MOVE IN: Receipt of a copy of this form is acknowledged by:

Tenant _____ Date _____
Tenant _____ Date _____
New Phone Service Established? ☐ Yes ☐ No   New Phone Number _____
Landlord (Owner or Agent) _____ Date _____
Landlord _____
   (Print Name)

THIS SECTION TO BE COMPLETED AT MOVE OUT: Receipt of a copy of this form is acknowledged by:

Tenant _____ Date _____
Tenant _____ Date _____
Tenant Forwarding Address _____
_____
Landlord (Owner or Agent) _____ Date _____
Landlord _____
   (Print Name)

MIMO REVISED 11/07 (PAGE 5 OF 5)

Reviewed by _____ Date _____

EQUAL HOUSING OPPORTUNITY

MOVE IN / MOVE OUT INSPECTION (MIMO PAGE 5 OF 5)

Source: Reprinted with permission of California Association of REALTORS®.

rent for an unfurnished unit and up to three months' rent for a furnished unit.

When the tenant vacates, the landlord is only allowed to retain as much of the tenant's deposit as is reasonably necessary to remedy tenant defaults. Any unused portion of the deposit must be returned to the tenant at her last known address within three weeks after the premises are vacated. If the landlord fails to comply with this statute, she may be legally liable to the tenant through a small claims court action, through an attorney, or through a complaint filed by the tenant with the Consumer Protection Bureau.

Exculpatory Clause

Leases frequently contain an **exculpatory clause** (hold-harmless clause), whereby the tenant relieves the landlord of any and all liability for personal injury or property damage that results from the owner's negligence or the condition of the property. These clauses are invalid in residential leases, even if the tenant has agreed to one of them, and her legal rights are still intact.

Right of Entry

Most leases contain a provision that allows the landlord to enter the premises for specific purposes. If a lease is lacking such a provision, the landlord can enter only when:

- An emergency requires entry.
- The tenant consents to an entry.
- The tenant has surrendered or abandoned the premises.
- The landlord has obtained a court order permitting entry.
- The entry is during normal business hours after reasonable notice (twenty-four hours is considered reasonable notice) to make necessary or agreed-upon repairs, alterations, or improvements or to show the premises to prospective or actual purchasers, mortgagees, tenants, workers, or contractors.

Tenant's Responsibilities

According to the California Civil Code, a tenant must:

- Keep the living unit clean and sanitary.
- Use all utility fixtures properly.
- Use the property only for its intended lawful purpose.
- Pay rent on time.
- Dispose of garbage and other waste in a sanitary manner.
- Abide by all rules and regulations.

- Give a thirty-day notice when vacating.
- Return door and mailbox keys when vacating.
- Leave the unit in a clean condition when vacating.

Landlord's Responsibilities

A residential lease has an implied warranty of habitability. This does not extend to issues caused by a lack of tenant cleanliness. The landlord must keep the property in reasonably good order and repair, including the plumbing, heating, electrical systems, and all areas under the landlord's care. The roof must be kept free of leaks and all health and safety issues (for example, loose railings) should be corrected in a reasonable time frame.

If the landlord allows the property to fall into a state of *uninhabitable* disrepair or the property becomes uninhabitable because of health and safety issues, the landlord cannot collect any rents. Violating this ordinance subjects the landlord to actual damages suffered by the tenant and special damages of not less than $100 or more than $1,000. A tenant can also raise the defense of habitability against any eviction notice.

If a landlord fails to make a timely correction of a repair that is her responsibility, the tenant has three options:

1. The tenant may abandon the property and not be held liable for back rents or an unfulfilled lease.
2. The tenant may refer the problem to a mediator, an arbitrator, or, for serious problems, small claims court.
3. The tenant may notify the owner in writing of an emergency situation that must be taken care of. If the owner fails to respond, the tenant may call her own repair people and offset the repair costs with up to one month's rent on the next rent check. However, tenants may do this only twice in each year of tenancy.

Note that a tenant cannot be prohibited from installing a satellite dish within the area under tenant control.

Assignment Versus Sublease

A tenant has the right to assign or sublease her interest in a property unless the lease specifically prohibits it.

An assignment transfers the entire leasehold rights to a third party. The third party pays her rent directly to the original lessor and the original lessee is eliminated.

A **sublease** of property transfers only a part of a tenant's interest. The sublessee pays her rent to the original lessee who in turn

is still responsible for payment of rent to the lessor. The original lessee has what is referred to as a "sandwich lease."

A lease should clearly indicate whether or not it may be assigned or subleased. Leases often state that no subletting or assignment shall take place without the express written permission of the lessor, which shall not be unreasonably withheld.

Termination of a Lease

A tenancy for a specified period, such as an estate for years, requires no notice of termination because the date has already been specified. A month-to-month tenancy necessitates a written thirty-day notice because of its perpetual existence. Always check with your broker as termination notice laws are constantly changing.

Evictions and Unlawful Detainer Action

A landlord may evict a tenant and bring an **unlawful detainer action** against her for failure to pay rent when due, violation of provisions contained in the lease or rental agreement, or failure to vacate the premises after termination of thirty days' written notice. To remove a tenant for nonpayment of rent, a landlord must:

- Serve the tenant with a **three-day notice** to pay rent or quit the premises.
- If the tenant fails to heed the notice, the landlord files an unlawful detainer action in municipal court.
- If the landlord wins, the court awards the landlord a judgment. The landlord then asks for a writ of possession authorizing the sheriff to evict the tenant.
- The sheriff sends the tenant an eviction notice. If the tenant fails to leave, the sheriff then physically removes the tenant.

The state of California legislature has authorized several city attorneys and prosecutor offices to bring unlawful detainer actions to abate drug-related nuisances. The landlord is charged fees and costs.

If a small claims court action is necessary to recoup money from a tenant for lost rent or property damage, an owner or property manager may do so without the aid of an attorney. The maximum amount of a small claims court suit is $7,500.

REO and Forclosed Homes

A major provision of the "Helping Families Save Their Homes Act" of 2009 sets the required notice of termination as follows: A REO lender or buyer who acquires title to property through

foreclosure must provide at least a 90-day notice to terminate for a bona fide tenant. Sufficient notice is considered 90 days for a month to month tenant where a new owner will occupy the property as her primary residence. Tenants with a one-year or fixed-term lease of longer duration who have a remaining term in excess of 90 days may stay in the property until the end of the existing lease.

Retaliatory Eviction

A landlord cannot decrease services, increase rent, or evict a tenant within 180 days after the tenant exercises a right protected under the law, including:

- Lawfully organizing a tenant association.
- Complaining to a landlord about the habitability of the premises.
- Complaining to a public agency about property defects.

A tenant cannot waive her rights against retaliatory eviction.

Prohibition of retaliatory eviction is a defense against eviction. If a landlord has been shown to have acted maliciously, the tenant is entitled to actual damages and punitive damages from $100 to $1,000.

16.3 LICENSED REAL ESTATE ASSISTANT
The Value of a Licensee's Time

Currently, most **licensed assistants** earn an hourly wage, depending on their experience, overall skill level, and familiarity with various computer programs. Many are also paid performance **bonuses** that are either tied to gross commission earnings received by the employing licensee from the broker or tied to a dollar value bonus of, say, $200 for every million dollars in closed business by the employing licensee. Many licensees who are seeking to expand their market presence and income will hire a combination licensed assistant (to do escrows, inspections, and so on) and **buyer's representative** or "buyer's rep."

Someone acting as a combination buyer's rep and licensed assistant is often paid as follows. Remember that all commissions are paid to the "hiring" or "employing" broker.

- A salary is paid for the time spent as a licensed assistant.
- If the buyer's rep produces the client, he or she receives a percentage of the commission received by the employing licensee.

- If the employing licensee refers a buyer to the buyer's rep, the buyer's rep receives a percentage of the commission paid to the employing licensee.

If you are acting as a buyer's representative only, then you should receive a percentage of the total compensation received by your office per the employment contract you signed with your broker. The commission split or compensation is always negotiable when you are hired.

To determine if a licensee needs a licensed assistant, she must determine the value of her time. If a licensee's level of production is such that she is earning about the same amount of money on an hourly basis as an assistant, then a choice must be made. Where does the licensee want her career to go and what level of earnings does the licensee wish to attain? If a higher per-hour standard is the answer, a new business plan is in order that will, at some point, include a part-time or full-time licensed assistant to handle the growing amount of "behind-the-scenes" work involved in processing an escrow. Remember, if you do not have an assistant, you are one.

The Right Time to Hire an Assistant

Hiring an assistant isn't always about money. Sometimes it's about having a life. When you have a licensed assistant working for you, you are "in business" fifty-two weeks a year, even when you are on vacation. When you don't have one, you are out of business when you are away or must pay large referral fees to another licensee to handle your business for you.

Often, the first sign that it is time to add a licensed assistant to a licensee's team is when the **seventy-hour syndrome** becomes the norm. Often licensees "ramp up" their activities to earn higher incomes, only to find that the new level of activity necessary to achieve the desired income requires seventy or more hours of work per week and they have all but forfeited most of the other important things in their life. This is a sure sign that an assistant is needed.

The Art of Transitioning

Letting go isn't easy. Most licensees who work at a level requiring an assistant are driven individuals. They tend to want things done their way and often don't have a lot of patience. If you take a

position as a licensed assistant, you must demand that you be given a written but flexible job description and adequate training. Ask also that you have a high level of **communication** between you and your employing licensee. You must be up-to-date on the laws and regulations of the various state and federal agencies that govern real estate and business practice, the policies and regulations of the company that you and the licensee work for, and the licensee's particular way of doing business. Learning this "on the fly" is a sure invitation to disaster, so you must be demanding about proper training.

Licensed assistant duties often include:

- Setting up and maintaining listing and escrow files.
- Scheduling appointments with inspectors, appraisers, and support people.
- **Escrow coordinator** (opening and maintaining escrow files).
- Maintaining contact with lenders and escrow licensees during the escrow and through the after-escrow period until all issues are finalized.
- Keeping the employing licensee advised of missing paperwork.
- Building and maintaining a list of quality service providers.
- Drafting addendums under the employing sales associate's direction.
- Negotiating repair requests.
- Sending copies of inspections and documents to escrow and the co-op broker as needed.
- Preparing informational binders for each new listing taken by the employing licensee.
- Copying entire files and submitting them to the broker.
- Adding clients' names to the employing licensee's database.
- Entering new listings into the MLS (with the company's permission) or submitting them to the company for input.
- Answering calls for and giving general assistance to the clients of the employing licensee when she is away from the office or on vacation.
- Checking and restocking property brochure bins on listings.
- Installing and removing keyboxes on listings.
- Being responsible for all monthly mailings.
- Writing and submitting ads.
- Handling all faxes and advising the licensee of them as necessary.

Hiring/Interviewing

The scope of work of an unlicensed assistant is so narrow that it really doesn't pay to hire someone, especially when combined with the danger of performing licensed activities without a license, which can subject a licensee to sanctions by the California DRE. There is also a distinct difference in the awareness of responsibilities the assistant has to the employing licensee and the general public. It is really a "standard of care" issue that can make or break a licensee's reputation.

Note: If you are seeking a position as a licensed assistant, prepare a professional-looking resume and have it available as necessary. Even if you mailed one to a broker or licensee in advance of an employment interview, bring another copy with you for reference. Be prepared to talk about the strengths you bring to the position and how the licensee would benefit from them. Talk about your organizational skills and your ability to deal effectively with people. If you have good phone skills, make a point of it. If you have no desire to be a full-time real estate salesperson, be sure to explain why, as this is an important issue with employing licensees. After each employment interview, follow up with a handwritten thank-you note to the broker or licensee you spoke with.

Training

As a licensed assistant, you must be trained in two ways. You must be familiar with the licensing laws and regulations of the state of California and the California DRE. Also, ensure that you are fully trained in the policies and procedures of the real estate company you work for and the way your employing sales associate does business.

It can be frustrating taking on a new support position of that nature only to receive constant criticism from the employing sales associate because you aren't doing the activities required of you, especially when your training may have been vague to nonexistent. Be clear about your need for a written job description, a reasonable time to get up to speed, and good, constant communication.

If you are a new or newer licensee, you would be wise to consider taking the course of study necessary to obtain the **Real Estate Professional Assistant (REPA)** designation offered by the National Association of REALTORS®. This comprehensive course is given in four, three-hour segments over two weeks for a cost of about $200.

Talk to your employing sales associate about the value of receiving ongoing training, especially field training in which you accompany the licensee on appointments when an offer is presented to a seller or a listing is taken.

How to Work Effectively with a Licensee

As a licensed assistant or buyer's representative, you serve a vital function in expanding the effectiveness of another licensee's productivity. This is a team effort, and you should expect to be treated as a valued team member. Nothing will take the place of good on-going communication between you to enhance this.

Many experienced licensees find it hard to delegate responsibility to others, and you will need to constantly communicate the importance of your ability to handle your responsibilities to your employing licensee. After experiencing what you can do for her, the employing licensee will become comfortable with you and learn to delegate more and greater responsibility to you. Have patience, but ask for additional duties.

The Four Deadly Sins

Praise in Public, Criticize in Private: There will be times when something just doesn't go as planned and you or your employing sales associate get irritated with each other. Never air your grievances in a public forum. Ask for a meeting in private. Have a written agenda if necessary and openly talk out your differences. There is no faster way to lose a good assistant or get fired by an employing sales associate than to berate her in a public forum. This is embarrassing and should not be done under any circumstances.

Your Bad Day Is Yours, Not Theirs: All of us who have worked in the real estate field know there can be good days and bad days. Both business and personal issues can come to play that are emotional in nature and can cause a person to become sad, grouchy, or even angry. If something happens to you that causes you to be in a miserable mood, don't take it out on your assistant. It is a tough enough job just keeping your escrows current and your clients happy. This is the primary reason assistants quit. Both assistants and sales associates must be ready and willing to talk through problems and frustrations, but neither should use the other as a dumping ground for frustrations or hostility toward others.

Expect Excellence, but Train Thoroughly: Your licensed assistant should be keenly aware of the standard of care you maintain with

the public and your clients and she should be expected to do the same. The only way to maintain this level of care and service is to ensure that your assistant is thoroughly trained in all aspects of the job necessary to fully support you at that level. Someone cannot be expected to maintain a level of service or conduct that she has not been thoroughly trained to meet or exceed.

Keep the Workload Reasonable to Avoid Burnout: As your business expands, the demands placed on you and your licensed assistant to maintain your **standard of care** become more challenging. Be watchful that you do not expand your business beyond what one assistant can reasonably handle. As the employing licensee, you must see that things are done on time and your assistant is working reasonable hours to get them done. If your business is obviously growing and you suddenly start to experience issues, such as late paperwork, files not maintained properly, signs of fatigue in your assistant, many late nights worked, or an unpleasant change of attitude, stop long enough to evaluate your assistant's workload. Ask carefully if she has too much to do. You may find it is time to add another part-time assistant or even a buyer's representative. The point is to stay aware of your operation and if it is growing, keep enough staff to handle it properly. This will avoid costly turnover of assistants. It may be necessary to build an extra cash reserve before hiring an addition to your team, so be watchful and, at the first sign of overwork of your existing support team, check your finances.

It's a Family Affair

One of the fastest growing and most effective types of partnerships occurring in real estate brokerage today is the **husband/wife team**. The advantage is that if both are licensed, each can hold a separate Open House on any given Sunday and double the chances of acquiring a new client, or both people can hold one Open House and double the chances that potential clients will like one of them and want to work with him or her.

Usually either the husband or the wife is more detail oriented and assumes the role of the licensed assistant. If he or she is good with buyers, he or she will assume the dual role of assistant and buyer's representative. In this case, there is a full commission check to the family if one of them sells something.

Communications are usually good between husband/wife teams as well. One drawback is that vacation coverage usually entails using outside help.

SUMMARY

In this chapter you learned about three careers available to people who hold real estate licenses. These include jobs as commercial real estate brokers, property management and leasing, and licensed real estate assistants or buyer's representatives. The commercial real estate practitioner can start in residential real estate and slowly transition into commercial real estate by "time blocking" commercial real estate activities in her daily activities or work for a large commercial real estate firm. Although the latter method usually requires the licensee to have greater financial reserves as it normally takes considerably longer to earn commission checks, the licensee often receives better training and has greater credibility with her commercial clients.

Commercial real estate valuation should always start with a rent survey to evaluate a property's current rental income with pro forma rents that may be available.

The National Association of REALTORS® has several professional designations available such as the CCIM and CPM designations that will greatly enhance a licensee's knowledge and ability to earn a better income and give better service to the public.

Some examples of commercial real estate investments are self-storage facilities, office buildings, apartment complexes, retail shopping centers, and land. Because each takes specialized knowledge, commercial practitioners are wise to specialize in one product type if the size of their community warrants it.

Licensees involved in property management often act as leasing specialists as well and tend to provide services for one particular type of commercial property such as apartment or office buildings. An AMO designation is given by the IREM to firms that meet specific professional standards. The three types of property managers include licensed property manager, individual property manager, and resident manager. Although similar, each performs a different function.

The California DRE's *Reference Book—A Real Estate Guide* defines and lists specific duties that each property manager is charged with, including collecting rents, paying bills, keeping abreast of economic and market conditions, and establishing rent schedules, among other duties. This and other DRE publications are available at www.dre.ca.gov. A trust account is necessary in a property management company and great care must be used to keep it current and accurate.

Great care should be exercised in drafting leases. A lease or rental agreement creates a leasehold estate that may be an estate for years, an estate from period to period, an estate at sufferance,

or an estate at will. The three basic types of leases include the gross lease, net lease, and percentage lease. Each is used with a different type of commercial property. Many percentage leases contain a recapture clause indicating that a landlord may terminate the lease if the tenant does not generate a certain amount of minimum rent.

For a lease to be valid, it must include the names of the parties, be in writing if for longer than one year, show the amount of rent and when and to whom it must be paid, state the duration of the lease, adequately describe the property, be between parties who are capable of contracting, and show any automatic renewals in bold-face type.

Licensees must be careful not to violate any fair housing or ADA rules and regulations when leasing property.

Most leases contain a right of entry provision, whereby the landlord or property manager can enter the premises for specific and lawful purposes. With written consent, leasehold estates may be sublet or assigned. Evictions are started with a notice of violation to the tenant and escalate to an unlawful detainer action by the landlord and, potentially, removal by the county sheriff's office. Retaliatory evictions are not allowed by state law.

Licensees who are considering hiring licensed assistants should assess the value of their time to determine if a licensed assistant is warranted. Some licensees hire a combination licensed assistant/ buyer's representative. This has the advantage of providing a needed part-time assistant and a licensed assistant to refer buyers to and still retain much of the commission income. Salaries and commission rates are negotiable.

If a licensee hires a licensed assistant, the new assistant must be thoroughly trained in governmental, company, and the employing associate's policies, and a complete job description must be created for the assistant to use as an operational guide. Licensed assistant's duties may include setting up and maintaining escrow and listing files, maintaining good client communication throughout an escrow, scheduling appointments on behalf of the employing sales associate, negotiating repair requests, and maintaining the employing sales associate's database.

The hiring interview should include the use of forms and checklists (see Appendix B) and the review of a complete resume. Licensed assistants must be treated with respect, have a fair amount of work to do, and be thoroughly trained. An assistant should be praised in public and criticized in private; they should not be the brunt of an employing sales associate's anger or frustration with things they had nothing to do with. An assistant's workload should be kept to a reasonable level to avoid burnout. Husband/wife teams can make excellent and efficient partnerships.

CLASS DISCUSSION TOPICS

1. Discuss the reasoning behind conducting a rental survey before placing a value on an office building.

2. You have listed two retail shopping centers. One has thirty tenants that are all prospering but there's no anchor tenant; the other has seven tenants including a national chain supermarket that is near the end of its lease with declining sales. Which is the better investment and why?

3. Why must a property manager be so concerned with constantly evaluating area conditions and rental rates of competing properties?

4. You are a property manager. The apartment complex you manage has several leases about to expire. You have just confirmed that a high-tech firm is moving to town in two months and will employ 600 people. What should you do about the upcoming lease renewals?

5. You are an excellent listing licensee and always carry a number of listings. A new marketing system you put in place has started generating even more buyers than you have time to work with. You enjoy your listing activities but don't like working with buyers much. You are currently working over seventy hours a week just to keep up, and your spouse is really getting angry. What action should you take?

CHAPTER 16 QUIZ

1. Which of the following defines CCIM?
   A. Certified Capital Investment Manager
   B. Confirmed Commercial Inventory Manager
   C. Certified Commercial Investment Member
   D. None of the above

2. Which of the following is true about going to work for a large commercial real estate brokerage firm?
   A. It gives you more credibility with your commercial clients.
   B. It requires a large savings account or other source of income.
   C. It usually provides better training than a residential company would offer.
   D. All of the above.

3. Which of the following is defined by a lease under which a tenant is to pay $1,500 per month for five years and none of the operating expenses?
   A. Net lease
   B. Percentage lease
   C. Gross lease
   D. Month-to-month lease

4. Which of the following businesses would likely pay the highest percentage on a percentage lease?
   A. National chain drug store
   B. Men's clothing store
   C. Parking lot
   D. Restaurant

5. A percentage lease contains which of the following?
   A. A minimum rental rate.
   B. An annual CPI increase clause.
   C. A covenant to remain in business clause.
   D. A and C.

6. Which of the following businesses is likely to pay the lowest percentage on a percentage lease?
   A. Tobacco shop
   B. Music store
   C. Real estate office
   D. Supermarket

7. Which is an untrue statement concerning security deposits?
   A. Nonrefundable cleaning deposits are allowed if stated in bold print.
   B. Deposits for unfurnished rentals cannot exceed three months' rent.
   C. Waterbed insurance is not allowed to be mandatory by a landlord.
   D. All of the above.

8. An unlicensed assistant can do which of the following activities?
   A. Call the licensee's sellers and give them Open House results and recommend a price change based on the results.
   B. Telephone prospect for the licensee.
   C. Draft an addendum for the licensee and have the buyers sign it.
   D. None of the above.

9. Which of the following indicates that you need a licensed assistant?
   A. Your children ask who you are.
   B. You work more than seventy hours per week.
   C. Some of your sellers have complained they never hear from you.
   D. All of the above.

10. Which of the following is a good way to lose a licensed assistant?
    A. Criticize the assistant in front of several licensees and the branch manager.
    B. Yell at the assistant because an appraisal on your listing just came in $30,000 low.
    C. Both a and b.
    D. None of the above.

Appendix A
Quiz Answers

Chapter One

1. d.	3. c.	5. c.	7. d.	9. d.
2. b.	4. d.	6. d.	8. d.	10. d.

Chapter Two

1. d.	3. b.	5. d.	7. a.	9. a.
2. d.	4. a.	6. a.	8. d.	10. d.

Chapter Three

1. a.	3. d.	5. d.	7. d.	9. b.
2. d.	4. c.	6. d.	8. a.	10. d.

Chapter Four

1. d.	3. d.	5. a.	7. b.	9. c.
2. d.	4. a.	6. c.	8. d.	10. d.

Chapter Five

1. b.	3. d.	5. b.	7. d.	9. a.
2. b.	4. a.	6. c.	8. d.	10. d.

Chapter Six

1. c.	3. c.	5. a.	7. a.	9. c.
2. c.	4. d.	6. b.	8. b.	10. d.

Chapter Seven

1. a.	3. d.	5. d.	7. a.	9. b.
2. d.	4. c.	6. d.	8. d.	10. d.

Chapter Eight

1. c.	3. d.	5. d.	7. c.	9. b.
2. a.	4. a.	6. d.	8. d.	10. a.

Chapter Nine

1. c.	3. d.	5. c.	7. d.	9. c.
2. d.	4. d.	6. d.	8. d.	10. a.

Chapter Ten

1. b.	3. d.	5. a.	7. c.	9. d.
2. a.	4. d.	6. d.	8. d.	10. b.

Chapter Eleven

1. c.	3. b.	5. c.	7. a.	9. d.
2. d.	4. c.	6. a.	8. d.	10. d.

Chapter Twelve

1. d.	3. d.	5. d.	7. d.	9. c.
2. a.	4. a.	6. b.	8. d.	10. b.

Chapter Thirteen

1. d.	3. c.	5. b.	7. d.	9. c.
2. c.	4. c.	6. a.	8. b.	10. d.

Chapter Fourteen

1. c.	3. d.	5. d.	7. b.	9. c.
2. d.	4. d.	6. b.	8. b.	10. a.

Chapter Fifteen

1. d.	3. c.	5. c.	7. d.	9. b.
2. d.	4. a.	6. a.	8. d.	10. d.

Chapter Sixteen

1. c.	3. c.	5. d.	7. d.	9. d.
2. d.	4. c.	6. d.	8. d.	10. c.

Appendix B

Licensed Assistant Pre-employment application

Full name _____

Address

_____

City, State, Zip _____

Telephone numbers: Home _____ Cell _____

E-mail address _____ DOB (D/M ONLY) _____

Driver's license # _____ Soc. Security # _____

(You will be required to present both if you are offered employment)

How far do you live from this location? _____

Do you have your own transportation? _____

EMPLOYMENT HISTORY (Start with most recent and provide at least two years).

Employer name/phone   From   To

_____

Duties:

_____

_____

_____

_____

Employer name/phone   From   To

_____

Duties:

_____

_____

_____

_____

Employer name/phone   From   To

_____

(continued)

Duties:

_____

_____

_____

_____

By initialing below, you are giving us permission to contact your previous employers.

_____

Initial here

PERSONAL REFERENCES:

Name _____

Address _____

Telephone number _____

Relationship _____

Years known _____

Name _____

Address _____

Telephone number _____

Relationship _____

Years known _____

Name _____

Address _____

Telephone number _____

Relationship _____

Years known _____

By initialing below, you are giving us permission to contact your references.

_____

Initials

Licensed Assistant Interview Sheet

1. Are you currently licensed in this state? If yes, for how long?

2. Are you licensed in any other state? If so, do you plan to return there?

3. Tell me about your real estate career if you've had one, and why you decided on a real estate career.

4. Are you currently employed? If so, where, and for how long?

5. Why are you making the transition from sales to a licensed assistant position?

6. What is the best job that you've ever had, and what did you like the most about it?

7. What former job did you like the least and why?

8. Are you aware of the many duties that are required of a licensed assistant?

9. How do you feel about working some weekends?

10. Would you be willing to show property to some of my clients and write offers for me for a bonus if it was necessary?

11. If you are selected, you will need to supply me with at least two former clients and two agents as references; will you do that?

12. If an angry client called and was verbally abusive to you, how would you handle it?

13. What questions do you have for me at this time?

Glossary

A

abatement of judgment A document containing a condensation of the essential provisions of a court judgment.

abatement of nuisance The act of ending or terminating a nuisance; a type of legal action brought to end a nuisance.

abstract of judgment A summary of money judgment. The summary is usually prepared so that it may be recorded, thereby creating a (judgment) lien on real estate owned by the judgment debtor.

abstract of title A summary of the instruments affecting title to a parcel of real property as shown by the public records.

acceleration clause
1. A clause in a deed of trust or mortgage giving the lender the right to call all sums owing her to be immediately due and payable upon the occurrence of a certain event. It is also a clause that permits a debtor to pay off a loan before the due date.
2. A clause in a promissory note, deed of trust, or mortgage that provides that upon default of a payment or some other stated event, the entire unpaid balance becomes immediately due and payable.

acceptance An essential element of every contract, it is the consent to be bound by the offer. In deeds, it is the consent to accept a grant of real property.

access right The right of an owner to go into and out of her property.

accommodation party A person who, without receiving value, signs a promissory note to help another person borrow money or get credit.

accord and satisfaction The discharge of an existing contract by accepting the performance under a substitute contract. Generally, consideration under the new contract is different from and of lesser value than under the original contract, and satisfaction is the performance of that contract; the combination discharges the original contract.

accretion A gradual addition to land from natural causes; for example, from gradual action of ocean or river waters.

accrued depreciation
1. For purposes of appraisal, accrued depreciation is the difference between the cost of replacement as of the date of the appraisal and the present appraised value.
2. The accumulated loss in value that has affected the improvements on real property.

acknowledgment A formal declaration before an officer duly authorized as a notary public by a person who has executed an instrument, stating that the execution is her act and deed. A formal statement (usually before a notary public) by the person signing a deed or document that the instrument was actually and freely signed.

acoustical tile Blocks of fiber, mineral, or metal with small holes or a rough-textured surface to absorb sound, used as covering for interior walls and ceilings.

acquisition The act or process by which a person procures property.

acre A measure of land equaling 160 square rods, 4,840 square yards, 43,560 square feet, or a tract about 208.71 feet square.

ad valorem According to value.

ADA Refers to the Americans with Disabilities Act. The ADA applies to equal access to employment, public services, public accommodations, public transportation, and telecommunications.

adjacent Located next to or near an object or parcel of property.

adjoining Located so as to touch an object or share a common property line.

adjusted cost basis For tax purposes, it is the original cost of the property plus improvements and minus allowable depreciation, amortization, and depletion.

administrator A person appointed by the probate court to administer the estate of a deceased person who has died without a will (intestate). Her duties include making an inventory of the assets, managing the property, paying the debts and expenses, filing necessary reports and tax returns, and distributing the assets as ordered by the probate court. (See also Executor.)

adverse possession A method of acquiring property based on open and notorious possession, under a claim of right, color of title, continuous use for five years, and the payment of taxes. A method of acquiring property through continuous use of that property while paying taxes on it.

advertising The process of calling attention to something to arouse a desire to buy the product or service being promoted. (See Truth in Lending Act) (TILA).

affidavit A statement or declaration reduced to writing, sworn to or affirmed before some officer who has authority to administer an oath or affirmation, such as a notary public or a commanding officer in the service.

affirm As relating to contracts affirm means to confirm, swear, ratify, verify, or accept a contract that could otherwise be cancelled.

agency A special relationship of trust by which one person (agent) is authorized to conduct business, sign papers, or otherwise act on behalf of another person (principal). This relationship may be created by expressed agreement, ratification, or estoppel. In California, only a licensed real estate broker may represent another in the purchase, sale, or lease of real property for compensation.

agent One who represents another, called a principal, and has authority to act for the principal in dealing with third parties. The relationship is referred to as an agency relationship. Someone authorized to act for another (the principal) in business matters. In California, only a licensed real estate broker may represent another in the purchase, sale, or lease of real property for compensation. (See Real Estate Agent.)

agreement of sale
1. A written contract between a buyer and seller setting out the terms of sale.
2. An installment sales contract covering real property, especially a long-term contract.

AIDS The sellers of real property, their agents, or their subagents may not disclose that somebody died of AIDS or had AIDS in said property.

alienation The transferring of property to another. Conveyance or transfer of title to real estate from one person to another person.

alienation clause In a deed of trust or mortgage, a provision that if the secured property is sold or transferred, the lender has the option of accelerating the loan and declaring the entire unpaid balance immediately due and payable. Also called a "due on sale" clause.

alligator Purchasing lower-priced properties will limit the appetite of the alligator. The alligator is an expensive piece of property that gobbles up all the profits. Negative cash flow on a keeper property is referred to as an alligator.

all-inclusive trust deed (AITD) A form of seller financing that is subordinate to but including the original debt or encumbrances. Similar to a wraparound mortgage but uses trust deed instead of a mortgage.

alluvion (alluvium) Soil that has been deposited by accretion on the shore of a river or body of water and that increases the real property.

ALTA policy The title insurance policy issued to institutional lenders. The initials stand for American Land Title Association, an organization that regulates and standardizes the provisions within title policies.

alternate fee listings Also called "flat rate or fixed fee MLS listing," it refers to the practice

used by some limited agency firms of unbundling their compensation schedule to charge only for individual services rendered, such as signs, brochures, MLS listing, and so forth. (See MLS access only listings.)

ameliorating waste Improvements to property that, while not damaging the value of the property, technically qualify as waste. For example, an apartment building constructed on property designated only for single-family structures is considered ameliorating waste.

amenities As used in the real estate business, the features that make a piece of real property, especially a home, enjoyable.

amortization
1. The liquidation of a financial obligation on an installment basis, which includes both principal and interest.
2. Recovery of cost or value over a period of time. The method or plan for the payment of a debt, bond, deed of trust, and so on by installments or sinking fund.

amortization schedule A list of the due dates and amounts by which the principal sum of an obligation will be reduced by partial payments.

annual percentage rate (APR) The cost of credit as determined in accordance with Regulation Z of the Board of Governors of the Federal Reserve System for implementing the Federal Truth in Lending Act.

annuity A sum of money received or paid yearly or at other fixed periods.

anticipatory breach Advance notice of intention to violate the terms of a contract.

appeal The review or rehearing by a higher court of a low (inferior) court's decision.

appraisal An estimate and opinion of value. An opinion or estimate of the fair market value of a property.

appraiser One qualified by education, training, and experience who is hired to estimate the value of real and personal property on the basis of experience, judgment, facts, and use of formal appraisal processes.

appurtenant Attached to or considered part of land, because of being considered necessary and incidental to the use of that land. Commonly applied to easements that are considered part of property.

assemblage The act of assembling smaller contiguous parcels of land or improved property to create a larger and more valuable single parcel.

assessed value Value placed on property as a basis for taxation. A value used by the tax assessor before July 1978. It represented 25 percent of the assessor's fair market value. After deducting any exemptions from assessed value, one applied the tax rate to the net figure to determine annual property taxes.

assessment An official valuation of property for the purpose of levying a tax, or the amount of tax levied.

assessor The official who has the responsibility of determining the assessed values.

assignee One to whom property is assigned or transferred.

assignment A transfer of any property or right to another. The transfer of one's entire interest in property. Generally, the term is limited to intangible personal property (that is, stocks, bonds, promissory notes) and to leasehold estates.

assignment of rents clause A clause in a deed of trust or mortgage, providing that in the event of default, all rents and income from the secured property will be paid to the lender to help reduce the outstanding loan balance.

assignor One who assigns or transfers property.

assumption Acceptance of personal liability for another's debt or obligation. In the case of the sale of real estate, the buyer personally accepts and promises to pay off the existing deed of trust.

assumption of agreement A contract by which a person agrees to pay a debt or obligation owed by someone else.

assumption of mortgage or deed of trust The taking of title to property by a grantee in which she assumes liability for payment of existing note secured by a mortgage or deed of trust against the property.

attachment Seizure of property by court order before judgment, usually done to have it available in the event a judgment is obtained in a pending lawsuit. The actual or constructive

seizure of property by court order during a lawsuit. The usual purpose is to hold the assets as security for the satisfaction of a judgment.

attachment lien A lien on property arising because of an attachment of that property.

attorney in fact An agent authorized to perform certain acts for another under a power of attorney. (See Power of Attorney.)

avulsion The sudden tearing away or removal of land by the action of water flowing over or through it.

B

backfill The replacement of excavated earth in a hole or against the side of a structure.

balance sheet A financial statement showing a person's assets, liabilities, and net worth.

balloon payment When the final payment on a note is greater than the preceding normal installments, the final installment is termed a balloon payment. An installment promissory note providing for the last payment to be much larger than any previous payment. By statute, any payment more than twice the smallest payment is a balloon payment, although in practice generally the term refers only to the last payment.

bankruptcy A state of adjudicated insolvency per federal bankruptcy law. Will not eliminate all loans secured by real property.

base and meridian Imaginary lines used by surveyors from which they find, measure, and describe the location of lands.

base molding Molding used at the top of the baseboard.

base shoe Molding used at junction of baseboard and floor, sometimes called a carpet strip.

baseboard A board that goes around the room against the wall and next to the floor.

batten Narrow strips of wood or metal used to cover joints on the interior or exterior of a building; they are also used for decorative effect.

blockbusting The illegal practice of trying to lower property values through the instigation of panic selling in a neighborhood.

bearing wall or partition A wall or partition that supports any vertical load, in addition to its own weight.

benchmarks A location indicated on a permanent marker by surveyors.

beneficiary
1. One entitled to benefit from a trust.
2. The lender on the security of a note and deed of trust. The creditor (lender) under a deed of trust.

beneficiary statement (See Offset Statement.)

betterment An improvement on real property that increases the value and is considered a capital asset.

bilateral contract A contract in which the consideration given by each party is a promise, that is, a promise for a promise.

bill of sale A written instrument given by the seller to the buyer to pass title to personal property.

binder A written statement that binds the parties to an agreement until formal contracts can be drawn; an agreement to cover a down payment as evidence of good faith.

blanket trust deed A deed of trust binding more than one parcel of property as security. It is frequently encountered in subdivisions, where every lot in the subdivision is bound by the same deed of trust. As the lots are sold, they are released from the deed of trust by a partial release provision.

blanket mortgage One mortgage that covers more than one piece of real property.

blighted area An area in which real property is declining in value because of destructive economic forces.

blog An online journal allowing discussion, reflection, and the sharing of opinions on various topics.

board foot A unit of measurement for lumber: 1 foot wide, 1 foot long, 1 inch thick (144 cubic inches).

bona fide A Latin term meaning "in good faith."

bona fide purchaser (BFP) A purchaser who pays fair value for property in good faith, and without notice of adverse claims.

book value An accounting term that is the difference between cost and the total amount of depreciation that has been taken. Net worth of a property as carried on the corporate balance sheet.

bracing Frame lumber nailed at an angle in order to provide stability to the structure.

breach The breaking of or failure of duty, violation of or failure to perform an obligation.

broker An agent who earns income by arranging sales and other contracts. A real estate broker is an individual licensed by the state of California to arrange the sale or transfer of interests in real property for compensation.

broker's trust fund account Withdrawals from this account may be made only by the broker.

brownfields Refers to the Small Business Liability Relief and Brownfields Revitalization Act (2002). A federal law relating to contaminated properties where future use may be complicated by hazardous substances. (See www.epa.gov/brownfields/index.html)

BTU British Thermal Unit; the quantity of heat required to raise the temperature of one pound of water one degree Fahrenheit.

building line Often called a setback line, a building line is a line running a certain distance from the street, in front of which an owner cannot build. These lines are set by law.

building paper A heavy waterproofed paper used as sheathing in exterior walls or in roof construction as insulation and protection against moisture.

business and professions code One of the twenty-five California codes containing the laws passed by the state legislature. It contains the statutes regulating the conduct of real estate brokers and establishes the Department of Real Estate.

business opportunity A term used to describe a business including its stock-in-trade, fixtures, and goodwill.

C

C.A.R. Abbreviation for the California Association of REALTORS®

C.C. & R. Abbreviation for covenants, conditions, and restrictions. Often used synonymously with general plan restrictions on a subdivision.

CAL VET LOAN (California Veterans Farm and Home Purchase Program) A program administered by the State Department of Veterans Affairs for the direct financing of farms and homes for veterans who qualify. The funds for these loans come from the sale of state bonds.

capital assests Assets of a permanent nature used in the production of income. Examples would include land, buildings, and equipment.

capital gain The gain recognized for federal and state income tax purposes when a taxpayer disposes of a capital asset.

capital gain—short term An asset held for one year or less. The holding period is determined by the date of acquisition and the date of sale. Capital gains are taxed differently according to the length of time held. Short-term capital gains are currently taxed at ordinary income rates.

capital gain—long term An asset held for more than one year. At this time the tax rate may be 5 percent or 15 percent, depending on your marginal tax rate.

capitalization In appraising, a method of determining value of property by considering net income and a reasonable percentage of return on the investment.

capitalization rate The percentage rate or rate of interest considered a reasonable return on the investment. It is used in the capitalization method of determining value based upon net return.

casement window Windows set in frames of wood or metal that swing outward.

cash flow The new amount of cash a property produces when all cash income and other cash generated are added together and all cash expenses and other cash payments are deducted.

cause of action A legal right; facts giving rise to an enforceable claim.

caveat emptor A Latin phrase meaning "let the buyer beware"; the legal maxim stating that the buyer must examine the goods or property and buy at her own risk.

certificate of reasonable value (CRV) The Veterans Administration's written appraisal of the value of a property.

certified property manager (CPM) A member of the Institute of Real Estate Property management of the National Association of REALTORS®

chain of title A series of conveyances, encumbrances, and other instruments affecting the title from the time original patent was granted, or as far back as records are available. A history of the recorded ownership of real estate and claims against title to real estate.

chattel
1. Personal property.
2. This term is sometimes used in a law to describe any interest in real or personal property other than a freehold.

chattel mortgage A personal property mortgage. (See Security Agreement.)

chattel real In real estate, an estate less than a freehold estate, such as a lease.

circuit breaker An electrical device that automatically interrupts an electrical circuit when an overload occurs. Circuit breakers can be reset and, today, are used instead of fuses.

civil code One of the twenty-five California codes containing the statutes passed by the state legislature. The most important code relating to contracts and real estate, the Civil Code defines the nature and requirements for contracts and real estate transactions, among its many other provisions.

civil law A system of jurisprudence, sometimes called Roman law, wherein all the laws are set forth in advance to regulate conduct (as opposed to common law, where the principles of law develop on a case-by-case basis). In California the term also refers to the law relating to and between individuals, as opposed to criminal law.

client One who pays an agent to perform a service for a fee. Real estate has traditionally referred to the seller as the client and the buyer as the customer unless the buyer has entered into a Buyer Representation Agreement.

cloud on title A claim or document that affects title to real estate. The actual cloud may ultimately prove invalid, but its existence mars the title.

CLTA policy The title insurance policy issued to homeowners and noninstitutional lenders. The initials stand for the California Land Title Association, which regulates and standardizes the provisions within title policies.

code of civil procedure One of the twenty-five California codes that contain the statutes passed by the state legislature. It contains most of the procedural requirements for enforcing rights granted by other codes, including the procedures for evictions, foreclosures, and lawsuits.

codicil An amendment to a will.

collar beam A beam that connects the pairs of opposite roof rafters above the attic floor.

collateral Property subject to a security interest; property used as security for a debt. (See Security Agreement.)

collateral security The transfer of property of other valuables to ensure the performance of a principal agreement; an obligation attached to a contract to guarantee its performance.

collusion A secret agreement between two or more persons wishing to defraud another for a wrongful purpose or to obtain an object forbidden by law.

color of title That which appears to be a good title but, in fact, is not; for example, a forged deed. A document that appears to convey title but in fact is ineffective, conveying no title at all. It is one of the requirements for adverse possession and easement by prescription.

commercial acre A term applied to the remainder of an acre of land after the area devoted to streets, sidewalks, curbs, and so on has been deducted from the acre.

commingling The mixing of different funds so that they can no longer be distinguished. In domestic law it refers to the combination of separate property and community property, so that the separate property and community funds can no longer be distinguished; in such cases all property is considered community property. For brokers it refers to the mixing of clients' money with the broker's separate bank accounts.

commission An licensed broker's compensation for performing the duties of her agency agreement. In the real estate business, this fee is usually a negotiated percentage of the selling price of a home or a percentage of the lease or rents.

common law The body of law that grew from customs and practices developed and used in England. A body of unwritten law that developed from the general customs and usage. It was adopted in the United States and exercised by court decisions following the ancient English principles and the recorded law of a state.

community property All property acquired by a husband and wife living together, except separate property. (See Separate Property.) Property owned in common by a husband and wife as a kind of marital partnership.

compaction Packing or consolidation of soil. When soil is added to a lot to fill in low places or to raise the level of the lot, it is often too loose to sustain the weight of buildings. Therefore, it is necessary to compact the added soil so that it will carry the weight of the building without the danger of settling or cracking.

comparative (or competitive) market analysis (CMA) One of the three methods in a appraisal process. A means of comparing similar type properties, which have recently sold, to the subject property to determine a selling price range.

compound interest Interest paid on the original principal and also on the accrued and unpaid interest that has accumulated as the debt matures.

condemnation
1. The act of taking private property for public use by a political subdivision.
2. A declaration by proper governmental authorities that a structure is unfit for use. The takeover of private property for public use through the exercise of the power of eminent domain.

condition
1. A provision in a contract stating that the contract will not go into effect or that it will terminate upon the occurrence of some specified future event.
2. A restriction added to a conveyance that, upon the occurrence or nonoccurrence of some act or event, causes the estate to be defeated.
3. A contractual provision that upon the occurrence or nonoccurrence of a stated act or event, an obligation is created, destroyed, or defeated.

condition precedent A condition that must occur before an estate is created or enlarged, or before some other right or obligation occurs.

condition subsequent A condition that, upon its failure or nonperformance, causes the defeat or extinguishment of an estate, right, or obligation.

conditional commitment A loan commitment for a definite amount under certain terms and conditions. It is subject to an unknown purchaser's satisfactory credit rating.

conditional sale contract A contract for the sale of property whereby the seller retains legal title until the conditions of the contract have been fulfilled. The buyer has an equitable interest in the property. (See Security Agreement.) A contract for the sale of property by which possession is delivered to the buyer, but title remains with the seller until full payment or the satisfaction of other stated conditions.

conditional use permit An exception to or relief from the application of a zoning ordinance, because of special authorization granted by the zoning authorities. The issuance rests on public policy benefits and prior authorization in the zoning ordinance.

condominium A system of individual ownership of units in a multifamily structure, combined with joint ownership of common areas of the structure and the land. The ownership of an individual unit in a multiunit structure, combined with joint ownership of common walkways, land, and other portions of the property.

confirmation of sale A court approval of the sale of property by an executor, administrator, guardian, or conservator.

consideration Anything of value, or that is legally sufficient, given to induce someone to enter into a contract. The inducement for

entering into a contract—usually involving money, services, or a promise—although it may consist of a legal benefit to the promisor or any legal detriment to the promisee.

constructive eviction A breach of the landlord's warranty of quiet enjoyment. Any acts by the landlord that substantially interferes with the tenant's use and enjoyment of the premises.

constructive notice A notice given by the public records; that is considered equivalent to actual notice even though there is not actual notice.

1. Notice given by a recorded document.
2. Notice imputed by a law because a person could have discovered certain facts upon reasonable investigation, and a "reasonable man" in the same situation would have conducted such an investigation.

Consumer Credit Protection Act (See Truth in Lending Act.)

contingent Conditional; uncertain; conditioned upon the occurrence or nonoccurrence of some uncertain future event.

continuation statement A statement filed to extend the time limit on a financing statement that had been filed earlier.

contract of sale (See Conditional Sale Contract.)

convenant A contractual agreement whereby one of the parties promises to perform or to refrain from doing certain acts.

conventional loan A loan that is made using real estate as security; that is not federally insured or guaranteed.

conversion The misappropriation or misuse of trust funds.

convertible adjustable rate Allows the borrower to adjust to a fixed interest rate.

cooperative apartment A form of ownership in which each individual owner becomes a shareholder of a corporation that holds title to the apartment. This coop owner is granted a proprietary lease to a specific unit. Such interest is treated as personal property. Each coop shareholder is responsible for her share of corporate expenses including property taxes and maitenance.

cost basis (See Adjusted Cost Basis.)

cotenancy Where two or more individuals have rights to an undivided interest in the same property.

counteroffer The rejection of an offer by the submission of another offer, different in terms from the original offer. Any purported acceptance of an offer that introduces new terms is a rejection of that offer and amounts to a counteroffer.

coversion The wrongful appropriation of another's goods to one's own use; to change from one character or use to another.

1. In tort, an unauthorized claim of ownership over another's personal property.
2. In property, the change of character of property from real to personal, or vice versa.

credit unions A growing source of funds for real estate loans.

CRV Abbreviation for Certificate of Reasonable Value.

D

dealer As it relates to real estate, a dealer is a person who holds property primarily for sale to her customers in the ordinary course of her business.

debt service The sum of money needed to amortize the loan or loans during each payment period.

debtor

1. A party who "owns" the property that is subject to a security interest.
2. A person who owes a debt.

declaratory relief A court's decision on the rights of the parties in a question of law, without ordering anything to be done.

dedication An appropriation of land by its owner for some public use and accepted for such use by authorized public officials on behalf of the public. A gift of privately owned land to the public or for public use. It may be voluntary or involuntary.

deed A written instrument that, when properly executed and delivered, conveys title.

deed of trust A security instrument transferring title to property to a third person (trustee) as security for a debt or other obligation.

default
1. Failure to fulfill a duty or promise, or to discharge an obligation.
2. Omission or failure to perform any act. Failure to perform a legal duty or to discharge a promise.

default judgment A judgment obtained because the defendant failed to appear and defend her case.

defeasance clause The clause in a mortgage or deed of trust that gives the borrower the right to redeem her property upon the payment of her obligations to the lender.

defeasible Capable of being defeated. A defeasible estate is one that has a condition attached to the title that, if broken, causes the termination of that estate.

defendant The party being sued in a lawsuit; the party against whom an action is filed.

deferred maintenance Maintenance and accumulated repairs that have been postponed.

deficiency judgment A judgment given for the unpaid balance of a debt remaining after the surety is sold. A court decree holding a debtor personally liable for the shortage or insufficiency realized on the sale of secured property. The debtor owes the difference between the sale price of the property and the amount of the secured debt.

delivery (of a deed) The unconditional, irrevocable intent of a grantor immediately to divest (give up) an interest in real estate by a deed or other instrument.

deposit Money offered by a buyer to a seller usually in conjunction with a purchase offer to indicate good faith. Also known as earnest money. The money is usually intended to be applied toward the purchase price of property, or forfeited on failure to complete the contract.

deposit receipt A contract used in the real estate business that includes the terms of the contract and acts as a receipt for "earnest money" to bind an offer for property by the prospective purchaser. The name given to most real estate contracts containing the terms of the sale of real estate and receipt for earnest money (deposited).

depreciation A loss in value from any cause. This loss in value to real property may be caused by age or physical deterioration, or by functional or economic obsolescence.

desist and refrain order An order that the Real Estate Commissioner is empowered by law to issue; orders individuals to refrain from committing an act in violation of the Real Estate Law.

deterioration The process of gradual worsening or depreciation.

devise A gift of real property by deed.

devisee One who receives real property under a will.

directional growth The direction in which the residential sections of a city seem destined or determined to grow.

disclosure statement A statement that the Truth in Lending Law requires a creditor to give a debtor showing the finance charge, annual percentage rate, and other required information.

discount To sell a promissory note before maturity at a price less than the outstanding principal balance of the note at the time of sale. It may also be the amount deducted in advance by the lender from the face of the note.

discount points A fee charged by the lender when making an FHA or VA loan to offset the lower interest rate the lender will receive compared with conventional loan interest rates. One point is equal to 1 percent.

discount rate The interest rate that is charged on money borrowed by banks from the Federal Reserve System.

discounted trust deed A trust deed that is sold at less than its face value. An investment in this kind of deed can be a perfect investment.

discriminatory conduct Conduct that negatively impacts a person of a protected class. The DRE Regulations state that discriminatory conduct is a basis for disciplinary action and civil litigation.

district court The main trial court in the federal court system and the lowest federal court. It has jurisdiction in civil cases where the plaintiffs and defendants are from different states (diversity of citizenship) and the amount in

controversy is over $10,000, and in cases involving a federal question.

dominant tenement The tenement obtaining the benefit of an easement appurtenant. The parcel of land that benefits from an easement across another parcel of property (servient tenement).

double escrow An escrow that will close only upon the condition that a prior escrow is consummated. The second escrow is contingent upon and tied to the first escrow. While double escrow is not illegal, unless there is full and fair disclosure of the second escrow, there may be a possibility of fraud or other actionable conduct by the parties.

due on encumbrance clause A clause in a deed of trust or mortgage that provides that upon the execration of additional deeds of trust or other encumbrances against a secured parcel of property, the lender may declare the entire unpaid balance of principal and interest due and owing.

due on sale clause An acceleration clause that grants the lender the right to demand full payment of the mortgage or deed of trust upon sale of the property. A clause in a deed of trust or mortgage that provides that if the secured property is sold or transferred, the lender may declare the entire unpaid balance immediately due and payable. Its use has been severely limited by recent court decisions. Also called an alienation clause.

E

earnest money A deposit of money paid by a buyer for real property as evidence of good faith. The primary purpose of earnest money is to serve as a source of damages in the event of buyer breach or default.

easement A right, privilege, or interest that one party has to use the land of another. Example: A right of way. A legal right to use another's land for one's benefit or the benefit of one's property (right of way).

easement appurtenant An easement created for the benefit of a particular parcel of property. There is both a dominant and a servient estate. The easement is annexed to and part of the dominant property.

easement in gross An easement that benefits a particular individual, not a parcel of property. It involves only a servient estate. A public utility easement is an example.

economic life The useful life of an improvement or structure; that period during which an improvement will yield a return on the investment.

economic obsolescence The loss in value to property due to external causes such as zoning or a deteriorating neighborhood. It is also referred to as social obsolescence.

effective gross income The amount of net income that remains after the deduction from gross income of vacancy and credit losses.

E.I.R. Abbreviation for Environmental Impact Report.

emblements Things that grow on the land that require annual planting and cultivation.

eminent domain The right of the government and certain others, such as public utilities, to acquire property for public or quasi-public use by condemnation, upon payment of just compensation to the owner. The constitutional or inherent right of a government to take private property for public good upon the payment of just compensation.

encroachment The projection of a structure onto the land of an adjoining owner. A structure or natural object that unlawfully extends into another's property.

encumbrance Any claim, interest, or right improperly possessed by another that may diminish the true owner's rights or value in the estate. Examples include mortgages, easements, or restrictions of any kind. A claim, lien, or charge on property.

endorsement
1. The act of signing one's name on the back of a check or a note, with or without further qualification.
2. The signature described above.

environmental impact report A report that must be prepared whenever any agency or individual considers a project that may have a significant impact on the environment, as directed by the California Environmental Quality Act.

Equal Credit Opportunity Act Prohibits discrimination among lenders.

equal housing opportunity Prohibits discrimination in the listing, sale, lease, rental, or financing of real property due to race, creed, religion, sex, marital status, or handicap. Should apply exactly the same in all real estate transactions.

equal protection The Fourteenth Amendment to the U.S. Constitution and similar provisions in the California Constitution require each citizen to receive equal protection of the laws. There are no minimum standards of protection; all equally situated individuals must simply be treated equally. (The due process clause of the Constitution imposes certain minimum standards of protection.)

equity
1. The interest or value that an owner has in real property over and above the liens against it.
2. A part of our justice system by which courts seek to supplement the strict terms of the law to fairness under the circumstances, rather than on fixed legal principles or statutes.
3. Ownership in property, determined by calculating the fair market value less the amount of liens and encumbrances.

equity buildup The increase of the owner's equity due to mortgage principal reduction and value appreciation.

equity of redemption The right to redeem property during the foreclosure period. In California the mortgagor has the right to redeem within twelve months after the foreclosure sale.

erosion The wearing away of the surface of the land by the action of wind, water, and glaciers, for example.

escalator clause A clause in a contract that provides for the upward or downward adjustment of certain items to cover the specific contingencies set forth. A clause in a promissory note, lease, or other document that provides that upon the passage of a specified time or the happening of a stated event, the interest rate shall increase.

escheat The reversion of property to the state when there are no devisees or heirs capable of inheritance. Reversion of property to the state upon the death of an owner who has no heirs able to inherit.

escrow The deposit of instruments and funds with a third neutral party with instructions to carry out the provisions of an agreement or contract. A complete or perfect escrow is one in which everything has been deposited to enable carrying out the instructions. The neutral third party (stakeholder) who holds money, deeds, or other documents pursuant to instructions for delivery upon completion or occurrence of certain conditions.

estate The degree, quantity, nature, and extent of the interest that a person has in real property.
1. Ownership interest in real estate.
2. The quality and quantity of rights in property.

estate at will The occupation of real property by a tenant for an indefinite period. One or both parties may terminate it at will. A leasehold tenancy which at common law could be terminated by either party at any time without advance notice. Thirty days' notice is now required to terminate this type of estate in California.

estate for life A freehold estate whose duration is measured by and limited to the life or lives of one or more persons.

estate for period to period A leasehold tenancy that continues indefinitely for successive periods of time, until terminated by proper notice. When the periods are one month in duration, it is often called a month-to-month tenancy.

estate for years A lease that will expire at a definite time or date. A leasehold tenancy of a fixed duration, being a definite and ascertainable period of a year or any fraction or multiple thereof. It has a definite beginning and ending date, and hence a known and definite duration. A six-month lease would be an estate for years because it has a beginning and ending date.

estate of inheritance An estate that may go to the heirs of the deceased. All freehold estates are estates of inheritance, except life estates.

estop To ban, stop, or impede.

estoppel A doctrine whereby one is forbidden to contradict or deny her own previous statement, act, or position. The doctrine that prevents a person from exercising a legal right, because that person previously acted in an inconsistent manner, so that a third person detrimentally relied on the earlier acts. An agency is created this way when an individual knowingly allows another individual to act as their agent without authorizing such acts.

estoppel certificate (or clause) The assertion in a contract that mortgage debt and collateral pledged are correct as of the date of the agreement. A written statement by tenants of the amount of rent they pay, the amount of any other funds held by the landlord on their behalf and a statement that they are not withholding any rent due to condition of property issues.

ethics A standard of conduct that all members of a given profession owe to the public, clients or patrons, and other members of that profession. Refers to a branch of philosophy that deals with moral science and moral principles. It is a debatable subject and cannot be legislated. It is based on what each individual feels is good or bad.

ethnic Pertaining to a group of people sharing a common or distinctive culture, religion, or language. The seller of a property is not allowed to ask the buyer their ethnic background.

eviction Dispossession by legal process, as in the termination of a tenant's right to possession through reentry or other legal proceedings.

exclusive agency listing A written agreement giving one agent the exclusive right to sell property for a specified period of time, but reserving the right of the owner to sell the property himself or herself without liability for the payment of a commission.

exclusive authorization and right to sell listing A written agreement giving one agent the exclusive right to sell property for a specified period of time. The agent may collect a commission if the property is sold by anyone, including the owner, during the term of the listing agreement.

exculpatory clause A provision in leases and other instruments seeking to relieve one party of liability for her negligence and other acts. In residential leases such clauses are invalid, and in other leases the courts have limited the landlord's ability to escape liability for intentional acts, and for acts of affirmative negligence.

execute To complete, make, perform, do, or follow out. To sign a document intending to make it a binding instrument. The term is also used to indicate the performance of a contract.

executor A person named by the testator of a will to carry out its provisions as to the disposition of the estate. A personal representative appointed in a will to administer a decedent's estate.

F

fair market value The amount of money that would be paid for a property offered on the open market for a reasonable length of time with both the buyer and the seller knowing all uses to which the property could be put and with neither party being under pressure to buy or sell. (See Market Value.)

Fair Housing Amendments Act of 1988 Important piece of legislation that further extends protection against housing discrimination to families and handicapped persons.

Facebook A social networking website owned by Facebook, Inc. Users connect with friends, relatives, and others to share social or other contacts.

false promise A statement used to influence or persuade.

Fannie Mae (See Federal National Mortgage Association.)

farm A specific geographical area that a licensee focuses on for listings and sales.

Federal Deposit Insurance Corporation (FDIC) An independent agency of the federal government whose purpose is to insure deposits in banks and savings banks entitled to federal deposit insurance. For a more detailed description go to www.fdic.gov.

Federal Fair Housing Act Established under Title VIII of the United States Civil Rights Act of 1969 and amended in 1988. It was created to provide fair housing throughout the United States.

Federal Home Loan Mortgage Corporation (FHLMC) A government-sponsored enterprise (GSE) created by Congress to support liquidity and stability in the secondary mortgage market. It is also known as Freddie Mac.

Federal Housing Administration (FHA) Established as a federal agency under the National Housing Act in 1934, its purpose was and is to stabilize the mortgage markets by insuring housing mortgages and credit.

Federal National Mortgage Association (FNMA) A federal corporation that provides lenders with a secondary mortgage money market.

Federal Reserve System The central banking system of the United States under the control of a central board of governors (Federal Reserve Board). It involves a central bank in each of twelve geographical districts, with broad powers in controlling credit and the amount of money in circulation.

fee simple An estate in real property by which the owner has the greatest possible power over the title. In modern use it expressly establishes the title of real property with the owner without limitation or end. She may dispose of it by sale, trade, or will, as she chooses. In modern estates the terms "fee" and "fee simple" are substantially synonymous.

fee simple absolute The highest estate known at law. A freehold estate of indefinite duration, incapable of being defeated by conditions or limitations. Sometimes simply called fee or fee estate.

fee simple defeasible A fee simple estate to which certain conditions or limitations attach, such that the estate may be defeated or terminated upon the happening of an act or event. Also called a fee simple subject to a condition subsequent estate.

fiduciary A person in a position of trust and confidence, as between principal and broker. A fiduciary owes complete allegiance to her principal including the duties of confidentiality, full disclosure, loyalty, obedience, accounting for all monies, and the use of skill care and due diligence. A fiduciary may not make a profit from her position without first disclosing it to the beneficiary.

financing statement The instrument filed to perfect the security agreement and give constructive notice of the security interest, thereby protecting the interest of the secured parties. (See Secured Party, Security Agreement, and Security Interest.) The security interest in personal property. It is analogous to a mortgage on real property, except that it secures personal property. Under the UCC, it may be filed in Sacramento with the secretary of state.

finder's fee Compensation paid to a person for finding someone interested in selling or buying property. In general, finder's fees are illegal in California since a commission may only be paid to a licensed real estate broker. When a transaction involves a federally related loan, such fees are prohibited by the Real Estate Settlement Procedures Act (RESPA)

First Amendment The constitutional amendment guaranteeing freedom of speech, press, assembly, and religion.

fixtures Items that were originally personal property but that have become part of the real property, usually because they are attached to the real property more or less permanently. Examples: store fixtures built into the property and plumbing fixtures.

flipper property Any property bought for immediate resale and profit.

footing The base or bottom of a foundation wall, pier, or column.

foreclosure A legal proceeding to enforce a lien, such as a mortgage or deed of trust. The process by which secured property is seized and sold to satisfy a debt. A mortgage or involuntary lien must be sold by a court-ordered sale; a sale under a deed of trust may be either by court action or through a private trustee's sale.

formal will A will signed by the testator in the presence of two or more witnesses, who must themselves sign the will.

Fourteenth Amendment The constitutional amendment that directs that no state can deprive a person of life, liberty, or property without due process or equal protection of the law.

fraud Deception that deprives another person of her rights, or injures her. False representation

or concealment of material facts that induces another person to justifiably rely on it to her detriment.

Freddie Mac (See Federal Home Loan Mortgage Corporation.)

freehold An estate of fee. An estate in real property that is either a life estate or an estate in fee.

front foot Property measurement for sale or valuation purposes. The property measurement is along the street line, and each front foot extends to the depth of the lot. It is usually used in connection with commercial property. Front foot is usually more important than depth in retail stores due to added street exposure.

fructus Fruits, crops, and other plants. If the vegetation is produced by human labor, such as crops, it is called fructus industrials; naturally growing vegetation is called fructus naturales.

future advances Future (additional) loans made by a lender and secured under the original deed of trust. The advances may either be optional or obligatory, but the deed of trust or mortgage must provide in the security instrument that it will cover any such future advances.

future interest Interest in land or other things where possession or other rights occur at some future date.

G

gable roof Pitched roof with sloping sides.

gambrel roof A curb roof, having a steep lower slope with a flatter upper slope above.

garnishment A legal process to seize a debtor's property or money in the possession of a third party.

general plan restrictions Covenants, conditions, and restrictions placed on a subdivision or other large tract of land, designed to benefit and burden each lot in the tract.

Government National Mortgage Association (Ginnie Mae) A federal corporation within the Department of Housing and Urban Development (HUD) that assists mortgage lenders in gaining access to capital for mortgage loans. Ginnie Mae securities are the only mortgage-backed securities guaranteed by the full faith and credit of the U.S. government.

graduated lease Usually a long-term lease that provides for adjustments in the rental rate on the basis of some future determination. For example, the rent may be based upon the result of appraisals to be made at predetermined times in the future or the rise or fall of the consumer price index.

grant deed In California, a deed in which the word grant is used as a work of conveyance and therefore, by law, implies certain warranties. The deed used to transfer property in California. By statute it implies only two limited warranties.

grantee The buyer; a person to whom a grant is made.

grantor The seller; one who signs a deed. The seller or person who executes a grant.

gross income Total income before expenses are deducted.

gross rent mutiplier A number that reflects the ratio between the sales price of income property divided by gross annual rental income. It is useful in estimating the market value of income-producing property.

ground lease An agreement leasing land only, without improvements, ordinarily with the understanding that improvements will be placed on the land by the tenant.

ground rent
1. Earnings from the ground only.
2. Earnings of improved property after allowances are made for earnings of improvements.
3. A perpetual rent that grantors in some states may reserve to themselves and their heirs when they convey real property.

H

handicap Includes but is not limited to a physical or mental impairment that substantially limits one or more of a person's major life activities.

hazard insurance Insurance that protects the owner and lender against physical hazards to property such as fire and windstorm damage.

header A beam placed perpendicularly to joists and to which joists are nailed in the framing

of openings such as windows, doors, and stairways.

heirs Persons who succeed to the estate of someone who dies intestate (without a will). It sometimes indicates anyone who is entitled to inherit a decedent's property.

highest and best use An appraisal phrase that means that use of real property that is most likely to produce the greatest net return on land or buildings, or both, over a given period of time.

hip roof A pitched roof with sloping sides and ends.

Holden Act (Housing Financial Discrimination Act) Bars discrimination based on ancestry, color, race, marital status, national origin, or sex. Specifically states that "redlining" is illegal in California.

holder in due course One who has taken a negotiable note, check, or bill of exchange in due course before it was past due, in good faith, without knowledge that it has been previously dishonored and without notice of any defect at the time it was negotiated to her, or for value. Someone who acquires a negotiable instrument in good faith and without any actual or constructive notice of defect. The acquisition must occur before the note's maturity. Such a holder takes the note free from any personal defenses (such as failure of consideration, fraud in the inducement) that may be available against the maker.

holographic will A will that is entirely written, dated, and signed by the testator in the testator's handwriting. No witnesses are needed.

homeowner's exemption An exemption or reduction in real property taxes available to those who reside on their property as of March 1. The current amount is $7000 off the assessed value of the home.

homestead
1. A home upon which the owner or owners have recorded a Declaration of Homestead, as provided by California statutes that protects the home against judgments up to a specified amount.
2. A probate homestead is a similarly protected home property set aside by a California probate court for a widow or minor children. A special, limited exemption against certain judgments available to qualified homeowners.

hundred percent location A retail business location considered the best available for attracting business.

I

IDX Internet Data Exchange.

illusory contract An agreement that gives the appearance of a contract but in fact is not a contract because it lacks one of the essential elements.

implied Not expressed by words, but presumed from facts, acts, or circumstances.

impound account A trust account established by the lender to pay property taxes and hazard insurance.

income approach An appraisal technique used on income-producing properties. Also known as the capitalization approach.

incompetent Someone incapable of managing her own affairs by reason of age, disease, weakness of mind, or any other cause determined by a court of law.

indebtedness A debt or obligation.

indemnification Compensation to a person who has already sustained a loss. For example, an insurance payment for a loss sustained under a policy.

ingress The act of or avenue for entering property.

injunction
1. An order issued by a court to restrain one or more parties to a suit or proceeding from performing an act deemed inequitable or unjust in regard to the rights of some other party or parties in the suit or proceeding.
2. A court order prohibiting certain acts, or ordering specific acts.

installment note A note that provides that payments of a certain sum or amount be paid in more than one payment on the dates specified in the instrument.

installment sales contract Also known as an agreement of sale or a land contract.

installment sale method A method of reporting capital gains by installments for successive tax years to minimize the impact of capital gains tax in the year of the sale.

institutional lender Lenders who make a substantial number of real estate loans, such as banks, savings banks, and insurance companies.

interest deduction interest paid on real estate loans is partially or fully deductible on an individual's income tax return, subject to certain limitations. The amount of a home equity loan that qualifies for an interest deduction cannot exceed $100,000 at this time.

interest rate The percentage of a sum of money charged for its use.

interest rate cap A limit on the rate of interest that can be charged by a lender. The majority of all adjustable rate mortgages do contain an interest rate cap.

Internet A system of worldwide, interconnected computer networks.

interpleader A court proceeding initiated by a stakeholder, such as a broker or escrow agent, that decides the ownership or disposition of trust funds.

intestate Dying without a will or leaving a defective will.

involuntary conversion The loss of real property due to destruction, seizure, condemnation, eminent domain, foreclosure sale, or tax sale.

involuntary lien Any lien imposed on property without the consent of the owner.

irrigation districts Quasi-political districts created under special laws to provide for water services to property owners in the district.

J

joint note A note signed by two or more persons who have equal liability for payment.

joint tenancy Joint ownership by two or more persons with right of survivorship. Four unities must be present: time, title, interest, and possession. Property held by two or more people with right of survivorship.

judgment debtor A person who has an unsatisfied money judgment levied against her.

judgment lien A money judgment that, because it has been recorded, has become a lien against the judgment debtor's real property.

junior lien A lien lower in priority or rank than another or other liens.

junior mortgage A mortgage subordinate in right or lien priority to a previous mortgage.

L

laches Unreasonable delay in asserting one's legal rights.

land contract A contract used in the sale of real property when the seller wishes to retain legal title until all or a certain part of the purchase price is paid by the buyer. It is also referred to as an installment sales contract or an agreement of sale.

land sales contract A contract for the sale of property, by which possession is delivered to the buyer, but title remains with the seller until full payment or the satisfaction of other stated conditions.

landlocked Property totally surrounded by other property with no means of ingress or egress.

landlord The person who leases property; the owner of the property.

lands, tenements, and hereditament Inheritable lands or interest.

late support The support that the soil of an adjoining owner gives to her neighbor's land.

lease A contract between owner and tenant, setting forth conditions upon which the tenant may occupy and use the property and the term of the occupancy.

leasehold estate The estate of a tenant under a lease. (See Estate for Years.)

legal description A description recognized by law; a description by which property can be definitely located by reference to government surveys or approved recorded maps.

lender guidelines Most lenders use FannieMae and Freddie Mac underwriting guidelines.

lessee A tenant; the person who is entitled to possession of property under a lease.

lessor A landlord; the property owner who executes a lease.

letter of intent An expression of intent to invest, develop, or purchase without creating any firm legal obligation to do so.

lien A lien makes the debtor's property security for the payment of a debt or the discharge of an obligation.

life estate An estate in real property that continues for the life of a particular person. The "life" involved may be that of the owner or that of some other person. An estate in property whose duration is limited to and measured by the life of a natural person or persons.

limited partnership A partnership composed of some partners whose contribution and liability are limited. There must always be one or more general partners with unlimited liability and one or more limited partners with limited liability. A special partnership composed of limited and general partners. The general partners have unlimited liability and total management, whereas the limited partners have to voice in the management and their only financial exposure is to the extent of their investment. In some ways the limited partners' interest is similar to that of stockholders in a corporation.

liquidated damages clause An agreement between the parties that in the event of a breach, the amount of damages shall be liquidated (set or fixed). The amount is set before the breach, usually at the time of making the contract, on the assumption that the exact amount of damages is difficult to determine because of the nature of the contract.

lis pendens A notice of pending litigation recorded to give constructive notice of a suit that has been filed. A recorded notice that a lawsuit is pending, the outcome of which may affect title to property.

listing An employment contract between a broker and her principal (client). A listing is automatically canceled upon the death of the agent (real estate broker) or the principal (owner). Another real estate broker must negotiate a new listing with the owner upon the death of the real estate broker.

listing agreement An employment contract authorizing a broker to sell, lease, or exchange an owner's property.

loan committee The committee in a lending institution that reviews and approves or disapproves the loan applications recommended by a loan officer.

loan correspondent A loan agent usually used by distant lenders to help the lender make real estate loans.

loan package A group of documents prepared along with a loan application to give the prospective lender complete details about the proposed loan.

loan value The lender's appraised value of the property.

loss mitigation department A division of a financial institution or lender whose purpose is to minimize losses from foreclosures or defaults.

LTV Abbreviation for "loan to valuation."

M

MAI A member of the Appraisal Institute. A real estate designation earned by members of the Appraisal Institute after meeting strict prerequisites and passing a rigorous examination.

marginal land Land that barely pays the cost of working or using it.

market data approach (See Comparative Market Analysis.)

market price The price paid regardless of pressures, motives, or intelligence.

market value
1. The price at which a willing seller would sell and a willing buyer would buy, neither being under abnormal pressure.
2. As defined by the courts, it is the highest price estimated in terms of money that a property would bring if exposed for sale in the open market, allowing a reasonable time to find a purchaser with knowledge of the property's use and capabilities for use.

marketable title Title free and clear of reasonable objections and doubts; also called merchantable title.

material fact A fact that would be likely to affect a person's decision in determining whether to enter into a particular transaction. Any

information that will influence the judgment or decision of the customer.

mechanic's lien A lien given by statute to persons supplying labor, materials, or other services to improve real property. Whenever a contractor, laborer, or materialman provides labor or materials to improve real property and is not paid, that person is entitled to a lien against the property as a means of securing payment. Certain statutory steps must be taken to file, record, and foreclose the lien.

merchantable title (See Marketable Title.)

merger of title The combination of two estates. Also refers to the joining of one estate burdened by an encumbrance and another estate benefited by the encumbrance. Whenever a benefit and a burden are merged, the encumbrance is extinguished.

meridians Imaginary north and south lines that intersect base lines to form a starting point for the measurement of land.

metes and bounds Terms used to describe the boundary lines of land, setting forth all the boundary lines together with their terminal points and angles. Metes means measurements. Bounds means boundaries.

minor A person under the age of majority. In California all persons under eighteen years of age, the age of majority in California.

misrepresentation An intentional or negligent suggestion or statement of a material fact in a false manner with the intent of deceiving someone into taking a course of action she would not otherwise normally pursue. A licensee may be disciplined for misrepresentation even though that misrepresentation did not result in a loss to the principal.

mitigation Facts or circumstances that tend to justify or excuse an act or course of conduct.

MLS access only listings A service provided by limited agency brokers offering only MLS access to sellers. (See Alternate Fee Listings.)

mobile home (Manufactured Home) A stationary, prefabricated type of housing designed and equipped for human habitation. It may be transported to a home site by special equipment.

month-to-month tenancy A lease of property for a month at a time, under a periodic tenancy that continues for successive months until terminated by proper notice, usually thirty days.

monument A fixed object and point established by surveyors or others to establish land locations.

moratorium The temporary suspension, usually by statute, of the enforcement of liability for debt.

mortgage A contract by which property is hypothecated (pledged without delivery) for the repayment of a loan.

mortgage convertible adjustable rate Allows the borrower to adjust to a fixed interest rate.

mortgage conveyance The transfer of the title of real property from one to another. Also an instrument that transfers an interest in real property from one person to another.

mortgage guaranty insurance Insurance against financial loss available to mortgage lenders from the Mortgage Guaranty Insurance Corporation, a private company organized in 1956.

mortgage loan broker A person or corporation who acts as an intermediary between borrower and lender for compensation.

mortgagee One to whom a mortgagor gives a mortgage to secure a loan or performance of an obligation; the lender under a mortgage. (See Secured Party.) A creditor (lender) under a mortgage.

mortgagor One who gives a mortgage on her property to secure a loan or assure performance of an obligation; the borrower under a mortgage. (See Debtor.) A borrower (property owner) of money under a mortgage.

multiple listing A listing, usually exclusive right to sell, taken by a member of an organization composed of real estate brokers with the provisions that all members will have the opportunity to find an interested client; a cooperative listing. A listing taken by a broker and shared with other brokers through a specialized distribution service, usually provided by the local real estate board. Generally, such listings are exclusive right to sell listings.

mutual assent An agreement between the parties in a contract. The offer and acceptance of a contract.

mutual water company A water company organized by or for water users in a given district, with the object of securing an ample water supply at a reasonable rate. Stock is issued to users.

N

NAR National Association of REALTORS®

negative amortization

1. Occurs when normal payments on a loan are insufficient to cover all interest then due, so that unpaid interest is added to principal. Thus, even though payments are made on time, the principal grows with each payment.
2. Occurs when the debt service is not sufficient to cover the interest amount of the loan. This note should only be used in an area that is appreciating in value.

negligence Either the failure to act as a reasonable, prudent person or the performance of an act that would not be done by a reasonable, prudent person.

negotiable instrument A check or promissory note that meets specified statutory requirements and is therefore easily transferable in somewhat the same manner as money. The negotiable instrument can be passed by endorsement and delivery (or in some cases by mere delivery), and the transferee takes title free of certain real defenses (such as failure of consideration, fraud in the inducement) that might exist against the original maker of the negotiable instrument.

NEPA National Environmental Protection Act, a federal statute requiring all federal agencies to prepare an Environmental Impact Statement and meet other requirements whenever a major federal action is anticipated that could significantly affect the environment.

net listing A listing that provides that the agent may retain as compensation for her services all sums received over and above a stated net price to the owner. An employment agreement that entitles the broker to a commission of only the amount, if any, that the sales price of the property exceeds the listing price.

nonfreehold estate A lease tenancy. (See under Estates for the types of leasehold estates.)

nonjudicial foreclosure Foreclosure and sale of property without resorting to court action, by private sale. For deeds of trust the foreclosure provisions are outlined by the statutes and the requirements in the security instrument, which include a notice of default, right to reinstate, publication of sale, and trustee's sale.

notary public An individual licensed by the state to charge a fee for acknowledging signatures on instruments.

note A signed written instrument promising payment of a stated sum of money. Shortened name for a promissory note.

notice of completion A notice recorded after termination of work on improvements, limiting the time in which mechanic's liens can be filed against the property.

notice of default A notice that is recorded in the county recorder's office stating that a trust deed is in default and that the holder has chosen to have the property sold. The trustor (property owner) has three months after the date of recording to reinstate the loan. Recorded notice that a trustor has defaulted on her secured debt.

notice of nonresponsibility A notice provided by law designed to relieve a property owner from responsibility for the cost of work done on the property or materials furnished for it when the work or materials were ordered by a person in possession. Notice relieving an owner from possession. Notice relieving an owner from mechanic's liens for work on property not ordered by that owner.

notice to quit A notice to a tenant to vacate rented property. Also called a three-day notice. Notice given to tenants in default of their lease terms or on their rent, which directs them to either cure the default or to vacate the premises.

novation The acceptance of a new contract in substitution for the old contract, with the intent that the new contract will extinguish the original contract. Sometimes encountered in transfers of deeds of trust, where the new owner assumes the debt and the lender, through novation, releases the former owner from any

liability under the original promissory note and deed of trust.

nuisance Anything that is injurious to health or indecent or offensive to the senses, or any obstruction to the free use of property so as to interfere with the comfortable enjoyment of life or property or unlawfully obstructs the free passage or use, in the customary manner, of any navigable lake or river, bay, stream, canal, or basin, or any public park, square, street, or highway. A legal wrong arising from acts or use of one's property in a way that unreasonably interferes with another's use of her property.

O

obligee A promisor; a person to whom another is bound by a promise or another obligation.

obsolescence Loss in value due to reduced desirability and usefulness of a structure because its design and construction become obsolete; loss because of becoming old fashioned and not in keeping with modern needs.

offer A proposal to create a contract, which signifies the present intent of the offeror to be legally bound by her proposal.

offeree A person to whom an offer is made.

offeror A person who makes an offer.

offset statement Statement by owner of a deed of trust or mortgage against the property, setting forth the present status of the debt and lien. Also called a beneficiary statement.

open house The common practice by brokers, of showing listed properties to the public. Also, an opportunity for a licensee to meet potential buyers and sellers, and for buyers and sellers to get an idea of relative value in the current market.

open listing An authorization given by a property owner to a real estate broker in which the broker is given the nonexclusive right to secure a purchaser. Open listings may be given to any number of brokers without liability to compensate any except the one who first secures a buyer ready, willing, and able to meet the terms of the listing or who secures the acceptance by the seller of a satisfactory offer.

open-end mortgage or deed of trust A mortgage containing a clause that permits the mortgagor or trustor to borrow additional money without rewriting the mortgage or deed of trust.

option A right to have an act performed in the future; a right given for a consideration to purchase or lease a property upon specified terms within a specified time; a contract to keep an offer open for a particular period of time. The right of a person to buy or lease property at a set price at any time during the life of a contract.

option listing A listing that also includes an option, permitting the broker to buy the property at the stated price at any time during the listing period.

orientation Placement of a house on its lot with regard to its exposure to the rays of the sun, prevailing winds, privacy from the street, and protection from outside noises.

or more clause A simple prepayment clause that permits the borrower to make a normal payment or any larger amount, up to and including the entire outstanding balance, without a prepayment penalty.

ostensible agency An agency implied by law because the principal intentionally or inadvertently caused a third person to believe someone to be her agent, and that third person acted as if that other person was in fact the principal's agent. This can lead to an unlawful undisclosed dual agency and should be avoided in all cases.

overages in trust account Any unexplained overages in the trust account must be held in trust by the licensee and must be maintained in a separate record. An overage is every bit as bad as a shortage in a trust account.

P

parity wall A wall erected on the line between two adjoining properties that are under different ownership for the use of both owners.

parquet floor Hardwood flooring laid in squares or patterns.

part-time status Many real estate licensees have other full-time jobs. A part-time licensee cannot devote a full-time effort to represent a client; therefore the failure to disclose a part-time status is considered unethical real estate practice.

partial reconveyance In a deed of trust or mortgage, a clause that permits release of a parcel or part of a parcel from the effects and lien of that security instrument. The release usually occurs upon the payment of a specified sum of money.

partition action A legal action by which co-owners seek to sever their joint ownership. The physical division of property between co-owners, usually through court action.

partnership An association of two or more persons to unite their property, labor or skill, or any one or combination thereof, in prosecution of some joint business, and to share the profits in certain proportions. An agreement of two or more individuals to jointly undertake a business enterprise. If it is a general partnership, all partners have unlimited liability and, absent other agreements, share equally in the management and profits of the business.

patent The instrument that conveys title to government land.

payment clause A provision in a promissory note, deed of trust, or mortgage, permitting the debtor to pay off the obligation before maturity.

percentage lease A lease on property, the rental for which is determined by the amount of business done by the tenant, usually a percentage of gross receipts from the business, with provision for a minimum rental.

periodic tenancy A leasehold estate that continues indefinitely for successive periods of time, until terminated by proper notice. When the periods are one month in duration, it is often called a month-to-month lease.

personal property Any property that is not real property. (See Real Property.) Property that is movable, as opposed to real property, which is immovable; also includes intangible property and leasehold estates.

pier A column of masonry used to support other structural members.

pitch The incline or rise of a roof.

plaintiff The party who initiates a lawsuit; the person who sues another.

pledge Deposition of personal property by a debtor with a creditor as security for a debt or engagement.

pledgee One who is given a pledge as security. (See Security Party.)

pledgor One who gives a pledge as security. (See Debtor.)

plottage increment The appreciation in unit value created by joining smaller ownerships into one large single ownership. (See Assemblage.)

plywood
1. Laminated wood made up in panels.
2. Several thicknesses of wood glued together with grains at different angles for strength.

pocket listing When a real estate licensee convinces a seller that she can procure a buyer for the property and wants to withhold the information from the multiple listing services. This is considered unethical.

points Points paid for refinancing must be spread out over the life of the loan to be deductible on a person's income tax.

police power The right of the state to enact laws and regulations and its right to enforce them for the order, safety, health, morals, and general welfare of the public. The power of the state to prohibit acts that adversely affect public health, welfare, safety, or morals. (Zoning and building codes are examples of exercise of police power.)

power of attorney An instrument authorizing a person to act as the agent of the person granting it. A special power of attorney limits the agent to a particular or specific act, as a landowner may grant an agent special power of attorney to convey a single and specific parcel of property. Under a general power of attorney, the agent may do almost anything for the principal that the principal could do himself or herself. A document authorizing a person (an attorneyinfact) to act as an agent.

prefabricated house A house manufactured, and sometimes partly assembled, before delivery to the building site.

prepayment penalty Penalty for the payment of a note before it actually becomes due. A fee or charge imposed upon a debtor who desires to pay off her loan before its maturity. Not all prepayment clauses provide for a penalty, and

in many real estate transactions the law regulates the amount of penalty that may be charged.

prescription Securing of an easement by open, notorious, and uninterrupted use, adverse to the owner of the land for the period required by statute, which, in California, is five years. A method of obtaining a right in property by adverse use over a prescribed period of time.

present interest An estate in land that gives the owner the right to occupy her property immediately, as opposed to a future interest, which grants only the right to occupy the premises at some future date.

principal The (client) employer of an agent. Someone who hires an agent to act on her behalf. The term also refers to the amount of an outstanding loan (exclusive of interest).

priority That which comes first in point of time or right. Superior, higher, or preferred rank or position.

probate Court supervision of the collection and distribution of a deceased person's estate. This takes place in Superior Court within the county where the property is located.

procuring cause The event originating from another series of events that, without a break in continuity, results in an agent's producing a final buyer. Proximate cause. A broker is the procuring cause of a sale if her efforts set in motion an unbroken chain of events that resulted in the sale.

profit a prendre An easement coupled with a power to consume resources on the burdened property.

promissory note A written promise to pay a designated sum of money at a future date.

property Anything that may be owned. Anything of value in which the law permits ownership.

proration of taxes Division of the taxes equally or proportionately between buyer and seller on the basis of time of ownership.

puffing Exaggerated comments or opinions not intended as factual representations. Putting things in their best perspective is not subject to disciplinary action. Exaggerated puffing may be a violation of the Code of Ethics for REALTORS®

punitive damages Money awarded by the court for the sole purpose of punishing the wrongdoer, and not designed to compensate the injured party for her damages.

purchase money mortgage or purchase money deed of trust A mortgage or deed of trust given as part or all of the consideration for the purchase of property or given as security for a loan to obtain money for all or part of the purchase price.

Q

quasi-contract A contract implied by law, that is, the law will imply and consider certain relationships as if they were a contract.

quiet enjoyment The right of an owner to the use of property without interference with her tenant's possession or use.

quiet title action A lawsuit designed to remove any clouds on a title to property. It forces the claimant of an adverse interest in property to prove her right to title; otherwise she will be forever barred from asserting it.

quitclaim deed A deed to relinquish any interest in property that the grantor may have, but implying no warranties. A deed that transfers only whatever right, title, or interest, if any, the grantor owns, without implying any warranties.

R

range A strip of land six miles wide, determined by a government survey, running in a north-south direction.

ratification The adoption or approval of an act performed on behalf of a person without previous authorization.

ready, willing, and able buyer A purchaser of property who is willing to buy on terms acceptable to the seller and who further possesses the financial ability to consummate the sale. Producing such a buyer sometimes earns the broker a commission, even though a sale is not forthcoming.

real estate agent Since the only one authorized to represent buyers and sellers in the purchase,

sale or leasing of real property for compensation in California is a licensed broker, that principal broker is, by definition, the "real estate agent." All licensees acting under that broker's employ are "agents" of that broker, not agents of the buyer or seller directly.

real estate association An organization whose members consist primarily of real estate brokers and salespersons.

real estate investment trust (REIT) A specialized form of holding title to property that enables investors to pool their resources and purchase property, while still receiving considerable tax advantages, without being taxed as a corporation.

real estate licensee When used without modification, refers to a person, whether broker or salesperson, licensed under any of the provisions of the California BPC.

real estate trust A special arrangement under federal and state law whereby investors may pool funds for investments in real estate and mortgages and yet escape corporation taxes.

real property Land and anything affixed, incidental, or appurtenant to it, and anything considered immovable under the law. Land, buildings, and other immovable property permanently attached thereto.

REALTOR® Pronounced: Real tor. A real estate broker (or Associate REALTOR®, salesperson) who is a member of the National Association of REALTORS®

recapture
1. An event whereby an owner of income property pays a tax on depreciation deductions taken on her income taxes at the time of sale.
2. A provision in tax laws that reduces certain benefits from claiming depreciation.

receiver A neutral third party, appointed by the court to collect the rents and profits from property, and distribute them as ordered by the court. Often used as a remedy when mere damages are inadequate.

reconveyance A conveyance to the landowner of the legal title held by a trustee under a deed of trust. The transfer of property back from a lender who holds an interest as security for the payment of a debt. In a deed of trust, the beneficiary reconveys property upon satisfaction of the promissory note.

recordation Filing of instruments for record in the office of the county recorder. Once recorded, the instrument gives constructive notice to the world.

redemption Buying back one's property after a judicial sale.

reformation A legal action to correct a mistake in a deed or other document.

reinstatement A right available to anyone under an accelerated promissory note secured by a deed of trust or mortgage on property. If a deed of trust is foreclosed by trustee's sale, the debtor may have up to three months from the recording of the notice of default to pay the amount in arrears plus interest and costs, thereby completely curing the default (reinstating) without penalty.

REO department (REO Real Estate Owned) The division or department of a lending institution that handles Real Estate Owned properties acquired through foreclosure or default.

rejection Refusal to accept an offer. Repudiation or rejection of an offer automatically terminates the offer.

release clause A stipulation in a deed of trust or mortgage that upon the payment of a specific sum of money to the holder of the deed of trust or mortgage, a particular lot or area shall be removed from the blanket lien on the whole area involved.

reliction The gradual lowering of water from the usual watermark.

remainder An estate that vests after the termination of the prior estate, such as after a life estate. Example: a life estate may be granted to Adams, with the remainder granted to Baker. Most commonly, an estate (future interest) that arises in favor of a third person after a life estate.

remedy The means by which a right is enforced, preserved, or compensated. Some of the more common remedies are damages, injunctions, rescission, and specific performance.

rent The consideration paid by a tenant for possession of property under a lease.

rental property Rental income from a smaller property may show a higher rate of profit than from a more expensive property.

renunciation The cancellation of an agency relationship by the real estate agent; requires written notice to the principal.

rescission The unmaking of a contract and the restoring of each party to the same position each held before the contract arose.

reservation A right or interest retained by a grantor when conveying property; also called an exception.

residue The portion of a person's estate that has not been specifically devised.

RESPA Real Estate Settlement Procedure Act. Generally prohibits the giving and receiving of kickbacks and unearned fees.

respondent The person against whom an appeal is taken; the opposite of an appellant.

restriction A limitation on the use of real property arising from a contract or a recorded instrument. An encumbrance on property that limits the use of it; usually a covenant or condition.

retaliatory eviction A landlord's attempt to evict a tenant from a lease because the tenant has used the remedies available under the warranty of habitability.

reversion The right a grantor keeps when she grants someone an estate that will or may end in the future. Examples: the interest remaining with a landlord after she grants a lease, or the interest an owner of land has after she grants someone a life estate. Any future interest (estate) left in the grantor. The residue of an estate left in the grantor after the termination of a lesser estate.

revocation Withdrawal of an offer or other right, thereby voiding and destroying that offer or right. It is a recall with intent to rescind.

ridge board The board placed on edge at the ridge of the roof to support the upper ends of the rafters; also called rooftree, ridge piece, ridge plate, or ridgepole.

right of ownership The evidence of a person's ownership or interest in property.

right of survivorship The right to acquire the interest of a deceased joint owner. It is the distinguishing feature of a joint tenancy.

right of way The right to pass over a piece of real property or to have pipes, electrical lines, or the like go across it. An easement granting a person the right to pass across another's property.

riparian rights The right of a landowner with regard to a stream crossing or adjoining her property.

riser
1. The upright board at the back of each step of a stairway.
2. In heating, a riser is a duct slanted upward to carry hot air from the furnace to the room above.

Rumford Act Prohibits discrimination in employment and housing. Is enforced by the Department of Fair Employment and Housing.

S

safety clause In a listing agreement, a provision that if anyone found by the broker during her listing period purchases the property within a specified time after the expiration of the listing, the broker receives her full commission.

sale lease back A situation in which the owner of a piece of property sells it and retains occupancy by leasing it from the buyer.

sales contract A contract between buyer and seller setting out the terms of sale.

salesperson When used without modification, refers to a person licensed as a salesperson under Calif. BPC. A real estate salesperson must, at all times, be under the supervision and direction of a licensed broker.

sandwich lease A leasehold interest that lies between the primary lease and the operating lease. Example: A leases to B; B subleases to C; C subleases to D. C's lease is a sandwich lease.

satisfaction Discharge of a mortgage or deed of trust lien from the records upon payment of the secured debt. Discharge of an obligation or indebtedness by paying what is due.

secondary financing A loan secured by a second mortgage or a second deed of trust.

secondary money market Where loans are purchased and sold.

section A square mile of land, as established by government survey, containing 640 acres.

secured debt An obligation that includes property held as security for the payment of that debt; upon default, the property may be sold to satisfy the debt.

secured party The party having the security interest in personal property. The mortgagee, conditional seller, or pledgee is referred to as the secured party.

security agreement An agreement between the secured party and the debtor that creates a security interest in personal property. It replaced such terms as chattel mortgage, pledge, trust receipt, chattel trust, equipment trust, conditional sale, and inventory lien.

security deposit A deposit made to ensure performance of an obligation, usually by a tenant. A sum of cash given as collateral to ensure faithful performance of specified obligations.

security interest A term designating the interest of a secured creditor in the personal property of the debtor.

senior lien A lien that is superior to or has priority over another lien. Also, the first deed of trust or lien on a property.

separate property Property that is owned by a husband or wife and that is not community property. It is property acquired by either spouse prior to marriage or by gift or inheritance after marriage; also, in California, it is the income from separate property after marriage. Property held by a married person that is not community property; it includes property owned before marriage and property acquired after marriage by gift or inheritance.

servient estate The parcel of property that is burdened by and encumbered with an easement.

servient tenement An estate burdened by an easement.

setback ordinance An ordinance prohibiting the erection of a building or structure between the curb and the setback line. (See Building Line.)

severalty ownership Ownership by only one person; sole ownership.

shake A handsplit shingle, usually edge grained.

sheathing Structural covering, such as boards, plywood, or wallboard, placed over the exterior studding or rafters of a house.

sheriff's deed A deed given by court order in connection with the sale of property to satisfy a judgment.

short sale listing The listing of a property where the anticipated proceeds from the sale are not sufficient to pay the outstanding balance owed on the property.

sinking fund
1. A fund set aside from the income from property that, with accrued interest, will eventually pay for replacement of the improvements.
2. A similar fund set aside to pay a debt.

small claims court A branch of the Municipal Court. The rules of this court forbid parties to be assisted by attorneys, dispense with most formal rules of evidence, and have all trials heard by judges. The monetary limit of cases before the court is $1,500.

social networking Interaction between groups who share a common interest.

soil pipe Pipe carrying waste from the house to the main sewer line.

sold to the state A bookkeeping entry on the county tax rolls indicating that the property taxes are delinquent. The entry begins the five-year–redemption period, after which the property may be physically sold to the public for back taxes.

sole or sole plate A structural member, usually two by four, on which wall and partition studs rest.

special assessment Legal charge against real estate by a public authority to pay the cost of public improvement, as distinguished from taxes levied for the general support of government.

specific performance A legal action to compel performance of a contract; for example a contract for the sale of land. A contract remedy by

which one party is ordered by the court to comply with the terms of the agreement.

square footage of building An appraiser always uses the exterior dimensions to calculate the square footage of a building.

staging a property Preparing a property for sale.

statute of frauds The state law that provides that certain contracts (including most real estate contracts) must be in writing in order to be enforceable in the courts. Examples: real property leased for more than one year or an agent's authorization to sell real estate.

statute of limitations A statute that requires lawsuits to be brought within a certain time to be enforceable. The basic periods are one year for personal injury, two years for oral contracts, three years for damages to real or personal property, four years for written contracts, and three years from date of discovery for fraud.

steering An illegal procedure where individual buyers are shown properties only in specific neighborhoods with the intention of directing their purchase to specific regions or areas.

stepped-up basis A higher, increased tax value of property given as the result of most sales or taxable transfers. The tax basis is used in computing capital gains and losses on the transfer of property.

stop notice A notice served on the owner of property or custodian of funds. It requests, with certain penalties for noncompliance, that any funds due to a general contractor be paid to the claimant, laborer, or materialman.

straight mortgage or deed of trust A mortgage or deed of trust in which there is no reduction of the principal during the term of the instrument. Payments to interest are usually made on an annual, semiannual, or quarterly basis.

straight note A promissory note that is unamortized. The principal is paid at the end of the term of the note.

straightline depreciation An accounting procedure that sets the rate of depreciation as a fixed percentage of the amount to be depreciated; the percentage stays the same each year.

subchapter-s corporation A corporation that, for federal tax purposes only, is taxed similarly to a partnership. The corporate entity is disregarded for most federal tax purposes, and the shareholders are generally taxed as individual partners.

subjacent support Support that the soil below the surface gives to the surface of the land.

subject to Burdened by and liable for an obligation. A method of taking over a loan without becoming personally liable for its payment.

"subject to" mortgage or deed of trust When a grantee takes a title to real property subject to a mortgage or deed of trust, she is not responsible to the holder of the promissory note for the payment of any portion of the amount due. The most that she can lose in the event of a foreclosure is her equity in the property. In neither case is the original maker of the note released from her responsibility. (See also Assumption of Mortgage or Deed of Trust.)

sublease A lease given by a tenant.

subordinate To make subject or junior to.

subordination agreement In a mortgage or deed of trust, a provision that a later lien shall have a priority interest over the existing lien. It makes the existing lien inferior to a later lien, in effect exchanging priorities with that later lien.

subordination clause Senior lien that makes it inferior to what would otherwise be a junior lien.

subrogate To substitute one person for another's legal rights to a claim or debt.

succession The inheritance of property.

successor in interest The next succeeding owner of an interest in property. The transferee or recipient of a property interest.

superior court The principal trial court of the state; a court of unlimited monetary and subject matter jurisdiction, and an appeal court for decisions of municipal courts and small claims courts.

supreme court The highest court in California and the federal court structure. This court is almost exclusively an appeals court, accepting (by certiorari) only those cases that, in the court's

discretion, involve issues of significant magnitude and social importance.

surety One who guarantees the performance by another, a guarantor.

swing loan A short-term loan using a borrower's equity in her unsold home to buy her new home.

syndication A group of individuals pooling their resources to purchase property through the holding vehicle of a partnership, corporation, or other association. Each individual owns share in the legal entity formed to acquire and hold title to the property. This is an alternative method to finance and purchase real estate. This allows an investment in real estate without having to do any of the work.

T

tax basis The tax value of property to the taxpayer. It is a figure used to compute capital gains and losses.

tax deed Deed issued to the purchaser at a tax sale.

tax sale Sale of property after a period of nonpayment of taxes.

tenancy A leasehold estate. (For specific types of leases, see under Estates.)

tenancy in common Ownership by two or more persons who hold an undivided interest in real property, without right of survivorship; the interests need not be equal.

tenant One who leases real property from the owner.

tenements All rights in real property that pass with a conveyance of it.

tentative map The Subdivision Map Act requires subdividers to initially submit a tentative map of their tract to the local planning commission for study. The approval or disapproval of the planning commission is noted on the map. Thereafter, the planning commission requests a final map of the tract embodying any changes.

tenure in land The manner in which land is held.

termite shield A shield, usually of noncorrodible metal, placed on top of the foundation wall or around pipes to prevent passage of termites.

testament The written declaration of one's last will.

testamentary disposition A gift passing by will.

testate A person who dies leaving a will.

testator A person who makes a will. Technically, a testator is a male and a testatrix is a female, although in common use testator refers to anyone who makes a will.

thirty-day notice A notice terminating a periodic tenancy without cause, by ending a tenancy thirty days from date of service.

three-day notice A notice giving a tenant three days in which to cure a default or quit the premises. It is the first step in an unlawful detainer action, as the means of terminating a lease for cause. When rent is delinquent, it is sometimes called a notice to quit or pay rent.

"time is of the essence" These words, when placed in an agreement, make it necessary that all time limitations and requirements be strictly observed.

title Evidence of the owner's right or interest in property.

title insurance Insurance written by a title company to protect a property owner against loss if title is defective or not marketable. A special policy of insurance issued by a title company, insuring the owner against loss of or defects in title to the insured property. The policy may be either a CLTA policy, issued to the property owner and to noninstitutional lenders, or an ALTA policy, issued to institutional lenders.

topography Nature of the surface of the land. Topography may be level, rolling, or mountainous.

tort A wrongful act. A wrong or injury. Violation of a legal right. A civil wrong, not arising from a breach of contract. Most torts lie in negligence, although they could also be intentional torts (such as assault and battery, trespass) or strict liability torts.

township A territorial subdivision that is six miles long and six miles wide and that contains thirty-six sections, each one mile square.

trade fixtures Articles of personal property that are annexed to real property but that are

necessary to the carrying on of a trade and are removable by the owner. Fixtures installed to further one's trade, business, or profession. They are an exception to the general rule that fixtures are part of a building. Such fixtures installed by a tenant may be removed before the expiration of the tenancy.

transfer Conveyance; passage of title.

transfer disclosure statement (TDS) seller and real estate broker disclosure statement. The law also allows the buyer the right to cancel her offer on disapproval of the TDS. Though there are a number of exceptions to the TDS requirement (see text) licensees are not exempt from doing their portion of the disclosure.

transferee The person to whom a transfer is made.

transferor The person who makes a transfer.

trespass An invasion of an owner's rights in her property. Unauthorized entry onto another's land.

trespasser One who trespasses. The importance of this classification of individuals on property is created by the methods for removal and the liability of the property owner if the trespasser is injured on the owner's property.

trust A right of property, real or personal, held by one party called the trustee for the benefit of another party called the beneficiary. Arrangement whereby one person holds property for the benefit of another under fiduciary (special confidential) relationship.

trust deed Deed given by a borrower to a trustee to be held pending fulfillment of an obligation, which is usually repayment of a loan to a beneficiary. A deed of trust. Foreclosure of this deed may be at a foreclosure or at a trustee's sale. The lender in the trust deed is referred to as the beneficiary. Trust deed investments should be on improved property rather than on unimproved property.

trust funds Consists of money or property received by a real estate licensee on behalf of others. Cannot be given to the seller without the permission of the buyer. Must be in writing. These funds may not be commingled. It is against the law. Protects the money in case a legal action is taken against the broker. These records are subject to audit and examination by the D.R.E. All records and corresponding instruments must be kept for a period of three years.

trustee The person who holds property in trust for another. In a deed of trust, the person who holds bare legal title in trust.

trustee's deed The deed issued by the beneficiary after the foreclosure and sale under a deed of trust.

trustee's sale The private sale of property held by a trustee under a deed of trust as part of the foreclosure proceedings. This sale must be conducted in approximately four months.

trustor One who conveys her property to a trustee. The borrower or debtor under a deed of trust.

trustor's reinstatement rights These rights continue for five business days prior to the date of the trustee's sale.

Truth in Lending Act (TILA) A complex set of federal disclosure statutes and part of the Consumer Credit Protection Act implemented by Regulation Z as amended by the Truth in Lending Simplification and Reform Act designed to provide a borrower with a means of discovering and comparing the true costs of credit. This is strictly a disclosure law and does not set maximum or minimum interest rates or charges for credit.

Twitter A web-based social networking and micro-blogging service.

U

undue influence
1. A compulsory charge on property or individuals, the payment of which supports a government.
2. Taking any fraudulent or unfair advantage of another's necessity or weakness of mind. Using a position of trust and confidence improperly to persuade a person to take a course of action. By relying on the trusted confidant, the decision maker fails to exercise her free will and independent judgment.

Uniform Commercial Code (UCC) A group of statutes establishing a unified and comprehensive scheme for regulation of security

transactions in personal property and other commercial matters, superseding the existing statutes on chattel mortgages, conditional sales, trust receipts, assignment of accounts receivable, and other similar matters.

unique visitor A statistic describing a unit of traffic to a website.

unjust enrichment A legal doctrine that prevents a person from inequitably benefiting from another's mistake, poor judgment, or loss. In a land sales contract the vender may no longer keep both the property and the buyer's excess payments (over her damages) in the event of breach, because to do so would unjustly enrich her at the buyer's expense.

unlawful detainer An action to recover possession of real property. A lawsuit designed to evict a defaulting tenant, or anyone unlawfully in possession of property, from premises. It is summary in nature, entitled to a priority court trial, and litigates only the right to possession of property (and damages resulting there from).

Unruh Civil Rights Act Deals with equal rights in business establishments, prohibits age limitations in housing, and sets age limitations necessary for senior housing. It states that all persons within California are free and equal no matter what their sex, race color, ancestry, national origin, or disability, they are entitled to full and equal accommodations.

unsecured debt A debt not backed by specific property to satisfy the indebtedness in case of default.

urban property City property; closely settled property.

usury Claiming a rate of interest greater that that permitted by law. Charging a greater rate of interest on loans than the rate allowed by law.

V

veterans administration loan (VA Loan) A government-sponsored mortgage assistance program. This loan does not contain a "due on sale" clause.

valuation Estimated worth or price. The act of valuing by appraisal.

variable interest rate (VIR) An interest rate that fluctuates in a set proportion to changes in an economic index, such as the cost of money. Extensive regulations cover use of VIRs in loans on residential property.

variance An exception or departure from the general rule. An exception granted to a property owner, relieving her from obeying certain aspects of a zoning ordinance. Its granting is discretionary with the zoning authorities and is based on undue hardship suffered by the property owner because of unique circumstances affecting her property.

vendee Purchaser or buyer or real property.

venue The location in which a cause of action occurs; it determines the court having jurisdiction to hear and decide the case. For real estate, the court having proper venue is one in the county in which the property is located.

verification A sworn statement before a duly qualified officer as to the correctness of the contents of an instrument. Written certification under oath and/or penalty of perjury, confirming the truth of the facts in a document.

vested Bestowed upon someone, such as title to property. Absolute, not contingent or subject to being defeated.

Veteran's Exemption A deduction from the annual property tax allowed to a qualified veteran residing on residential property. However, the normal Homeowner's Exemption is greater than the Veteran's Exemption and the law allows the taxpayer to use only one.

void To have no legal force or effect; that which is unenforceable. Unenforceable, null, having no legal effect.

voidable An instrument that appears to be valid and enforceable on its face but is, in fact, lacking some essential requirement. May be declared void, but is valid unless and until declared void.

voluntary affirmative marketing agreement A voluntary commitment by real estate licensees to promote fair housing by using methodology that is fairer than government regulations.

voluntary lien Any lien placed on property with the consent of the owner or as a result of the voluntary act of the owner.

VOW Virtual Office Website.

W

waiver Giving up of certain rights or privileges. The relinquishment may be voluntary and knowing, or it may occur involuntarily through action of the parties. The action resulting in the waiver is unilateral and requires no action or reliance by the other party.

warranty An absolute undertaking or promise that certain facts are as represented. Occasionally used interchangeably with guarantee.

warranty deed A deed that is used by a grantor to warrant clear title. It is commonly used in other states, but in California the grant deed with title insurance has replaced it.

warranty of habitability Implied warranty in residential leases. The landlord covenants by implication that the premises are suitable for human occupancy. The implied warranties are found in the statutes and implied by common law.

waste The destruction, or material alteration of or injury to premises by a tenant for life, or tenant, or tenant for years. Example: a tenant cutting down trees or mining coal. The destruction, injury, material alteration, or abusive use of property by a person rightfully in possession, but who does not own the fee or entire estate (for example, by a lessee or life tenant).

water table Distance from the surface of the ground to a depth at which natural groundwater is found.

web page A document on the World Wide Web.

website Pages on the World Wide Web accessible from the same URL (Uniform Resource Locator) and typically located on the same server.

will A document that directs the disposition of one's property after death.

witnessed will A formal will, signed by the testator in the presence of two or more witnesses, each of whom must also sign the will.

wraparound mortgage (See All-Inclusive Trust Deed.)

writ A process of the court under which property may be seized. An order from the court to the sheriff or other law enforcement officer directing and authorizing a specific act.

writ of attachment A writ authorizing and directing the physical attachment (seizure) of property.

writ of execution An order directing the sheriff to seize property to satisfy a judgment.

writ of immediate possession An order authorizing a landlord to obtain immediate possession of a tenant's premises, pending the outcome of an unlawful detainer action or other court proceeding.

Y

YouTube A website owned by Google, Inc. where users may upload and share videos.

Z

zoning Act of city or county authorities specifying the type of use to which property may be put in specific areas. A government's division of a city or other geographic area into districts, and the regulation of property uses within each district.

Index

M